D0480159

OPERATIONS
MANAGEMENT

OPERATIONS MANAGEMENT

Steve Paton, Ben Clegg,
Juliana Hsuan and Alan Pilkington

McGraw-Hill
Higher Education

London Boston Burr Ridge, IL Dubuque, IA Madison, WI New York San Francisco
St. Louis Bangkok Bogotá Caracas Kuala Lumpur Lisbon Madrid Mexico City Milan
Montreal New Delhi Santiago Seoul Singapore Sydney Taipei Toronto

Operations Management
Steve Paton, Ben Clegg, Juliana Hsuan and Alan Pilkington
ISBN-13 9780077126179
ISBN-10 0077126173

**McGraw-Hill
Higher Education**

Published by McGraw-Hill Education
Shoppenhangers Road
Maidenhead
Berkshire SL6 2QL
Telephone: +44 (0)1628 502 500
Fax: +44 (0)1628 770 224
Website: www.mcgraw-hill.co.uk

British Library Cataloguing in Publication Data
A catalogue record for this book is available from the British Library

Library of Congress Cataloging in Publication Data
The Library of Congress data for this book has been applied for from the Library of Congress

Acquisitions Editor: Leiah Batchelor
Development Editor: Leonie Sloman/Jennifer Yendell
Production Editor: James Bishop
Marketing Manager: Alexis Thomas

Text design by Hardlines
Cover design by Adam Renvoize
Printed and bound in Italy by Rotolito Lomborda S.P.A.

ISBN-13 9780077126179
ISBN-10 0077126173

Dedication

"To Mandy, Karli and Ethan" – SP

"Thanks to my wife Anna and my children,
Harry and Ella for their support and encouragement" – BC

"To my mom Lina for her endless love" – JH

"To my family in all the places I call home" – AP

Brief Table of Contents

Detailed Table of Contents

Guide to Case Studies

Guide to Case Studies continued

Preface

There are numerous operations management textbooks in publication, and coming up with something new and different is a daunting task. Before writing this book we felt it was important to understand what the purpose of this book would be and where it would fit in the already busy market. It is always best to practise what you preach and luckily for us writing a textbook is itself an exercise in operations management and, like all good operations managers, at the outset we realized we needed an operations strategy to guide the book.

One of the key strategic activities when designing something is to understand the trade-offs. Designing a product is an exercise in compromise as no product can be everything to everyone. We discovered there are several trade-offs in designing an operations management textbook; between the need for a compact text and the need for comprehensive coverage; between the use of older, established and still relevant material and the inclusion of newer, less well-known but more useful material; between theoretical rigour and ease of practical application; and between depth of detail for the specialist student versus scope of coverage for the generalist.

The decisions taken in balancing these trade-offs are made more difficult by the way the field of operations management is currently evolving. It is moving away from a discrete and manufacturing-focused subject (concerned with materials control, capacity planning and production scheduling), towards a more service-focused, wide-ranging subject that encompasses pretty much all the activity of a modern business. We believe that by considering these trade-offs we have made the correct decisions for this textbook.

In our choices we believe that we have added some new content that is becoming increasingly important to the field of operations management and so deserves to be brought into the fold. First, the recognition of the larger strategic context and the increasing importance of operations strategy and its strong links with corporate strategy; and the inclusion of innovation as a practice. Secondly, we have emphasised the importance that design plays in product, process, supply chain and services, and how it affects the costs and value created for customers. Thirdly we treat the management of operations with fresh topics such as the need for increasing integration, lean and agile thinking, good project management and the use of technological solutions for planning. And fourthly, we look into the future of operations management by providing an insight into improvement approaches and tools, performance measurement and provide an emphasis on careers of operations managers and the profession of operations management as a whole.

This book is therefore intended to be: accessible to the student with no prior knowledge of operations but still useful to the experienced operations manager; contemporary in its approach but respectful of the classics; and theoretically rigorous but useful to practitioners.

The key aims of the text are to:

- Explore fundamental operations management principles that are applicable to both manufacturing and service situations
- Offer a contemporary and novel treatment of the core subject areas in operations management
- Reflect recent developments in operations management theory and practice
- Provide a balanced approach to services vs manufacturing and qualitative vs quantitative coverage
- Integrate theory and practice throughout via the use of plentiful practical examples, worked examples and superior cases
- Encourage students to read/engage with the material in an interactive way through pedagogical punctuation

- Highlight key developments and practices in the last 5–10 years by recognizing the changing world of operations management and in particular emphasising the themes of Globalization, Business Integration and Corporate Social Responsibility (CSR).

Our intention has been to provide well-chosen content that maps easily and directly onto a typical course in operations management, thereby conveying a sense of value and relevance to students and lecturers alike. This text is targeted at both undergraduate and postgraduate audiences and offers a complete course in operations management, without requiring any prior knowledge. It is designed to be used in standalone shorter courses or as an integral part of a contemporary degree in business and management.

This book therefore seeks to overcome the main challenges lecturers and instructors face in delivering an operations management module, which are: what subjects to teach, what level to teach them at and how to make them relevant and interesting.

Overview of the Book

This book is organised into 4 sections Directing, Designing, Managing and Improving to reflect the current nature of operations managers' roles:

Section 1 Directing

This section introduces the principles, theory and concepts and in operations management. Broadly speaking, it deals with the strategic issues which senior operations managers must consider in their decision making. It therefore interfaces with other management disciplines such as Strategic Management, Marketing and Innovation. This book takes the view that Operations is the 'engine' that drives the business, therefore to guide the business effectively senior management must have a good understanding of the capabilities of that 'engine'.

Chapter 1 introduces the strategic environment that operations exists within and aims to provide an understanding of the decision-making processes that guide the company and that operations managers must support. Only by understanding the techniques used at corporate level can operations managers shape activity at the operational level to fit coherently with the company strategy.

Chapter 2 while strategic in theme, this chapter focuses more closely on the strategic dimension of operations management itself looking at the concepts that will help operations managers to formulate useful strategies and take the correct decisions about the shape of the conversion process that will in turn support and enable the overall corporate strategy.

Chapter 3 deals with the topic of innovation, an area that is quickly becoming strategic in nature, and a strong understanding of this is crucial to formulating strategy at both at the operational and corporate levels. These days in many industries a good innovation strategy is becoming critical to organizational success.

Section 2 Designing

All operational systems, simple or complex must be designed. This section includes the practices and methods which help put together the systems, processes, products and services that operations management is based upon:

Chapter 4 looks at supply chain management in a more contemporary way. It introduces supply networks and how they are designed and also considers the management of enterprises. First, it presents the differences between supply chains, networks and enterprises. Then the theoretical background is discussed and practical techniques introduced to help in decision making, both strategically and tactically. Trends such as outsourcing and supplier rationalization are also dealt with.

Chapter 5 takes a closer look at how products and services can be designed in order for companies to stay competitive. It covers strategies and techniques that companies use to develop innovative product and service solutions and also looks at more contemporary approaches, such as modularity and service architecture. Only by understanding the new product and service development processes can organizations devise the best strategies to ensure that the correct solutions can be introduced to the market. Strong design capability is a key advantage in the struggle to stay ahead of the competition.

Chapter 6 introduces the importance of process thinking in operations management. It describes the theoretical background to processes and how they impact upon order processing, operations layout and operational practices. Techniques for modelling, designing and improving business processes are given and the role of technology is explained.

Section 3   Managing

This section explains the tools and techniques which ensure an operation, once up and running, will continue to operate smoothly and efficiently on a day-to-day basis:

Chapter 7 discusses the concepts of capacity and how an organization deals with constraints on what it can produce. It discusses the nature of capacity and how it can be matched with varying or unpredictable demand. Methods of forecasting are considered and the chapter evaluates strategies for services and queuing techniques.

Chapter 8 focuses on issues that operations managers need to consider when managing supply chains and supply relationships, and looks at various strategies to balance agility and efficiency in supply relationships and supply chain management of services and products. It is crucial for the managers to have an overview of the activities and processes that take place when goods and services are produced, from the suppliers to the final customers. As the goal of all companies is to ensure that their customers are satisfied, it is important that the flow of goods and services take place as smoothly as possible in the supply network.

Chapter 9 extends the ideas of the supply chain and looks at how to manage the flow of materials in the internal part of the operation. Today this is largely achieved using highly computerized and integrated systems under the heading Enterprise Resource Planning (ERP).

Chapter 10 examines the contribution of lean techniques to the operational system and how they can help develop highly responsive dependent demand systems, which essentially respond to variations in demand. So we can define a lean system as a highly efficient process which produces products and services in the desired quantities, exactly when they are needed. It also discusses the limitations of the lean approach and so allows a more realistic assessment of what can be applied by managers in the real world.

Chapter 11 introduces project management and deals with a unique set of problems facing those organizations which instead of repeating the same operations each day, find themselves undertaking just one activity before moving onto something completely different. In order to manage projects effectively, project managers rely on administrative skills to ensure the time, cost and performance criteria of the project are met and also teamwork and leadership. It moves away from just focusing on the tools of project management and allows the reader to adopt frameworks and learn the organizational and leadership elements of project management.

Section 4   Improving

No operation can succeed by standing still. A key feature of operations management is the need to continually adapt to changing market conditions while improving performance and enhancing the competitiveness of the firm – this section deals with the issues that arise due to these requirements:

Chapter 12 introduces performance management as a process and a tool for decision making and action taking specifically related to the identification and achievement of quantifiable goals, from corporate to individual. It demonstrates how operations management links to corporate strategy delivery. It illustrates how suitable measures and systems are created, and how they can be used effectively to engender performance improvement.

Chapter 13 introduces some key concepts of quality management and illustrates why quality performance is important and a central issue for all organizations. It illustrates why quality is becoming more challenging to manage as the demands from customers and the environment become more complex. Companies seek to incorporate all aspects of quality into the products and services they offer, and in doing so; they rely on quality management tools so they can monitor, control and improve the operational processes. This chapter also investigates the various approaches and tools used in quality management, performance and improvement, and in doing so provides a comprehensive introduction to nominal distribution and application of SPC charts.

Chapter 14 is a summary chapter that brings together the important themes in the book – which are corporate social responsibility (CSR), business integration and globalization. This chapter investigates these themes more comprehensively before discussing their future impact on careers and the profession of operations management.

About the Authors

Dr Steve Paton, University of Strathclyde

Steve began his career as an engineer in the Aerospace industry before progressing through various Operations and Project Management roles until reaching executive level within the Defence industry. Steve has an MBA from Glasgow University and on gaining his PhD in the area of knowledge workers and the labour process from the University of Strathclyde; he entered academia and now works in the Strathclyde University, Department of Management where he teaches in the areas of Operations and Project Management on a range of courses including MBA. Steve's main focus at present is in executive education and he manages a portfolio of corporate programmes for the university. He has published in journals including the *International Journal of Project Management*, *Journal of General Management* and *Journal of Knowledge Management* and is also co-author of *Management: An Introduction* by David Boddy published by Prentice Hall.

His current research interests include the management of intellectual labour, the profession of project management and high-value operations.

Contact: steve.paton©strath.ac.uk

Dr Ben Clegg, Aston Business School

Ben has over 20 years experience in operations management. He holds a BSc (Hons.) in Management Science from Loughborough University, a PhD in Systems Engineering from De Montfort University and is a Chartered Engineer. He is a member of the Institute of Engineering and Technology (IET) and the Higher Education Academy (HEA) and is an active participant in the European Operations Management Association (EurOMA) and the Production and Operations Management Society (POMS). Ben joined Aston Business School in 2003 and previously taught at the University of Central England, EM Lyon Business School in France and was a visiting scholar at Stanford University's Centre for Integrated Facilities Engineering, USA. Prior to entering academia Ben undertook a university sponsorship and graduate apprenticeship with GEC in operations and project management, worked as a practising manager in both the private and public sector and worked for a university start-up company. As well as teaching, Ben regularly consults and trains others in operations management and has won awards for his teaching and research.

Dr Clegg has contributed towards many books and has published in leading journals such as the *International Journal of Operations and Production Management*, *International Journal of Production Research*, *International Journal of Production Economics* and the *IEEE Systems, Management and Cybernetics*. He reviews for the *International Journal of Productivity and Performance Measurement*, the *Journal of Manufacturing Technology Management* and the Information Resource Management Association. His latest book is *Sustainable Supplier Management in the Automobile Industry* and he has also produced a government sponsored report, *The Ten Myths of Manufacturing*. Ben's interests include process improvement, strategic thinking for operations management and improvement methodologies.

Contact: b.t.clegg@aston.co.uk

Dr Juliana Hsuan, Copenhagen Business School

Juliana is an Associate Professor of Operations Management at the Copenhagen Business School (CBS), Denmark. She obtained her PhD in operations management from CBS and Licentiate of Science degree in logistics from the Helsinki School of Economics, Finland. She worked as an automotive electrical design engineer and executive trainee (with Motorola in the USA) before joining academia. She serves as an officer for INFORMS (Institute for Operations Research and the Management Sciences) — Technology Management Section, as a member of the board of EurOMA (European Operations Management Association), and as a faculty member of CEMS (Community of European Management Schools and International Companies) — Logistics Group. Her research has been published in well respected journals such as *Decision Sciences, Journal of Product Innovation Management, IEEE Transactions on Engineering Management, Production Planning & Control, Technovation, R&D Management* and *Supply Chain Management: An International Journal,* among others. Her teaching and research interests include product and service design, supply chain management, modularization strategies, and portfolio management of R&D projects.

Contact: jh.om@cbs.dk

Dr Alan Pilkington, Royal Holloway

Alan Pilkington is a Senior Lecturer in Operations and Technology Management at the School of Management, Royal Holloway, University of London. He holds a B.Eng. (Hons.) degree in Engineering from Leicester Polytechnic University and a PhD in Manufacturing Strategy from Aston University. Prior to his time in academia, he spent six years as a manager for a UK automobile producer working on introducing new manufacturing systems and on joint venture projects with Japanese car makers.

Dr Pilkington is Chair of the IEEE Technology Management Society, a Senior Member of the IEEE, and member of the IET, European Operations Management Association, and Production and Operations Management Society. He has published many articles in the *Journal of Operations Management, California Management Review; Technovation;* and *International Journal of Operations and Production Management.* His most recent book, *Transforming Rover: Renewal against the Odds, 1981–1994,* looks at the rise and decline of the UK car industry. His current research involves patent analysis techniques to explore inventor and technology networks in the fuel cell industry; analysing bibliometric data to define emerging research streams; and the adoption of process improvement methodologies for strategic advantage.

Contact: a.pilkington@rhul.ac.uk

Guided Tour

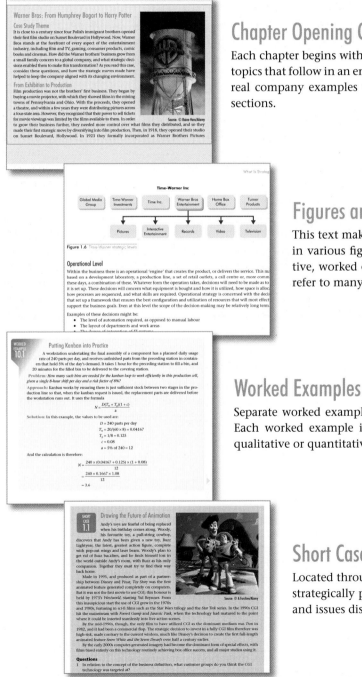

Chapter Opening Case Studies

Each chapter begins with an opening case study introducing the key topics that follow in an engaging way for students. In many instances, real company examples will be discussed and highlighted in these sections.

Figures and Tables

This text makes extensive use of data, and presents them in various figures and tables. Explanations in the narrative, worked examples and end-of-chapter problems will refer to many of these exhibits.

Worked Examples

Separate worked examples are integrated throughout the chapters. Each worked example illustrates an intuitive way to solve either qualitative or quantitative problems in a step-by-step format.

Short Case Studies

Located throughout the chapters are short case examples strategically placed to demonstrate how the key theories and issues discussed translate into the real world.

CRITICAL PERSPECTIVE

Innovation out of Control

The early life of the bicycle, in the development of large-penny-farthing, took a brief but relatively harmless evolution we have not been as lucky: too much innovation has someti impacts on our society. Many high-profile innovations have reached mar as a result of poor process control. One of the most prolific innovators in people have never heard of. Thomas Midgley Jr (1889–1944) was an Ar turned chemist. It could be said that Midgley has had more impact o other single organism in Earth's history. Midgley held over 100 patents, being chlorofluorocarbons (CFCs), the ozone-layer-depleting chemicals th aerosols. As if this gigantic mis-step was not enough, and with an astonishi he also developed the tetra-ethyl lead (TEL) additive to gasoline, which fumes. He was lauded at the time for his discoveries, but today his legacy considering the serious negative environmental impacts of these innovatio rate social responsibility has increased in profile, and some companies regar from history should highlight how important it is to behave responsibly endeavour.

The problems that recently Enron wo

Critical Perspective Boxes

These separate sections are distributed throughout the text to demonstrate an alternative theoretical perspective, to encourage and promote critical thinking.

Contemporary Thinking: Dynamic Capabilities

The resource-based view (RBV) that we have been discussing assumes that be sustained over time. Indeed, the whole concept of sustainable competiti of the market (Locket, 2009).

The RBV and competence literature therefore does not really address the current resources can be refreshed or future resources created to meet the a characteristic of most markets, and – it could be argued – is becoming increasingly competitive. If long-term market equilibrium does exists at markets such as the whisky industry, or to luxury markets such as jewellery that change is slow to happen. For most companies, however, this benign s resources and competitive advantage are critical concerns for managers.

Teece and Pisano (1994) and Teece *et al.* (1997) were the first to move beyo lished RBV when they proposed that it couldn't explain how some firms timely and rapid reaction to changing market conditions. They coined the te **capability** to describe a firm's ability to integrate, build and reconfigure c to address rapidly changing environments. A dynamic capability is not a r lem-solving event in spontaneous response to a stimulus; it is intentional,

probably incremental, and so is less risky to implement, and less costly to pacts upon resources low-risk ventures, it may not yield a large return. If we need to revise our stand totally new markets, then we can consider the innovation as radical.

The story of the bicycle indicates that, after a few early, **radical innovat mental innovation** has taken over, and has produced a large number o improvements.

It could be argued that, these days, most innovation is incremental. In serv it may be doing something a little differently, and a little better. In physica may be a small improvement in performance, or a small increase in functio

Innovations can be radical or incremental in each of the four Ps, as indicat must consider each innovation in these terms if we are to understand its fu

Contemporary Thinking Sections

These sections of text introduce and bring to the fore the latest academic thinking on a particular topic.

ⓘ **Stop and Think**

1 We are surrounded by so-called innovative products. Consider everyda mobile phone. Use Table 3.2 to try to identify the radical innovations th and the incremental innovations that matured the product to its current

Stop and Think Questions

Students are invited at regular intervals to 'stop and think' about a particular concept or issue through these reflective questions, encouraging them to apply their own ideas and analysis, thus promoting critical thinking and reinforcing concepts.

viduals. Organizations facing high levels of uncertainty in their markets and to seek to develop their own internal resources, and look for low-risk proje (e.g. hospitals often have their own back-up power plants to ensure that th electricity). However, such risk aversion usually means more expense, and s

The key point is that all the above assumptions affect transaction costs. If when an organization's overall transaction costs with external organization transaction costs, it will often grow. This is because it is cheaper and easier Conversely, if internal transaction costs are higher than external transactior benefit from downsizing or outsourcing its operations, because it is cheape organization to perform these activities.

TCE is often criticized for:

• Failing to explain clearly situations when suppliers should collaborat relationships
• Focusing too much on cost minimization rather than on value maxi

Resource-based View

As explained in Chapter 1, the *resource-based view* (RBV) traditionally focuses organization. We also saw how the traditional RBV has, more recently, been ifferent organizations

The Key Point is....

These short summary statements highlight and reinforce the key aspects that students should have understood, following a particular text section.

Source: 2007 Getty Images

passenger ew market of longer- e meeting ntal regu- the plane passenger- head with ial aircraft o Jet. any EADS is double- ane – which can carry up to 853 people. In contrast, their main ed to invest in mid-sized passenger jets that are faster, cheaper

art of the project until operators got their first planes. Pre-orders ge project (estimated at €11 billion) in order to start generating nt venture with Airbus to ensure that their planes were designed

the design and manufacturing process. For instance, Rolls-Royce

Key Theme Icons

Located throughout the text in the margins', these icons highlight the important trends and themes in operations. *Business Integration* icons highlight the cross-functional areas of business operations. *Globalization* icons indicate passages that relate to the nature of international/global operations, or where globalization is affecting business. *Corporate Social Responsibility (CSR)* icons highlight key sections that relate operations management to this increasingly important topic.

Discussion Questions

1 Corporate strategy is normally formulated at the top of the organization, but who do you think needs to be involved with formulating operations strategy, and what contribution do they each bring?

2 In relation to the external value matrix, reflect on how the consideration of these factors may affect achievement of the prime operations objective of efficiency.

3 Apply the operations strategy generation process to a charity. Consider who the customers and the competitors are, and discuss how an understanding of them would influence the charity's operation.

4 Consider the concept of trade-offs. What trade-offs might a police force have to think about when planning its operational activity?

5 Discuss the product life cycle model. Can you think of a product that does not follow these phases?

Visit the Online Learning Centre at
www.mcgraw-hill.co.uk/textbooks/paton for a range of resources to
support your learning.

Further Reading

Buttle, F. (1996) 'Servqual: review, critique, research agenda', *European Journal of Marketing*, **30**(1), 8–32.

Hayes, R., Pisano, G., Upton, D. and Wheelwright, S.C. (2005) *Operations Strategy and Technology: Pursuing the Competitive Edge*, Wiley, Hoboken, NJ.

Parasuraman, A., Zeithaml, V. and Berry, L. (1994) 'Reassessment of expectations as a comparison standard in measuring service quality: implications for future research', *Journal of Marketing*, **58**(1), 111–124.

References

Hayes, R.H. and Wheelwright, S.C. (1988) *Restoring Our Competitive Edge: Competing through Manufacturing*, Wiley, New York.

Hill, T. (1993) *Manufacturing Strategy: Text and Cases*, Macmillan.

Johnston, R. (1995) 'The determinants of service quality: satisfaction and dissatisfaction', *International Journal of Service*

End of Chapter Questions

These are separated into three assessment sections: Review Questions, Discussion Questions and Problem Questions. Each section enables either independent and/or group learning with plentiful opportunities to practise concepts and ensure understanding of key topics; and, where relevant, reinforce qualitative or quantitative material and methods.

The location decision for any operation is therefore determined by the relative strengths demand-side factors.

Centre of gravity method: approach that uses the physical analogy of a 'balancing point' to determine the geographical location of an operation relative to others that it has a direct relationship with.

Weighted score technique: technique for comparing the attractiveness of alternative operational locations that allocates a weighted score to each relevant factor in the decision.

Operations managers need to draw on their skills and experience decisions, although there are some basic quantitative steps that ca process. We describe two here: the **centre of gravity method**, w transportation-based decisions, and the **weighted score techniq** to assess wider managerial factors in an outsourcing decision.

Centre of Gravity Method

Minimizing transportation costs for an operation is usually an i factor in locating an operation. The **centre of gravity method** ca mize these costs. It is based on the idea that all possible locatio assigned a numeric value, based on the sum of all transportation location. The best location is the one that minimizes the overall

All locations are represented on a scale map that has square gridlines on it, rather like a st centre of gravity of the map is found, and this represents the coordinates of the lowest-c The x and y coordinates of this location are calculated using the following formulae:

$$x = \frac{\sum x_i V_i}{\sum V_i}$$

$$y = \frac{\sum y_i V_i}{\sum V_i}$$

where x_i is the x coordinate of the source or destination i, y_i is the y coordinate of the sour

Key Terms

These are highlighted in boldface throughout the chapters, and are defined in the margin notes for easy reference.

Summary

In this chapter we have provided some tools that can be used to explore the strategic landscape at the corporate level. The understanding gained can then be used to set the context within which the operational engine that drives the business can be placed. We have shown that the strategic landscape that operations managers must consider consists of both the market environment within which their organization exists and the strategic direction that is set by the top level of the organization. This strategic direction may simply be a set of financial objectives, or it may be more elaborately described by mission statements and strategic plans.

Strategy has been presented from two viewpoints: the market-based view, which suggests that an organization should align itself with market need, and the resource-based view, which suggests that the organization should understand what it is good at, and develop competencies in these areas that will allow it to gain a competitive advantage. The strategy process is therefore as follows:

1 Understand what your business is – business definition model.

2 From the MBV:
  (a) Investigate your overall market environment – PESTEL
  (b) Define your immediate competitive position – Porter's Five Forces
  (c) Understand what your customer wants – value theory.

3 From the RBV:
  (a) Define what you need to be good at to exist in the market – core competencies
  (b) Leverage your competencies to create a competitive advantage – distinctive competencies.

4 Analyse the nature of your competitive advantage to understand how sustainable it is, and therefore how your competence must change to maintain advantage – dynamic capabilities.

Although we have argued that a balanced approach to strategy must take into consideration aspects of both the MBV and the RBV, we have concentrated on the RBV, as this is the 'wrapper' within which the operations strategy is packaged.

The next chapter will continue the RBV journey by looking more closely at what can be done at the more detailed operational level to shape and configure activity, and so leverage operational competencies to achieve competitive advant

Summary

This section briefly reviews and reinforces the main topics covered in each chapter, to ensure students have acquired a solid understanding of the key topics.

Key Theories

The key theories discussed in this chapter were:

- **The model of operations contribution** – the four stages of performance that operations can achieve in support of corporate strategy, which are defined as internally neutral, externally neutral, internally supportive, and externally supportive.

- **The five dimensions of service quality** – those aspects that customers value and must be delivered. These are tangibles (including price, functionality and performance, variety and customization, and quality), responsiveness, reliability, assurance, and empathy.

- **Order-winning and order-qualifying criteria** – those features that customers see as the key reasons to buy or not to buy a product or service.

- **Performance profiling and prioritizing** – the process of measuring the performance of the operation against that of the competition to identify what improvements must be carried out to create an advantage.

- **Operational trade-offs** – the prioritizing of important performance objectives over those that are less important.

- **The product life cycle** – the five stages that a product will pass through from the point of introduction to the point of withdrawal. These are birth, growth, maturity, decline, and withdrawal. Each stage requires a change of emphasis in operations strategy.

- **Value propositions** – those generic operations strategies that help focus the process of strategy-making to create competence in specific areas. The six propositions introduced are innovators, brand managers, price minimizers, simplifiers, technological integrators and socializers.

Suggested Answers to Stop and Think Questions

1 **Corporate strategy:** It could be argued that no corporate strategy should be devised without a good understanding of the core operational competencies of the business, and how well they are

Key Theories and Equations

These sections briefly recap and summarize the key theories and equations covered in the chapter, to aid revision and student learning.

Technology to Enhance Learning and Teaching

Visit www.mcgraw-hill.co.uk/textbooks/paton

Lecturer support – Helping you to help your students

In addition to the assignments, questions, problems and activities McGraw-Hill provides within Connect, we also offer a host of resources to support your teaching.

- **Faster course preparation** – time-saving support for your module
- **High-calibre content to support your students** – resources written by your academic peers, who understand your need for rigorous and reliable content
- **Flexibility** – edit, adapt or repurpose; test in Connect or test through EZ Test. The choice is yours.

The materials created specifically for lecturers adopting this textbook include:

- *PowerPoint presentations to use in your lecture presentations*
- *Image library of artwork from the textbook*
- *Solutions manual providing answers to the problems in the textbook*
- *Case Notes with guide answers to case questions, written to help support your students in understanding and analyzing the cases in the textbook*
- *Additional case studies – longer length cases not found in the textbook, accompanied by questions and teaching notes*
- *Additional exam style questions*
- *Exclusive videos created for the textbook to engage, illuminate and educate your students*
- *Test Bank*

To request your password to access these resources, contact your McGraw-Hill representative or visit:

www.mcgraw-hill.co.uk/textbooks/paton

EZ TEST ONLINE

Test Bank available in McGraw-Hill EZ Test Online

A test bank of hundreds of questions is available to lecturers adopting this book for their module. For flexibility, this is available for adopters of this book to use through Connect or through the EZ Test online website. For each chapter you will find:

- A range of multiple choice, true or false, short answer or essay questions
- Questions identified by chapter, type and difficulty to help you to select questions that best suit your needs

McGraw-Hill EZ Test Online is:

- **Accessible** anywhere with an internet connection – your unique login provides you access to all your tests and material in any location
- **Simple** to set up and easy to use
- **Flexible**, offering a choice from question banks associated with your adopted textbook or allowing you to create your own questions
- **Comprehensive**, with access to hundreds of banks and thousands of questions created for other McGraw-Hill titles
- **Compatible** with Blackboard and other course management systems
- **Time-saving-** students' tests can be immediately marked and results and feedback delivered directly to your students to help them to monitor their progress.

To register for this FREE resource, visit www.eztestonline.com

Connect

 Want an online, **searchable version** of your textbook?

Wish your textbook could be **available online** while you're doing your assignments?

 ### Connect™ Plus Operations Management eBook

If you choose to use *Connect™ Plus Operations management eBook*, you have an affordable and searchable online version of your book integrated with your other online tools.

Connect™ Plus Operations Management eBook offers features like:

- Topic search
- Direct links from assignments
- Adjustable text size
- Jump to page number
- Print by section

 Want to get more **value** from your textbook purchase?

Think learning operations management should be a bit more **interesting**?

Check out the STUDENT RESOURCES section under the *Connect™* Library tab.

Here you'll find a wealth of resources designed to help you achieve your goals in the course. Every student has different needs, so explore the STUDENT RESOURCES to find the materials best suited to you.

connect™

OPERATIONS MANAGEMENT

STUDENTS...

Want to get **better grades**? *(Who doesn't?)*

Prefer to do your **homework online**? *(After all, you are online anyway...)*

Need **a better way** to **study** before the big test?
(A little peace of mind is a good thing...)

 With **McGraw-Hill's** *Connect™ Plus Operations Management,*

STUDENTS GET:

- **Easy online access** to homework, tests, and quizzes assigned by your instructor.

- **Immediate feedback** on how you're doing. (No more wishing you could call your instructor at 1 a.m.)

- **Quick access** to lectures, practice materials, eBook, and more. (All the material you need to be successful is right at your fingertips.)

- A Self-Quiz and Study tool that **assesses your knowledge** and **recommends** specific readings, supplemental study materials, and additional practice work.*

*Available with select McGraw-Hill titles.

Less managing. More teaching. Greater learning.

INSTRUCTORS...

Would you like your **students** to show up for class **more prepared**?
(Let's face it, class is much more fun if everyone is engaged and prepared...)

Want an **easy way to assign** homework online and track student **progress**?
(Less time grading means more time teaching...)

Want an **instant view** of student or class performance? *(No more wondering if students understand...)*

Need to **collect data and generate reports** required for administration or accreditation? *(Say goodbye to manually tracking student learning outcomes...)*

Want to **record and post your lectures** for students to view online?

With **McGraw-Hill's** *Connect™ Plus Operations Management,*

INSTRUCTORS GET:

* Simple **assignment management**, allowing you to spend more time teaching.

* **Auto-graded** assignments, quizzes, and tests.

* **Detailed Visual Reporting** where student and section results can be viewed and analyzed.

* Sophisticated **online testing** capability.

* A **filtering and reporting** function that allows you to easily assign and report on materials that are correlated to learning outcomes, topic and level, of difficulty.

* An easy-to-use **lecture capture** tool.

* The option to **upload course documents** for student access.

Custom Publishing Solutions: Let us help make our **content** your **solution**

At McGraw-Hill Education our aim is to help lecturers to find the most suitable content for their needs delivered to their students in the most appropriate way. Our **custom publishing solutions** offer the ideal combination of content delivered in the way which best suits lecturer and students.

Our custom publishing programme offers lecturers the opportunity to select just the chapters or sections of material they wish to deliver to their students from a database called CREATE™ at www.mcgrawhillcreate.com

CREATE™ contains over two million pages of content from:

- Textbooks
- Professional books
- Case books – Harvard Articles, Insead, Ivey, Darden, Thunderbird and Business Week
- Taking Sides – debate materials

across the following imprints:

- McGraw-Hill Education
- Open University Press
- Harvard Business Publishing
- US and European material

There is also the option to include additional material authored by lecturers in the custom product – this does not necessarily have to be in English.

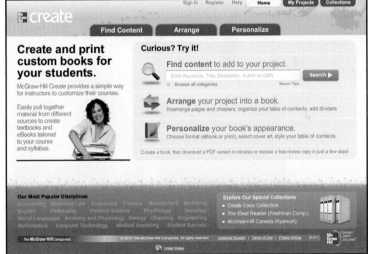

We will take care of everything from start to finish in the process of developing and delivering a custom product to ensure that lecturers and students receive exactly the material needed in the most suitable way.

With a **Custom Publishing Solution**, students enjoy the best selection of material deemed to be the most suitable for learning everything they need for their courses – something of real value to support their learning. Teachers are able to use exactly the material they want, in the way they want, to support their teaching on the course.

Please contact your local McGraw-Hill representative with any questions or alternatively contact Warren Eels e: warren_eels@mcgraw-hill.com.

Make the Grade!

Acknowledgements

We hope you enjoy this book, and are inspired to go on to become the great strategic and operations managers of the future. There are a number of individuals we must acknowledge who contributed at various stages in one way or another to this textbook.

First we should mention those who helped us from the initial planning stages right through to the development and final publication of the book: Rachel Gear, Leiah Batchelor, Leonie Sloman, Jennifer Yendell and all those others working behind the scenes at McGraw-Hill for helping to develop this book. We'd like to extend our thanks to Briony Boydell (Portsmouth University) and Olga Matthias (University of Bradford), who contributed to the textbook by providing chapter content, for chapters 7 and 12 respectively; as well as Tom Mullen (University of Strathclyde) for providing suggestions and content to include. Other people who have also helped shape the book include: William Ho, Prasanta Dey and Tim Baines (Aston Business School); Jill MacBryde (Strathclyde Business School); and Peter Ball (Cranfield University).

The authors and publishers would like to pay special thanks to all those who participated at various stages in the text's development, be it by completing one of our surveys, reviewing chapters, attending our focus group or participating in our video series; each has made a positive contribution to the final product:

Dotun Adebanjo, University of Liverpool
Malcolm Afferson, University of Bradford
Eamonn Ambrose, University College Dublin
Amr Arisha, Dublin Institute of Technology
Gilbert Aryee, Cardiff University
Ozlem Bak, University of Greenwich
S. Balabani, King's College London
James Baldwin, University of Sheffield
P. Barbonis, Radboud University Nijmegen
Nick Barnett, University of Westminster
Anu Bask, Aalto University
Nicola Bateman, Loughborough University
Jens Bengtsson, Norwegian School of Economics and Business Administration
John Bicheno, Cardiff Business School
Heidi Bjorstad, Bergen University College
Thorsten Blecker, Hamburg University of Technology
Jürgen Bode, International School of Management
Lennart Bogg, Malardalen University
Tommy Bood, Karlstad University
Owen Brady, Institute of Technology, Carlow
Louis Brennan, Trinity College Dublin
Naomi Brookes, Aston University
Martin Butler, University of Stellenbosch

Peter Byrne, Dublin City University
Declan Carew, Dublin City University
Luc Chalmet, Ghent University
Alfred Chinta, University of Bolton
Mary Dempsey, NUI, Galway
Stephen Disney, Cardiff University
Alexander Douglas, Liverpool John Moores University
Veronica Earle, University of Hertfordshire
Roy Edwards, Staffordshire University
Helgi Gestsson, University of Akureyri
Stein Erik Grønland, Norwegian School of Management
Jane Guinery, University of Nottingham
Mark Hall, Bristol University
Graham Heaslip, Institute of Technology, Carlow
Alex Hiller, Nottingham Trent University
William Ho, Aston University
Julie Hodges, Durham University
Ian Holden, University of Lincoln
Jeffery Holden, University of Westminster
Bill Hollins, University of Westminster
Donal Hughes, University College Dublin
Ola Hultkrantz, Chalmers University of Technology
Stanley Hutchinson, Saxion University
Alessio Ishizaka, University of Portsmouth

Hing Kai Chan, University of East Anglia
Christer Karlsson, Copenhagen Business School
Phil Kelly, Liverpool John Moores University
Bruce Kibler, Cologne Business School
Yearnmin Kim, University of Ulsan, Korea
Katri Karjalainen, Manchester Business School
Ronald Klingebiel, Anglia Ruskin University
Gyöngyi Kovács, Hanken School of Economics
John Lamb, University of Aberdeen
Björn Lantz, University of Gothenburg
Benn Lawson, Queen's University Belfast
Reda Lebcir, University of Hertfordshire
Moren Levesque, York University
Kevin Maher, Institute of Technology Tralee
Morag Malins, University of Warwick
Patmond Mbeke, University of KwaZulu Natal
Thomas McNamara, Rennes School of Business
Anne-Marie McTavish, Coventry University
Eðvald Möller, University of Iceland
Jan Mouritesen, Copenhagen Business School
Michael Nelson, University College Dublin
Michael O'Mahony, Cork Institute of Technology
Leonard O'Sullivan, Limerick University
Jonathan Owens, University of Lincoln
Hosein Piranfar, University of East London
Garry Priddis, University of Brighton
Rosalind Rae, Robert Gordon University
Vijayender Reddy, Nyenrode Business University
Amanda Relph, University of Hertfordshire
James Rowell, University of Buckingham

Gwenny Ruël, University of Groningen
George Ruthven, Stellenbosch University
Anders Segerstedt, Luleå University of Technology
Chris Seow, University of East London
Karin Smidt-Destombes, Vrije Universiteit A'Dam
James Smith, Coventry University
Ebrahim Soltani, University of Kent
Jan Stentoft Arlbjørn, University of Southern Denmark
Mark Stevenson, Lancaster University
Mikko Tarkkala, Helsinki School of Economics
Brian Terry, Richmond University
Rudd Teunter, Lancaster University
Anders Thorstenson, University of Aarhus
Markku Tinnilä, Alto University
Sandra Transchel, University of Mannheim
Norbet Trautmann, University of Bern
Joris Van de Klundert, Maastricht University
Karl Van der Merwe, Nelson Mandela Metropolitian University
N. Van der Zee, NHL University
Allard Van Riel, Radboud University Nijmegen
V. Venugopal, Nyenrode Business University
Chris Voss, London Business School
Stephen Wagner, Otto Beisheim School of Management
Nigel Wild, University of Greenwich
Biao Yang, University of York
Ying Yang, University of Aberystwyth
Tie Xu, University of Sunderland
Linda Zhang, University of Groningen

We would also like to thank the following contributors for the material that they have provided for this textbook and its accompanying resources:

Briony Boydell, University of Portsmouth
Garry Copeland, British Airways
Curt Corneliussen, J. Lauritzen
Martijn De Lange, TNT Post UK
Bang Gun Je, STX
Graham Jones, Farnborough International Ltd
Y.S. Kim, Hyndai Heavy industries Co., Ltd
Olga Matthias, University of Bradford
Tom Mullen, University of Strathclyde

Dave Piper, Lightning Source UK Ltd
Steffen Ring, Motorola
James Rowell, University of Buckingham
Soroosh Saghiri, Kingston University
Jan Sjulstok, J. Lauritzen
Steve Sutton, Intel PLC
Carl Wegeberg, J. Lauritzen
Choi Yeon Woo, Hyndai Heavy Industries Co., Ltd
Kim Young Jum, Hyndai Heavy Industries Co., Ltd

We would also like to thank the following students for their feedback and help in developing this book:

Intikhab Akhtar, Royal Holloway, University of London
Alexandra Bosova, Aston University

Gabriela Krasteva, Aston University
Gabriela Veselinova, Aston University

Every effort has been made to trace and acknowledge ownership of copyright, and to clear permission for material reproduced in this book. The publishers will be pleased to make suitable arrangements to clear permission with any copyright holders whom it has not been possible to contact.

Introduction

Learning Outcomes

After reading this chapter you should be able to:

- Define the term 'operations management'
- Describe the conversion process model of operations management
- Use the conversion process to analyse the operations of organizations
- Discuss the impact of tangible and intangible products on the conversion process
- Discuss the role of the operations manager
- Reflect on the practice of operations management

Heathrow Terminal 5: A Turbulent Take-off

Case Study Theme

Terminal 5 was officially opened on 14 March 2008, following thirteen years of planning, seven years of construction, months of trials involving thousands of members of the public, and four public enquiries into poor performance during the build project. The terminal handled its first flight with the landing of British Airways flight BA026 from Hong Kong at 4:50am on 27 March 2008. Barely hours after this initial flight Terminal 5 had become one of the country's biggest news stories. Within three days British Airways been forced to cancel 208 flights, and had lost more bags than any other airline. By the end of the first week BA was facing a bill for £25 million in costs caused by disruption.

Source: © Adapt Design and Advertising / iStock

As you read this case study, think about the operational problems that combined to create this crisis, and how much responsibility the operations management of the airport should take for these events.

One Man's Experience

Standing in Edinburgh Airport departure lounge one fine, spring morning, on route to Lyon via London, Karl looked up at the information screen as delays began to appear against the BA flights bound for Heathrow. Soon every flight indicated a delay. In a short while, notices of delays were replaced by notices of cancellations. Not long after that, notices of cancellation were replaced by . . . well . . . notices of nothing at all. Business travellers with deadlines to meet began to show signs of unease, while tourists with families

1

became downright annoyed. More significantly, however, members of staff were looking positively confused. With no information forthcoming, questions were asked, and these questions were met with shrugs and blank faces. No news was coming out of Terminal 5 – indeed, nothing at all was coming out of Terminal 5. With no flights entering or leaving, the entire system of airline travel was quickly breaking down as the knock-on effects of aircraft not being where they should have been were felt across the country.

Finally, after the eternity of time that exists only while waiting for delayed flights in departure lounges, an announcement was made. Apparently there were de-icing problems at Heathrow, problems that seemed to exist despite the pleasant, spring morning, and problems that seemed to be affecting the aircraft at Terminal 5 more severely than any of the other terminals. A freak microclimate perhaps? A localized blizzard? An alien invasion? – or perhaps something rather more mundane and operational.

After many hours of inactivity, flights to Terminal 5 began to move again, slowly and randomly; information on timing was frequently, wrong and communication was still sporadic and contradictory.

Karl finally secured himself passage on one of the few outgoing planes. Once Karl was on board, the captain's welcome was unusual, in that it contained much non-standard information. His theme seemed to be the inadequacies of the operational performance of Terminal 5, and how embarrassed he was personally about this. Most importantly, however, it was to be understood that it was not his fault (nor the fault of his crew), that there was nothing he could do about it, and that, despite this, passengers should have a pleasant flight, and should enjoy the extensive choice of fine beverages and tasty pastries on offer. This announcement also solved the Terminal 5 icing mystery: it turned out that, although there had been a small amount of ice, a fully operational process for de-icing stationary aircraft would have coped easily with this condition. Terminal 5, it seemed, wasn't furnished with such a working process at this point.

On finally arriving at Terminal 5 extremely late, but miraculously still on the same day, Karl was confronted by a brand new and impressive building that was extremely busy, yet totally devoid of any useful activity. Numerous passengers were wandering around aimlessly with vacant looks; some were camping on floors; others were standing hopefully in vast queue's that snaked back and forth as far as the eye could see. Few members of staff were available (or even visible), and those who were available seemed trained specifically to say 'I am very sorry, but we have no information at this time.' Soon the loudspeaker system began to call for anyone without a ticket or boarding pass to: 'Please clear the building immediately!' Civilization was apparently beginning to break down.

Karl was an experienced traveller. He realized that since leaving Edinburgh his situation had not improved. He had been stuck 4 miles from home in a functioning terminal, now he was stuck 400 miles from home in a non-functioning one. He was not safely within the processes of a well-oiled, operational machine, as is normally the case at airports, but lost within the labyrinth of a vast and broken system.

As there was no information on any of the flight information boards, with a sinking feeling in his heart Karl approached a tired and lonely member of the airport staff, who was looking the worse for wear, having spent his shift repeatedly claiming to know nothing, and being continually lambasted for his efforts by irate, would-be travellers. Presenting a friendly face, Karl attempted to reason with this individual. The show of friendship was worth while, as Karl quickly ascertained that neither the manual nor the automated check-in systems were working. He was welcome to try the web-based check-in system, but unfortunately that wasn't working either. The functionality of these systems, it seemed, was largely irrelevant, as there were no flights leaving to be checked in for anyway. Obviously sensing in Karl a sympathetic soul, and desperate to unburden himself, the airline employee then volunteered that it was his first day on the job, and that he, like many other new employees, had been given minimal training (limited, it seemed, to that single, oft-repeated phrase). So even if the systems were working, few people knew how to operate them.

Offering thanks for this small piece of help, and stopping only to advise the member of staff that he was doing a good job, Karl parted company with the airport employee who offered one last piece of advice: 'Whatever you do, if you ever finally get onto a plane, don't under any circumstances check your baggage in!'

This advice Karl duly took – advice that was to prove strangely prophetic, and which would have been extremely useful to thousands of other passengers.

Introduction

Air travel is arguably one of the most complex operations in existence today. It is a service that utilizes the most complex technology and the highest-value assets; works to challenging and relentless schedules, 24 hours a day, 365 days of the year; spans the entire planet, regardless of political or environmental conditions; and is responsible for the lives of millions of customers.

Air travel includes activities that touch every area thought of as operations management.

- It is supported by a supply chain network that comprises many suppliers, including the aircraft manufacturers that supply the planes, the airport authorities that manage the infrastructure, and the travel companies that provide passengers.
- Its quality and safety standards must be of the highest order, to ensure fault-free operation of all parts of the process.
- The design of its processes is extremely challenging, with large numbers of passengers, multiple destinations, and complex security and legal constraints.
- The planning of capacity in this low-profit, highly competitive arena leaves little margin for error. An empty aircraft seat cannot be inventoried and resold, because the same seat on the next flight is a separate sale.

The story of Heathrow Terminal 5 is an extreme example of what can go wrong when operations management is poorly done. Many factors were to blame for the problems that occurred – badly trained staff, incomplete building work, poorly tested IT systems, and incomplete processes – but at the end of the day the blame was laid squarely at the door of the operations management team, as both the operations director and the customer services director subsequently lost their jobs.

Operations management was once the poor relation in managerial work, wiped with the oily rag of manufacturing and hidden in the shadow of other, more glamorous and highly paid roles, such as marketing, strategic management, finance and human resources. But now, with the application of operations management methods outside the arena of production, there has been a rise in the number of opportunities related to operations, and an accompanying increase in the value placed on operations skills and the kudos associated with being an operations manager. In addition, with the penetration of operations management into the service sector, operations managers can no longer lurk in the background, their mistakes hidden within the 'black box' of the production line. As the case study shows, good operations management is not only crucial to success in business, but is also highly visible.

The purpose of this chapter is threefold. First, to introduce the basic concepts and language that underpin operations management, and so create an understanding that will enable you, as a student of management, to 'think like an operations manager' within any industry sector. Second, to create the foundation for effective study of the material within the chapters to come. And last, and possibly most important, to stimulate your interest in what – we would argue – is becoming the most ubiquitous area of contemporary management.

What Is Operations Management?

Today's Management Challenges

The Matrix is a system, Neo. That system is our enemy. But when you're inside, you look around, what do you see? Businessmen, teachers, lawyers, carpenters – the very minds of the people we are trying to save . . . Many of them are so inured, so hopelessly dependent on the system, that they will fight to protect it.

Morphues to Neo, *The Matrix*

In making the statement above, Morpheus is attempting to open the mind of his student Neo to the true nature of life in *The Matrix*, and the shocking revelation that reality is a fabrication, a virtual world created to enslave the human race. The challenge Morpheus faces is that Neo, like the rest of humanity, is so familiar with the current situation that he cannot imagine another state of being.

Society in the 21st century exists in a similar way: the state of organization of our everyday lives is so pervasive that it is difficult for most people to conceive of a different way of existing. Our lives are lived in a state of systematization, from the moment we wake to the moment we go to sleep. When we leave our beds, we engage in personal processes for cleaning, dressing and feeding. When we leave our homes, we step into processes for transport and security. When we arrive at our places of work, we fit into processes for producing products or delivering services. We are never free of process. Our lives are continually 'managed' within the system that is our society.

Whereas the fictional Matrix is a system for exploiting and enslaving the human race, the processes and systems in our everyday lives exist (possibly) with the opposite purpose. They are there to make our lives easier – to enable us to be more efficient and productive. Transport systems get us to where we want to be, quickly and easily; health care systems keep us fit and well; security systems keep us safe from harm; and manufacturing systems produce goods that are reliable and affordable, and meet our needs.

Therefore, simplistically, it could be argued that the overall challenge we face as managers is to increase the systematization in society. This challenge lies squarely within the remit of operations management.

The Operations Challenge

Let's investigate this overall challenge in a bit more detail. Operations management can be defined as *the activity of managing the resources of the organization that deliver goods and services.*

The way to perform this activity is to implement systems and processes that are:
- *repeatable* – can be done over and over again
- *consistent* – produce the same result every time
- *reliable* – do not break down randomly.

The achievement of these three objectives in organizational systems has been the goal since the first factories were established, but these days the standard of performance required against each objective is driven mainly by the following factors.
- Increased competition in terms of cost and quality, due to:
  - The globalized world, with more companies operating in each market, pushing the boundaries of operational performance
  - Advances such as automation and information technology that constantly invent new ways of doing things, more cost-effectively and to a higher quality standard.
- Increased complexity due to:
  - Customer pull – the market demand for differentiated, higher-functionality products to fill every need, such as higher-capability mobile phones that carry features such as web access and satellite navigation
  - Technology push – science and engineering's ability to create more sophisticated products, such as intelligent fabric and microchips.
- Increased environmental regulation due to:
  - Increased focus on ethical issues, such as exploitation of labour in the developing world
  - Tightening environmental restrictions, such cutting pollution and reducing the emission of greenhouse gases
  - Growing legal constraints, such as employment law.

So it is not enough to have processes that are repeatable, consistent and reliable; they must also be efficient to be successful in the competitive arena in which they operate, and compliant with the restrictions in the overall environment. This means that they must produce the greatest output for the least input, while not breaking any laws or codes of practice. And the standard of performance achieved by this efficient system must be at least as good as that of the processes used by the competition, to gain a cost advantage.

The key point is that operations management is based on the belief that, to achieve efficiency and therefore advantage over the competition, you need to introduce and operate the most reliable, consistent and repeatable processes for utilizing organizational resources. These processes should be applied to all aspects of organizational activity.

Slicing Up the Profits

SHORT CASE

One of the original skills developed by early humans was hunting animals for food. In tandem with this came the skill of cutting up the catch into edible chunks. Part of the trick here was in producing as much food as possible from a single carcass, to sustain the tribe for as long as possible. Today much the same logic applies, but now the key driver towards an efficient process is not survival, but profit. As you read this case study, consider how little waste there is in modern food production processes.

Source: © Mike Dabell/iStock

The Sharp End of the Food Industry

In the meat industry, like every other, efficiency is measured by how much output is gained from a given input. In this case the output is the price that can be commanded for selling the cuts of meat, and the input costs are the cost of buying the carcass, the cost of the butcher's labour, and the overheads of running the facility. The main factors influencing this process are the speed of work, the skill of the worker, and the effectiveness of materials utilization.

The need for speed is obvious, as the quicker the activity is carried out, the higher the throughput will be, and the greater the number of units that are processed.

The skill of the butcher is critical: a highly skilled butcher will be more precise in his activity, resulting in less waste and a larger proportion of high-quality meat, which can be turned into more desirable cuts that can be sold for a premium price.

High materials utilization in this context means reducing to a minimum the parts of the carcass that cannot be sold. In the meat industry the process produces very little waste. What cannot be sold as steak will be sold as minced beef, what cannot be sold as minced beef will be sold as sausages, and what cannot be sold for human consumption will be sold as animal food.

The process for butchering animals has evolved over many centuries, with techniques, skills and tools being upgraded as technology and facilities have changed. Repeatability, consistency and reliability are key factors in the success of this industry. The process must be repeatable, as it must happen numerous times, over and over again; it must be consistent, in that it must result in the same quality of output each time an animal is processed; and it must be reliable, in that it must not break down. Failure to meet any of these objectives will result in reduced efficiency and therefore loss of profit.

What, once upon a time, saw groups of hunters huddled around a fire, with flint axes and crude knives, has turned into a multimillion-pound industry that is crucial to society, with a supply chain stretching from farm to high street, in a process that utilizes the latest technology, automation and management principles in the search for the most efficient and profitable process for converting meat to money.

Question

1 The process of producing fresh meat is a long one, beginning essentially with the birth of the animal. Think of the number of opportunities within this journey for the process to break down, by becoming inefficient or inconsistent.

The Conversion Process

The first step in achieving a process-based organization is to understand the overall work of the organization as a *conversion process* – so called because it represents the conversion of a specific set of input resources into the specific output (or set of outputs) that is the product.

Figure 1 represents a model of the conversion process. In its most basic form, a set of input resources – raw materials, people, information and money – enter a 'black box' representing the processes of the organization.

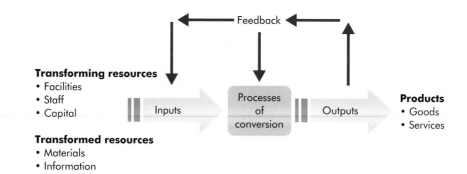

Figure 0.1 The conversion process

Transforming resources: facilities such as buildings, equipment and tools and process technology; all the staff involved in the conversion process; and the capital that is needed to buy materials, and pay for the facilities and staff.

Transformed resources: materials to be converted into products for sale, and information.

Here the organization converts these inputs to an output that is the product or service to be sold. These resources can be categorized into two types: **transforming resources** are the elements that carry out the conversion process, and **transformed resources** are the elements that are converted by the process to become the product.

Transforming resources are:
- *Facilities*: buildings, equipment and tools and process technology
- *Staff*: all the people involved in the conversion process working to complete conversion activities, operate machinery or maintain the equipment.
- *Capital*: needed to buy materials, and pay for the facilities and staff.

Transformed resources are:
- *Materials*, such as metal, wood and plastic, which can then become parts such as nuts and bolts, structures, or printed circuit boards, which can be built into the final product such as cars, buildings or computers. As the input materials move through the conversion process, their physical form will be changed in some way to form the eventual product.
- *Information*, such as design specifications, assembly instructions, scientific concepts or market intelligence. Information is useful in two ways in the conversion process: first, where it informs the process of conversion, for example in design specifications and diagrams, without which the product could not be built; and, second, where it is part of the product, and is sorted, recombined or repackaged to form different information. Accountants do this with financial information, which is converted from its raw form into published accounts, and journalists do this when news is reconfigured and packed into a newspaper or television format.

Figure 0.1 also shows a feedback system. This monitors the conversion process, and captures any deviations from process norms that may occur. Feedback is needed to ensure that the process performs the way it should, repeatably, reliably and consistently. As nothing is perfect, and things are subject to change over time, even the best processes must be constantly monitored and measured to ensure they do not deviate from their required norm.

Feedback broadly falls into two categories:
- Feedback that is *internal* to the conversion process. This ensures that the process produces exactly the same product, over and over again. This feedback is usually quantitative: for example, the number of units produced; the dimensions of the product, such as the weight of a chocolate bar – too high, and product is being given away; too low, and the customer is being short-changed; or oven temperature in a cooking process – too high and the food may be burned, too low and it may be raw.
- Feedback that is *external* to the conversion process. This can be either qualitative, such as how the customer enjoyed the product, or quantitative, such as what percentage of the market buys the product. This feedback can inform the design of the product: a poorly selling product, or one that generates a lot of complaints, may need to be modified to make it more successful.

Figure 0.2 illustrates the conversion process in terms of the manufacture of a motor car.

To understand this concept further we must put the 'black box' of the conversion process under the microscope. Figure 0.3 shows how the operation is actually made up of linked chains of conversion processes.

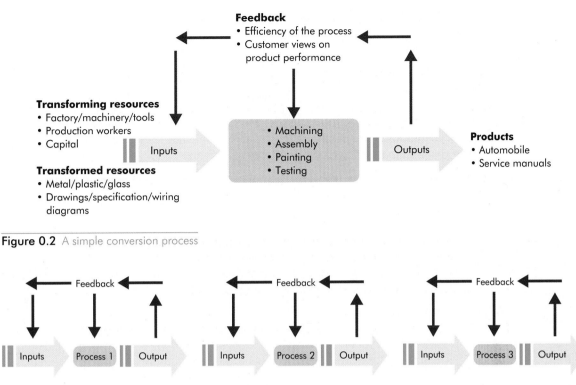

Figure 0.2 A simple conversion process

Figure 0.3 The conversion process expanded

We can view the conversion process as a series of processes, with the output of one process becoming the input of the next, and all working to produce the end goal that is the product to be sold. Of course, in most industries the overall process will comprise many parallel process chains, all converging to create the final product. It is critical to this idea to see the next stage of the process as a 'customer', because the output from one stage becomes the input to the next, and it must be correct, or the next stage cannot be performed properly.

As operations managers – regardless of the industry sector or product – we must see the work of the organization as a set of linked processes that take a set of inputs and reconfigure these into something that the organization can sell to the market.

When Is a Process Not a Process?

In simple terms, operations management argues that the utilization of robust processes will create the most efficient mode of business operation. This argument has been proved time and time again, as evidenced by everything from the production lines of car companies (first popularized by Henry Ford) to the customer and product management systems utilized in fast-food outlets such as McDonald's, or in the modern airport terminal.

As managers analyse their business, and attempt to implement greater systematization, the question that emerges is therefore: how much process is too much process? Put another way, which activities cannot be process based? There is no easy or universal answer to this, but fundamentally the answer must be based on the amount of randomness that will remain within the work process, despite our best attempts to remove it.

For example, in building a car, it should be possible to create a process that is totally non-random. If the design is robust, if all the processes of manufacture are well thought out, if the facilities are well constructed and immune from external influence, if the feedback loops are correct and the workforce well disciplined, then every unit of output should come together in exactly the same way, with no surprises.

▶ Any breakdown in the process will be due to external, unanticipated events such as labour strikes, or to extreme environmental conditions, such as earthquakes, that impinge on the closed environment of the factory.

But now consider, for example, the process of carrying out common surgical procedures, such as cataract operations or appendectomies. These processes are repeatable, and – some might argue – no more complex than the build of a car, but they are subject to more randomness. Variations in the physical features and underlying health conditions of the input resource – the patient – may necessitate decisions during the process of surgery that lead to its being changed, or even abandoned.

This means that the workers in the car assembly process should be expected simply to follow the process, as any decision taken by them would disrupt it, but in the surgery example the surgeon must posses both knowledge and the responsibility to take decisions as they arise, to deviate from the process in order to ensure the ultimate success of the operation.

> **The key point is** that although the ultimate goal in any business should always be the implementation of consistent, repeatable and robust processes, when we are choosing such things as the detail of the steps, the flexibility of the process, and the knowledge held by, and responsibility given to, the worker, we need to consider the nature of the work done, the requirement for retained knowledge in the worker, and the ability to make decisions that this enables.

❶ Stop and Think

1 Surgery is performed by a skilled surgeon, supported by a team of people, who complete the entire operation. What prevents routine surgery being performed on a production line basis, with each worker trained in only a small part of the procedure?

The Nature of Products

It is common to associate the term 'product' with something tangible – a physical artefact that can be seen, held, and used. Until very recently this association was correct; very little of what was bought and sold did not have some sort of physical or tangible presence. These days, though, with the growth of the service sector, the word 'product' is increasingly applied to intangibles, such as financial services, package holidays, health care or legal advice. A mortgage is no less a product than a car or a watch. It is designed for a purpose, sold, paid for, and used. It is important that as operations managers we see the 'production' process of these intangible products in the same way that we see the production process of tangible products, in that there are still inputs, outputs, processes and feedback loops.

Indeed, in restaurants the product that is bought is the experience of the meal. Although eating out is considered a service, it is a combination of the physical product that is the meal and the service experience that is provided by the attentiveness of the staff and the ambience of the surroundings.

It is becoming increasingly difficult to draw a distinction between physical product and service delivered. Nowadays, very few physical products are sold without some form of service package attached. For operations managers this means that the conversion process model is as applicable to settings such as restaurants, banks, schools and hospitals as it is to production factories.

Figure 0.4 shows a conversion process for a typical service: the service of education provision. Although the operational philosophy of the conversion process applies to both production and service delivery, there are nevertheless some differences between them. The main one is that in service delivery the customer is present in the conversion process at all times; indeed, the customer can be considered as one of the raw materials that is 'transformed'. This might be from a non-graduate to a graduate (as shown in Figure 4); or from a customer with long, untidy hair to one with styled hair; or from a patient with a disease to one who is cured.

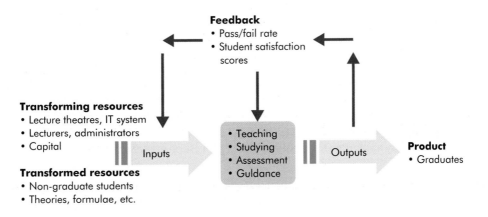

Figure 0.4 The conversion process of education

The customer's presence in the conversion process has consequences for operations managers. First, and most importantly, in the manufacture of physical products most of the work is done in a factory, closed to interference by the eventual customer, but in services such as hairdressing, education or policing, the customer is an integral part of the process – and customers have the potential to behave unpredictably. So the process needs to be able to handle the *randomness* that this brings. The way to deal with this tends to be to build more flexibility into the process, and staff it with more knowledgeable and empowered staff.

There is a second problem, though – that of *heterogeneity*. The customer's presence will cause inconsistencies in the delivery of a service, and this means that each customer may have a slightly different experience. This is easy to recognize where a dining experience may be better or worse depending on the atmosphere created by the presence or absence of other customers.

There are other differences between production and service delivery that also cause problems. For example, the intangible nature of the service experience makes it more difficult to ensure that a quality service is being produced. It is more difficult to measure the service experience than it is to measure the utility or functionality of a physical product.

Also, services tend to be difficult to store. If a hotel room misses a night's occupation, then this revenue is lost, as the next night is a different revenue-generating opportunity. Similarly, the experience of going to a theatre show or a rock concert cannot be wrapped and mass-produced. The closest thing might be the product equivalent that is the DVD of the show or the CD of the rock concert, but this is always a poor imitation of the actual experience.

These issues affect several aspects of operations management, and we shall explore them further, later in the book.

> ❗ **Stop and Think**
>
> 2 Have you ever sought legal advice for any reason? Perhaps buying a house, claiming compensation, or even defending a criminal charge? From a lawyer's perspective, how can consistency, reliability and repeatability be guaranteed in the process of delivering legal services?

How Is Operations Management Practised?

Let's Think More about Process

When we walk into McDonald's we enter a process for queuing, we are served by someone who is not a trained waiter, we purchase a meal that is cooked by someone who is not a trained chef, and we eat in an environment that can only by quite a stretch of the imagination be called a restaurant. Moreover, the meal we buy has been designed to specific standards of quality, is the product of a process of manufacture, and will be produced in exactly the same way, regardless of where or when it is bought. McDonald's is the ultimate in systematization.

Organizational processes evolved in different places and at different rates throughout history, but the father of process design is usually recognized as Fredrick Winslow Taylor (1911). In the late 19th and early 20th centuries the United States experienced rapid industrialization. Driven by new technologies, more complex forms of organization emerged, and many of the world's best-known companies were founded, including Esso, General Motors and Ford. Skilled workers were scarce, and even basic language skills were difficult to find. Taylor, and his idea of *scientific management*, solved this problem by making the attributes of the worker mostly irrelevant. Taylor and his supporters believed in *rationalism* – the view that if you understand something, you should be able to state it explicitly, and write a rule or law for it. The effect of applying rules and procedures is to replace uncertainty with predictability. By applying this thinking to the process of manufacture, reliability, consistency and repeatability would result.

Before Taylor, work was based on the craft system, where individuals controlled the work process, as they knew what to do and how to do it. However, this left managers and owners with a level of control over the production process similar to the control that a beekeeper has over the productive capacity of a beehive. In addition, to take full advantage of the rise in mechanization, all of the activities within a particular conversion process had to be fully understood by those who controlled the factory. Taylor advocated five principles that were to transform the manufacturing world.

1   A clear division of task and responsibility between worker and manager – the manager planned and organized; the worker carried out the tasks.

2   The use of scientific methods to determine the best way of doing the job – the separation of *conception* (the planning of the work) and *execution* (the doing of the work). In effect this meant that the craft knowledge possessed by the worker was taken by the management, formalized, improved, and assimilated into the process of production.

3   Scientific selection of the person for the newly designed job – simply the right person for the right job.

4   The training of the worker to do the job in a specific way – implementation of the division of labour to the point where each worker was specialized in an extremely small area of work. Whereas a craft system might see specialization as all of the skills and activities of mechanical work, for Taylor, in the assembly of a car, specialization would be limited to the activity (and associated skill) of fitting a single part.

5   Surveillance of workers – the implementation of rudimentary performance management systems and feedback loops to keep everything on track.

Taylor's five principles were based on experiments he carried out almost exclusively in the steel industry in 19th-century America, but his ideas have endured and spread, and have become the basis of operations management in all industries today. They were initially developed by Henry Ford into the production line system that came to dominate manufacturing work, and more recently have been applied in the service sector, as evidenced in McDonald's and other global fast-food outlets.

! Stop and Think

3   Look around at the organizations that you come into contact with in your daily life. Try to identify the processes that they use. Can you find any that are not underpinned in some way by Taylor's principles?

Characteristics of Operations Management

All operations have similarities, in that they transform input resources into output products, but they also differ in various ways. The four most important characteristics – the *4Vs of operations management* – are:

- The *volume* of the output – how many units of a given type of product are produced. Fast-food delivery and the production of consumer goods are examples of high volume where the large number of similar products to be produced justifies a high investment in specialized facilities, equipment and process planning.

- The *variety* of the offering – how many types (or versions) of a product have to be manufactured by the same facility. If a standard product such as a mass-produced car is to be built numerous times, the process can become very specific, both in equipment used and staff skills; but if the factory has to produce many types of custom car, then more general hand tools and more highly skilled staff are needed, to provide the necessary manufacturing flexibility.

- The *variation* in demand for the output – how the required number of products may differ from day to day, or week to week. The best example of this is in holiday resorts, where the facilities have to cope with vast differences in throughput, depending on the time of year. A ski resort, for example, will be working at full capacity throughout the winter months, but may have no business at all during the summer.
- The degree of *visibility* – how much customers can see of the manufacture of the product, or the delivery of the service. This applies mainly to the service sector, because for most services the customer's presence as a transformed resource is vital to the process. But even in service delivery, some aspects of the process are out of sight of the customer. Airport terminals such as Heathrow Terminal 5 are a good example of a mix of high-visibility and low-visibility processes. After check-in, your baggage disappears until it emerges (or, as we have seen, quite possibly doesn't emerge) at your destination. The customer does not see the process for moving it. By contrast, production systems are generally low visibility – closed to the eyes of the public, locked behind factory doors. This means that the customer is only aware of the finished product. This is not always the case, though; many companies are now opening their factories to the public. A particularly popular example of this is provided by food-processing plants, where the public are invited to come and view the conversion process. Some companies, such as high-profile drinks manufacturer Guinness, are taking this further and making their factories into a sort of theme park experience, where customers can tour, view, taste and buy. In cases like this the process of manufacture has become highly visible.

Who Is the Operations Manager?

The Role of the Operations Manager

Much has changed since the time when the operations managers of Taylor and Ford were inward facing, concerned only with the minutiae of process implementation, and the single-minded drive for efficiency. Those in operations roles in the mid-20th century, if transported forwards in time to the early 21st, might experience a mix of emotions, confronted with what their role has become.

Would the overwhelming sense be one of pride? Operations management, previously a member of the minor nobility in the hierarchy of management disciplines, has now risen in status to management royalty. It commands large numbers of employees, is seen as the engine driving the organization, and may be critical in strategy generation. Where once it was imprisoned in the production line, it has now broken out and travelled extensively, emigrating to all industries and companies.

Accompanying this sense of pride might be a feeling of satisfaction that the techniques of system and process have been vindicated, and have become the new management religion, with disciples in all management specialisms attempting to implement systems wherever possible throughout the organization in areas such as sales, recruitment, training and finance.

But such optimism might be tempered by feelings of unease at the size of the current role. These days, it could be argued, the operations role is much more challenging, both in content and in scope. The nature of the operations manager's role will depend on the type of organization and the characteristics of the industry, but in addition to the traditional tasks such as process design and capacity planning, many of the following responsibilities will be found:

- *Strategizing*: aiding in the development of corporate strategy, and devising and implementing operations strategies to support it
- *Performance management*: devising methods to increase the performance of the entire organization
- *Change management*: engaging in initiatives to continually update and improve the organization and re-engineer processes to meet ever-increasing competitive pressures
- *Design of products and services*: where once the scope of operations was limited to the manufacture of products to an existing design, these days it is increasingly absorbing the design work, because the design of the product and the design of the process of manufacture are carried out concurrently.

CRITICAL PERSPECTIVE

No Place for the Operations Function!

The drive towards process began in the Industrial Revolution, where new technology in the form of steam-driven machinery enabled products to be manufactured faster, and more consistently. This new system supplanted the previous craft-based system; large factories were built, where people and machines worked together in the process of manufacture. Early management systems, based on the division of labour and scientific management (Taylor, 1911), were quickly established to shape the labour force around the needs of the machine, and of the process.

These factories became characterized by the process of the production system. The term 'operations management' did not come into use until the mid-20th century, and was coined in association with the manufacture of products. Manufacturing at this time dominated the industrial landscape, and companies were structured in discrete functions such as production, marketing, finance and sales. This, combined with the historical legacy, associated the operations function with production activity. This situation still persists today within some companies, and indeed some textbooks still use this terminology. But as industrial activity in the service sector has grown, there has been a consequent association of the term 'operations' with a far wider variety of industries. Operations management has been adopted by many companies that do not produce any physical product. It is now associated more with techniques such as process thinking and problem solving, which can be applied to any organization in any industry. Nowadays banks label call centres as operations hubs, and retailers associate operations with the movement and sale of merchandise.

The key point is that operations management is no longer confined to one organizational 'function', but can be applied as process and method across the organization in a far wider arena.

Operations Management Skills

With the role of the operations manager growing, it is difficult to distil a specific set of the skills needed to be an effective operations manager from the seemingly endless set of general management skills that make up the toolkit of the 21st century manager. As the scope of operations widens, merging and overlapping with other areas of the organization, operations managers are increasingly seen as mini-general managers, expected to have skills across the organizational piste. Planning, both at detailed and strategic levels; organizing of resources; influencing and communicating; leading and motivating; implementing change and shaping culture; making decisions and problem solving – all fall under the remit of the operations manager. It is not easy to make sense of this jigsaw, but it is possible to tidy up some of these skills, and hence gain a better sense of what is required to make a success of the operations management role.

If we assume the basic activity of management is decision-making, then we can think of the foundation of the operations role as deciding:
- *What* resources will be needed: material, skills, information and capital
- *When* each resource will be needed: scheduling and sequencing of tasks
- *Where* the work will be done: in company or externally
- *How* the work will be done: process, system and activity
- *Who* will do the work: types of worker.

To build on this, though, it is not enough to merely list what an operations manager does. The following *bundles of skill* should provide a clearer picture of what the operations manager needs to be good at.
- *Managing process*: This is still the keystone of the operations manager's role. It requires skills in process planning and systems thinking, coupled with an understanding of technology and the ability to utilize it effectively, in addition to the ability to manage the people elements that facilitate any process.
- *Managing complexity*: With the size and diversity of today's operations, the challenge is not in the individual tasks or decisions that are taken, but in how they interact as a whole, and the complex relationships that result.

- *Linking conception and execution*: For Taylor the designer designed the process and the worker worked within the process. These days, in many organizations, both conception and execution are carried out under the banner of operations. The management of the design process, with its inherent creativity and randomness, will require a different approach from management of the production process, with its repetition and discipline.
- *Balancing today and tomorrow*: The short-term focus is key, as it is the efficiency and discipline within the current conversion process that provide the profit and keep the organization afloat, but the longer term must not be neglected. A balance must be struck between doing what is important today and planning for what may be important tomorrow. Operations is possibly unique, in that its view of life must have one eye on survival, and the other on what is important for success tomorrow.

The key skills that pull these bundles together are the abilities to:
- Process large amounts of varied and complex information
- Coordinate large numbers of tasks
- Prioritize effectively in both timescale and criticality
- Solve complex and varied problems

And above all, remain calm, under the pressure of doing all the above and still meeting time, cost and quality targets.

The Evolving Nature of Operations

Operations management has undergone much change since the days of F W Taylor, but the discipline's evolution is not complete. When the external environment influences the organization, ultimately the organization will look to operations management to deal with the resulting changes. There are three external themes that serve to alter the way operations management is practised.

GLOBALIZATION

Globalization

There has been international commerce since the earliest times, with merchants trading spices and materials across the expanding known world. By the 19th century many businesses were operating across the globe. More recently this tendency to operate internationally has grown much more quickly: a much greater proportion of business than ever before is done across national boundaries, and many more companies see their markets on a global scale. Indeed, for many companies – such as travel or logistics firms – their sole purpose is to operate internationally.

> **Globalization:** the increasing integration of internationally dispersed economic activity, and the extension of an organization's operational activity to cover the whole world.

Several factors are driving this exponential rise in global business, and have now come of age: market factors, such as homogeneous customer requirements, international distribution channels, and more comprehensive transportation networks; economic factors, such as international economies of scale and resource cost differentials; and environmental factors, such as the reduction in trade barriers and increasing sophistication in communications technology.

Operations management has been at the forefront of this trend, where (mainly) lower labour costs in the developing nations have caused a large-scale shift of low-skill manufacturing activities, such as mass production, and service activities, such as call centre work, from Europe and the USA to developing nations such as China, India and South America.

Globalization therefore results in a larger-scale canvas on which to practise operations management and a greater need for an external operational perspective.

Business Integration

While globalization is serving to expand the geographical boundaries that businesses operate within, there is a complementary effect whereby organizations are integrating more effectively with other organizations through supply chain relationships, to better capture the expanding opportunities provide by these global markets.

BUSINESS INTEGRATION

External integration is seen mainly in the creation of longer, larger supply chains, with companies specializing more in a smaller number of capabilities and then partnering with other companies to produce the final product or provide an integrated service. This requires new ways for companies to communicate and interface with each other.

Similarly, as globalization drives up efficiency and shortens product life cycles, companies need to work more effectively at breaking down internal barriers between functions, departments and culturally diverse groups. The prime example of this is the interface between the R&D and production functions. There is no longer time for these traditionally separate units to adopt abrasive relationships leading to lengthy times for a new idea to be ready for sale. Closer teamworking is required, removing boundaries and building relationships.

Corporate Responsibility

CSR

Milton Friedman the economist believed:

> *In a free economy there is one and only one social responsibility of business – to use its resources and engage in activities designed to increase its profits so long as it stays within the rules of the game.*
>
> Friedman (1962: 133)

This simplistic notion was limited to obeying the rules of free competition, and therefore the 'rules' referred mainly to the crimes of deception and fraud. This was a view based on the notion that a free economy, with all parties behaving in their own self-interest, would ultimately lead to the greater good. As has been evidenced in the banking crisis, and in the recent environmental oil disaster in the Gulf of Mexico, this thinking has been shown to be flawed. These days responsibility extends to more than the economic and legal imperatives. Carroll (1999) adds, first, *ethical responsibility*, which encourages companies to do the right thing in relation to the wider social interest, such as supporting the environment or a disadvantaged group; and, second, *discretionary responsibility* to contribute to the community in any way possible.

> **Corporate responsibility:** the awareness, acceptance, and management of the wider implications of management decisions.

Corporate responsibility therefore encourages a more even balance of public good and private gain.

As you read through this book, each theme will be signalled as it appears in the text. This will allow you to consider the ways in which these forces are shaping the theories, tools and techniques of operations management.

Key Theories

The key theories discussed in this chapter were:

- **Conversion process** – the system of operational activity that takes a specific set of inputs and turns them into a specific output (or set of outputs) that is the product

- **The 4Vs of operations management** – volume of output, variety of offering, variation in demand for the product or service, and visibility to customers of the production or service delivery process

- **Scientific management** – a management philosophy associated with Fredrick Winslow Taylor that encouraged the use of rational methods to plan operational processes in great detail

Suggested Answers to Stop and Think Questions

1 **Process of surgery:** In simple terms it should be possible to design a process of surgery for routine operations that could be done by semi-skilled staff rather than a fully qualified surgeon, much as a car is built by semi-skilled staff rather than by a fully qualified mechanic. In practice, though, there are reasons why this does not happen. The main one is that the input – that is, the patient – is not always the same in terms of underlying health and severity of condition to be operated on. Therefore

decisions will have to be taken during the process of the operation, and these require a skilled surgeon. Also, if an emergency occurs, the surgeon must be skilled in techniques beyond those required for the operation, in order to deal with the emergency safely. In reality there is also another, less practical, reason in that the profession of surgery is highly enclosed, with a governing body that would not look kindly on the profession being diluted by the introduction of operations management methods beyond a certain level. By contrast, in Russia the production line approach was implemented by the late Dr Svyatoslav Fyodorov, in operations to cure myopia.

2   **Legal services:** A legal service must be based on a defined process, but it differs from the production of goods or the delivery of more standardized services such as transport or fast food, in that the key element is not how well the process is defined; it is the knowledge displayed by the professional delivering the service.

Specialization is important. Much as the medical profession is build upon specialist knowledge areas, so too is the legal profession.

Process is not a key factor, but it still has a part to play. Those elements of the service that can be systematized and managed, such as the process of interaction with the customer (the meetings, communications and so on), should be standardized. Likewise, maintaining the same lawyer throughout a particular case will result in a more consistent approach for the client.

People skills are important in this process, too: they will provide a degree of empathy between the parties involved, and make for a more supportive and comfortable experience for the client.

3   **Taylor's principles:** It is difficult to find an organization that does not employ some measure of scientific management. The important thing to consider is the degree of systematization. Large companies engaged in large volumes of repetitive, low-skill activities such as production lines, call centres or travel will have embraced process management as much as possible. Conversely, a smaller organization with less repetitive activity that requires a high level of decision-making, such as R&D or legal services, will be less process based.

Online LearningCentre

Visit the Online Learning Centre at **www.mcgraw-hill.co.uk/textbooks/paton** for a range of resources to support your learning.

Further Reading

Ackroyd, S. and Thompson, P. (1999) *Organisational Misbehaviour*, Sage, London.

Bhagwati, J. (2005) *In Defence of Globalization*, Oxford University Press, Oxford.

Blowfield, M. and Murray, A. (2008) *Corporate Responsibility: A Critical Introduction*, Oxford University Press, Oxford.

Sprague, L.G. (2007) 'Evolution of the field of operations management', *Journal of Operations Management*, **25**(2), 219–238.

References

Carroll, A.B. (1999) 'Corporate social responsibility', *Business and Society*, **38**(3), 268–295.

Friedman, M. (1962) *Capitalism and Freedom*, University of Chicago Press, Chicago.

Taylor, F.W. (1911) *Scientific Management*, Harper & Row, New York.

Directing

Contents

JOBS

WANTED
Operations Director

We are looking for an operations director to play a central role in running the critical processes and systems to support the achievement of our global mission.

This position has primary responsibility for planning and implementing our operational routines including; making decisions about the location and capacity of our facilities, working with our partner firms to procure and manage the flow of parts and services and develop our systems to world class levels through implementing lean principles.

The right candidate will be a self-starter and team player with at least 10 years' relevant experience and proven success in operational and strategic management.

What does it take to become an Operations Director?

We talk to Grahame Jones at Farnborough International Ltd to find out.

Name: Grahame Jones

Current Position: Operations Director Farnborough International Ltd (FIL)

Previous: Group Operations Director Haymarket & BBC Haymarket Exhibitions Ltd

Years in operational role: 22

How did you get into Operations Management, what about the career attracted you and what other jobs have you done?

I joined FIL in 2009, prior to that I'd been working for the Haymarket Publishing Group. In that role the awareness of schedules, managing teams and working varying hours were crucial to ensuring publications were on sale at the right time. These skills seemed to fit with the role at FIL which is more events orientated. Before working at FIL a career in operations management/events was not obvious to me, but I had the opportunity to work on Top Gear Live, Gardener's World Live and Match of the Day which opened up a new area to me and encouraged me to continue my career in this area. I was headhunted to FIL where the challenge of working on the air show was too hard to refuse! After all, how many people get the chance to virtually build a small town every two years!

What was the most useful experience that prepared you for your current role?

The most useful experience would have to be the relaunch of Gardener's World Live. The exhibition was at the NEC and without real outdoor show gardens, the challenge was to change a car park from a concrete landscape to an area befitting 40 show gardens, 10,000m2 of hall exhibition space for RHS floral displays and approx 10,000m2 of outdoor exhibition space. This involved a team of civil engineers', quantity surveyors, an architect, landscaping experts and designers. Farnborough International Air-show (FIA) is almost completely modular and temporary; so civil engineering and planning applications are all part of the air-show delivery.

What's a typical day in the life of an Operations Director?

A typical day involves keeping up to date with the team to be aware of critical dates within the project plans, especially those that are further into the future, as they can be easily forgotten. I attend regular planning meetings and keep in touch with outside influences within the industry.

What aspects do you like most about your job?

Being challenged. Hearing new ideas from the sales, marketing or flying teams that make you think, these things stop you becoming complacent. Visiting other events to see how well we perform is useful because if we're not this helps us put systems in place to rectify and improve. And of course, the satisfaction of delivering a successful event!

What are biggest challenges in your role?

Having the foresight to predict events that will not come to fruition until two years into a project, such as the supply chain and procurement. In these days of economic uncertainty we need to be more aware of the stability and sustainability of our suppliers. It's increasingly important to have a list of B and C preferred suppliers to call upon and constantly looking to see who replacements could be.

What changes have you seen in your time in the industry?

More legislation in health and safety and the introduction of the Equality Act (DDA), which are required to assist us in performing better. There is now a better and more cohesive alliance between the Organizer and the Venue and the joining of the professional bodies to form SAG's (Safety Advisory Groups).

Where do you see yourself in 10 years time?

Hopefully a Non-Executive Director to an assortment of companies that require the experience and knowledge that I have.

What do you consider the ideal skills for your role?

Experience of managing projects/exhibitions; willingness and ability to initiate change; the ability to plan strategically and have an eye for detail. You need to have good knowledge of lean/Six Sigma, understand how to analyse data; be a good communicator, negotiator and be able to manage people effectively.

Business Strategy and Customer Orientation

Learning Outcomes

After reading this chapter you should be able to:

- Define what is meant by strategy and strategic management
- Define an organization's business by identifying who their customers are, what they want, and how the organization satisfies those wants
- Effectively use key strategic terms
- Explain how strategy exists at different levels in the organization
- Describe the difference between market-based and resource-based approaches to strategy
- Discuss the nature of organizational competencies and capabilities
- Explain the nature of competitive advantage

Warner Bros: From Humphrey Bogart to Harry Potter

Case Study Theme

It is close to a century since four Polish immigrant brothers opened their first film studio on Sunset Boulevard in Hollywood. Now, Warner Bros stands at the forefront of every aspect of the entertainment industry, including film and TV, gaming, consumer products, comic books and cinemas. How did the Warner brothers' business grow from a small family concern to a global company, and what strategic decisions enabled them to make this transformation? As you read this case, consider these questions, and how the strategic moves made have helped to keep the company aligned with its changing environment.

From Exhibition to Production

Film production was not the brothers' first business. They began by buying a movie projector, with which they showed films in the mining towns of Pennsylvania and Ohio. With the proceeds, they opened a theatre, and within a few years they were distributing pictures across a four-state area. However, they recognized that their power to sell tickets for movie viewings was limited by the films available to them. In order to grow their business further, they needed more control over what films they distributed, and so they made their first strategic move by diversifying into film production. Then, in 1918, they opened their studio on Sunset Boulevard, Hollywood. In 1923 they formally incorporated as Warner Brothers Pictures

BUSINESS INTEGRATION

Source: © Raine Vara/Alamy

Incorporated, and the first major stars to work with the studio included John Barrymore, Douglas Fairbanks Jr, and curiously enough a dog called Rin Tin Tin. This trend continued with Bette Davis, James Cagney, Humphrey Bogart, and even the future American president, Ronald Reagan.

Strategic Directions

By the end of 1924 Warner Bros was arguably the most successful independent studio in Hollywood. As the studio prospered, it grew initially through strategic acquisition, with the purchase of the Vitagraph Company, which had a nationwide distribution system, and further diversification, with the establishment of a successful radio station, KFWB in Los Angeles.

Determined to embrace new technology – a strategy that continues to this day – Warner Bros signed a contract with the sound company Western Electric, established the Vitaphone sound process, and began making films with music and effects. These included *The Jazz Singer*, starring Al Jolson, which signalled the end of the silent era and the birth of 'the talkies'. All this was done despite the misgivings of Harry Warner, who famously wondered, '*Who the hell wants to hear actors talk?*'

Further acquisitions followed, with additional theatre chains, a string of music publishers (which later formed Warner Bros Music), and several radio companies. So began a period of success in films that saw Warner Bros follow market trends, beginning with the production of musicals before shifting into swashbucklers, then gangster movies, war epics and westerns. This period also saw possibly their most significant strategic acquisition so far with the purchase of Schlesinger's cartoon unit, and the introduction of Bugs Bunny and Daffy Duck, characters that came to define the company's image.

Innovation

As time passed, Warner Bros came to rely more on innovation as a way to stay ahead of the competition. Examples of this included the first colour newsreel in 1948, and the introduction of Cinemascope in the 1950s. Then came the realization in the 1960's that the soundtrack to a film could be sold as a separate product, and so they began distributing the studio's film soundtracks through the Warner Music Company, in effect creating a new market and making use of the synergies within Warner's company portfolio.

More recently, further synergies were found in the opportunities provided by linking the latest technology in special effects – originally blue screen and then computer-generated image – with the comic-book characters supplied by the Warner-owned DC Comics. Prior to the introduction of this type of technology, the comic-book world had been all but impossible to recreate satisfactorily for live-action film. This new strategy culminated in 2008 with the release of *The Dark Knight*, the Academy Award winning Batman film that became the second highest grossing movie of all time, and the ongoing production of the *Harry Potter* franchise, the most successful film series of all time.

Strategic Threats

With the coming of television as a competitor to theatre movie distribution in the 1950s and 1960s, Warner made a difficult attempt at diversification into this emerging market. This was initially delayed by anti-trust issues, with concerns that Warner might become too dominant in the entertainment market. However, Warner finally achieved a foothold with early shows such as *Maverick*, and television is now part of Warner's core business. This strategy continues today with the ongoing growth of cable, and the facility to download movies from the Internet.

Lasting Success

Although by the late 1960s movie audiences were shrinking, Warner Bros continued to believe in the public's affinity for stars, signing deals with big names such as Paul Newman, Robert Redford, Barbra Streisand and Clint Eastwood, and so carrying the studio successfully through the 1970s and 1980s. This period also saw the relabelled Warner Communications engage in joint ventures for distribution with Columbia Pictures and Walt Disney Pictures, and diversify further into video games and theme parks. To the surprise of many, glitzy Warner Communications merged in 1989 with the conservative publishing company Time Inc. to form Time-Warner. In 2008 Warner Bros celebrated its 90th anniversary in a year that saw it break the all-time studio box-office record, grossing $1.753 billion.

Sources: www.timewarner.com; www.boxoffice.com; C. Warner-Sperling and C. Milner (1999) *Hollywood Be Thy Name: The Warner Brothers Story*. University Press of Kentucky, Lexington, KY, USA.

Introduction

During its history, Warner Bros has been forced to shift strategic direction more than once, because of changes in:

- Consumer taste, driven by fashion and world events
- Available technology, with the introduction of sound, Technicolor and more recently digital effects
- The competitive arena, with the rise of television, and home music and entertainment systems
- The economic and legal environment, with changes in consumer spending patterns, global downturns, growth in actor's pay, and anti-trust laws.

One cynical interpretation of the Warner Bros story is that it has been a series of managerial knee-jerk reactions: discrete decisions taken at points in time in response to opportunities and situations that emerged. Another interpretation is that each decision was part of a larger strategy that was coherent and clear, designed to pre-empt changing conditions and so sustain and grow the company. In reality the true situation lies somewhere between these two extremes: a mixture of planned action and necessary reaction. The company today is vastly different in size and scope from that which was born nearly a century ago. The journey is of course not complete, with further reshaping no doubt already planned and under way.

This case is not unique: all firms undergo some form of evolution during their lifetime. While this case is possibly larger in scale than most, the changes – and the situations that initiated and fuelled them – exist to varying degrees for all companies.

The concern of this book is operational rather than strategic, with a focus on the activities that generate the product or service that the customer 'buys', but in today's organizations the operational and the strategic cannot be totally separated. The organization must have an operational 'engine' that is capable of executing the business that it strategically chooses to undertake; conversely, the organization must understand its operational capability in order to decide which business to pursue.

Think of this as a journey: the company strategy will dictate the destination and the overall direction, whereas operations will be the vehicle that takes the company there. The vehicle must be appropriate to the journey; there would be little point in using a boat to cross a desert. This is a rather long-winded way of saying that a company's operations cannot be considered separately from its strategy.

Overview

The purpose of this first chapter is to create a foundation of understanding in strategic management against which the operational activity of the organization can be placed, to enable an understanding of how operational activity can be aligned with strategic direction.

This chapter therefore aims to:

- Create an understanding of the market and company environment within which operations management exists
- Provide an understanding of strategic management that will enable further study of it as a subject area
- Introduce the strategic planning process
- Propose methods that will help build company strategy
- Explain the role of operations management in the generation of competitive advantage.

The treatment of business strategy in this chapter is aimed at providing a foundation for the treatment of operations strategy in Chapter 2, where the emphasis on strategy is internal to the company, with the main focus on how the organization's resources are important in the strategy-making process. The present chapter also deals with external influences in the market, such as competition, and political and economic conditions, to ensure some degree of completeness and balance in the coverage of this subject.

This chapter will begin by presenting a way to define and understand your business, because the first step in strategy-making is to understand what your business is about. We explore the characteristics of strategic decisions, before looking at how organizations can gain some kind of advantage over their competition. The language of strategy is then presented, because this is the terminology that allows us to understand strategy, and communicate it easily. Different ways of approaching strategy are then introduced, dealing with such issues as what the company should be good at to be successful, and how this fits in with what the market wants. Finally, the role of operations in contributing to business strategy is examined, as the link to the operations strategy content in Chapter 2.

CRITICAL PERSPECTIVE

Product and Service Organizations

The story of Warner Bros touches upon many of the areas that are understood to be within the strategic domain, such as the geographical spread of the company, its product range and its scope of activity. But it also illustrates a more fundamental point, which lies at the core of defining what a company is actually about, and causes some confusion for both academics and practitioners. At first glance it would seem that Warner Bros provides a service that provides entertainment. However, this service is based on the manufacture of a product – initially the feature film. This product was then joined by other 'products', such as radio shows, television programmes, computer games and recorded music. At some point the product/service boundary became increasingly blurred: the manufactured product – whether it be a game, a film or a soundtrack – is no longer sold as a service on the cinema or TV screen, but as a physical product in the form of a DVD or CD. More recently, digital technology has further muddied the waters, as the physical manifestation of the product (the DVD) is now becoming obsolete, with the advent of downloadable music and pictures. Does this make the film or music producer a service provider or a product provider?

This product–service mix can be applied to most of what we would consider to be traditional production, or product-based, companies. For Warner Bros, the media and delivery route of the product changed and this altered the product/service emphasis. A different example is provided by the car industry, where, as well as supplying the car itself, it is now the norm for car companies to provide finance and maintenance packages as well. This provides a one-stop-shop service to the customer, where the car is only one part of that service. The offering to the market is less about the product and more about an affordable and risk-free transport package.

Most companies exist somewhere in the middle of the continuum between pure product and pure service (see Figure 1.1). Pure service companies do exist – professional practices such as legal and accounting firms, for example – most companies are a combination of product and service providers. A restaurant is considered as a service, but it is supported by the manufacture of food products; and, as mentioned, the entertainment experience provided by a cinema would not be possible without the production of a film. Most consumer goods are products that are wrapped in a service package. Ironically, pure product companies are the most difficult to define, because most products need some form of service and support.

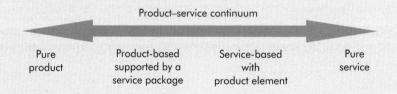

Product–service continuum

| Pure product | Product-based supported by a service package | Service-based with product element | Pure service |

Figure 1.1 Product–service continuum

In business-to-consumer relationships, examples of products that don't need support might be fully disposable products such as razor blades, for example, or a child's balloon; here the support element is limited to disposal, an activity that is taken care of by societal infrastructure rather than the supplying company.

In business-to-business transactions, all physical products – even relatively simple ones, such as single-unit, machined parts – must be supported by some sort of repair or replacement service, as defined by legislation and encouraged by accepted quality management practice.

An understanding of the nature of the business that you are in, and of what the customer wants, is something that is central to strategy. If a company defines itself as either a product or a service provider, more often than not it will be ignoring the opportunities that might emerge from recognizing the link between product supply and service provision – opportunities that may only require a slight shift of emphasis in operational activity to exploit.

The key point is that, these days, the customer is often looking for a package from a single company that meets a need, is all inclusive and problem free, and is procured with the least effort from a single supplier.

What Is Strategy?

Defining our Business

Strategy can be daunting, both to implement within the business and to study as a subject. This is due to the numerous concepts and terms that are involved in the academic treatment of the subject; the ever-increasing complexity of organizations, products and business environments; and the difficulty in finding a useful starting point for the task of making strategy, and a coherent route through that process. This chapter provides a simple inroad to the subject, focusing on the areas that will allow operations managers to implement the resulting strategy.

At its most simple, a business can be defined by the model shown in Figure 1.2. Here there are only three sets of strategic considerations. Those decisions relate to defining:

1   Who the customers are – what the market is, what customers exist within it and how they are grouped

2   What the customer wants – what they value and will therefore pay to receive

3   How your organization can deliver a product or service that will meet and satisfy that customer want.

All other strategic thinking comes as a result of addressing these three basic areas.

This model is a mix of questions that are *external* to the organization – the 'what' question and the 'who' question – and *internal* to the organization – the 'how' question. Simply speaking, strategy is the process of decision-making that provides the answers to these questions. Figure 1.3 illustrates the use of this model with an example from the banking industry.

Expanding on this simple view, strategy has been defined by Johnson *et al.* (2005) as:

the direction and scope of an organization over the long term which achieves advantage in a changing environment through its configuration of resources and competencies with the aim of fulfilling stakeholder expectations.

Therefore decisions are made with the aim of:

- Providing a product or service that the customer wants in preference to all competitor products
- Guiding the organization throughout its lifetime by defining its scope of activity
- Configuring its resources to carry out this scope of activity

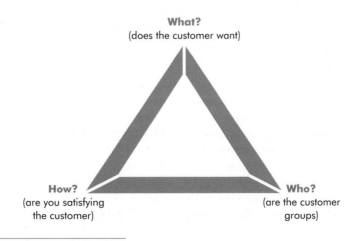

What?
(does the customer want)

How?
(are you satisfying
the customer)

Who?
(are the customer
groups)

Figure 1.2 The business definition (Abell, 1980)

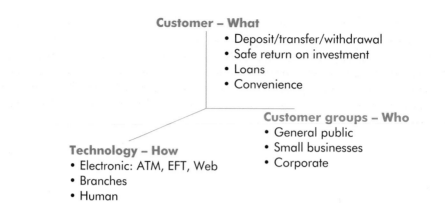

Customer – What
- Deposit/transfer/withdrawal
- Safe return on investment
- Loans
- Convenience

Customer groups – Who
- General public
- Small businesses
- Corporate

Technology – How
- Electronic: ATM, EFT, Web
- Branches
- Human

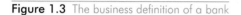

Figure 1.3 The business definition of a bank

and so achieving greater market share and profits, to satisfy those with a stake in the business, and in addition doing all this within a changing social, political, economic and technological environment.

The point of this is to show that strategy need not be complex; it can be approached by answering some fundamental questions about the business. Jack Welch, Managing Director of the General Electric Company for many years, has a similar approach to strategy. He describes it simply as:

- Understanding where the business is at the moment
- Creating a clear view of where it wants to be
- Working out how it will get where it wants to be.

Making Strategic Decisions

The decisions to be made that follow from these fundamental questions are rather conveniently termed *strategic decisions*. These decisions tend to differ from operational decisions in the following ways.

- *Time horizon*: Strategic decisions are concerned with the long term – maybe years or decades – whereas operational decisions tend to be more immediate – maybe weeks or months. What 'long term' means, though, will differ, depending on the industry and the organization. Within the aircraft and defence industries, for example, projects tend to last for many years: so for companies such as BAE Systems or Boeing, strategic timescales may be measured in decades. For smaller companies, such as SMEs, partnerships or sole traders, strategic timescales may be measured in single years or even months.
- *Scale of consequence*: Strategic decisions may fundamentally alter the direction of the entire business, and therefore have an impact on all areas of the organization, whereas operational decisions may be limited to only one department, process or activity. For Warner Bros the strategic decisions taken altered the shape of the company, its market, and its product portfolio.
- *Scope of activity*: Strategic decisions tend to define the areas of activity and the geographical locations that the organization should concentrate on; operational decisions are concerned more with how the activities should be carried out, including the processes, tools and skills required. For Warner Bros the portfolio of activity has changed, in relation both to the markets operated in, with the acquisition of games companies, and to the activities undertaken, with the move to producing TV and music. Many companies will operate within a more limited scope than this, but all companies need to define where the boundaries of their organization lie.
- *Level of complexity*: Strategic decisions will be concerned with a multitude of diverse and seemingly unrelated factors, including the organization's capability, competitors' activities, the customer's needs, and the political and economic landscape. For Warner Bros, several changes are occurring simultaneously; technology push is changing the products; fashion and culture are changing customer requirements; and social trends are changing the economic situation. All companies, regardless of size, need to understand and manage many random, interacting factors.
- *Level of certainty*: Strategic decisions tend to rely on information that is unclear and uncertain. This is partly because the vast, complex nature of the industrial landscape means it is difficult to construct

a complete picture, even if all the information is available. But it is usually because the required information simply cannot be found, as companies will guard against disclosing any details that might be of strategic significance to their competitors. Also, strategic decisions are highly speculative in nature. They tend to rely on 'guesses' about the future, because it is impossible to know what the world will be like in years to come. Prior to the invention of the microchip, who would have guessed that films based on computer-generated images, such as *Toy Story*, would be so successful? But the decision to invest in CGI technology had to be made before a single film had been made in this format, based on the prediction that this route would lead to success.

Drawing the Future of Animation

Andy's toys are fearful of being replaced when his birthday comes along. Woody, his favourite toy, a pull-string cowboy, discovers that Andy has been given a new toy, Buzz Lightyear, the latest, greatest action figure, complete with pop-out wings and laser beam. Woody's plan to get rid of Buzz backfires, and he finds himself lost in the world outside Andy's room, with Buzz as his only companion. Together they must try to find their way back home.

Made in 1995, and produced as part of a partner-ship between Disney and Pixar, *Toy Story* was the first animated feature generated completely on computers. But it was not the first movie to use CGI; this honour is held by 1973's *Westworld*, starring Yul Brynner. From this inauspicious start the use of CGI grew in the 1970s

Source: © A Farchive/Alamy

and 1980s, featuring in sci-fi films such as the *Star Wars* trilogy and the *Star Trek* series. In the 1990s CGI hit the mainstream with *Forrest Gump* and *Jurassic Park*, when the technology had matured to the point where it could be inserted seamlessly into live action scenes.

By the mid-1990s, though, the only film to have utilized CGI as the dominant medium was *Tron* in 1982, and it had been a commercial flop. The strategic decision to invest in a fully CGI film therefore was high-risk, made contrary to the current wisdom, much like Disney's decision to create the first full-length animated feature *Snow White and the Seven Dwarfs* over half a century earlier.

By the early 2000s computer-generated imagery had become the dominant form of special effects, with films based entirely on this technology routinely achieving box office success, and all major studios using it.

Questions

1   In relation to the concept of the business definition, what customer groups do you think the CGI technology was targeted at?
2   Do you think this technology was filling a gap in the market, or was it creating its own market?

Sources: www.disney.co.uk; S. Watts, *The Magic Kingdom: Walt Disney and the American Way of Life*, Houghton-Mifflin, Boston, MA, 1997.

If strategic decisions are taken correctly, initially they will help in defining the business model that is to be adopted, and then they will help in crafting the strategy that will support its achievement.

For example, consider Polaroid's business definition:

Perfecting and marketing instant photography to satisfy the needs of more affluent US and West European families for affection, friendship, fond memories, and humor.

From this simple sentence, Polaroid's business can be understood from a strategic viewpoint.

- Question: what are the customer needs (or what is being satisfied)? Answer: affection, friendship, fond memories and humour.
- Question: who are the customer groups (or who is being satisfied)? Answer: more affluent US and West European families.
- Question: how are customer needs being satisfied (or what are the technologies used and functions provided)? Answer: instant photography.

Strategic decisions can therefore be seen as searching for the fit between the organization and the environment that will result in the most successful operation possible.

CRITICAL PERSPECTIVE

The Taxonomy of Decisions

In our drive to organize, we tend to want to categorize everything around us. Sometimes this is useful – when cataloguing plants, animals or rocks, for example – but sometimes it is not, as when we try to label decisions as one type or another. In the organizational context, a decision is really the process of selecting one option from a range of options, and then committing resources to pursue it. Decisions get labelled variously as strategic or operational, high level or low level, long term or day to day.

This labelling system can sometimes be misleading. For a small building firm, a high-level, strategic, long-term decision might involve a small shift from home extensions into loft conversions; it might only affect a handful of people, and be relevant only for a few months (or until the next extension job comes along); and it might not be very complex at all. For a large multinational, an operational decision might involve much analysis of complex information, be in effect for years, and direct the activity of thousands of staff.

The key point is that decisions, and their consequences in terms of timescale and scope of activity, should be evaluated in terms of the context that they exist in, rather than on any absolute scale that defines decisions as either strategic or operational.

Competitive Advantage

Competitive advantage: what sets a firm apart from its rivals, making it the supplier of choice for customers within a particular market.

Achieving fit between organization and environment is necessary for success, but it is not sufficient, if your company cannot do better than the competition. There is one overarching characteristic of all organizational decision-making that rests mainly (but not exclusively) in the arena of strategy, and that is the search for **competitive advantage**.

Competitive advantage is what sets a firm apart from its rivals, making it the supplier of choice for customers within a particular market. Only by achieving competitive advantage can a firm hope to gain the required market share that will allow it to succeed, and meet its strategic purpose.

To gain competitive advantage it is essential for an organization to understand the competitive environment within which it exists. Porter (1979) summarized the competitive environment in his Five Forces Model (shown in Figure 1.4).

The Five Forces Model was originally developed as a way of assessing the attractiveness of different industries, but it can equally well be used to identify the forces of competition within a particular industry environment. The key insight with this framework is to expand the focus of competitive analysis from purely rival companies to encompass all factors within the environment. In addition to direct rivals, Porter identifies four further factors or 'forces' that influence the competitive arena. The resulting five forces, each one representing a particular threat, can be summarized as follows.

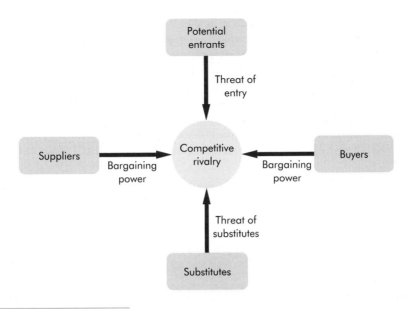

Figure 1.4 Five Forces Model (Porter 1979)

Direct Rivals

An organization's direct rivals are those with products or services that compete directly for the same customers' business. The intensity of the competition between direct rivals tends to be shaped by the following factors:

- The *size and capability of competing companies*: similarity will tend to make competition more intense.
- *Market maturity* in terms of growth or contraction in customer demand: in a growing market there may be enough business to support several competing organizations in a relatively benign environment, whereas in a stable or contracting market there may be more intense competition for the limited business available.
- *High fixed costs*: a high investment by a company in a particular product will leave it subject to greater loss if the venture is not successful. This therefore creates a greater motivation to succeed. High investment is effectively a barrier to both entry into and exit from a market.
- *Lack of differentiation between products and services*: this results in more intense competition, as no organization can gain an advantage purely as the result of product or service features.

None of these elements exists in isolation; they are all interconnected. For example, two companies of similar size, operating in a mature market, each having invested a considerable sum in what turns out to be relatively undifferentiated products, will experience a different type of competitive situation from that of two companies of differing sizes that have invested relatively small amounts on differentiated products, within a growing market.

Potential Entrants

The threat of entry by other competitors will shape the competitive environment. The size of this threat will depend upon the existence of barriers to entry into the market. If the barriers are high, then potential competitors should be less able to enter the market. Barriers to entry tend to be shaped by the following factors:

- *Size of investment*: the requirement for a large amount of up-front capital spend on tools, infrastructure or technology will deter rivals from pursuing that market.
- *Specialist knowledge*: if this is difficult to gain quickly, it will be hard for a rival to climb the learning curve and become effective in the new market.
- *Supply chain loyalty*: if the suppliers and customers within the market are reluctant to deal with new companies, it will be difficult for a rival company to gain a foothold in the market.
- *Legislation or quality approvals*: if these are cumbersome and extensive, it may be time consuming and costly to gain compliance, making it difficult to begin operating in the market.

These factors can exist in combination, so creating further barriers. For example, if profitable activity can be found only at large volumes, then economies of scale must quickly be obtained. Therefore a high level of investment, access to a robust supply chain and the necessary know-how must be in place at a very early stage.

Substitutes

These represent the threat that a product may be replaced by a different product that provides the same or increased functionality, leading to increased perceived benefit for the customer. The substitution could be:

- *Product for product or service for service*: for example, the plane replaced as a mode of transport by the train.
- *Change of requirement through obsolescence*: for example, the car phone replaced as a mode of communication by a mobile phone.
- *Change of priority due to changing customer circumstances*: for example, a holiday abroad replaced by a holiday nearer home.

Suppliers

The bargaining power of suppliers will affect the shape of the market. Porter suggests that suppliers are more powerful when the following conditions are present.

- *There are a limited number of possible suppliers*. This means that it will be difficult to swap from one to another, resulting in greater reliance on a particular supplying company.
- *The cost of the supplied product forms a large part of the final product cost*. This means that an increase in supplier cost will result in an impact on profitability.
- *A supplier has a similar operational capability*. This will make it easy for them to move up the supply chain and do business with the end customer.

Buyers

The bargaining power of buyers, or customers, will affect the shape of the market. Porter suggests that buyers are more powerful when the following conditions are present.

- *There are a limited number of possible buyers*. This means that the market is restricted, a condition that is especially difficult if there are a lot of competitor companies attempting to supply these few customers.
- *Products are relatively undifferentiated from those of rivals*. This means that the customer can shop around for the best deal on similar products.
- *A buyer has a similar operational capability*. This makes it easy for them to move down the supply chain and carry out the activities themselves.

WORKED EXAMPLE 1.1

Small-town Sandwiches: Eating Up the Market!

Problem: *Small-town Sandwiches is a small, sit-in/take-out, food business with two outlets, both well placed: one in the main shopping area of Small-town and the other in the business district. It specializes in freshly made sandwiches, salads, and fresh fruit products. It employs 20 people, all food is prepared daily within each shop, and most of the raw materials (fruit, vegetables, eggs, milk, etc.) are sourced locally from neighbouring farms. Small-town Sandwiches has enjoyed a relative monopoly throughout its 20-year history, due partly to its position as the first such business in the area, and partly to its good reputation as the 'local, quality, food supplier'.*

Until recently Small-town was a relatively sleepy village, with little to recommend it to other food businesses. However, last year Big-city Broadcasting, attracted by low property values in Small-town, invested in a regional call centre and administration office, bringing many new jobs to Small-town. With the larger consumer market and demand for fast food, Small-town Sandwiches, is currently benefiting from the increased volume of business, but it is nervous of the likely effect on the food industry in Small-town, and wants to carry out an analysis of its changing market.

Use Porter's Five Forces Model to help Small-town Sandwiches understand the potential threats that these changes to its environment might create.

Approach: The competitive environment has changed. From a stable monopoly position, Small-town Sandwiches is now operating in a growing market, which may be attractive to other players. Porter's Five Forces Model can be used to help Small-town Sandwiches understand this changing market.

Solution:

Direct rivals: Until recently the market could not support another similar food business, so it currently has no direct rivals.

New entrants: With the increase in the size of the market, conditions may now be sufficiently attractive for another business to set up. The Small-town Sandwiches business model is not difficult to replicate, as there are no intellectual property rights or protected supply, and set-up costs are relatively low. This means there are few barriers to entry to prevent either a new local rival or an existing franchise such as Subway from setting up.

Substitutes: The market here is for food of all types. Small-town Sandwiches has traded on quality and healthy eating, but other fast-food outlets such as McDonald's may see an opportunity, as the market requirement created by these new, more dynamic consumers may shift from quality to speed. The influx of new people to Small-town may bring a 'coffee shop' culture, where franchises such as Starbucks may further crowd the market with their brand of lunch and pre- and post-work offerings. And with a growing population, Small-town may become attractive for the larger supermarkets, and this increased provision of inexpensive food may discourage consumers from buying take-out.

Suppliers: All produce is sourced locally: therefore the farms may consider selling direct to the public.

Buyers: With a high volume of workers located in a single area, Big-city Broadcasting may consider providing its own food outlets, or inviting a franchise to operate directly within its site.

It is clear from this analysis that the change in the market will have considerable ramifications for Small-town Sandwiches' business.

Packaging a Strategy

So far we have looked at the definition of the business, the decisions that need to be made that will shape the direction of the business, and the issues surrounding how to gain the competitive advantage that the company needs to succeed. We now turn our attention to the elements that make up a strategy, and how that strategy can be communicated to others. Some form of framework for organizing the outcomes of strategic decisions is necessary to allow these to be captured and communicated to the rest of the organization. Terminology varies among books and authors, but the following terms provide a useful framework for analysing an organization's strategy, and so creating coherence and commonality.

Mission Statement

This encapsulates the overriding purpose of the organization that is in line with the shareholders' expectations. An example could be: 'to provide quality cars to drivers who appreciate the ultimate driving experience'. This makes a statement both on the type of product that will be produced, and on the customer that is being targeted.

Vision

This is the desired future state to be achieved by the organization. Extending the automotive example, the associated vision statement might be 'to be the number 1 mass manufacturer of quality cars in the world.' This adds detail on the competitive positioning that is being sought.

Values

These are statements that guide how the organization will behave while attempting to achieve the vision. 'Robust and safe engineering', 'fault-free construction', 'superior service' and 'environmentally aware' are phrases that, if understood, should both inform the behaviour of the staff and help shape the perception of the customer.

Strategic Objectives

These are more detailed, precise statements, illustrating what needs to be achieved to meet the organizational vision. They can be organized in various ways, but a useful framework that will help in the creation of operational strategy is the Kaplan and Norton (2004) Strategy Map framework, which categorizes objectives in four quadrants:

- Financial – to return a profit of x%; to increase revenue by y% per year; to reduce costs by £z.
- Customer – to understand our customers' priorities; to produce cars that exceed environmental standards.
- Internal – to achieve error-free production; to exploit the latest technologies.
- Learning and growth – to employ the best people; to maintain accurate information.

This framework, if populated correctly, will result in a balanced set of strategic objectives, allowing easier flow-down to operational level and therefore a more actionable strategy.

Strategic Plans

These are high-level statements of how the company will achieve its strategic objectives, and of the actions that will lead to achievement of the vision. Examples might be 'to capture the sports car sector', 'to develop a strong brand' or 'to be the first mover into a particular new market'. Such plans, although high level, should be specific enough to allow managers to create more detailed operational-level plans that can be actioned by the organizations. Each of these plans forms a piece of the jigsaw that is the overall strategy.

Strategic Priorities

These are high-level guides to what the organization should concentrate upon. If the business is large and complex, some sort of coherent action must be taken across divisions, business units and departments. Strategic priorities help focus the organization in achieving its strategic objectives. They could include:

- Focus initially on the home market before going overseas
- Concentrate on reducing loss-making business before expanding activity
- Ensure all activity is supported by a quality system.

Not all companies use all the elements we have discussed above to package their strategy. The defence company BAE Systems, however, follows this framework quite closely in its corporate strategy package:

Our vision is to be the premier global defence, security and aerospace company.

Our mission is to deliver sustainable growth in shareholder value through our commitment to total performance for all our customers.

Strategic objective: total performance through:
- *Customer focus*
- *Financial performance*
- *Programme execution*
- *Responsible behaviour.*

Strategic action plans:
- *Grow our electronics, intelligence and support business both organically and via acquisitions, and improve our efficiencies*
- *Implement our global land systems strategy and deliver on our efficiency and rationalization plans*
- *Establish in the UK sustainably profitable-through-life business, in air, land and sea*
- *Grow our home markets in the Kingdom of Saudi Arabia, Australia and India*
- *Implement our global initiatives in security, readiness and sustainment, and unmanned aircraft systems*
- *Continue to develop our global markets*

The Earth and Space Foundation packages its strategy in a slightly different way. The simple mission statement below makes the vision of this organization clear; it is easy to understand what objectives the Foundation may have.

The Earth as an oasis, cared for by a space-faring civilization.

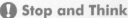 **Stop and Think**

2 Strategy can be packaged in different ways, as the examples above show. Consider how the packaging of strategy will help to communicate the message to employees. Will a formal or informal structure and tone help to get the message across, or is the approach context specific?

Where Is Strategy Carried Out?

Decisions are taken at all levels of the organization, but we tend to associate strategic decisions with those taken by more senior managers, and operational decisions with those at levels further down. The complexity of many organizations makes it difficult to determine the point in the hierarchy at which the strategic decisions stop and the operational decisions start. Moreover, some decisions that are taken for purely operational reasons have a significant impact on the organization's capability, and therefore take on a more strategic dimension. Some companies, especially large multinationals, may have extremely complex structures, such as that shown in Figure 1.5, but it is generally accepted that three levels of organizational strategic decision-making are sufficient to work with.

BUSINESS INTEGRATION

Corporate Level

This is usually the top level of the organization – maybe a main board of directors representing shareholders, or the owner of the company and his advisers. The larger and more diversified the organization, the more general the strategy will be at this level, as it must be relevant to all the diverse divisions or business units that may be operating in different markets, delivering widely varying products and services. Within a large conglomerate, strategy at corporate level may be described purely by a mission statement that is supported by a vision, a set of values, and a set of overall targets. Strategic planning activity will be mainly about shaping the portfolio of businesses that the corporation has interests in. The main activity will therefore be in the acquisition and divestment of businesses.

Although the size of the company is a factor in the strategic activity that is carried out at corporate level, the degree of diversity of business that the company undertakes is more significant. The more diverse the business,

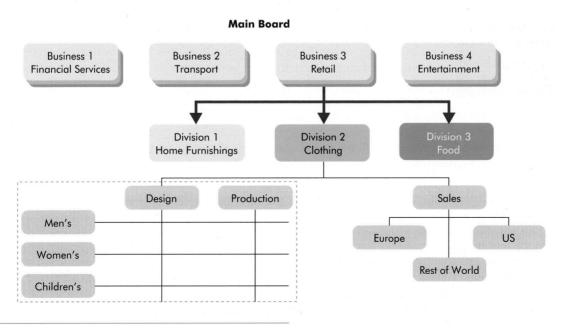

Figure 1.5 An example of a complex organizational structure

the less able the corporate decision-makers will be to create high-level strategy that is applicable to all the business units. Companies with very streamlined businesses are able to be more prescriptive at the top level, with more detailed mission statements that can be more readily translated into action.

An example of a high-level corporate strategy that is generalized for a diversified business is that of the Babcock International Group:

Babcock International Group Corporate Strategy Package

Mission: To be recognized as the leading technical support service business in the UK and selected overseas markets

Strategic Objectives:
- *To be top three in the marketplace*
- *To hold long-term contracts with infrastructure owners, primarily government, regulated bodies and blue chip companies*
- *To be customer focused, and work collaboratively with customers*
- *To provide a technical service that is important to supporting the customer's assets and operations*
- *To balance risk and reward*
- *To sustain annual double-digit growth at a minimum of 6% operating profit*
- *To maintain an excellent safety record*

This company operates in a range of markets, including transport, estates management, marine and energy: therefore the corporate strategy package must be relevant to all the divisions, to provide an overall direction.

An example of a more specific corporate strategy is that of Google:

Mission: to organize the world's information and make it universally accessible and useful.

This business is more focused: therefore the statement is clear and relevant to all employees, regardless of level.

Business Level

The next significant level is the business unit level, sometimes called the divisional level. The actual label does not matter; the key thing is that at this level decisions are made in relation to a discrete and homogeneous business, where strategy is applicable to the specific market within which the business is operating.

Another way to look at this is that corporate strategy defines what industries and markets an organization works within, whereas the business strategy will deal more with how the organization competes in these chosen industries and markets.

> **Strategic alignment:** the alignment of all decisions made at different levels of the organization with the overall strategic goals.

Like the corporate-level strategy, the business level strategy will tend to have a vision statement, showing where the company wants to be in a specific period of time, and a set of strategic targets to be met in support of that vision, which are aligned with the vision and targets at corporate level (**strategic alignment**). Remember that the company's values and overall mission as defined at corporate level should apply equally at business level. The strategic planning carried out at business level will differ from that at corporate level, as it will be concerned more with taking decisions on specific market-based factors, such as:

- The customers' requirements, and what product or service should be provided to meet them
- The threat of competition, and how to gain an advantage
- The changing nature of the market environment, and how to stay abreast of it.

Like corporate strategy, business strategy is therefore also concerned with the long term, and with the scope of the business, but it must provide enough short-term detail and clarity to allow the organization to create processes and systems that support the achievement of the higher-level vision and goals. This middle-level business strategy can therefore be thought of as providing a link between the corporate-level and the operational-level strategies.

Warner Bros, because of its size, is an example of a company that needs to devolve strategy-making to lower levels. Here, for example, is the mission statement of its theme parks business:

To bring people together of all ages, cultures and backgrounds to enjoy the highest international theme park standards of quality, fun and entertainment.

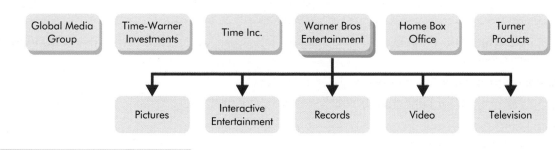

Time-Warner Inc

Global Media Group | Time-Warner Investments | Time Inc. | Warner Bros Entertainment | Home Box Office | Turner Products

Pictures | Interactive Entertainment | Records | Video | Television

Figure 1.6 Time-Warner strategic levels

Operational Level

Within the business there is an operational 'engine' that creates the product, or delivers the service. This may be based on a development laboratory, a production line, a set of retail outlets, a call centre or, more commonly these days, a combination of these. Whatever form the operation takes, decisions will need to be made as to how it is set up. These decisions will concern what equipment is bought and how it is utilized, how space is allocated, how processes are sequenced, and what skills are required. Operational strategy is concerned with the decisions that set up a framework that ensures the best configuration and utilization of resources that will most effectively support the business goals. Even at this level the scope of the decision-making may be relatively long term.

Examples of these decisions might be:
- The level of automation required, as opposed to manual labour
- The layout of departments and work areas
- The degree of integration of IT systems
- The organization of work – empowered teams or direct supervision.

These decisions exist above the day-to-day level, providing a framework for and guidance on how things should be done. They are below the business level, but support the achievement of its goals. In Chapter 2 we shall look at operations strategy in more detail.

Time-Warner is typical of a large multinational company with a complex structure, operating across a number of markets, and with many levels where strategic thinking may be carried out. Figure 1.6 illustrates the top three levels of the overall company. Each business has its own area of responsibility: for example, Time Inc. publishes magazines, and Warner Bros Entertainment is active across all current and emerging media and platforms, including feature film, television, video games and international cinema.

CRITICAL PERSPECTIVE

The Scope of Operations

Once upon a time the operations function was found mainly in production companies, and existed as one of a number of functions that made up the organization. Other functions might have been:

BUSINESS INTEGRATION

- *Human resource management*: responsible for recruitment, training and selection of staff
- *Engineering*: responsible for the development of products and technology
- *Finance*: responsible for controlling the money
- *Procurement*: responsible for the control of suppliers
- *Marketing*: responsible for the external interface of the company with the market.

This is not an exhaustive list – functions, and how they are named, vary by industry and by convention – but it serves to illustrate the demarcation lines that existed within the structures of companies. The operations function tended to be responsible for the internal activity that led to the creation of the product. More recently, though, the characteristics that differentiate functions have become less clear. This has expanded the scope of what is considered to be operations. This trend is the result of:

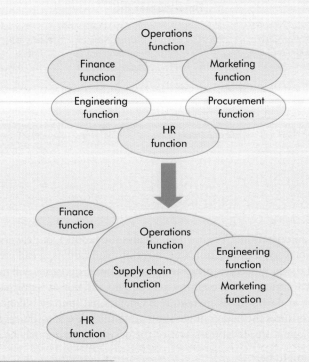

Figure 1.7 The changing scope of operations

- The recognition that operations management principles – efficiency and quality – are not limited to production activity, but can apply across the organization
- The development of management structures that emphasize integration rather than the separation created by discrete functions
- The adoption of the term 'operations' by companies that are not production focused, and its subsequent application to a wide variety of activities, such as call centre or distribution work.

This has led to the growth in scope of activity that is commonly referred to as operations.

Figure 1.7 shows how the functional groupings, and their relationship with what is considered to be 'operations', have changed. Some of the functions have been absorbed completely, and some have become tied more closely to Operations.

BUSINESS INTEGRATION

- Engineering and development activity has become more closely connected to production, as a result of the need to engineer products that are practical and efficient to manufacture. Therefore in many companies engineering is considered to be a central part of operations.
- Marketing activity, or the understanding of customer need, has become more closely linked to the development of products or services, and the eventual fulfilling of that need.
- Procurement has been relabelled 'supply chain management', and has been absorbed into operations, as the growth in complexity of products and services requires the resources of several companies to be combined. In essence, the supply chain has become a geographically diffuse operations unit.

Some functions are still discrete, but their scope of activity has been altered as some, but not all, of their activity has been absorbed into operations:

- Human resources management has seen much of its people-related activity, such as workforce performance development reviews and recruitment, taken over by operations. The operations managers have adopted these activities, as they are closest to both the tasks and the employees, and therefore they understand the needs best. The human resources function is often reduced to housekeeping activities, such as record-keeping and compliance work, or setting up cycle-to-work schemes.
- Finance is often devolved into operational departments, with the responsibility for cost centre profit and loss. Much to the annoyance of accountants, the finance function is often reduced to a single department that collates the information generated by the rest of the business.

This is only one interpretation of the changing scope of operations. It is difficult to generalize about what operations is considered to be across industry sectors, but what can be stated is that our understanding of what operations is has changed in recent years.

The key point is that the scope of operations will vary, depending upon the industry sector and the company, therefore for managers it is more useful to think of the type of operational activity, such as material controls, purchasing or assembly, and how it is carried out, rather than how it is labelled within the functional and departmental structure of the company.

Stop and Think

3 As operations have grown in scope to encompass other organizational functions, consider how this affects the job of the operations manager.

SHORT CASE 1.2

Operations in the Finance Industry

Operations was once the domain of the manufacturing company, and had a language all of its own. As you read this press release from The Royal Bank of Scotland (RBS), consider how the terminology of operations has become more commonplace in the finance industry.

Source: © Iain Masterton/Alamy

RBS to Locate Global Banking Operations Centre In Amsterdam

The Royal Bank of Scotland Group today announced that it would locate a new Global Banking Operations Centre in Amsterdam as part of its investment in the Netherlands if the RBS-led consortium banks are successful in completing their bid to acquire ABN AMRO. The centre will act as a hub for the enlarged RBS Group's international cash management and euro-currency processing. The proposed transaction with ABN AMRO would give RBS the opportunity to grow its presence in the Netherlands. The first stage in this process is to locate a new Global Banking Operations Centre in Amsterdam.

The new centre would form the hub for a number of functions critical for the success of the combined RBS/ABN AMRO group. The new centre is expected to become the base for:

The international cash management and euro-clearing activities for the combined RBS/ABN AMRO group worldwide, and be a centre of excellence for euro-denominated treasury functions.

A key component of RBS euro-denominated middle and back-office activities, supporting the enlarged RBS Global Banking and Markets business, and complementing its existing global operating model.

In addition to the set-up of 'operations centres', the adoption of 'operating models' and the recognition and use of the language of process in the finance industry, companies have gone further, labelling the items they sell, such as mortgages, loans and investments, as 'products'. Like physical products, these need to be designed, and features such as lifetime, interest rate and flexibility need to be built in.

Question

1 How much further does the financial sector need to go for its products to meet the quality and level of performance achieved by the best engineering and manufacturing companies?

Sources: www.rbs.co.uk; RBS press release, 25 September 2007.

Table 1.1 Summary of strategy levels

Strategy level	Questions	Purpose	Concerns
Corporate	Why does the organization exist? What should the organization do? Where does the organization do it?	Set overall mission vision and purpose	Building a successful corporation Ensuring a balanced portfolio of businesses Creating synergies between businesses Satisfying the shareholders
Business	What should the business do? Where does the business do it? How does the business do it?	Create a business that is aligned with the corporate strategy	Building a successful business Ensuring the business unit contributes to corporate goals Responding to changing market conditions Maintaining a competitive product or service portfolio Coordinating the various operational groups
Operational	How does the operation do it? Who within the operation does it? When is it done?	Provide and sustain the competencies that result in a competitive advantage.	Setting up systems and processes that are best in class Maintaining a resource base that meets operational needs

Strategic Alignment

Table 1.1 summarizes how each level of strategic decision-making fits in. Note the change in emphasis from the more philosophical 'why' questions at the corporate level to the more practical and detailed 'what', 'how', 'who' and 'when' questions further down. This changing emphasis helps to create some degree of vertical strategic alignment through the organization.

BUSINESS INTEGRATION

Whereas the business-level strategy can be thought of as the link between the corporate goals and how these are met, the operations-level strategy can be thought of as the link between the business strategy and what is done on the 'shop-floor' to achieve it.

Strategy begins at the top, and progressively adds detail at each of the lower levels. This layering is crucial, because:

- The vague principles defined at the top level need to be made clear so that they can be implemented, and this is more effectively done progressively, in a series of small, logical jumps rather than a single leap of faith.
- The diversity of the business means strategy must allow for different conditions in each area of the business, and this incremental translation process makes this possible.
- The size of the strategic task means that it cannot be done by one set of people but must have the involvement of a number of levels, utilizing a range of experience: the layering process makes this possible.

Alignment is the key feature. This is easiest to see at the operational level: if each department or function is working in isolation, they will not achieve the integration necessary to operate effectively. For example, a marketing department might demand a particular product, but the design department creates a slightly different product, which the production department does not have the capability to build. Alignment is also important at the business and corporate levels, though: if each business unit is moving in a different direction, then the corporate goals will never be achieved. This situation will be akin to a set of cottage industries working autonomously, neither contributing directly to the overall goals nor achieving any of the benefits of being part of a larger unit.

How Is Strategy Approached?

External (Market-based) and Internal (Resource-based)

There are two overall approaches to strategy:

- The external **market-based view** (Porter, 1980), which encourages understanding of all aspects of the external or market environment, in an attempt to guide the firm safely through the terrain
- The internal **resource-based view**, sometimes called *resource-based theory*, which concentrates on the firm's capability, and how it can be configured and used to achieve success.

> **Market-based view:** the strategic approach that prioritizes what the market wants in its decision-making.
>
> **Resource-based view:** the strategic approach that prioritizes the capability of the firm in its decision-making.

These schools of thought approach strategy-making from different ends of the spectrum, but it is clear that they both have a part to play. Regardless of which approach is preferred, some understanding of the other must be present, as this is necessary to engage in a balanced, strategic, decision-making process.

The concern of this book is operational, and therefore the focus here will be on the internal resource-based view, and the management of the firm's resources to create a competitive advantage. However, first we shall draw from the market-based view, because resources must be managed against the backdrop of the external environment.

The Market-based View

This approach prioritizes market conditions in the strategic decision-making process. Here we shall concentrate on two aspects of this: the wider market environment (Figure 1.8), and the needs of the customer.

First, how do we define exactly what the market is? It could encompass the entire external environment that your company exists within. Obviously, some awareness of all levels of the environment is beneficial, but it is impossible to take into consideration absolutely everything that may impact on your company. Here we shall define the market as that which exists within your industry, and is immediately external to your firm.

Once we have defined the market, two levels of analysis are important: identifying the features in the macro-environment that may affect how your specific market behaves; and identifying the factors that are directly related to your company's operation.

Porter's Five Forces Model is one tool that we can use to analyse the direct market, but for the wider environment we need a broader-brush approach.

PESTEL Framework

The PESTEL method of analysis considers six factors in the macro-environment that might affect your organization.

- *Political factors*, including changes in government, and associated ideologies:
  - ○ Financial priorities – tax and spending
  - ○ Global stability and inter-country relationships
- *Economic factors* that affect the cost of operations and the spending patterns of potential customers:
  - ○ Exchange, interest and inflation rates
  - ○ Economic cycles in geographical regions and industry sectors

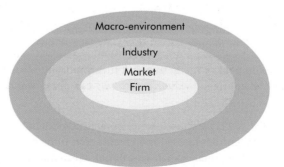

Figure 1.8 The environment

- *Social factors*, including demographic and cultural aspects that affect patterns of customer taste:
  - Population structure, including demographics such as age and ethnic mix
  - Lifestyle trends, such as health awareness, increasing leisure time and attitudes towards work
- *Technological factors* that can reshape markets, products and modes of production:
  - New discoveries and developments, and rates of obsolescence
  - New purchasing mechanisms, such as the Internet
  - IT and automation, which create new modes of production and service delivery
- *Environmental factors* that shape the way business is done:
  - Global warming and pollution
  - Energy consumption
- *Legal factors* that set the framework that businesses have to operate within:
  - Trade regulation, such as barriers, tariffs and quotas
  - Industry regulation, such as quality and safety standards.

These factors are not independent of one another; they interact. For example, a politically motivated decision may have an effect on the economic situation, or on the legislative framework. By investigating each of these areas, and relating the findings to your immediate market context, you will unearth a range of general environmental factors that may have a significant impact on your strategy. It is particularly important to look at the future impact of these factors, rather than at what may have happened in the past.

In addition to these six factors, there are three more you can use that will add to the power of this analysis. These factors are different: they can be applied to each of the previous factors to make the PESTEL analysis less static, and better able to cope with the time dimension:

- *Novelty factors*: the degree to which the environment presents the organization with new things
- *Predictability factors*: the degree to which the new things happen in a random and unforeseen way
- *Dynamic factors*: the speed (or rate of change) of the environment.

Customer value proposition: statement of precisely what the customer values and will therefore buy in the form of a product.

The Customer Value Proposition

When you have defined your market, have identified the significant factors in the wider environment, and understand the influence they have on your company, the key thing that the market can tell you is the customer need.

To create a product or service that will sell, it is critical to understand what the customer's values are, and to do this we must understand what value means from a customer perspective.

A model first proposed by Gutman in 1982 to define how customers categorize products in their memory has been adapted by Woodruff and Gardial (1996) into a hierarchy that defines what customers prioritize in terms of value. The hierarchy has three levels. From top to bottom, they are:

1   Goals and purposes that they want to meet that the product or service may help with. For example, a package holiday may be about meeting new people, or finding a partner.

2   Desired consequences in use situations that will have an impact on goal achievement. A large number of nightclubs in a holiday resort will consequently provide more opportunities to socialize.

3   Desired product and service attributes that will contribute to the desired consequence. The provision of cheap alcohol and dark surroundings in the nightclub will provide customers with the chance to get to know each other better – and in many cases lay the groundwork for an unwelcome surprise once sober.

This thinking is drawn from the domain of marketing, but it is important to understand the process by which customers arrive at their understanding of value, before we can understand what the operations system must deliver.

Customer value elements: factors that, when combined, define the value proposition.

Sheth *et al.* (1991) proposed a more practical model that relates mainly to the consumer market. It identifies five value elements that influence customer choice, as described in Table 1.2: functional, social, emotional, epistemic and conditional value. The various markets will place different importance on each of these **customer value elements** or, more commonly, a combination of elements, as a proxy of value.

Table 1.2 Customer value elements

Value	Definition	Example
Functional	Based on physical performance; measured on choice attributes	Automobile, based upon fuel economy and maintenance record
Social	Achieved through association with particular demographic group	Clothing/jewellery/gifts for others' consumption
Emotional	Acquired when product arouses emotional states	Certain foods associated with particular settings
Epistemic	Refers to the seeking of new varieties of offerings, arousing a sense of novelty or interest	Trying a new brand of product, moving away from the familiar
Conditional	Utility received, based upon the result of a specific set of circumstances	Extreme: seasonal products such as Christmas cards. Subtle: popcorn at the movies

Table 1.3 The resources of the organization

Resource category	Tangible	⟷	Intangible
Physical	Plant and equipment Geographical location Access to raw materials		
Human			Skill and experience Judgement and insight Intelligence and creativity Relationships
Organizational	Systems and processes	Management structure	Culture

Woodruff (1997: 142) offers a definition that consolidates all the alternative definitions of value:

> a customer's perceived preference for and evaluation of those product attributes, attribute performances, and consequences that arising from use that facilitate (or block) achieving the customer's goal and purposes in use situations.

Regardless of the nature of your customer – be it a government, another company, or a consumer group – it is essential that you understand their value proposition. Only by understanding the attributes of the product or service that the customer values, and the process that they use to decide what to buy, can the product or service package be defined. It is then a matter of configuring the resources of your organization to deliver this value.

The Resource-Based View

It is generally recognized that the resource-based view (the RBV) began with Penrose (1959), who proposed that what happened inside the firm was as important as what happened outside it. Over the last 20 years. it has been argued, the RBV has risen to the pre-eminent position in strategy research (Locket *et al.*, 2009).

The RBV describes the firm as a collection of assets or resources that are tied semi-permanently to it (Wernerfelt, 1984). The definition of resources is necessarily wide. Daft (1983) defines them as all assets, capabilities, organizational processes, firm attributes, and information knowledge controlled by the firm that enable it to conceive and implement strategies that improve its efficiency and effectiveness. Although such a comprehensive definition should be applauded, it is of little use from an operational perspective. Table 1.3 includes some examples of what can be considered organizational resources, and shows that they can vary in both form and substance.

From an operations point of view, resources can be either tangible or intangible. Tangible resources are those that can be seen or touched or formalized, such as plant and equipment, systems and processes. Intangible resources exist informally, and are therefore more difficult to define. They might include culture, skill and experience.

Resources should be thought of as 'potential to create value for the customer', and ultimately they contribute to competitive advantage, so securing the business within the market. Tangible resources tend to be easiest to manage in support of the creation of value, but intangible resources will be more difficult for competitors to replicate. The mobilization of these resources, and how they can be made to support the organization, is termed operational strategy, and will be explored further in Chapter 2.

❗ Stop and Think

4 Tangible resources may be easier to manage than intangible resources, but which resource type has the potential to make the most impact on operational performance?

BUSINESS INTEGRATION

SHORT CASE 1.3	## The Hammer Comes Down on eBay

To some extent all strategy-making must be both resource based and market based; attempting to capture a market while not investing in the necessary resources, or investing in resources with no market in mind, will lead to failure. Here is an example of an attempt to follow the market without fully backing up this strategic play with the necessary resource infrastructure.

Source: © Sergey Mironov/iStock

Founded in 1995, eBay connects a diverse and passionate community of individual buyers and sellers, as well as small businesses. With more than 88 million active users globally, eBay is the world's largest online marketplace, where practically anyone can buy and sell almost anything. The website is part car-boot sale, part auction house, part local market, part high street store, with the cost determined by how much people are prepared to pay.

eBay's strategy in recent years has been to move into other lucrative markets, evolving from a bid-only auction site to one that also sells fixed-price goods from other retailers, much like other online sellers such as Amazon. During the strategic shift, though, this aspiration has not always been matched by eBay's operational capability to deliver. In 2009 the site experienced technical difficulties, because its operational processes and systems were unable to cope with the increased volume and variety of orders that were the result of this strategic move. These difficulties resulted in the site being unavailable for periods of time, and a consequent loss of revenue.

Questions
1 What customer need is being met by eBay?
2 Do you consider the strategic decision to move from auctioning to retailing as an extension of the current business or a move into an entirely new market sector?

Sources: www.ebay.co.uk; *Financial Times*, 23 November 2009.

Resources and Competitive Advantage

For a resource to have the potential to result in some sort of competitive advantage it needs to have four attributes. These attributes were originally expressed by Barney (1991) as *valuable, rare, imperfectly imitable* and *non-substitutable* (VRIN).

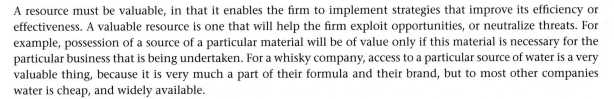

A resource must be valuable, in that it enables the firm to implement strategies that improve its efficiency or effectiveness. A valuable resource is one that will help the firm exploit opportunities, or neutralize threats. For example, possession of a source of a particular material will be of value only if this material is necessary for the particular business that is being undertaken. For a whisky company, access to a particular source of water is a very valuable thing, because it is very much a part of their formula and their brand, but to most other companies water is cheap, and widely available.

A resource must be rare, in that not many (or, preferably, not any) other companies have access to it. The more abundant the resource, the less valuable it will be, and so the less it will contribute to competitive advantage. How rare must the resource be to remain valuable? This is a tricky question. If the resource is unique, then it is easy to see that it will provide a considerable advantage, but the effect of its availability to some other companies will depend on the competitive environment existing in the market, as described by Porter's Five Forces. To put it another way, as long as the number of firms who possess this resource is small enough to prevent the occurrence of perfect dynamic competition within the sector (Hirshleifer, 1980) then the resource is still rare enough to be useful. In the whisky example, if the source of water was plentiful, and the recipe and process for distilling the whisky were freely available, then the market would be 'flooded' with equivalent products, making the product almost valueless. As it stands, the whisky industry is crowded with products that are differentiated by the subtleties of such things as water source.

For a resource to remain rare, it must either be difficult to imitate, or be difficult to substitute. This may be the case if:

- It has been obtained through unique historical conditions – for example, a scientific breakthrough leading to intellectual property that can be protected, or the location of a factory in a geographical position that subsequently turns out to be uniquely valuable.
- Its source, or how it leads to advantage, is intangible. This may be the case, for example, in companies with a strong culture that is difficult to formalize, leading to unique social relationships, such as a particularly strong management team.
- It is made up of several resources in combination – for example, an organization with a strong R&D function that is made up of people, processes and infrastructure. The discrete resources, such as the scientists, their skills and their relationships, and how they use the processes and tools, will be difficult to duplicate.

The degree to which a resource can be imitated or substituted is always difficult to determine. The key thing to consider is not how similar the equivalent resource is, but what it can create in terms of competitive advantage for a rival that may erode or neutralize your own market position. History is littered with examples of substitute products: from the replacement of the horse by the car, to the valve by the transistor, and more recently to the cathode ray tube by the liquid crystal display. And now the same is happening to services in retailing, as web-based shopping starts to replace high street shopping.

We can think of these VRIN distinctions as a filter:

- First, does your resource neutralize a threat or exploit an opportunity?
- If so, is it rare enough that it is available either only to you or to a small enough number of competitors that the advantage it provides is not marginalized?
- If so, how long can this advantage be protected? Or, put another way, how long before it is imitated or substituted?

If this timescale is significant in terms of the industry life cycle and your strategic horizons, then the competitive advantage gained may be sustainable.

Using this system, and referring back to Table 1.2, we can seen that resources that are more intangible, such as skills and culture, will tend to be more difficult to imitate. Tangibles such as equipment and tooling tend not to be key resources, as they can be bought and sold with relative ease.

CSR

CRITICAL PERSPECTIVE

Sustainable Competitive Advantage

A firm is said to have a **sustainable competitive advantage** when it is implementing a value-creating strategy that is not simultaneously being implemented by any current or potential competitors. For this advantage to be sustained two things must apply:

- The resources within a market, and available to the firms competing within it, are not equally spread.
- These resources are not mobile: that is, they are company specific in some way, and are likely to remain that way.

> **Sustainable competitive advantage:** competitive advantage that is based on a valuable, rare, imperfectly imitable and non-substitutable resource that is specific to the company, and cannot be transferred.

Therefore the resources must not only be VRIN for a short period; they must stay VRIN for an undefined, and possibly indefinite, period. Some authors have suggested that an advantage is sustainable simply if it lasts for a 'long' period of time. This suggestion is attractively simple, but it is unsatisfactory, because it raises the question: how long is long enough for a firm to be sure that competitive advantage is safe, and can be sustained? The answer will vary by industry and by sector. To attempt to define a time period, we would need to understand both the product life cycle and the nature of the competition.

Another suggestion is that that competitive advantage is sustainable only if it continues to exist after all efforts to duplicate it have ceased. This is a bit more useful, in that it does not rely on the specification of a time period, but it is no less difficult to define, as it requires complete knowledge of what the competition is doing.

The key point is that while the characteristics of competitive advantage and the resources required to achieve it are clear, the perpetuation (sustainability) of this advantage over time is more difficult to achieve. So, from a practical perspective, it is important to understand how long an advantage, once achieved, will last, and then work on its perpetuation or its replacement.

Competencies: Bundling of Resources

So far we have dealt with resources mainly as discrete entities. But although some resources may create a competitive advantage on their own, such as a unique supply of a raw material (water in the whisky industry) or a piece of intellectual property (a formula for a drug), it is more useful to think of resources in combination. Resources working together create a more powerful force, which leads to a better competitive advantage.

This bundle of resources is commonly called a *competence* (Hamel and Prahalad, 1990).

A competence in organizational terms might be the combination of its human resources, such as the skill and knowledge within a production department, and its physical resources, such as the IT infrastructure and the process tooling that allow the company to manufacture a product or deliver a service within a particular market. Or it might be the combination of the skills of kitchen staff in producing a certain type of food, the abilities of customer-facing staff and the décor of the restaurant (the infrastructure) that create a certain type of themed dining experience for a particular customer group.

Defining the scope of a competence – how many resources it comprises, or how much of the organization it encompasses – is not an exact science. The general rule is that it should be more than just one resource, but less than all the resources of the entire organizational system.

To unpack this concept further, we can understand competencies better in terms of their relationship with competitive advantage. Over the past few years a hierarchy of competencies has emerged from the literature that helps to define the nature, and more importantly the value, of competencies – that is, how much a particular competence contributes to competitive advantage.

Threshold Competencies

At the basic level are **threshold competencies**. These are competencies that allow the firm to exist and operate, but provide no competitive advantage. Without these competencies no level of operation is possible. Returning to our restaurant example, threshold competencies would be the basic package of resources that, when combined, allow the basic production and serving of food.

> **Threshold competencies:** competencies that allow the firm to exist and operate, but provide no competitive advantage.

In the VRIN framework, at the threshold level competencies will provide little value, because all companies in the market should be able to do these basic things.

Core Competencies

At the next level exist what are termed **core competencies**. Hamel and Prahalad (1990) propose that for a competence to be core to the business, it must:
- Provide open access to a variety of markets
- Contribute significantly to performance
- Be difficult to imitate.

> **Core competencies:** competencies that contribute directly to business goals.

This adds some clarity, but Eden and Ackerman (2005) further propose that, unlike a threshold competence, a core competence contributes directly to the business's strategic goals.

First, the resources must be identified and bundled together to create such a core competence. Then some differentiation must be created so that this core competence also leads to a competitive advantage.

SHORT CASE 1.4

Korry: We Package Light

One of the basic technologies mastered by early humans was harnessing the power of fire, and the light and heat it provided. Arguably, this was the single most significant event in the history of technological development. Now artificial light surrounds us – one of the most taken-for-granted features of modern life. Since early human beings created the first candle, the generation of light has moved on through many levels of sophistication, and now embraces many complex and diverse technologies. As you read this case consider the composition of the competencies: what skills, infrastructure and processes are needed to create light for today's sophisticated applications?

Company vision: To be the supplier of choice with our customers. When they think of electro-optical control and display components and subsystems, we want them to think of Korry first.

Korry Electronics was founded in 1937 by Boris Korry to manufacture and distribute his invention, the first front-relampable, illuminated indicator for aviation. Today, Korry's product lines include the most advanced switches and indicators, as well as custom interface and lighting solutions, integrated switch panels, displays, and controls for all forms of vehicle. Korry continues to pioneer new technologies, including high-performance, active-matrix liquid crystal displays.

For Korry the competence is in the 'packaging of light' for specific applications. This competence will therefore comprise a knowledge of physics (specifically heat and light), electrical and mechanical engineering, design capability, and the processes and skills used in manufacture.

Questions
1 What attributes would a customer value in a supplier such as Korry?
2 What is the key resource that supports Korry's core competence?

Source: www.korry.com

Distinctive Competencies

The term 'distinctive competence' has been coined to describe a competence that is so valuable, rare, inimitable and non-substitutable, and so aligned with business goals, that it creates a clear competitive advantage. Quite simply, a competence is distinctive if others are unable to emulate it.

Distinctive competencies: competencies so unique that they create competitive advantage.

Distinctive competencies are sometimes difficult to understand, so this idea is probably best explained by an example. WL Gore and Associates is possibly best known to the general public for its brand Gore-Tex, the waterproof and breathable (and eye-wateringly expensive) fabric that is seen as the industry standard in high-performance garments. Gore, however, sees its core competence as being the development of fluoropolymer-based technologies. This competence allows it to operate in many diverse product markets, including medical devices and electrical cable assemblies, as well as the well-known clothing market. From this general core competence sprang the distinctive competence that is the ability to manufacture the Gore-Tex fabric, and the range of garments that this product is used in.

It could be argued that Gore-Tex is the perfect product. The manufacturing process is so rare that it is unique to WL Gore; it generates enormous value in the form of revenue to the company; although there have been many imitators, none has come close to breaking the Gore-Tex dominance; and it is difficult to think of a product that will replace clothes in most of the applications that Gore-Tex is used in.

Competencies in Service Provision

In this chapter we have proposed that most companies deliver a combination of physical products and services. We now need to look further into the characteristics of core competencies in relation to service delivery.

There are several factors that make the operation of delivering a service different from that of producing a product:

- *Simultaneity of production and consumption.* A service cannot be inventoried or stored; it is created and consumed at the same time. For example, a theatre show is performed and viewed at the same time; the next show is a different service episode. This means that a service generally has no shelf life. If a ticket is not sold on a particular night, the show will take place anyway; there is no subsequent opportunity to sell that ticket.
- *Presence of the customer in the conversion process.* Most manufactured products are made in a factory, isolated from the view of the eventual customer. Most services are delivered in the presence of the customer: therefore there is little insulation between what the customer sees and what the delivery process does. In a theatre show, if a mistake is made (in operations terms, a quality error) this cannot be corrected before the service is dispatched to the customer.
- *Intangibility of services.* Unlike a physical product, service features are not easily defined, as they cannot be 'touched'. Also, each customer may have a slightly different perception of the service experience. Some customers may enjoy the theatre show, while others may be more ambivalent, but all have experienced the same service.

Companies that provide products must develop competencies in engineering and manufacture, generally within a closed environment. The elements of competencies here may include:

- The possession of intellectual property
- The achievement of process excellence
- The ability to manipulate technology

By contrast, Van Looy *et al.* (2003) have suggested that competence in services is all about developing a *customer orientation*. This concept is perhaps more abstract than competence in the production environment, and the elements that make it up are consequently more difficult to define, but here are some suggestions:

- The capacity to understand the customer's priorities
- The ability to speak the customer's language
- The ability to empathize with the customer
- The ability to show consideration for the customer
- The ability to de-risk the customer's business

As has been argued, most companies are a combination of product and service providers. They must therefore develop some form of customer competence, in addition to their product-based competence. The importance of this service-based competence – whether it is threshold, core or distinctive – will depend very much on the nature of the business.

The key point is that the service environment has some distinguishing features that need to be considered in the creation of a core competence.

Contemporary Thinking: Dynamic Capabilities

The resource-based view (RBV) that we have been discussing assumes that resources are heterogeneous, and can be sustained over time. Indeed, the whole concept of sustainable competitive advantage is based on a static view of the market (Locket, 2009).

The RBV and competence literature therefore does not really address the dynamic nature of markets, or how current resources can be refreshed or future resources created to meet the changing environment. But change is a characteristic of most markets, and – it could be argued – is becoming more prevalent as markets become increasingly competitive. If long-term market equilibrium does exists at all, it is limited to some specialized markets such as the whisky industry, or to luxury markets such as jewellery, where product life cycles are so long that change is slow to happen. For most companies, however, this benign state does not exist, so developing new resources and competitive advantage are critical concerns for managers.

Teece and Pisano (1994) and Teece *et al.* (1997) were the first to move beyond the established RBV when they proposed that it couldn't explain how some firms demonstrate timely and rapid reaction to changing market conditions. They coined the term **dynamic capability** to describe a firm's ability to integrate, build and reconfigure competencies to address rapidly changing environments. A dynamic capability is not a reactive, problem-solving event in spontaneous response to a stimulus; it is intentional, planned, and deliberate. A dynamic capability is a process that impacts upon resources or bundles of resources (competencies) to change them to meet a perceived future state.

Dynamic capability: a firm's ability to upgrade and reconstruct its capabilities in response to the changing environment, therefore attaining and sustaining its competitive advantage.

Ambrosini and Bowman (2009) state that dynamic capabilities comprise four main processes:
- *Reconfiguration*: the transformation and recombination of assets and resources. This may occur after a merger or acquisition, where the new shape will realize new synergies that previously didn't exist.
- *Leveraging*: the replication of processes or systems across operational units
- *Learning*: the increase in effectiveness and efficiency that is the outcome of reflection on failure and success
- *Integration*: the pulling together of resources to create new competencies

They then give some examples:
- The R&D process, where the effective use of creativity and innovation can continually alter the nature of the game
- The strategic acquisition process, where the buying up of other businesses can both refresh the resource portfolio and change the shape of the competitive environment
- The knowledge deployment process, where the effective use of knowledge assets can leverage competencies
- The organizational restructuring process, where the reconfiguration of the firm can release previously untapped capability

Dynamic capabilities can therefore be seen as those that enable firms to keep pace with their changing environment, by developing resources and competencies that will continue to 'hit a moving target'.

It could be argued that dynamic capabilities exist at the opposite end of the spectrum from sustainable competitive advantage, as they enable a firm in a fast-moving market, where sustainability is impossible to achieve, to gain advantage by achieving a series of temporary, short-lived advantages.

Summary

In this chapter we have provided some tools that can be used to explore the strategic landscape at the corporate level. The understanding gained can then be used to set the context within which the operational engine that drives the business can be placed. We have shown that the strategic landscape that operations managers must consider consists of both the market environment within which their organization exists and the strategic direction that is set by the top level of the organization. This strategic direction may simply be a set of financial objectives, or it may be more elaborately described by mission statements and strategic plans.

Strategy has been presented from two viewpoints: the market-based view, which suggests that an organization should align itself with market need, and the resource-based view, which suggests that the organization should understand what it is good at, and develop competencies in these areas that will allow it to gain a competitive advantage. The strategy process is therefore as follows:

1 Understand what your business is – business definition model.

2 From the MBV:
    (a) Investigate your overall market environment – PESTEL
    (b) Define your immediate competitive position – Porter's Five Forces
    (c) Understand what your customer wants – value theory.

3 From the RBV:
    (a) Define what you need to be good at to exist in the market – core competencies
    (b) Leverage your competencies to create a competitive advantage – distinctive competencies.

4 Analyse the nature of your competitive advantage to understand how sustainable it is, and therefore how your competence must change to maintain advantage – dynamic capabilities.

Although we have argued that a balanced approach to strategy must take into consideration aspects of both the MBV and the RBV, we have concentrated on the RBV, as this is the 'wrapper' within which the operations strategy is packaged.

The next chapter will continue the RBV journey by looking more closely at what can be done at the more detailed operational level to shape and configure activity, and so leverage operational competencies to achieve competitive advantage.

Key Theories

The key theories discussed in this chapter were:

- **Competitive advantage** – gained by being better than the competition in key areas of performance that are important to the customer.

- **Porter's Five Forces Model** – a framework that helps to identify the influences that shape competition in an industry sector. These forces come from immediate rivals, new entrants, substitute products, buyers and suppliers.

- **Market-based view** – an external-facing view of strategy-making that prioritizes the needs of the market in the strategic decision-making process, so shaping the operation to meet these needs.

- **Resource-based view** – an internal-facing view of strategy-making that prioritizes the capabilities of the organization as the most important factors in achieving competitive advantage.

- **Organizational competencies** – the activities and processes through which the organization deploys its resources effectively to ultimately achieve competitive advantage. These can be classed as threshold, core and distinctive.

- **Customer value proposition** – a combination of the attributes of the product or service that the customer values and the processes that they use to decide what to buy.

- **Dynamic capabilities** – the organization's abilities to develop and change competencies to meet the needs of the rapidly changing environment, and so sustain competitive advantage.

Suggested Answers to Stop and Think Questions

1 **Product–service continuum:** Very few companies exist that can be considered as concerned purely with production. The closest to this extreme may be those that produce very high volumes of very simple and disposable products such as plastic pens or newspapers. These products cannot break down, and even if they did they would be replaced rather than repaired. At the opposite extreme, companies that supply the service of advice-giving, such as legal practices or business consultants, may have little in the way of a tangible product, but even they may need to produce documentation in the form of reports. The overwhelming majority of companies therefore are hybrids, with both product and service elements.

2 **Strategy packaging:** This issue is context specific. In large companies with large numbers of employees who do not have an overview of the business or are not knowledgeable enough to understand the concept and process of strategy, a simple and straightforward message communicated informally may be useful. In smaller, more knowledge-based companies, such as professional practices, the mission and vision statements may be more sophisticated, containing more information designed to provide direct guidance to employees.

3 **The job of the operations manager:** In the past, the operations manager was concerned purely with scheduling, logistics and other production matters. Now the skill set required has grown to include other areas such as design and development, and the supply chain. It also requires knowledge of peripheral functions such as recruitment and training, and the sales and marketing processes. The operations management job has therefore broadened. It also requires a greater level of interaction with the other parts of the organization.

4 **Resource impact:** Clearly, the source of organizational capability is the people in the organization, and their ideas. All aspects of the more organic elements of the organization should be considered to have the most impact. However, this resource will be marginalize if the information that they require is not available, and the culture that they exist within is not supportive.

connect

Review Questions

1 Consider how the time horizon, level of complexity and scope of strategic decisions will differ between a large multinational and an SME.

2 For your local rail company, analyse the competitive environment using Porter's Five Forces model.

3 Consider a successful company that you are familiar with. Can you identify the competencies that it has, and categorize them as threshold, core or distinctive?

4 List the differences between a core competence and a distinctive competence. Can you think of examples of each?

5 Explain what dynamic capabilities are.

Discussion Questions

1 Using the vocabulary introduced – mission, vision, objectives, priorities, etc. – create a corporate strategy package for an organization that you are familiar with.

2 For a highly diversified company such as the Virgin Group, discuss how the top level of the company can implement strategic control over each business unit.

3 Consider and discuss how, as the scope of the operations function increases, the relationship between marketing and operations should be managed.

4   Contrast and compare the resource-based and market-based approaches to strategy-making. Which is more aligned with operations management?

5   Conduct a PESTEL analysis for a large company that operates in your local area.

Visit the Online Learning Centre at **www.mcgraw-hill.co.uk/textbooks/paton** for a range of resources to support your learning.

Further Reading

Augier, M. and Teece, D.J. (2007) 'Dynamic capabilities and multinational enterprise: Penrosean insights and omissions', *Management International Review*, **47**(2), 175–192.

Cepeda, G. and Vera, D. (2007) 'Dynamic capabilities and operational capabilities: a knowledge management perspective', *Journal of Business Research*, **60**(5), 426–437.

Fitzsimmons, J.A. and Fitzsimmons M.J. (2006) *Service Management: Operations, Strategy, and Information Technology*, McGraw-Hill, London.

Griffiths, D.A. and Harvey, M.G. (2006) 'A resource based perspective of global dynamic capabilities', *Journal of International Business Studies*, **32**(5), 597–606.

Helfat, C.E., Finkelstein, S., Mitchell, W., Peteraf, M., Singh, H., Teece, D. and Winter, S. (eds) (2007) *Dynamic Capabilities: Understanding Strategic Change in Organizations*, Blackwell, Oxford.

References

Abell, D.F. (1980) *Defining the Business: The Starting Point of Strategic Planning*, Prentice Hall, Englewood Cliffs, NJ.

Ambrosini, V. and Bowman, C. (2009) 'What are dynamic capabilities and are they a useful construct in strategic management?', *International Journal of Management Reviews*, **11**(1), 29–49.

Barney, J. (1991) 'Firm resources and sustained competitive advantage', *Journal of Management*, **17**(1), 99–120.

Daft, R. (1983) *Organisation Theory and Design*, West, Cengage, OH.

Eden, C. and Ackermann, F. (2005) 'Discovering core competences: working with patterns of distinctive competences and competences', *Proceedings of the British Academy of Management Conference*, Oxford (CD-ROM).

Gutman, J. (1982) 'A means-end model based on consumer categorization processes', *Journal of Marketing*, **48**(2), 60–72.

Hamel, G. and Prahalad, C.K. (1990) 'The core competence of the corporation', *Harvard Business Review*, **68**(3), 79–91.

Hirshleifer, J. (1980) *Price Theory and Applications*, 2nd edn, Prentice Hall, Englewood Cliffs, NJ.

Johnson, J., Scholes, K. and Whittington, R. (2005) *Exploring Corporate Strategy*, 7th edn, FT/Prentice Hall, Harlow.

Kaplan, R.S. and Norton, D.P. (2004) *Strategy Maps: Converting Intangible Assets to Tangible Outcomes*, Harvard Business School Press, Cambridge, MA.

Locket, A., Thompson, S. and Morgenstern, U. (2009) 'The development of the resource–based view of the firm: a critical appraisal', *International Journal of Management Reviews*, **11**(1), 9–28.

Penrose, E.T. (1959) *The Theory of the Growth of the Firm*, Wiley, New York.

Porter, M.E. (1979) 'How competitive forces shape strategy', *Harvard Business Review*, March/April, 86–93.

Porter, M.E. (1980) *Competitive Strategy: Techniques for Analyzing Industries and Competitors*, Free Press, New York.

Sheth, J.N., Newman, B.I. and Gross, B.L. (1991) 'Why we buy what we buy: a theory of consumption values', *Journal of Business Research*, **22**(2), 159–170.

Teece, D.J. and Pisano, G. (1994) 'The dynamic capabilities of firms: an introduction', *Industrial and Corporate Change*, **3**(3), 537–556.

Teece, D.J., Pisano, G. and Shuen, A. (1997) 'Dynamic capabilities and strategic management', *Strategic Management Journal*, **18**(7), 509–533.

Van Looy, B., Gemmel, P. and Van Dierdonck, R. (2003) *Services Management: An Integrated Approach*, 2nd edn, FT/Prentice Hall, Harlow.

Wernerfelt, B. (1984) 'A resource based view of the firm', *Strategic Management Journal*, **5**, 171–180.

Woodruff, R.B. (1997) 'Customer value: the next source for competitive advantage', *Journal of the Academy of Marketing Science*, **25**(2), 139–153.

Woodruff, R.B. and Gardial, S.F. (1996) *Know Your Customer: New Approaches to Understanding Customer Value and Satisfaction*, Blackwell, Oxford.

2 Operations Strategy

Learning Outcomes

After reading this chapter you should be able to:

- Define the term 'operations strategy'
- Develop an operations strategy using the model provided
- Explain the concept of trade-offs in operations management
- Explain how the product life cycle might inform operations strategy
- Discuss the utility of generic operations strategies

Harley-Davidson: From Cubic Inches to Cult Status

Case Study Theme

In relation to loyalty, how many organizations can boast of having the company name tattooed on the bodies of both customers and employees? In terms of longevity, how many companies can boast of over 100 years of life, essentially from a single product? And in terms of exposure, how many companies can boast products so iconic that they are considered an integral part of some of the most famous movies ever made? Despite these factors, the road to success for Harley-Davidson has been a bumpy one. Harley-Davidson has been close to bankruptcy, and has seen its market invaded by foreign competition. More recently the global recession has necessitated changes in the way it operates, in order for it to survive.

Source: © R.W. Spitzenberger/Getty Images

Harley-Davidson is a company that, during its long history, has generally stayed within a single area of business, concentrating on doing what it does well. As you read this case, consider the relationship between operations and corporate strategy; more particularly, think about whether operations strategy must always be subordinate to corporate strategy.

Origins

In 1901 William S. Harley, aged 21, drew up plans for a small engine with a displacement of 7.07 cubic inches (116 cc) to be used in a regular pedal-bicycle frame. Over the next two years he and his friend Arthur Davidson laboured on their motor-bicycle. It was finished in 1903, but unfortunately the boys found their powered cycle unable to conquer Milwaukee's modest hills. Work began on an improved, second-generation machine, and this motorcycle was finished by September 1904. This is the first documented appearance of a Harley-Davidson motorcycle.

By April 1905 complete motorcycles were in limited production, and in 1906 Harley-Davidson built its first factory. Then, in 1907, it extended and increased production to 150 motorcycles a year. So began a period of growth that would see the company dominate the market for domestic heavy motorcycles. By 1914 production had risen to over 16,000 motorcycles a year, and Harley-Davidson had emerged as the clear leader in the American motorcycle market.

Strategic Changes

After continued growth throughout the 1920s, the Great Depression slowed Harley-Davidson's success, with sales plummeting from 21,000 in 1929 to less than 4,000 in 1933. In order to survive, the company made its first truly strategic move, and diversified into the manufacture of industrial power-plants based on its motorcycle engines. This helped the company weather the storm and emerge as one of only two American motorcycle manufacturers to survive the Depression. In the Second World War, Harley-Davidson produced over 90,000 motorcycles for the US Army and the Allies, receiving two awards for production excellence. High levels of civilian production resumed afterwards and success continued until the end of the 1950s.

Challenges

In the 1960s Honda, Kawasaki and Yamaha invaded the American market. When sales at Harley-Davidson dropped, as a result of increasing competition, the company began to look for a buyer, and was finally sold in 1969 to American Machinery and Foundry (AMF), which streamlined production and slashed the workforce. This tactic resulted in a labour strike and a lower quality of bikes. Harley-built cycles were now more expensive than Japanese motorcycles, and inferior in performance, handling and quality. The Harley-Davidson name was mocked as 'Hardly Ableson' and 'Hardly Driveable'.

The 1960s and 1970s saw strategic moves into the production of (rather surprisingly) golf carts in 1963 and (less surprisingly) snowmobiles in 1971, and the purchase of 60% shares in the Tomahawk Boat company. Sales were maintained throughout the 1970s, but the company still struggled with profitability, as AMF was unable to manage the business efficiently. In 1981, with the aid of Citibank, a team of former Harley-Davidson executives began negotiations to reacquire the company from AMF and rescue it from bankruptcy. In a leveraged buyout they pooled $1 million in equity and borrowed $80 million from a consortium of banks.

Operational Changes

Harley's rescue team knew that the Japanese motorbike manufacturers were far ahead in quality management, and they made a bold decision to tour a nearby Honda plant. Ironically, the Japanese had learned total quality management from the Americans Deming and Juran, and soon after their tour of the Honda plant the Harley-Davidson Motor Company decided to put this quality management approach into practice. This, and the implementation of just-in-time inventory (JIT) and an employee involvement scheme, saw costs drop significantly and efficiency rise.

Rather than trying to match the Japanese, a strategy that had been attempted in the 1960s and 1970s with the introduction of smaller cycles, the new management deliberately exploited the 'retro' appeal of the brand, building larger motorcycles that deliberately adopted the look and feel of their earlier machines.

GLOBALIZATION

In addition to operational initiatives such as quality management and JIT, the management introduced a supply chain strategy in which many components, such as brakes, forks and shock absorbers, were outsourced to foreign manufacturers. As quality increased and technical improvements were made, the buyers slowly returned. Further strategic moves were made, including a partnership with Ford, which in 1999 added a Harley-Davidson edition to the Ford F-Series truck, complete with the Harley-Davidson logo.

More recently . . .

In order to counter the economic challenges of the 21st century, Harley-Davidson is executing a strategy to deal with the impact of the recession and the worldwide slowdown in consumer demand, with the intent of strengthening its operations and financial results. This strategy is to invest in strengthening the Harley-Davidson brand and, operationally, to get the cost structure right.

To strengthen the brand, Harley-Davidson is gearing up its marketing to reach out to emerging rider groups. It is also continuing to focus on product innovations targeted at specific growth opportunities with its strong core customer base and new riders. Outside the US the company continues to support dealer development and marketing activities that, over recent years, have helped drive strong retail sales growth.

As the economy has slowed, operationally Harley-Davidson has reduced production and implemented smaller motorcycle shipments, to help the dealerships across the country by not having to carry large, unsold inventory loads. Operations decisions have been taken to consolidate engine and transmission build in Milwaukee, and paint and frame operations at the New York assembly facility, and to outsource parts, accessories and general merchandise distribution through a third party.

Source: www.harley-davidson.com

Introduction

Unlike Warner Bros, Harley-Davidson did not rely on corporate strategy, with methods such as diversification into new product markets and acquisitions of other companies. Throughout its long life Harley-Davidson has tended to stay within one arena, basing its strategy on its core competence in the design and production of motorcycles and small internal combustion engines.

It could be argued that Harley-Davidson prioritized operational strategies over corporate ones, embracing a resource-based approach that emphasized the building and strengthening of core competencies. But this is not the whole story. More recently this internal focus has been supported by a market awareness that suggested it would be difficult to beat the Japanese at their own game, and that the key to success was in the brand. Today Harley-Davidson sells a lifestyle choice that is seen as far more valuable than the physical product alone.

GLOBALIZATION

This case serves to illustrate that there needs to be a balance between the internal and external views of strategy. With Warner Bros the external view has been paramount, with operations shaped to fit the needs of the customer. With Harley-Davidson the product and resources that created it have always been at the forefront, driving the company forward.

The concern of this chapter is operational. It assumes that a strategic direction and goal have been set at the corporate level, and the priority is now to set up the most effective and efficient operational system to enable the organization to meet this goal.

Overview

The purpose of this chapter is to pick up where corporate strategy ends, and investigate how the operational systems and processes are conceived that will support the company in reaching its strategic goals.

This chapter therefore aims to:
- Clarify what operations strategy is
- Explain how operations strategy fits with and complements business strategy
- Introduce a process that will aid in generating operations strategy
- Discuss the contingencies that affect operations strategy.

The treatment of operations strategy in this chapter is aimed squarely at providing a model to guide the creation and operation of the more detailed processes and systems that are the concern of the remainder of this book.

This chapter will begin by investigating what operations strategy actually is, and how it can contribute to meeting overall business objectives. It will continue by introducing a process that can be used to create operations strategy, and then go on to discuss the contingent factors that impact on the work that operations needs to do. It will then look at more generic strategies that can be adopted to simplify the work of operations.

What Is the Role of Operations Strategy?

What Is Operations Strategy?

Operations strategy: the set of major decisions about core competencies, capabilities and processes, technologies, resources and key tactical activities necessary in the function or chain of functions that create and deliver product and service combinations.

Operations strategy, like higher-level corporate strategy, is about decision-making. Slack and Lewis (2002) define it as the pattern of decisions that shape the long-term capabilities of an operation, and their contribution to an overall strategy.

Unlike higher-level strategic decisions, operational decisions tend to be short term and tactical, concerned more with the initiation and directing of action at the lower levels of the organization.

Like higher-level strategic decisions, the decision-making process must be guided towards the achievement of a common purpose, and the 'signposts' that inform the decision-making process may be formalized in statements similar to those used in higher-level strategy-making.

The definition proposed by Slack and Lewis is a reasonable starting point, but it is incomplete; it does not hint at the nature of the decisions to be taken, or set operations strategy within the context of the resource-based view.

Lowson (2002) expands on Slack's view by proposing that operations strategy can be defined as:

> *Major decisions about, and management of: core competencies, capabilities and processes, technologies, resources and key tactical activities necessary in the function or chain of functions that create and deliver product and service combinations and the value demanded by the customer.*

This expanded statement sits well within the resource-based view. It captures the various elements that operations may call upon to support strategy; it highlights the tactical level of operation; and it emphasizes the integration of functional activity into a single entity that aims to satisfy the customer.

It is also useful to think of the purpose of an operations strategy. Why is it necessary? We propose that an operations strategy exists to:

> *Enable the operational unit to create a distinctive competence by effectively blending the resources of the organization and guiding its tactical activities so creating a competitive advantage.*

For those of us with a more straightforward view of the world, the nature of operations strategy can be illustrated by the following anecdote:

> *A body of soldiers sits, far from home, outgunned and completely surrounded by the enemy. The General sits at the entrance to his tent for some considerable time, staring into the blue sky. Eventually he summons the Colonel, and orders him to get the troops back to base.*
>
> *'Can you suggest how I might do that sir?' asks the Colonel.*
>
> *The General replies: 'That's your responsibility. I decide strategy; you implement it.'*

How Can Operations Contribute to Strategy?

We have proposed that operational activity is the engine that drives the business. Extending this analogy, if 'operations' is the engine, the organization is the vehicle, and strategy is the map and destination, then the performance of the organization is based on the efficiency of the engine and how effectively it drives the organization towards the strategic destination. The efficiency of this operational engine is the concern of Parts 2, 3 and 4 of this book. The concern of this chapter is how effectively the operation aligns with strategy and therefore drives the organization. It is therefore worth spending some time understanding how operations can help the organization to pursue and achieve its strategy.

Figure 2.1 separates operational activity into four categories, each representing a different level of contribution that the operational engine makes in support of the business strategy.

Stage 1: Internal Neutrality

At the basic level, operations does the minimum to support the business. It is not aware of the overall business strategy, or of its performance in relation to comparable operations in other organizations, or to overall industry

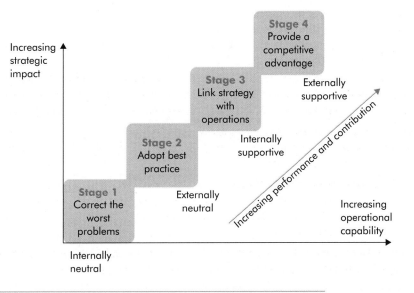

Figure 2.1 The contribution of operations to strategy (Hayes and Wheelwright, 1988)

standards. It is internally facing, not only in relation to the external environment, but also in relation to its position within the organization. There is little attempt to improve performance, and the view of the rest of the organization is that operations is a source of problems rather than of solutions. Any success achieved by the organization is in spite of operations rather than because of it. From a resource-based viewpoint, a company with an operational engine working at this level has no foundation upon which either to plan or to implement strategy. The perception of senior management when questioned about operations would be that it is a source of problems; isolated and uncooperative. It is, in effect, preventing the company from achieving its goals. This can be compared to the 'unconscious incompetent', who is performing poorly and is not even aware of it.

Stage 2: External Neutrality

To move on from Stage 1, even before consideration is given to the business strategy, the operational engine must become self-aware, conscious of its own performance limitations. It will do this by gaining an external perspective, and so begin to compare itself with other, similar operational units that exist within the market. This awareness, coupled with management determination to change, will begin to move the operation to a higher level of performance. Initially this will be seen as 'conscious incompetence', where performance is poor but recognized as being poor, but there is a will to change, and a level of improvement to aim for. The perception of senior management when questioned about operations would be of a group making some effort and achieving some level of improvement. At this stage operations is, in a limited way, able to implement the strategy of the company.

Stage 3: Internally Supportive

Here operations has achieved a level of excellence in terms of the activities that it carries out. It is efficient, and can be relied upon. The key thing is alignment, because at this stage operations has become aware of the business strategy and has aligned itself with it, mobilizing its now considerable capability in pursuit of the overall business goals. Operations is a conscious competent: good at what it does, and aware of what it needs to do to sustain and improve. Operations will begin to generate its own strategy to guide it in the execution of the activities that are required of it in pursuit of the overall company strategy. It may be that some competitive advantage is achieved through excellent operation. Senior management will be confident in the ability of operations to support the direction that the business takes.

Stage 4: Externally Supportive

This stage resonates most clearly with the resource-based view. Here operations has moved further. The change in state from that achieved in Stage 3 is a subtle but significant one. The level of performance reached at Stage 3 has made it best in class, achieving a competitive advantage, but now at Stage 4 operations is innovating, proactively driving forward towards future markets by creating products and services that are one step ahead of the competition. Here senior management is so confident of operations that it can base future business strategy around it: operations is truly in the driving seat.

! Stop and Think

1   Corporate strategy should never be developed without taking operations management into consideration. Think about this statement. Do you agree with it?

Operations Contribution and Competencies

BUSINESS INTEGRATION

From a resource-based perspective it is critical that the maturity of operations is clearly understood, because it will be impossible to build a strategy around the creation of operational competencies if the operations of the company are not performing at least at Stage 3. In the language of competencies, Stages 1 and 2 can be likened to threshold competencies, where just enough is being done for the organization to be present in the market. Stage 3 moves these threshold competencies forward to become core and perhapseven distinctive. Then, at Stage 4, competitive advantage should be gained, with distinctive competencies achieved that may be coupled with some degree of Dynamic Capability. All parts of the business are 'joined up', and operations now has the flexibility to alter its shape in response to, or in anticipation of, changing market conditions.

SHORT CASE 2.1

Teekay Corporation: The Marine Midstream Company

When you turn on a control on your cooker, gas will flow and ignite on the ring. When you insert the nozzle of a petrol pump into the filler of your car and pull the trigger, petrol flows into the tank. The journey of these fuels from deep underground to kitchens and garage forecourts is generally invisible to us unless an ecological disaster and the resulting news story forces it onto our TV screens. Without energy, though, society would be unable to function. Energy powers industries, fuels transportation systems, and generally improves the quality of our lives. But first , that energy must be moved from where it is produced to where it is consumed. You will probably not have heard of the Teekay Corporation, but it is an essential link in the global energy supply chain, serving the world's leading oil and gas companies by transporting more than 10% of the world's seaborne oil and gas. With a fleet of over 155 vessels, offices in 16 countries and 5,600 employees, Teekay helps its customers link their upstream energy production seamlessly to their downstream processing operations.
- Teekay's mission: To be the premier provider of marine services in the oil and gas industry.
- Teekay's core purpose: To be the first choice for customers in the shipping industry; and to uphold the Teekay standard as a respected symbol of quality.

Teekay's reputation for safety, quality and innovation has earned it a position as the Marine Midstream Company; the strength and flexibility of its fleet create a significant competitive advantage for the corporation, and for its customers. With approximately 7,000 loadings and unloadings a year, Teekay's activity is intensive and complex. At the heart of operations, multifunctional ship teams are fully responsible for the day-to-day operations of the fleet, with each team focused on a dedicated group of vessels. Every team is equipped to efficiently deliver the entire service process of vessel operations. Supporting these teams are dedicated competence and performance management systems, including centres of excellence with expertise focused on ensuring compliance, continuously improving performance and developing innovative projects and programmes for every aspect of operations, including marine and technical services, health, safety, quality and information technology.

These systems are the foundation of Teekay's service to its customers. Teekay is a company where success is built upon a core competence in seaborne transportation of fuels. For Teekay the performance of its operations must be externally supportive of the overall company strategy. Every effort is therefore made to achieve operational excellence in everything that the company does.

How Is Operations Strategy Generated?

The Strategy Generation Process

The literature contains several similar approaches to generating operations strategy (Platts and Gregory, 1990; Hill, 1993; Slack *et al.*, 2007). The approach presented here uses elements of each to create a more integrated process that is firmly embedded within the corporate strategy package. This approach is based on a five-step framework, as detailed in Table 2.1.

This process of generating operations strategy provides the bridge between the higher-level strategy dealt with in Chapter 1 and the operational activity that delivers the value proposition.

Step 1: The Corporate View

The company's overall strategic direction should have been defined as an output from the higher-level strategy-making activity. This step therefore links the operations strategy to the corporate strategy. The output of the corporate strategy-making process will have been packaged as mission, vision and objectives, as discussed in Chapter 1. These need to be translated into similar operational statements:

- *Operational vision*: articulates the desired state of performance that the operational unit wants to achieve.
- *Operational objectives*: define the level of performance that needs to be achieved to meet the vision. This will be in terms of quantifiable targets, such as units of output, quality standards to be met, etc.

Table 2.1 Operations strategy-making process

Step	View	Activity description	Purpose
1	Corporate	Translate top-level strategy package into operationally usable terms	To ensure that the content of the corporate (top-level) strategy package is understood, so that any operational activity is totally aligned with the corporate mission, vision and objectives
2	Customer	Define the product and service features that operations must deliver that are important to customers	To ensure that the customer value proposition is fully understood and focused upon
3	Performance	Determine the performance levels that the operation must achieve	To understand the performance of the competition that operations must exceed in order to be successful
4	Process	Plan the operational processes that form the basis of the competence of the operation	To ensure that the operational processes are coherent with the value proposition
5	Infrastructure	Plan the infrastructure required to support the effective and efficient execution of the processes	To ensure that the infrastructure provision supports the operational processes

- *Operational plans*: detailed sequences of activity that if undertaken will lead to the objectives being met and, ultimately, the vision being achieved.
- *Operational priorities*: set the focus by defining what is important in the short term (perhaps weeks or months, depending on the business) as the plans progress. For example, the focus at an early stage within an immature operation might be in training and tooling up, whereas in a more mature operation it might be to attain a better level of quality from an existing process.

The output of this first step, in the form of these statements, is a 'signpost' that ensures that operations does not deviate along a path that is not in line with the overall corporate strategy.

CSR

CRITICAL PERSPECTIVE

Operations and CSR?

Operations management, at its core, is all about creating the correct product or delivering the correct service as efficiently as possible. The key drivers of efficiency are cost of labour, material and utilities. In the 1970s and 1980s efficiency levels tended to be driven by increasingly progressive management and engineering practices, such as kaizen (continuous improvement) and lean manufacturing.

However, since the turn of the century the emphasis has changed. There has been much debate about the ability of the 'high-cost' economies of the West to compete with the 'low-cost' economies of the emerging nations. The lower cost of labour in places such as China, India and South America has resulted in many high-profile companies such as Mattel and Apple taking strategic operational decisions to outsource the manufacture of their products to these countries. Although this has resulted in cheaper costs to produce, and therefore lower consumer prices, there are increasing concerns about the control of these factories and the working practices adopted. Often low cost is achieved by compromising on health and safety, with workers forced to work long hours in poor conditions, leading to ill health and accidents. Child labour is common, with workers as young as six years of age toiling for long hours in factories.

The key point is that decisions in operational strategy are not always based solely on the practical aspects; they must also consider the ethical and social aspects of the factory system.

Step 2: The Customer View

Whereas Step 1 was considered wholly within the corporate strategy-making exercise, Step 2 is more of an overlap between the corporate and operational strategy levels. The elements that make up the customer value proposition will have been considered at the corporate level, but now the detail must be clarified, to define the exact product or service that is to be created and delivered. The features that make up the value proposition presented in Chapter 1 are useful at the corporate level, but at the operational level we must be more specific, and define clearly what can be produced that the customer will buy. The following list contains generally accepted elements that customers may value in a product or service. These elements may not all be applicable in all cases, but some combination of them will feature in all buying decisions.

In relation to both physical products and the delivery of services, the following tangible elements will be important:

- *Price* – or how much the product costs. In most cases this will carry some weight in the customer's decision-making process. For undifferentiated products such as airline travel, or many consumer goods and services where convenience is important, the price will be paramount, as many customers will reason that cheapest is best.
- *Functionality* – or what the product does. Where price is less of a consideration, products that do more may be more attractive to customers. This is especially true for technology-based products such as the iPhone, where the variety of features and the extent of its functionality are the prime considerations in choosing it over a rival product.

- *Performance* – or how well the product does what it is meant to do. This element will feature more strongly in higher-value 'statement' products, such as a Porsche car, or in products that help in the completion of work tasks, such as Snap-on tools.
- *Variety/customization* – or how well the product fits the need. This is more relevant where additional features may be added to a core set of functions, in products such as a mobile phone, or in financial services such as mortgage and investment provision.
- *Quality* – or how closely the product meets its intended purpose. There are various meanings attributed to the word 'quality'; here it is defined as conformance to requirements, and in situations where the customer has a very clear requirement, a quality product will be one that meets that requirement most closely. This is applicable to any product or service, and is an overall measure of how robust it is and how much functionality it has in relation to what the customer specified it should have.

Five Dimensions of Service Quality

In relation to service delivery, all the above elements apply, and are commonly labelled the *tangibles*. In service operations the tangibles tend to take a slightly different emphasis, representing:
- The appearance of the physical facilities and personnel
- The quality of the tools or equipment used to provide the service
- The artefacts used in provision of the service, such as cutlery or credit cards

In addition to the tangibles, the following intangibles must also be considered:
- *Responsiveness* – or willingness to help a customer and provide prompt service. This element is applicable to all service encounters, but it is most powerful in a less-structured service environment, where there is more opportunity for the customer to request something random, or outside the normal scope of operation. For example, a high-class restaurant with a varied menu might be expected to be more responsive than a fast-food outlet, where the customer would not think to request an alteration to the service on offer.
- *Reliability* – or the consistency of performance and dependability. Here the promises that the customer has been given are honoured correctly, and consistently, over numerous service encounters.
- *Assurance* – or the ability of the operation to inspire confidence. This element is most easily illustrated in the provision of professional services. For example, in a dental surgery the ambience of the surroundings, the infrastructure and tooling, and the knowledge and expertise displayed by the staff make the client feel secure in the experience.
- *Empathy* – or the understanding and attentiveness shown to customers. Here the focus is mainly on the skills of the staff, their awareness of others, and their ability to communicate effectively. This is most easily seen in relation to the emergency services, where empathizing with the victim is both a key feature of the service experience and a critical factor in the effective performance of the task.

The collective group of tangibles and the four intangible factors above have become commonly known as the *five dimensions of service quality*.

The output of this step provides a clear understanding of what the operational processes must be set up to deliver. In other words, it represents a signpost pointing at what the customer wants, and thus ensures that operations has a clear view of what it is aiming to do.

CRITICAL PERSPECTIVE

Dimensions of Service Quality

For a physical product the features used to describe what the customer wants tend to be discrete, absolute, and easy to measure. The features of service quality are often less easy to define. Some criticism has been generated in the following areas:
- *Independence*: the four intangible dimensions are relatively easy to understand and 'handle', but they may not be as discrete as they first seem. It has been suggested that assurance is a combination of competence, courtesy and credibility, and that empathy may be broken down into access and understanding.

▶
- *Completeness*: there are many behaviours that customers may look for in a good service, such as care, friendliness and integrity, but it is not clear how these fit into the model.
- *Calibration*: there are no universal dimensions for measurement, such as metres, volts or degrees Celsius. Each element has to be calibrated for the specific situation.
- *Universal usage*: each element may have a slightly different meaning in different contexts. With tangibles a centimetre is a centimetre, regardless of context, but in service settings assurance will mean something different in the accident and emergency department of a hospital, for example, than in a fast-food outlet.

The key point is that in service situations the elements used to define the performance required must be specific, and must be selected and calibrated to suit the industry context.

Order-Winning and Order-Qualifying Criteria

Order-winning criteria: the key reasons to buy a product or service.

Order-qualifying criteria: the required standards that, if not achieved, will disqualify a product or service from consideration by the customer.

A good way to determine the relative importance of each element is to distinguish between **order-winning criteria** and **order-qualifying criteria** (Hill, 1993).

Order-winning criteria are features that the customer regards as key reasons to buy the product or service. Improving these elements will directly affect the business that is won. Order-qualifying criteria will be less key to winning business, but will play a part in *losing* it. In other words if an element of these criteria is not present at the required standard, it may disqualify the product or service from consideration by the customer.

Satisfiers and Dissatisfiers

Another way to look at this has been proposed by Johnston (1995), who suggests that each dimension of service quality can be categorized in three ways, as follows:
- Predominantly a *satisfier*: deficiency in these elements results in negative customer feelings (complaining behaviour), but excess performance does not lead to positive feelings.
- Predominantly a *dissatisfier*: excess performance in this area leads to positive feelings in the customer, but deficiency does not lead to negative feelings.
- A *mixture of both*.

Johnston found that, in a bank, attentiveness, care and friendliness were satisfiers; integrity, reliability and functionality were dissatisfiers; and responsiveness could be both.

Step 3: The Performance View

In Step 2 we considered the features of the product or service that the customer required, and how they could be quantified. In Step 3 we consider the performance of the operation as it attempts to build the required features into the products it manufactures, or the services it delivers.

Once all the product and service features are understood (Step 2), the key consideration is the performance of competitor operations, as this must be exceeded if the market is to be captured.

Some way of measuring operational performance and some understanding of the mechanisms that deliver that performance are required. There is a distinction between tangible and intangible elements that must be considered.

Tangible elements tend to be easier to quantify and measure – the mechanisms (process and system) within operations that create the product or deliver the service more directly connected to the performance of the output. For example, reducing production costs through efficiency gains will have a direct effect on the price of the product or service.

The intangibles are more abstract, and tend to be measured indirectly – in the same way as the mechanisms that support delivery of these elements also tend to act more indirectly. For example, it is more difficult to take direct action to increase elements such as assurance or empathy, because these are closely related to the skill of the front-line staff and the perception of the customer.

Tangible Performance Measures

> **Performance measures:** factors that the customer will use to judge the performance of a product or service.

Cost

- *Operational priority*: providing tradable products/services while still returning a profit.
- ***Performance measure***: numerical measures of efficiency such as labour utilization, cost of goods, work in progress.
- *Operational delivery mechanism*: process excellence leading to high levels of efficiency and low-cost operation.
- *Rationale*: here the ability of the organization to perform well in relation to cost is directly related to how efficient (cost-effective) the conversion process is.

Functionality and performance

- *Operational priority*: providing goods or service that embody the correct level of functionality and product features.
- *Performance measure*: numerical measure of compliance with customer requirement.
- *Operational delivery mechanism*: design, development and technology processes.
- *Rationale*: the organization's ability to embody functionality and features in the product or service delivery system in a more innovative, comprehensive or useful way will result in the customer perceiving greater utility.

Variety/customization

- *Operational priority*: provide a range of goods or services that fit the needs of a wide range of market segments with the minimum of functional redundancy.
- *Operation performance measure*: numerical measure of the number of discrete products or product families based on a core concept.
- *Operation delivery mechanism*: design, productionization and configuration control processes.
- *Rationale*: the cost-effective provision of a variety of customized products or services from a core concept will increase the size of the market, as niches will be catered for. Here the emphasis is on the elimination of over-engineering by excluding all but the required functionality, and on the use of processes that enable additional variants to be created at a small incremental cost.

Quality

- *Operational priority*: provide a product or service that exactly meets the customer requirements and is fit for purpose.
- *Operational performance measure*: numerical measure of number of defects occurring in the conversion process, customer returns or complaints, scrap rates, warranty repair costs, etc.
- *Operation delivery mechanism*: total quality management system.
- *Rationale*: consistent adherence to customer expectation will result in repeat business.

CRITICAL PERSPECTIVE

What Is Quality from a Customer's Viewpoint?

Which is the better-quality car: a Ferrari or a Ford? The answer to this question from many car buyers would probably be 'a Ferrari' – but the logic for this answer is not entirely clear. Some reasons might be the sophisticated styling, the exclusive brand, certain aspects of the performance, and the high price. This typifies the general perception of quality. In some circumstances, though, the Ferrari may not fit the purpose that a car as a mode of transport is required for. It may lack storage space and therefore be unfit for the weekly shop or the school run; it may be thirsty for fuel and therefore unfit for the environmentally minded motorist; and it may be uncomfortable to travel in for long journeys. This introduces the concept of quality as *fitness for purpose*.

▶

▶ In operations terms, quality is a measure of how well the product or service fits the purpose for which it is intended. From this perspective almost any product can be considered a quality product, so long as 'it does what it says on the tin'. To define fitness for purpose, all aspects of the product or service must be specified at the design phase, and the product or service must then be delivered to meet these specifications exactly. Therefore if the specification is for a car that carries five people, delivers economy of 50 miles per gallon, has a top speed of 70 mph, needs servicing every 20,000 miles and has a warranty covering five years of trouble-free usage, then the Ferrari would probably not fit the specification, and therefore could not be considered a quality car. The same is true in the provision of a service. Many people would consider McDonald's, with its simple, cheap food, to be low quality in comparison with a Michelin star-rated restaurant; but if the customer is in the market for cheap, functional food delivered with the minimum of fuss, and McDonald's delivers this consistently to the standard promised by their specification, then it can also claim to be a quality food outlet – which some may find difficult to 'swallow'.

The key point is that quality for operations managers is considered as an absolute measure of conformance to requirement, and not a more nebulous measure of comparison or perception.

Intangible Performance Measures

Tangible measures of the performance of products are fairly easy to quantify and measure, but the intangibles present in services – responsiveness, reliability, assurance and empathy – are more problematic.

Reliability:
- Promises to do something by a certain time, and then does so
- Shows a sincere interest in solving your problems
- Performs the service right, first time

Responsiveness:
- Always willing to help customers
- Always gives prompt service to customers
- Is never too busy to respond to customer requests

Assurance:
- The behaviour of employees instils confidence
- Employees are always courteous
- Employees always have the knowledge required

Empathy:
- Employees give customers individual attention
- Has operating hours that are convenient to customers
- Understands specific customer needs

The key to thorough measurement is to ensure that the questions are correct for the market context, and relevant to the customer and the service being offered.

So intangibles must be measured indirectly. The mechanisms that drive performances are similarly indirect. Some processes can be implemented to ensure responsiveness, but elements such as empathy can be provided only through the skill of the staff. Therefore the selection, recruitment and training of staff will indirectly contribute to higher performance in this area.
- *Operational priority*: providing a professional and reassuring customer experience
- *Performance measure*: mixture of quantifiable measures (usually time-based) and unquantifiable measures gauged by customer satisfaction questionnaires or verbal feedback
- *Operational delivery mechanism*: processes and skill of the front-line staff
- *Rationale*: the organization's ability to manage the customer through the service delivery process as professionally as possible will result in repeat business.

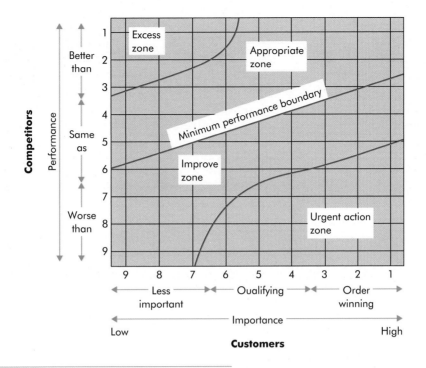

Figure 2.2 Performance prioritizing source (Slack *et al.*, 2007)

Although we are dealing here with the making of operations strategy, it is important to understand the nature of the products and services that are being provided. Chapters 12 and 13 will deal with these dimensions in more detail, in relation to how the process can be managed to create a quality product or service.

> **❶ Stop and Think**
>
> **2** Operations management is primarily about consistency and conformity, and the creation of a repetitive process that doesn't diverge from a preset norm. Consider the effect not only of 'unpredictable' customers within the service process, but also of 'empowered' employees.

Performance Prioritizing

To help understand the performance levels that are required in each of the elements above, Slack *et al.* (2007) extend this model by creating a performance matrix that also takes the competition into account. This is a more complex model, but it also provides an understanding of which factors need the most work. It can therefore help in prioritizing operational effort, in relation both to the order-winning criteria and to which elements are most deficient in relation to the competition. This model is shown in Figure 2.2.

This model has four steps in its use:

1   Define the elements that are an important part of the value proposition.

2   Plot these in the matrix in relation to competition and customer, as defined in Table 2.2. For example if an element is a 1 on 'importance to customer' but a 9 in 'performance against competition' then urgent action is needed to move it above the competition.

3   Prioritize the action areas by analysing the gaps between the performance of your company and the required performance.

4   Formulate plans to change the performance for each element to meet the required performance target.

Table 2.2 Performance criteria

	Performance against competition	**Importance to customer**
1	Considerably better	Provides a crucial advantage
2	Clearly better than	Provides an important advantage
3	Marginally better	Provides a useful advantage
4	Sometimes better	Needs to be above industry standards
5	Same	Needs to meet industry standards
6	Slightly worse than some	Needs to be on par with competition
7	Worse than most	Not important but may become so in future
8	Worse than all	Rarely considered by customers
9	Considerably worse than all	Never considered by customers

There are four zones in the matrix:

- *Appropriate*: here the balance of importance to customer against performance as compared with the competition is about right. Any effort to improve here may be a waste of resources.
- *Improve*: the elements in question are important enough to be worthy of consideration, and the performance in this area, compared with the competition, is deficient enough to warrant action.
- *Urgent action*: these elements are critical to the customer, and the competition has a significant advantage, so action must be taken immediately.
- *Excess*: elements in this zone are performing well, but if the importance to the customer is sufficiently low, it may be that excessive effort and resource are being expended. Perhaps some reduction in performance could be accepted, with the associated reduction in cost.

**BUSINESS
INTEGRATION**

**SHORT
CASE
2.2**

Linn Products: We Start with the Music . . .

Linn Products was established in 1972 by Ivor Tiefenbrun. Born in Glasgow, he was passionate about two things – engineering, and listening to music. When he couldn't buy a hi-fi good enough to satisfy his needs, he decided to make one himself.

In 1972 Linn introduced the Sondek LP12 turntable, the longest-lived hi-fi product still in production anywhere in the world, and still the benchmark by which all turntables are judged.

Source: © Galina Dreyzina/iStock

The Linn Sondek LP12 turntable revolutionized the hi-fi industry, proving categorically that the source of the music is the most important component in the hi-fi chain. Linn then set out to make the other components in the hi-fi chain as revolutionary as the first, setting new standards for performance over the years with each new product.

Today, Linn is an independent, precision-engineering company uniquely focused on the design, manufacture and sale of complete music and home theatre systems for customers who want the best. Linn systems can be found throughout the world – in royal residences, and on board super-yachts.

At Linn, operations is an integrated process, from product development through to after-sales service. All aspects of Linn's products are designed in house, and all the key processes are controlled by Linn people. Linn believes that everything can be improved by human interest and attention to detail. So the same

person builds, tests and packs a complete product, from start to finish. They take all the time necessary to ensure that every detail is correct.

Only then will the person responsible for building the product sign it off and pack it for dispatch. Every product can be tracked all the way from that individual to the customer, anywhere in the world. Linn systems are sold only by selected specialist retailers who have a similar commitment to quality products and service.

Question

1   In the production of its goods, Linn does not embrace a traditional Fordist production line philosophy, where numerous workers do very small pieces of the process in a highly controlled environment. Linn relies on skilled, empowered workers, who take responsibility for all aspects of build and test. What are the advantages and disadvantages of this production method?

Sources: www.linn.co.uk; in-company research.

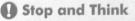 **Stop and Think**

3   Most organizations strive for excellence in some way or other. Consider the operational challenges in actually becoming and remaining a world leader.

Step 4: The Process View

Having understood all aspects of the product to be manufactured, or the service to be delivered, and having then defined the required performance of the operation, we must plan the individual processes that make up the overall conversion process. Finding answers to the following questions will help with this.

- How is the conversion actually carried out – a mix of technology and human labour?
- What are the basic operations principles of the system – leanness, flexibility, etc.?
- What competencies will form part of the system – extent and use of supply chain?
- What are the limits of the system – capacity and time?
- Where is the system located – proximity to suppliers or customers?
- How is the system organized – layout and arrangement for movement of parts and/or people?
- How is quality ensured – what methods are to be used?

Making such decisions at this stage will help in guiding the design of the individual processes. The detail of how to design these processes is dealt with in Part 2 of this book.

Step 5: The Infrastructure View

The tactical decisions around the shape of the conversion process that were taken in the previous step now need to be supported by similar decisions on the support infrastructure. Decisions should be taken here in the following areas:

- *Management structure*: hierarchical, flat or matrix
- *Management system*: autocratic or empowered
- *Job design*: tasks highly divided and deskilled, or craft based
- *Enterprise control system*: discrete systems for inventory, accounts, manufacturing, etc. or all integrated within a single business system
- *Automation*: level and type of technology employed
- *Shape of the supply chain*: suppliers used, and how they are managed.

Making Operations Strategy: Summary

The five-step process outlined above begins at the level of corporate strategy, and progresses through increasingly detailed decisions until all the tactical decisions that make up an operations strategy have been taken. With this level of operations strategy now in place, the detailed activity of designing the products and processes can begin.

However, there are various contingencies that need to be considered when generating operations strategy. The two most important are the concern of the next section.

WORKED EXAMPLE 2.1

Big-town Builders: Laying the Foundation for Success

Sandy Concrete gazed expectantly across the boardroom table at his operations director, Will Shovel, hoping to be surprised and delighted by his response to Sandy's question. But after a few seconds of awkward silence, 'surprised and delighted' gave way to 'mildly hopeful', which in turn stood aside for 'disappointed as usual'. Counting to ten, Sandy resisted the temptation to let 'disappointed as usual' hand over the baton to 'mildly annoyed'.

Will was not a bad operations director. A fully skilled builder with 30 years on the job, he had vast experience of construction, he was hardworking, a good planner, and respected by those around him. Will's problem was that he had no strategic vision. Give him a job to do and, like a Duracell bunny, he would do it and do it until the job was done, or he died trying. But ask him to operationalize a corporate strategy and he would slump dejectedly in his chair and stare off vacantly into space. You might as well ask a dog to play a trumpet.

Sandy gazed around the table at the board of Big-town Builders: Johnny Cash, Financial Controller; Lottie Stuff, Procurement; Sheila Wheels, Transport and Logistics; Wilma Sackem, Human Resources; and finally Jim N. Tonyx, Sales and Marketing, sitting, as always, in stylish sunglasses and sharp suit, proudly nursing his latest hangover.

Sandy pushed on, determinedly repeating himself, this time aiming at the wider audience.

'Ladies and gentlemen, we are the top management team. We need to think about the future. The current economic situation has caused our traditional market for affordable, small housing to dry up. Normal people can no longer afford to buy houses – only rich people can.'

Nods of sad agreement rippled round the table at this last point.

'We need to change strategy to survive. Our marketing people have done some research. The way forward is luxury dwellings, fitted to the highest standard with the newest technologies, and built using the latest in environmental and sustainable materials and processes.'

At this point Sandy paused, before taking a deep breath and continuing.

'With, of course, the highest-specification security system to keep the increasing numbers of desperate homeless people out.'

A man of some morals, but mainly not wanting to dwell on a negative, Sandy moved hastily on.

'Our corporate slogan will no longer be "Big-town builds bright, budget and bijou". From now on it will be "Big-town homes – big, bold, beautiful and blissful".'

At this Jim N. Tonyx stirred in his seat, sat up, and beamed around the table, making sure he gained his rightful credit for coming up with this catchy yet business-like slogan.

Ignoring him, Sandy concluded: 'We need to make this vision into a reality – has anyone any ideas on how we can approach this?'

Problem: *Use the operations strategy-making process to help Big-town Builders achieve their strategic vision.*

Approach: The issue here is that this company is set up operationally for one type of activity – the design, build and support of small, traditionally built, budget homes. They now need to change, to

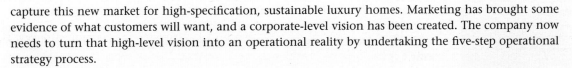

capture this new market for high-specification, sustainable luxury homes. Marketing has brought some evidence of what customers will want, and a corporate-level vision has been created. The company now needs to turn that high-level vision into an operational reality by undertaking the five-step operational strategy process.

Solution:

Corporate: Here the vision is relatively clear: budget and small is out, large and luxurious is in. From an operational point of view this needs to be translated into what is actually going to be done. The operational vision must be set. Here the signal is clear: quality is the most important thing. Objectives must then be set in relation to cost, quality and volume. Then plans must be made and priorities set.

Customer: Further research must be carried out to define exactly what a luxury sustainable dwelling actually looks like. What price, quality, functionality and variety of features do customers want in their house? All customer requirements must be understood. There are some clues in the case: security system as standard, high-tech equipment, green materials, and so on. This list must be expanded to include the number of rooms, the choice of fixtures, fittings and features, and the size of the garden. In essence, what does the affluent citizen of Big-town require of a home? From this information, a range of house types can be designed. In addition to the physical product, Big-town builders must set up a support operation that includes selling and after-sales service. Think of the intangibles. How would customers want to be treated as they purchase, move into and live in their new home?

Performance:

Product performance must be set in terms of building regulations to be met. For example, how thermally efficient are the buildings? Will they meet the required environmental standards?

Operational performance must be considered; targets must be set for efficiency in all aspects of the operation – how quickly things are done, and how well the construction activities are performed.

Process:

Do the core competencies for this work exist in the business? The processes required to build using 'green' rather than traditional and high-tech rather than standard materials need to be developed. Luxury homes may have home entertainment systems and IT provision, all of which needs to be designed and built in, with the necessary fabrication and installation processes. Sales and service processes for customer care will need to be more robust, capable of dealing with a more demanding customer and a more sophisticated product.

Infrastructure:

In addition to the tools and equipment to build the homes, Big-town also need to create an organizational infrastructure to support the activity: a supply chain of companies for the additional materials and expertise required; an IT support system capable of scheduling the larger bills of materials, and controlling the configuration of different house types; and possibly a change of management structure to control this new business.

Contingencies in Operations Strategy Generation

Trade-offs

When creating an operations strategy, it must be kept in mind that an operations system can be designed to do some things well but at the expense of others; one element of performance must be traded off against another. This has parallels in other pursuits. For example, in athletics, to achieve a certain speed over a long distance a good marathon runner must trade off strength in muscle mass against weight to be carried. Or to achieve super-sonic flight a jet fighter trades off size and fuel efficiency against maximum speed.

Trade-offs: factors that cannot exist concurrently in their best state; the optimization of one necessitates a compromise in another.

In operations systems, possible **trade-offs** are:

- *Low price against available variety*: systems that have to operate at low cost will normally be set up to produce a small number of configurations at a high volume of product. Here the requirement for change of configuration or product type adds cost.
- *Speed against flexibility*: changes to the requirement will reduce the speed of service. For example, any change to the timing or destination of a package may affect the speed of the delivery.
- *Personalized attention against volume of customers*: a call centre, for example, may set time limit targets for its operators specifying a maximum call length. This action may force the operator to be dismissive with the customer, and therefore reduce the quality of the service experience.

Trade-offs are impossible to ignore. The key thing is to understand where the operational focus should rest, and ensure that the element being compromised in the trade-off is less important to the customer than the element being prioritized.

SHORT CASE 2.3

Zara: The Need for Speed . . .

Amancio Ortega Gaona began working as a delivery boy for a shirt-maker when he was only 13 years old. He later managed a tailor's shop, where he made nightshirts and pyjamas. In 1963, when still in his 20s, he started Confecciones GOA in La Coruña, to manufacture women's pyjamas (and later lingerie products), initially for sale directly to garment wholesalers. In 1975 the firm opened its first Zara retail shop in La Coruña, Spain. Then in the 1980s the company established retail operations in all the major Spanish cities. In 1988 the first international Zara store opened in Porto, Portugal, followed shortly by New York City in 1989 and Paris in 1990. But the real 'step up' in foreign expansion took place during the 1990s, when Zara entered Europe, the Americas and Asia.

Source: © Kevin Foy/Alamy

Zara is now present across the world, with a network of over 1,500 stores. Zara claims to move with society, dressing the ideas, trends and tastes that society itself creates. It is claimed that Zara needs just two weeks to develop a product and get it into stores, compared with the industry average of nearly six months. Zara has a large design team, and its design process is closely linked to the public. Information travels from the stores to the design teams, transmitting the demands and concerns of the market. The vertical integration of operational activities (design, production, logistics and sales in the company's own stores) means Zara is flexible and fast in adapting to the market. Its operational strategy is characterized by speed and continuous product renovation.

Question

1 Zara's operations strategy is clearly built around speed and agility. What key enablers do you think it relies on to achieve this level of performance?

Sources: www.zara.com; Strathclyde University teaching case.

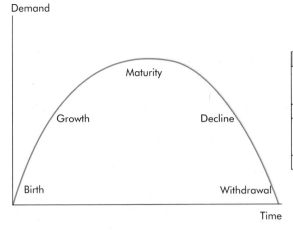

Stage	Birth	Growth	Maturity	Decline
	Product/service just introduced to market	Gains acceptance	Market saturates	Alternatives available
Volume	Low	Rapid growth	Level	Rapid decline
Order winners	Functions, capability and reputation	Availability and quality	Cost and dependability	Cost
Customers	Innovators	Early adopters	Main market	Late adopters

Figure 2.3 Product life cycle

Product/Service Life Cycle Model

The **product life cycle** model, originally formulated by Vernon (1966), and illustrated in Figure 2.3 is an attempt to generalize customer behaviour over the lifetime of a product. From an operations perspective it is important to have some appreciation of the part life cycles play in your market, because each stage will require a change in emphasis of the operations strategy. Factors that may change and affect how operations behave are summarized and understanding of how these factors interact within a specific market will provide a context for the generation and subsequent evolution of the operations strategy.

> **Product life cycle:** generalized model of the buying behaviour of customers over time; used to predict demand for a product or service.

How Can Operations Strategy Be Simplified?

What is clear about strategy-making, at both the corporate and operational levels, is the number and complexity of the decisions that need to be made. Michael Porter (1985) proposed a shortcut in the form of three different *generic strategies* that firms could use to achieve competitive advantage:

- *Differentiation*: an emphasis on providing products and services that are different from and more desirable than those offered by the competition
- *Overall cost leadership*: an emphasis on providing a comparative level of utility at a lower cost than the competition
- *Focus*: an emphasis on serving niche markets

These strategies have been criticized heavily, as they are not totally discrete. Each must contain elements of the others: for example, low price alone will not sell a product or service, and a differentiation strategy may result in a greater focus on specific markets. However, although these proposals may break down under scrutiny, from an operations point of view it is useful to think of them as an overall guide to the emphasis that operations must adopt when creating the conversion process.

Contemporary Thinking: Value Disciplines

Porter's strategies were developed as a tool to assist higher-level strategy-making, but work has been done to translate similar ideas into the operational arena. Treacy and Wiersema (1993) approached the idea of generic strategies from the viewpoint of value for the customer. They argued that a value proposition is a combination of the elements that the customer wants and will pay for – both tangible (price, functionality/performance, variety/customization, and performance) and intangible (reliability, responsiveness, assurance and empathy). In this view, the first three steps of the operations strategy-making process outlined previously will be aimed at defining exactly what the value proposition is composed of.

Treacy and Wiersema propose three generic operations strategies, or *value disciplines*, that inform the set-up of the operation: operational excellence, product leadership and customer intimacy.

Operational Excellence

The focus here is on the lowest overall cost to the customer. The key point is that the overall cost to the customer does not consist only of the price paid; it includes other intangible costs that the customer may experience, such as the inconvenience levels that result from problems with the product, or the wasted time associated with a poor service.

The concept of operational excellence is based upon the principles of efficiency. As a result, products and services are standardized, with little variety, as this would have a detrimental impact on the efficiency of the organization.

Operationally, the aim is to reduce waste through programmes such as lean manufacturing, reducing cost at all opportunities within the production process. Growth comes from a constant steady volume of business, discovering new ways to use existing assets, and identifying opportunities to repeat their excellence in new markets. Operational excellence tends to be at the heart of many service businesses, where high volumes of customers are routinely dealt with. Transport companies such as train operators must prioritize this: customers prioritize reliability and speed above the aesthetic appeal of the train and the track, and seldom have any allegiance to one company over another. Banks and other companies that use call-centre-based operations also operate on this model. If the call centre does not work well, frustrated customers will consider taking their business elsewhere.

BUSINESS INTEGRATION

SHORT CASE 2.4

'S Baggers — Bagging a meal

It's fair to say we live in a technological age – the latest gadgets, such as iPhones, iPads and Blackberries, dominate our world. The food industry has kept pace with modernity, embracing trends such as fast food and designer meals. However, 'S Baggers restaurant in Nuremberg, Germany, has taken things a step further, by incorporating the latest technology in the process of food delivery.

The proprietor of the restaurant, Michael Mack, decided to remove waiters and staff from the front of house, allowing the humans in the operation to

Source: © Vario images GmbH & Co.KG/Alamy

focus on preparing exceptional food. 'S Baggers is the world's first fully automated restaurant. At 'S Baggers you don't need waiters to order food. Customers use touch-screen TVs to read the menu and select their meal. The dishes are delivered over a patented, gravity-fed, conveyor belt system. The inside of the restaurant resembles a theme park rollercoaster ride, with tracks running all the way from the kitchen high up in the roof down to the tables, twisting and turning as they go. The food whizzes down the tracks in little 'cars' to the customers' tables.

Unlike fast-food outlets, in the kitchen it is man, not machine, that makes the food. Everything is prepared from fresh ingredients, with high-quality dining in mind. When it is ready, the meal is given a sticker in a colour to match the customer's seat, and dispatched downhill to the correct table.

As an operations strategy this allows 'S Baggers to combine the quality inherent in a meal prepared by a fully skilled chef with the low cost and convenience associated with a fully mechanized delivery system.

Questions

1 What do you think are the disadvantages of removing people from the process of serving food?
2 Do the advantages of the low-cost mechanized system outweigh the disadvantages?

Sources: www.sbaggers.de; in-company research.

Product Leadership

The focus here is on the ability to make products and deliver services that customers recognize as superior. Innovation is the key process, which relies on the talents and creativity of employees. Therefore research and development is the operational focus in the pursuit of the next breakthrough.

Markets must be educated when breakthrough products and services are developed, because customers must realize their potential value before they can be expected to buy them. Once educated, customers are willing to pay premium prices for these products. Intangible value here may be found in the social acceptance gained from buying a leading brand or the lifestyle that is associated with owning the product. From an operations perspective a flexible structure, with the ability to focus resources on the most successful projects, is key. High-technology offerings such as the iPhone, or the latest games console, must be the leading product in their arena, or the discerning customer will move on to the 'next big thing'. High-quality items such as Rolex watches or branded jewellery must similarly be seen as the best in class, or the customer will move on to another class.

Customer Intimacy

The aim in this value discipline is to offer a total solution service to the customer. The value is therefore primarily in the overall service offered, of which the product may only be a part. Customer-intimate organizations form strong relationships with their customers. They focus on learning as much as possible about their customers' business, and so ensure that they can serve them in the most effective way. The services on offer are tailored to customer requirements, to ensure that the client feels that they receive the best service available. Such organizations exploit their customer relationships to ensure that they achieve the full business potential from their client, to the extent where the customer becomes dependent upon their organization for their service. The development of such relationships results in these organizations taking on the responsibilities of their clients, with the aim that the two parties will achieve mutual success.

Operationally, all departments must be aligned to provide a total solution, as employees are required to adapt to the changing needs of the customer. All companies must have a certain relationship with their customers, but large engineering and construction companies have recently discovered the utility of this strategy. For example, partnering arrangements between governments and large engineering contractors in the procurement of defence equipment such as planes and submarines create a seamless relationship. Here success is based on knowing your customer better than they know themselves, predicting new requirements, managing their risks, and proactively solving their problems.

Value Matrix

Martinez and Bititci (2001, 2006) developed the value disciplines further in their model called the **value matrix**. This is based on the proposal that there can be organizations that have the same value proposition (operational excellence, product leader or customer intimacy), but differ in their operational configuration.

> **Value matrix:** a framework of generic operations strategies called value propositions that informs the set-up of the operation.

The value matrix therefore introduces *hard* and *soft* factors that provide further focus on how the overall operational strategy can be implemented by the organization. Hard characteristics are based on the technology used by the organization, whereas the soft characteristics are based on intangible activities (Table 2.3).

- *Innovators*: invest significantly in the R&D function of the business, having high levels of design skills that can make use of this investment in their pursuit of breakthrough products. Operationally, they aim to reduce the time to market of their products, and dedicate resources to educating their potential markets. The customers of innovative organizations are prepared to pay premium prices for such products, expecting them to be technologically superior to any other comparable product.
- *Brand managers*: invest in the brand of their products by creating a status that becomes associated with their brand name. They achieve this with a mix of physical and non-physical attributes. The operational focus of brand managers is market orientated, developing streamlined distribution channels and fast delivery. The markets of brand managers often pay premium prices to gain the status that accompanies the product, so achieving social acceptance or recognition.

Table 2.3 The value matrix

	Hard	**Soft**
Product leadership	Innovators: • Customers buy new products never seen before, and value advanced technology applied in new devices • Microsoft and Intel	Brand managers: • Customers pay a premium for the status brought by the product, and value the feelings of superiority and well-being that it brings • Harley-Davidson and Nike
Operational excellence	Price minimizers: • Customers buy ordinary products, and value adequate performance at low prices • Toyota and Casio	Simplifiers: • Customers buy convenience at a relatively low price, and value easy-to-do business transactions. • EasyJet and Amazon
Customer intimacy	Technological integrators • Customers buy tailored products and services configured to their needs; they value total care • IBM and Cisco Systems	Socializers: • Customers buy flexible service, and value good relationships • Sales Consultancy Service and DHL

Source: Martinez and Bititci (2001).

- *Price minimizers*: aim to offer products to their customers at the lowest price on the market. They do so by operating a low-cost facility that is focused on optimizing process performance and reducing waste, made possible through the adoption of lean techniques. The customers of such organizations focus primarily on the price, combined with acceptable features, when making purchasing decisions. Here other factors such as performance are traded off against cost.
- *Simplifiers*: attempt to make the buying process accessible and convenient for their customers. This involves the coordination of production and distribution activities, requiring no other members of the supply chain. Customers who buy products from simplifiers seek a purchasing process that is straightforward, and requires little input.
- *Technological integrators*: tailor their offerings to customer requirements. They have a wide variety of skills as their capability that allows them to adapt to consumer demands. These organizations tend to have selection criteria for their customers, on the basis that they will form long-term relationships with them, presenting the potential for repeat business.
- *Socializers*: offer a flexible service to customers, who have confidence in the ability of the organization. The customer seeks a reliable service, and trusts the organization to deliver its offerings, fulfilling the standards set by previous experiences of the organization and so perpetuating the relationship.

Although the value disciplines are still quite wide in scope, they are more specific than Porter's generic strategies. Externally they focus more closely on a single market segment or customer group, and internally they inform the configuration of the operational activity, and therefore are more useful when applied to the business unit rather than at the corporate level.

CRITICAL PERSPECTIVE

Value for All

Operations strategy, by its nature, is focused more narrowly in scope than corporate strategy. Indeed, until very recently the operations function was considered to be totally inward-facing, concentrating completely on what went on 'within the factory', with little concern about the external environment, because what went on in the outside world was the domain of the external-facing functions such as marketing. The increasing scope of what is considered operations, and the dominant role that operational activity now plays within the firm, necessitates some consideration of the impact of the way operations does its work. The matrix shown in Table 2.4 demonstrates that operations must be responsible for more than just the creation of value for the customer in the most efficient way, as the generation of the value proposition must necessarily take into account the concept of value for all.

Table 2.4 External value matrix

	Financial	**Strategic**	**Social**
Country	GDP impact	Employment Intellectual capital	Environmental impact
Investors	Return Growth	Sustainability	Ethics
Employees	Wages Pensions	Career progression Lifelong learning	Personal development Working conditions

Source: adapted from Livesey (2006).

The key point is that organizations have responsibilities for adding value to society as a whole, and this must be taken into consideration within process of generating operations strategy.

Summary

In this chapter we have presented a model for creating operations strategy that can be used to link the overall corporate strategy to the day-to-day operational activity of the business. We have argued that the operational activity undertaken by the organization is critical to strategic success, and that competitive advantage can be gained only by obtaining a robust operational capability. We have further proposed that in today's organizations the scope of operations is wider than ever before, with most of the value-adding activity taking place as part of the responsibility of operations managers.

We have presented the making of operations strategy as a sequence of five steps:

- The *corporate view*, which translates top-level strategy into operationally usable chunks

- The *customer view*, which ensures that what the customer requires from the product or service is fully understood

- The *performance view*, which ensures the level of performance to be achieved by the operation to please the customer and beat the competition is understood

- The *process view*, which ensures that the processes and activities that are used are fully in line with the corporate, customer and performance views

- The *infrastructure view*, which ensures the organization is built to support the operational processes in achieving their performance targets

We have shown that the achievement of a perfect operations system is not possible, and that any system is subject to compromise, where some performance goals can be achieved only by trading off performance in others. Further we have suggested that it may be sensible to decide on a generic operations strategy, where the critical performance criteria are prioritized at the outset and therefore guide the strategy-making process.

The intention here is to present strategic activity as a seamless process connecting the objectives set at the highest level with the activity that occurs at the lowest. Only by achieving this linkage can the organization take full advantage of its competencies, and achieve the standard of performance that it needs to create and maintain competitive advantage.

▶ # Key Theories

The key theories discussed in this chapter were:

- **The model of operations contribution** – the four stages of performance that operations can achieve in support of corporate strategy, which are defined as internally neutral, externally neutral, internally supportive, and externally supportive.

- **The five dimensions of service quality** – those aspects that customers value and must be delivered. These are tangibles (including price, functionality and performance, variety and customization, and quality), responsiveness, reliability, assurance, and empathy.

- **Order-winning and order-qualifying criteria** – those features that customers see as the key reasons to buy or not to buy a product or service.

- **Performance profiling and prioritizing** – the process of measuring the performance of the operation against that of the competition to identify what improvements must be carried out to create an advantage.

- **Operational trade-offs** – the prioritizing of important performance objectives over those that are less important.

- **The product life cycle** – the five stages that a product will pass through from the point of introduction to the point of withdrawal. These are birth, growth, maturity, decline, and withdrawal. Each stage requires a change of emphasis in operations strategy.

- **Value propositions** – those generic operations strategies that help focus the process of strategy-making to create competence in specific areas. The six propositions introduced are innovators, brand managers, price minimizers, simplifiers, technological integrators and socializers.

Suggested Answers to Stop and Think Questions

1 **Corporate strategy:** It could be argued that no corporate strategy should be devised without a good understanding of the core operational competencies of the business, and how well they are executed. The resource-based view prioritizes core competencies, arguing that a company should develop capability and then find markets that will allow them to succeed, whereas the market-based view prioritizes finding a market, and then working out how to be successful in it. Whichever way strategy is approached, little success will be gained without an efficient and effective operational engine driving the business.

2 **Empowered employees:** Empowered employees will have the discretion to take decisions on behalf of the customer, to optimize the customer experience. Although this is a good thing, in some cases it may result in the wrong decision being taken, which may disrupt the conversion process, or be out of line with the company's overall operations strategy. This may set a precedent that, while appropriate in specific circumstances, may not be sustainable for every customer all the time. Empowerment requires a level of knowledge, skill and judgement that may not be present in all employees.

3 **World-leading operations:** Most markets are occupied by numerous companies, all attempting to gain the greatest share. The pace of technology change creates a challenge, because it is making it increasingly difficult to gain a leadership position and, more importantly, maintain it, because a new process or device may soon be invented that will displace the previous best, either by direct replacement or by substitution. Communication and information availability creates a challenge, as it helps to distribute best practice, and so creates a more level operational playing field: for example, Japanese manufacturing methods are no longer confined to Japan. Another challenge is presented by mobility of labour, as this means that companies can bid for the best people regardless of location, so removing the employee skill and knowledge advantage.

connect™

Review Questions

1 Contrast operations strategy and corporate strategy, and try to identify each within organizations that you are familiar with.

2 What do you think are the order-winning and order-qualifying factors for the UK supermarket chain Tesco?

3 In relation to the product life cycle, choose some products that you are familiar with, and identify which stage of the life cycle they are at.

4 How might speed of production and variety of product require a trade-off decision?

5 What changes in the set-up of the production line may be required as the product moves from the birth stage to the growth stage of the product life cycle?

Discussion Questions

1 Corporate strategy is normally formulated at the top of the organization, but who do you think needs to be involved with formulating operations strategy, and what contribution do they each bring?

2 In relation to the external value matrix, reflect on how the consideration of these factors may affect achievement of the prime operations objective of efficiency.

3 Apply the operations strategy generation process to a charity. Consider who the customers and the competitors are, and discuss how an understanding of them would influence the charity's operation.

4 Consider the concept of trade-offs. What trade-offs might a police force have to think about when planning its operational activity?

5 Discuss the product life cycle model. Can you think of a product that does not follow these phases?

Online LearningCentre Visit the Online Learning Centre at **www.mcgraw-hill.co.uk/textbooks/paton** for a range of resources to support your learning.

Further Reading

Buttle, F. (1996) 'Servqual: review, critique, research agenda', *European Journal of Marketing*, **30**(1), 8–32.

Hayes, R., Pisano, G., Upton, D. and Wheelwright, S.C. (2005) *Operations Strategy and Technology: Pursuing the Competitive Edge*, Wiley, Hoboken, NJ.

Parasuraman, A., Zeithaml, V. and Berry, L. (1994) 'Reassessment of expectations as a comparison standard in measuring service quality: implications for future research', *Journal of Marketing*, **58**(1), 111–124.

Skinner, W. (2007) 'Manufacturing strategy: the story of its evolution', *Journal of Operations Management*, **25**(2), 328–335.

Treacy, M. and Wiersema, F. (1996) *The Discipline of Market Leaders*, HarperCollins: London.

Waters, D. (2006) *Operations Strategy*, Thomson, London.

Wortman, B. (2005) 'Value changing behaviour: getting the habit', *Journal of Business Strategy*, **26**(4), 38–45.

References

Hayes, R.H. and Wheelwright, S.C. (1988) *Restoring Our Competitive Edge: Competing through Manufacturing*, Wiley, New York.

Hill, T. (1993) *Manufacturing Strategy: Text and Cases*, Macmillan.

Johnston, R. (1995) 'The determinants of service quality: satisfaction and dissatisfaction', *International Journal of Service Industry Management*, (6)5, 53–71.

Livesey, F. (2006) *Defining High Value Manufacturing*, University of Cambridge Institute for Manufacturing, Cambridge.

Lowson, R.H. (2002) *Strategic Operations Management: The New Competitive Advantage*, Routledge, London.

Martinez, V. and Bititci, U. (2001) 'The value matrix and its evolution', *Proceedings of the 8th International EurOMA Conference: What Really Matters in Operations Management*, Bath, UK, pp. 118–130.

Martinez, V. and Bititci, U. (2006) 'Aligning value propositions in supply chains', *International Journal of Value Chain Management*, **1**(1), 6–19.

Platts, K.W. and Gregory, M.J. (1990) 'Manufacturing audit in the process of strategy formulation', *International Journal of Operations and Production Management*, **10**(9), 5–26.

Porter, M.E. (1985) *Competitive Advantage: Creating and Sustaining Superior Performance*, The Free Press, New York.

Slack, N. and Lewis, M. (2002) *Operations Strategy*, Prentice Hall, Upper Saddle River, NJ.

Slack, N., Chambers, S. and Johnston, R. (2007) *Operations Management*, 5th edn, Prentice Hall/Financial Times, Harlow.

Treacy, M. and Wiersema, F. (1993) 'Customer intimacy and other value disciplines', *Harvard Business Review*, **71**(1), 84–94.

Vernon, R. (1966) 'International investment and international trade in the product cycle', *Quarterly Journal of Economics*, **80**(2), 190–207.

3 Innovation

Learning Outcomes

After reading this chapter you should be able to:

- Define what innovation is within the context of operations management

- Identify different types of innovation

- Distinguish between the process of innovation and the outcome of the innovation process

- Explain how organizations can harness innovation both strategically and operationally

- Discuss where innovations come from

- Appreciate the importance of innovation to contemporary organizations

Recycling the Bicycle: Orville and Wilbur Would Be Proud . . .

Case Study Theme

There is still some debate around who invented the bicycle, although curiously enough there is little debate about the bicycle-makers who invented the airplane. Since its invention, few products have undergone as much change as the simple bike. With a basic design that has endured for nearly two centuries the bicycle, now packed full of innovation, exists at the cutting edge of technology and occupies one of the fastest-changing and most competitive markets in the world.

As you read this case study, think about the sources of the innovation that preceded each episode in the story of the bicycle.

Did You Know That . . .

- The fastest speed achieved on a bicycle is an amazing 245 km/h (152 mph)
- There is enough energy in a slice of pizza for a person to cycle 16 kilometres (although not at 245 km/h)
- About 100 million bicycles are manufactured worldwide each year.

Source: © Duncan Walker/iStock

The First Rides

In 1817 Baron Karl von Drais invented a walking machine, a kind of pre-bicycle, to help him get around the royal gardens. This early invention embodied design principles that have endured until today: two same-size, in-line wheels, with the front wheel steerable, that are mounted in a frame straddled by the rider. This early device was made entirely of wood, and was propelled by pushing the feet against the ground.

The evolution of the two-wheeled walking machine began in 1865 when, with an innovative leap, pedals were applied directly to the front wheel. This machine was known as the velocipede, or 'fast foot'. Hard on the heels (or toes) of pedals came two further innovations, when in 1870 a more comfortable all-metal machine appeared with solid rubber tyres. And so the modern bicycle was born.

Revolutions in Technology

Then, in what became a major innovative cul-de-sac (because unfortunately no one had thought to invent a gearing system), the front wheels became larger and larger, as makers realized that the bigger the wheel, the farther you could travel with one rotation of the pedals. Luckily this rather dangerous and ungainly route was short-lived as again innovation, this time in metallurgy, came to the rescue with the development of robust processes for making metal light and strong enough to manufacture the precision parts that make up the chain-set. From this point, with bicycle design firmly back on the straight and narrow, there was no turning back. Dunlop in 1888 invented the first inflatable tyre (which in the course of time found a more lucrative application on the automobile). Gearing systems evolved through the first half of the 20th century until the appearance in the 1960s of the derailleur (external) gearing system we know today. More recently came disc brakes from the auto industry for better stopping, and carbon fibre from the aero industry for strong, lightweight frames.

Revolutions in the Market

> 'In the early 1990s Giant produced 3 new models a year; today it is nearer 10. Each model usually includes an incremental improvement as these bikes are sold on their embodiment of the latest innovation.'
>
> Antony Lo, CEO of Giant Bicycles (Upham, 2006)

From a simple start, bikes' designs have evolved to occupy every application, creating markets as they go: BMX bikes for stunt riding, mountain bikes for going uphill, downhill bikes for going downhill, touring bikes, commuter and hybrid bikes, racing bikes that vary in design, with numerous, subtly different features and components to suit a variety of distances, events, surfaces and terrains.

Innovation Spreads

But technology is not the prime force at work here; it is the riders, who constantly strive to find new places and innovative ways to ride a bike. The invention of mountain bikes and BMX bikes in the 1970s spawned entirely new markets and new sports, as each has since become an Olympic event. In sport sometimes innovation can go too far, and this is never better epitomized than by Graeme Obree, the Scottish racer who, in his pursuit of success, built an innovative new competition bike that included bearings from an old washing machine and went on to record-breaking success before falling foul of cycling legalities because he was 'too innovative'.

Customer Information Becomes Innovation

GLOBALIZATION

Most companies tend to favour manufacturing in low-cost economies such as the Far East, but Giant Bicycles, itself a Taiwanese manufacturer, maintains a factory in the Netherlands to satisfy the European market, because it believes the detail-oriented construction of bikes and the highly incremental nature of technical innovation in bike manufacturing make it crucial to keep production close to the customer for speeding up innovation, so that the factory can meet the needs of each regional market. In addition, Giant forgoes the supply chain approach (the use of specialist suppliers) as much as possible; instead it favours vertical integration, with all the processes involved in manufacturing a bike, including welding, fabrication, painting and heat treatment, under one roof.

Orbea, the Spanish cycle-maker, takes this approach one step further, ensuring its bikes remain a product of skilled craftsmanship and personal pride. From concept to manufacture, an Orbea bicycle can take between six months and two years to create, and each bike carries a lifetime guarantee. Orbea is certain that its success is based largely on the creativity and innovation that drives improvement in both the design and the manufacture of its bikes.

So the evolution of bicycles has been driven by innovations in many different areas, including technology, manufacturing processes, lifestyle and sport. It is difficult to see where the next innovation will come from – but then that statement could easily have been made at any time in the last 100 years.

Sources: www.giant-bicycles.com; www.orbea-usa.com; D.V. Herlihy, *Bicycle: The History*, Yale University Press, New Haven, CT, 2004.

Introduction

A stand can be made against invasion by an army; no stand can be made against invasion by an idea.

Victor Hugo, *History of Crime* (1852)

Innovation, it would seem, is the opposite of operations management. Operations management is concerned with the 'Taylorist' creation of order, the implementation of process, and the reduction of variability. Innovation is disordered and random. Ideas are unpredictable, and difficult to plan but when they come, they are impossible to quell. Everything that we see in our society around us – technology, fashion, art and culture – is in some way a product of innovative ideas. For most of history this has been a disordered process. Real innovation, especially these days, is like a rare animal – difficult to spot, as it tends to be camouflaged within the wrapper of a larger, more complex product or service offering. Innovations are dressed up as additional functionality or increased performance, but greater utility within the product is not in itself the innovation but the outcome (the result) of the **innovation process**. Real innovation is arguably one of the few sources of competitive advantage left to companies, and to harness it they must develop processes to help them innovate. The ownership of innovation is therefore very much in the arena of operations management. The challenge that operations managers face is in squeezing the randomness and creativity associated with innovation into a consistent and robust operational process.

> **Innovation process:** the sequence of activities that generates an idea.

Bicycles are easy to understand; everyone is familiar with them. They are found in the velodromes of high-performance sporting institutes and in the shanty towns of the developing world. Their functionality is simple, and does not hide the technological and market innovation that has driven their evolution. Innovation is an integral part of the story of the bicycle:

- Initially the need for a faster, human-powered method of getting around
- Complemented by the huge growth in interest in engineering and its application
- Fuelled by the later rise in the popularity of sports and exercise
- Supported throughout by rapid advances in technology
- And more recently embraced as a lifestyle choice and environmental imperative.

Bikes are a prime example of the customer-driven 'pull' of the market linked to the technology-driven 'push' of industry.

Overview

The purpose of this chapter is not to study the nature of innovation, but to investigate how it happens, and how it can be encased within the framework of the organization to allow us to manage it as part of our operations.

This chapter therefore aims to:

- Create an understanding of what innovation is
- Propose methods that will help build innovative capacity
- Introduce ways in which innovation can be managed operationally
- Show what is required of innovative organizations in the future

This chapter will begin by defining what innovation is, before exploring where innovation comes from. It will go on to analyse the role of innovation within the organization, the factors that encourage it, and the processes that can be used to manage it.

CSR

Innovation out of Control

CRITICAL PERSPECTIVE

The early life of the bicycle, in the development of large-wheeled models such as the penny-farthing, took a brief but relatively harmless evolutionary wrong turn. In other cases we have not been as lucky: too much innovation has sometimes resulted in very negative impacts on our society. Many high-profile innovations have reached markets they should not, mainly as a result of poor process control. One of the most prolific innovators in recent times was a man most people have never heard of. Thomas Midgley Jr (1889–1944) was an American mechanical engineer turned chemist. It could be said that Midgley has had more impact on the atmosphere than any other single organism in Earth's history. Midgley held over 100 patents, one of his most 'successful' being chlorofluorocarbons (CFCs), the ozone-layer-depleting chemicals that found their way into most aerosols. As if this gigantic mis-step was not enough, and with an astonishing talent for the unfortunate, he also developed the tetra-ethyl lead (TEL) additive to gasoline, which creates highly toxic exhaust fumes. He was lauded at the time for his discoveries, but today his legacy is seen as a bit more mixed, considering the serious negative environmental impacts of these innovations. These days, when corporate social responsibility has increased in profile, and some companies regard it as a constraint, this lesson from history should highlight how important it is to behave responsibly while engaging in scientific endeavour.

The problems that result from uncontrolled innovation are not limited to manufactured products. More recently Enron won the *Fortune* magazine award for innovation for six consecutive years between 1996 and 2001. But, despite this, in 2001 it was forced to file for bankruptcy protection. Much of this failure was due to what could charitably be called their 'innovative' accounting methods; much criticism was also aimed at the innovation employed in their financial products. One view is that Enron's problems may have been caused by management pressure for an innovative, fast-paced, loosely controlled, ideas-based organization.

The key point is that both of these tales illustrate the importance of harnessing and controlling the innovation process without unnecessarily strangling it. In the first case, the dangers of lead were known at the time by Midgley. In relation to Enron, part of the blame was directed at the 'uncontrolled culture of innovation' that the management encouraged within the company. Short-term financial gains were pursued and rewarded at the expense of longer-term financial prudence and sustainable business practice.

Enron provides a stiff and very public lesson from recent history on the perils of innovating in finance – a lesson, it seems, that was lost on many of the world's leading banks.

The Nature of Innovation

Dealing with Definitions

Capital isn't so important in business. Experience isn't so important. You can get both these things. What is important is ideas. If you have ideas, you have the main assets you need, and there isn't any limit to what you can do with your business and your life.

Harvey S. Firestone (1868–1938)

Although this chapter deals with an operational process, it is different from most of the others in this book in that it is concerned with a concept that is immediately recognizable, in some way, to us all. We are constantly confronted with innovation in our daily lives. It is everywhere. It is a lazy salesman's first and last choice of label for all 'new' products and services. The word is almost made valueless by its ubiquity.

Most people, if asked what innovation is, would probably say something like 'the act of coming up with something new'. This definition is close to what is contained in most dictionaries. For our purposes, though, we need more precision, and we can find it in the definition given by Van de Ven (1986: 591):

> *Innovation is a new idea, which may be the recombination of old ideas, a scheme that challenges present order, a formula, or a unique approach which is perceived as new by the individuals involved.*

It is worth unpacking this statement. Innovation is closely associated with the idea of newness, but we need to look at what 'new' actually means. 'New as the recombination of old ideas' is possibly the most common manifestation of innovation today. The engineering of cars has evolved over the last 100 or so years, but much recent innovation has been in the mixing of existing technologies into different packages that can be used in the automotive application. The satellite navigation system is a good example of this. Although it was considered innovative when it was introduced by car makers a few years ago, there was little here that was actually new. The silicon chip and database software that provide the memory had been common for many years in IT applications; the liquid crystal display used for information presentation had been around in many audio-visual products; and the Navstar satellite system that provides the positional information had been operating in the aerospace industry since the late 1970s, with the original idea thought of years before.

The above definition of innovation is useful, but it limits innovation to the act of coming up with the new idea. Some authors go beyond this definition, and believe it to be the process through which new ideas, objects, behaviours and practices are created, developed or implemented (Robertson, 1967; Zaltman *et al.*, 1973).

To make this definition more useful we need to find a contextual (i.e. industrial) understanding, and this was helpfully provided by the UK Department of Trade and Industry's Innovation Unit in 2004: it stated simply that 'innovation is the successful exploitation of new ideas'.

To achieve this exploitation, operations managers Isaksen and Tidd (2006) add that innovation must be concerned with the organizational systems and tools necessary to translate ideas into new processes, products, services or businesses.

Innovation: Process, Outcome and Type

Now that we have a grasp of the term 'innovation', we need to understand how it is used. There are three separate concepts that we need to understood when talking about innovation:

- *Innovation as a process*: the steps and activities that need to happen in sequence to generate an idea, and turn it into something that can be sold for profit
- *Innovation as an outcome*: the feature that is new and different that can be sold or used as a differentiator. These **innovation outcomes** can be categorized in four ways: *process* (that is, the manufacturing process or service delivery process – not to be confused with 'process of making the innovation happen' mentioned above), *product*, *paradigm* and *position*

> **Innovation outcome:** the output that is new or different.

- *Type of innovation*: the form the innovation takes. This is generally spoken of in two ways: *incremental* and *radical*

Innovation as an Operations Process

In simple terms this can be viewed as a filter where ideas are gathered, channelled and focused before those ideas with potential are selected. This is shown in Figure 3.1. The beginning of the process is the generation of an idea, and this stage is necessarily random and disordered (the source of ideas will be discussed later). The key here is to create order from this randomness as quickly as possible. To do this, resources and effort are applied to these high-potential ideas to develop them into something that can be implemented as a product, process of manufacture or service delivery, position or paradigm. Each idea must be assessed for its practicality – can it be done? And for its commercial potential, will it make money?

The high-potential ideas are then selected for further work. These 'lucky' selected ideas will go through a process of design to develop the concepts further. If this is successful, and no problems are encountered, the ideas can be implemented within the company's portfolio of offerings.

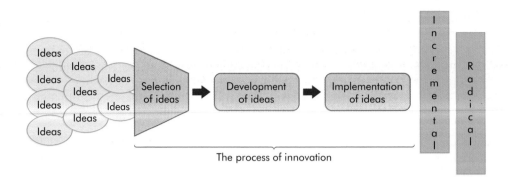

Figure 3.1 The general process of innovation (developed from Tidd and Bessant, 2009)

The same process steps will always occur, but their duration and complexity will vary, depending on the idea and its potential application. For example, an idea for a new product based on a new technology may require a high level of R&D effort to bring it to the point of market implementation, whereas an idea for repositioning an existing product in the market may require only a refocused sales effort.

Outcomes of Innovation: The Four Ps

Product Innovations

These are changes in the things that the organization offers for sale. We said in Chapter 1 that products can be either physical goods, such as cars and phones, or intangible service offerings, such as finance or transport. An innovation in a physical product would be a change in a function or feature of it – for example the incorporation of a global positioning system in a sports watch such as the Garmin Forerunner, to allow accurate speed and distance to be measured when training. In relation to a service, it might for example be incorporation of the facility to check-in online for a flight. Such innovations enhance the utility of the physical product or the service offering, making the customer more likely to buy them.

Process Innovations

These are changes in the processes that create the product that is sold. An innovation here might be the addition of a self-service checkout at the supermarket, where customers can scan their own purchases using a barcode reader; or it might be a web-based account management system to allow customers to control their personal finances. In the design and manufacturing processes for products, innovations might take the form of computer-aided design software that allows products to be designed on-screen, without the use of prototypes or physical models; or new tools and equipment that lead to higher-quality, more efficiently produced products.

CRITICAL PERSPECTIVE

Service Delivery Process vs Product Manufacturing Process

The difference between a change in the service delivery process and the service outcome that the customer will experience is often more noticeable to the customer than the difference between the change in a manufacturing process and the outcome embodied in the product. This is because manufacturing processes are usually hidden from customer view. For example, if an innovative change is implemented in a production process to make the process slightly quicker, then there will be no change to the product itself, and so the customer will not be aware of the innovation. A change in a service delivery process to make it quicker, however, should manifest itself to the customer as improved service.

The innovative improvements in the production process that allow a car, plane or bicycle to be manufactured more quickly, or more cheaply, may not be apparent to the customer, except possibly in a reduced cost. The bicycle market provides a useful example here. Innovations such as the development of light-emitting diode technology, and the resulting processes for mass-producing LEDs, have led to lighting systems for cycles that are not only cheaper, but brighter, more robust and less power hungry than the previous filament technology. But the innovations in the technology and the manufacturing process are still largely invisible to the cyclist who buys the light, as these innovations have taken place in the factory or laboratory.

If we apply the same logic to services, we can see a difference. In service delivery the customer is very much part of the process, as it is not closed within a factory. So although the incorporation of an innovation such as the barcode reader for customer use is part of the process of moving customers through a supermarket, it is immediately obvious as a desirable outcome to the customer, as it should result in fewer queues. The customer not only experiences the outcome (shorter queues and less time spent in the supermarket) but also experiences the innovation that has resulted in this outcome (the barcode reader).

The key point is that the difference between product innovation and process innovation is not always clear. When talking about processes we need to distinguish between the process for manufacturing a product, which is not visible or important to the customer, and the process for delivering the service, which is directly visible to the customer.

Position Innovations

These are changes in the way the product or service offering is targeted. Put another way, it is the targeting of a product or service at a different use or customer base. For example, Lucozade was once thought of as a convalescence drink for sick people, but it has subsequently moved market position and been retargeted as a sports drink for fit and healthy people (the more astute of us may find this marketing ploy a bit ironic). This repositioning strategy then led to innovations in the product in terms of flavouring and composition – for example, to drink as an energy source or for rehydration/electrolyte replenishment.

Another example of extreme repositioning is in the automobile market, where large, thirsty and cumbersome four-wheel-drive vehicles were once considered off-road workhorses. They have now become fashionable as on-road, safe (for passengers, though possibly less so for other, less affluent, road users) family cars for picking up the kids from school.

Paradigm Innovations

These are changes in how companies might frame what they do – for example, the reframing of a supermarket such as Tesco from a simple seller of food products to a provider of all the family's needs, including petrol, clothing and financial products. Here the reframing has created synergies, where shoppers will buy food, then go for petrol, and then pay for it all on their Tesco credit card. (This might one day lead to a further process innovation whereby your salary could be paid directly from your employing company to Tesco, so missing out the middle man.) Another more sophisticated example is BAE Systems, which was reframed from an engineering company to a customer solutions company that not only designs and manufactures defence equipment, but also takes care of all aspects of the customer's needs, including servicing, training and spares provision, supply chain management – even partnering in strategy formulation and risk management.

Mid-town Medical: Fit to Innovate

Dr Foster slumped forward dejectedly over his desk in his consulting room in the Mid-town health centre at the end of another long day spent treating the ailments of the town's inhabitants. Another day packed with frustrating conversations with a stream of patients, all seemingly proud to be in receipt of mainly preventable health issues that, in their eyes, were due to either bad luck or their being in possession of a truly unique physiology that made them more susceptible to health problems than the average person.

High cholesterol, high blood pressure, diabetes, obesity and all manner of other lifestyle-related problems were all the fashion in Mid-town. The doctor's last patient, a certain Mr Roland Poly, was a typical example. His only exercise consisted of walking daily to one of the numerous fast-food outlets that Mid-town boasted, before stopping at the off-licence for a tasty beverage to wash down the inevitable pies, burgers or fish and chips that made up his diet. Healthy cooking? Dr Foster sometimes wondered whether anyone in Mid-town even possessed a kitchen.

Treatments prescribed were helpful in the short term, but did little to combat lifestyle-related health issues in the long term. After 20 years of medical experience Dr Foster felt like a refuse collector, cleaning up the mess left by bad diet, lack of exercise, and generally poor lifestyle. The main products consumed in Mid-town seemed to be junk food, tobacco and alcohol, with no health food shops or sports facilities within 20 miles. Worse still, patients took little notice of his advice. They wanted a quick fix – a pill to clear away the conditions brought on by years of excess and sloth.

Dr Foster gloomily wondered what could possibly be done to halt this destructive trend.

Problem: *Use the 4Ps framework to generate solutions to Mid-town's health problems.*

Approach: Health care provision has undergone changes in recent years, driven mainly by budgetary constraints. It is now seen as cheaper to prevent illness, through the adoption of a healthy lifestyle, than to treat the resulting condition once it has established itself. This, coupled with the growth of companies in the service sector offering lifestyle and exercise products, has served to change how health is viewed.

Innovative thinking in four areas can be identified that can help to initiate this change in Mid-town.

Solution:

Paradigm: The emphasis needs to move from cure to prevention – from medical services to health care and well-being. The paradigm has to shift to a holistic approach, with medical provision aimed at supporting patients who take responsibility for their well-being, rather than relying on medical science to fix problems after they have arisen.

Position: The target market should therefore shift from reactive treatment of already ill people to a focus on keeping healthy people healthy.

Product: In the service sector it is sometimes difficult to define what the product is. Medical services are very much associated with the physical product that is the treatment delivery mechanism – perhaps an injection, a bottle of medicine, or a course of pills. The product needs to be expanded to include advice and associated products, such as health food and exercise provision, that support the paradigm shift. This product can be offered by a supply chain of companies, including the medical services, providers of training facilities and fitness advice, health food manufacturers and retailers, and the education system.

Process: The process within the system of medical provision is generally initiated by the patient when a health problem arises. A more proactive process could be adopted that includes a sequence of steps to prevent the potential patient arriving at the point of requiring treatment.

Table 3.1 Competence and Innovations

Core competence	Potential innovation
Largely preserved	Incremental
Destroyed or requires significant rework	Radical

Source: developed from Westland (2008).

Innovation Types: Radical and Incremental

Not all innovations are the same in terms of scale and scope. Some, such as the internal combustion engine and the microprocessor, have fundamentally changed society. Others, such as the fabric Gore-Tex or the ballpoint pen, while very successful, have made less of an overall impact.

It is difficult to classify innovation in terms of their impact. Many innovations, although very sophisticated, may have a low impact due to how they are applied, what they are replacing, or when they come along. For example, the invention of a practical hydrogen-fuelled engine as a replacement for the fossil-fuelled internal combustion engine might be an extraordinary and very useful technological leap, but fundamentally it would change very little about the way we drive our cars. There might be an incremental improvement, but not much more. The Honda FCX Clarity is the first such car, and part of its appeal is that it drives very much like a normal car. However, in terms of the environment the widespread use of this technology may have a massive and radical impact. So for drivers the innovation is incremental, but for environmentalists the innovation may be viewed as radical.

So why is this important for us as operation managers? The point here, as we have said, is that innovations are not all the same in terms of scale, scope or impact; the same innovation can have a different impact depending on how it is framed. We as managers must assess the innovation's commercial potential in terms of revenue, profitability and risk before investing large amounts of capital in its development. It is therefore useful to categorize innovations along a scale from *radical* (those innovations that have a large impact) to *incremental* (those that have a smaller impact).

A review of commercialized innovations can tell us whether an innovation was incremental or radical, and what impact it has had, but this historical analysis is not forward-looking, and therefore is not particularly useful for us as managers. We need a method for carrying out a more proactive assessment, to understand how the pursuit of an innovation will affect our organization. Here it is useful to return to the strategy that we studied in Chapter 1: specifically the resource-based view, and the theory of competencies. If we assume that all firms have developed a range of competencies to undertake their business, and that it would be useful to understand the radical–incremental continuum in relation to these, then we can draw up Table 3.1.

As managers, we can use this table to categorize the potential innovation, and decide how we may have to reframe our internal competence. If the innovation does not require significant change to our competencies it is probably incremental, and so is less risky to implement, and less costly to pursue. But, as with many low-cost, low-risk ventures, it may not yield a large return. If we need to revise our competencies significantly, or understand totally new markets, then we can consider the innovation as radical.

The story of the bicycle indicates that, after a few early, **radical innovations**, **incremental innovation** has taken over, and has produced a large number of small-step improvements.

It could be argued that, these days, most innovation is incremental. In service delivery it may be doing something a little differently, and a little better. In physical products it may be a small improvement in performance, or a small increase in functionality.

> **Radical innovation:** extreme, game-changing progress.
>
> **Incremental innovation:** change that moves things on in small steps.

Innovations can be radical or incremental in each of the four Ps, as indicated in Table 3.2, and as managers we must consider each innovation in these terms if we are to understand its full potential.

---

❶ Stop and Think

1 We are surrounded by so-called innovative products. Consider everyday items such as the iPod or the mobile phone. Use Table 3.2 to try to identify the radical innovations that made the technology possible, and the incremental innovations that matured the product to its current level of sophistication.

Table 3.2 Innovation outcomes and types

	Incremental	Radical
Product	Turbocharger fitted to a car engine	Hydrogen-powered cars
Process	Banking carried out by phone, rather than face to face in branch	Internet banking replaces human contact completely
Position	Lucozade offered in a range of flavours	Lucozade marketed as a sports drink rather than a convalescence drink
Paradigm	Tesco becomes a one-stop shop for all consumer goods	Tesco becomes a provider of financial services

CRITICAL PERSPECTIVE

A Patently False Patent Myth

Is innovation and creativity limitless? For more than a century there has periodically appeared in print the story about an official of the US Patent Office who, in the 19th century, resigned his post because he believed that all possible inventions had already been invented. Did a patent official really resign over a century ago because he thought nothing was left to invent? This mystery was investigated by the D.C. Historical Records Survey. The investigator, Dr Eber Jeffery, published his findings in the July 1940 Journal of the Patent Office Society.

> *Jeffery found no evidence that any official or employee of the US Patent Office had ever resigned because he thought there was nothing left to invent. However, Jeffery may have found a clue to the origin of the myth. In his 1843 report to Congress, the then commissioner of the Patent Office, Henry L. Ellsworth, included the following comment: 'The advancement of the arts, from year to year, taxes our credulity and seems to presage the arrival of that period when human improvement must end.'*
>
> Adapted from *The Skeptical Inquirer*, vol 13 (spring 1989), pp. 310–313.

Although the language used in the above excerpt may be somewhat impenetrable and difficult to follow, what is being discussed is the view that, given the acceleration in scientific and technical achievement that began around 300 years ago, we may come to a point quite soon where there is nothing left to invent.

Although this famous and rather attractive myth seems to have been proven to be false, it does raise questions for industry about the continuous and perpetual nature of innovation. It could be argued that, as technology progresses, each additional advance will be more difficult to make. The Moon is relatively easy to reach in comparison with Mars, which in turn is relatively easy to reach in comparison with the nearest star. Indeed, it may be impossible to reach the nearest star, no matter how innovative we are.

At a more practical level, mobile phones can only become smaller and lighter, and be increasingly packed with functionality, before the law of diminishing returns sets in. Many would argue we have gone past that point already, with phones able to do far more than anyone would ever need. A phone that fits in your palm may be better than one the size of a house brick (all the rage back in the 1980s), but would we really need one the size of a thimble?

There is a limit to the speed at which a service can be provided. Twenty years ago it might have taken a week to set up a mortgage; these days it can be done in a matter of hours. Would there really be any benefit to being able to do it in a matter of minutes? Customers and markets can only be served so well, or in so many different ways.

Does this mean that in future there will be less radical innovation and more incremental innovation? Or less product and process, and more position and paradigm? Put another way, will innovation be less about substance and more about how we view things? In current entertainment the latest so-called 'innovation' is in talent shows such as *The X Factor*. But, in reality, these shows are little more than a reinvention of the holiday camp talent competitions that have existed for as long as we can remember.

Each show has a similar format, and each strives (and often fails) to differentiate itself from the others, more often than not resorting to cheap shocks and revelations as opposed to real substance and true creativity. Are we on the verge of an era of the 'emperor's new clothes' where very little is actually new?

The key point is that, some time soon, innovation may not be the key to the strategy of product and service differentiation that it once was.

Where Do Innovations Come From?

Eureka Moments

It is commonly thought that the word 'eureka' is derived from the Greek word *heúrēka* (εύρηκα), meaning 'I have found it', made famous by the ancient Greek thinker Archimedes, who is believed to have shouted it while jumping into a bath of water. The reason for this strange behaviour was that his observation of the displacement of water resulted in an insight on how to measure the purity of gold. This was an exercise given to him by Hiero of Syracuse, who was worried about the authenticity of his crown (and evidently the trustworthiness of his crown-maker). Regardless of the truth of this, the word 'eureka' has since come to be associated with the act of having an idea.

The classic view of innovation is the eccentric inventor, often of pensionable age, being struck by an impromptu idea – often accompanied by the famous shout, a lot of excited arm-waving and irresponsible jumping up and down – before running off to spend the next couple of years in the garden shed, turning his brilliant idea into a working prototype. This might have been the case in times gone by, but these days innovation is usually the product of considerable investment in capital, manpower and equipment within the auspices of a large company's R&D department or a university laboratory.

There are famous cases of genuine 'eureka' moments, though. Probably the most famous is Percy Shaw's idea for the road safety device, which occurred when he noticed how light reflected from a cat's eye. Although simple in concept, this idea underwent a process of design and development before becoming the innovative product that we all know today. A more recent and obscure, but possibly more inspirational, example is described in the case study below.

SHORT CASE 3.1

Plugging a 'Mole' in the Market

Sharon Wright's appearance on Dragon's Den was a master-class in how to spot a gap in the market and gain investment.

SME Business News, 27 July 2009

Sharon Wright, a young mum from Scunthorpe, England, had her eureka moment while having a phone line installed in her home. Under pressure for time she offered to help the phone engineer thread the cable through the wall of her house. To Sharon's surprise, to do this the engineer produced a makeshift tool made out of a wire coat-hanger. Sharon's previous experience in Health and Safety management told her that, as well as being difficult to use, this device wasn't suitable – and even slightly hazardous. Research into the market showed there were no alternative tools available for cable threading. Within hours she had sketched out the design of the Magnamole tool, a plastic rod with a magnet at one end and an accompanying metallic cap for attaching to the wire to be threaded through the wall. She soon had a prototype built, and orders followed from large customers around the world.

What is remarkable about Sharon is that she didn't really have any prior knowledge or experience of the area of business she was moving into, but that didn't stop her from taking advantage of an obvious gap in the market.

Questions
1 There must be thousands of cables being installed every day around the world, and thousands of people employed in electrical installation. Why do you think it took someone from outside this market to spot the gap and invent a solution?
2 After the initial idea, what do you think the next step is in turning an idea into a product?

Source: www.magnamole.co.uk

Sources of Innovation

Despite the attraction of romantic and inspirational stories of unlikely individuals with brilliant ideas overcoming all odds, in reality the eureka moment is only one of a number of ways in which innovation can occur. Figure 3.2 illustrates the main sources that may trigger the innovation journey for an organization.

Knowledge Push

The Resource-based Approach: Research and Development as a Competence

Apart from eureka moments, the most obvious source of innovation has always been the laboratories of formalized scientific research. History conjures images of individual laboratories, but these days, increasingly, it is large companies investing in research and development centres that yield the most innovation. Some companies, such as ICI, Bell, DuPont and Apple, have made their reputation through the public's acknowledgement of their commitment to innovation.

> **Knowledge push:** innovation driven by advances in technology that create new products.

These days innovation is less the result of freewheeling ideas generation, and more the result of a systematic commitment of specialist staff, equipment and facilities to solving specific problems (**knowledge push**).

To produce consistent innovation, it is critical to specialize in one area. DuPont Australia's Technical Centre advertises itself as 'your portal to our network of highly skilled professionals, knowledge, expertise and resources', boasting 'a technical team of specialists with a range of expertise in many areas including physical and chemical testing of chemicals and materials such as: engineering polymers, industrial polymers, fluoropolymers, elastomers and rubbers'. Similarly, Audi has three specialist centres for R&D – the Aluminium Centre, the Electronic Centre and the Wind-tunnel Centre – each working on specific areas.

The important thing to note here is that the resource must be focused on one area of expertise, so the key thing for managers is to define that area in terms of its scope, and develop it as an organizational competence.

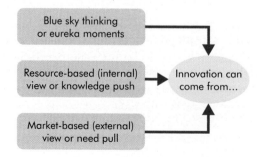

Figure 3.2 Sources of innovation

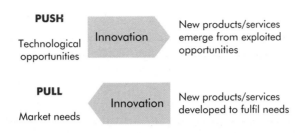

Figure 3.3 Push and pull innovation

Need Pull

The Market-based Approach: Market Scanning

Need pull: customer identification of gaps in the market that provide an opportunity to innovate and create a product.

The complement to creating an innovative new product is finding a gap to fill in the market (**need pull**). There is little point in investing significant resources in finding a solution to a problem that doesn't exist. Sometimes, though, the application of products is difficult to assess. Digital music players and lightweight headphones are now an essential part of a runner's or cyclist's training kit, but could this method of combating boredom translate to a product for swimmers? Some companies obviously think so, as evidenced by products such as the Aquapac waterproof headphones for swim training. This application may sound like a joke (it isn't), but the key question is – will it make money?

Many products we see in the market today, especially in the area of IT, were inconceivable a few short years ago. Whereas it is logical that the typewriter could pave the way for a product such as Microsoft Word, it is less conceivable that it would lead to a product such as PowerPoint or Access. Whereas the home phone could lead to the mobile phone, there was a giant leap to the functionality embodied in the iPhone.

There have been some notable innovative failures, such as the Sinclair C5 electric vehicle for personal transportation. Despite this misfire, it has been followed more recently by more successful innovations in the area, such as the Segway people transporter, a two-wheeled, self-balancing electric vehicle invented by Dean Kamen and produced by Segway Inc.

It is important to be aware of the driving forces in the external environment that may yield an opportunity.

Technological innovations, such as those noted above, do not always lead to a single product exploited by a single company. Technology spreads like a virus. There are many examples of this, but possibly the most ubiquitous in recent years has been touch-screen technology, which has found its way into all kinds of products such as mobile phones, cameras and iPads. Awareness of what the market is doing with technology application is therefore critical.

Scanning the market by analysing what competitor products exist may be useful, but there are other, more specific, external areas that may yield the opportunity for an innovative product or service.

SHORT CASE 3.2

Spreadshirt: Innovative E-commerce

Founded in Leipzig, Germany, by graduate students Lukasz Gadowski and Matthias Spiess, Spreadshirt is an online platform for apparel merchandising that allows Internet site operators to create their own online shops for free, and sell customized products. Spreadshirt lets anyone integrate these online shops with their own websites. These shop partners can then earn commissions on each sale through Spreadshirt. Requirements for using Spreadshirt are minimal: you need only an Internet connection, and design/logo graphic files for products. Spreadshirt does the rest by handling the production, shipping, payment processing and customer service. For people who just want to create and order personalized shirts with a design and text of their choice, Spreadshirt also has the Spreadshirt Designer shop available on its website. Since its origination in Germany, the company has expanded its market to the rest of Europe and the US. It has received acclaim globally, winning the Hewlett-Packard Innovation Award in 2004, and being named in *Business Week*'s Europe Top 500 Growth Companies.

Question

1   Do you think that the growing sophistication of technology and its implementation in information systems such as the Internet is making society and individuals more innovative; or do you think that technology-based applications are purely an additional outlet to channel the output of existing innovative individuals?

Source: www.spreadshirt.co.uk

Regulation Changes

We are surrounded by regulation. We live our lives within frameworks that seem to become more sophisticated and all-encompassing as time goes on. Regulation can restrict, but it can also trigger innovation by mandating change. Environmental legislation on pollution, for example, has paved the way for innovation in the development of renewable forms of energy – an industry that was for many years neglected because of the dominance of fossil fuels. On a smaller scale, the drive for reduced speed and greater safety on our roads has led to the development of speed cameras and airbags. Ironically the Gatso road safety camera was originally invented by a rally driver, Maurice Gatsonides, to help him increase his speed around corners.

As well as direct opportunities resulting from the passing of laws, legal changes have also led to some elliptical paths to innovation. Tobacco use has not yet been directly regulated against, but the new focus on health, combined with legal restrictions in advertising and lawsuits against tobacco companies, has forced the larger companies to devote increasing resources to creating innovative, 'safer' products, such as the Philip Morris Accord cigarette holder and the RJR Eclipse cigarette. Ironically, these attempts at product innovation have caused some difficulties for the tobacco companies, because the introduction of a cigarette that is 'safe' represents an implicit admission that the previous products were 'not safe' – an admission that (amazingly enough) tobacco companies have yet to make.

So we can see that understanding the legal and social climate can produce a handy signpost to where new products and services may be needed in the future.

Accidents and Unplanned Events

Many innovations have been the result of an 'accident' in the lab, such as Alexander Fleming's discovery of penicillin, or alternative applications for discoveries such as 3M's reuse of 'sticky but not too sticky' adhesive in Post-it notes. We mentioned the Segway above. The innovative gyro that makes it possible was developed in the defence labs of BAE Systems before it found application in this alternative market.

Unplanned events such as terrorist attacks have also paved the way for innovation in safety and security products. Biometric scanning devices represent one such industry that has benefited from this unfortunate opportunity. Applied Biometrics Products is a company with a core technology that combines proprietary software and hardware designs to produce portable biometric scanning devices. But this is only part of their offering, as they use it in combination with their expertise in assessing the needs of a customer to provide a service developing innovative customized security solutions to meet those needs.

One of the largest service industries in the world – personal insurance – developed around the need to guard against unplanned events. From the initial innovation that set up Scottish Widows (the first Scottish personal insurance company), the insurance industry has continued to innovate, and now covers almost everything that one can think of. Famous insurances include Bruce Springsteen's voice and Jennifer Lopez's bottom. Lloyd's of London is said to have sold insurance against werewolf attacks and vampire bites. How much do you think it would cost to insure Jennifer Lopez's bottom against a vampire bite?

The insurance industry, old and stuffy as it may seem, still continues to innovate, with the latest incarnation being the infamous hedge funds that are a method of insuring against negative movements in the investment markets.

SHORT CASE 3.3	## Dying to Be Innovative . . .

In 1906 the German insurance expert Alfred Manes defined insurance as:

Source: Scottish Widows

an economic institution resting on the principle of mutuality, established for the purpose of supplying a fund, the need for which arises from a chance occurrence whose probability can be estimated.

Two Church of Scotland ministers, Robert Wallace and Alexander Webster, are given credit for inventing the first true personal insurance fund based on correct actuarial and financial principles in 1743. This fund, the Scottish Ministers' Widows Fund, was set up to take care of the widows and children of deceased clergymen. There were two innovations here: first, the creation of a fund with premiums that were profitably invested to ensure a growing value; and second, the use of mathematics to allow projections to be made (with surprising accuracy, as it turned out) on the future finances, such as rate of growth of the fund.

Within a few years similar funds were springing up, using the same model, all over the English-speaking world spreading throughout the professions. One of these funds was conceived in 1812, when a number of eminent Scotsmen gathered in Edinburgh, to consider setting up a general fund for securing provisions to widows, sisters and other females. As a consequence of this, the Scottish Widows Fund Life Assurance Society – Scotland's first mutual life office – opened for business in 1815. Today, as part of the Lloyds banking group, Scottish Widows has over £100 billion under management. Insurance premiums in developed countries have risen steadily from 2% of gross domestic product at the beginning of the 20th century to just under 10% today.

It is a curious fact about this industry that the most insured people tend to live in the safest places, and be least at risk from unplanned events.

Questions
1 Where do you think the next innovation will come from in the insurance industry?
2 Do you think most innovations in finance are radical or incremental?

Source: www.scottishwidows.co.uk

Users as Innovators

Users are sometimes viewed as passive recipients of innovation, but they can also be a useful source of ideas. When a product is in the market, there is potential for everyone who buys it to find a new application.

There are three categories of users who are particularly important for innovation:
- *Lead users*: people who not only use the product but also help in its development. Indeed, like Michelle Mone (see case study below), they may even be the innovator who has an idea after using a similar product, and develops it into a competing and more successful product.
- *User communities*: groups of users who congregate around a product or product platform such as iTunes and find new and innovative ways to use it.
- *Extreme users*: users who push products to their limit, creating a need for improved performance. The story of the bicycle is an example of this, with the relentless drive for more durable and higher-performing machines. The modern clockwork radio is another example. it was designed and patented in 1989 by British accountant Trevor Baylis using existing technologies. He envisaged it as a radio for use by people in developing countries without access to batteries, or electrical supplies.

SHORT CASE 3.4

Comfort and Joy

Michelle Mone grew up in Glasgow, Scotland. She began her career as a model, and later moved into sales and marketing. In October 1996, while attending a dinner-dance wearing a very uncomfortable, cleavage-enhancing brassiere, she decided that she could design something that was more comfortable and better looking, but would still create the all-important enhanced cleavage.

Source: © 2010 Getty Images

MJM International Ltd was set up in November 1996, and three years of research, design and development resulted in the patented Ultimo bra, which achieved the aims Mone had set out to accomplish.

Once patented, the Ultimo bra then launched at Selfridges department store in London in August 1999. Selfridges sold the pre-launch estimate of six weeks of stock within 24 hours, and over 10 years later this is still known as the biggest ever bra launch in the UK, where photographers and camera crews from all over the world were in attendance. In April 2000 Mone won the World Young Business Achiever Award in the Epcot Centre, Florida. Ultimo subsequently expanded into the United States, and in May 2000 Ultimo was launched at the Saks Fifth Avenue store in New York.

In September 2003 MJM launched another invention – the Ultimo Miracle Body. Mone said that she was given the challenge from her celebrity customers to create a backless and frontless bra. Her technical team said it was impossible – 12 months later it was achieved, and the product was aptly called the Miracle Body.

Question

1 Research this case further. Do you think that product innovation is the important success factor here, or is it the marketing of the brand that has created this success?

Sources: www.ultimoco.uk; MJM Limited; Wikipedia.

🛈 Stop and Think

2 After getting an idea for an entirely new product, or an improvement to an existing one, what would you do next?

Innovation and Operations Management

The Innovation Life Cycle

It is clear that it is important to identify innovation opportunities, either by utilizing internal knowledge resources or by finding external gaps in the market. To help in this, Abernathy and Utterback (1978) have identified how innovation opportunities in relation to products may change over time, as shown in Figure 3.4.

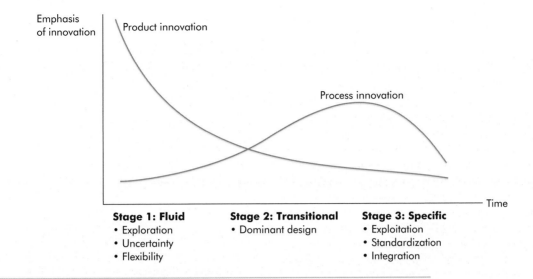

Figure 3.4 The product innovation life cycle (adapted from Abernathy and Utterback, 1978)

Stage 1: The Fluid Phase

Initially, as a new technology emerges or a new idea for a product begins to take shape, there is a lot of uncertainty. This uncertainty can be categorized into the *target* – what the application of the technology will be – and the *technical* – how the technology can be harnessed to meet this application. This phase will be characterized by extensive experimentation and learning, and will end when the dominant design emerges, or – put another way – when the configuration emerges that will characterize the product for most of the remainder of its life cycle.

For example, the dominant design that emerged for a family car is: four wheels, one at each corner, with engine in the front, steered by hand using a wheel, and clutch, brake and accelerator operated by foot, and arranged from left to right in that order.

At the end of this stage the target will be defined, and the technical issues in relation to reaching that target should have been mostly overcome. The focus of innovation in this stage is very much on the technology and its application.

Stage 2: The Transitional Phase

Here activity becomes less random and more planned, with the product configuration becoming ready for sale. The focus of activity is on maturing the product platform by finalizing functionality, and improving quality and reliability. Innovation in product and technology is becoming more incremental, aimed at squeezing in as much functionality as possible, and achieving the greatest degree of differentiation in the market. This is evident in the automobile, where the configuration is now standard, but manufacturers are packing in features and additional functionality, such as electric windows, in-car entertainment systems and navigation aids. Innovation in process begins to become important, as the ideas will partly define the operations and production processes.

Stage 3: The Specific Phase

The focus is now on cost, with innovative behaviour squarely aimed at the production process, realizing economies of scale and improving efficiency. The product is considered mature in the market, and may be hanging on to its position with a combination of historical customer loyalty, low price and high quality. Despite continuing strong sales, at this stage the product will be ripe for replacement by a newer product. Again, the car industry is a prime example of this, as the mass production systems used are among the most efficient in the world.

From a product development point of view, as time progresses innovation will move from the radical to the incremental, with each successive innovation becoming less and less impactful as the 'well of innovation' dries up. Similarly, from a process point of view, as the product becomes more mature the innovations that squeeze the final few drops of efficiency out of the manufacturing process may become more incremental. Therefore the emphasis of innovation changes over time, not only in terms of its nature (radical or incremental) but also in its emphasis on the process of manufacture as opposed to the technology and functionality that are embodied in the product.

The Four Ss: Organizational Factors in Managing Innovation

BUSINESS INTEGRATION

The need to innovate is clear, but an organization's ability to be innovative may be less well developed. In the absence of any usable form of artificial intelligence, innovation and ideas must come from a company's employees, whether they are directly employed to be innovative (in the case of R&D staff), or just part of the general workforce. Whatever the employee's role, the organization must do everything it can to create an innovative environment.

Smith *et al.* (2008) have defined the features of the organization that will impact on the effectiveness of the process of innovation. These have been distilled here into four Ss: *strategy, structure, style* and *support*.

- *Corporate strategy*: Above all, a corporate strategy must be developed and cascaded down from the top to communicate shared vision and goals (Jager *et al.*, 2004). If the organization is relying on innovation as part of its competitive advantage, then the strategy must state this explicitly, so that all employees will be encouraged to behave in the correct way.
- *Management style*: The management team must act on the strategy, to reinforce its effect on the employees. A 'facilitate and empower' style will foster innovation better than a 'command and control' style; employees who are empowered and autonomous will act more innovatively when not constrained (Muthusamy *et al.*, 2005). It would seem logical that, to be innovative, employees need a greater level of managerial support. Clearly, they need to be given sufficient resources and the space to allow ideas to emerge. So there is a delicate balance to be struck here between controlling and empowering – particularly with employees who are working within a highly regulated system such as a production line or a call centre.
- *Organizational structure*: This generally dictates the nature of jobs, and must be coherent with the management style used within the organization. A high degree of division of labour and extreme specialization of tasks are detrimental to innovation. Task variety and cross-functional communication are advantageous. Although lone employees can be innovative, teams of employees working together are more likely to be more successful over the long term.
- *Technology and knowledge management support*: Technology directly affects employees, as it is commonly used as a facilitator of knowledge transfer, drawing together fragmented knowledge resources to develop a single knowledge repository (Jantunen, 2005). Technology, in the form of IT systems, can be used to pull together and centralize information from many sources making it easier to find and use. This means that employees can quickly and easily gain access to the information they need to generate ideas. Supporting the organization with the correct IT-based tools results in a more integrated approach to new idea development.

When considering the four Ss, it is clear that innovation can be better supported in an integrated business, where all parts are aligned, and innovative employees are working to a *strategy* enabled by the appropriate management *structure*, facilitated by the correct management *style*, and *supported* by the provision of the best tools, equipment and information.

Staff as Innovators

Enabling innovation within organizations is all about making maximum advantage of employees as innovators – not only those who are directly employed for this purpose, but all workers, regardless of their role. 'With every pair of hands a brain comes free' was the mantra of the 'new' management of the 1980s and 1990s. The philosophy here is that every idea, however small, is useful, because in a large company the accumulation of ideas can, over time, reap significant rewards.

This journey begins by designing an organizational structure that emphasizes communication and flexibility, supported by an empowering management style and the appropriate information technology, but these must be supplemented by other mechanisms. Recently much has been made of employee participation. This initially emerged with the 'quality miracle' of the Japanese manufacturers, which was enabled by the system of *kaizen* or *continuous improvement* (Imai, 1986). Employees were encouraged to question work processes and look for incremental improvements in all that they did, leading to a better production process and therefore better product quality and organizational efficiency. Suggestion schemes are not new – indeed, Denny's Shipyard in Dumbarton, Scotland, implemented one back in the mid 19th-century – but the more systematic and proactive approach of the Japanese was a key factor in their success. Kaizen has been joined by other systems, such as *total quality management* (Bounds *et al.*, 1994) and *lean manufacturing* (Womack and Jones, 1996). The emphases differ, but the key to all these systems is in getting employees involved in the thinking behind the product and process of delivery, and encouraging them to generate ideas that lead to improvements that ultimately benefit the overall revenue and profit of the company in which they work.

The utility of these systems is not restricted to manufacturing, and they are now being applied equally to the service sector.

As a framework it is useful to think of areas where employees can contribute ideas. Tonnessen (2003) has identified places where staff can be encouraged to innovate. These are within their immediate work area and activity, within the overall process that they are involved in, within their group or department and in relation to the overall company operation and strategy.

Contemporary Thinking: From Continuous Improvement to Continuous Innovation

The previous section discussed the role of employees in innovation and proposed that schemes such as continuous improvement (CI) were useful in maximizing employee innovative behaviour. Traditional 'CI' is still useful for improving operational efficiency, but theorists are now proposing that something more is needed. Figure 3.5 depicts how the necessary competencies that firms must possess have evolved over time. Note that the model indicates an accumulation (rather than a displacement), driven by increasingly demanding customers and markets. Where efficiency was once enough, it must now be supplemented by good quality, flexibility, and the ability to be innovative. The question is therefore how can companies move on from continuous improvement and develop a competence in **continuous innovation**.

> **Continuous innovation:** the ability to repeatedly generate new ideas.

Boer and Gertsen (2003) define two arenas in which a company must innovate:
- Operational effectiveness – the ability to satisfy today's customers' demands in terms of cost, quality and functionality. This they term *exploitation*, and the objective of innovation here is to exploit what the company already has. Activity here is therefore very much in line with the methods used in CI.
- Strategic flexibility – the capability to find and develop new configurations of products and markets. This they term *exploration*.

Competence in only one arena will always be sub-optimal, because a firm that specializes in exploitation will become better and better at milking an increasingly obsolete technology, whereas a firm that specializes in exploration will never realize the full advantage of its discoveries. A combination of innovation in exploitation and innovation in exploration is crucial to a firm's survival, and this is what is meant by *continuous innovation*.

The challenge here is to build an organization that can simultaneously exploit and explore. There are two ways to do this. Traditionally, firms have used the separator of organizational structure: exploitation and exploration activities are done in different parts of the organization, using different staff, working with different processes

	1960s	1970s	1980s	1990s	2000s
Customer demands	Low price	+ High quality	+ Product variety	+ Product uniqueness	
Organisation optimized for:	Efficiency	+ Quality	+ Flexibility	+ Innovation	

Figure 3.5 The evolution of firms (adapted from Boer and Gertsen, 2003)

and tools, and sometimes management philosophies – e.g. R&D located separately from production. This can create tensions in communication, in the use of common processes, and in labour relations.

Another solution is time-based separation. There are two ways this can be achieved:

- The *ambidextrous model* – which can behave both organically in an empowered, flexible and creative way when the situation needs radical innovation to come up with new ideas, and then more mechanistically when the situation requires incremental innovation to realize increased efficiency.
- The *punctuated equilibrium model* – which plans for a period of radical innovation in the development of a product, and then re-forms for a longer period of incremental change as the product of the technology is exploited.

The achievement of continuous innovation is closely related to the dynamic capabilities discussed in Chapter 1. Both concepts are seen as solutions to the increasingly dynamic environment that organizations find themselves faced with, where the more static models – such as developing a core competence and staying with it, or the use of incremental models for improvement – need to be supplemented by methods of moving the company forward in a more radical way.

CRITICAL PERSPECTIVE

Freedom or Constraints

The goal of operations management is to achieve operational excellence. This is traditionally defined in terms of efficiency, measured as a ratio of some form of output to some form of input. Simplistically this could be x number of widgets produced using y number of labour-hours: more widgets for fewer hours means greater efficiency. Traditional thinking shows us that the path to efficiency is through repetition, conformance to a fixed system, and reduction in variation. Even in new product design, efficiency is the goal, with project management techniques put in place to measure the achievement of time, cost and quality targets. Efficiency is easy to measure in manufacturing, and possible (but not so easy) to measure in product design, but it is almost impossible to measure when radical or breakthrough innovations are being worked towards, because this type of innovation includes more substantial components of 'newness, uncertainty and ambiguity' (Magnusson *et al.*, 2009).

The need to balance innovation and efficiency is not new, and was once labelled 'the paradox of administration' (Thompson, 1967); but today's competitive landscape requires firms to reach new levels of performance. This results in them being forced to reach a delicate compromise between longer-term exploration – with its demands for the development of new ideas, and the flexibility this requires – and short-term exploitation, with its needs for efficiency and profitability that can be optimized only within the constraints of an operational system. Indeed, the attempt to systematize innovation may be counterproductive. Styhre (2008), in his analysis of R&D in the pharmaceutical industry, indicates that providing the time and space for employees to 'play' may be a factor in the innovation process. He further suggests that advanced scientific exploration can be a process of skill and chance as much as of method and management. For operations managers this raises the obvious question: how do we create a process for play?

The key point is that when managing innovation, where new ideas and blue sky thinking are the output, then traditional operations management techniques may not apply. Sometimes the advantages gained by tightly controlling a process may be outweighed by the advantages of allowing a team of creative people free rein to generate and develop ideas.

SHORT CASE 3.5	Singapore: Innovating as Policy

Singapore is an island city-state off the southern tip of the Malay Peninsula. It has few natural resources, and yet is recognized as one of the most prosperous regions on earth. It is one of the world's leading financial centres, and the main Asian logistics hub. Its economy is often ranked amongst the world's top ten most competitive and innovative. Originally a British colony, it gained sovereignty in 1965, and has since grown to become the fourth wealthiest country in the world in terms of GDP per capita.

Source: © Oksana Perkins/iStock

Singapore was already successful in logistics, finance and manufacturing, but its government realized that something more was needed, and made attempts to develop high-value industry, with a focus on innovation and creativity. In support of this they adopted a three-pronged policy:

- *Knowledge and skills development.* While other countries were moving towards efficiency by automation and process, Singapore adopted a high-skills strategy aimed at creating a population ready to embrace knowledge-intensive industries.
- *Infrastructure and institutions.* Industrially, the first technology plan (1991–1995) invested S$2 billion in technology infrastructure. The government further recognized that critical mass was needed in each sector, so industry clusters were set up in areas such as biotechnology and pharmaceuticals.
- *Engage stakeholders and promote a creative culture.* The government realized that, in addition to skills and infrastructure, the cultural and social environment needed to be attractive to professional knowledge employees, so they embarked on a process of improving the cultural and social infrastructure to make Singapore a more attractive place in which to live and work. For example, an initiative called Creative Community Singapore was established in 2005 to provide opportunities for Singaporeans to channel their creative energies for the larger good of the community.

Record 15.5% growth in Q1

The Straits Times, 21 May 2010

As this headline indicates, Singapore seem to be successfully bucking the world trend, with innovation a critical success factor in its economic performance.

Question

1 Traditionally, Asian societies are known for their individual discipline and ordered way of life. Do you think this is an advantage or a disadvantage in stimulating innovation?

Source: J. Gwee, 'Innovation and the creative industries cluster: a case study of Singapore's creative industries', *Innovation: Management, Policy & Practice*, 2009, **11**(2), 240–252.

Summary

In this chapter we have defined innovation as both the creative process of coming up with a new idea and the more operational process of implementing it and producing a product that can be sold in the market. We have shown that, as managers, we must distinguish between the innovation process – that is, the series of steps taken to produce an outcome – and the outcome itself, as the embodiment of innovative features or functions in a product or service offering.

We have shown that innovation outcomes can be embodied as:

- New *products* or changes to existing products
- Improvements in *processes* of manufacture or service delivery
- Changes in the market *position* of a product to increase sales
- Changes in company *paradigms* to open up new markets.

In each of the above forms, innovation can take the form of radical, game-changing steps, or incremental – smaller or more subtle – changes.

We have shown that innovations can come from three sources:

- Genuine eureka moments gained as the result of blue-sky thinking
- Resource- and competence-based knowledge push generated internal to the company
- Market-based need pull identified externally to the company.

As the focus here is operations management, this chapter then went on to outline some methods that can be used to manage innovation in the organization. We showed that innovation is subject to a life cycle, with highly creative processes – characterized by uncertainty and randomness, and aimed at producing new ideas – being replaced by more manageable processes, aimed first at defining the product or service offering and then at exploiting the potential of this offering. In addition, features of the organization such as strategy, structure, style and support systems can be configured to produce a more creative environment, where employees who are the source of innovation can be encouraged to behave innovatively. It has been demonstrated that the control required in operations management is often not compatible with the freedom required to encourage innovation, and that a balance must be found.

Finally we suggested that, in future, successful companies will need to excel at both exploration (identifying and developing innovative ideas) and exploitation (extracting as much from them as possible). The critical success factor for these companies will be in effectively changing their mode of operation to be effective at both practices.

Key Theories

The key theories discussed in this chapter were:

- **The four Ps of:**
  - o Product innovation: the changes in the things that the organization offers for sale
  - o Process innovation: the changes in the process that creates the product
  - o Position innovation: the changes in the way the product is offered or targeted
  - o Paradigm innovation: the changes in how a company frames what it does.

- **'Knowledge push' or 'need pull':** where innovation is driven by advances in technology that create new products and markets where none existed before, or where customers identify a need and companies strive to fill the need.

- **The innovation life cycle:** a time-based representation of how innovation is carried out, from the discovery of a new technology until it becomes mature and fully developed.

- **The four Ss of facilitating innovation:**
  - o Strategy: innovation is explicitly called for in the corporate strategy
  - o Structure: roles and jobs are defined to aid in innovative behaviour
  - o Style: management empowers the workforce to behave innovatively
  - o Support: IT systems are available to support innovative behaviour.

- **Exploitation** – the capability to satisfy today's customers' demands in terms of cost, quality and functionality versus **exploration** – the capability to find and develop new configurations of products and markets.

Suggested Answers to Stop and Think Questions

1 **Incremental and radical:** All electronic devices are made possible by the radical invention that was the transistor, followed by the radical repackaging of a large number of these in the microchip configuration. Incremental innovation is then the use of the microchip in different applications. In electronics technology the process of miniaturization that makes the density of functionality within a small product possible could be considered an incremental improvement. It may be useful to think of the radical innovation as the invention of the technology and the incremental as the steps in its application to products.

2 **Gaps in the market:** This is one of the paradoxes in innovation, where sometimes familiarity breeds blindness so a problem is overlooked. Also, those who work in a particular job will generally find their own ways of doing things, which may be sufficient for them but are not a universal solution. Finally, it may be that some people are just better at coming up with new ideas than others.

connect

Review Questions

1 What do you think is meant by the phrase 'recognizing the potential of an innovation'?

2 What do you think efficiency means in the early 'fluid' stages of the innovation life cycle?

3 What are the differences between the process of bringing an innovation to market in a physical product such as a car, and the process of bringing an innovation to market in a service offering such as finance or travel?

4 Explain the differences between 'knowledge push' and 'need pull' in relation to innovation.

5 Explain the difference between 'continuous improvement' and 'continuous innovation'.

Discussion Questions

1 Discuss the disadvantages of creating an innovative organization where all employees are encouraged to be creative and produce new ideas.

2 Analyse a cutting-edge product such as a Garmin Forerunner training aid. Discuss the innovations in technology and marketing that were required to make this a success.

3 Consider the issues associated with managing innovative people. Discuss how this can be challenging in the operational environment.

4 'Innovation in the last century was based on finding a market need that was not filled, and then using innovation to fill it. In the current century, innovation is creating needs that have never been thought of before.' Discuss this statement.

5 Think of a product or service for which users have driven innovation in its development. Discuss how the product started, and where it may be heading.

 **Online Learning Centre**   Visit the Online Learning Centre at **www.mcgraw-hill.co.uk/textbooks/paton** for a range of resources to support your learning.

Further Reading

Benner, M.J. and Tushman, M.L. (2003) 'Exploitation, exploration and process management: the productivity dilemma revisited', *Academy of Management Review*, **28**(2): 238–256.

Bessant, J. (2003) *High Involvement Innovation: Building and Sustaining Competitive Advantage through Continuous Change*, Wiley, Chichester.

Bessant, J., Lamming, R., Noke, H. and Phillips, W. (2005) 'Managing innovation beyond the steady state', *Technovation*, **25**(12), 1366–1376.

Burns, T. and Stalker, G.M. (1961) *The Management of Innovation*, Tavistock, London.

Hyland, P. and Beckett, R. (2005) 'Engendering an innovation culture and maintaining operational balance', *Journal of Small Business and Enterprise Development*, **12**(3): 336–352.

Tidd, J. and Bessant, J (2001) *Managing Innovation: Integrating Technological, Market and Organisational Change*, 4th edn, Wiley, Chichester.

References

Abernathy, W. and Utterback, J. (1978) 'Patterns of industrial innovation', *Technology Review*, **80**(7), 40–47.

Boer, H. and Gertsen, F. (2003) 'From continuous improvement to continuous innovation: a (retro)(per)spective', *International Journal of Technology Management*, **26**(8), 805–827.

Bounds, G., Yorks, L., Adams, M. and Ranney, G. (1994) *Beyond Total Quality Management: Toward the Emerging Paradigm*, McGraw-Hill, New York.

Imai, M. (1986) *Kaizen: The Key to Japan's Competitive Success*, McGraw-Hill, New York.

Isaksen, S.G. and Tidd, J. (2006) *Meeting the Innovation Challenge: Leadership for Transformation and Growth*, Wiley, Chichester.

Jager, B., Minnie, C., Jager, J. and Welgemoed, M. (2004) 'Enabling continuous improvement: a case study of implementation', *Journal of Manufacturing Technology Management*, **15**(4), 315–331.

Jantunen, A. (2005) 'Knowledge processing capabilities and innovative performance: an empirical study', *European Journal of Innovation Management*, **8**(3), 336–349.

Magnusson, M., Boccardelli, P. and Börjesson, S. (2009) 'Managing the efficiency–flexibility tension in innovation: strategic and organizational aspects', *Creativity and Innovation Management*, **18**(1): 2–7.

Muthusamy, S.K., Wheeler, J.V. and Simmons, B.L. (2005) 'Self-managing work teams: enhancing organisational innovativeness', *Organisational Development Journal*, **23**(3): 53–67.

Robertson, T.S. (1967) 'The process of innovation and the diffusion of innovation', *Journal of Marketing*, **31**(1), 14–19.

Smith, M., Busi, M., Ball, P. and Van Der Meer, R. (2008) 'Factors influencing an organisation's ability to manage innovation: a structured literature review and conceptual model', *International Journal of Innovation Management*, **12**(4), 655–676.

Styhre, A. (2008) 'The element of play in innovation work: the case of new drug development', *Creativity and Innovation Management*, **17**(2): 136–147.

Tidd, J. and Bessant, J. (2009) *Managing Innovation: Integrating Technological, Market and Organisational Change*, 4th edn, Wiley, Chichester.

Thompson, J.D. (1967) *Organisations in Action*, McGraw-Hill.

Tonnessen, T. (2003) 'Continuous innovation through company-wide employee participation', *The TQM Magazine*, **17**(2), 195–207.

Upham, S.P. (2006) 'Innovation and interrelatedness of core competencies: how Taiwan's Giant Bicycles broke into the US bicycle market', *Managing Global Transitions*, **4**(1): 41–62.

Van de Ven, A.H. (1986) 'Central problems in the management of innovation', *Management Science*, **23**(5): 590–607.

Westland, J.C. (2008) *Global Innovation Management: A Strategic Approach*, Palgrave Macmillan, Basingstoke.

Womack, J.P. and Jones, D.T. (1996) *Lean Thinking: Banish Waste and Create Wealth in Your Corporation*, Simon & Schuster, New York.

Zaltman, G., Duncan, R. and Holbek, J. (1973) *Innovations and Organizations*, Wiley, New York.

Designing

Contents

JOBS

WANTED
Strategic Supply Chain Manager

A strategic supply chain manager is needed to head our growing European network. As part of a global organization delivering products and services to businesses you will need to be dynamic and resourceful.

You'll have the ability to draw on experiences from most business functions but particularly project management, new product/service development, purchasing, logistics and operations. You should have a strong first degree, relevant professional qualifications and at least a proven 10 years' record of delivering successful strategic change.

What does it take to become a Supply Chain Manager?

We speak to Steve Sutton at Intel to find out.

Name: Steve Sutton

Age: 48

Current position: Supply Chains Programs Manager

Years in role: 3

How did you get into Operations Management?

I joined Intel after graduating as an Engineer with a degree in Electrical & Electronic Engineering. After a restructure in 2000 an opportunity came up for me to run the Supply and Pricing side of Intel's Business Operations. I took the role to extend my experience within the company and move closer to the heart of Intel's business in EMEA (Europe, Middle East and Africa).

What about the career attracted you?

I moved into supply chain management part way through my career and was attracted by the central nature of the role — working with customers, Finance, Sales, Logistics, Marketing and factories to satisfy product demand without building excessive inventories.

What other jobs have you done?

I started at Intel in 1984 as a quality engineer, and moved up through the ranks to engineering management. I later moved into marketing before joining the Business Operations team in 2000 where I ran the factory facing supply group. In 2003 I took responsibility for the customer facing team working with customers on their supply needs, before moving into my current role as Supply Chain Programs manager — improving the tools and processes we use to run the business. It's not a typical pathway, but it demonstrates that over a long career, the path can twist and turn many times.

What was the most useful experience that prepared you for your current role?

Working in the other Business Operations groups was the best experience I could have had before moving into Programs as I had a clear idea of the challenges faced by users and customers. This enabled me to help steer the efforts of IT to produce tools and systems that aligned with user needs.

What's a typical day in the life of a Supply Chain Programs Manager?

Much of my day is spent in meetings where my role is to oversee and steer different groups towards a common set of goals. I also attend various review meetings for updates on different projects. As a manager I will often have one to one meetings with those who work for me and also key stakeholders within the company. Towards the end of the day I speak on the phone with colleagues in the US as they are starting their day. Sometimes I need to attend early morning (6 a.m.!) or late night meetings where Intel counterparts from around the world get together to make decisions on specific projects.

What aspects do you like most about your job and why?

I love solving problems and helping others achieve their aims. I have found that these interests are very portable across the different roles I have had and this has enabled me to maintain my personal motivation working for the same company for the last 26 years.

What do you consider the ideal skills for your role?

In my current role the key skills are probably experience in people management, project management and a thorough understanding of the core business. On top of that, it is vital to have a strong network especially in a large company like Intel, in order to be able to effectively influence world wide projects.

What are the biggest challenges in your role?

One area where I spend significant time is aligning stakeholders from across the company to maintain momentum on key projects. Customers, Business Operations, Sales, Factories, Logistics and IT all have a stake in the supply chain and it's important that we maintain alignment without delaying projects.

If you weren't in Operations Management, what would you be?

If I were not working at Intel, I probably would have been a teacher. Within Intel I satisfy this need by being a trainer on a number of internal courses we run and I enjoy helping people in the class to develop new skills.

4 Designing Supplier Relationships

Learning Outcomes

By the end of this chapter, you should be able to:

- Define what a supply chain, a supplier network and an enterprise are

- Appreciate how suppliers and their customers often work together in an increasingly integrated way

- Describe why and how outsourcing takes place

- Apply simple models to help locate an operation and its suppliers

- Design an agile enterprise based on the theories of the resource-based view of an organization, and transaction cost economics.

More Power for More Passengers

The Airbus A380 is the largest commercial passenger jet ever built. It was designed to meet new market requirements for an increasing number of longer-haul flights between major airports while meeting more stringent security and environmental regulations. From an industrial perspective, the plane needed to save the ailing European large-passenger-aircraft industry by competing head to head with some of the most successful commercial aircraft ever built, such as the Boeing 747 Jumbo Jet.

Source: © 2007 Getty Images

Arguably, Airbus and its parent company EADS gambled the future of the company on this double-decker, monster-sized, 'super-jumbo' plane – which can carry up to 853 people. In contrast, their main competitor, Boeing in the USA, continued to invest in mid-sized passenger jets that are faster, cheaper and easier to own.

It was nearly seven years from the start of the project until operators got their first planes. Pre-orders for the planes were essential for this huge project (estimated at €11 billion) in order to start generating revenue. Singapore Airlines formed a joint venture with Airbus to ensure that their planes were designed and built exactly to their requirements.

Key suppliers were also included in the design and manufacturing process. For instance, Rolls-Royce Aerospace Group was one of only two engine suppliers. Rolls-Royce built the new Trent 900 engines – one of the most powerful jet engines ever built. The other engine (the GP2700) was built by the American

CSR

BUSINESS
INTEGRATION

Engine Alliance (EA), whose parent companies are General Electric and Pratt & Whitney. Rolls-Royce and AEA are the main partners in the joint venture, investing time, money and knowledge right from the beginning.

In turn, Rolls-Royce joined up with its key suppliers in risk- and revenue-sharing arrangements, where suppliers invested in the development of the new engine in exchange for a percentage of their sales revenue. Seven companies participated as risk- and revenue-sharing partners (from Spain, the USA, Italy, Sweden and Japan). Three other companies were included as programme associates (from South Korea and Japan). These companies had an input into some design decisions, but did not share in the overall risk-and-revenue partnership. In addition, hundreds more suppliers were engaged in conventional, openly competitive arrangements.

Much responsibility rested with the supplier management team at Rolls-Royce. They managed the huge network of global suppliers, to try to ensure that parts and services were delivered on time, every time, at acceptable costs. This involved recruiting new suppliers, developing new processes, planning and scheduling, materials management, manufacturing, assembly, and final delivery to the customer. In short, the supplier team provided the links that kept the supply chain together. As a result, the Trent 900 was officially certificated as airworthy on time, in October 2004, and the first A380 flew in April 2005. Rolls-Royce is now a major player in Singapore's aerospace industry, accounting for over 10% of the country's aerospace output via joint ventures with local industry. Eight out of the first 11 airlines to order the A380 chose the Trent 900 engine.

Source: Ben Clegg, Aston Business School

Introduction

This chapter focuses on how internal organizational and external competitive forces interact and influence the design and management of operations, and particularly on how organizations come together to form different types of supplier relationship. Supplier relationships can most simply be thought of as a *chain* of organizations working together. Or, if the relationships are more complicated, they can be thought of as a *network* of organizations working together. Sometimes, if relationships are even more highly integrated, they may be considered as a joint *enterprise*.

A chain of suppliers is normally thought of as one organization supplying another in a simple, openly competitive set-up, such as a farmer supplying a grocery store, or a manufacturer of paper supplying a newspaper company. A network of suppliers is a collection of organizations that collectively deliver parts and services to an end customer. This arrangement can arise simply because an element of collaboration between organizations can often be better than purely open competition. An enterprise arises when organizations work so closely together that it becomes hard to differentiate them.

The opening case describes a sophisticated form of supplier relationship, best thought of as an enterprise. Even Airbus itself is a collaboration of aircraft manufacturers, spanning a number of European countries. In this case supplier relationships have to work at all levels throughout the enterprise (i.e. strategic, tactical and operational). Relationships have been successfully forged with customers (e.g. Singapore Airlines) and with suppliers (e.g. Rolls-Royce), who work very closely with Airbus using their processes, working to their objectives, and sometimes sharing in their risks and rewards. In this case the types of relationship have arisen because the design and manufacture of the product (the Airbus 380) are too complex to be controlled by a single organization; they require the expertise and buy-in of many different partners at all levels.

Supplier relationships between organizations cover not only elements that are bought and sold, such as materials or services; they also include intangibles such as competencies, processes, decisions and strategies. Supplier relationships will usually focus on the delivery of a family of products, such as aircraft, or a group of services, such as package holidays. Sometimes relationships are set up to encourage innovation, as a new product or service can be created more easily than by a single company working alone.

Supplier relationships are an important part of the operational strategy (Chapter 2) of the organization. This chapter begins by looking at the basics of supplier relationships, including the terminology that is used. It will also look at why different types of supplier relationship arise, and at the decisions that are taken in designing effective networks.

Different Perspectives on Supplier Relationships

Three different views or perspectives on supplier relationships are introduced in this section. They range from a simple *supply chain*, through the more complicated but increasingly common *supplier network*, to the sophisticated *enterprise management* perspective.

Supply Chain Relationships

A 'supply chain' is a metaphor used to describe a simple, linear relationship between a series of different organizations such as a raw materials supplier, a product manufacturer, a distributor, and an end customer. Supply chains are concerned with the flow of three things between participating organizations: information, money, and materials. This is illustrated in Figure 4.1. Within each organization there are activities and processes related to each of these flaws.

The flow of activities might be triggered by a customer order – for example a bicycle from Halfords, a large UK retailer of bicycles and car accessories. The information about the order is transmitted to the distributor, in this case the Halfords warehouse; then to the manufacturer, which might be DBS, a Norwegian bicycle producer; and then, in turn, to the manufacturer's suppliers. As goods are moved along the supply chain, the firms involved incur transaction costs. These are the extra costs involved in buying goods or services (e.g. employing people to negotiate contracts, and the costs involved in moving items from one place to another). The management of these activities are referred to as *supply chain management*.

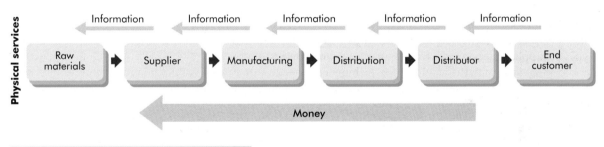

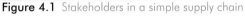

Figure 4.1 Stakeholders in a simple supply chain

Historically, business processes within individual firms in a traditional supply chain have operated relatively independently of each another. There was little sharing of information between the customers and the suppliers. Firms tended to rely on their immediate stakeholders for demand information, and therefore the information flow was slow. In order to make sure the supply chain operated smoothly, the stakeholders focused on maintaining buffers (excess stock) of materials, and capacity and lead times were based on forecast rather than actual demand.

Globalization, deregulation (the removal of government control), increasing customer demand and advances in both information and transportation technology have all contributed to make the design and management of supply chains increasingly complex. Shorter product life cycles and competitive pressures have forced firms to find new ways to work together, improve their operational efficiency, and make supply chains increasingly integrated. Figure 4.2 shows the contrast between traditional supply chains and integrated supply chains.

Supplier Network Relationships

A **supplier network** has a supply side and a demand side, as illustrated in Figure 4.3. On its *supply side* an operation has its suppliers of parts, information and services. These

> **Supplier network:** loose group of organizations that collectively delivery parts and services to an end customer.

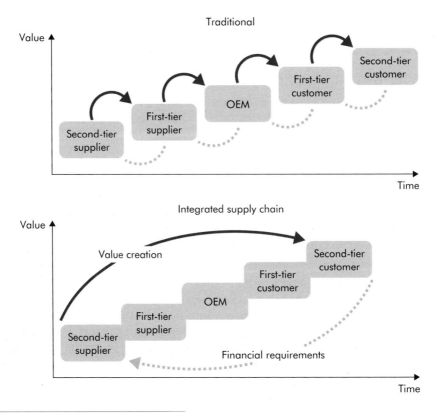

Figure 4.2 Traditional versus integrated supply chain

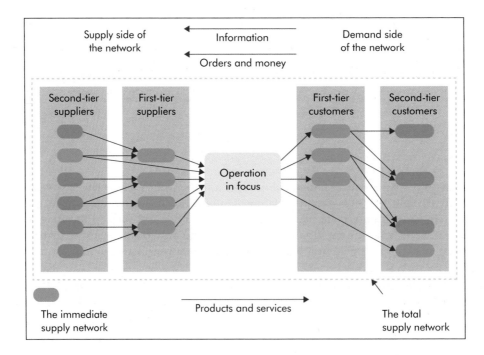

Figure 4.3 A simple supplier network

suppliers themselves have their own suppliers, who in turn may also have their own suppliers, and so on. On the *demand side* the operation has its customers. These customers might not be the final customers for the operation's product or services; they might have their own set of customers, and so on until the end user or consumer is reached.

On the supply side are a group of companies that supply the operation directly. These are called *first-tier suppliers*, and they are supplied by the *second-tier suppliers*. Some second-tier suppliers may also supply directly to the company that sells to the end customer, thus missing out some tiers in the network. For example, a second-tier supplier of nuts and bolts might supply its product both to the first-tier supplier, which might be an engine manufacturer, and to the operation in focus, which might be a car maker.

Similarly, on the demand side of the network, *first-tier customers* are those that receive inputs directly from an operation. In turn, first-tier customers may also supply *second-tier customers*, and so on. Customers who receive inputs directly from an operation are referred to as the *immediate supply network*, and customers that receive inputs indirectly from an operation, are referred to as the *total supply network*.

Occasionally a second-tier customer may receive inputs from an operation directly, as well as from its first-tier supplier. If this practice is unplanned, it can cause confusion in the network (most often over pricing), but if it is carefully planned it can be advantageous. For example, if the central operation were a golf club maker, its first-tier customers would include wholesalers, who in turn supply would supply retail outlets, the second-tier customers. However, it might also supply some retailers directly with made-to-order products, such as expensive custom-made clubs for professionals. On the supply side, most of the second-tier suppliers will provide only raw materials such as metal and rubber to manufacturers in the first tier, who may carry out other work such as machining and assembly. However, occasionally they might provide the golf club maker directly with simple products such as rubber hand-grips.

Along with the flow of goods and services in the network, each link in the network will feed back orders and information to its suppliers. When stocks run low, the retailers will place orders with the wholesaler or directly with the brand owner or manufacturers, who will in turn pass on these orders to their suppliers, and so on. It is a two-way process, with goods and services flowing one way – *downstream* – towards the end customer, and information, such as order quantities, and financial payments flowing the other way – *upstream* – towards the suppliers.

Enterprise Relationships

The European Commission (2003) defines an *enterprise* as

> *any entity engaged in an economic activity, irrespective of its legal form. This includes, in particular, self-employed persons and family businesses engaged in craft or other activities, and partnerships or associations regularly engaged in an economic activity.*

Enterprise management is the management of these enterprises.

In its simplest form, an enterprise could be a single integrated organization, but enterprises are normally thought of as being made up of parts of different organizations. The structure of an enterprise will depend upon many different, business-related factors, and its success will depend on its ability to acquire *core competencies* and integrate them into its products and services. In other words, the peripheral activities of one organization should be a core competence of another organization within an overall enterprise structure focused on delivering a particular family of products or services. However, even when an enterprise has been set up, it may need to be reconfigured and adapted to meet changing needs. For example, the construction of the Channel Tunnel was carried out by an enterprise that, throughout its lifetime, had many different structures and member companies, depending on the phase of work that was under way. When the tunnelling phase was complete, the tunnelling company would leave the enterprise relationship.

Different Supplier Relationships

The term *supply chain management* (SCM) was introduced by consultants during the 1980s, buts its roots can be traced back to the 1920s, when mass production philosophies began to dominate industry. In the 1970s supply chain management was known primarily as

▶ *distribution*, which focused on the integration of warehousing and transportation within the firm. The focus was on ways in which firms could make internal changes that would reduce inventories and distribution costs.

In the 1980s the focus of SCM shifted towards re-engineering firms' supply chain processes in order to lower supply chain operating costs. This included a change in thinking, from *pushing* goods to customers towards being more market focused, and letting customers *pull* what they wanted, as and when they needed it, from their suppliers. This was achieved mainly through real-time interaction with customers, and having wider product ranges, with more emphasis on modular products and customization. SCM also made extensive use of computers and information technology in planning, delivery and control. By the end of the 1980s the goal of many firms had become reduction of SCM cost to improve customer service; this was often achieved by giving activities and responsibilities to other organizations.

In the 1990s new management concepts emerged, most notably that supplier relationships are best thought of as networks rather than as chains. This is because SCM also aimed to achieve better linkages and coordination between the processes of other organizations throughout the supply chain. From the 1990s the view was that SCM could become a strong competitive advantage for many firms. This would require a firm to align its SCM strategy (sourcing, demand flow, and customer service) with its business strategy.

With an increasing focus on services and satisfying customer needs, supply chain management had also become known as *demand chain management*. Demand chain management emphasizes market needs and customers, while the supply chain focuses on suppliers. Together, demand and supply chain management are thought of as parts of the supply network. Since the turn of the 21st century the term *enterprise management* has arisen: this is concerned with the management of companies that have become so closely integrated that it is difficult to think of them as networks of separate companies, or simple supply chains.

> **Enterprise:** group of different companies, or group of parts of different companies, working together to deliver a product or service in a highly integrated way.

Contemporary thinking in operations management usually considers the supply chain or network metaphors to be an oversimplification. Supplier management theory is focusing increasingly on the **enterprise** as an operational entity, rather than on the traditional concept of supplier networks. For those of us who like a straightforward view of the world, though, an enterprise can be thought of as a group of different companies, or a group of parts of different companies, working together in a highly integrated manner to deliver a family of products and services to an end customer.

The key point is that different terms are used to describe the relationships between companies. You must decide which one is most appropriate in any given situation.

ⓘ Stop and Think

1 Managers often use metaphors to help explain complicated ideas. Do you think these are helpful, or do they add to the complexity? How else could complicated ideas be conveyed more easily?

Transferring Activities to Suppliers

> **Outsourcing:** process of giving part of your operations to another organization.

Outsourcing is the process of giving another organization the responsibility to deliver part of your products or services rather than doing it from within your own organization (known as *in-house* delivery). The term 'outsourcing' also means setting up a *procuring* and *purchasing* process for products and services. By outsourcing, a company enters into a contractual agreement, typically with a supplier for the supply of a certain capacity that has previously been carried out in house. The ownership, responsibility and decision-making power are shifted – partly or wholly – to the supplier.

SHORT CASE 4.1	**Banking on Outsourcing**

Barclays is one of the world's biggest banks. In the early 2000s Barclays Global Retail Bank was attracted to outsourcing and offshoring (i.e. moving work out of the home country in favour of another) to India, because of the low labour rates. According to David Skillen, Chief Operating Officer of Barclays Global Retail Bank, the original driver for outsourcing was labour arbitrage (i.e. taking advantage of different labour rates around the world), delivering as much as 40% savings compared with the UK.

Source: © Bloomberg via Getty Images

Barclays initially outsourced its non-voice back-office services (i.e. its Internet services) for both its commercial and retail banks to Intelenet in 2003. Skillen explains that 'There was no reason for us to own our servicing call centres, since they were really a commodity.' In addition to reducing labour costs, the ability to serve customers 24/7, 365 days a year, was another attraction. Also, outsourcing helped the UK call centre to balance its workload by providing more flexibility.

As the relationship evolved, Barclays learned how to manage it for best value. In the early days of offshoring, Barclays just sliced off the mechanical aspects of a particular process, such as data entry, and only outsourced that. However, it eventually came to understand that service providers can deliver more value at a strategic level if they control the whole process from start to finish. As trust and understanding grew, Barclays began to outsource the end-to-end delivery of its core processes, such as new information technology development, finance and accounting, and human resources management.

Questions

1 How have Barclays and Intelenet built a good relationship?
2 How can service providers add more value to a buying organization?
3 Do you think the buyer or the seller of the service should have most influence?

Source: http://www.outsourcing-center.com, 13 September 2010

Outsourcing is typically used to improve an organization's financial position, operational productivity or structure. Financially driven reasons include improving return on assets, gaining access to new markets and customers, reducing overall costs, and turning long-term fixed costs into costs that are more variable in the short term. Productivity-driven reasons include improving quality, shortening cycle time, obtaining new expertise and technologies, and reducing risks. Organizationally and structurally driven reasons include being able to focus on what the firm does best (i.e. its core competencies), increasing flexibility to meet changing demand patterns, helping to improve customer responsiveness, and joining up with other successful companies. These reasons are summarized in Table 4.1.

Offshoring is a specific form of outsourcing in which companies transfer some of their activities to other countries outside their country of origin. The main drivers behind offshoring have been access to new markets worldwide, and lower labour costs in developing countries. It has been estimated that labour rates in developing countries can be 90% lower than those in developed countries. For example, the average salary of a radiologist in 2006 was US$35,000 in India, US$95,000 in Singapore, US$140,000 in the UK with the National Health Service, and US$340,000 in the USA (Yu and Levy, 2010).

The reverse of offshoring is known as *onshoring*. This is when organizations bring their suppliers back to their home country, to reduce risk or increase supply certainty.

Single Sourcing

In *single sourcing* the buyer relies on one source for the supply of an item or service. The arrangement between the firms is like a partnership, and often results in a strong, durable and trusting relationship. Price will

Table 4.1 Reasons for outsourcing

Financially driven reasons	• Improve return on assets by reducing inventory and selling unnecessary assets • Generate cash by selling low-return entities • Gain access to new markets, particularly in developing countries • Reduce costs through a lower cost structure • Turn fixed costs into variable costs (or vice versa) depending on the situation
Productivity driven reasons	• Improve quality and productivity • Shorten cycle time • Obtain expertise, skills, and technologies that are not otherwise available • Improve risk management • Improve credibility and image by associating with superior providers
Organizational/structurally driven reasons	• Improve effectiveness by focusing on what the firm does best • Increase flexibility to meet changing demand for products and services • Increase product and service value by improving response to customer needs

Source: adapted from Jacobs and Chase (2008, p. 189).

not necessarily be the most important criterion. Single sourcing often requires that the partners trust each other, especially regarding the sharing of confidential knowledge about the outsourced products and services, which can be complex and specialized. The strong dependence, in turn, encourages more commitment and effort from both parties.

Single sourcing also has its disadvantages. The buyer might be more vulnerable to disruption if a failure to supply occurs. For instance, this can happen when a supplier files for bankruptcy, and has no means of fulfilling the contract. Too much dependence on a particular supplier also makes the firm vulnerable to price demands. The extreme version of this occurs when the supplier is the sole source of the product or service: there are no other suppliers with the capability to deliver it – a monopoly situation (e.g. the supply of piped water to homes in a particular area of the UK).

Multiple Sourcing

In order to avoid the supply risks associated with single sourcing, companies can use *multiple sourcing*, establishing a wide supply base, where the suppliers are encouraged to compete with each other – often on price. The buyer can then drive down the price by *competitive tendering*. Multiple sourcing strategies also allow the buyer to switch sources in case of supply failure, as well as tap into wider sources of knowledge and expertise. If such a practice becomes too adversarial, though, it can be difficult to encourage commitment from suppliers. They will also be less willing to invest in new technologies and processes if they know their customer may be sharing confidential details with their competitors.

Sourcing from two parties (or *dual sourcing*) combines the advantages of single sourcing and multiple sourcing by building strong relationships without the danger of a monopoly occurring. Some guidelines for sourcing decisions, adapted from Burt *et al.* (2003), are as follows:

Single sourcing is appropriate when:
- Lower total cost results from a much higher volume (economies of scale)
- Quality considerations dictate
- The buying firm obtains more influence or 'clout' with the supplier
- Lower costs are incurred to source, process, expedite, and inspect
- The quality, control, and coordination required with just-in-time manufacturing require a single source
- Significantly lower freight costs may result
- Special tooling is required, and the use of more than one supplier is impractical or excessively costly
- Total system inventory will be reduced
- An improved commitment on the supplier's part results
- More reliable, shorter lead times are required
- Time to market is critical

Multiple sourcing is appropriate:
- To protect the firm during times of shortage, strikes and other emergencies
- To maintain competition and provide a backup source
- To meet local content requirements for international manufacturing locations
- To meet customers' volume requirements
- To avoid lethargy or complacency on the part of a single-source supplier
- When the customer is a small player in the market for a specific item
- When the technology path is uncertain
- In areas where suppliers tend to leapfrog each other technologically

If organizations decide to outsource their products and services, and there is a choice between different possible suppliers, they need to decide which one to go for. The next section looks at choosing suppliers, based on their location.

Location Decisions and Supplier Relationships

It is often said that, when buying a house, there is nothing as important as location: the same might be said for locating a business. Unfortunately, not all businesses have good reasons for their location choice. Often they are there for historical reasons, and find it difficult to justify the cost and disruption of moving unless compelled by very strong reasons. Strong reasons might include changes in demand for their goods and services, or in changes in their supply of inputs.

The Impact of Demand Changes

Demand changes can be driven by a change in the location of a customer, in frequency of purchases, or in the total number of customers in a particular area. For instance, if there is a boost in the construction activity in a particular area of a country – Beijing's new airport, for example – then a cement manufacturer may choose to locate there. Similarly, if there is growth in the student population in a certain area of a city, then more fast-food outlets may locate there.

Demand-based location is heavily influenced by the suitability of the site itself. For instance, luxury holiday hotels are often located next to a sandy beach in a beautiful bay. If a hotel were located in a back street industrial area, it would have little appeal, and demand for its service would inevitably be low. The same is also true for retailers, who compete for high-profile sites in the high street, where demand from passing traffic is high; such sites can fetch a premium price in comparison with back streets that have little passing traffic. Quite often a particular address is sought after, such as Wall Street in New York for trading companies, Harley Street in London for medical practices, or Sunset Boulevard in Los Angeles for swanky restaurants. At other times the site is determined by convenience: for example, public services such as fire stations, hospitals and schools have to be located near the population that will use them.

The Impact of Supply Changes

Supply changes can be driven by the cost or availability of inputs supplied to an operation. For example, a mining company or a forestry company may need to relocate as resources become depleted, or an energy company may need to relocate to where there is a plentiful and reliable supply of water to drive its hydroelectric turbines.

A manufacturing or software engineering company may choose to relocate to parts of the world where the labour force is relatively cheap, in terms of cost per hour of employment, or beneficial exchange rates, or lower overheads. (Overheads in this case refer to the extra costs of employing someone, e.g. pension, fringe benefits and sick pay.) Other labour-related issues include the availability of the right sort of labour. For example, science parks are often located close to universities because they hope to recruit the people that the university has educated.

A company may also choose to relocate to areas where land and business rates are cheaper, and so can be influenced by wider governmental, political, societal and economic forces.

Making the Location Decision

The aim of making a good location decision is to achieve an appropriate trade-off between the costs associated with the geographical location, the level of service an operation is able to deliver to its customers, and the potential the location has to generate revenue. In different scenarios some factors are more important than others. For instance:

- Commercial manufacturers are concerned mainly with minimizing the variable costs due to geographic locations associated with the transportation of supplies and finished goods, while maximizing their revenue and customer service levels
- Commercial service providers are concerned mostly with the direct costs of renting or leasing premises (such as offices, conference centres or retail units) and their potential to attract clients, as clients usually place a lot of weight in *where* they go for services such as a meal or a haircut
- Non-profit organizations are concerned mainly with a location's ability to provide an acceptable level of service to its customers, sometimes despite its costs of leasing, renting or any associated transportation costs to and from it. For instance, the location of a school is often chosen for easy access by its pupils and their parents.

The location decision for any operation is therefore determined by the relative strengths of its supply-side and demand-side factors.

Centre of gravity method: approach that uses the physical analogy of a 'balancing point' to determine the geographical location of an operation relative to others that it has a direct relationship with.

Weighted score technique: technique for comparing the attractiveness of alternative operational locations that allocates a weighted score to each relevant factor in the decision.

Operations managers need to draw on their skills and experience when making location decisions, although there are some basic quantitative steps that can help rationalize the process. We describe two here: the **centre of gravity method**, which is most useful for transportation-based decisions, and the **weighted score technique**, which can be used to assess wider managerial factors in an outsourcing decision.

Centre of Gravity Method

Minimizing transportation costs for an operation is usually an important contributing factor in locating an operation. The **centre of gravity method** can be used to help minimize these costs. It is based on the idea that all possible locations can be scored and assigned a numeric value, based on the sum of all transportation costs to and from that location. The best location is the one that minimizes the overall transportation cost.

All locations are represented on a scale map that has square gridlines on it, rather like a standard road map. The centre of gravity of the map is found, and this represents the coordinates of the lowest-cost location for a site. The x and y coordinates of this location are calculated using the following formulae:

$$x = \frac{\sum x_i V_i}{\sum V_i}$$

$$y = \frac{\sum y_i V_i}{\sum V_i}$$

where x_i is the x coordinate of the source or destination i, y_i is the y coordinate of the source or destination i, and V_i is the volume to be transferred from source or destination i.

WORKED EXAMPLE 4.1

Putting the Centre of Gravity Method into Practice

A local authority operates four schools, which currently each have a small storeroom for their foodstuffs (e.g. tins, vegetables, milk). The local authority has decided to get rid of these small storerooms and build a large new central distribution centre to try to cut costs and create more space in the schools for the pupils. Each school is a different size, and needs a different volume of supply, and hence a different number of deliveries (i.e. trucks) travelling to and from them per week. Table 4.2 shows the volumes transported each week.

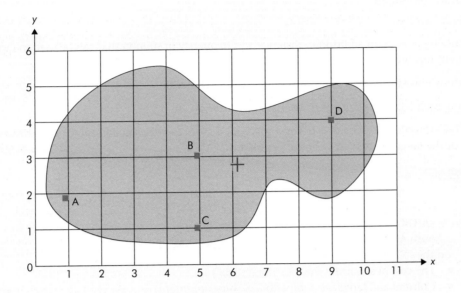

Figure 4.4 Centre of gravity model for the local authority

Table 4.2 **Weekly deliveries to the schools**

	Deliveries per week
School A	5
School B	10
School C	15
School D	20
Total	50

Problem: *Where should the new distribution centre be located?*

Approach: The local authority region is sketched out on a grid – which is represented by the blue area in Figure 4.4. In the figure the schools' locations are also plotted, and the above formulae are applied.

The calculation is therefore:

$$x = \frac{(1 \times 5) + (5 \times 10) + (5 \times 15) + (9 \times 20)}{50} = 6.2$$

$$y = \frac{(2 \times 5) + (3 \times 10) + (1 \times 15) + (4 \times 20)}{50} = 2.7$$

This means that the minimum-cost location, or the 'centre of gravity', for the new distribution centre is at point (6.2, 2.7) – which is shown by the red cross on the map.

In practice the optimum location will also be influenced by other factors, such as the transportation network, or the geography of the land. So if the optimum location was at a point with poor access to a suitable road, or at some other unsuitable location, such as in a river or in a graveyard, then the chosen location would need to be adjusted. Therefore this technique is used only as a guide, suggesting general locations.

Weighted Score Technique

This technique involves:

1   identifying criteria (in addition to distance and frequency of supply) that can be used to evaluate different locations

2   assigning a weighting of relative importance to each criterion

3   scoring each location's suitability against each criterion.

This technique can also be extended beyond physical factors to wider management considerations, such as cultural fit, or the language capability of the population.

WORKED EXAMPLE 4.2

Putting the Weighted Score Technique into Practice

A UK Internet service provider (ISP) has decided to set up a new call centre in Poland, or South Africa, or India. In order to choose the correct location, it has decided to evaluate them on the following criteria:

• The cost of acquiring the location (crucial)
• Cultural and language compatibility (very important)
• The site's access to the international airport (very important)
• Local taxation rates or subsidies (important)
• The availability of suitable skills in the local labour force (important)
• Time zone difference from Greenwich Mean Time (minor importance).

There are three sites to consider that may work. These are known as sites P (Poland), SA (South Africa) and I (India). After investigating each in detail, the operations managers allocate a score between 0 and 100 that they believe represents the usefulness of each site in relation to each criterion; this is shown in Table 4.3.

Problem: *Where do you think the ISP should locate its new call centre, and why?*

Approach: Allocate a weighting between 1 and 5 to each of the criteria to indicate how important they are. Then multiply each usefulness score by the importance weighting. Finally add up the adjusted scores (Table 4.4).

Solution: The preferred outsourcing option is the South African site (see Table 4.4), as the weighted total score is the highest: $(90 \times 5) + (50 \times 3) + (50 \times 3) + (80 \times 4) + (70 \times 4) + (50 \times 1) = 1,400$.

Using the same method, the Polish site has scored lowest, and the Indian site has achieved the middle rank.

Note: The ISP company can use this technique to reassess the scenario should any factors become more or less important; or if other factors need to be considered later on.

Table 4.3 Usefulness scores for new call centre outsourcing decision

Criterion	Usefulness scores for sites		
	P	SA	I
Cost of the site	80	90	95
Rate of local property taxation	40	50	80
Availability of suitable skills in the labour force	50	50	50
The site's access to the international airport	50	80	25
Cultural and language compatibility	30	70	25
Time zone difference from Greenwich Mean Time	30	50	40

Table 4.4 Weighted usefulness scores for new call centre outsourcing decision

Criterion	Importance weighting	Weighted usefulness scores for sites		
		P	SA	I
Cost of the site	5	400	450	475
Rate of local property taxation	3	120	150	240
Availability of suitable skills in the labour force	3	150	150	150
The site's access to the international airport	4	200	320	100
Cultural and language compatibility	4	120	280	100
Time zone difference from Greenwich Mean Time	1	30	50	40
Total weighted scores		1,020	1,400	1,105

Supply Base Rationalization

From the late 1990s onwards, supplier management practices have shown a strong trend towards increasing supplier integration, which in turn reduces the overall number of suppliers. This practice is often called **supply base rationalization**, and can be seen as a backlash to the tendency of organizations to outsource during the preceding decades.

> **Supply base rationalization:** reduction of suppliers in order to become more efficient.

The underlying purpose of supply base rationalization is simple: it involves working more closely with fewer suppliers. The practice builds on the idea that an individual organization has only a limited amount of resources, and by reducing the number of suppliers an organization has to manage *directly*, it becomes easier for it to focus its management efforts. But although supply base rationalization may achieve short-term cost savings, and complement other practices such as *lean management* (as described in Chapter 10), it can bring its own problems. These are described below.

The financial effect of supply base rationalization can be demonstrated by looking at cost structures. Broadly speaking, there are three levels of cost:

- *Strategic costs* – which are best thought of in terms of commercial risks incurred and lost business opportunities. They are typically intangible, indirect, and very hard to measure
- *Tactical costs* – which are management costs associated with things such as visiting suppliers, holding quality audits and supplier conferences. These are usually overheads that can be attributed to particular products or services
- *Operational costs* – which are the costs of making the products or delivering the service, such as materials, and salaries of employees. Relatively speaking, these are direct costs and are the easiest to measure.

Often when organizations move from a large supply base to a smaller one, the cost structure seems to turn upside down, as demonstrated in Figure 4.5. Strategic costs increase relatively as the buying organization becomes increasingly dependent on fewer firms, and has more strategic activities to participate in, such as the co-development of new products and services. In contrast, operational costs *should* decrease relatively, because the overall number of transactions should decrease (e.g. moving from ten suppliers to one can mean raising 10 times fewer purchase orders). The overall intention of supplier rationalization, by the dominant organization, is to reduce overall cost (as implied in Figure 4.5 by the smaller triangle post-reduction) and management complexity. This is achieved by reducing the number of suppliers managed, by either encouraging first-tier suppliers to

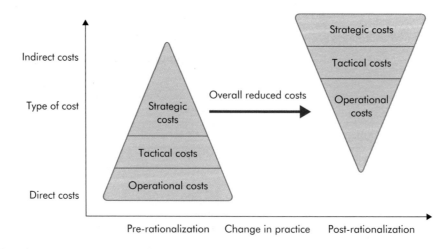

Figure 4.5 The effect of cost on supply base reduction (adapted from Cousins, 2005)

merge, or encouraging some first-tier suppliers to manage other first-tier suppliers, who, as a result, effectively become second-tier suppliers.

We should treat the practice of supplier rationalization with caution, though, because it is difficult to demonstrate clearly *overall* cost savings, owing to the problems of measuring the indirect cost element accurately.

WORKED EXAMPLE 4.3

Costing Supply Base Rationalization at EuroCook

A large European industrial catering company known as EuroCook is looking to outsource some of its food production in an effort to reduce its overall supply costs and their variable cost component. EuroCook has five different non-meat food production lines that it wants to outsource (bread, cakes, pastries, biscuits and cereals), as it wants to concentrate on meat-based products, which will continue to be made in house. It has invited FoodFactory to bid for the work. The costs should be based on 1,000 units of output per month over a 12-month period, and need to be broken down and attributed to strategic, tactical and operational activities.

EuroCook's management accountants have calculated what it costs the company currently to produce its non-meat product lines; these are shown in the 'Pre-rationalized suppliers' column in Table 4.5. FoodFactory's accountants have costed the bid; their costs are given in the 'Post-rationalized suppliers' column in Table 4.5.

Problem: *Will it be cheaper for EuroCook to keep managing its non-meat product lines in-house, or let another company (FoodFactory) manage them?*

Approach:

Pre-rationalized suppliers total annual costs (€s):

$$= 100,000 + (5 \times 10,000 \times 12 \text{ months}) + (1000 \times 1.2 \times 12 \text{ months})$$
$$= 100,000 + 600,000 + 14,400$$
$$= €714,400$$

Post-rationalized suppliers total annual costs:

$$= 300,000 + (5 \times 5,000 \times 12 \text{ months}) + (1000 \times 0.8 \times 12 \text{ months})$$
$$= 300,000 + 300,000 + 9,600$$
$$= €609,600$$

Solution: It can be seen that at 1,000 units of production per month it is far cheaper (€714,400 − €609,600 = €104,800 savings per year overall) to let FoodFactory manage its suppliers.

Table 4.5 Supply base rationalization for EuroCook's non-meat product lines

Level at which cost is incurred	Example	Supplier management costs	
		Pre-rationalized suppliers managed by EuroCook	**Post-rationalized suppliers managed by FoodFactory**
Strategic	Whole company (e.g. EuroCook or FoodFactory) on an annual basis	€100,000 per year Variable costs	€300,000 per year Fixed costs
Tactical	Particular production line (e.g. bread) on a monthly basis	5 lines × 12 months × €10,000 per month Variable costs	5 lines × 12 months × €5,000 per month Fixed costs
Operational	Unit of output (e.g. one tray of bread)	1,000 units per month × €1.2 cost per unit Variable	1,000 units per month × €0.8 cost per unit Variable

Note: Rationalization means that EuroCook is effectively dealing with only one supplier (FoodFactory) for all its non-meat products, rather than with many individual suppliers. This should make management of suppliers simpler. This decision will also reduce its risk, as some of its variable costs have been turned to fixed costs, which makes budgeting and financial planning easier.

The key point is that, by practising supply base rationalization, an organization has costs that are arguably more certain, and easier to measure and manage.

Stop and Think

2 If you were a senior manager in a small organization supplying a large organization, which was conducting a supplier rationalization programme, what steps would you take to ensure that your company was not adversely affected?

Supply Base Rationalization at Sony

SHORT CASE 4.2

Sony makes innovative products, such as the Walkman music player and the PlayStation game console. It has built a valuable global brand. However, in the financial year ending 2009, the Japanese company made its first annual loss in 14 years (nearly £0.5 billion) as it was hit by declining global demand, a strong Chinese yuan, and reducing product prices. In response, under a turnaround plan led by Chief Executive Officer (CEO) Howard Stringer, Sony halved the number of parts suppliers, to reduce its costs by 20%. This was achieved because it was less costly to manage fewer suppliers.

Sony reduced the number of parts makers from about 2,500 to about 1,200 in a single year.

GLOBALIZATION

Source: © 2009 Getty Images

BUSINESS INTEGRATION

After supplier rationalization, Sony became more focused, improved its efficiency, boosted its earnings and profits, expanded its demand-side distribution network, and increasingly shared its parts makers' processes with its suppliers.

Another closely related issue was that the various internal divisions of Sony needed to work together better. Stringer said that their business units often didn't communicate well with each other, and even hinted that they were territorial. Stringer said that 'we must transform Sony into a more innovative, integrated and agile global company,' which is an essential step to take before rationalizing the external supply base.

Questions

1   What further steps could the CEO of Sony take to save supply costs?
2   What would you do if you were a supplier to Sony?
3   What are the downsides to the supplier reduction that Sony is implementing?

Source: The Associated Press, 2009. Adapted.

CRITICAL PERSPECTIVE

Why Do Organizations Outsource and Rationalize?

Outsourcing is concerned with finding alternative external supply sources for an organization, and supply base rationalization is about ensuring that the organization does not have too many external supply sources. If an organization has too many suppliers, this can generate a burdensome overhead and unnecessary complexity.

Often businesses go through cycles of outsourcing followed by periods of supplier rationalization, which is then repeated as organizations drop certain suppliers and subsequently look for new ones. Although this may be seen as wasteful and iterative, it often stops an organization from stagnating, by bringing in fresh ideas and approaches.

The key point is that an organization must make sure that it has enough external suppliers to keep costs and internal bureaucracy down and innovation up, but not so many that they begin to become burdensome and counterproductive.

The Design of Enterprises for Closer Supplier Relationships

Enterprise management is an emerging idea about how organizations are designed, structured and managed. Contemporary thinking sees an enterprise as an inter-organizational structure that links the operations of separate companies very closely.

There are three basic types of enterprise:

Virtual enterprise: temporary group of organizations exploiting a short-term, high-risk opportunity.

Extended enterprise: semi-permanent group of organizations working towards joint strategic objectives.

Vertically integrated enterprise: almost permanent and extremely well-integrated group of organizations; very similar to a single legal entity.

- **Virtual enterprise (VE):** a short-term temporary group of (parts of) organizations exploiting a specific short-term, often high-risk opportunity
- **Extended enterprise (EE):** a semi-permanent group of organizations working towards joint strategic objectives
- **Vertically integrated enterprise (VIE):** an almost permanent and extremely well-integrated group of organizations; similar to a single legal entity.

These three types exhibit different characteristics and are suited to different operational contexts, as described in Table 4.6.

Table 4.6 Enterprise types: virtual, extended, and vertically integrated

	Virtual enterprise	Extended enterprise	Vertically integrated enterprise
Philosophy	Agile	Lean and agile	Lean
Foundation of relationship	Based mainly on technical competence features; emphasis on high innovation; allocation of resources depends on competitive and comparative advantage	Based mainly on social competence features; past relationship experience important; emphasis on strategic sourcing of critical products	Based mainly on efficiency factors; emphasis on transaction costs (e.g. prices)
Core competencies	Newly emerging, speculative, untested, high risk, requires many members to spread risk; high asset specificity; high transaction costs	Tested to some extent, medium risk, understood by innovators; medium asset specificity; medium transaction costs	Mature, well-accepted, tested and widely usable; low asset-specific investments; low transaction costs
Scope of relationship	Project-based activities that exploit specific opportunities across organizational boundaries; present a unified face to externals; partners involved in many other collaborative activities simultaneously to lessen their risks	Mid-term strategic thinking; often spans whole product life cycle across organizational boundaries	Standardization, high production volumes and corporatization of structures; focus on scales of economies rather than on scope of economies
Longevity of relationship	Short-term temporary alignment of operations	Medium to long term	Foreseeable as permanent (as long as competitive)
Proximity and depth of relationship	No stability; dynamic and unpredictable environment; collaboration improves agility and flexibility; low degree of interdependence and integration	Strategic collaboration; relationships, technology and knowledge management become critical; medium degree of interdependence and integration	Tend towards industrial dominance; emphasis on removal of IT legacy systems; high interdependence and integration
Governance of relationship	Loose and flexible; temporary and reactive to emerging trends; right balance of control and emergence (i.e. co-opetition)	Strategic sourcing and partner development; design and implementation of co-owned processes; proactive governance aiming for efficiency	Single command and control; focused on monitoring and control through standardization and corporatization
Strategic role of enterprise integrator	Incubator; scouting for potential value members; initiates collaborative activities	Integrator; coordination of collaborative activities; supports value members in competence development	Incumbent; in-house development of proprietary systems; relying on power and authority
Strategic role of value members	Innovative suppliers; deploying specific competencies for innovating new technologies and solving complex R&D problems	Integrator; integrating parts to more complex systems and managing and coordinating sub-supplier base	Volume production; value creation through cost-efficient making and delivery of parts to high quality
Main collaboration points	Mainly new product and service planning and concept design	Mainly concept, early delivery design and mass delivery planning	Mainly high-volume design and delivery

Enterprise integrator/ orchestrator: organization that takes the lead role in transforming a loose supply network into a tightly integrated enterprise.

In an enterprise there is always one dominant – most strategically influential – organization, known as the **enterprise integrator** or **orchestrator** (Brown *et al.*, 2002). This organization is predominant in the design of the enterprise, and it is critical that operations managers within this organization understand suppliers' motives capabilities and structures, in order to be able to design an appropriate *enterprise structure*. The enterprise should contain the most useful parts of the most suitable organizations. This requires managers in the integrator organization to combine an 'outside, looking in' view, known as an *exogenous view*, of each partner with an 'inside, looking out' view, known as an *endogenous view* of their organization. This is based on the resource-based view of an organization described in Chapter 1 and the theories of transaction cost economics described in the section below.

Endogenous theories: theories about an organization that focus on the organization and its links to the business environment.

Exogenous theories: theories about an organization that focus on its internal workings, resources and skills.

Endogenous theories or views and **exogenous theories** or views should be used to complement one another; excessive focus on either one can result in a poor operations strategy. For instance, too much internal focus can mean that an organization does not develop strong enough links with its suppliers and customers, implying that it might be hard for it to buy or sell products and services easily. Conversely, too much external focus can mean that the organization may not develop internal skills and resources adequately, implying that it risks losing its unique competitiveness or innovative features. We shall now build on these ideas to show how enterprises should develop over time.

Transaction Cost Economics

Transaction costs: the price associated with buying or selling goods or services.

If you bought a new coat, you might spend time and money choosing it, and have to pay delivery costs if you bought it through the Internet, or pay petrol and parking costs if you drove to a shopping centre. These costs are all **transaction costs**. Another example would be buying a house. As well as the cost of the house, there is the time spent with estate agents, fees to estate agents and legal fees, and the costs of moving.

Transaction cost economics (TCE) has emerged as a *de facto* economic explanation for the existence and scope of a commercial organization. Nobel Prize Laureate Ronald Coase (1937) stated that commercial organizations exist because of these 'transaction costs' – in other words, the price of using the open market mechanism. An organization has to use this thinking all the time when buying new products or services. For example, buying new computer services for students' residences or a university library will incur transaction costs. These may include the time taken to do research (e.g. spending time researching what type of server is needed, and who provides them), bargaining (e.g. spending time negotiating with potential suppliers) and enforcement (e.g. maintenance of the servers, and extra costs for fixing problems). There will be similar costs involved for the computer service provider (e.g. time putting together a proposal, delivering a sales pitch, etc.).

TCE is based upon the interplay of four behavioural assumptions: bounded rationality, opportunism, asset specificity and uncertainty.

Bounded rationality is the assumption that, although most human behaviour is intended to be rational, it is often limited by knowledge, behaviour and language (Simon, 1957). For instance, we may try to choose the cheapest or most waterproof coat we can, but we have no sure way of knowing this, as we cannot check *every* coat that is for sale.

Opportunism is the assumption that 'actors' (organizations or individuals) will try to improve their own standing in comparison with others. For instance, if we saw a coat that was fashionable and good value, and we really wanted it, we would buy it regardless of any other actors' needs or desires. Opportunism could be described as 'self-interest seeking with guile' (Williamson, 1975). This is self-centred behaviour, and is often how free markets operate. However, it is difficult to distinguish between those who act like this deliberately, those who act like this from bounded rationality, and those who may actually want to collaborate. Higher competitive pressures and levels of mistrust between organizations will cause more opportunism.

Asset specificity considers how specialized assets (e.g. core competencies for design, manufacture or branding) are dedicated to delivering certain products or services. In successful times these are often the source of competitive advantage. These specialized assets are risky to own, though, as they cannot be fully utilized if the particular application for which they were acquired is no longer required. This is because they cannot be easily transferred to another application. For example, a general-purpose sewing machine that is used to make coats will have low specificity, because it can easily be used for making a variety of other clothing, whereas a machine that can be used for only one task (e.g. a fabrication plant for PC processors) will have high specificity, as it will have expensive retooling and changeover costs. The four main types of asset specificity are *location* (e.g. restriction to a particular place), *physical properties* (e.g. speed of a machine), *human limitations* (e.g. limited skills) and *degree of dedication* (e.g. the amount of different things that can be done at any one time). In adverse conditions, assets with highly specific properties are believed to increase the opportunism, or, if conditions allow, may result in organizations collaborating.

Uncertainty relates to the business environment, and the behavioural limitations of organizations and individuals. Organizations facing high levels of uncertainty in their markets and the external environment will tend to seek to develop their own internal resources, and look for low-risk projects and organizations to work with (e.g. hospitals often have their own back-up power plants to ensure that they always have a reliable source of electricity). However, such risk aversion usually means more expense, and slower rates of innovation.

> **The key point is** that all the above assumptions affect transaction costs. If other factors are favourable, then when an organization's overall transaction costs with external organizations are higher than its internal transaction costs, it will often grow. This is because it is cheaper and easier to do activities in house. Conversely, if internal transaction costs are higher than external transaction costs, an organization can benefit from downsizing or outsourcing its operations, because it is cheaper and easier to get another organization to perform these activities.

TCE is often criticized for:

- Failing to explain clearly situations when suppliers should collaborate as partners in jointly strategic relationships
- Focusing too much on cost minimization rather than on value maximization.

Resource-based View

As explained in Chapter 1, the *resource-based view* (RBV) traditionally focuses on the internal resources of a single organization. We also saw how the traditional RBV has, more recently, been extended to recognize that resource bases vary over time and require collaboration with different organizations, leading to the *dynamic capabilities view* (DCV) of organizations (Teece *et al.*, 1997) discussed in Chapter 1. The main difference between the DCV and the RBV of organizations is that DCV considers a number of simultaneously collaborating organizations working towards joint business objectives, instead of individual organizations being purely opportunistic. This is also recognized by the managers of enterprises.

The core competencies of an organization (which are endogenous resources) are difficult to transfer, because of high transaction costs, dependence on tacit knowledge, and high asset specificity. Because of this, core competencies can usually only be deployed effectively internally within single organizations. However, under certain conditions organizations may prioritize development of their core competencies over and above the minimization of transaction costs – for instance when engaging in a new collaborative venture (such as a long-term research project with a university to develop a new technology). This challenges the notion of competitive advantage, and suggests that *cooperative advantage* or *collaborative advantage* (Dyer and Hatch, 2004) can sometimes be more appropriate. Collaboration should occur when the minimization of operational transaction costs has become less significant than gaining new external core competencies in new collaborative enterprises.

In other words, to remain competitive, new meta-core competencies (those that are a property of the whole enterprise, rather than just one company) need to be built by the enterprise integrator alongside existing traditionally valued ones to reconfigure operational competencies and organizational structures. The enterprise integrator's role is assumed by the most significantly influential member of the enterprise. For example, the Canadian company Magna Steyr attempted to acquire parts of the former European General Motors as it almost became strategically and financially more dominant than GM, the original equipment manufacturer.

SHORT CASE 4.3

Virgin: Come Together

Source: © Photogenix/Alamy

The Virgin Festival (or 'V Festival') is a groundbreaking music festival, as it was the first to be delivered over two days at two different UK venues – Hylands Park in Essex and Weston Park in Staffordshire. Originally, the festival was the brainchild of the pop group Pulp's lead-man, Jarvis Cocker, who wanted to play two live festivals on consecutive days, one in the north and one in the south of England. The festival contrasts with other big summer music festivals, such as Glastonbury, that are held over several days, at a single location.

BUSINESS INTEGRATION

In the UK, SJM Concerts promotes the festival. The planning involves many different types of organization, such as caterers, radio stations, ticket agencies, mobile phone companies, engineers, sanitation providers, security, emergency services – and, of course, the musical artists. They must come together for a short time span to deliver a service to the festival-goers and then part until, perhaps, participating again the following year.

GLOBALIZATION

The V Festival concept has been so successful that it is now also staged in Australia (over four sites in Sydney, Melbourne, Perth and the Gold Coast), where it is sponsored by Virgin Mobile, Virgin Blue (local airline) and MTV. What makes this festival so successful is that the key partners in it have a shared long-term vision for what should be delivered, and how to deliver it. Even the short-term stakeholders (e.g. the food stalls, and the artists) become part of the bigger picture.

Questions

1   Who do you think are the most powerful organizations in this enterprise, and what core competencies do you think they have?
2   Name aspects of the festival that have high and low transaction costs.
3   Are there any advantages to be gained from having multi-site festivals?

Source: Ben Clegg, Aston Business School

❗ Stop and Think

3   Why don't organizations cooperate all the time, if there are potential gains to be made from doing so?

Collaborative enterprise governance: method of controlling parts of many different organizations simultaneously, in order to deliver products and services with agility and efficiency.

Contemporary Thinking: Collaborative Enterprise Governance

Designing and integrating collaborative enterprises is rather like putting together a jigsaw puzzle where each piece is owned by a different organization. **Collaborative enterprise governance** (CEG) is an approach to designing enterprises. It considers enterprises to be made up of parts of different companies (i.e. the pieces of the puzzle), known as *enterprise modules*, where each individual enterprise module is built around highly specific core competencies belonging to an individual organization. For instance, an enterprise module could be the engines on a ship such as the new *Queen Mary 2*, or a military vessel such as the new BAE Systems Astute Class nuclear submarine; or the provider of ticketing services for a train company such as Eurostar.

Often the enterprise module provider gives a unique and valuable proposition distinct to the rest of the enterprise, such as an in-house design and engineering specialism, or is a provider of additional capacity, such as an additional

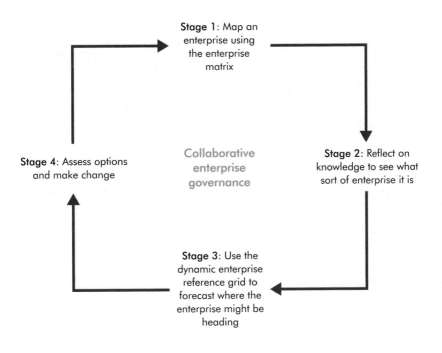

Figure 4.6 Collaborative enterprise governance

assembly plant in another country. The core competencies of any enterprise module are combined with other less specific resources, such as communication technology, cooperative contracts, and shared processes (which are relatively easy to share across a whole enterprise), to form an enterprise structure with economically acceptable transaction costs.

Enterprise integrators help overcome the traditional adversarial view, and help promote the ideas of inter-company collaboration instead. This means connecting enterprise modules (parts of one organization) with other enterprise modules (parts of another organization) to create *agile enterprises*. These agile enterprises often meet the demands of rapidly changing business environments, while operating with acceptable costs, more easily than single large traditional organizations. The role of enterprise integrator is often fulfilled by companies such as information technology consultancies, which provide the skills and technology to design shared processes and technology (e.g. companies such as SAP, Capgemini or Accenture). Sometimes, if it is necessary and if the enterprise is agile enough, the jigsaw can be remade with different pieces, to create a new picture (e.g. a new enterprise). The four main stages of CEG are shown in Figure 4.6, and are explained below.

Stage 1: Mapping the Enterprise

First we have to decide on a particular product or service family on which to focus the enterprise, and then map the enterprise using the *enterprise matrix* shown in Figure 4.7.

The members of the enterprise, who create value for it in some way or another, should be listed on the vertical axis; they are listed in order of significance, from the most important at the top to the least important at the bottom. There can be any number of these value members, which may reach into the hundreds for a complex product such as an aircraft or a complex service such as a long-distance luxury air flight. But the different types of value member can usually be classified into just a handful of different types, in order of the most significant: enterprise integrator, joint partners, design-make-and-deliver, and make-to-print suppliers:

- An *enterprise integrator* will be the most influential, as it brings all the other companies together (like Airbus in the opening case study).
- A *joint partner* will usually have made some up-front investment in the project, and will share in the revenues and losses of the whole enterprise (like the Rolls Royce Aerospace Group in the opening case study).

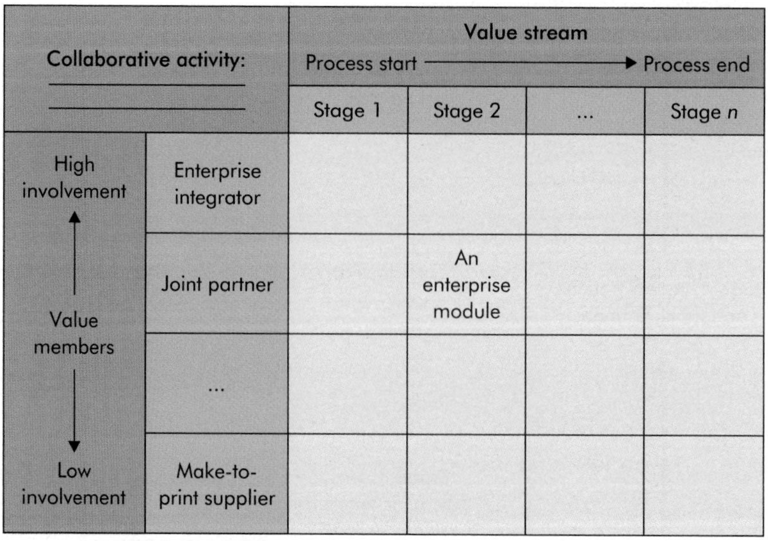

Collaborative activity:		Value stream			
		Process start ———————————► Process end			
		Stage 1	Stage 2	...	Stage n
High involvement ↑ Value members ↓ Low involvement	Enterprise integrator				
	Joint partner		An enterprise module		
	...				
	Make-to-print supplier				

Figure 4.7 The enterprise matrix: a mapping tool

- *Design--make-and-deliver suppliers* could be employed by the enterprise integrator or joint partner to design and deliver items or services, and so are skilled members (like the programme associates in the opening case study), and will usually be hired through an invited competitive tendering process to participate.
- *Make-to-print suppliers* are relatively low-skilled organizations, delivering standard low-risk and low-value items that are easily available.

Design-make-and-deliver and make-to-print suppliers are likely to get paid whether the whole enterprise is successful or not (as long as it does not become bankrupt), as they have not invested in it up front, and do not share directly in its profit.

Each stage of the value stream in the enterprise is then mapped along the horizontal axis, with the first stage on the left-hand side and the last stage on the right-hand side. There can be any number of stages, but the whole value stream can usually be described adequately in a few key stages.

What each member of the enterprise does at each stage of the value stream is then described in the appropriate place in the enterprise matrix. This is a description of:
- What the enterprise module has as specific assets, and how they differentiate it from the others
- What processes it uses, and what they deliver
- How its performance is measured
- How it can be efficiently linked with other modules
- The transaction costs that are incurred by using it

By describing the enterprise like this, we can begin to understand how the whole enterprise is built and governed.

Stage 2: Reflecting on Knowledge

This stage compares practice with theory to decide which sort of enterprise structure a particular scenario is currently best suited to. Table 4.6 characterized the three main types of enterprise: *virtual enterprises* (VEs), often found in research and development situations; *extended enterprises* (EEs), often found in knowledge transfer and product or service derivation situations; and *vertically integrated enterprises* (VIEs), found in commercially proven situations with stable markets. These different types do not result from different strategies, but are actually part of the same overall strategy, focused on inter-organizational collaboration at different times of the enterprise's development. Virtual enterprises are preferable in rapidly changing environments, and are typically used for experimental products and services; extended enterprises are preferable in environments that are fairly predicable, and deliver products and services with some proven track record; and vertically integrated enterprises are preferable in very stable operational environments, when organizations compete mainly on cost.

Remember that each enterprise is focused around the delivery of a particular family of products or services (e.g. mp3 players, or a mobile device payment services). Therefore an enterprise module is likely to be part of many different enterprises simultaneously. For example, an enterprise module making parts for Sony music players is also likely to be able to supply other consumer brands; and Visa will have payment-processing modules operating in many different organizations, each operating quasi-autonomously, but drawing upon the same specific competencies. It is therefore useful to perceive enterprises as a collection of quasi-autonomous modules, where each module is simultaneously able to contribute value to a number of coexisting enterprises.

Stage 3: Using the Dynamic Enterprise Reference Grid

It is important to recognize that competencies are strategic resources which need to be developed and managed. The number and type of enterprise engagements for any one organization depend on the value placed on its enterprise modules by other companies and, the capability to deploy them; this is known as an enterprise module's **engageability**. The engageability of a module may increase over time as value members become

> **Engageability:** the ability to attract partners and the means to deliver value.

more integrated, transaction frequency increases, and costs reduce (exogenous factors). In a similar way, the low marketability of a new competence (exogenous factor), due to its untested market value, will initially result in low attractiveness and low engageability. However, this may change through further development of the competence, leading to higher maturity and less risk.

Figure 4.8 shows the *dynamic enterprise reference grid* (DERG). It summarizes the four main types of enterprise and their engageability, ranked simply as 'high' or 'low'. In each of the quadrants, the most suitable enterprise structure is shown. The DERG is important because it is the basis of how dynamic changes in an enterprise can occur. Below we give a description of each of the quadrants (Q) of the DERG, with examples.

Quadrant 1 (Q1): Low Current Engageability but High Future Potential Engageability

Enterprises in this quadrant are managed and governed 'virtually', and show a prevalence of modules with competencies that have low current but high future engageability potential. This is because they usually have many

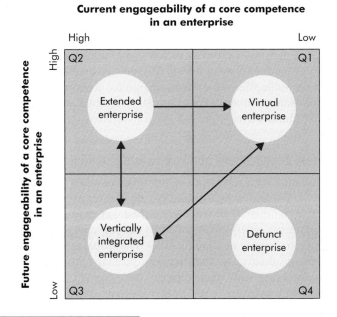

Figure 4.8 Dynamic enterprise reference grid (DERG)

newly emerging competencies – for example, the initial enterprise that developed the prototype Bluetooth short-range, hands-free communications protocol for mobile devices, which at the time was untested on consumer markets. In this situation, the enterprise governor and the value members will be reluctant to make long-term plans and investments until they start to produce revenue. So, here, collaboration arrangements will often be temporary, intended to exploit market opportunities and spread the risk over many different value members. In addition, the cost of collaborating may be very high, owing to the fragmented resource base, the high specificity of the competencies, and the high transaction costs. These are all characteristics of a *virtual enterprise*. In a virtual enterprise it is usual for value members to deliver very specific and limited value to the overall value stream. The selection of value members is based on their ability to solve complex technological problems, and their capability to bring them to market quickly.

Quadrant 2 (Q2): High Current Engageability and High Future Potential Engageability

Enterprises in this quadrant are governed as extended enterprises, and show a prevalence of competencies that are currently highly engageable, owing to their relatively mature nature and market success; this makes them highly attractive to other value members. eBay, an Internet site that has proven ability to sell products, or an ability to deliver a market-ready Bluetooth chip for mobile devices, are good examples. Such competencies involve relatively low levels of uncertainty and risk during their deployment. They are also perceived to have high potential engageability in the future, based on an ever-increasingly universal application of their value proposition. In this situation the enterprise integrator will seek a more stable, medium- to long-term co-developmental supply strategy with value members in order to minimize commercial opportunism. This decreases the costs of collaboration, and increases the ability to integrate these competencies into efficiently operating enterprises. These are characteristics of an *extended enterprise*. In an extended enterprise the value members tend to be involved in collaborative activities spanning many steps of the value stream. Their selection is based primarily on their good interface capabilities, making it relatively easy to use their competencies in an increasing number of different enterprises at relatively low transaction costs.

Quadrant 3 (Q3): High Current Engageability but Low Future Potential Engageability

Enterprises are governed in a *vertically integrated* way; they are currently highly engageable, thanks to their mature, well-established and widely usable competencies and capabilities. However, on the downside, they may become less attractive in the future, because of fears that profit margins are eroding, or that their technologies may become obsolete. This may cause the enterprise governor to seek whole-ownership of capabilities to minimize transaction cost. This leads towards a merging of organizations or permanent acquisitions of enterprise modules within a *vertically integrated enterprise*, and a control-based governance structure. An example of this is Chinese auto manufacturer NAC's purchase of MG Rover's Longbridge production plant. By taking this course of action, the once collaborative enterprise begins to closely approximate the traditional vertically integrated organization. In vertically integrated enterprises a single significant member (or small number of significant members) will cover most of the value stream in order to maximize economies of scale and standardization. In this situation, the selection of value members is based primarily on their ability to be highly efficient, and not necessarily on their ability to be innovative.

Quadrant 4 (Q4): Low Current Engageability and Low Future Potential Engageability

Enterprises found in this quadrant have a prevalence of enterprise modules that are perceived as undesirable for current and future engagement. The enterprise integrators seek to disengage them from the rest of their organization before an unrecoverable commercial situation is reached. For example, Hewlett-Packard sold the major shareholding in its PC manufacturing enterprise in 2004 to a Chinese company (Lenova Group). Recovery from this situation is possible by simultaneously developing other new virtual engagements, such as Hewlett-Packard partnering with management consultancies so that they can provide high-value IT business services. Another example is the ISP PlusNet partnering with small software development companies to become a high-value online business applications service provider (ASP). In this way, the collaborative enterprise governance cycle begins again.

Stage 4: Assess Options and Make Changes

This stage occurs when enterprise managers need to redesign and implement changes to an enterprise, based on new understanding of any given context. The dynamic enterprise reference grid shown in Figure 4.8 indicates how one enterprise structure may change into another as a result of different factors acting upon it. This is a two-way dependency, as the chosen enterprise structure will affect the development of future potential competencies, just as the development and deployment of competencies will influence the emergence of enterprise structures. Proactive strategies are shown in Figure 4.8 by the arrows, and are based largely on controllable endogenous factors.

It is important to note that all enterprises are at risk of becoming defunct, and could fall into Quadrant 4 if they do not closely monitor internal and external factors, act upon changes affecting them, and proactively seek to modify their enterprise type to best suit their situation.

The key point is that at different points of a product and service life cycle different enterprise structures and methods of governance are required.

SHORT CASE 4.4 — A Smart Car Needs a Cleverly Designed Enterprise

BUSINESS INTEGRATION

The Smart car is one of the most innovatively designed and produced cars of recent years. The production of the Smart was initially a temporary collaboration, with weak ties between parts (enterprise modules) of Daimler-Benz (DC) and SMH, manufacturer of Swatch watches, to exploit market opportunities for very small cars. As the market grew the relationship strengthened, and it became longer term and more permanent.

These changes were accompanied by a change in the role of DC, which grew from a coordinator of manufacturing and logistics operations (relationship and technology management) to include the coordination of strategic information (knowledge management). DC began to act as the enterprise integrator. These changes saw the enterprise move from a virtual enterprise (Q1) into an extended enterprise (Q2).

Because of problems of achieving further market penetration for the Smart, tension between DC and Swatch grew, and led to the buyout of the two-seater Smart from Swatch by DC. This signified a transition from a extended enterprise (Q2) structure towards a vertically integrated enterprise (Q3) as major parts of the know-how and competencies of the venture became 're-insourced' into parts of DC. DC became an overwhelmingly dominant force, controlling the collaborative relationship that once had been a virtual and then an extended enterprise.

As a vertically integrated enterprise (Q3) DC also deployed its core competencies in other directions, which gave birth to the production of the new Smart Forfour car jointly designed with Mitsubishi, in another separate inter-company enterprise where parts would be supplied by Mitsubishi and the engines by Mercedes-Benz. This initially formed a new virtual enterprise (Q1) that quickly became successful and moved towards an extended enterprise structure (Q3). And so the cycle goes on.

The Smart is the result of effective enterprise management, and by being proactive the enterprise has avoided becoming defunct.

Questions

1 Using the collaborative enterprise governance concept, describe how careful enterprise management has helped Smart.
2 Why do you think these changes have helped effective innovation and efficient production?

Source: Ben Clegg, Aston Business School

Using the Enterprise Matrix

Isobel has chosen to do her dissertation on medieval history, and urgently requires a rare book that is currently out of print for her research. She finds it on the website of a popular online bookseller, who promises to print and deliver it within 24 hours by using their on-demand print supplier. The enterprise for the on-demand print company is mapped out using the enterprise matrix, as shown in Table 4.7.

Problem:

Using Table 4.7:

1 *State how many key steps there are in their value stream, and how many different types of value stream members they have. What does the 'development partner' do?*

2 *What sort of enterprise do you think it is? Who is the systems integrator? Why?*

Approach:

Read the above section (Collaborative enterprise governance) carefully, and then refer to the enterprise matrix example in Table 4.7.

Solution:

1 Table 4.7 shows five key stages in the value stream, starting with new process development and ending with delivery. It also shows five main types of supplier/value member: the most significant are the customers, and the least significant are the open-source suppliers. The development partner is responsible for making the special printing machines and making sure they are well maintained.

2 One might consider the printer to be the systems integrator in this extended enterprise. This is because using an on-demand print supplier of books (i.e. they do not begin to make the book until it has been sold) requires a highly integrated process. To deliver this requires a collaborative and competitive enterprise strategy, developing strong semi-permanent links with their immediate customers (the publishers), a good understanding of their end customers' needs (i.e. Isobel, the buyer and reader of the book), access to a large distribution of wholesalers, retailers and booksellers, and unprecedented inventory control via electronic links (Internet and electronic data interchange).

Table 4.7 The enterprise matrix for an on-demand book-printing service

Value members	Book-printing value stream				
	New process development	Scheduling	Printing	Finishing	Delivery
Publishers (customers)	Electronic data links				
On-demand printing company	Electronic data links	On-demand electronic data links scheduling	High-technology printing	Binding and finishing	
Development partner	Company that co-develops the printing machines		Contract maintenance		
Strategic/dual-source supplier		Paper suppliers			
Open-source supplier				Other materials (e.g. glue and card)	Logistics company

Stop and Think

4   From your experience, can you think of other examples that the collaborative enterprise governance concept could be applied to?

Summary

This chapter has focused on how supplier relationships are formed. It started by providing a background to different ways of thinking about supplier relationships – chains, networks and enterprises – and emphasized that these give us metaphors and models to help us understand different types of relationship. It showed how these relationships can change and evolve due to internal and external factors.

It then examined how operational activities can be transferred to and from firms by outsourcing, and outlined the advantages and disadvantages of doing this, and also the benefits and costs of using multiple-source and single-source supply chain strategies. Decisions on site location were considered with two tools – the centre of gravity method and the weighted score technique – introduced to help in making these decisions. Finally the characteristics of enterprises were studied in more detail, and a method of designing them (collaborative enterprise governance) was explained.

Outsourcing is not a panacea for all operations management problems; too much uncoordinated outsourcing can itself cause problems. Sometimes in an industry or company there is a trend to rationalize, and bring the supply base back into control, which can mean a reduction of suppliers overall, or the use of other organizations to manage suppliers for you.

Key Theories

- **Transaction cost economics (TCE)** – an economic explanation for the existence and scope of a commercial organization. TCE is based on the interplay of four behavioural assumptions; *bounded rationality, opportunism, asset specificity* and *uncertainty*.

- **Resourced-based view (RBV)** – an organization theory that focuses on the internal resources of a single organization. RBV explains how competitive advantage within organizations is achieved and sustained over time. RBV assumes that each organization (i.e. a single legal autonomous entity) is thought of as a bundle of resources in its own right.

- **Enterprise management** – the management of companies that have become so closely integrated that it is very difficult to think of them as networks of separate companies, or simple supply chains.

- **Supply base rationalization** – management practice that reduces the number of suppliers an organization has to deal with. The objective is often to reduce management costs and complexity.

Suggested Answers to Stop and Think Questions

1   **Management metaphors:** There probably is no easier way of doing this, although managers sometimes develop metaphors, models, frameworks and formulae to help develop generic principles for managing. Most metaphors need to be treated with caution, though, as they will only get you so far before they fail.

2   **Combatting supplier rationalization:** Seek to 'move up the value chain' by becoming a module supplier rather than a component supplier, develop meta-competencies of integration yourself in addition to traditional ones, seek to understand the end customer better, and cease competing only on a cost basis.

3 **Cooperation:** Cooperation and collaboration between organizations are suitable only when complementary competencies are being used. At other times, when similar competencies are being used, organizations will be in competition with one another. Sometimes there is a grey area between these juxtapositions that require organizations to work together within strict legal arrangements; these often focus on the delivery of specific product and services.

4 **Collaborative enterprise governance:** The concept could be applied to the delivery of any complex product or service that uses a variety of different organizational roles. It is especially relevant where the business environment, role and membership of the enterprise are rapidly changing. For instance, services would include air flights, Internet service provision, and mobile phone services; products would include big budget films, large buildings and construction projects.

connect

Review Questions

1 Can organizational relationships be accurately explained using a simple 'chain' metaphor, or is this an oversimplified view?

2 Why is it important for companies to work together more closely than before?

3 What are outsourcing, in-sourcing and offshoring?

4 Under what circumstances would you practise supply base rationalization?

5 What are TCE and RBV? What are they used to explain?

6 What is an enterprise, within the context of supplier management? What different sorts of enterprise are there, and how do they differ?

Discussion Questions

1 What effects do you think good supplier–buyer relationships have on an industry overall? How can they be encouraged?

2 Map out a supply network for a product such as a car or aircraft, or a service such as hotel accommodation. State and discuss the complexities that you come across in trying to do this. What do you think are the success factors?

3 Try to map an enterprise for a product or service that you are familiar with, using the enterprise matrix. State who you think are the relatively major and minor members of the enterprise, and what their roles are. Using the dynamic enterprise reference grid, describe what you think are the dynamic changes occurring in it.

Problems

1 A fire service serves three different cities – A, B and C – in a region. There are located at coordinates (35, 47), (12, 25) and (86, 72) respectively. The fire service needs to build a new fire station, D, to serve all three cities, taking into account how often they are called out (V). The details for each city and their frequency of callouts are given in Table 4.8.

Table 4.8 Locations of cities A, B, C and their frequency of callout

City	Location		Frequency
	x	y	V
A	35	47	50
B	12	25	70
C	86	72	80

Required: *Using the centre of gravity method, locate the new fire station, D.*

Use the following formulae:

$$x = \frac{\sum x_i V_i}{\sum V_i}$$

$$y = \frac{\sum y_i V_i}{\sum V_i}$$

where x_i is the x coordinate of the source or destination i; y_i is the y coordinate of the source or destination i, and V_i is the amount to be 'transferred' from source or destination i.

2   A European English-speaking university is thinking of setting up a new teaching facility overseas. It needs to take into account:

- Number of local students (crucial)

- Rent of the site (very important)

- Availability of suitable teaching staff in the area (important)

- Accessibility from the home nation (minor importance).

The university is considering two sites, one in Hong Kong (HK) and one in East Africa (EA). After some research, the university allocates usefulness scores (out of 100) to each potential teaching facility, shown in Table 4.9.

Table 4.9 Usefulness scores for the new teaching facility decision

Criteria	Usefulness scores for sites	
	EA	HK
Number of local students	70	90
Rent (note: high score means it is cheap)	60	20
Availability of suitable teaching staff in the area	50	70
Accessibility from the home nation	50	80

Required: *Using the weighted score technique, calculate which site you think the university should choose for its new teaching facility, and why.*

3   The Washing Machine Company wants to rationalize the number of its suppliers, as it believes there are too many, which creates unnecessary complexity and costs in the supply network. It is considering outsourcing the management of all its suppliers to one of two possible companies: Supply Chain Management Company A or Supply Chain Management Company B. Table 4.10 shows the current supplier management costs in the 'Pre-rationalized suppliers' column and bids from the potential alternative options in the other two columns.

Table 4.10 Cost comparisons for three possible outsourcing solutions for the Washing Machine Company

Level at which cost is incurred	Example	Supplier management costs		
		Pre-rationalized suppliers	Supply Chain Management Company A	Supply Chain Management Company B
Strategic	Whole-company costs on a annual basis	€1,000,000 Fixed costs	€1,500,000 Fixed costs	€500,000 Fixed costs
Tactical	Different production lines: (e.g. domestic washing machines, and industrial launderette machines) on a monthly basis	2 lines × 12 months × €200,000 per month Variable costs	2 lines × 12 months × €100,000 per month Fixed costs	2 lines × 12 months × €400,000 per month Fixed costs
Operational	Unit of output: one washing machine	500 units per month × €100 cost per unit Variable	500 units per month × €50 cost per unit Variable	500 units per month × €150 cost per unit Variable

Required: *Using the supplier rationalization approach in described in the chapter, and a planned output of 500 washing machines per month, calculate whether The Washing Machine Company should continue to manage its own suppliers, or rationalize them by giving the management of them to Company A or to Company B, if it is going to reduce their overall annual supply costs.*

Visit the Online Learning Centre at **www.mcgraw-hill.co.uk/textbooks/paton** for a range of resources to support your learning.

Further Reading

Baldwin, C.Y. and Clark, K.B. (2000) *Harvard Business Review on Managing the Value Chain*, Harvard Business School Press, Boston, MA.

Binder, M. and Clegg, B.T. (2010) *Sustainable Supplier Management in the Automotive Industry: Leading the 3rd Revolution through Collaboration*, Nova Science Publishers, New York.

Doz, Y.L. and Hamel, G. (1998) *Alliance Advantage*, Harvard Business School Press, Boston, MA.

Dyer, J.H. (2000) *Collaborative Advantage: Winning Through Extended Enterprise Supplier Networks*, Oxford University Press, Oxford.

Fine, C.H. (1998) *Clockspeed: Winning Industry Control in the Age of Temporary Advantage*, Perseus Books, Reading, MA.

Hamel, G. and Prahalad, C.K. (1994) *Competing for the Future*, Harvard Business School Press. Boston, MA.

Fung, V.K., Fung, W.K. and Wind, Y. (2008) *Competing in a Flat World: Building Enterprises for a Borderless World*, Wharton School Publishing, Philadelphia, PA.

References

Brown, J.S., Durchslag, S. and Hagel III, J. (2002) 'Loosening up: how process networks unlock the power of specialization', *The McKinsey Quarterly*, Special edition: Risk and Resilience, 59–69.

Burt, D.N., Dobler, D.W. and Starling, S.L. (2003) *World Class Supply Management: The Key to Supply Chain Management*, 7th edn, McGraw-Hill/Irwin, Boston, MA.

Coase, R. (1937) 'The nature of the firm', *Economica*, **4**(16), pp. 386–405.

Cousins, P.D. (2005) 'The alignment of appropriate firm and supply strategies for competitive advantage', *International Journal of Operations and Production Management*, **5**(3), 143–155.

Dyer, J.H. and Hatch, N.W. (2004) 'Using supplier networks to learn faster', *MIT Sloan Management Review*, **45**(3), 57–63.

European Commission (2003) 'Commission recommendation of 6 May 2003 concerning the definition of micro, small and medium-sized enterprises', *Official Journal of the European Union*, C(2003) 1422, L124/36–41.

Gartner, C.A. (2004) 'Offshoring in the service sector: economic impact and policy issues', *Economic Review – Federal Reserve Bank of Kansas City*, **98**(3), 5–37.

Jacobs, F.R. and Chase, R.B. (2008) *Operations and Supply Management: The Core*, McGraw-Hill/Irwin, New York.

Simon, H.A. (1957) *Models of Man: Social and Rational*, Wiley, New York.

Teece, D.J., Pisano, G. and Shuen, A. (1997) 'Dynamic capabilities and strategic management', *Strategic Management Journal*, **18**(7), 509–533.

Williamson, O.E. (1975) *Market and Hierarchies: Analysis and Antitrust Implications*, Free Press, New York.

Yu, K.-H. and Levy, F. (2010) 'Offshoring professional services: institutions and professional control', *British Journal of Industrial Relations*, **48**(4), 758–783.

5 Product and Service Design

The First Generation of Chrysler Jeep's WIPERs

As you read this case, please consider how a new product is created, and the various processes the designers have to go through in order to meet the customer's requirements.

The Jeep Grand Cherokee was first introduced in the US in 1993 as a high-end, sport utility vehicle (SUV). The commercial success of this new family of Jeeps was uncertain, as it had numerous new concepts and innovations that were not present in former Jeeps (i.e. the Cherokee and Wrangler). Moreover, a large portion of the development responsibilities for these innovations was outsourced.

Soruce: © Bloomberg via Getty Images

For example, both the design and manufacturing of the wiper controller module (co-named WIPER) was outsourced to Motorola. The WIPER system (shown in Figure 5.1) links the switch (which is connected to the steering wheel) to the motor, wash pump and wiper blades. It translates the driver's command into the desired wiper mode. Although this is a simple function that many drivers take for granted, the new system took three years to progress from concept development to production.

The Concept

The controller used by older Jeep families applied relay-based technology, which made a 'clicking' sound when switching from ON to OFF – an annoying feature that Chrysler wanted to eliminate. Just imagine driving a car in rainy weather for hours, with the wiper controller clicking at you continuously! So Chrysler asked Motorola to develop a 'quiet' WIPER controller. One plausible technical solution was to create a fully electronic controller. Because there were no radical innovations involved in the process, the development of the electronic 'el-WIPER' was carried out independently of Chrysler's involvement.

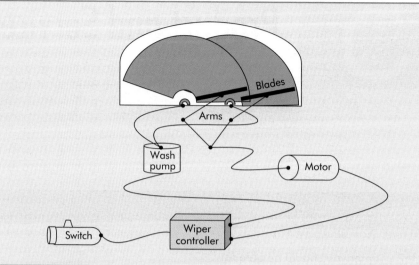

Figure 5.1 The WIPER system

Challenges

Motorola faced some challenges. Not only was it working with Chrysler for the first time, but it had a tight budget, and short development and manufacturing lead times. Although all the modules of the wiper system (i.e. motor, wiper arms, blades and wiper switch) had predetermined specifications set by Chrysler, how they would function as an integrated wiper system in relation to the rest of the vehicle was not known. At this stage this was a new design, and there were no cars available for testing the concept at the time, so the designers had to rely on lab testing. Finally, when Grand Cherokees were available for testing, el-WIPERs would catch fire when tested under certain conditions, even though they worked flawlessly in lab simulations and tests.

Learning from Failure

Because of these failures, interface specifications and compatibility issues had to be re-examined. As a consequence, the design team went back to the drawing board, and started redesigning the system from scratch. Several solutions were assessed. This process provided Motorola and Chrysler with a valuable learning experience. Everybody gained a much better understanding of the windscreen wiper system as a whole, in terms of its functionality and interfaces with other elements of the vehicle. Most importantly, a great deal of the WIPER's specifications for the Grand Cherokee Jeep were redefined. This step was made possible through an active collaboration between Motorola and Chrysler to share and solve technical problems. Face-to-face meetings and daily phone calls became a habit.

What could the design team do to solve this problem as quickly and effectively as possible without having to change the manufacturing processes that were already in place? The ideal solution was to redesign the WIPER with a 'silent' relay. One of the advantages of relay-based technology for this application was that it would increase the robustness of the WIPER. The only problem was that all the relays available at the time were considered very noisy, as they all made clicking sounds. Major relay suppliers in the world were invited to develop a silent relay, based on detailed technical requirements specified by Motorola. An innovation competition took place among the suppliers.

Solution

In less than a year, around 15 prototypes were tested and evaluated. In the end, a Japanese manufacturer was chosen as the sole supplier, because it was able to offer the best-performing silent relay at the most competitive price. The silent relay proved to be the key factor for economies of scale and scope, as it could also be used with other Jeep families (such as Cherokee and Wrangler). This meant that one common WIPER could be mounted on any Jeep without degradation in functionality and performance, and additional savings could be gained from economies of scale of components, universal tooling, and common assembly and manufacturing processes.

Source: Juliana Hsuan, Copenhagen Business School

Introduction

As we saw from the Jeep Grand Cherokee's experience, there were various uncertainties Motorola had to face when designing the WIPER system. Although the design concept was a simple one, the transition from lab test to on-car test added other dimensions of complexity and uncertainty. Even with a well-devised concept, a design that worked well at one stage of development (in the lab) had to be abandoned because of problems at the next stage (on the car). This also highlights the pressure that the design team had to face in terms of lead times, cost, and design options. As the case shows, the amount of money already invested in the design and manufacturing did not allow the team to redesign the WIPER system from scratch. They had to find solutions within the existing design. When introducing new designs to an existing systems it is important to test how the innovation performs with the rest of the system. Another issue that many manufacturers have to consider is how to create economies of scale from the innovations. This WIPER system ended up replacing the Wrangler and Cherokee's wipers systems too, effectively standardizing the system across the product range.

There is increasing pressure for firms to be competitive in the marketplace. They have to bring out products and services faster, and offer the customers a wider range of choices. For instance, mobile phone makers must introduce at least two new models each year, with an array of new functionality such as cameras, Internet access or video, for example.

Firms need to respond to the challenges of introducing new products and services into the market before their competitors, making sure they are defect-free, and guaranteeing the desired level of services. So how should firms organize their development strategies? This chapter will begin by taking a look at the *new product development (NPD)* process, where product concepts are created and turned into designs. We shall learn about product design strategies that firms pursue in order to achieve a balance between cost and performance. These strategies include product platforms, modularization, and mass customization. Next, we link NPD processes to the management of manufacturing and services. Here we learn about how products and services are interlinked. We shall also learn about how services can be designed, and the implications for an organization's front- and back-office processes.

The New Product Development Process

It often takes a long time for new products to be developed, evaluated, tested, manufactured, marketed, and then sold into the market. Positive return on investment may not show up in the corporate accounting books until many years later. Take mobile phones, for example. The first commercial portable cellular phone, Motorola's Dyna TAC8000x, took more than 10 years to develop, with an investment of over $100 million.

Research and Development

New product development is often regarded as a part of the *research and development (R&D)* process (see Figure 5.2). **Research** is often referred to as a scholarly or scientific investigation. It is generally categorized as either basic or applied. In natural sciences, for instance, the main activity of *basic research* is to obtain a more complete understanding of the subjects under study (for example, superconductivity, the properties of chemical

> **Research:** scholarly or scientific investigation or inquiry; generally categorized as either basic or applied.

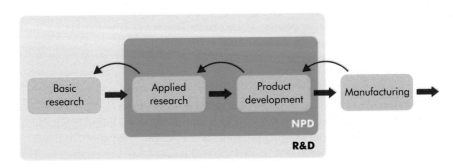

Figure 5.2 Relationship between R&D and NPD.

Table 5.1 Management challenges of research and development

	From research . . .	**. . . to development**
Cooperation	Informal	Formal
Knowledge	Tacit	Explicit
Criteria	Qualitative	Quantitative
Evaluation	Subjective	Objective
Business goal	Strategy alignment	Operational feasibility
Risk focus	Risk	Payback period
Cost focus	Opportunity costs	Cash flow
Financial focus	Option value	Contribution margin

Source: adapted from Nixon and Innes (1997).

reactions, quantum physics, or materials science), often with no implications for commercial applications. *Applied research* is directed primarily towards a specific practical aim (commercially or scientifically), with the goal of finding possible applications for the existing basic research. For example, silicon can be found in both semiconductors and cosmetic implants.

In many industries the goal of research is to apply scientific knowledge to a company's business, enabling it to lay the technological foundation for the development of new products or processes. Not all firms have the capability or resources to undertake research, and these companies tend to seek cooperation with universities and research centres.

> **Development:** an activity that involves systematic but non-routine technical work directed towards producing new or improved materials, products or services.

The **development** (D) part of R&D, also referred to as *experimental development*, involves systematic but non-routine technical work that is often directed towards producing new or improved materials, products or services. Development also seeks to shift product or process concepts through a series of stages to prove, refine, and ready them for commercial application. Many firms do not see a distinction between applied research and NPD, as many undertake both of these activities.

The high degree of uncertainty and risk inherent in R&D and NPD projects poses enormous decision-making difficulties for managers. Furthermore, R&D activity often includes other members of the supply chain, and so requires cross-company collaboration. These factors make it extremely difficult to assess the return on investment of NPD projects. The transition from research to development can be incredibly challenging, as listed in Table 5.1.

It is not surprising that the success rate of R&D projects tends to be low. Out of 60 ideas, typically only one project passes through all the NPD hurdles – technical evaluation, market research analysis, development, prototyping, and product launch – a success rate of 1.67%. Figure 5.3 illustrates this drop-out rate for R&D projects.

Phases of Development

The NPD process can be divided into six phases, as shown in Figure 5.4. The marketing, manufacturing, and finance departments are also involved with various tasks, as detailed below.

Phase 0: Planning

Planning is generally referred to as the initial phase of an NPD process. Often the designers consider the amount of innovation that is to be incorporated in the new product, and consider the following questions: is the product simply an upgrade of or increment to an existing product? Is it a radical innovation? What is the target market? Does the firm have the capability to develop it? How long will it take? Can the product be distributed and sold with the current supply chain? To what extent does the product capture the key elements of customer value (i.e. functional, social, emotional, epistemic, and conditional)?

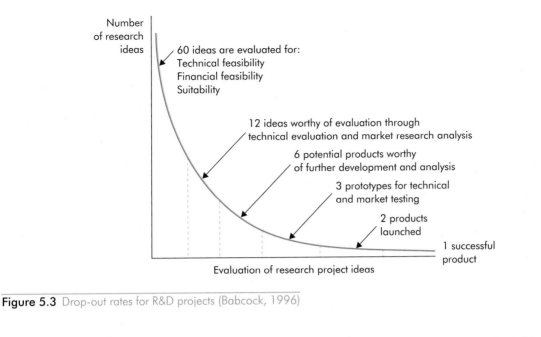

Figure 5.3 Drop-out rates for R&D projects (Babcock, 1996)

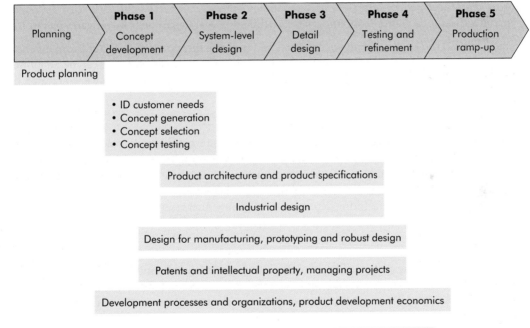

Figure 5.4 The new product development process (adapted from Ulrich and Eppinger, 2008)

At this stage, marketing activities usually include the articulation of market opportunities and definition of market segments. Manufacturing identifies production constraints, and sets up the supply chain strategy. In addition, the R&D department provides an overview of available technologies, and the finance department provides the financial goals. Most importantly, the general manager, and sometimes the chief executive officer (CEO), is likely to allocate resources to the project.

Phase 1: Concept Development

Concept development is the phase when the designers investigate the feasibility of product concepts, develop industrial design concepts, and build and test experimental prototypes. At this stage, the marketing department is in charge of collecting customer needs and identifying lead users and competitor products. This means that

Table 5.2 Customer roles in NPD

Customer role	NPD phase	Key issues/managerial challenges
Customer as resource	Ideation	• Appropriateness of customer as a source of innovation • Selection of customer innovator • Need for varied customer incentives • Infrastructure for capturing customer knowledge • Differential role of existing (current) and potential (future) customers
Customer as co-creator	Design and development	• Involvement in a wide range of design and development tasks • Nature of the NPD context: industrial/consumer products • Tighter coupling with internal NPD teams • Managing the attendant project uncertainty • Enhancing customers' product/technology knowledge
Customer as user	Product testing	• Time-bound activity • Ensuring customer diversity
	Product support	• Ongoing activity • Infrastructure to support customer–customer interactions

Source: Nambisan (2002, p. 395).

manufacturing costs need to be estimated, and production processes checked for feasibility. Moreover, the finance department has to facilitate economic analysis, while the legal department investigates patent issues.

The early stages of NPD can be messy, and are often referred to as the *fuzzy front end*. One of the main challenges during this stage is to understand how to capture and integrate customer requirements. This can be a daunting task, as the customers can have many roles in the NPD process (Table 5.2), including as a resource, co-creator, or user.

Phase 2: System-level Design

In the system-level design phase the designers typically generate alternative product designs and systems. The marketing department is usually responsible for developing marketing plans for product options and extended product families. The procurement department is responsible for deciding whether it would be more cost-effective to make key components in house or to source them from external manufacturers, and for identifying suppliers for outsourced components. The manufacturing department will define final assembly schemes, and set target costs.

Phase 3: Detailed Design

In the detailed design phase the designers define each part, choose materials, and assign specification limits for the components. This means that, at this stage, the manufacturing department has to define piece-part production processes, design tooling, define quality assurance processes, and begin procurement of tooling.

Phase 4: Testing and Refinement

In the testing and refinement phase, the designers typically have to perform reliability, life, and performance tests. They are also responsible for obtaining regulatory approvals, and implementing design changes. Concurrently, the marketing department has to develop promotion and launch materials, and facilitate field testing. In addition, the manufacturing department has to facilitate supplier ramp-up, refine fabrication and assembly processes, train the workforce, and refine quality assurance processes. The sales department will develop a sales plan.

Phase 5: Production Ramp-up

In the production ramp-up phase, production methods are likely to change from small-scale prototyping and pilots to higher-volume production methods, often requiring expensive dedicated machinery and workers. The design department has to evaluate early production units, and the marketing department has to place early promotion with key customers. This is when the entire production system starts its full operation.

❗ Stop and Think

1   Why do good designs sometimes become bad products?

SHORT CASE **5.1**

Recyclable Mobile Phone?

Nokia is a world leader in mobile communications, and continuously produces top-quality handsets. In the mobile phone industry, in 2008, it enjoyed a healthy market share of 40%. Nokia makes a huge effort to involve consumers in its technology development projects, and one such project is the design of phones for recyclability.

The Nokia 6650 is Nokia's first 3G mobile phone, and is designed for recyclability. Different substances can be traced at the component level so that they can be handled in the appropriate way at the end of the product's life cycle. This is possible via a detailed examination of the material content of the phone. This also allows for the estimation of recycling costs for different logistics and recycling alternatives.

The development of the Nokia 6650 involved the R&D team, operations, marketing and sales, logistics, and environmental teams. Nokia also involved its external partners, such as suppliers, recycling service providers and accessory teams. The knowledge gained from the product development of Nokia 6650 is now shared with other product programmes.

Source: © Getty Images

CSR

Questions
1   Can you identify some key challenges for Nokia in designing phones for recyclability?
2   How should Nokia plan its NPD processes for the future generations of its phones?

Source: www.nokia.com

Product Platforms

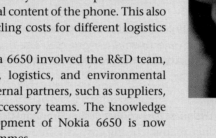

GLOBALIZATION

Product life cycles are getting shorter for many products, such as mobile phones, cars and video games, and many firms are relaying on their NPD capabilities to develop products quickly, and to cover a wide range of markets. These products have to be designed to function as specified, and meet all regulations of the target markets. One strategy that can help firms to achieve this goal is through creating **product platforms**.

> **Product platform:** a set of interconnected subsystems that form a common structure, from which a stream of derivative products can be developed and produced.

Platform strategy is basically a foundation for designs that can be used to build a large variety of products. It forms a structure from which a stream of *derivative products* can be developed. With a platform strategy, designs can be shared and reused, so that the designers don't have to start from scratch each time they create a new product. One of the first successful companies to pursue platform thinking on a large scale was Sony. Between 1980 and 1990, Sony introduced more than 160 variations of Walkman, based on a platform strategy. Sony continues to apply platform strategy in its current products. Sony, in partnership with Ericsson, is refining its gaming products on Google's mobile platform with the Android gaming platforms.

In car manufacturing, the platform shared between different car models might be a set of common designs, engineering and production processes. Major components, such as chassis, steering and suspension, are shared across models. For example, the platform for the Audi A4 is the basis for the VW Golf, the new Beetle and the

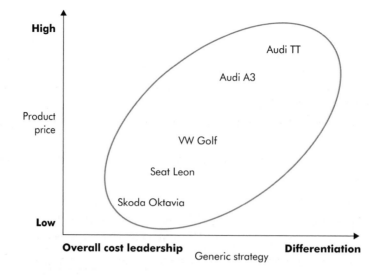

Figure 5.5 VW inter-firm product platform development (Trott, 2008)

Bora product families (Lung *et al.*, 1999). The Volkswagen Group also applies platform strategy to support its brand strategy with different strategic objectives: see Figure 5.5. The brands are segmented according to cost strategy or differentiation strategy in relation to the product price, which can range from low to high. The Skoda Oktavia, for instance, has a low price tag, and is produced based on cost leadership. Conversely, the Audi TT is expensive and highly differentiated.

Platform strategy originated from the quest for product design simplifications in the early 1990s. Many firms were facing tremendous pressure to reduce manufacturing costs, shorten product development lead time, and bring products to the market faster than before. There are many advantages associated with platform strategy, including:

- Reduced development and manufacturing costs
- Reduced incremental costs of addressing the specific needs of a market segment
- Reduced fixed costs of developing individual product variants
- Reduced development time
- Reduced systemic complexity
- Improved ability to upgrade products
- Lowered investment risks
- Greater degree of component and subsystems reuse
- Increased responsiveness of partners and suppliers
- Higher product variety offered to customers.

As the product life cycles of many products, such as mobile phones and computers, get ever shorter – new models are being introduced to the market much faster than before – many firms find that implementing platform strategies can be extremely difficult. This means that they have to be able to capture customer needs and market changes faster than before. One strategy to tackle this challenge is to increase the number of product variants, so that customers have more options to choose from. But too much product variety can create coordination problems for the firms. As a consequence, many firms are shifting their strategy towards reducing the number of platforms while increasing the number of derivative models and products.

This trend tells us that derivative products will be developed from fewer platforms. Reducing the number of platforms, while increasing the number of product variants (i.e. more options for customers to choose from), requires that there be components that can be shared with other platforms. Some of the key decisions firms consider when configuring platforms include:

- How to make sure that the platform is compatible with complementary products
- How to create technology competencies that prevent imitation
- How to share components and designs effectively
- How to maintain platform leadership – that is, how to maintain its market leadership in its core technical area.

> **WORKED EXAMPLE 5.1**

Platform Reduction Decision

Yamaha has £500 million to invest in new models of motorbike for the next 10 years. It knows it costs £100 million to develop a platform, and then £10 million to develop each separate model from the basic platform.

Problem: *If Yamaha needs 10 new motorbikes (or new models) to sell over the 10 years, how many platforms would you advise it to develop?*

Approach: Start by working out the total development cost for all 10 motorbikes, then work out how many platforms Yamaha can afford to invest in.

Solution:

$$\text{Development cost of 10 new bikes} = (10 \text{ new bikes}) \times (£10 \text{ million to develop})$$
$$= £100 \text{ million to develop 10 new bikes}$$

$$\text{Investment left for platforms} = \text{total investment} - \text{development cost of new bikes}$$
$$= £500 \text{ million} - £100 \text{ million} = £400 \text{ million}$$

$$\text{Number of platforms} = \frac{\text{Investment left for platforms}}{\text{Development cost per platform}} = \frac{£400 \text{ million}}{£100 \text{ million}} = 4 \text{ platforms}$$

Yamaha needs to develop four platforms.

Modularization

One of the main factors that influence the management of platforms is how to simplify the complex processes related to the platform. This process is called *modularization*, and it starts by partitioning the complex processes into simpler processes so that each portion can be dealt with separately. For instance, a mobile phone platform has both hardware and software, and it would be much easier for the designers to be able to work on the development of these two processes independently. They can specialize in their own knowledge, hence making the design and production processes more efficient. This can shorten the NPD cycle and reduce manufacturing costs.

Many people don't even bother to upgrade their computers any more; they just buy a new one. This is made possible because IBM-compatible PCs are modular systems that comprise key modules (operating system, keyboard, mouse, monitor, etc.) that can be easily mixed and matched. These modules are manufactured by various suppliers. As long as the interfaces of the modules comply with the industry standards, so that when they are plugged together the PC works, any company can make and sell them in the market.

Virtually all systems can be modularized. The first step to understanding how modularization works in a system is to identify how the system can be decomposed – that is, how it can be broken down into simpler, smaller portions. This process of simplification is referred to as *modularization*. For example, an automobile (a much more complex system than a PC) can be decomposed into four levels of complexity (Figure 5.6):

1 *System* – this is the level before deconstruction starts. For example, automobile systems can be passenger cars, sports cars, vans, etc.

2 *Subsystem* – the automobile system can be broken down into various subsystems, such as windshield wiper system, braking system, intelligent transportation systems (ITS), anti-lock braking system (ABS), engine, etc.

3 *Module* – each subsystem is further decomposed into modules. For example, the windscreen wiper subsystem is decomposed into wiper motor, motor, wipers controller, etc.

4 *Component* – each module is further decomposed into components. For example, the wipers' controller is made of various components, such as nuts, bolts, capacitors and resistors.

There may be many layers of decomposition, depending on the complexity of the system, but the component level is considered the lowest level of decomposition, as a component is a discrete item that cannot be broken down further.

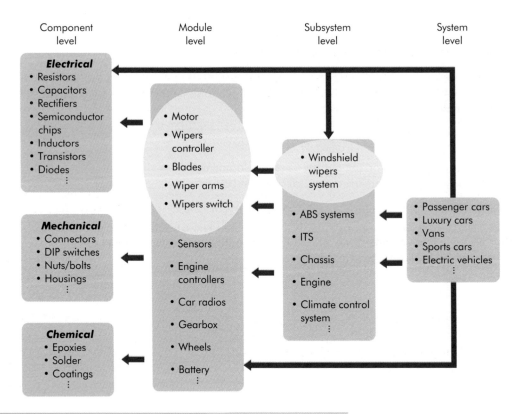

Figure 5.6 Modularization levels in automobiles (adapted from Hsuan, 1999)

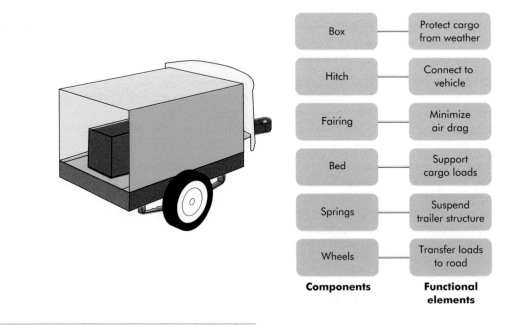

Figure 5.7 Example of a modular design (Ulrich, 1995)

Modular Product Architectures

Modular product architectures enable firms to minimize the physical changes required to achieve a functional change. The design of the trailer in Figure 5.7 illustrates an example of modular design. The physical components, such as the box, hitch, fairing, bed, springs and wheels, each have independent functions, as shown in the figure. Changes made to one of the components should not affect the function of the other components. For instance, the purpose of the box is to protect the cargo from weather. Making changes to the box does not affect the function of other components, such as the wheels or the hitch.

Modular product architecture designs provide the foundation for flexible platforms, as they allow for product variations. These designs intentionally create independence between components by standardizing interface specifications. That is, the components can be disassembled and recombined into new configurations. Product variants can be realized with less difficulty, as changes in one component do not lead to changes in other components. Physical changes can be implemented more easily without adding tremendous complexity to the manufacturing system.

The motivation behind this strategy is to gain cost savings through economies of scale from component commonality, inventory and logistics, and to introduce technologically improved products more rapidly. It also allows the firm to make easily product changes such as upgrades, add-ons, product line extensions and cosmetic adaptations. This in turn enables the firm to make use of customer feedback and alter its systems accordingly by substituting some components while retaining others. Other examples of products with modular product architectures include LEGO toys, bicycles, elevators, and mobile phones.

Integral Product Architectures

With *integral product architectures*, modifications to any one component cannot be done without the redesign or reconfiguration of the other components, which can be expensive and time consuming. Figure 5.8 provides an illustration of the integral design approach to the trailer example. In contrast to the modular trailer design, the integral design exhibits a more complex relationship between components and the functional elements. The function of protecting cargo from weather is dependent on three components: upper half, lower half, and spring slot covers.

Examples of integral designs include Formula One cars, satellites, the human body, and even computers. The Apollo computer of the 1980s, for example, was considered more integral than IBM PCs or Sun Microsystems. High performance was emphasized, and the workstation was designed with a proprietary architecture based on Apollo's own operating and network management systems. Much of the hardware was designed in-house. Apollo's designers believed that it was necessary for various parts of the design to be highly interdependent in order to achieve high levels of performance in the final product (Baldwin and Clark, 1997).

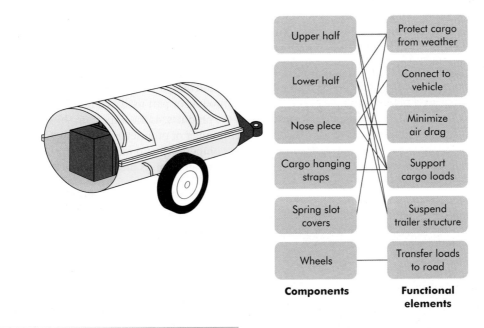

Figure 5.8 Example of an integral design (Ulrich, 1995)

Table 5.3 The trade-offs between modular and integral designs

Benefits of modular designs	Benefits of integral designs
• Task specialization • Platform flexibility • Increased number of product variants • Economies of scale in component commonality • Cost savings in inventory and logistics • Lower life cycle costs through incremental improvements such as upgrades, add-ons and adaptations • Flexibility in component reuse • Independent product development • Outsourcing • System reliability due to high production volume and experience curve	• Interactive learning • High levels of performance through proprietary technologies • Systemic innovations • Faster access to information • Protection of innovation from imitation • High entry barriers for component suppliers • Craftsmanship
Examples: elevators, mobile phones, IBM PCs, LEGO toys	Examples: Formula One cars, Apollo computers, satellites

Source: adapted from Mikkola and Gassmann (2003).

Managing Product Architectures

Similar systems produced by different companies undoubtedly have different product architecture designs, as a result of different design and technology choices. For instance, although Sony's and Philips's high-definition TVs are similar, the way they are designed and manufactured is specific to each company, dependent on the firm's NPD and manufacturing strategy, as well as on how its relationships with suppliers and customers have evolved over time. Depending on market needs and the technological core competencies of the firm, the trade-offs between modular and integral architecture strategies should be assessed carefully. Some trade-offs are summarized in Table 5.3.

If the firm's goal is to reach as many customers as possible with many product variants, then it should follow a modular product design strategy. Modular architectures try to use as many standard and generic components as possible. These components allow the firm to gain from economies of scale in component commonality, as the same components can be shared with other products. This leads to cost savings in inventory and logistics, as components can be bought and shipped in large quantities. The modular nature of the design allows specialization of individual tasks to take place independently of other tasks (e.g. software development does not have to be carried out together with hardware development). Modular products typically rely on manufacturing processes that can support the production of high volumes of products.

If, however, the firm's goal is to create state-of-the-art innovation, where performance is the key criterion, then integral product design strategies may be the better option. Integral design tends to avoid the compromises that are required when using a modular approach. For example, a module or part used in a number of products may not be optimized, in terms of its performance, for any one of the products, as the important thing is that it works in them all. Also, integral architectures tend to have a higher number of proprietary technologies than modular architectures. This protects the firm from quick imitation by competitors, and raises the entry barrier for component suppliers, especially when the firm wants to control the progress of its proprietary technologies.

> **❶ Stop and Think**
>
> **2** What kinds of challenge might a firm face when changing its NPD strategy from integral product design to modular product design, or vice versa?

The Role of Interfaces

Interfaces are basically devices that connect one component to another, such as plugs. Take the PC, for instance. The keyboard is connected to the operating system via a cable, and the power supply for the operating system is connected to the outlet via a plug. The latter connector comes in various shapes (e.g. flat pins for the US and round pins for mainland Europe). The interfaces have to be compatible in order for the system to work.

Interface specifications define the protocol for the fundamental interactions across all components of technological systems. The setting and development of interface specifications have a huge impact on setting industry standards. Consider, for instance, the smartphone industry. Virtually all handset manufacturers in the world (e.g. Nokia, Motorola, Samsung, Sony, Apple) are developing devices based on the 3G standard. (3G refers to a family of standards for wireless communications, especially for mobile telephony or cellular technology.) The purpose of the standard is to facilitate growth, increase bandwidth, and support more diverse applications. For example, GSM (global system for mobile communications), the most popular standard for mobile telephony systems, could deliver not only voice, but also circuit-switched data at faster speeds. But to support mobile multimedia applications, 3G had to deliver packet-switched data with better spectral efficiency, at far greater speeds.

> **Interface specifications:** define the protocol for the fundamental interactions across all components constituting a technological system.

The 3G standard has a strong influence in shaping the competitive landscape of the wireless communication industry. The technological development of the mobile devices, in terms of platform and product architecture design, has to comply with industry standards and specifications. This means that interfaces linking different systems with the 3G standard have to be specified and standardized in order to ensure compatibility. Standardization of interfaces allows the makers of components to concentrate their capabilities narrowly and deeply, and thus to improve their part of the system independently of others. It encourages supplier specialization, and hence fosters the emergence of network organizations. The rate at which interface specifications change influences the way product architecture is controlled, and hence impacts on how firms organize within the industry, to compete or cooperate around the new set of interface specifications.

Organizing Product Designs for Manufacturing

During a product's design, its manufacturing processes must also be considered. Some simple products are made from just one part – a drinking glass, for example. However, most products are made from many parts, which in turn might be made from different parts. For example, consider all the different materials needed to make a wheeled desk chair. A product design must include a **bill of materials (BOM)** listing all the materials and components needed to make the product, and the quantities required. The BOM may also be referred to as the *product structure* or *product tree*.

> **Bill of materials (BOM):** file (or product structure or product tree file) that lists the description of the product (such as the material, components and quantity) and the sequence in which the product is to be assembled.

Figure 5.9 illustrates the product structure of a swivel chair, portraying its product hierarchy, from the lowest level (Level 4) to highest level (Level 0) of assembly order.
- The swivel chair (Level 0) needs one seat and one base (Level 1).
- The seat is assembled from one back, one frame, two arms, and one button (Level 2).
- The back is assembled with moulded back and padded back cushion (Level 3).
- Finally, the padded back cushion comprises of one batting, one fabric, and three buttons (Level 4).

Similar logic applies for the base (Level 1) and the bottom (Level 2), and its subassemblies in Levels 3 and 4.

The BOM provides the foundation for linking the final product design to the design guidelines or methods for other processes – what is known as the *design for X* (DFX). Here X denotes the various criteria that affect the characteristics of a product, such as reliability, robustness, serviceability, environmental impact, assembly, or manufacturing. The design guidelines provide methods and information that help designers and managers to make decisions in order to control and improve the characteristics of a product. The most common DFX method is *design for manufacturing* (DFM), as it provides the information for estimating the manufacturing costs directly. The decision process of the DFM method is illustrated in Figure 5.10.

Mass Customization

Mass customization emerged as a concept in the late 1980s. Generally, it emphasizes the need to provide products that can meet customers' individual needs through unique combinations of modular components. The goal is to produce customized products (to achieve economies of scope) at low costs (to gain from

BUSINESS INTEGRATION

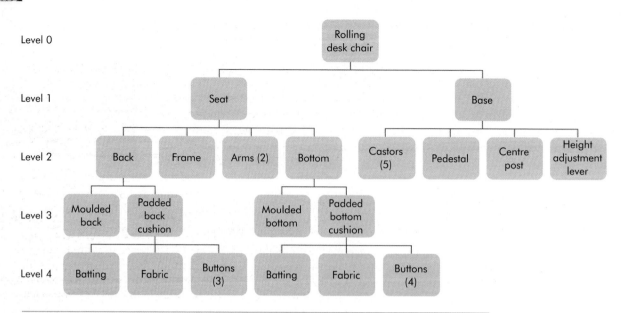

Figure 5.9 Product structure for a swivel chair (adapted from Davis and Heineke, 2005, p. 548)

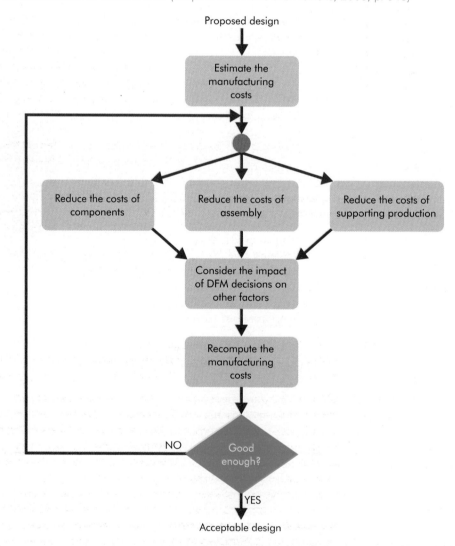

Figure 5.10 Decisions related to the DFM method (Ulrich and Eppinger, 2008, p. 213)

economies of scale). It allows companies to penetrate new markets and capture customers whose special needs could not be met with standard products. Da Silveira *et al.* (2001) identified six success factors of mass customization:

- *Customer demand for variety and customization*: successful mass customization depends on the trade-offs between the potential sacrifices that the customer makes and the firm's ability to produce and deliver customized products
- *Appropriate market conditions*: being the first to develop a mass customization system can provide competitive advantage for the firm
- *Value chain readiness*: successful mass customization depends on the willingness and readiness of suppliers, distributors and retailers to match the demands of the firm (mass customization is discussed in Chapter 8)
- *Technology availability*: the implementation of advanced manufacturing technologies (AMTs) is fundamental to enable the development of mass customization systems
- *Customizable products*: successful mass-customized products must be modularized, versatile, and renewable
- *Shared knowledge*: successful mass customization depends on the firm's ability to translate customer demands into new products and services. The implementation of mass customization involves product configuration, value chain network, process and information technology, and the development of a knowledge-based organizational structure.

Product variety is driven by customer demand. The capability to design and produce products in collaboration with customers provides mass-customizing firms with the ability to capture valuable new knowledge. Mass customization strategy has been implemented with computers, Levi's jeans, bicycles, Nike shoes, Smart cars, and many other products. The National Bicycle Industrial Company (NBIC) of Japan, for instance, has focused on its manufacturing competence to create customized bicycles. Over 11 million combinations were available, with production times ranging from eight to ten days. The company was able to produce 50 to 60 semi-customized bikes per day (Bell, 1993).

WORKED EXAMPLE 5.2

Product Complexity

Customers of a car dealer were given a free choice of combining 15 paint colours, four interior fabrics, three engines (4, 8 and 12 cylinder), a choice of manual or automatic gearbox, and a list of 10 different optional extras that could be chosen independently of each other.

Problem: *How many different options can the customers choose from?*

Approach: Each choice can be combined with other options independently: hence, the total number of options is the arithmetical product of the number of option choices.

Solution:

$$\text{Number of options} = (15 \text{ paint colours}) \times (4 \text{ interior fabrics}) \times (3 \text{ engines}) \times$$
$$(2 \text{ gearboxes}) \times (10! \text{ optional extras})$$
$$= 1,306,368,000$$

(Note: 10! is the factorial of 10:
$$10! = 10 \times 9 \times 8 \times 7 \times 6 \times 5 \times 4 \times 3 \times 2 \times 1 = 3,628,800)$$

Mass customization can be realized in many ways (Pine, 1993), as shown in Figure 5.11:

- Create products and services that are customizable by customers by involving them in the design phase
- Modularize components to customize end products and services (e.g. postponed manufacturing involving design, manufacturing, and distribution phase)
- Provide quick response through the supply chain (involving the distribution phase)
- Customize services around standard products or services (involving the distribution and sales phase)
- Provide point-of-delivery customization (involving the sales phase).

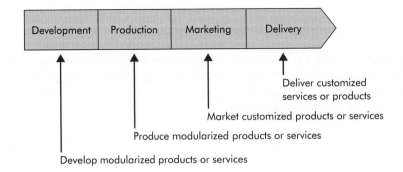

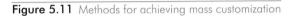

Figure 5.11 Methods for achieving mass customization

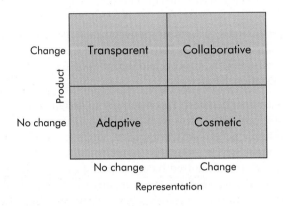

Figure 5.12 Four approaches to customization (Gilmore and Pine, 1997)

By using mass customization, firms can exploit their capabilities in NPD through market intelligence, so that customers' needs can be translated into individually tailored products.

Approaches to Mass Customization

Gilmore and Pine (1997) proposed four approaches to customization (Figure 5.12): collaborative, adaptive, cosmetic, and transparent.

- *Collaborative customization* helps the customers to articulate their needs, and to identify the precise offering that fulfils their needs, such as with cars and kitchens.
- In *adaptive customization*, the product is designed so that users can tailor, modify or reconfigure it themselves to suit different occasions. For example, we can customize mobile phone features ourselves (ringing tones, address lists, display patterns, etc.)
- With *cosmetic customization*, a standard product is presented differently to different customers, such as with the design of promotional items, where the individual customer's name is printed on the product.
- In *transparent customization* the individual customers are offered unique goods or services from a standard package. For example, based on a customer's previous purchase records, Amazon.com is able to recommend books and gifts that the customer might consider buying.

Mass Customization

You have just been hired as the product-marketing manager of a fashion jeans company. In order to increase customer satisfaction, the company is devising strategies to create customized jeans for individual customers. Your job is to figure out how to create unique value for the customers through mass customization.

The company sells three types of jeans:
- High fashion jeans: low sales volume, supplied directly by fashion factories, no option to make changes in stores
- Standard design jeans: high sales volume, supplied by the company, final tailoring added at the stores (e.g. name printing, special graphics printing, special buttons, final tailoring)
- Tailored jeans: varied sales volume according to season, supplied by the company, customers can order the jeans to their specific designs

Problem: *Apply the product–representation matrix in Figure 5.12 to define the type of customization needed. What type of customization should you adopt?*

Approach: The first step is to classify the jeans according to the right customization strategy. Consider whether each type of jean can be customized by a change to the product, and whether it can be customized by a change to how the product is represented.

Solution:

Table 5.4

	Product		Representation		Type of customization
	Change	**No change**	**Change**	**No change**	
High fashion jeans		X		X	Adaptive
Standard design jeans		X	X		Cosmetic
Tailored jeans	X		X		Collaborative

High fashion jeans fit best with adaptive customization, as there are no options to change the design of the jeans from the supplier (the product) or their visual appearance (the representation). The customers, however, can add accessories and make alterations themselves.

Standard design jeans fit best with cosmetic customization, as there are no options to change the design of the jeans (the product), but the final design of the jeans is tailored to customers' individual needs at the stores during the final purchase (the representation).

Tailored jeans call for collaborative customization, as there are changes both in the design of the jeans (the product) and in how the jeans should look (the representation). Customers need to articulate their design requests and needs before the jeans are produced.

There is another opportunity for the company to satisfy its customers through transparent customization. Although not practised by the company at the moment, it is possible for the company to offer new designs of jeans to its preferred customers based on their previous purchasing records.

🛈 Stop and Think

3 Consumers might be pleased to know that there is a wide range of product variety to choose from when purchasing a product, but what kinds of problem could they face when there are too many options? What kinds of problem does it present for the producers and retailers?

Oticon's Sumo Hearing Aid

Source: © U. Bellhaeluser/Getty Images

Most people with severe hearing problems tend to be conservative, and stick to the same instrument for as long as possible. Some users are still wearing 30-year-old hearing instruments, as it takes a long time for the brain to adapt to new sounds and patterns.

Oticon, a Danish-based company, designs and manufactures a full range of hearing aids and fitting systems. Its most powerful behind-the-ear instrument is the Sumo, based on an analogue design, which has better power performance than digital design. This is especially important for one niche of customers: those with profound hearing loss.

The development lead time for the Sumo (from concept generation to final production) was a little over three years. The Sumo has been in production since 2002, and its product life cycle is estimated to be between 10 and 15 years, complemented with new versions approximately every 18 months. The trend in hearing aids, however, is changing from analogue to digital, so Sumo will probably be Oticon's last analogue product.

People have different shapes of ears, and hence cannot all wear the same style of hearing aid. Hearing aids have to perform as specified, but also have to be adapted for each individual. Oticon applies the platform approach, with as many standardized components as possible. However, standardization needs to be balanced with innovation, as it is crucial for the company to prevent competitors from copying its innovation.

Questions

1 In what ways can the organization of NPD processes shape and influence the success of Sumo?
2 What type(s) of mass customization strategy is/are pursued with Sumo?
3 What kinds of process are involved in mass-customizing the SUMO?
4 How should Oticon plan for the future generations of its hearing aids?

Source: Mikkola and Skjøtt-Larsen (2006)

BUSINESS
INTEGRATION

Product Service Systems

The service sector is becoming ever more important in industrialized economies. Service industries continue to dominate the UK economy. In 2000, public services accounted for 70% of the UK gross domestic product; for the private sector, it was over 50% (National Statistics, 2000). Virtually everything we do, from buying goods to eating in restaurants, has service elements in it. When we buy a high-end video camera, for instance, we want to make sure we learn how it works. Sometimes the instruction manual is not clear enough. We also want to have access to a virtual help desk and other services. Inevitably, firms need to extend intangible aspects of products in order to satisfy various customer needs. Similarly, service providers such as restaurants, consultancies and banks are becoming increasingly dependent on products (especially with the help of new technologies) to enhance the perceived quality of the services offered.

Can services be designed so that they look like products? One of the biggest challenges of selling services is that they are intangible and heterogeneous. Services can't be touched, smelled, tasted or tried before purchase. Customers' requirements and needs also differ. *Productization* of services attempts to make intangible services more tangible. For example, a professional consulting firm might enhance its services to its clients by packaging the services with product documentation, such as executive materials, templates, worksheets, and other tools. With service productization, the consulting firm can provide differentiation of its services, and establish credibility with new clients.

Products should be designed with services in mind, and vice versa. The convergence process of creating products with a higher service content is referred to as **servitization of products**. Conversely, the convergence process of developing services to include product content is referred to as the **productization of services**. Together, servitization of products and productization of services form the *product–service system* (Figure 5.13).

The key point is that the design of products and that of services have to be interlinked.

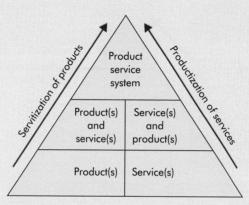

Figure 5.13 Evolution of product–service systems (Baines et al., 2007)

Service Design

Now that we have a better understanding of how products can be developed and designed for mass customization, let's find out about the role of service design.

A **service** is any activity or benefit that one party can offer to another that is essentially intangible, and does not result in the ownership of anything. The production, delivery and consumption of services all take place at the same time. Services are also perishable: that is, they cannot be stored. When a service is designed, managers need to be aware of how it affects customer contact, the front- and back-office activities, its management processes, and the bottom line.

A characteristic of many services is that they are extended, with elements or modules of the service consumed consecutively over a period of time. Examples of this type of service include air travel and sea cruises. In such services there are more complex relationships between elements of the service. An airline may provide different services for its coach class passengers and its business class passengers. On a cruise liner, passengers may choose which services to use and when to use them over the course of the cruise.

Whether the services are extended, or consumed consecutively, all the service system elements must be designed in a way that creates a consistent service offering that achieves the strategic service vision of the organization. The service delivery system design considers three interrelated elements (Roth and Menor, 2003), as illustrated in Figure 5.14:
- Strategic service design choices
- Service delivery system execution, renewal and assessment
- Customer-perceived value of the total service concept.

The strategic design choices include choices related to structural, infrastructural and integration aspects of the system. Structural choices involve decisions related to the physical aspects of the delivery system, including

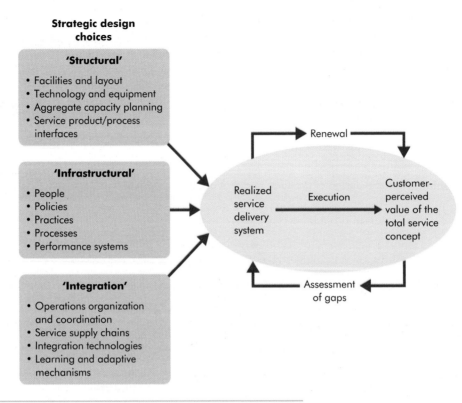

Figure 5.14 Elements of service delivery systems (Roth and Menor, 2003)

facilities and layout, technology and equipment, aggregate capacity planning, and service product/process interfaces. Infrastructure choices relate to the people, policies, practices, processes and performance aspects of service design. Integration choices are concerned with issues related to operations organization and coordination, service supply chains, integration technologies, and learning and adaptive mechanisms aspects of the service design.

The strategic choices, in turn, influence how the realized service delivery system is executed or renewed into customer-perceived value of the total service concept. These choices also impact on the possible gaps that might exist between the service delivered and customer perception.

Customer Contact

Customer contact: refers to the physical presence of the customer in the system, or the percentage of the time that the customer is in the system relative to the total service time.

Because services involve **customer contact**, there are two elements that organizations need to consider when designing new services: the customer, and the communication channel with the customers. The *degree of customer contact* refers to the physical presence of the customer in the system, or the percentage of the time that the customer is in the system, relative to the total service time (Fitzsimmons and Fitzsimmons, 2008):

$$\text{Degree of customer contact} = \frac{\text{Percentage of time the customer is in the system}}{\text{Total service time}}$$

In high-contact services (e.g. reception at hotels), the quality of service is determined by the perception of the customer's experience, as the customer participates directly in the process. In low-contact services (e.g. maintenance of trains), the customer has very little or no influence on the production process. Table 5.5 lists the major design considerations that an organization should consider in high- and low-contact systems.

Front-office activities: activities where there is direct customer contact, whether face to face, or by email, telephone, or letter.

Front and Back Office

The impact of customer contact on a service delivery system is often conceptualized in terms of front-office and back-office activities. **Front-office activities** are those where

Table 5.5 Major design considerations in high- and low-contact systems

Decision	High-contact system	Low-contact system
Facility location	Operations must be near the customer	Operations may be placed near supply, transportation, or labour
Facility layout	Facility should accommodate the customer's physical and psychological needs and experience	Facility should enhance production
Product design	Both the environment and the physical product define the nature of the service	Customer is not in the service environment, so the product can be defined by fewer attributes
Process design	Stages of production process have a direct, immediate effect on the customer	Customer is not involved in most of the processing steps
Scheduling	Customer is in the production schedule, and must be accommodated	Customer is concerned mainly with completion dates
Production planning	Orders cannot be stored, so smoothing production flow will result in loss of business	Both backlogging and production smoothing are possible
Worker skills	Direct workforce constitutes a major part of the service product, and so must be able to interact well with the public	Direct workforce need have only technical skills
Quality control	Quality standards are often in the eye of the beholder	Quality standards are generally measurable
Time standards	Service time depends on customer needs, and therefore time standards are inherently loose	Work is performed on customer surrogates (e.g. forms), and time standards can be tight
Wage payment	Variable output requires time-based wage systems	'Fixable' output permits output-based wage systems
Capacity planning	To avoid lost sales, capacity must be set to match peak demand	Storable output permits setting capacity at some average demand level
Forecasting	Forecasts are short term, time oriented	Forecasts are long term, output oriented

Source: Chase (1978, p. 139).

there is direct customer contact, whether face to face, or by email, telephone or letter. **Back-office activities**, on the other hand, are activities that are hidden from the customers. The back office can also be interpreted as a platform from which many different front-office services can be managed. Front-office services will have a higher degree of customer contact than back-office services. The line of customer visibility separates the front- and back-office activities. Figure 5.15 provides an example of front- and back-office activities in processing a retail loan. Soliciting a loan application usually requires customer contact in the form of an interview. After the loan interview is completed and the application form filled out, a significant amount of back-office work is required to process the application. After the application process is checked, there is customer contact again as the customer is invited back to sign the document. Once the document is signed, the back-office proceeds on the post-loan processing activities.

Back-office activities: activities that are hidden from the customers.

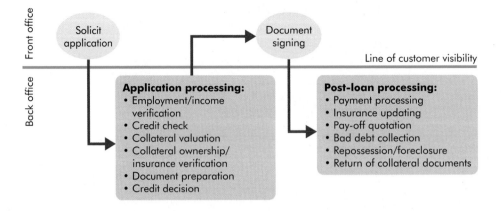

Figure 5.15 Activities in processing a retail loan (adapted from Metters and Vargas, 2000)

SHORT CASE 5.3

Fashion Service at Open Clips

Open Clips was founded in Goiânia, in the middle region of Brazil, by two oral surgeons who had a passion for fashion. Contrary to the main fashion brands targeting large Brazilian cities such as Rio de Janeiro and São Paulo, Open Clips wanted to bring modern and innovative fashion with exclusive styles to other cities. Its unique style, combined with bright colours, became so popular that it grew from one small boutique to 19 large shops in well-reputed shopping centres.

Its success was attributed to its dedicated team, its inspirational leaders, its top fashion designer, its creative services, and its ability to respond to market needs faster than its competitors.

Its success brought in many competitors in the market, who started to copy its designs, and soon Open Clips was losing market share. With the global economic recession that started in 2007, the company faced huge financial strain, and so it had to rethink its strategy. As a result, it decided to make a radical change in its approach to selling fashion. The company closed down all its stores and became a wholesaler for exclusive fashion stores located in Brazilian regions with warm temperatures.

The owner, one of the co-founders, believes that having happy and loyal employees and customers is the key to a successful enterprise, so Open Clips offers unique services to its employees, to its suppliers, and to its customers. Many of its employees come from poor families, so Open Clips educates them to become skilled in the production of garments, and in sales management. It also offers freshly cooked meals for its employees every day, free of charge. The designer workshop is located inside the production factory. After receiving the customer order, the designer and the production manager plan the production schedule for the exact number of garments to be produced. Although the number of employees has been reduced since the reorganization, the team support each other in all the tasks of new service development activities, from design to full production.

The owner believes that personal contact is an important part of customer satisfaction, so he visits the company's customers (the exclusive shops) regularly. He and his management team often help and educate their customers on how to make financial plans and create marketing campaigns. For customers located in more remote places, the owner also helps them to find the most effective mode of transport, so that the garments are delivered on time and in good condition.

Whereas most of the fashion houses in Brazil offer two collections per year, Open Clips offers three, in January, May and August. Many European fashion houses have noticed its unique design styles, and have started to source designs from Open Clips.

Questions
1 What challenges might Open Clips face when designing its services for European clients?
2 Discuss how the reorganization of Open Clips' strategy affected its front- and back-office activities.
3 To what extent should front- and back-office activities be integrated?

Source: Juliana Hsuan, Copenhagen Business School

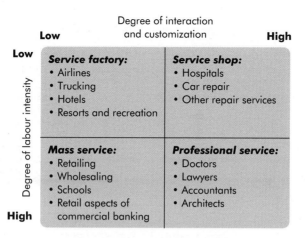

Figure 5.16 Service process matrix (Schmenner, 1986).

Service Process Matrix

The *service process matrix*, developed by Schmenner (1986), is a classification of service industry firms based on the characteristics of their service processes in terms of degree of interaction and customization versus the degree of labour intensity (Figure 5.16). The **degree of interaction and customization** describes the customer's ability to affect the nature of the service being delivered. The **degree of labour intensity** is defined as the ratio of labour cost to capital cost, such as plant and equipment costs.

> **Degree of interaction and customization:** the customer's ability to affect the nature of the service being delivered. Degree of labour intensity: the ratio of employee cost to capital cost.

The service process matrix provides four classifications of services: *mass service, service factory, service shop* and *professional service*. Customers seeking service from professionals such as physicians, lawyers and architects will probably require individual attention, but the customers of mass service such as volume retailing, fast food and low-cost flights receive a less differentiated service. The services provided by a service factory are standardized services with high capital investment (e.g. budget airlines and low-cost hotels). Service shops, on the other hand, allow for customization, but they also require high capital investment (e.g. hospitals and private education).

Most services change over time. We can see changes taking place in many service industries. For instance, a Dutch network of care providers for the elderly delivers a variety of care and service packages, with three kinds of service: a basic service common to all customer groups; a set of services that can be configured by customer segment; and a set of services that allows for customization at an individual level (de Blok *et al.*, 2007).

As the amount of customization and labour intensity changes over time, managers encounter new challenges, as illustrated in Figure 5.17.

Contemporary Thinking: IT (ERP) Implications: Virtual Service (e-Service)

BUSINESS INTEGRATION

With the increasing application of Internet technologies, virtual services are becoming a major competitive strategy for many service organizations. **e-Service** is the provision of service using online media, which can be delivered in a virtual environment with little or no human interaction (Voss, 2003). A range of services with respect to *customer relationship management* (CRM) is portrayed in Figure 5.18. CRM can vary between e-service, such as the provision of pure services (e.g. computer services), and e-commerce, which is the sale of physical goods, such as CDs, through an environment such as Amazon. Other CRM includes selling information (e.g. infomediaries – intermediaries for information transaction), selling value-added service (e.g. online travel agents), and selling a bundle of service and goods (e.g. PCs).

> **e-Service:** the delivery of service using online media, which can be delivered in a virtual environment with little or no human interaction.

> **❗ Stop and Think**
>
> 4 Recall an experience you had when you were dissatisfied with a service. What caused it, and who was to blame?

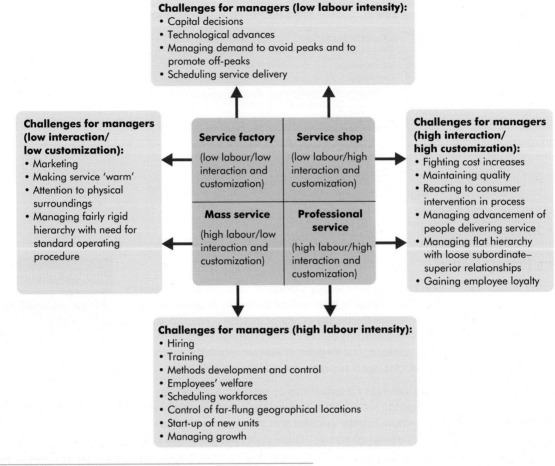

Figure 5.17 Challenges for service managers (Schmenner, 1986)

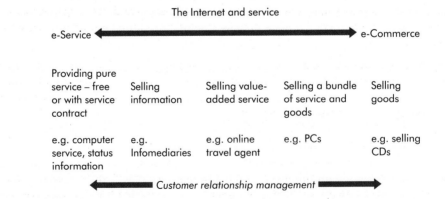

Figure 5.18 A spectrum of virtual service strategies (Voss, 2003, p. 89).

Contemporary Thinking: New Service Development

Stages of Service Development

Although services and products differ in many aspects, the process of *new service development* (NSD) is not very different from that of NPD. Recall that the NPD process of physical products goes through six phases: planning, concept development, system-level design, detail design, testing and refinement, and production ramp-up.

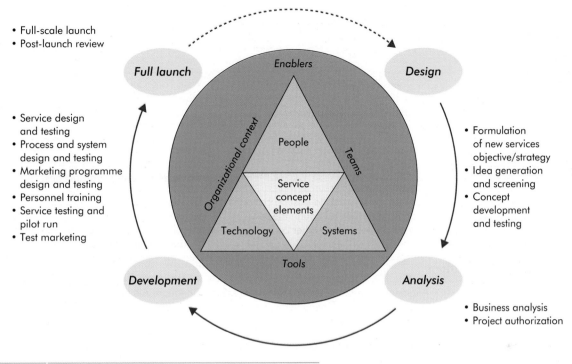

Figure 5.19 New service development cycle (Menor et al., 2000).

Figure 5.19 shows that the NSD cycle also go through similar stages: design, analysis, development, and full launch (Menor *et al.*, 2002).

The NSD cycle shows that the service design process is iterative and non-linear. When new services are being designed, the organization needs to focus on the formulation of new services objectives, idea generation and screening, and concept development and testing. During the analysis stage, managers need to analyse the business and obtain project authorization. After the analysis stage, the actual development of the service starts. During this stage the new service is designed, and the related processes are tested. Organizations also need to train the personnel to deliver the service. Full launch does not happen until all the processes from the design stage are in place.

New services can also represent either a radical or an incremental upgrade on previous services, as described in Table 5.6. For instance, major service innovation is needed when the services are intended for markets that have not been defined, such as with Wells Fargo's Internet banking that was launched in 1995. Since then the evolution of Internet banking could be described as incremental.

Service Architecture

New service development can be designed using the principles of product modularity. If we view a set of services as a system (just like a product system), then a service system can be broken down into different levels of complexity. What we have now is a service architecture instead of a product architecture. A service system can be decomposed into four levels of analysis:

Level 0: Industry

Level 1: Service company/supply chain

Level 2: Service bundle

Level 3: Service package/component

The holiday industry provides an apt illustration of the four levels of service architecture decomposition (Figure 5.20):

Table 5.6 Levels of service innovation

New service category	Description	Example
Radical innovations		
Major innovation	New services for markets as yet undefined. These innovations are usually driven by information- and computer-based technologies	Wells Fargo Internet banking, launched in May 1995
Start-up business	New services in a market that is already served by existing services	Mondex USA, a subsidiary of MasterCard International that designs and distributes smartcards for retail transactions
New services for the market currently served	New service offerings to existing customers of an organization (although the services may be available from other companies)	Freestanding bank branches or kiosks in supermarkets or other retail establishments (e.g. Wells Fargo kiosks in Starbucks coffee shops).
Incremental innovations		
Service line extensions	Augmentations of the existing service line, such as adding new menu items, new routes, or new courses	Singapore Airlines' first-class airport check-in in a special, exclusive lounge
Service improvements	Changes in features of services that are currently being offered	Delta Airlines' use of ATM-like kiosks to distribute boarding passes to passengers
Style changes	The most common of all 'new' services, these are modest forms of visible change that have an impact on customer perceptions, emotions, and attitudes. Style changes do not change the service fundamentally, only its appearance	Funeral homes, such as Calvary Mortuary in Los Angeles, now offer abbreviated ceremonies that celebrate life instead of mourn death, full-service flower shops, and facilities with more pastels, brighter walls, and more windows and lights

Source: Fitzsimmons and Fitzsimmons (2008, p. 66).

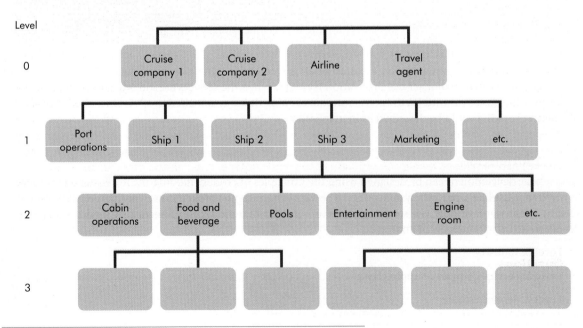

Figure 5.20 Decomposition of sea cruise services (Voss and Hsuan, 2009)

- Level 0 features the various players in the industry, such as cruise ship operators or airlines.
- Level 1 is the individual company. A firm may operate a number of cruise ships, and has marketing services and port operations services, as well as back-office, procurement, and other services. Some of these services may be outsourced, building a service supply chain.
- Level 2 reflects the level of the ship itself. Each ship has an architecture consisting of a variety of guest services such as swimming pools, restaurants, night clubs, and cabins. There are further services associated with the running of the ship and its interface with shore visits, and so forth. These guest services may be standardized and thus easily replicated across all the ships of the fleet, or they may be custom-designed for that ship. Further, these services may be unique to the company and not easily imitated, or they may be standard – that is, similar across all firms operating in the industry.
- Finally, at Level 3, each of these services can be broken down into a further set of service components such as the individual elements of cabin operations, from cabin design to specific service personnel.

The key point is that service systems can also be decomposed into simpler pieces (modules).

SHORT CASE 5.4

Restaurant Fuego: Standardization of the Processes as a Venue to Franchising

Restaurant Fuego opened in 2003, and was the first Argentinian restaurant in Copenhagen. It is an elegant restaurant with a friendly and welcoming Latin-Argentine atmosphere, enhanced with a lounge for cocktails with open fires. It serves only Argentinian wines and meats. In 2008 Fuego performed well economically, and the owners' next goal was to expand the restaurant as a franchise, with outlets in the Scandinavian capitals of Oslo and Stockholm. However, in order to optimize resources and transfer the know-how gained from Fuego, various tasks and processes needed to be simplified and standardized.

Source: © Koray Nik ISIK/iStock

The first step was to map a detailed process flowchart of the activities. This provided a visualization of all processes and activities performed in the restaurant. It identified bottlenecks, wastes and mistakes. Next a manual of operations was created as a way to standardize service and reduce mistakes. The manual of operations was divided into three parts. The first part covered the operations for the processes in the kitchen and service floor. The second part included a guide for the preparation of the different cocktails. The last part provided a detailed description of the different types of grape and Argentinian wines.

As a result, the overall efficiency improved. For instance, specific storage labels were assigned for every item in the restaurant, including wines. The new wine strategy enabled higher wine inventory rotation, and better placement of wines that are not sold often. The various improvement initiatives were able to reduce inventory mistakes by as much as 40%.

Questions
1 Why is standardization of processes needed for franchising in a business such as Restaurant Fuego?
2 How can standardization be planned during the service development process?
3 What stage of the development cycle is Fuego Restaurant in?

Source: Nissen (2009)

> **❶ Stop and Think**

5 Are there major differences between innovation in services and innovation in products?

Customers' Input in Service Development Process

Customer satisfaction is one of the most important goals when developing new services, as we have learned that customers can act as resource, co-creator, and/or as user during the NPD process. Similarly, because services are consumed immediately after production, it is possible for customers to participate during the NSD process, as listed in Table 5.7.

CSR

SHORT CASE 5.5	**Hotel Guldsmeden**

Hotel Guldsmeden is one of the first hotel chains in Denmark to embrace the concept of ecology and high-quality organic foods and products. The hotel offers services tailored to environmentally conscious and health-conscious customers. One of its hotels has recently become a member of Green Globe, an international certification organization with the strictest standards in environmental tourism.

The hotels recycle as much as possible. For instance, the organic coffee scrub used in the spa is made of the coffee grounds left over from breakfast mixed, with Epsom salt and essential oil. The keycards are made of 100% biodegradable and sustainable materials, such as corn and other plant materials. In order to save energy, soon there will be solar panels installed on the roofs of the hotels.

At its hotels located in Denmark, there are no plastic bottles with water in any of the rooms and cafés. Instead, there are reusable glass bottles with the inscription 'Great water straight from the tap'.

Everything else in the hotels is organic, including the food, drinks, sanitary products, beauty and health products, cleaning products, linen and towels. The hotel chain promises that every single item of the food it serves to its customers is 95% organic.

Questions
1 In what ways do the services provided by Hotel Guldsmeden differ from ordinary hotels?
2 What challenges does Hotel Guldsmeden face in its new service development process in order to be the leader in providing an ecological and organic experience for its customers?
3 How could Hotel Guldsmeden involve its customers in the development of its services?

Source: www.hotelguldsmeden.com

Table 5.7 Customers' input in the NSD process

NSD processes	Activities performed by customers
Strategic planning	• Provide feedback on financial data
Idea generation	• State needs, problems and their solutions, criticize existing service • Identify gaps in the market • Provide a wish list (service requirements) • State new service adoption criteria
Idea screening	• Suggest rough sales guide and market size • Suggest desired features, benefits and attributes • Show reactions to the concepts • Provide input on liking, preference and purchase intent of all the concepts • Help the producer in go/kill decision
Business analysis	• Provide feedback on financial data, including profitability of the concepts, competitors' data
Formation of cross-functional team	• Join top management in selecting team members
Service design and process system design	• Review and jointly develop the blueprints • Suggest improvements by identifying fail points • Observe the service delivery trial by the firm personnel
Personnel training	• Observe and participate in mock service delivery process • Suggest improvements
Service testing and pilot run	• Participate in a simulated service delivery processes • Suggest final improvements and design change
Test marketing	• Provide comments on the marketing plan • Provide detailed comments about their satisfaction with marketing mixes • Suggest desired improvements
Commercialization	• Adopt the service as trial • Feedback about overall performance of the service along with desired improvements, if any • Word-of-mouth communications to other potential customers

Source: adapted from Alam and Perry (2002).

Summary

In this chapter we introduced some theories and tools for managing the design of products and services. Understanding the new product development (NPD) process provides the foundation for the development of innovative products and services. One current competitive strategy pursed by many firms is platform development, which enables them to offer higher product variety to customers at lower costs. How a platform is configured, in terms of the technology composition and organization, is dependent on product architecture design strategies (which can range from modular to integral).

One purpose for devising modular designs is to create flexibility and changeability of product configurations. If the product strategy is to offer a wide range of products at the lowest cost possible (such as mass customization), then modular product architecture designs might be the right strategy. The best way to achieve mass customization is with modular components – that is, with components that can be mixed and matched and configured into a wide variety of new products and services. However, if the goal is to be

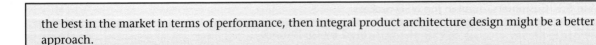

the best in the market in terms of performance, then integral product architecture design might be a better approach.

Development of services is equally crucial for the survival and competitiveness of the firms. We highlighted some key issues related to service design, such as how to measure the degree of customer contact, and the value created by the front- and back-office activities. The service process matrix is a tool to assess the degree of interaction and customization with respect to degree of labour intensity. The design and development of new services go through several stages similar to those used in designing products. However, with services, the customers become the key part of the new service design (NSD) process, and whether they are involved in the design process or not can affect the outcome of the service system.

Key Theories

The key theories discussed in this chapter were:

- **Platform design** – the creation of a foundation design that can be used in a number of products, and upon which the remainder of the design can be based.

- **Modularization** – an approach to organizing complex products and processes efficiently by decomposing complex tasks into simpler portions to allow the tasks to be managed independently and yet work together as a whole without compromising performance.

- **Mass customization** – a strategy that emphasizes the need to provide outstanding service to customers in providing products that meet their needs (through maximizing individual customization) at a low cost (e.g. through modular components).

- **Service process matrix** – a framework that provides a classification of service industry firms based on the characteristics of a firm's services processes, in terms of degree of interaction and customization versus the degree of labour intensity.

Suggested Answers to Stop and Think Questions

1 **Good designs; bad products:** It takes a long time for good design ideas to become commercialized. The various NPD stages that any product has to go through make the success of the product even more uncertain. During the NPD journey, there are numerous trade-offs to be considered. Once in production, engineering changes cannot be made without lengthy procedures. When the product reaches the market, it becomes completely impossible for firms to control how the customers use the product. Often the final product sold in the market is very different from the concept idea. Firms typically discover that the real needs of their customer are not met with what the product is intended for (e.g. sleek mobile phones with touch pads – high tech, but unusable for blind people or people with big fingers). In other instances, customers may find innovative ways to use the products that the firms did not think of (e.g. using a cheese slicer as a vegetable slicer, or using a cooking spatula as an ice scraper). These end up being perceived as bad products.

2 **NPD strategy:** The challenges can be discussed from many perspectives: organizational, manufacturing, and supply chain management.

Challenges from an integral design to a modular design: how to decompose the system. Once the product is decomposed, the management has to consider how to change the manufacturing processes and job designs accordingly. The manufacturing process has to be able to accommodate high-volume production and repetitive processes. The management has to consider how to divide the labour so that each design unit can work independently. If outsourcing is the motivation for pursuing a modular design strategy, then sourcing decisions have to be devised (i.e. low cost versus partnership strategies).

Challenges from a modular design to an integral design: how to integrate the various modular components of the product to create a new product so that the firm can gain control of its technology. The manufacturing process has to be redesigned to accommodate lower volumes. The management has to think about how to create synergy among the team members across various departments so that they can work harmoniously. The supply chain managers have to consider how to share knowledge of specialized technology with key suppliers, or to integrate vertically.

3 **Product variety:** Psychological studies suggest that humans are able to process only up to nine different types of information in short-term memory. Too many options cause the consumer to become sidetracked from what they really want from the product. They may get lured away by options that they do not really need.

For the retailers and producers, high product variety could create forecasting problems related to consumer preferences. Coordination problems in the supply chain might arise from stockouts, overstocking, and product return policies. Overstocking translates into high inventory costs.

4 **Service quality:** The perception of service quality varies from person to person. A bad service for one person can be a good service for another. In order to understand the service delivery process and customer satisfaction, we need to look at the number and types of services delivered. The scale and scope of the services delivered are the outcomes of how the service system is designed, linking the front-office and back-office activities together. As customers, we are in contact only with the front-office part of the service system. However, the back-office activities provide the support and foundation for the success of the front-office activities.

5 **Innovation:** Basically there is not much difference between innovation in services and innovation in products, apart from the fact that services are intangible and consumed at the same time as they are produced, and products are tangible. We can apply the theories of innovation to analyse innovation in services. In most cases, though, service innovation cannot take place without products, and vice versa. The degree of integration between services and products can be analysed from the servitization of products and the productization of services perspectives.

connect

Review Questions

1 Describe the current market situation of the music industry. How do innovation and standardization of technological development influence the way music is distributed and sold?

2 Check the mobile phones you and your colleagues have. Which brands do they have? Do they have same functions? What are the common and distinct features of phones within the same brand? How can you apply the new product development and platform design theories to answer these questions?

3 Select a product or service that has some sort of customization. What kind of product (or service) configuration does it have? How is customization realized? Apply modularization strategies to this problem.

4 You have just opened a restaurant in a posh area of your city. How would you organize its activities to ensure that the processes between the front office and the back office are aligned?

5 Your country is devising a new ticketing system for its trains. How would you design the service system? What kinds of challenges do you expect to encounter?

Discussion Questions

1 Discuss why it is important for firms to be at the forefront of technological development. Where do ideas for new product development come from?

2 Think about the last holiday you took. Which services impressed you most? Discuss the link between front- and back-office activities that might have taken place.

3 Consider a job that requires high levels of customer contact. Discuss how the management could design the service to create a great experience for the customers and job satisfaction for the workers.

4 You have just been hired by the health care director of a major hospital. The hospital wants to provide better care for its patients, such as the quality of the treatment received, and the sophistication of medical equipment used in the care. Discuss the factors you need to consider to make this process a success, through the perspective of the product–service system.

5 Imagine you are working for an IT company that is expanding into new markets. Discuss how you would design the service, and whether the customers should be involved in the process.

Problems

1 Philips has £700 million to invest in new models of its high-definition TVs (HDTV) for the next six years. The management estimates that it costs £150 million to develop a basic platform. It also costs another £15 million to develop each model that is derived from the basic platform. Philips wants to introduce eight new HDTV models over the next six years.

Required: *Calculate the number of platforms Philips needs to develop.*

2 A new, trendy shoe shop is offering customized shoes to its customers. The customers have the choice of combining three types of heel (high, short or stiletto), two types of leather (suede or plain), and four colours (black, brown, tan or beige). Customers can also add ornaments (buckles, clips, etc.) from a list of nine options that can be chosen independently of each other.

Required: *Calculate the number of options the customers can choose from.*

3 You are the supplier of hair care products (shampoos, conditioners, hair creams, etc.) to hair salons all over Europe. You have three main categories of customer:

High-end beauty shops: these sell all kinds of beauty products, including the standard hair care bottles from your company.

Professional salons in the UK: the hairdressers want two types of product: large bottles to be used on customers' hair, and standard bottles that can be displayed and sold to customers.

Professional salons in Nordic countries: the requirements for these are the same as for the hairdressers in the UK, expect that the bottles have to be translated into Nordic languages: Danish, Swedish, Norwegian and Finnish.

Required: *Apply the product–representation matrix to categorize the type of customization needed to satisfy your customers.*

Visit the Online Learning Centre at **www.mcgraw-hill.co.uk/textbooks/paton** for a range of resources to support your learning.

Further Reading

Binder, M., Gust, P. and Clegg, B.T. (2008) 'Frontloading: a means to improving the competitiveness of R&D collaboration in automotive supply networks?', *Journal of Manufacturing Technology Management*, **19**(3), 315–331.

Cooper, R. and Kleinschmidt, E. (1994) 'Determinants of timelines in product development', *Journal of Product Innovation Management*, **11**(5), 381–96.

Menor, L.J., Tatikonda, M.V. and Sampson, S.E. (2002) 'New service development: areas for exploitation and exploration', *Journal of Operations Management*, **20**(2), 135–157.

Zomerdijk, L.G. and Vries, J.D. (2007) 'Structuring front office and back office work in service delivery systems', *International Journal of Operations and Production Management*, **27**(1), 108–131.

References

Alam, I. and Perry, C. (2002) 'A customer-oriented new service development process', *Journal of Service Marketing*, **16**(2), 515–534.

Babcock, D.L. (1996) *Managing Engineering Technology: An Introduction to Management for Engineers*, 2nd edn, Prentice Hall, Upper Saddle River, NJ.

Baines, T.S., Lightfoot, H.W., Evans, S., Neely, A., Greenough, R., Peppard, J., Roy, R., Shehab, E., Braganza, A., Tiwari, A., Alcock, J.R., Angus, J.P., Bastl, M., Cousens, A., Irving, P., Johnson, M., Kingston, J., Lockett, H., Martinez, V., Michele, P., Tranfield, D., Walton, I.M. and Wilson, H. (2007) 'State-of-the-art in product-service systems', *Journal of Engineering Manufacture*, **221**(10), 1543–1552.

Baldwin, C.Y. and Clark, K.B. (1997) 'Managing in an age of modularity', *Harvard Business Review*, (September–October), 84–93.

Bell, T.E. (1993) 'Bicycles on a personalized basis', *IEEE Spectrum*, **30**(9), 32–35.

Chase, R.B. (1978) 'Where does the customer fit in a service operation?' *Harvard Business Review*, **75**(5), 137–142.

Da Silveira, G., Borenstein, D. and Fogliatto, F.S. (2001) 'Mass customization: literature review and research directions', *International Journal of Production Economics*, **72**(1), 1–13.

Davis, M.M. and Heineke, J. (2005) *Operations Management: Integrating Manufacturing and Services*, 5th edn, McGraw-Hill, Boston, MA.

De Blok, C., Meijboom, B., Luijkx, K., and Schols, J. (2007) 'Modularity in health care: towards cost-efficient and client-focused service provision', *Proceedings of the 14th Annual EurOMA Conference*, Ankara, Bilkent University.

Fitzsimmons, J.A. and Fitzsimmons, M.J. (2008) *Service Management*, 6th edn, McGraw-Hill, Boston, MA.

Gilmore, J.H. and Pine, B.J. (1997) 'The four faces of mass customization', *Harvard Business Review*, **75**(1), 91–101.

Hsuan, J. (1999) 'Impacts of supplier–buyer relationships on modularization in new product development', *European Journal of Purchasing and Supply Management*, **5**(3), 197–209.

Lung, Y., Salerno, M.S., Zilbovicius, M. and Dias, A.V.C. (1999) 'Flexibility through modularity: experimentations with fractal production in Brazil and in Europe', in *Coping With Variety: Flexible Productive Systems for Product Variety in the Auto Industry*, Y. Lung, J.J. Chararon, T. Fujimoto and D. Raff (eds), Ashgate, Aldershot, pp. 224–257.

Menor, L.J., Tatikonda, M.V. and Sampson, S.E. (2002) 'New service development: area for exploitation and exploration', *Journal of Operations Management*, **20**(2), 135–157.

Metters, R. and Vargas, V. (2000) 'A typology of de-coupling strategies in mixed services', *Journal of Operations Management*, **18**(6), 663–682.

Mikkola, J.H. and Gassmann, O. (2003) 'Managing modularity of product architecture: towards an integrated theory', *IEEE Transactions on Engineering Management*, **54**(1), 57–69.

Mikkola, J.H. and Skjøtt-Larsen, T. (2006) 'Platform management: implications for new product development and supply chain management', *European Business Review*, **18**(3), 214–230.

Nambisan, S. (2002) 'Designing virtual customer environments for new product development: toward a theory', *Academy of Management Review*, **27**(3), 392–413.

Nissen, H.C.A. (2009) 'Standardization of work processes on the service floor of Restaurant Fuego', unpublished master thesis, Copenhagen Business School.

Nixon, B. and Innes, J. (1997) 'Research and development performance measurement: a case study', paper presented at the 1997 R&D Management Conference, Manchester, 14–16 July.

Pine, J. (1993) *Mass Customization: The New Frontier in Business Competition*, Harvard Business School Press, Boston, MA.

Roth, A.V. and Menor, L.J. (2003) 'Insights into service operations management: a research agenda', *Production and Operations Management*, **12**(2), 145–164.

Schmenner, R.W. (1986) 'How can service business survive and prosper?', *Sloan Management Review*, **27**(3), 21–32.

Taylor, F. (1911) *Principles of Scientific Management*, Harper, New York.

Trott, P. (2008) *Innovation Management and New Product Development*, 4th edn, Financial Times/Prentice Hall, Harlow.

Ulrich, K.T. (1995) 'The role of product architecture in the manufacturing firm', *Research Policy*, **24**(3), 419–440.

Ulrich, K.T. and Eppinger, S.D. (2008) *Product Design and Development*, 4th edn, McGraw-Hill, New York.

Voss, C. (2003) 'Rethinking paradigms of service: service in a virtual environment', *International Journal of Operations and Production Management*, **23**(1), 88–104.

Voss, C. and Hsuan, J. (2009) 'Service architecture modularity', *Decision Sciences*, **40**(3), 541–569.

Process Design

Learning Outcomes

After studying this chapter you should be able to:

- Use the techniques of systems thinking

- Appreciate the value of the process perspective over the functional perspective

- Decide which type of process is best suited to a particular operation

- Use process mapping tools effectively to design and redesign processes

- Appreciate the use of technology in processes

- Select a suitable layout for a particular process.

Take a Welcome Break

Driving long distances can be arduous at the best of times. The Bolt family were driving from Manchester in the North West of England to Paris, France, via the Channel Tunnel and the Eurostar train. The weather was bad, the roads were snowy, and the journey had been slow. They had already had to queue and pay for tunnels and toll roads, and needed to stop for a break after four hours of driving. As the family travelled frequently, the four of them knew the 'pit stop' process well.

Source: © David Gee/Alamy

As they came into the service area just off the main highway they were filtered into the 'cars' lane away from the 'trucks long-stay parking', and the 'fuel only' lanes. Once they had parked, the first things to do were to find the toilets and then some food. As these particular services were new, the layout of the facility was very efficient: there were lots of clean toilets with the latest 'cyclone' hand-drying machines, automatic taps and flushing toilets. The food and shopping court had been designed so that people wanting to eat different foods – fast-food burgers or healthier snacks – could sit together. After eating, the two children went to the nearby indoor play area to get some exercise, and Mr Bolt logged onto the Internet using the free WiFi connection to catch up on his emails, and then used the ATM to get some cash. Meanwhile Mrs Bolt went to do a spot of shopping to buy gifts for the family they were visiting.

Outside, the snow was falling thick and fast, and Mr Bolt was keen to get going as the traffic bulletin boards in the food court were warning of potential road closures. They all got back into the car, and after Mr Bolt had checked that the car was safe to drive, he drove to the on-site fuel station a few hundred metres away to fill up and get some de-icer for the windscreen. Once the car had been sorted out they tried to set off. Unfortunately the snow had worsened so, changing plan, Mrs Bolt suggested that they abandon the journey for now and check into the on-site Days Inn hotel before it filled up with similarly minded people. Mr Bolt thought this was a good idea, as he could use his loyalty card and earn points by staying there. It would also be quick and easy, as he knew this hotel had an express check-in-and-out, and an 'open all hours' self-service breakfast bar, which meant they could get going as soon as possible in the morning.

The process that the Bolts had followed was similar to that of any other visiting family. Other types of customer, such as truck drivers or lone business travellers, would follow different paths through the services to meet their differing requirements. Truck drivers might wish only to use the showers, and the overnight 'park and sleep' facility. Business travellers, on the other hand, might just want to stop for a quick coffee, or use the free WiFi lounge to send some urgent work messages, or even use the on-site 'pay by the hour' business conference facilities.

Source: Ben Clegg, Aston Business School

Introduction

The opening case demonstrates that we experience operations and operational processes every day, whether through travel, work or leisure. We experience so many that we often forget that they are operations and operational processes, and that someone, somewhere, has consciously designed them and is responsible for managing them. This chapter will demonstrate the importance of operations and operational processes for an organization, how they are designed, and how they are managed.

The design and management of processes are fundamental to establishing any operation. Common practice is to innovate, standardize and then optimize a process before beginning again with any new requirements. Process thinking is a radical departure from traditional thinking, which is more concerned with optimizing business functions, and is known as *functional thinking*. Process thinking is more about optimizing **business processes** that cross functions within an organization and deliver goods and services for the end customer. Functional thinking can be an inefficient and ineffective practice. Process thinking can replace functional thinking and make organizations work better from the customer perspective.

Business process: a sequence of tasks to get things done.

Effective process management is the basis for many modern operations management practices, such as quality management and lean thinking, and therefore it is important to fully understand it. Process-oriented thinking is also the basis for successful supply chain management, which is the practice of joining up the processes of different organizations as seamlessly as possible.

This chapter begins by briefly outlining systems thinking in the context of process management. It then explains the different generic types of process and order, and the different sorts of process mapping used to support process design. It finishes by discussing the implications that physical layouts have for operations.

Systems Thinking

System: a complex whole, the functioning of which depends on its parts and the interactions between those parts.

In order for us to discuss processes in a meaningful way, we need to briefly turn our attention to *systems thinking*. Simply defined, a **system** is a complex whole, the functioning of which depends on its parts and the interactions between those parts. We can easily think of many different types of system: natural systems, such as rivers

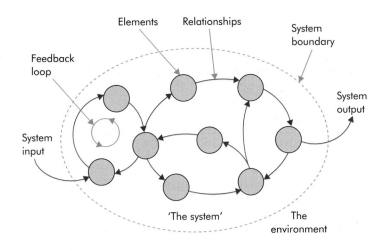

Figure 6.1 Systems properties

and waterways; biological systems, such as living organisms or ecosystems; designed complex product systems, such as ships and IT networks; and human activity systems, such as businesses and organizations. Understanding how these systems work is known as *systems thinking*.

All too often, studies of systems are too reductionist. *Reductionism* sees the parts of a system as more important than the whole. However, the whole emerges from the interactions between those parts. A good understanding of the whole system cannot be gained from studying each of the parts in isolation, but must be gained by studying the whole system, and how its parts work together. The alternative to reductionism is **holism**, which is endorsed by those who use systems thinking (which is also known as **holistic thinking**). Holism considers a system to be more than a sum of its parts. This type of thinking is used widely in philosophy, biology, engineering, physical sciences and organizational and management theory. In this chapter we are interested in using holistic systems thinking for the design and management of business processes.

> **Holistic thinking/holism:** considering a system to be more than a sum of its parts.

Figure 6.1 shows the essential parts of a system. Notice that a boundary separates the system from the wider environment. There is a defined route for inputs into the system, and another for its outputs. Also, the elements interact with each other in different ways: some react with just a few other elements, some with many, and some are involved in feedback loops.

Table 6.1 provides an example of how both a service provider (a high street bank) and a manufacturer (of washing machines) can be viewed as a system. Systems thinking should underpin all that operations managers do, if an operation is going to work well. It is possible to think of countless other operational examples and apply systems thinking to them. The opening case was an example of one such system.

Many techniques for process design and improvement are derived from systems thinking, and learning these techniques is rather like learning a modern language. In contrast, learning systems thinking is like learning the root language from which they are derived (e.g. Italian and Spanish, which are both derived from Latin). Therefore, appreciating systems thinking can help one to understand process improvement tools better. It is useful to keep the systems thinking perspective in mind throughout this chapter, because all business processes and operations are systems.

❶ Stop and Think

1   How do you think operations management would benefit if everyone applied systems thinking to it?

Table 6.1 Systems properties in service and manufacturing processes

	Organization	
	High street bank	**Washing machine manufacturer**
System	Customer relationship management (CRM) system	Production system
System inputs (resources to be transformed, e.g. people, items or information)	New customers with no profile	Sheet metal
Feedback loops (keep the system in control)	Data-mining techniques to check the effectiveness of marketing promotions	ISO 9000 quality procedures, ISO 14000 environmental regulations, total productivity maintenance, shareholder meetings, health and safety regulations
Elements Transforming resources – those that do not become part of the final product or service but are used to make and deliver them	People – marketing department; financial – employee incentives; tangible – computer hardware; intangible – intellectual property, CRM software	Human – machine operatives; financial – working capital; tangible – machines; intangible – operating procedures
Transformed resources – those that are being processed and may end up as part of the final product and service	Personalized and updated customer profiles to facilitate a more personalized service	Parts, materials and sub-assemblies to make finished products for the consumer
Relationships between elements (these make activities occur)	Customers (system inputs) are transformed by employees (who are a transforming resource): e.g. customer profiles are updated by the CRM software every time a transaction is made	Tangible materials (system inputs) are transformed by humans and machines (transforming resources): e.g. people use machines and materials to make other machines
System boundary (establishes authority and influence)	Limit of channel interfaces with customers and bank that can produce valuable communication	The interface with suppliers at one end, the interface with customers at the other end
Environment (to link a system with the rest of the world – which is itself made up of other systems)	Competition, and regulation of the high street banking sector	Competition, and regulations (e.g. health and safety, European laws)
System outputs (the creations of the systems – which are hopefully value-adding)	Transformed resources – e.g. loyal customers with a fully customized profile	Transformed resources – e.g. parts and materials become washing machines

Processes

Processes are typically designed and operated to perform transformations; a transformation (or conversion) is something that adds value to the entity being processed (e.g. materials or people). A process is normally designed around two major factors; the *volume* (high or low) and the *variety* (small or large) of what needs to be delivered.

Figure 6.2 shows an input–output diagram, which is a very simple representation of a process: there are inputs, a transformation, and outputs, which all need to be controlled and resourced. This representation can be used for a whole company, for part of a company, or even for a single task.

Different stages (or tasks) in a process are often the responsibility of different functional areas (departments or business units) within an organization. Functions such as marketing, operations and finance are important for

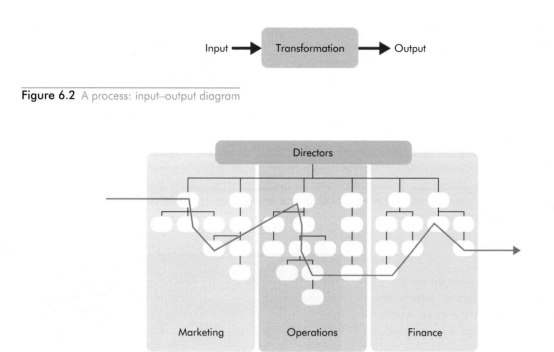

Figure 6.2 A process: input–output diagram

Figure 6.3 Processes and functions

internal purposes – such as setting budgets, career development, and measuring performance. But external customers are rarely interested in the internal structure of an organization; they are far more interested in factors that affect them directly, such as speedy delivery, good quality, dependability and flexibility. It is factors such as these that can be improved by taking a process view of an organization rather than a functional view. Figure 6.3 shows the functional view of the organization, with the vertical columns representing marketing, operations and finance.

In Figure 6.3 the business process is represented by the horizontal red line, going from left to right across the organization, that links together various activities carried out by different functions. This represents the path that a transformed item (e.g. people, data or material) would take through an organization. For example, the red line might be a business process for planning and executing a 'buy one, get one free' sales promotion in a brewery.

Figure 6.3 shows that processes often have *hand-offs* between one function and another; these are marked by the responsibility for the process activity changing. Because of these, time and information can be lost. In some cases, the number of hand-offs is immense, and an organization performs badly as a result. For instance, a US study into the manufacture of a fighter aircraft revealed huge wastes as 'the typical subassembly goes through four plants, four states and 74 organizational "hand-offs" between engineering, purchasing and fabricating operations. It goes 7,600 miles and takes darn near forever' (Deming, 1999, p. 123).

Types of Process

There are four main types of process: continuous, assembly line, batch, and project. In manufacturing, the product flow will be the same as the flow of materials, since materials are usually being converted into the end product. In services it is more usual to have a flow of information or people – customers or clients – that are being processed.

Continuous

Continuous processes are most applicable to so-called *process industries*. Process industries are those in which products or services are made continuously, and they tend to be highly standardized and automated, with very high volumes of production. Examples are standard beer brands, paper, oil, and the production of electricity. Production may run 24 hours a day, seven days a week. Delivery may stop only for maintenance activities. For example, a nuclear power station may run without stopping for 50 years. It is often very hard to differentiate the product or service from that of competitors, and low cost becomes the order winner in an unregulated market. For instance, a house owner will usually choose the cheapest power supplier for their electricity and gas, as the service will often be indistinguishable between providers; few of us think about or measure the quality of our electricity.

Continuous operations tend to be highly automated, have high set-up costs, operate at very high volumes, and usually produce non-discrete products such as liquids (water, petrol or beer), semi-solids (paint or concrete), or services such as gas or electricity. It is often very difficult to change over quickly from delivering one type of service or product to another. For these reasons a high degree of certainty and predictability is needed for it to be worth setting up a continuous process.

Assembly Lines

Assembly lines are characterized by a prede-fined sequence of operations which move items from one step to the next. Assembly lines are set up to deliver discrete products such as cars, fridges, computers and mobile phones. The transformed resources (parts) are often moved from one step to the next in a semi-automated way on mechanisms such as conveyor belts or automatic guided vehicles (AGVs).

Traditional assembly lines are designed to be very efficient, and produce high volumes of fairly standardized products; this is often referred to as *mass production*. The main advantage of an assembly line process is efficiency. The downside of an assembly line is that it can be difficult to change from delivering one type of output to another, and so flexibility needs to be built into the line if possible. For instance, it can take weeks to change over from producing one type of car to another on a car assembly line. The changeover time is wasted (non-value-adding) time, as during changeover the operation does not produce any saleable output.

Batch

Batch flow processes are characterized by batches (or 'lots') of work being produced together (e.g. a particular customer order, or a particular product or service derivative). Batches of work typically move between different functions or *work cells* throughout a process.

Work cells are particularly useful for batches, because they are relatively flexible, and can achieve acceptable economies of scale. For instance, a large fairground ride can process a specific group of people, a baker's oven can bake batches of specific varieties of bread or cakes, and a clothes factory may have a work cell to make a certain type of clothing. The people and equipment in a work cell should be set up to handle batch sizes that match the demands of customers.

Batch flow allows more flexibility than an assembly line, as its machines and people are more adaptable – that is, they have lower task specificity. However, batch processing is difficult, because it requires careful *layout* of the work cells and *sequencing* of activities.

Batch operations are most useful when an organization has many different products that are processed similarly, and are required frequently at relatively low volumes. In such situations the batch operation is the most economical type of process, and incurs the least risk. Other examples of products made in batches are ceramic crockery, fashion clothing, wooden furniture and boats, as these are all products with high variety, made in relatively low volumes.

Job Shop

The *job shop* is a very adaptable and highly skilled work cell that may deliver an entire product by itself. In a job shop the output will still be made in batches, but it will be customized to specific customer orders, which are typically received intermittently. Like batch processing, the job shop uses standard equipment, but will have higher flexibility to deliver a variety of products and volumes of production. Costs are generally higher, since the volume of output and degree of standardization are lower. Typical products manufactured in a job shop are machine components or prototypes. Typical services delivered in a job shop include revision sessions for university courses, and monthly drop-in clinics at doctors' surgeries for mothers and babies.

Project

The *project* type of process is typically used for large, unique products and services. Examples of service-based projects are concerts and large sporting events; examples of product-based projects are the construction of bridges, hospitals and stadiums. Technically speaking there is little product flow in a project, since materials and labour are brought to the project site, and the project itself is stationary. The unique nature of projects means that they are characterized by complex planning and scheduling, they are hard to automate, and they need highly skilled and motivated staff to work on them.

In a project-type process each delivery is often made individually, and is differentiated from other deliveries. Projects often result when a customer requires large amounts of customization and uniqueness. Generally speaking, the cost of unit production for projects is high, and sometimes difficult to control. This is because projects are often difficult to define fully at the beginning, and changes commonly occur during their delivery – which can have negative implications for timescales and cost.

Table 6.2 summarizes the different types of process and their characteristics, as described above. A process should ideally have characteristics that are suited to the nature of the product or service that it is delivering; if it does not, then this may result in process inefficiencies, high costs, and loss of competitive advantage.

Volume and Variety

Figure 6.4 provides an overview of the four process types, differentiated by volume and variety demands – which are, arguably, the two most important factors determining process design. Note that job variety, process flexibility and unit cost are highest for a project, and get progressively lower moving from project processes towards continuous processing. Conversely, volume of output is lowest for a project, and gets progressively higher, moving towards continuous processing. Note, too, that all these types fall along a diagonal. The implication is that the diagonal represents the ideal choice of process for the given set of circumstances. For example, if the goal is to be able to process a single job involving a unique output (e.g. building the London Eye), then a project management process is most appropriate. However, for more volume, a job shop or a batch process would be more suitable, and so on. Note that any combinations too far from the diagonal should not normally be considered. For instance, using a job shop for high-volume and low-variety jobs may result in long lead times; or using a continuous processing process for low-volume and high-variety jobs could result in higher-than-necessary costs due to the number of times the process needs to be reconfigured to make a different product.

Often, the processes shown in Figure 6.4 do not exist in their 'pure' form. Instead, hybrid processes that have elements of different process types embedded in them are usually found. For instance, organizations that operate primarily in a repetitive mode, or a continuous mode, will often have specialist *repair shops* (i.e. job shops) incorporated to be able to fix or make new parts for equipment that fails. Similarly, if a volume increases for some items, an operation that once began in a job shop or as a batch process may develop into an assembly line process. However, it is unlikely that any other type will evolve into a continuous process, as this process type tends to be suitable only for specific types of product and service with highly predictable demand patterns. Figure 6.4 shows examples of product (blue) and service (red) processes for each type.

Table 6.2 Summary of types of process, layout and order – explained throughout this chapter

Process characteristics	Process type				
	Continuous	Assembly line	Batch	Job shop	Project
Description	Highly standardized goods or services	Standardized goods and services	Partly customized outputs to customer requirements	Made to order, custom-made specification	Highly customized and often unique output
Output	Continuous flow	Discrete	Discrete	Discrete	Discrete
Advantages	Very efficient, very high volume	Low unit cost, high volume, efficient	Flexibility	Able to handle a wide variety of work	Dedicated adaptable team and resources
Disadvantages	Very rigid, lack of variety, costly to change, very high cost of downtime	Low flexibility, high cost of downtime	Moderate cost per unit, moderate scheduling complexity	Slow, high cost per unit, complex planning and scheduling	High risk and cost uncertainty, takes time to establish
Cost estimation	Routine	Routine	Fairly routine	Specific costing – but relatively simple	Specific costing – simple to complex
Cost per unit	Low	Low	Moderate	High	Very high
Equipment used	Dedicated	Dedicated	General purpose	General purpose	Varied
Fixed costs	Very high	High	Moderate	Low	Varied
Variable costs	Very low	Low	Moderate	High	High
Labour skills	Low to high	Low	Moderate	High	Low to high
Marketing	Promote standardized goods and services	Promote standardized goods and services	Promote flexibility	Promote capabilities	Promote capabilities
Scheduling	Routine, interdependent and sequential	Routine, interdependent and sequential	Moderately complex	Complex	Complex, continually subject to change
Work in process inventory	Low	Low	Medium to high	High	Varied
Longevity of operation	Ongoing and indefinite	Ongoing for whole product/service life cycle	Short individual deliveries – repeated often	Fixed duration – short to medium	Fixed duration – medium to very long
Probable type of order	MTS (make to stock)	MTS/ATO (assemble to order)	ATO	ATO/MTO (make to order)	MTO
Probable type of layout	Product-service dominant	Product-service dominant	Process dominant	Work cell	Fixed position

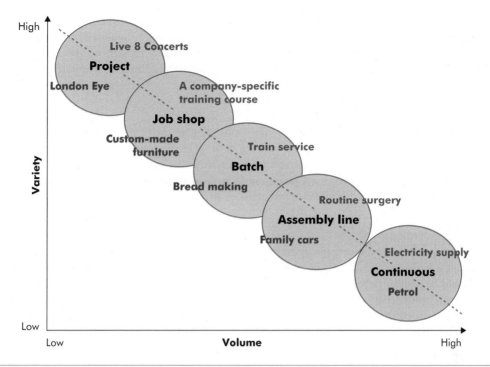

Figure 6.4 Volume and variety: the impact upon process definition, with service and manufacturing examples (adapted from Hayes and Wheelright, 1979)

🛈 Stop and Think

2 What happens if the process that you design falls into the 'dead zones' either side of the diagonal line in Figure 6.4?

Types of Order

A factor that greatly influences process design is the type of order. Orders can be fulfilled in different ways. The main types are *made to order* (MTO), *made to stock* (MTS) and *assembled to order* (ATO), which is an in-between hybrid of MTO and MTS. There are advantages and disadvantages to each practice. An MTS process can provide faster service to customers by taking a product from available stock, but there is an associated stockholding cost. The additional stockholding cost may be offset by a lower unit production cost, as the product will be manufactured in the most economical batch quantities. The MTO process will provide flexibility to customize the product or service to a customer's requirement, and also avoid the cost of stockholding. The ATO practice attempts to use a process that has the best parts of MTO and MTS practices. The type of process most suited to each type of order is shown in Table 6.2.

Make to Order

In the MTO process, individual customer orders are identified during production. As each order is made to a particular customer specification, each job in the process is associated with a particular customer. For instance, when you buy a new BMW you will be given a unique number that will enable you to see your car being configured in the factory. BMW has even made this available to view on the Internet, using a webcam. One can always identify an MTO process by simply looking at who the job is for. In the MTO process the cycle of production and order fulfilment begins with the customer order, in this case from the car salesman in the BMW dealership. Only after receiving an order will the work begin – with the ordering of the necessary materials. Once the materials arrive, the order can be processed – assuming the necessary machines and people are available. When the order is complete, it can be delivered to the customer.

Lead time: the time it takes to design, make and deliver a product or service.

The key performance measure of an MTO process is the time it takes to design, make and deliver; this is referred to as the **lead time**. Although the idea of an MTO process applies mostly to products, an equivalent service would be something like a tailor-made personalized service – rather like having a chauffeur and limousine at your beck and call.

Make to Stock

The MTS process is a standard process used to make items that are put into inventory, which can then be used immediately to fulfil customer demand. Everything in an MTS process is geared towards having the right items in stock when a customer places an order, so that it can be fulfilled straight away. In contrast to MTO, MTS processes build products only for inventory stock, and the jobs in process are not linked to any particular customer. Classic examples are standardized homogeneous products such as foodstuffs, and consumer goods such as kettles and refrigerators.

The critical management tasks with MTS are forecasting, inventory management and capacity planning. The MTS process begins with the producer specifying the product or service. The customer then requests a product from inventory. If the product is available in inventory, it is delivered to the customer. If it is not available, a *back order* signal should be sent to production to make some more items to put into stock. In the MTS process, customer orders do not influence production; the production cycle is driven by the need to replenish stock. In other words, the customer-ordering cycle follows a completely independent cycle from the production cycle. Therefore what is being produced may have little bearing upon what is required by customers at any point in time.

Performance measures for an MTS process include the percentage of orders filled from inventory; this is called the *service level*, and is typically targeted above 90%. Other measures are the length of time it takes to replenish inventory, inventory turnover, capacity utilization, and the time it takes to fill a back order. The objective of an MTS process is to meet the desired service level at a minimum cost. Although the idea of MTS is applied mostly to products, the equivalent idea in services is to have a standard service that you have to wait for, and which is non-negotiable – rather like having your car oil changed at a Kwik Fit or Jiffy Lube type of service garage.

Assemble to Order

Assemble to order (ATO) processes are a growing trend that has been facilitated largely by the use of Internet-based ordering systems that can make processes increasingly customer focused. The ATO process builds sub-assemblies in advance of demand, and then puts them together to make the final product when a specific customer order is received. ATO is a hybrid of make to order and make to stock. Whereas the sub-assemblies are made to stock, the final assembly is made to order. When a specific order arrives, the sub-assemblies are taken from inventory and assembled to fill the customer's order. But, of course, the product must be designed in a modular fashion for ATO to be used. For instance, Benetton initially makes all its jumpers in an 'un-dyed' neutral colour, and then dyes them afterwards once an order has been received from a retailer. By doing this, Benetton is able to balance its inventory with customer demand better, while still providing quick 'final assembly' of the product and delivery to the customer.

There are other variations on ATO, including mass customization, in which every single product could potentially be different (explained in more detail in Chapter 5). For instance, Mattel offered Barbie dolls that could wear any item of clothing from a choice of thousands, and any hairstyle from a choice of hundreds. Although ATO is usually applied to products, the service equivalent would be buying a package holiday and selecting different options to tailor your own holiday package.

The differences between the three main types of order are described in Table 6.3.

Customization point: the point where a process output becomes linked to a specific customer order.

The type of customer order determines the **customization point** in the ordering process. This is defined as the point where the product becomes linked to a specific customer order, and the customer becomes involved in the process. There are three main points where customization can occur: these are shown by the shading in Figure 6.5.

For MTS the customization point is after the design and make is completed: therefore any customization has to be limited to delivery and packaging only. For ATO the customization point is after design, but before final assembly: therefore the ATO process gives the customer more choice, since the product is assembled after the

Table 6.3 Characteristics of different order types

	Make to stock (MTS)	**Assemble to order (ATO)**	**Make to order (MTO)**
Product/service	Producer specified Low variety Inexpensive	Part customer and part producer specified Mid expense Mid variety	Customer specified High variety Expensive
Objectives	Balance inventory, capacity and service	Quick assembly – needs balanced inventory and quick delivery	Manage delivery lead times and capacity
Main operations problems	Forecasting, planning production, control of inventory	Designing products and services that are modular	Specification Quality levels Delivery time

order is placed. For MTO processes the customization point is during the design phase, and may even include ordering in unique, bespoke parts (e.g. new materials for a tailor-made suit, new paint for an unusual car colour, or a special birthday cake for a celebratory restaurant meal). For MTO the maximum amount of customization is possible, but the lead time to the customer can be longer, and the product typically costs more.

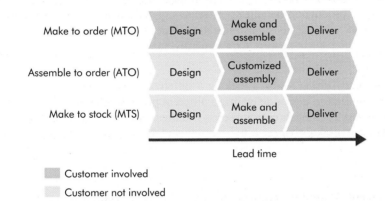

Make to order (MTO) — Design | Make and assemble | Deliver

Assemble to order (ATO) — Design | Customized assembly | Deliver

Make to stock (MTS) — Design | Make and assemble | Deliver

Lead time

■ Customer involved
□ Customer not involved

Figure 6.5 Customer involvement in different types of order

SHORT CASE 6.1

Diamonds Are for Ordering

Buying an expensive piece of jewellery such as an engagement ring can be a big decision, and it is important to get it just right. For instance, mass-produced diamond rings can be bought in any high street jewellery chain, but if you want something more individual you have to go to a jeweller who can design and make bespoke items.

Online jewellery companies such as Blue Nile are an alternative. These e-retailers offer a choice of band shapes and styles, diamond cuts, shapes and quality, which can be selected and ordered over the Internet.

Source: © Mark Evans/iStock

Alternatively, one could also try renowned diamond centres such as Amsterdam, which have led customized jewellery design and manufacture for hundreds of years. There are many shops in such areas that possess the skills to design and make rings from scratch. Customers can have anything they desire . . . as long as they can afford it!

Questions

1   Which scenario is most likely to work on MTS, MTO and ATO ordering?
2   What implications are there for designing the manufacturing process?

Source: Ben Clegg, Aston Business School

Contemporary Thinking: Design for Mass Customization

Up to this point we have been discussing traditional process strategies and order types that map neatly onto Figure 6.4. However, there have been major developments in process and product technologies recently, such as computers, robotics, and the Internet, which are facilitating a change in thinking. New technologies have driven process strategy towards *mass customization*.

Mass customization is a process strategy that can repeatedly deliver products or services in very small batch sizes, often involving just one item or one service delivery. In the volume and variety figure (Figure 6.4) mass customization is placed in the top right-hand corner, which is a strategy that is not normally financially sustainable. This is because traditional mass production is built on *economies of scale*, delivering high volumes of standardized output with few options. By contrast, mass customization depends on *economies of scope*, which can provide a high variety of outputs from a single process. Consequently, mass customization has a common *process* rather than a common *product* or *service*.

Customization (or 'customer-ization') means making a different product for each customer (usually at high cost), whereas mass customization means delivering a different product or service for each customer at approximately mass production cost levels. Mass customization is difficult to do, though, as it requires the whole process to be flexible – from the order taking, through to assembly and delivery. For instance:

- The production process must be rapid, flexible, and able to accommodate changes in specification. This means that batch (or 'lot') sizes of one are possible, such as pizza production at a takeaway pizza house.
- Inventory control needs to be tight, and there should be no finished stock held and therefore no obsolescence; nobody wants yesterday's pizza.
- Delivery requires careful tracking and tracing of every order; there may be many different pizzas going to many different customers, all at the same time.

The key point is that mass customization is difficult to achieve consistently, and requires mass collaboration along the supply chain. The advantages are that customers' demands are met quickly, and forecasting errors and risks are reduced.

SHORT CASE 6.2   Mass Customization at Dell

Dell has recently become the number one maker of file servers in the United States (computers used to serve up files on a computer network – as found in a university library, for example), and holds the number two position worldwide. Dell builds servers efficiently, and their customers know exactly where their server is during every step of the production process.

The production process begins when the customer orders the server. This information is placed in a production queue that itemizes every component to be built into the server. The required inventory is then sent to the assembly area to make sure that it is queued. Dell collaborates closely with its suppliers to provide them with real-time production data, so it can have inventory available on the loading docks connected to the factory floor. This allows Dell to keep only two hours' worth of inventory on the factory floor.

Assembly begins when the chassis, motherboard and memory are put together and moved to the 'kitting' area, where the other various internal components (such as drives, cards and connectors) from suppliers are added to the 'kit' tray. These kits are then moved to the assembly area, where they are automatically routed to the next available assembler. Each assembler can build a variety of servers (each is typically certified to build up to 15 different models). Once a server has been completed and tested, it is mechanically placed in a container and shipped out. Although production occurs very quickly, each server is customized specifically. The factory produces servers on a mass scale.

Questions

1   What is Dell's strategy and unique approach to order processing?
2   How has the design of its products helped mass customization?
3   What makes it possible to deliver high variation at competitive prices and lead times?
4   Why don't its competitors do the same?

Source: Ben Clegg, Aston Business School

❶ Stop and Think

3   What other products or services can you think of that would benefit from mass customization? How could this become feasible, and why hasn't it already been done?

Process Mapping

When we design and analyse processes, we need to ask questions such as:

- Is the process aligned with organizational strategy in order to achieve competitive advantage in terms of differentiation, response or low cost?
- Has the process got any non-value-adding steps that need to be eliminated?
- Does the process maximize customer value as perceived by the customer?
- Will the process help win orders?

BUSINESS INTEGRATION

There are many tools that can help us understand the complexities of process design and redesign. Many of these build on systems thinking, and focus on helping to develop a picture of the overall process; this is usually to help improve delivery of service, flow of information and management of materials. We shall now consider a few of these process-mapping tools, each of which has a slightly different purpose.

Flow Diagram

A **flow diagram** is a general-purpose diagram or schematic used to map the flow of people, material or progress. Figure 6.6 shows a very simple example of a flow diagram, using standard flow chart notation, for ordering a new sofa.

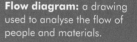

Flow diagram: a drawing used to analyse the flow of people and materials.

The main purpose of a flow diagram is to create a logical flow of activities (the sequence in which things are done), and indicate what the inputs and outputs are between them so that an awareness of the 'big picture' of an operation can be gained.

Swim Lane Map

Another general-purpose process visualization technique is the *swim lane map*; this is so called because it looks a bit like a swimming pool with lanes. A swim lane map is very similar to a flow diagram, but with more structure, as it has a time dimension along the horizontal axis and a functional dimension along the vertical axis that shows organization 'hand-offs'. Figure 6.7 shows an example of a swim lane map for the same simple ordering process shown in Figure 6.6.

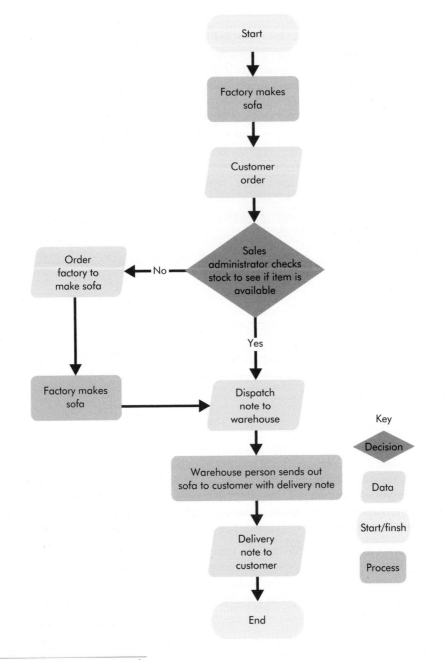

Figure 6.6 A flow diagram: ordering a sofa

The swim lane map is most useful when we are looking at process problems associated with functional divisions and waiting time.

Process Chart

A *process chart* is a general-purpose table, rather than a diagram, that uses symbols, time and distance to provide an objective and structured way to analyse and record activities in a process. It allows us to focus on value-adding activities. For instance, the process chart shown in Figure 6.8 is about making deliveries. The advantage of process charts over flow diagrams or swim lane diagrams is that there is no artistry involved, as they are always one-page tables produced on a standard template.

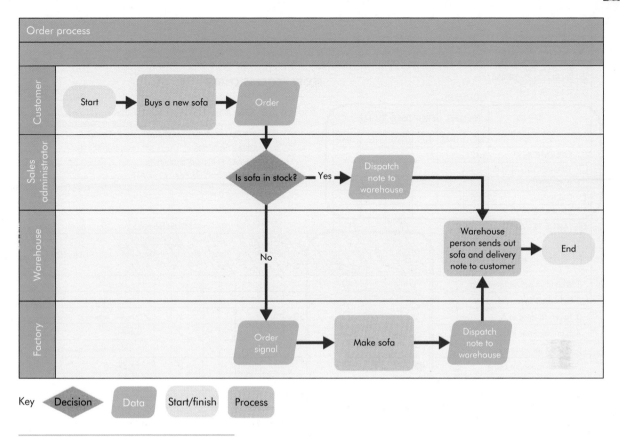

Figure 6.7 Swim lane map: ordering a sofa

The activities are listed in the left-hand column, and a line (threading vertically through the symbols) joins up symbols on a standard template shown in the central vertical columns (ringed in the figure). Each symbol represents a different type of activity, as defined in the top left table. Other attributes and notes about the activities can also be added in the right-hand columns. Taken together, the information depicts a process that can be followed by operatives rather like an instruction sheet.

Service Blueprint

Processes with a high service element are best suited to *service blueprinting* (Shostack, 1984). Service blueprinting is a process analysis technique that focuses on the customer, the provider's interaction with the customer, and on the activities of the provider. Service blueprints separate the service into physical evidence, customer/user actions, front-of-stage interactions (those actions by staff that interact directly with the customers or clients), backstage contact employee actions (those actions performed by customer-interfacing staff that do not involve the customer), and support processes that do not involve the customer. Figure 6.9 shows the service blueprint for the process of welcoming new students to a new course.

Value Stream Map

Perhaps one of the most sophisticated depictions of processes is the *value stream map* (VSM). A VSM requires a *current state* map to be produced, showing any present inefficiencies in the process, and a *future state* map that proposes how improvements can be made after waste in a process has been reduced.

Current State Value Stream Map

The current state VSM shows the process as it currently is, with all its inefficiencies. The most important icons used in this VSM are shown in Figure 6.10.

FLOW PROCESS CHART NO. 1 PAGE 1 OF 1

ANALYSIS — WHY? QUESTION EACH DETAIL — WHAT? WHERE? WHEN? WHO? HOW?

JOB Special Will Call & Mail Orders while in general office
MAN OR ☑ MATERIAL The Order Form
CHART BEGINS At receptionist's desk
CHART ENDS In mail chute
CHARTED BY H.F.G. DATE

SUMMARY

	PRESENT		PROPOSED		DIFFERENCE	
	NO.	TIME	NO.	TIME	NO.	TIME
○ OPERATIONS	12					
⇨ TRANSPORTATIONS	4					
☐ INSPECTIONS	3					
D DELAYS	5					
▽ STORAGES	–					
DISTANCE TRAVELED	140 FT.		FT.		FT.	

POSSIBILITIES

DETAILS OF PRESENT ~~PROPOSED~~ METHOD	Symbols (Operation / Transport / Inspection / Delay / Storage)	Distance in Feet	Quantity	Time	Eliminate	Combine	Change: Sequence	Change: Place	Change: Person	Improve	NOTES
1 Waited in box at reception	○ ⇨ ☐ D ▽										
2 Picked up by confid. clerk	○ ⇨ ☐ D ▽								✓		Use wire basket
3 Taken to desk at A	○ ⇨ ☐ D ▽	30'						✓	✓		To files instead; shorter distance
4 Examined (for information)	○ ⇨ ☐ D ▽							✓			At files
5 Waited (procure info.)	○ ⇨ ☐ D ▽				✓						Not necessary if taken to files
6 Prices written on order	● ⇨ ☐ D ▽							✓			At files
7 Taken to post. clerk at B	○ ⇨ ☐ D ▽	40'							✓		Shorter distance
8 Placed in desk tray	○ ⇨ ☐ D ▽										
9 Waited for clerk	○ ⇨ ☐ D ▽										
10 Picked up	○ ⇨ ☐ D ▽										
11 Examined (for information)	○ ⇨ ☐ D ▽										
12 Prices added (machine)	○ ⇨ ☐ D ▽										
13 Total written on order	● ⇨ ☐ D ▽										
14 Waited (clerk gets ledger)	○ ⇨ ☐ D ▽										
15 Total transferred to ledger	○ ⇨ ☐ D ▽										Taken directly to mail chute
16 Placed in special out box	○ ⇨ ☐ D ▽			✓							
17 Waited for routeing clerk	○ ⇨ ☐ D ▽			✓							Not necessary
18 Picked up	○ ⇨ ☐ D ▽			✓							Not necessary
19 Taken to desk (C)	○ ⇨ ☐ D ▽	40'		✓							Not necessary
20 Examined (determine route)	○ ⇨ ☐ D ▽						✓	✓			By B
21 Placed in envelope	○ ⇨ ☐ D ▽			✓							Not necessary; save cost of envelope
22 Addressed to proper dept.	● ⇨ ☐ D ▽			✓							Have B route and drop in mail chute
23 Taken to reception desk	○ ⇨ ☐ D ▽	30'						✓	✓		By B; shorter distance
24 Placed in mail chute	○ ⇨ ☐ D ▽										

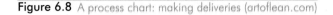

Figure 6.8 A process chart: making deliveries (artoflean.com)

Figure 6.11 shows a simple example of a current state VSM for the ACME Company, which makes spare parts (brackets) for tractors. The operation is currently very inefficient, as there is a great deal of waste in it, and it needs improving.

A VSM always places the customer in the top right-hand corner, and the suppliers are placed in the top left-hand corner. The tasks in the process are placed in white boxes with material flow going from left to right, and data about each of the tasks are placed in *data boxes* beneath them. Between each of the tasks lies an arrow indicating the direction of material flow, and a yellow triangle that indicates the amount of work in progress. Thick arrows between the tasks show material flow. Thin arrows are used to show information flow within a company, and

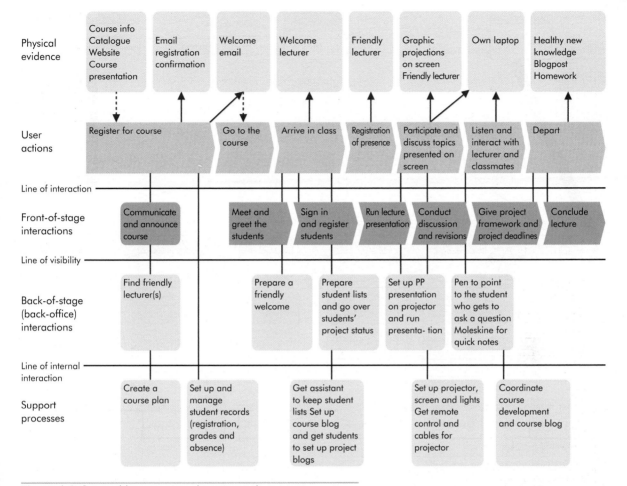

Figure 6.9 Service blueprinting: welcoming students to a new course

between its customers and suppliers. In the centre of the VSM at the top we show the method of production control. At the bottom of the diagram a *timeline* is calculated that shows all the waiting times and task cycle times in the process; these are summed up in the bottom right-hand corner.

The steps involved in producing a current state VSM are as follows:

1   Select a product or service family to focus on; this might be the food service in a hotel, or a postal service to a particular area.

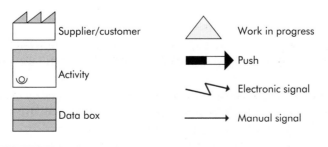

Figure 6.10 Value stream map icons

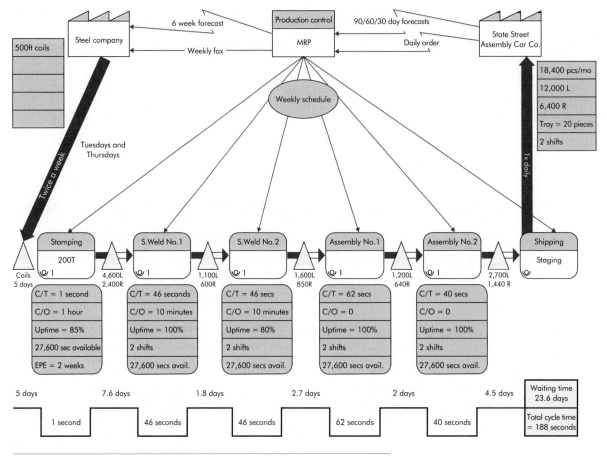

Figure 6.11 A current state value stream map for ACME: brackets for tractors

2   Capture the customer order requirements. For instance, how many of each type of service or item does the customer require, and how often do they want them to be delivered? These are recorded in a data box, at the top right corner, under the customer.

3   Starting at the end of the process, define each of the separate tasks, and measure their **cycle time**. The cycle time (C/T) is the *actual* time that it takes to produce a unit of output (sometimes known as *processing time*). Define the whole process by sequencing the separate tasks in the correct order.

4   It is also useful to collect other performance measures in the data boxes, such as:
   o   changeover time – time taken to change between producing different kinds of output
   o   uptime – the time a machine or person is available during a shift
   o   number of people required for each task (this is shown at the bottom of each task box – for instance, stamping uses one person)

These measures should be built into the calculation to help work out the *overall equipment effectiveness* (OEE) of a machine, or the *overall professional effectiveness* (OPE) of a person in a task.

5   Define the information flows in the process. This will be in the opposite direction to material flows (right to left). It will include the reorder signal from the customer to the operation, and the order the operations manager gives to people in the operations department; which could be via a manufacturing requirements planning (MRP) or enterprise resource planning (ERP) system (as described in Chapters 9 and 10), a kanban system, a manual instruction, or a combination of all these.

6   Measure the waiting time between each activity.

7   Work out the overall lead time in the process by adding up the cycle times of each task and the waiting times between each task.

Figure 6.11 shows an example that has a 23.6-day waiting time, and only 195 seconds of value added time. This is very wasteful, but it is typical of many operations. It clearly shows that improvements can be made in terms of waiting time. It also shows that there is a lot of work in progress (WIP) between each of the workstations, which could also be reduced.

WORKED EXAMPLE 6.1

Interpreting a Current State Value Stream Map

Problem: *Figure 6.11 shows a simple completed current state VSM for producing tractor spare parts (brackets). See if you can read some information from it.*

(a) *What are the customer's order requirements?*

(b) *What is the total cycle time for the tractor parts (in seconds)?*

(c) *What is the total lead time?*

(d) *Do you think that this is an efficient process? State why/why not.*

Approach: Carefully re-read the diagram and the notes about how it was constructed.

Solution:

(a) 18,400 pieces per month are required, including 12,000 left-hand brackets (LH) and 6,400 right-hand brackets (RH). These are to be delivered in trays of 20 using two shifts

(b) Stamping (1) + weld 1 (46) + weld 2 (46) + assembly 1 (62) + assembly 2 (40) + shipping (0) = 195 seconds' total cycle time.

(c) Total waiting time (in days) = 5 + 7.6 + 1.8 + 2.7 + 2 + 4.5 = 23.6 days.
Therefore ACME total lead time = 23.6 days waiting time + 195 seconds total cycle time.

(d) No. This is very wasteful, but is typical of many operations. It clearly shows that improvement can be made in waiting time. It also shows that there is a lot of work in progress (WIP) waiting between each of the workstations, which can be reduced. Also, the current VSM example in Figure 6.11 uses an MRP-controlled system using 90-, 60- and 30-day forecasts from the customer, and places daily orders. The ACME Company passes a six-week forecast and a weekly fax order to its supplier. Signals are sent to all steps in the process simultaneously; this is not a lean or efficient process.

Future State Value Stream Map

Once the current state VSM has been put together, the future state VSM has to be proposed. This is usually done by a team of people who know the process well, and know the principles and techniques of value stream mapping. The future state VSM is intended to show what a process could be like in the future, and how it could become leaner. The most important additional icons used in this future state VSM are shown in Figure 6.12.

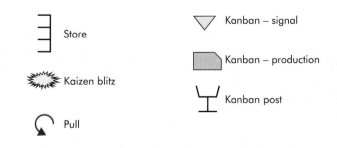

Figure 6.12 Further VSM icons

The main differences between the current state VSM and the future state VSM here are as follows:

- The customer is sending a more regular demand signal with smaller quantities to the manufacturer – in other words, the demand pattern is less 'lumpy'.
- The production controller or customer is sending one signal (a kanban signal – as detailed in Chapter 10) to the end of the process to create a 'pull' system.

> **Pacemaker task:** the task that dictates the speed of the overall process.

- Tasks have been consolidated and human resources reassigned to reduce waiting time. This results in the identification of the **pacemaker task**. This is the task that sets the pace of the overall process, and receives a signal direct from the customer through continually flowing processes – in other words, without any WIP held between it and the customer.
- 'Stores' are used only to help balance the production mix and volume, and not because tasks are overly fragmented.
- The supplier makes more frequent deliveries that are in smaller quantities – in other words, the deliveries are less 'lumpy'.

The steps taken to create this are as follows:

> **Takt time:** the time allowed by the customer for each unit of output to be produced.

1   Calculate the **takt time**. This is the time allowed by the customer for each unit of output to be produced; it is sometimes called the 'drumbeat' of the operation. It is calculated by using the following formula (which is explained further in Chapter 7):

Takt time = Overall equipment effectiveness / Average demand

2   Develop continuous flow in the process wherever possible – which is pulled directly by the customer's demand signal. This means that work in progress (WIP) and waiting times should both be reduced.

3   Use 'stores' only if necessary to control production where continuous flow cannot extend upstream any further back from the customer.

4   Try to send the customer demand to only one task in the production process. This should be as close to the end of the process as possible, to ensure that a customer driven pull system is established.

5   Distribute the production of different products/services evenly over time at the pacemaker task. At the pacemaker task the production mix of parts needs to be 'levelled' so that the customer gets what they have asked for when they asked for it.

6   Create an initial pull signal by releasing and withdrawing small, consistent increments of work at the pacemaker task to level the production volume.

7   Develop the ability to make 'every part every (EPE) day', then EPE shift, then EPE hour, in tasks further upstream from the pacemaker process.

8   Recalculate total lead time. Most savings will be made in the amount of waiting time. Steps 1–8 enable an operation to produce the smallest batch (or 'lot') size possible in the correct sequence (as shown in Figure 6.13 for ACME).

9   Finally, VSMs can also be used to identify further areas of improvement and levelling within the process – these are shown by the yellow 'kaizen burst' stars in Figure 6.13.

The main things to remember in relation to VSMs are that:

- An operation needs to work to the takt time set by the customer, and not the cycle times defined by an operation's actual capacity and capabilities.
- The most dramatic savings are often made by reducing wasted time between tasks, rather than in the actual tasks themselves, which is not always apparent prior to the mapping exercise.

For further details on VSM, read the guides by Rother and Shook (1999) and Bicheno (2004).

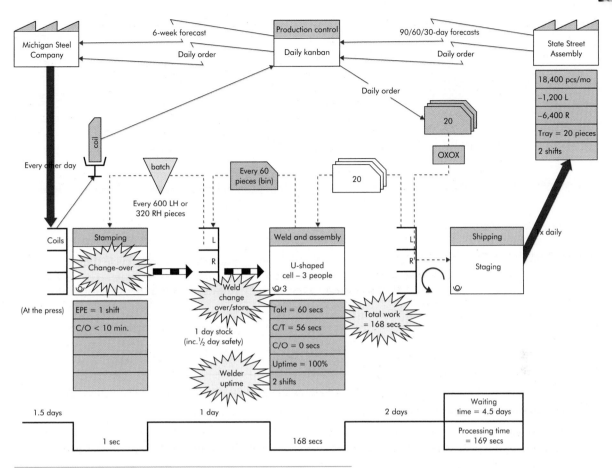

Figure 6.13 A future state value stream map: spare parts for tractors

---

WORKED EXAMPLE 6.2

Future State Value Stream Map for ACME Tractor Brackets

Problem: *Figure 6.13 shows a simple completed future state VSM for producing tractor spare parts (brackets). The waste in the process has been reduced. See if you can:*

(a) *Calculate the take time.*

(b) *Describe some ways in which the process has been made leaner.*

(c) *Calculate how much better the new lead time is in comparison with the old lead time in Figure 6.11.*

(d) *Say what other things ACME could do in terms of kaizen burst to make the process leaner.*

(a) **Approach:** Use the formula takt time = OEE / average demand

Solution: Assuming that ACME has 100% OEE we have 27,600 seconds in a working week, and the customer wants 18,400 pieces per month. Also, assuming that ACME has 20 working days per month with two shifts per day, then it has:

2 shifts × 20 days = 40 shifts

18,400 brackets / 40 shifts = 460 brackets per shift

or   27,600 seconds in a shift / 460 brackets = one bracket every 60 seconds

Therefore the takt time is 60 seconds.

(b) **Approach:** Carefully re-read the diagram and the notes on how it has been constructed.

Solution: The process has been made leaner by:

- Joining together the two welding and the two assembly tasks, and reducing the staffing requirement from four to three people
- Using kanban stores between the stamping and welding and assembly tasks, because the stamping machine works at a much quicker rate than any other tasks
- Sending the demand signal directly to the shipping task, which then pulls orders through the process as and when they are needed
- Creating a pacemaker task out of the newly created weld and assembly cell, because downstream is a continuous process pulled directly by the customer
- Achieving short production runs delivered in kanban trays of 20 parts in the ratio requested by the customer – 30 trays of LH brackets followed by 16 trays of RH brackets.

(c) **Approach:** Calculate the new lead time as in the previous worked example. Then calculate the difference.

Solution: ACME new total lead time = 4.5 days' waiting time + 169 seconds' cycle time

	Waiting time	Total cycle time (processing time)
Before	23.6 days	195 seconds
After	4.5 days	169 seconds
Difference	19.1 days	26 seconds

A significant improvement of 19.1 days' waiting time and 26 seconds' cycle time is achieved.

(d) **Approach:** Re-read the diagram and the notes on how it has been constructed.

Solution:

- Reduce changeover time and batch sizes at the stamping press, and aim to produce every part every shift.
- Eliminate the stores between stamping and welding to give an overall continuous flow of mixed production.
- Make the operators more efficient by making the welders and assemblers 100% OPE; this might be through training, better working conditions, or ergonomics.

Is Process Mapping Scientific Enough?

CRITICAL PERSPECTIVE

Some will say that process mapping is the single best way to apply **lean thinking** in an operation. It is an approach that analyses material and information flows with a view to eliminating time wastage and reducing the overall duration of the process lead time. The use of it has grown significantly in recent years.

Lean thinking: the elimination of waste.

Conversely, many people criticize process mapping for being too time consuming, and for producing nothing other than numerous pretty pictures. But those who make such criticisms are not necessarily seeing the wider purpose of the exercise, as the main purpose of a process-mapping exercise is not the process map itself, but the team building and organizational learning that come from having conducted the exercise. Many people working in operations find it difficult to think about the philosophical approach of systems thinking, and how to increase their process perspective on an operation; process modelling or mapping exercise can help overcome these obstacles.

It is true to say that process mapping uses a combination of science and art. Measurements of process performance can be taken using scientific equipment, but the representation, design and improvement of processes often fall to the experience, creativity and 'artistry' of operations managers. The real choice comes in deciding which particular sort of process map is most suitable for a particular process. For instance, if you are looking at a customer service process, then a service blueprint map may be best, or if you want to omit creative drawing, then use a process chart. Alternatively, if a measure of throughput is explicitly required, a VSM may be best the best option. Or if you are looking at a simple, low-volume process, a flow diagram may suffice.

The key point is that, whatever technique is used, process mapping must be a team exercise involving all the important stakeholders; process mapping is a tool to develop a collective vision for change, and needs to take a holistic, systems thinking approach.

Physical Layouts of Processes

Layout is a critical factor determining the long-term efficiency of an operation. Layout physically influences the organization's capacity, process operations, flexibility and cost, as well as the quality of work life, customer contact and image. Layout therefore has strategic implications: effective layout can help organizations achieve competitive advantage, whereas poor layout can have detrimental effects. Layout decisions include the best placement of machines (in production settings), of offices and desks (in office settings), or of service centres in hospitals, department stores, or local government offices.

> **Layout:** the physical configuration of departments, work centres, and equipment in an operation.

A good layout considers the following:

- *Materials handling equipment*: managers must make decisions about the equipment to be used, including conveyors, cranes, automated storage solutions and automatic vehicles. Materials handling costs should be minimized.
- *Capacity and space requirements*: only when personnel, machines and equipment requirements are known, can managers proceed with layout design and provide the necessary space for each part of the operation. Sometimes, though, extra space is used to create a feeling of opulence (as in the entrance to a bank, for example).
- *Environment and aesthetics*: factors such as air, noise, light, personal space, pollution and decor need to be considered. This is because a safe working environment is needed that keeps the morale of the workforce high.
- *Flows of information*: communication is important to any organization, and informal communication can be hindered or facilitated by a good physical layout. Where face-to-face communication is not possible, information technologies such as email and Internet-based systems must be used to complement physical communication and help the flow of information.
- *Cost of moving materials between work areas*: there may be special reasons for locating certain work areas together. For instance, there may be a high degree of traffic between them (e.g. customs and baggage collection in an airport), or it may be very difficult and expensive to move items between them (e.g. moving trucks between a paint shop and an assembly shop).
- *Appropriate levels of customer and employee interaction*: for example, a theme park should have highly visible, presentable and helpful staff.

Layout decisions are strategically important from an operational perspective because they can require large investments of time and money, which can result in long-term commitments to a particular configuration of machines and workspace. However, as the pace of industry quickens and product life cycles shorten, layout designs need to be viewed as dynamic. To make quick and easy changes in product ranges and production rates, operations managers must design flexibility into factory and warehouse layouts. This means considering small, movable, and flexible equipment – store displays need to be movable, office desks and partitions modular, and warehouse racks prefabricated and reconfigurable. To support this flexibility, managers must make sure their employees are multi-skilled, machinery is well maintained, and equipment is movable.

Different Types of Layout

There are three broad types of layout:

- *Fixed position layout*: where all activities cluster around the product or service being delivered. This type is used mainly in large-scale projects such as buildings, roads or ships, or large-scale events such as festivals or markets.
- *Product-service-dominant layout*: established to deliver one closely related group of products or services very efficiently, such as processing people through customs and immigration in an airport, or manufacturing LCD TV screens in a production facility. This layout type will deliver only one type of product or service, and so the product or service dominates the layout decision.
- *Process dominant layout*: concerned principally with setting up a generic process able to deal with a high variety of outputs, such as a general practitioner's surgery, or a mass customization production process. This layout type will deliver many different types of product and service, and so the process takes precedence over any one particular product or service.

A hybrid version of the above three is known as a *work cell layout*. Work cells are typically used to help balance load requirements on a facility while increasing variety and establishing a process around the most common or routine elements (e.g. a repair shop for items returned under warranty). They tend to use highly flexible machines and multi-skilled staff. Refer back to Table 6.2 to see a summary of how certain layouts are best suited to certain process and order types.

Fixed Position Layout

In a fixed position layout, the item being worked on remains stationary, and workers, materials and equipment are moved around as needed. The nature of the product generally determines this kind of arrangement; weight, size, bulk or fragility will make it undesirable or extremely difficult to move the product. Fixed position layouts are used for large products such as buildings, bridges and ships. This layout is also used in services such as open heart surgery and restaurant meals.

In fixed position layouts, attention is focused on the timing of deliveries of materials, equipment and people to the 'site' so that it does not become too hectic. The main requirements are that the fixed position layout has adequate space for its needs, supply and collection, and minimal movement of materials and people. Lack of storage space at the site can present significant problems – for example, at construction sites in crowded urban settings, or at banquets with large numbers of courses.

Because of the diverse range of activities carried out on large projects, and the wide range of skills required, special efforts are needed to coordinate the activities. For this reason a project management process is often preferred, as for the 2012 London Olympic Stadium, or the Virgin music festival case described earlier in Chapter 4.

Product-Service-Dominant Layout

Product-service layouts are used to achieve a smooth, rapid flow of high volumes of goods or customers through a process, such as people entering a cinema. This is made possible by high standardization and repetitive processing. Work is divided into a series of standardized tasks, permitting specialization of equipment and division of labour. The large volumes handled by these systems usually make it economical to invest substantial sums of money in equipment and job design.

Because only one (or a few closely related) product or service is being delivered by the process, it is possible to dedicate an entire layout to its processing requirements. For instance, if a portion of a manufacturing process required a sequence of cutting, bending and welding metal, the appropriate pieces of equipment could be arranged in that same dedicated sequence. Furthermore, because each item follows the same sequence of operations, it is often possible to utilize fixed-path material- or people-processing equipment, such as conveyor belts or moving walkways, between operations.

Product-service-dominant layouts are most applicable to continuous or assembly line processes (see Table 6.2 for a summary), such as car assembly. The main advantages with product-service-dominant layouts are efficiency and low unit cost. The main disadvantages are that they can create dull and repetitive working environments, require large capital investment, can be inflexible, and can be susceptible to breakdowns due to the high inter-dependency of tasks. Often, preventive maintenance and worker incentive schemes need to be put in place to help reduce the chance of breakdowns, worker boredom and output variations occurring.

In manufacturing environments, the layouts are referred to as *production lines* or *assembly lines*, depending on the type of activity involved. In a service environment, where people are usually being processed, these layouts are not always explicit, unless there is a visible queue of people (e.g. at airport security). However, the concept and principles of product-service layouts are just as valid in service environments.

Process-Dominant Layout

Process-dominant layouts are designed to process items or people that involve a variety of processing requirements. The variety of jobs requires frequent adjustments to equipment, such as retooling, and the use of operators with different skills. This causes a discontinuous (or discrete) workflow. Process-dominant layouts often feature departments or functional groupings.

A typical manufacturing example of a process layout is the machine shop, which has separate departments for milling, grinding, drilling, and so on. Items that require the same operations are usually moved in batches (or 'lots') to each departments in a sequence that varies from job to job. Consequently, variable-path materials-handling equipment (e.g. automatic guided vehicles, forklift trucks, hand carts) is needed to handle the variety of routes and items. The use of general-purpose equipment provides enough flexibility to handle the wide range of processing requirements. Workers who carry out the tasks and handle the equipment are usually skilled tradesmen.

Process layouts are also important for service environments. Examples include hospitals, universities, banks, garages, airlines, shops and public libraries. For instance, hospitals have departments specifically to handle surgery, maternity, paediatrics, physiotherapy, accidents and emergencies. Therefore, depending on the patient's condition, each one may take a specific route through departments. Another good example is given by IKEA, which has a very cleverly designed layout. From the moment customers arrive, to when they leave, the layout is designed to force them all to travel around every department in the store, including the restaurant.

In summary, process-dominant layouts are a 'jack of all trades and master of none' type of layout, as they can be used for many different products and services, but are not tailored to any particular one. The advantages of process-dominant layouts are that:
- They can handle a variety of processing requirements.
- They are not particularly vulnerable to equipment failures.
- General-purpose equipment is often less costly than specialized equipment.
- There is little interdependence between successive operations.

The disadvantages of process-dominant layouts are that:
- Inventory costs are high, as batch processing is often used.
- Routeing and scheduling pose continual challenges.
- Equipment utilization rates are low, because of routeing and scheduling complexities related to the variety of processing demands handled.
- Materials handling is slow and inefficient, relative to product-service-dominant layouts.
- Job complexity results in high supervisory costs.
- Special attention is necessary for each product in relation to routeing, scheduling, machine set-up, etc.

Work Cell Layout

A *work cell* is a hybrid version of product-service and process-dominant layouts. A work cell brings together people and machines that would normally be dispersed across various departments into a group, often known as a *job shop*, so that they can focus on making a single product or group of related products. Cellular work arrangements are used when volume warrants a special arrangement of machinery, people skills and equipment. The advantages of work cells are as follows:
- Work in progress inventory is reduced, because the work cell is set up to provide one-piece flow from task to task or machine to machine.

- Less floor area is required, because less space is needed between machines and tasks to accommodate work-in-progress inventory.
- Employee morale is better, because they feel more involved with the overall deliverables.
- Equipment and worker utilization is increased, because of quicker material flow, better scheduling, and more multi-skilled workers. This means that fewer machines and less capital investment are needed.
- Raw material and finished goods inventories are reduced, because reduced work in progress means more rapid movement of materials through the layout.
- Direct labour costs are reduced, because improved communication among employees, better material flow and improved scheduling are achieved.

The cellular production environment requires:

- Identification of families of products and services, often on the basis of shared processing equipment, parts or materials
- A high level of training, flexibility and empowerment of employees
- A self-contained facility with its own equipment, resources and quality.

A small restaurant could be considered a cell layout, where all the work is done in a specific area by a small team of people.

Designing Physical Layouts

Once the broad type of physical layout has been decided, the detailed design can take place. There are various techniques available, which are now discussed in more detail.

Fixed Position Layouts

In fixed position layouts, the location of resources will determined by how often the transforming resources such as equipment and workers can access the product being worked on. The detailed layout of some fixed position layouts, such as a building site, can become very complicated, especially if the planned schedule of activities is changed frequently. Imagine the chaos on a construction site if heavy machinery from different suppliers was continuously crossing paths, or if storage areas were put in inconvenient places.

Product-Service-Dominant Layouts

The goal of a product-service layout is to arrange workers or machines in the sequence in which they are needed for a specific product or service as efficiently as possible. The sequence is sometimes referred to as a *production line* or an *assembly line*; these can vary in length from short (e.g. making sandwiches) to long (e.g. making cars). The main benefit of assembly lines is the ability to divide work into a series of simple tasks, which may range from a few seconds to a few minutes. These tasks are typically bundled together and assigned to particular workstations and operators.

Deciding how to assign tasks to workstations is referred to as *line balancing*. The goal of line balancing is to obtain task groupings that represent approximately equal times. This minimizes the idle time along the line, and results in a high utilization of labour and equipment. Idle time occurs if task times are not equal among workstations, as some stations will be able to complete tasks quicker than others. The faster stations will experience periodic waits for the output from slower stations, or stand unutilized to avoid build-ups of work between stations downstream. Unbalanced lines are undesirable, as this situation leads to inefficient utilization of labour and equipment. Morale problems can also occur, as some workers may perceive they are working harder or faster than others.

Lines that are perfectly balanced will have a smooth flow of work, as activities along the line are synchronized to achieve maximum utilization of labour and equipment. The main obstacle to attaining a perfectly balanced line is the difficulty of forming task bundles that have the same duration. One cause of this is that it may not be feasible to combine certain activities into the same bundle, either because of differences in equipment requirements, or because the activities are not compatible (e.g. the risk of contaminating sensitive electrical equipment with dust). Line balancing can be achieved via calculation (see Chapter 10) or by value stream mapping.

Process-Dominant Layouts

The main issue in designing process-dominant layouts concerns the relative positioning of the departments involved. For example, some departments may benefit from adjacent location, whereas others need to be separated. For instance, a food preparation area should not be near a less sanitary area such as a packing bay. Conversely, two departments that share the same equipment or have high interdepartmental workflows would benefit from being close together. Layouts can also be influenced by external factors such as the location of entrances, loading docks, elevators, windows and areas of reinforced flooring. In some situations, such as super-markets or petrol stations, there may be a sufficient number of installations that a standardized layout will be defined.

Calculating a process-dominant layout requires the following information:
- A list of departments or work centres to be arranged, and their approximate sizes
- A projection of workflows and communication required between centres or departments
- An understanding of the distance between work centres or departments, and the cost per unit of distance to move loads between locations
- The size of the facility, and the amount of money to be invested in it
- Any special requirements, such as operations that need to be together or kept apart
- The location of key utilities or shared facilities such as access and exit points, toilets, or loading docks
- The sequence of flows.

If high-volume interactions or long distances are involved, for example moving thousands of items (or people) across a large site every day, the layout should be calculated mathematically using the formula

$$\text{Total cost of moving} = \text{Unit cost of moving} \times \text{Number of items to be moved}$$

WORKED EXAMPLE 6.3

Moving Items in a Process-Dominant Layout

An insurance company has two sites in a large town, and paper-based files have regularly to be moved between them. Every box of files that needs moving costs €20 (in time and petrol) to move. In an average week 100 boxes are moved.

Problem: *How much does it cost the insurance company per week to move these boxes around?*

Approach: Total cost of moving = Unit cost of moving × Number of items to be moved

Solution: 20 × 100 = 2,000

€2,000 per week is incurred

Note: Perhaps the company should think about relocating its offices onto a single site to save this cost.

If low volumes and small distances are involved, it often comes down to a heuristic management decision (i.e. an educated estimate or 'rule of thumb' decision).

Work-cell Layouts

The detailed design of cellular layouts first involves getting the right people and machines together, and then laying them out in the right shape. The basic variants for cell layouts are straight or U-shaped; see Figure 6.14. The main difference between these is in the placing of exit and entrance points, which may be influenced by the size and shape of the facility, and the overall operations that they are part of. U-shaped cells make it easier for people to share workstations, and may also be adapted into S-shaped or circular layouts.

Sometimes work cells can become large, and these are often referred to as *plants within a plant*; although these are an integral part of the overall organization, they may be capable of existing outside their parent organization, owing to their high level of autonomy and capability. Sometimes they may even be spun off to become separate new companies.

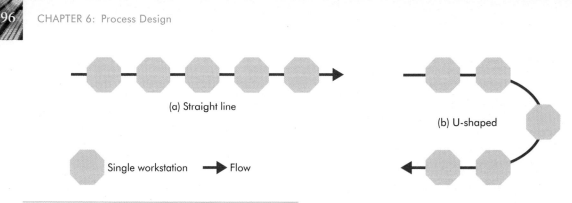

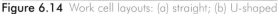

Figure 6.14 Work cell layouts: (a) straight; (b) U-shaped

SHORT CASE 6.3

Lay Out the Carpet

Source: © Lance Muil/iStock

Brintons Carpets has been a world-leading supplier of carpets to households and industrial clients across the world for over 200 years. Recent prestigious industrial clients include Changi Airport in Singapore, Cunard's *Queen Mary 2* cruise ship, and leading hotels and casinos.

Brintons' carpets are woven on looms that use a mixture of wool and other fibres. The looms are big, heavy machines that require careful set-up so that the products meet tight customer specifications. Each client will have provided exact specifications (shapes and sizes, colours and delivery requirements) for their carpet, all of which need to be met. The machines must be supplied with exactly the right type and colour of wool at the correct time.

After the carpet has been woven, it will be removed from the loom and transferred to another department for checking, trimming, backing and finishing, before being stored, delivered and installed at the client's site.

Questions

1   What type of process do you think Brintons uses for: (a) its domestic customers; (b) its industrial clients?
2   What types of order do you think Brintons typically gets?
3   What types of layout do you think Brintons uses during the design, manufacture and delivery of its carpets?

Source: Ben Clegg, Aston Business School and Phil Ellis, Brinton Carpets

---

❗ Stop and Think

4   What would be the consequences of using the wrong layout for a particular operation?

BUSINESS INTEGRATION

Technology in Processes

Operating a process will usually require the use of supporting technology. Whether it is a scanning machine for a hospital, a production robot for a factory, or a new IT system for an office, the decision to adopt the technology will need to consider cost, quality, capacity and flexibility. To make this decision, operations managers must carefully identify the necessary capacity, size, robustness and tolerances for the technology, as well as its ongoing maintenance requirements.

The correct selection of equipment for a particular type of process can provide competitive advantage for an organization. Many organizations develop unique process technologies to give added *flexibility*, lower cost or higher quality. Innovations and equipment modification may also allow for a more stable production process that requires less adjustment, maintenance and operator training.

Production Technology

In this section we shall introduce you to a range of production technologies. These are machine technology, automatic identification systems, process control, vision systems, robots, automatic storage and retrieval systems, automated guided vehicles, flexible manufacturing systems, and computer integrated manufacturing (CIM). It is common to find one or more of these technologies being used together in an integrated system.

Machine Technology

Machinery used for operations such as cutting, pressing and stamping, milling and drilling has made dramatic improvements in recent years. New machinery can cut metal components accurately to one micrometre (about 1/100th of a typical human hair), and assemble tiny *nano-machines* that can be used to operate inside our bodies. At the other end of the spectrum we have large powerful machinery, such as water-jet cutting tools so powerful they can be used to cut steel, or pneumatic hovering platforms so large that they can be used to move vehicles such as tanks along assembly lines. Machinery of the 21st century is considered to:

- Be five times more productive than that of previous generations
- Save more space and power
- Use more environmentally friendly materials, and allow for more recycling
- Be easier to control and operate quicker and more precisely.

Automatic Identification Systems and RFID

Most new processing technology (from manufacturing machinery to automatic teller/transaction machines) is controlled by digital signals. The challenge for operations management is to get data relating to physical items, materials and geographic locations accurate and up to date in computer systems. Until recently, data on physical things has been matched up manually with information in information systems; this can result in delays and errors. The first major advance in this area was the use of *bar codes* (labels with patterns that can be read by computers), which are attached to items or people. Typical applications have been stock control of materials, point-of-sale records in shops, and patient monitoring in hospitals. Bar codes require a visible line of sight between the reader and the object being read.

More recently, advances in technology have enabled *radio frequency identification* (RFID) to be used. RFID tags use integrated circuitry with their own aerials to send radio signals over a limited range (usually a few metres) to RFID readers. These tags can provide unique identification, which enables the tracking and monitoring of parts, pallets, people and pets – virtually anything that moves. Unlike a bar code reader, RFID requires no line of sight between the tag and the reader. Examples of RFID use include:

- The matching of records to patients, by including an RFID tag in their ID bracelet
- Tags on cars to locate where they are stored, and their product configuration (e.g. as used at Jaguar Land Rover)
- Tagging aircraft parts to monitor their history
- Finding out what is in a transportation container.

Process Control

Process control is the use of information technology to monitor and control a physical process. For instance, process control technologies can be used to measure the accuracy of printing, as printed material (such as stamps) can move over sensors at hundreds of metres per second to be automatically checked. Process control is also used to determine and control temperatures, pressures and qualities in petroleum refineries, cement plants, steel mills, nuclear reactors, and other process focused facilities. Process controlled systems operate as follows.

1   Sensors periodically collect data such as size, colour intensity and moisture.

2   This data is transmitted to a computer, which analyses it, and looks for variations in outputs and deviations from acceptable tolerances.

3   The output from the computer analysis may be a warning message on a computer screen, or a text to a personal digital device.

Process control is important to make sure that problems in the process are detected quickly.

Vision Systems

Vision systems combine video cameras and computer technologies, such as face, colour and shape recognition software. Visual inspection is an important task in most processing and manufacturing industries, but can be extremely monotonous, tedious, error prone, and even hazardous for humans to do. Vision systems enable visual inspection to be automated. Examples include inspecting the insides of brewing vats for beer making, gas pipelines, and parcel sorting on mail delivery systems.

Robots

Robots are mechanical devices controlled by computers. Today, robots can perform very complex tasks, at high speeds, very efficiently. They are best suited to highly repetitive, high-volume tasks that are monotonous, heavy, dangerous, or can be improved by the substitution of human effort. For example, Toyota uses robots to do welding on car bodies.

Automated Storage and Retrieval Systems

Warehouses can be computer controlled; computer and machinery can be used together to automatically store, record and retrieve items. These systems, known as *automated storage and retrieval systems*, often work without any human intervention. Such systems are operated by large logistic suppliers in their warehouses.

Automated Guided Vehicles

Automated guided vehicles (AGVs) are electronically controlled carts that are used to move parts and equipment around large facilities. They are used in car factories to move parts, in mail-sorting depots to move packages, and in hospitals to move meals around. They are often part of a wider automated system.

Flexible Manufacturing Systems

When a central computer is used to instruct each workstation and the materials handling equipment (which moves material between stations), the system is known as a *flexible manufacturing system* (FMS). An FMS is flexible because both the materials handling devices and the machines themselves are controlled by computer programs. Operators simply load new programs to manage different processes and produce different products. The result is a system that can economically produce low volumes and high varieties, as the cost associated with low utilization and changeover is substantially reduced. FMSs bridge the gap between product-service-dominant layouts and process-dominant layouts.

Computer-Integrated Manufacturing

Flexible manufacturing systems can be extended into the engineering and design, and inventory control departments. FMSs can also be electronically extended into the warehousing and shipping departments. In this way, *computer-aided design* (CAD) can generate the necessary electronic instructions to run a robot or an FMS. In a computer-integrated manufacturing environment, a design change to a part initiated at a CAD terminal can automatically result in changes being made to what is being manufactured on the shop floor in a matter of minutes. When this capability is integrated with inventory control, warehousing and shipping as part of a flexible manufacturing system, the entire system is called a *computer-integrated manufacturing* (CIM) system.

Table 6.4 Technology in services

Service industry	Example
Financial	Debit cards, electronic funds transfer, cash machines (ATMs), Internet based (e.g. stocks and shares, mortgages), paying-in machines
Education	Online journals, newspapers, virtual learning environments (VLEs) such as WebCT or Blackboard, classroom technology (e.g. classroom projectors)
Utilities and government	Online tax payments (e.g. car, company, TV), flood warning systems, congestion charges, variable road speed systems, public utility vehicles
Restaurants and foods	Wireless ordering, table booking and payment systems, robot butchering, air-conditioning, milking machines for cows, rotating tables or conveyor belts to access food
Communications	Electronic publishing, interactive TV, mobile devices (e.g. PDAs)
Hotels	Express check-in and out, automatic room billing, swipe keys
Wholesale/retail trade	Point-of-sale recording, e-commerce sites, use of bar codes and RFID tags, visual observation systems
Transportation	Public transport, automated toll booths, satellite navigation devices
Health care	Online patient health (e.g. blood pressure) monitoring
Airlines	Ticketless travel, Internet purchases, self-check-in, moving walkways, scanners for baggage and people
Leisure	Gym machines, wireless hotspots to access the Internet (e.g. social networking sites), video games

FMSs and CIM are reducing the distinction between low-volume/high-variety and high-volume/low-variety production. Information technology is allowing FMSs and CIM to handle increasing variety while expanding to include a growing range of volumes. Through the use of technology, mass customization is made possible.

Service Technology

Service technologies have also changed dramatically in recent years. Service technologies include diagnostic equipment at garages when cars are being serviced, security scanners at airports, and automatic machines in banks, hotels and restaurants. These are all aimed at either increasing flexibility or reducing costs. We can see self-check-in machines in low-priced hotels, self-service counters in fast-food restaurants, and many different types of self-service machine in banks.

Many of the fundamental technologies used in services are the same as in production, although their use is usually focused more on moving people (e.g. the customers) and information around, rather than parts and products. Table 6.4 summarizes some typical examples of service technologies.

We take many of these service technologies for granted, as they have become embedded into processes that we use all the time (there are many examples of service technologies in the opening case).

How the Mighty Amazon Flows

Jeff Bezos founded Amazon in 1994 in Seattle, USA. Since then Amazon has become one of the leaders in Internet-based shopping. Many people see Amazon as purely an online company that provides shopping services, but much of its success has been due to its extensive investment in technology – both front-end web technology and back-end process technology. This is essential for Amazon, as it predominantly retails physical products that need to be physically moved.

Amazon has software development centres, fulfilment and warehousing centres based all around the world, as well as many business partners, such as logistic carriers. Its online ordering process has to link seamlessly to its picking, packing and shipping operations. This requires it to have advanced information technology that drives the whole order fulfilment process.

Other companies, such as Webvan (a USA online grocery company), were not originally successful, as they did not anticipate the scale and complexity of the offline operations investment, and they went bankrupt quickly. Amazon learned quickly how to utilize process technology effectively, and has grown through research, development and implementation of new process technologies, as well as by partnering with other technology companies (e.g. print-on-demand book suppliers such as Lightning Source).

Questions

1   Could a company like Amazon have existed before Internet-based technology?
2   Which process technologies do you think Amazon uses for competitive advantage?
3   How do you think Amazon should use process technology to position itself against online competitors such as eBay, or retailers with stores such as Barnes & Noble?

Source: Ben Clegg, Aston Business School

Stop and Think

5   How many process technologies do you use in an average day that provide you with some kind of value?

Summary

The content of this chapter is fundamental to every operation, as it describes the process of how work gets done – or, to put it another way, how things become transformed from inputs into outputs, using various resources along the way. The chapter initially focused on designing processes to match the types of order they receive, and to ensure that they use the correct layout. Systems thinking is fundamental to good process management, because all processes are systems that need to be carefully integrated and controlled.

When designing and managing processes, factors such as volume, variety, order type, layout and the extent of mass customization all need to be taken into account. Often the best way to design or improve a process is to map it out using a process-mapping technique. These are used to develop group consensus, visualize the process, and debate future improvements.

Processes utilize people, knowledge and technology. How they are put together requires a mix of scientific principles, artistry, experience and technical know-how – all of which can have a fundamental impact on how well organizations perform.

Key Theories

- **Systems thinking** – a system is a complex whole, the functioning of which depends on its parts and the interactions between those parts. We can easily think of many different types of system: natural (e.g. river systems), biological (e.g. living bodies), designed (e.g. cars), abstract (e.g. religions), social (e.g. families), and human activity (e.g. business and organizations). Thinking about these systems is known as systems thinking. Operations management is founded upon systems thinking, as all processes are systems.

- **Volume and variety** – this is a simple but fundamental idea. It states that for an operation to work effectively and efficiently it must either be high-volume/low-variety or high-variety/low-volume. Any other combination, unless supported by advanced management thinking and technology, is likely to fail.

- **Order type** – the three basic order types are make to order, make to stock and assemble to order. Each type is suited to different types of physical layout and process management. Each order type fundamentally changes the way that the operation is run, and the philosophical approach of the managers. Mixing different types of order successfully is difficult to do, and requires careful planning.

- **Process layout** – there are three basic process layout types: fixed position, product-service dominant and process dominant. Each of these is suited to a certain type of order and process management approach. Getting the layout wrong can cause inefficiency.

Key Equations

$$\text{Takt time} = \frac{\text{Overall equipment effectiveness}}{\text{Average demand}}$$

$$\text{Total cost of moving} = \text{Unit cost of moving} \times \text{Number of items to be moved}$$

Suggested Answers to Stop and Think Questions

1 **Systems thinking:** Operations would become better. This is because a business operation is a complex organizational system that has many different elements, which cannot create value by themselves. It is important to ensure that all the parts work together, so that their total value is greater than the sum of their individual parts. This requires combining functional and process thinking to give a holistic, systems perspective, rather than a reductionist perspective that will tend to produce sub-optimal thinking.

2 **Dead zone:** If the process falls into the top right-hand corner, the chances are that it will be very complicated, and far too expensive to operate cost-effectively, unless a mass customization approach is adopted. This is because of the high-volume and high variety combination. If the process falls into the bottom left-hand corner then the chances are that scales of economies are not being met, owing to low volume and low variety, resulting in a high unit cost. The organization should either remain as a low-volume operator and offer more variety, or keep to low variety and increase volume.

3 **Mass customization:** Generally speaking, any product or service that has a high propensity for customers to want to tailor the specification to their own requirements, and to be willing to pay for that, is able to use a mass customization approach. Services might include, online shopping, wedding reception organization, car maintenance or home help services, for example. Products could include car, shoe or clothing manufacture. This is made feasible by using advanced IT (e.g. Internet-based systems that link up with 'back end' manufacturing operational systems), computer-controlled production machinery (e.g. assembly robots and electronic packing and sorting systems) and advanced operations management practices. Often mass production has not been adopted because one or more of the above factors is not known about or present.

4 **Wrong layout:** Using the wrong layout type could result in an inefficient process, producing poor-quality output. At best this could result in wasteful practices, overcrowding, confusion, etc. At worst it could endanger the people (employees and customers) who work in the operational layouts.

5 **Process technologies:** Start with any typical morning: there will normally be a process that you follow (e.g. get up, get dressed, eat, travel to college or work, etc.). This will probably use both stand-alone technologies (e.g. toaster, car, shower) and more complicated systems (e.g. TV, Internet, railway, Satnav). Without process technologies, our lives would be hugely different.

connect™

Review Questions

1 What is holistic thinking?

2 Name one product and one service that is suited to each of a (a) continuous, (b) assembly line, (c) batch, (d) job shop and (e) project type of production process, and state why they are suited.

3 Name one product and one service that is best delivered via (a) make to stock, (b) assemble to order and (c) make to order type of process. Why?

4 Name one product and one service that is best suited to (a) a product-service-dominant layout, (b) a process-dominant layout, (c) a work cell and (d) a fixed position layout. Why?

5 Describe what happens at the 'point of customization'.

6 List the reasons for conducting a process-mapping exercise.

7 State how different sorts of technology can help manufacturing and services operate more efficiently.

Discussion Questions

1 Discuss what would happen in an organization if there were no clearly defined operational processes.

2 (a) Think of an organization that you are familiar with (e.g. airport, college, or workplace) and then think of a particular product or service it supplies. Use Table 6.2 in this chapter to try to characterize the process that is used. Do you think it is effective? If not, how should it be improved?
   (b) Using the same organization, discuss the most suitable type of order, and state why it is suitable.

3 Have a go at sketching the layout of the organization you have used in question 2, and try to make it as efficient as possible. Discuss why you have sketched it as you have.

Problems

1 A process has three tasks, A, B and C. A takes 40 seconds, B 10 seconds and C 5 seconds. The waiting time between A and B is 10 minutes, and the waiting time between B and C is 2 hours. What is (a) the total cycle time, (b) the total lead time?

2 If a weekly shift is 2,400 minutes long, and a customer requires 9,600 units to be produced, what is the takt time?

3 A large electronics company has a head office and a semi-autonomous manufacturing cell on a single, large site. Large amounts of paperwork and product pass between them. One of the locations has to be removed and merged with the other. 100 parts per month are moved from the manufacturing cell to the head office, at a cost of €250 per 100 for final checking. 500 files of paperwork are moved between the head office and the manufacturing cell per week to help with the planning and production process, at €10 per 100. There are no conflicting layout issues.

   On the basis of this information alone, would you recommend closing the head office or the semi-autonomous manufacturing cell in order to minimize travel and its associated costs?

4 (a) If a process had a total cycle time of 30 minutes and a customer required a takt time of 20 minutes, would this be satisfactory to the customer?
   (b) If a process had a total cycle time of 30 minutes and a customer required a takt time of 50 minutes, would this be satisfactory to the producer?

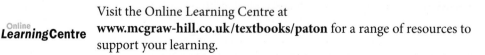

Visit the Online Learning Centre at **www.mcgraw-hill.co.uk/textbooks/paton** for a range of resources to support your learning.

Further Reading

Checkland, P.B. and Poulter, J. (2006) *Learning for Action*, Wiley, Chichester.

Hammer, M. (1997) 'Beyond the end of management', in *Rethinking the Future*, R. Gibson (ed.), Nicholas Brealey Publishing, London, pp. 95–105.

Pidd, M. (ed.) (2004) *Systems Modelling: Theory and Practice*, Wiley, Chichester.

Senge, P. (1990) *The Fifth Discipline: The Art and Practice of the Learning Organization*, Doubleday, New York.

References

Bicheno, J. (2004) *The New Lean Toolbox: Towards Fast Flexible Flow*, PICSIE Books, Buckingham.

Deming, W.E. (1999) *Metal Centre News*, **39**(6), 123.

Grover, V. and Malhotra, M.K. (1997) 'Business process re-engineering: a tutorial on concept, evolution, method, technology and application', *Journal of Operations Management*, **15**(3), 193–213.

Hayes, R.H. and Wheelwright, S.C. (1979) 'Line manufacturing process and product life cycles', *Harvard Business Review*, Jan–Feb, 133–140.

Rother, M. and Shook, J. (1999) *Learning to See: Value Stream Mapping to Add Value and Eliminate Muda*, Lean Enterprise Institute, Brookline, MA.

Shostack, G.L. (1984) 'Designing services that deliver', *Harvard Business Review*, **62**(1), 133–139.

PART THREE

Managing

Contents

Chapter 7: Capacity Planning and Management   207

Chapter 8: Supply Chain and Supply Relationship Management   239

Chapter 9: Inventory Planning and Management   275

Chapter 10: Lean Operations and Just in Time (JIT)   309

Chapter 11: Project Management   333

JOBS

WANTED
Managing Director

We are currently undergoing a period of rapid growth and have ambitious plans for the future. As Managing Director, you will play a central role in developing strategy and controlling operational activity. Leading a team of operations experts, your key challenge will be to create additional capability in our world-class manufacturing and service delivery.

This position has total responsibility for all operational activity including:

1) The translation of corporate strategy into operational activity while setting and meeting performance targets

2) Developing core competences and world-class operational processes

3) Management of all operational staff in design, production, supply chain and service delivery areas

The right candidate will have at least 10 years of proven success driving business improvement, experience of managing large budgets, and knowledge of current operations management methodologies and principles. Most importantly, you will be an inspirational leader, capable of motivating, coaching and getting the best from your team.

What does it take to become a Managing Director?

We speak to Dave Piper at Lightning Source UK Ltd to find out.

Name: Dave Piper

Age: 46

Current position: Managing Director, Lightning Source UK Ltd, an Ingram Content Group Inc. company

Years in role: 2

How did you get into Operations Management?

I qualified as a chartered management accountant while working for Smith and Nephew Ltd as a trainee accountant, and worked on well-known brands such as Nivea, Simple and Elastoplast. The desire to broaden my experience led me into roles in sales and marketing, project management and finally the supply chain, working as Operations Director for Beiersdorf UK Ltd.

What about the career attracted you?

Leadership has always been a passion of mine, from an early age, on sports pitches to today in business. Over the past 15 years, supply chain solutions that add value to the customer have become a critical differentiation between high-performing companies and those that cease to exist.

What other jobs have you done?

My career path from finance in a fast-moving consumer goods company to Managing Director of a print-on-demand company is not exactly typical! However, I have found a broad knowledge of different business functions, a passion for leadership, and knowledge of working in different industries has been a strong base for my career development.

What was the most useful experience that prepared you for your current role?

No single experience stands out, but having the ability to relate to people across the whole business certainly helps.

What's a typical day in the life of a Managing Director?

What I like most about my role is that no two days are the same. Each day brings new challenges and opportunities to improve the business, my team and myself.

What aspects do you like most about your job and why?

Engaging the minds of all our staff to find ways to enhance performance by improving quality, and producing books faster and more efficiently.

What do you consider the ideal skills for your job/role?

A willingness to listen, the ability to implement change, and a passion for leadership.

If you weren't in operations management, what would you be doing?

I would definitely be playing centre forward for West Bromwich Albion!

Where do you see yourself in ten years' time?

Hopefully touring the world watching England play cricket!

Waitrose and the Delia effect

The supermarket industry has regularly used advertising and special offers to increase both overall demand for its stores and also demand for individual and seasonal products.

Waitrose, the high-end supermarket chain, recently abandoned its policy of not working with celebrities to endorse its products, by signing two world-famous celebrity chefs on a three-year deal. Delia Smith, a recipe writer, leading author and TV presenter joined forces with Heston Blumenthal, a maverick chef, famed for egg and bacon ice cream, cooking with dry ice, and other such inventive creations in the kitchen, to front the advertising campaign.

The campaign involves Smith and Blumenthal filming a series of television advertisements, as well as appearing on billboards and in magazine features. The advertising strategy for Waitrose is to demonstrate a number of seasonal products being used in a recipe every week, in television commercials, backed up by a poster campaign and in-house special offers. Most of the ads are short cookery programmes, with one or both of the cooks demonstrating the various recipes; some ads last the whole advertising break of three and a half minutes. Richard Hodgson, Waitrose's

Source: © Waitrose

▶ commercial director, said: 'Every week will be a totally amazing new idea. Sometimes it will be a recipe, sometimes visiting a supplier or farmer, maybe even demonstrating a kitchen utensil.' He promised that viewers would not be bombarded with some of Blumenthal's more wacky recipes. 'Don't worry; we won't start selling snail porridge or liquid nitrogen. But I don't see why Heston couldn't demonstrate how a blowtorch can be used to get the top of crème brûlée crispy.'

Ocado, Waitrose's distribution partner, has restructured its website to allow customers to order products direct from the online recipe. Waitrose has allocated prime locations on the end of the refrigerated isles, with all the ingredients for the week's campaign grouped together and on a special offer price.

It has not all been plain sailing, though. The campaign received criticism for the timing of a particular ad for Delia Smith's rhubarb and ginger brûlée. The ad was screened so early in the year that British rhubarb growers were unable to meet the large resulting demand. The well-known phenomenon of the 'Delia effect' meant that Waitrose sold enough of the plant for 61,000 desserts in four days alone, or the same quantity that it usually sells in 12 weeks. British growers said they simply could not meet the spike in demand. Much of Britain's rhubarb is grown in a small area of West Yorkshire between Bradford, Wakefield and Leeds known as the Rhubarb Triangle. Early in the year growers 'force' it by growing the plant in heated sheds, but there is limited capacity. Janet Oldroyd, of the Yorkshire Rhubarb Growers' Association, said this season's crop had been delayed by cold weather, further reducing output. A Waitrose spokesman said that sales of rhubarb were 'so extreme' following the recipe being published online that it had to source from abroad.

A Delia recipe for fish risotto caused a backlash even from diehard Delia fans, when it was described as 'vile' on the discussion section of the Waitrose website. One customer wrote, 'I bought the very expensive ingredients for the seafood risotto, expecting to lay on a treat for my family. We all had one mouthful and gagged. It was disgusting, to say the very least. The entire meal went in the bin, and we all had toast instead.' Following the initial reactions to the recipe from news programmes, Waitrose appeared to be left with excess stock of the ingredients.

There is a requirement when planning these campaigns for Waitrose to have a greater understanding of what might impact upon supply of the products, and how much is likely to be demanded. This must be done within the supply chain, and the supermarket may need to be flexible within this plan to prevent further problems. Overall, however, Waitrose has seen an increase in demand for its products, and is encouraging customers to be more seasonal with their selection of goods. This enables the suppliers to meet the supermarket's demand more easily.

Sources: Telegraph online; Daily Mail online, BBC News

Demand: is the quantity of goods and services demanded by consumers.

Capacity: is the maximum goods or services that an operation can produce.

Introduction

The case demonstrates how complicated it can be to deal with the unpredictability of demand, and how difficult it can be to match this to the supply of goods and services and still have an efficiently run operation. The difficulty of meeting customer shopping patterns (**demand**) with what the suppliers and therefore the supermarket can provide (**capacity**) is a complicated timing issue (*forecasting*). Providing the right amount of product at the correct time requires careful planning and investment decisions.

There are three things an operation must consider when looking at production of goods and services:

- *Capacity*: How much can it make?
- *Demand*: How much does the market require?
- *Forecasting*: How can the operation match what is required with what it can make, without wasting resources?

These factors all impact upon each other. In order to fulfil the requirements of a market, an operation must be able to evaluate what capacity it can provide, and the options it has to increase or decrease this.

It is not just a case of offering the amount of goods or services wanted; it is also important to time when they are required. This can give an operation several problems when attempting to plan capacity.

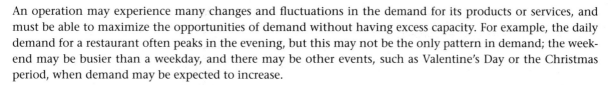

An operation may experience many changes and fluctuations in the demand for its products or services, and must be able to maximize the opportunities of demand without having excess capacity. For example, the daily demand for a restaurant often peaks in the evening, but this may not be the only pattern in demand; the weekend may be busier than a weekday, and there may be other events, such as Valentine's Day or the Christmas period, when demand may be expected to increase.

The provision of capacity is a decision that should not be taken lightly; once implemented it cannot easily be reversed, and the operation is then left to manage the choice it has made.

This chapter considers how capacity can be provided, adjusted and managed in order to satisfy the customer's demand and meet the operation's objectives, as efficiently as possible.

Capacity Management

Capacity management affects all areas of an operation. Capacity measures the rate at which the operation can transform inputs into outputs. Capacity is about the *quantity* of a product or service that can be delivered within a *given time period*. This could be, for example:

- The number of passengers per flight on an aeroplane
- The number of patients who can be seen in a surgery session at a doctors' practice
- The number of mobile phones that can be produced in a week by a factory.

Capacity is defined as the number of units (of goods and/or services) that an operation can produce over a given time period, under normal working conditions, without deploying additional resources.

Capacity is usually measured in convenient units, such as litres per hour or passengers per taxi. For instance, a domestic tap may be able to deliver 20 litres of water per minute; a bus may have a capacity of 53 passengers; a football stadium may be able to seat 50,000 spectators; or a branch of McDonald's may be able to serve 600 customers per hour.

Capacity may often be simple to calculate, but not always. More difficult questions might be, for example:

- How many fire engines should an airport have on standby?
- How many operations should a surgeon schedule?
- What service level should be offered to broadband customers?

When planning capacity, there are always two aspects to consider. First, there is the demand – the amount of the product or service that might be wanted. Second, there is the provision of the good or service. In providing products or services, the operation must evaluate the costs involved, and the trade-off between satisfying customers and the costs of production. Having too little capacity to respond to customer demand may mean missed opportunities and annoyed customers, but underutilized capacity is a waste of resources, resulting in higher costs.

Adjusting Capacity

Discrepancies between an organization's capacity and its customers' demands result in inefficiency, either in underutilized resources or in dissatisfied customers. The former may be a serious cost, but the latter may result in lost sales, lost customers, and loss of reputation. The operation's ability to adjust its key resources will minimize these discrepancies.

Some capacity changes can happen almost instantly, but others may take longer to put in place. An operation's capacity is a complicated mix of transforming resources. Resources are inputs to the process that allow capacity to be expanded or contracted, by changing the inputs into the process. How flexible the resource is depends on how much and how quickly it can be altered.

Capacity can be increased by various methods that involve adjusting the resources and inputs into an operation, such as:

- Introducing new approaches and materials
- Increasing the number of service providers or machines
- Increasing the number of operational hours
- Acquiring additional facilities.

It can be more difficult or expensive to decreasing capacity; it tends to rely on the operation's ability to sell or reduce resources as cost-effectively as possible. There are usually costs involved in reducing resources: for example, if the resource is staff, there may be redundancy costs; and closing facilities may incur significant costs.

Therefore the decision to alter capacity has to be taken carefully, in line with predictions of future demand.

Capacity Constraints

Constraint: is a restriction on the running of an operation.

A **constraint** on capacity is a resource that is less capable of increasing or decreasing its throughput over a given time period, in comparison with other parts of the operation. For example, in a sequence of machines on a manufacturing line, one may not be able to process as many units per hour as the others. Capacity will be constrained by this underproducing machine, creating a bottleneck in the process. It may be possible to increase the capacity of this machine by adding additional resources, or replacing the machine for a more effective one, which will increase the capacity of the overall facility.

Capacity is always constrained by the slowest or smallest-capacity task in a process: an operation will always go 'at the pace of the slowest walker'. Identifying restrictions in the process, and adding resources that can increase the output of the constraint, will improve the overall capacity of the operation.

The *resource mix,* made up of the individual transforming inputs, can potentially constrain an operation. The elements of the mix include:
- *Staff/skill levels*: Staff can be trained over time to be more flexible in their contribution to the process. A new employee can become more efficient at a given process over time and therefore become quicker at his or her job, which can increase the capacity of the operation.
- *IT facilities/technology*: This can provide a small or a very significant improvement to a process. Investment in IT can reduce process time, or even completely change the nature of the process itself. For example, online banking has been a significant improvement in the finance sector, by reducing the number of staff required to process individual transactions, and therefore massively increasing the bank's capacity to deal with its customers.
- *Materials availability*: A change in the supply of raw materials can affect the capacity potential of an operation. If there is a restriction in the availability of materials, or a timing problem, this can reduce capacity. Once this is remedied, the capacity can be improved.
- *Product or service mix*: Adjustments in other products or services that the operation delivers can restrict its capacity. This is because different products and services may use different quantities of resource per unit, and therefore a change in the product mix may result in a change in capacity.
- *Storage*: This can affect an operation's capacity if there is a resource constraint affected by timing in the process. If an operation has the ability to store work in progress, or finished goods it can improve the capacity of the process in the short term. The swings and fluctuations in demand can be mitigated by the ability to store products and allow the full capacity of an operation to flow.
- *Working schedules and access to facilities*: This can also dictate the full availability of capacity. A lecture theatre that can accommodate 100 students at a time could operate beyond a standard working day, but both staff and students might have a problem with 6 a.m. lectures!

These factors can be addressed in varying time frames. Some can be easily dealt with in the short term, but others can only be addressed in the long term. For instance, a short-term strategy for expanding a café's capacity would be to put a few extra tables outside, or extend staff working hours to cope with the extra demand. In the medium term the café owner would have more options available to increase capacity, such as hiring more staff, or installing additional cooking facilities in the kitchen to cope with extra demand. In the long term the possibilities can be much greater: the premises could be expanded, better equipment could be purchased, and more staff could be hired. The options available to an operation increase if there is more time to plan and implement them.

Theory of Constraints

The theory of constraints (TOC) was proposed by Eliyahu Goldratt in 1984. It is the practical results of his work on 'how to think'. TOC is a philosophy that suggests that any system always has *at least one constraint*, otherwise it would generate an infinite amount of output, and that constraints generally determine the pace of an organization's ability to achieve its goal, which is profit.

Goldratt emphasizes that constraints pose a significant threat to the well-being of an organization, and must be identified. He suggests that constraints may be labour availability, staff skills, machine availability, and capital or time available – or they may be more difficult to identify, such as organizational policies, guiding principles, or the rate of innovation.

There is rarely an equal flow of work within each work centre or task in a process. The constraint – the bottleneck – therefore controls the pace of the process. TOC reduces emphasis on maximizing all resources within a process, and instead prioritizes management of the bottleneck. Goldratt advocates a methodology he calls *drum–buffer–rope*. The bottleneck is the 'drum' that marks the time through the process; because of insufficient capacity in this section, this should be continually busy. The 'buffer' is required to make sure that the bottleneck is never short of work, and therefore the front end of the process should stockpile inventory to maximize throughput. The 'rope' is the communication device that makes sure the front part of the process does not *over*produce.

Goldratt's Five Focusing Steps

TOC sets out a five-step process that an operation should follow in order to free the system from the bottleneck that is slowing it down:

1   Identify the system's bottleneck and what exactly constrains the process.

2   Exploit the system's constraints, and establish the resources required to remove them.

3   Subordinate everything else to the above decision. This requires full management support to make sure that this remains the priority.

4   Elevate the system's constraints (identify the next constraint). Once this bottleneck is removed the next part of the process needs to be found.

5   If a constraint has been removed in a previous step, go back to step 1, but do not allow inertia to become the system's constraint.

By following these steps the operation identifies and clears the blockage. This will then in turn reveal a new bottleneck, and the five steps can start again.

Goldratt advises that the identification of any constraint is only transitional. When this constraint is removed, another will appear in its place.

Constraint analysis is a subject far larger than the subject of capacity management, but it does offer an important perspective on the question 'Is all capacity equally important?'

SHORT CASE 7.1

Wind Energy: Where's the Constraint?

According to the China Wind Energy Association, the power output generated by wind farms in China has not met expectations. Less than 80% of the power created has reached the national grid. The reason given for this underperformance is that, although new wind farms and turbines have been set up and are working as planned, their output has not been reaching the grid effectively for around the first three to four months

Differences in wind resources can partly explain the disparity, but insufficient investment in grid connections played a key part. The problem appears to be that the regions where wind resources are most abundant tend to have the weakest grid connections. In addition, some wind farms are generating more power than initial estimates, and their output has been rejected by the local grid companies because of concerns that it would overload their systems.

Wind farms generally have smaller generation capacity than coal-fired power plants, and their output is less stable, as they are subject to variable wind speed. As a result, the return on investment from wind power is lower for grid operators. The utilization rate of mainland wind farms in China is currently much lower than that of comparable projects operating in the UK or USA.

▶

The key point is a constraint will restrict the operation's capacity. If this constraint is reduced, or even removed, capacity will increase. A constraint can be reduced by increasing the resource in the bottleneck.

Measuring Capacity

When measuring capacity, the unit of measure can be either an input to or an output from the process. The key is to take the unit that best reflects the operation's ability to create and deliver its product or service. If inputs are too complicated to measure, then output measures may be more suitable. For example, factories are more often measured on units produced per day than on machine-hours utilized; and retail units can be measured on takings per day rather than on staff-hours employed. A suitable unit of measure could be volume, size, or rate of throughput, for example, but the unit of output and timescale needs to be *consistent*, i.e. if you start measuring your capacity in hotel *rooms* available it is not comparable to switch to number of *beds* available.

Input Measures of Capacity

Where the provision of capacity is fixed, it is often easier to measure capacity by inputs, for example, rooms available in a hotel or seats at a conference venue. When using input measures of capacity, the measure selected is defined by the key input into the process. Input measures are most appropriate for small processes, or where capacity is relatively fixed, or for highly customized or variable outputs, such as complicated services.

Output Measures of Capacity

Output measures count the finished units from the process, such as mobile phones produced in a day, or cars manufactured per week. They are best used when there is low variety in the product mix, or limited customization.

Capacity can be measured by looking at the operation as a whole, and then calculating the resources and facilities available and the process time. Table 7.1 shows examples of the alternatives that can be used for input and output measures.

For example, the measure of output capacity could be cars per shift, or tonnes per hour, or customers per day. However, the capacity of a surgeon or a university professor may not be measured in this manner: in these cases, capacity could be shown in the form of working hours per week.

Table 7.1 Examples of possible input and output measures

Process	Input capacity measure	Output capacity measure
Music festival	Square metres of land	Number of festival attendees
Hotel	Rooms available	Number of guests per week
Car-manufacturing plant	Machine capacity	Cars produced per month
Milk-bottling plant	Machine-hours available	Bottles filled per day
Lecture theatre	Number of seats available	Students on courses
Wedding planning service	Consultants available	Weddings per season

A simple formula for capacity is:

$$\text{Capacity} = \frac{\text{Time available}}{\text{Time needed for task}}$$

Calculating Output

A fitness instructor works an 8-hour day, takes two 15-minute coffee breaks, and has a half-hour lunch break. The time available for work is seven hours per worker per day.

Problem: *If the instructor spends 70 minutes with each customer (10 minutes for the consultation and booking, and 1 hour for the gym session), how many clients could the instructor process during a five-day week?*

Approach

$$\text{Capacity} = \frac{\text{Time available}}{\text{Time needed for task}}$$

where *time available* is the hours in the day for working (which excludes breaks), and the number of days worked in the week. The example has an eight-hour working day with an hour for breaks: this leaves 7 hours available, or 420 minutes per day. The instructor works a five-day week, so this is multiplied by 5.

The *time needed for task* is the number of minutes spent with each client, which in this case is 70.

Solution

$$\text{Number of clients per week} = \frac{(7 \text{ hours per day} \times 60 \text{ minutes per hour}) \times 5}{70 \text{ minutes per client}} = 30$$

The capacity of the fitness operation can be expressed as 30 clients per week.

This is a simplified measure, because it assumes that the fitness instructor doesn't have time off sick, or do any other activities such as maintain the gym equipment, or diversify into other areas such as taking classes.

Most processes will not have just one activity; many will have interlinking processes, with different capacity constraints on each. In such cases management will have to consider the capacity of the whole process, rather than individual constituent processes. Also, the individual process durations may differ. If stage 1 of a process takes 10 minutes, say, but stage 2 takes 20 minutes and stage 3 takes 10 minutes, then a backlog will appear at stage 2.

In Figure 7.1, the output of the process will be constrained by its slowest point. This is referred to as a *bottleneck* in the process.

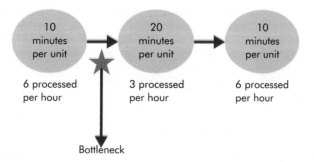

Figure 7.1 The bottleneck point in a simple process

Utilization: is the actual output shown as a percentage of the design capacity of the operation, this shows the percentage of time the facility is in actual use. And therefore demonstrates how well the resources are working.

Efficiency: is the actual output shown as a percentage of the effective capacity of the operation. It demonstrates how well the operation is working to expectations.

Design capacity: is the expected output of an operation when there are no stoppages

Effective capacity: is the expected output of an operation considering planned stoppages for maintenance, shift change over etc

Actual capacity: is the expected output of an operation considering both planned stoppages and unplanned stoppages.

Overall equipment effectiveness (OEE): is the actual capacity when applied to individual machines this tells the operation how well the equipment is being used.

Overall professional effectiveness (OPE): is the actual capacity when applied to the workers this tells the operation how well the employee is performing.

It is not always possible to predict accurately how long each stage is going to take. A hairdresser, for example, may allocate 30 minutes to each haircut, 40 minutes to each application hair colourant and 10 minutes to styling, but some individual customers may take more time and others less. In such variable processes it may not be possible to locate the bottleneck accurately.

This shows an important feature of capacity planning. In order to understand an operation's output, an hence plan the process, we need to make assumptions about what it is capable of, but often we find that these assumptions are inaccurate.

Defining Capacity

We can calculate an operation's **utilization** of resources, and the **efficiency** of its processes, by considering three categories of capacity: design capacity, effective capacity and actual capacity.

Design capacity is a theoretical number; it is not applied to the daily production of an operation. Design capacity is the output that an operation can produce continuously, at *maximum rate without stopping* for any shift changeovers, maintenance or other delays. It is what the process is capable of producing under perfect conditions. In some cases this might be interpreted as an operation's *maximum capacity*.

Effective capacity considers how the operation will run in the long term, how it will be staffed, and how it will be maintained. All *planned* stoppages in the normal working time frame are taken into consideration. It is also known as *available capacity*. The planned stoppages may include operational factors such as shift changeovers, lunch breaks, and set-up times.

Actual capacity is the same as effective capacity but contains *unplanned losses* as well as planned ones. These could include poor work rate, absenteeism, or new staff training, for example.

Actual output plus unplanned losses is the same as effective capacity (see Figure 7.2). Therefore an operation that is working its assets efficiently is minimizing unplanned losses.

The *actual capacity*, when applied to individual machines or tasks, is sometimes known as the **overall equipment effectiveness (OEE)**. This tells the operation how well the equipment is being used. By using such measures the equipment can be evaluated, and its contribution assessed. A similar measure can be applied to the contribution of people, and is sometimes known as the **overall professional effectiveness (OPE)**.

Efficiency and Utilization Calculations

The efficient use of the resources available is assessed by calculating output shown as a percentage of effective capacity:

$$\text{Efficiency} = \frac{\text{Actual output}}{\text{Effective capacity}} \times 100$$

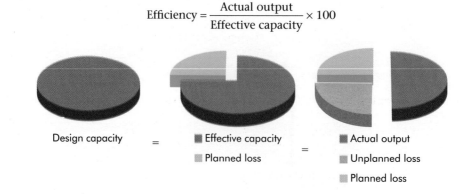

Figure 7.2 The proportions of capacity measures

In an operation that has been well designed, there will be minimal planned losses. This allows the resources to be used to the best of their ability. Capacity utilization is the measure of how much of the available capacity is used. Utilization is output shown as a percentage of the design capacity.

$$\text{Utilization} = \frac{\text{Actual output}}{\text{Design capacity}} \times 100$$

For example, if the fitness trainer in the previous example had only 24 clients who arrived at their appointments on time, the calculation would be:

$$\text{Utilization} = \frac{24}{30} \times 100 = 80\%$$

Therefore the utilization rate is 80%.

These measures of capacity can inform managers about how well resources are being utilized, and how efficient a process is.

WORKED
EXAMPLE
7.2

Calculating Capacity Measurements

Imagine you are managing a group of 10 electricians. They undertake in-home servicing of electrical systems, and are called by telephone for either emergency or pre-arranged visits. They charge a minimum call-out fee that covers the first 15 minutes of their visit plus travelling time. Beyond the first 15 minutes they charge in blocks of 15 minutes, plus the cost of any materials that they need to complete the job. The average call-out takes 1 hour.

The electricians are usually available for eight hours a day but, with two coffee breaks of 15 minutes each and a half-hour lunch break, they actually work a seven-hour day. Taking time off and illness into account, the electricians' available time reduces by 20%. This means the seven-hour day is reduced to a day of 5 hours 36 minutes (i.e. 5.6 hours)

Problem: *If actual work is only 200 billed hours in the week then: (a) What is the capacity utilization of the team? (b) What is their efficiency?*

Approach: First you need to calculate (a) the design capacity and (b) the effective capacity. Then use the actual output given above to calculate the capacity utilization and efficiency.

$$\text{Design capacity} = \frac{10 \text{ workers} \times 7 \text{ hours per day}}{1 \text{ hour per customer call-out}} \times 5 \text{ days of a working week}$$
$$= 350 \text{ customers per week}$$

$$\text{Effective capacity} = \frac{10 \text{ workers} \times 5.6 \text{ hour day}}{1 \text{ hour per customer call-out}} \times 5 \text{ days of a working week}$$
$$= 280 \text{ customers per week}$$

(a)   If actual work is only 200 billed hours in the week, then what is the capacity utilization of the team?

$$\text{Utilization} = \frac{\text{Actual output } 200}{\text{Design capacity } 350} \times 100$$
$$= 57\%$$

Solution: The utilization of the process is 57%.

(b)   If actual work is only 200 billed hours in the week, then what is their efficiency?

$$\text{Efficiency} = \frac{\text{Actual output } 200}{\text{Effective capacity } 280} \times 100$$
$$= 71\%$$

Solution: The efficiency of the process is 71%.

Takt Time and Cycle Time

In the above example, we suggested that the time taken to service each customer was 1 hour. This is often referred to as the *cycle time*, and can be applied to individual tasks or a whole process.

Takt time can be defined as the time allocated to each unit for making a product or providing a service in order to meet the customer demand. This is the rate at which the customer requires the product, and defines the speed of the manufacturing line.

Cycle time usually determines the output rate for manufacturing lines. For instance, in automobile manufacturing, cars are assembled on an assembly line, and are moved from station to station after a certain time: this is the cycle time. In a fast-food restaurant the service time for each order would also be called the cycle time.

Takt time can be used to compare with cycle time when balancing workloads. Ideally, the cycle time should be close to, but should not exceed, the takt time.

Takt time can be determined with the formula:

$$T = \frac{T_a}{T_d}$$

Where T is the takt time, e.g. rate at which work/unit should be produced; T_a is the time available to work, e.g. minutes of work/day; and T_d is the average (customer) demand (e.g. units required/day).

The available time is the amount of time available for work to be done. This excludes break times and any expected stoppage time (e.g. scheduled maintenance, team briefings); this is also referred to as overall equipment effectiveness (OEE) or overall professional effectiveness (OPE) as in Chapter 6.

WORKED EXAMPLE 7.3

Calculating Takt Time

An assembly line has a total of 8 hours available time in a shift. The employees working the shifts have a half-hour lunch break and two 15-minute tea breaks in each shift. The machines also require 10 minutes per shift in basic maintenance. At the start of each working day, the supervisor spends 10 minutes talking to the staff, and setting goals for the shift ahead.

Problem: *Calculate the available time to work for the line, and the takt time for 100 units per day.*

Approach: You will need to calculate the total time in the working shift, and then subtract the non-working time to determine the available time (i.e. the OEE or OPE).

Solution: 8 hours per shift is 480 minutes. Take away 30 minutes for lunch, 30 minutes for breaks (2 × 15 minutes), 10 minutes for a team briefing, and 10 minutes for basic maintenance work:

The available time to work (i.e. OEE or OPE) = 480 − 30 − 30 − 10 − 10 = 400 minutes.

If output demand was for 100 units a day, and you were running one shift, then the line would be allowed to spend a maximum of 4 minutes to make a product in order to be able to keep up with demand of 100 units per shift.

The *takt time* would be 4 minutes.

Capacity Planning

An operation has several ways in which it can respond to the changes in demand with its provision of capacity. The decision to provide capacity depends upon the selected strategy, the ability to store the product, and the timeliness of service production. The timing decisions of how and when to provide capacity need to be determined in line with demand.

Capacity Planning Methods

The organization has three main choices:

1   It can provide capacity ahead of the forecast, so that it is ready to respond immediately. This is known as a *capacity leads demand* strategy.

2   It can provide capacity as demand changes, so that it expands and contracts its capacity to follow demand. This is a *capacity matches demand* strategy.

3   It can wait to see what demand is, and then respond after it is confirmed. This is a *capacity lags demand* strategy.

Capacity Leads Demand

It is possible to have excess capacity ready to react to an increase in demand as *ready and available* capacity. This is therefore an opportunistic strategy with the purpose of attracting customers away from competitors.

This capacity strategy offers the advantage that the operation is ready to satisfy customer demand and meet short-term opportunities. However, there is a risk of demand not rising, in which case the operation is left with unnecessary costs and excess unused capacity.

It is an expensive way of providing capacity, as it requires investment to be made ahead of demand, but it is a useful strategy if the organization is trying to build market share and establish good customer relationships – benefits that can outweigh the cost of providing excess capacity.

An example of a capacity leads demand approach would be an extension to a lecture theatre before increased student numbers were confirmed.

Capacity Matches Demand

This strategy is adopted for the provision of capacity in line with demand. Capacity is increased in measured amounts in response to changing demand in the market. This is usually accomplished by flexible resources.

This strategy relies heavily on forecasting and accurate information, as investment decisions are made in line with the forecast. Incorrect forecasting will cause missed opportunities or wasted resources.

This strategy is often used in services, where staff are the flexible resource; they can be brought in to cover peak demand, and then sent home in quieter times – a toy store catering to the Christmas demand, for example, or a restaurant expanding and contracting its capacity in line with anticipated peaks and troughs in customer demand.

Capacity Lags Demand

Here increments of capacity are added after the demand has increased by providing capacity after the demand has risen. This allows the organization to provide capacity with certainty, and reduces the risk of unnecessary investment in capacity increases. However, this method does rely on the ability to provide products and services on short lead times, and assumes that the customer is prepared to wait.

This is less risky than providing investment ahead of demand. However, it has the disadvantage that customers may not be prepared to wait for the product or service, and opportunities can therefore be lost.

Capacity Timing

The ability to increase or decrease capacity can be planned over three time periods: short term, medium term and long term.

Short-term planning is predominantly reactive, and can be almost immediate, if capacity is adjusted on the same day, or may be over a period of up to 3 months (depending on the industry). Typically, only flexible resources can be applied to increase the capacity. It may be costly for the operation, because the cost of adjusting the resources may be higher on short-term timescales. In many cases, employees are the most readily available resource. Examples of this might include overtime for existing staff, or having multi-skilled staff who can be reallocated to where a bottleneck has occurred. An example of the latter could be the call on the PA system in a supermarket, requesting 'all till-trained staff to report to the checkout' in order to increase the capacity for payment when queues are backing up.

Medium-term planning changes are not implemented immediately; they typically have a horizon ranging between 3 and 12 months. In the medium term an operation has more time to make plans to adjust capacity, and therefore the changes tend to be more fundamental than short-term changes. They might include hiring or firing contract staff, or leasing additional facilities.

Long-term planning changes are typically over 12 to 18 months. Here the investment decisions tend to be more fundamental than the short or medium term, and will link to the strategy of an operation. The changes will take a long time to implement, and may also be difficult to reverse. They could include new full-time staff, new, faster processes, or investment in new machinery.

With each of these options the ability to make the adjustment depends on the nature of the individual process, and on the industry in which it is found. Some industries, such as the software industry, change very rapidly, and changes can be implemented much more quickly than in industries such as shipbuilding or oil production.

Staff training is another issue. A fast-food restaurant may be able to recruit and reassign staff easily, as training is relatively simple for a new employee, and investment costs are low. In comparison, a hospital may not be able to hire or reassign skilled surgeons, as they take many years to train.

 SHORT CASE 7.2

The City of Manchester Stadium

The stadium used by Manchester City Football Club was originally designed to be the central arena for the Manchester bid to host the 1996 Olympics. When the games were awarded to Atlanta, the City of Manchester refocused its efforts on the Commonwealth Games bid for 2002, which it won.

The stadium was originally planned as an 80,000-seat arena for the Olympics. This was revised down to a 60,000 capacity stadium for the Commonwealth Games. The Council's main concern, though, was

Source: © London Aerial Photo Library/Alamy

that the stadium should have a sustainable future, and so the plan was revised down again to accommodate a future for the stadium as the new ground for Manchester City FC, to replace its Maine Road stadium in Moss Side. The revised plan meant that the capacity for the Games in 2002 was 38,000, which then rose to 48,000 in 2003 when the stadium was handed over to Manchester City FC.

Construction of the stadium took 3,000 workers just over 2 years to complete, and it was handed over to the organizers four months ahead of the Games. The Commonwealth Games was a spectacular success, both for British athletes and for the City of Manchester. But no sentiment was shown when the bulldozers moved in, just hours after the closing ceremony. The track was removed, a third tier of seating was added, and the central pitch was lowered. The conversion costs of £30 million were met by the football club.

This plan was not without criticism, as there were many calls by leading athletes for a large athletics stadium to be retained, but there were parallels elsewhere: the stadiums from the Sydney and Atlanta Olympics became rugby and baseball grounds respectively. The City of Manchester Stadium has also been used as a concert venue, and has a capacity for 60,000 music fans, making it one of Europe's largest open air concert venues.

There are 2,000 parking spaces at the stadium, and a further 8,000 spaces provided locally. There are two train stations within a half-hour walk of the ground, and for concerts and special events a bus service is set up. The stadium is used twice weekly during the football season, and also hosts conferences, major sporting events, and even weddings.

Questions

1 How has long-term planning affected the final result for the City of Manchester Stadium?
2 Why was the original capacity for the Commonwealth Games stadium reduced from 60,000 to 38,000?
3 What other large facilities have changed use from their original purpose, and have they been as successful as the City of Manchester Stadium?

Sources:
http://www.gameslegacy.co.uk/cgi-bin/index.cgi/30
http://www.football-rumours.com/manchester_stadium.htm

Anticipating Changes in Demand

Demand can be volatile; it is something that tends to happen 'to' an operation. It exists outside the organization, and is therefore difficult to control. It is subject to many influences, which are summarized in Figure 7.3.

- *Changing tastes* – these can be hard to plan for. Fashions change, and new ideas occur. For example, the gradual trend towards a more environmentally friendly lifestyle has resulted in a slow and steady evolution of products and services to follow this trend. There can also be sudden unpredictable swings or changes of fashion that it is virtually impossible to plan for: for example, an influential celebrity may be seen using a product or service and create a sudden increase in demand.
- *Competition* – the demand for an organization's product or service will be highly dependent on the actions and reactions of its competitors. There may be a steady demand for the product the organization offers, but this can be severely affected if a competitor brings out a new, improved or even cheaper version of the product. The organization must be aware of its competitors, and how they may impact upon future demand.
- *Substitutes* – similarly, an alternative product may become available and divert the market demand for the product.

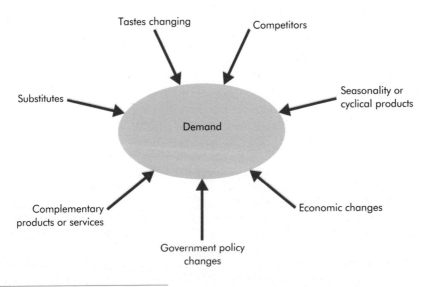

Figure 7.3 The external factors affecting demand.

- *Seasonality* – many products are naturally seasonal. For example, ice cream, fireworks and fluffy St Valentine's day teddy bears all have a time period where demand will peak. The nature of this peak relates to the particular product or service, and how much it will be demanded at a given time. For example, sunscreen sales in the UK peak in June and July, with a lower demand during the rest of the year for travel aboard, whereas Christmas cards have only the short window of demand in the months up to Christmas, before dropping to insignificant levels until the following Christmas. With a seasonal event, the previous year's demand can be used as an indicator for predicting future demand patterns.

- *Cyclical events* are similar to seasonal demand peaks, as they are regularly repeating events, but they may not necessarily occur at specific calendar dates – for example, daily commuter demands on transportation systems, or weekly shopping cycles that place high demands on shopping parks at weekends.

- *Special events* – these are one-off unique events that have very little or no demand pattern or history, such as the Olympics, or the football World Cup, which while appearing cyclical are actually unique events as the locations are a key factor. They are the most complicated to plan or predict demand for.

- *The external environment* may also affect demand patterns, with influences such as change in laws and government policy.

- *Economic changes.* Such as tax or mortgage rates, for example, will have a significant impact on demand for goods and services and will affect buying habits and behaviours.

The key point is . . . it is essential to try to understand demand patterns, and their predictability.

Unpredictable Demand

On 27 March 2007 the BBC's *Horizon* programme screened the results of a study of Boots' No7 Protect & Perfect Beauty Serum. A team of dermatologists, led by Professor Chris Griffiths, carried out an independent study into anti-ageing cosmetic products. The effect of No7 Protect & Perfect was compared with that of retinoic acid, a prescription drug used to treat severe photo-ageing of the skin, and the only product known to have a clinical effect on facial lines and wrinkles. The research revealed that in laboratory tests, pioneered by the research team, No7 Protect & Perfect Beauty Serum really could repair fine wrinkles damage associated with photo-aged skin.

Source: © Boots UK

In the days following the airing of the programme, the £16.75 Boots serum product sold out. Within 10 days of the show the sales volume – usually 1,000 pots of the lotion per week – reached 60,000. Ian Filby, the Beauty Director of Boots, said: 'We have been over-whelmed with the response following BBC's *Horizon*, with women literally racing each other to get hold of the last product in stores. We are getting more stock out to our stores on an hourly basis to meet demand.'

To cope with the sudden increase in demand, Boots issued a policy of *one product per customer* in order to dissuade consumers from reselling product on auction sites. A waiting list was then introduced; approximately 50,000 customers signed up for the product, and orders were being received from as far afield as the USA and Australia. Despite Boots' efforts to control sales, the product was being sold on eBay for up to five times its original price.

It took several months for supply to be fully restored. Despite other less optimistic studies, the product continues to be a top seller for Boots, and the range is sold around the world. Protect & Perfect Beauty Serum remains the fastest-selling product in Boots' history.

Questions
1 What action did Boots take to cope with this unexpected surge in demand?
2 What risks were there for Boots when undertaking this reaction to demand?
3 Think of other products or services for which there has been an unexpected surge in demand. What have been the successes and failures of the operations dealing with these surges?

Sources: 'Early rush for anti-ageing cream' (http://news.bbc.co.uk/1/hi/uk/6623709.stm); Finch, J. (2007) 'Serum to tackle age-old problem is here. Prepare for mayhem' (http://www.guardian.co.uk/lifeandstyle/2007/may/03/shopping.science); Poulter, S. (2007) 'The £17 cream even scientists say can banish wrinkles' (http://www.dailymail.co.uk/femail/article-445488/The-17-cream-scientists-say-banish-wrinkles.html#ixzz0rlcaXcTA)

Forecasting

Forecasting is the prediction of future demand, based upon qualitative and quantitative measures. It is an attempt to predict the future – which of course is an unknown. There are many different alternatives and hence forecasting can sometimes be little more than an educated guess.

A forecast is selected by a scheduler in an operation, and needs to be based upon the short, medium and long terms. Many subsequent decisions are dependent upon a forecast:

- *Material purchasing and expediting*: bought-in goods need to be ordered and allocated in line with the forecast. An incorrect decision may leave the operation with excess stock to be stored, or with the costs of extra material that may have to be purchased hurriedly.
- *The product mix*: this defines which products or services are to be made and when they are to be made. If the forecast is incorrect, the operation may be left with unsold finished goods, or missed sales opportunities.
- *Staff levels and overtime decisions*: staffing levels are based on the forecast, and recruitment decisions are made in line with medium- and long-term plans. Operations with skilled staff need to make decisions to increase capacity well in advance of increases in demand, as it will probably take longer to recruit a specialist than an unskilled worker.
- *Capital investment decisions*: these include facility, plant, and research and development issues. These will be made in line with forecast information.

The decisions to expand or contract facilities are not without risk, when based on a potentially uncertain future. Forecasting, when accurate, allows for timely planning of facilities and resources. But when it is incorrect, it can result in missed opportunities, or wasted capacity, or extra costs in expanding capacity. Organizations may invest heavily in information that may be relevant to future demand patterns or volumes.

Forecasting Models and Techniques

Forecasting models can be used to help predict future demand patterns. By understanding how the forecasting information will be used, for example in work plans, investment or supply chain information, it is possible to appreciate how much needs to be invested in forecasting models.

Questions that a manager should consider are:
- What is the time frame for the forecast? Is it for short- or medium-term decision-making, or for long-term planning?

- What decisions are to be based on the forecast?
- Who will be using the forecast?
- What is the risk exposure to the organization of an incorrect forecast?

A scheduler, who will be responsible for planning the production and capacity timing, will often use known or planned orders for the short-term element of the forecast, but for the medium- and long-term time horizons the information is based upon forecast and estimated data. If a product is sold on a four-week lead time, then the first four weeks of a schedule are dedicated largely to fulfilling these orders. Beyond this, though, the operation needs to plan what it is going to make, and this is where the management team will have to rely on a forecast to estimate future demand patterns, and plan capacity accordingly.

Methods of forecasting can be quantitative or qualitative. These two approaches can be used independently, but they are not mutually exclusive. Qualitative methods use appraisal, judgement and experience to estimate demand swings. These methods take into consideration factors that may be based on past experiences, opinions, or even hunches. Quantitative methods rely on data based on factors such as previous sales, which can help in identifying future trends. When combined, these methods can be very effective.

Qualitative Methods

The three main approaches to qualitative analysis are:
- Market surveys
- Delphi methods
- Scenario planning

Market Surveys

Here customers are surveyed for their future buying habits. From the resulting data, inferences can be drawn regarding future demand.

Surveys are especially useful when there is no previous information that can be used, most likely with new products or services that do not have a tested market or customer base.

Market data need to be collected from a representative sample of the target market, but this can be difficult to identify. Also, the reliability of the consumer response may be questionable, as the survey will ask for opinions, which may vary from person to person. Customer bias may be a problem if those surveyed customers tell interviewers what they think they want to hear, rather than their actual perceptions and intended buying habits. Collecting data and carrying out detailed analysis of the responses can be time consuming and expensive.

For a new form of technology, such as a new feature for a mobile phone, market surveys can test the reaction of potential customers as to how they would use such a product feature, and what they would value about it. This can give an indication of likely sales, and whether the new feature would be considered to be significant enough to increase current production volumes.

Delphi Methods

These are detailed interviews and studies of the opinions of a panel of experts in a particular area. Individual opinions are collected anonymously via questionnaires, and the results are circulated to other members of the group for interpretation and comment. This process is repeated until a group consensus is formed. Figure 7.4 shows the Delphi method process.

This is a useful method, because it evaluates different perspectives, and provides a wider commentary on collective opinion. The results from Delphi panels can be informative, and provide useful insights into future demand. The method is likely to consider a wide range of ideas and intangible factors that may be missed in quantitative data.

The entire process can be very time consuming and expensive, though. Also, it relies on a good selection of experts, and these can be difficult to identify. Sometimes their opinions do not reach a consensus, and then the process is of less use.

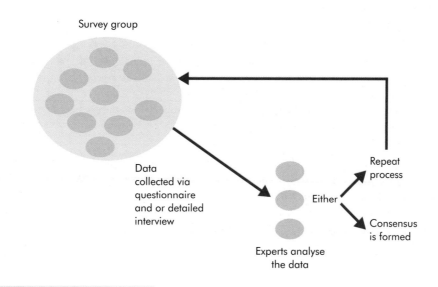

Survey group

Data collected via questionnaire and or detailed interview

Experts analyse the data

Either

Repeat process

Consensus is formed

Figure 7.4 The Delphi method of forecasting

Scenario Planning

This is a 'what if' approach. It considers the potential scenarios that an organization might face, and then analyses the demand pattern that might result from each scenario. A range of alternative outcomes are generated, and then the likelihood of each occurring and the risks involved are analysed.

This method can cover a wide range of possible futures, but there will always be scenarios that are not considered, and some of these might be significant.

An example of a scenario plan might be to consider the potential impact on demand for a building company if a general election is due. The scenarios could be related to the relevant policies offered by the political parties related to funding of housing projects, should they win the election. This can give information to the organization regarding the potential impact on their volumes.

Scenario planning works well when there is an established product or service, and when the variables and scenarios are understood. For new or emerging products there is too much that is unclear and unknown for this method to be of much value.

Quantitative Methods

Time series analysis is a mathematical model that uses past data to predict future demand. It attempts to establish a pattern from previous demand time periods, and then this is put on a curve to be extrapolated into a forecast of future demand.

Demand can be classified into four identifiable types:

- *Trend*: a gradual flow between selected time points, which is then carried on to the future. Factors contributing to a trend might include the economy, legislation, globalization, or the development of new Internet technology.
- *Seasonal demand*: a regular, year-on-year pattern. When these data are combined with qualitative data, such patterns can be simple to understand. Seasonality occurs as annual cycles, causing peaks and troughs of demand.
- *Cyclical demand*: a deviation from the trend line that might last for more or less than a year – it is the ebb and flow that is apparent. Cyclical demand may be affected by many factors, including economic or social conditions, fashion, and technology development.
- *Random variation*: an unexplained deviation from the trend line that follows no pattern or repetition. When all known causes for demand in a forecast that can be identified have been accounted for, then the remaining unexplained variations are referred to as *random* variations, error, or *noise*. Predictable variations fall into one of the previous categories, but may be classed as random if considered a true one-off event.

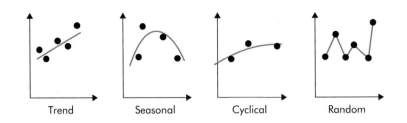

Trend   Seasonal   Cyclical   Random

Figure 7.5 Patterns of demand

Figure 7.5 illustrates the demand pattern for each of the following elements: average demand for the period trend, seasonal demand, cyclical demand and random.

If the time period under consideration is short, the forecaster's principal concern may be with random variations, short-term cyclical patterns or errors, whereas over longer timescales all trends become more detectable, and play a more important role.

Causal Relationship Forecasting

Causal methods are a form of mathematical analysis, used when historical data are available, and the relationship between the demand pattern to be forecast (referred to as the *dependent variable*) and other key related factors is known. The relationship between the variables is of interest because it is required in order to forecast demand based on it.

> **Dependent demand:** is reasonably predictable demand as it is linked or associated with another factor, which may have a clearer future pattern.
>
> **Independent demand:** is a less predictable demand pattern as it is not easily linked to other factors.

A **dependent demand** pattern is derived from such an association. This allows a level of predictability, and so demand isn't totally random. By contrast, **independent demand** means that there are few factors that can help in predicting demand patterns. The operator is almost 'working blind' as to the future, and has to take much more of a gamble when making future decisions. Examples of this could include the demand for umbrellas linked to rainfall, or the demand for New York City breaks linked to the exchange rate between the dollar and the pound or euro.

The first step in causal forecasting is to establish whether the relationship is actually linked, or whether occurrences are merely coincidental and unrelated. To discover this, the data need to be analysed for the irregular peaks and troughs in demand.

For example, the demand for baby essentials is closely linked to the birth rate. The dependent variable will be the demand for baby products. The independent variable will be the *birth rate*, for which there should be reliable current and past data. Figure 7.6 shows a simple relationship between baby products and the birth rate. The straight-line graph shown has been arrived at by analysing past sales data using a mathematical technique called *linear regression*.

Other Factors

Other factors need to be taken into account. One is the *product life cycle* (see Figure 2.4). Product demand typically follows four phases: birth, growth, maturity and decline. For products in the first two phases, longer forecasts are

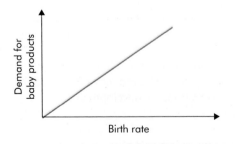

Figure 7.6 Relationship between baby products and the birth rate

necessary – e.g. sales of high-definition TV sets or the Microsoft Windows 7 operating system – whereas products in the latter two phases require shorter, more specific forecasts, usually of staffing levels, inventory levels or supply chain calculations.

Business cycles also are taken into account. Market growth or recession provides a general backdrop for forecasting estimates and time periods.

When creating a forecast, each factor must be carefully considered and evaluated for its expected impact on future demand. See Chapter 5 for more about the product life cycle.

Capacity Strategies

When an operation is planning how much capacity it needs, it must think about how it plans to react to the demand it faces. The operation must be aware of the options available to satisfy demand. There are three general strategies that can be used in the medium term:

- Level production
- Chase demand
- Demand management

These strategies are not mutually exclusive, and most organizations use a mix of them, but it is likely that one strategy will dominate. They are not reactions to small, daily swings in demand, but look at demand over an extended time frame. Such decisions require planning and investment.

Level Production

Level production largely ignores demand fluctuations, and works on producing units efficiently and then storing the finished goods, so that demand can be satisfied from stock. See Figure 7.7. Basically, it allows an operation to manufacture efficiently and optimize capacity, irrespective of the demand. There are two key conditions for this to work;

> **Level production:** this is where the operation produces to a consistent level, unsold product is stored and sold when demand peaks.

- The product must be suitable for storage, i.e. not highly customized, and non-perishable or with a reasonable shelf life.
- Demand must be relatively reliable, to avoid the risk of large stock-outs or excessive stock levels.

The level production strategy doesn't work for services.

This strategy forms part of a *cumulative plan*, where demand is satisfied over a period of time to suit the operation, and stockholding and selling from stock allow production to be effectively managed by stock control, allowing the operation to have the benefit of working to a less volatile plan.

Certain industries and products lend themselves to this strategy. For example, the demand for cigarettes is fairly consistent. Sales drop off in January and February as smokers make New Year resolutions to give up their habit, but demand returns to fairly consistent levels (as some fail to quit), and then peaks around Christmas time for the party season. The product is straightforward to store, and has a reasonable shelf life. As demand is fairly consistent the operation can feel confident about following such a strategy.

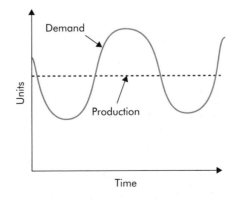

Figure 7.7 The level production strategy produces units to a consistent rate

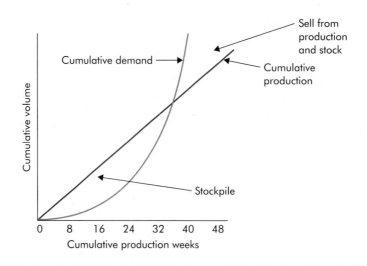

Figure 7.8 The level production strategy considers cumulative production ahead of cumulative demand

In **aggregate planning**, forecasts are set to be as capacity-efficient as possible, yet the aim is still to match the demand. See Figure 7.8. This style of planning rises above the detail of the product or service mix, and looks at capacity overall in line with the demand. It is a schedule that works in the medium term, and makes decisions based upon staffing and stockholding levels or leasing decisions. This works as part of a level production strategy, so that manufacturing is carried out to cover the demand, and stockpiling occurs ahead of selling from stock, rather than the other way round – it is hard to sell products if the warehouse is empty.

Aggregate planning: takes a top-level look at demand for the operation as a whole. It does not differentiate between different products and services.

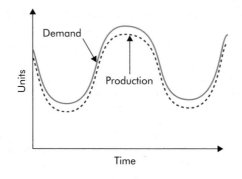

Figure 7.9 A chase demand strategy has production following demand

Chase Demand

Chase demand: is where the operation expands and contracts its capacity to follow demand changes.

In a **chase demand** strategy, the operation attempts to follow demand by expanding and contracting capacity (Figure 7.9). There will always be an element of fixed capacity that can be adjusted only over the long term, such as buildings or facilities, but other elements are flexible. By expanding and contracting these flexible resources the operation can minimize the costs of having excess capacity, yet still increase capacity to meet increases in demand.

A chase demand strategy requires considerable planning in process design and staff training. The operation needs to consider the question 'If demand goes up and then falls, how are we going to expand and then contract our capacity without wasting money?' In order to expand and contract capacity efficiently, the process needs to be adaptable. This can be achieved by designing a very simple process, so that staff can be hired and fired, or even be multi-skilled. Staff are not the only adjustable resource in the process, of course. Flexible machinery, or the ability to make other products in times of low demand, may help too. If a demand peak for one product can be combined with a demand slump in another, reallocation of resources can allow the demand to be followed.

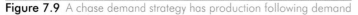

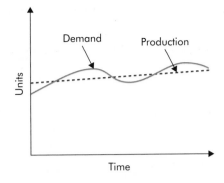

Figure 7.10 Demand management attempts to smooth demand fluctuations to allow a level production rate to be used

Demand Management

The level production and chase demand strategies are both supply-related solutions. The alternative approach is to manage or control demand by the customer and market – **demand management**.

> **Demand management:** is where the operation attempts to manipulate demand to smooth the peaks and troughs.

The concept of manipulating or controlling demand may be unfamiliar to an operations manager, but it is possible to use marketing tools to smooth demand in line with the required forecast for some products or services. Many of the tools may be short-term measures, and it is important that the adjustments made do not damage the potential long-term demand. Some methods of demand adjustment include:

- *Varying the price*. A discounted price for a product with an elastic demand curve, which is a product where its demand is affected by price, can be a strong incentive for the consumer to buy more. This happens regularly in supermarkets with price discounting, and it works well if combined with additional advertising.
- *Providing an incentive for off-peak services or products*. This works well with services to help smooth demand throughout a given time period. Good examples of this are an off-peak rate in the gym, or the early bird diner menu; both are used to flatten the peaks in demand, and increase utilization of wasted capacity at quieter times.
- *Additional marketing* can create awareness of a product that wasn't there before. This is most effective when combined with other methods, such as price discounting.
- Providing *alternative products or services*.

Demand management practices work in combination with the supply approaches mentioned above. It may not be possible to control demand to a level state, but it may help to smooth out the fluctuations of a chase demand strategy.

Contemporary Thinking: Yield Management

Yield management is widely regarded as an increasingly useful business tool. It is generally used in operations where the medium-term capacity is relatively fixed, and there is no straightforward way to expand and contract it. This is often the case in services with high investment in facilities, where variable costs are low, and where fixed capacity prevails. Examples are hotels, with a fixed number of rooms, or airlines, with their fixed number of seats.

> **Yield management:** is a group of methods that assist an operation with fixed capacity to maximize its revenue and utilize the capacity it has to its best advantage.

Yield management, or *revenue management* (as it is sometimes known), was first introduced as the option to choose to maximize returns from business assets. Revenue management is founded in pure economics, so craitically the curves of demand versus supply. This relationship has been studied in business using computer software that looks at historical trends, fixed capacities and revenues generated, and then forecasts the future, giving the business a set of rules to apply to its assets in order to maximize their financial potential.

This involves a set of strategies that an operation can employ to maximize revenue, either by charging individual customers as much as they are prepared to pay, or by extracting as much revenue from a process as possible. This asks the question: if one customer is prepared to pay more for a good or service, is it possible to charge them a higher price than another customer?

Certain conditions enable companies to use yield management. They include:
- Fixed capacity in the short and medium term
- The ability to sell the service at different times to different customers, and in advance of the service being delivered
- A market that has diverse customer requirements
- A service that has some unique characteristics to avoid a homogeneous market (this might be the destination or timing of an airline flight, or the facilities or location of a hotel).

The three key strategies for maximizing revenue through yield management are:
- Overbooking
- Price discounting
- Varying the service type.

In *overbooking*, the operation books more customers than it can accommodate, on the presumption that there will be some no-shows. It has the rather obvious disadvantage of the problems that may be caused if all the customers *do* turn up! A policy of overbooking is effective only if the take-up rate for the service is predictable, and if the costs of compensating a customer if they are unable to have their booked service are not too high. The advantages for the operation include maximum revenue and full capacity. This has been a popular policy of many airlines, which overbook their flights. They have a large volume of data from previous flights to predict rates of no-shows on various routes; customers who miss flights because of this policy are then compensated with alternative flights and possible upgrades. However, recent legislation has required airlines to compensate passengers financially as well as finding alternative flights, and this extra cost has led many of the budget airlines to discontinue this policy.

Price discounting has the same characteristics shown in demand management policy, in that it is aimed at optimizing the capacity at non-peak times. The top price that can be charged is set for the time of highest demand, and the price is then reduced for less attractive time periods. A high peak time price may also be used to deter people from booking at peak times, in order to control demand. Price discounting helps smooth demand over a given time period, and maximizes revenue. A good example of this is the holiday market: with a finite number of holidays available in Europe, peak times such as school holidays may incur heavy premiums, yet there are many bargains to be had 'off peak'.

Varying the service type allows an operation to 'grade' the services they are selling, and charge different prices accordingly. This allows them to charge extra from those who are prepared to pay more, with some justification. Seats in a theatre will be grouped in order of quality and price, with the dress circle seats being the best and most expensive, and the stalls being the cheapest. Upgrading a service can differentiate it from the standard service, and therefore higher prices can be charged. The advantage of this policy is that it is flexible in the short term; if an airline, say, has excess demand for economy class seats for a flight, but does not sell all its business class seats, then a business class seat can be 'converted' to an economy seat to maximize revenue. This is also a commonly used approach in selling on-demand software-as-a-service (SaaS) to businesses, or financial services to individual customers.

> ### ❶ Stop and Think
>
> 1 Today, some argue that this practice is not so much revenue management as price manipulation – altering the price that the business asks for a product or service at a particular point in time. It may help the company increase revenues, but is it always fair to customers who pay different rates depending on the time of purchase?

Queuing

Why Are We Waiting?

Several of the strategies for managing capacity described above require the ability to store products in order to follow the demand line. In times of low demand the product can be stockpiled; in peak times the rise in demand can be satisfied from stock.

Sometimes it is not possible to increase supply in advance, though. This is especially true of services: by their very nature, the production and consumption are simultaneous. In these cases *queuing theory* offers a more appropriate strategy. Queuing theory works on the basis that where the flow of consumers into a process is not regular, then there will be an element of waiting involved, where customers will have to queue.

This theory demonstrates that while some customers may be satisfied immediately, there will be periods of queuing for others, as the arrival time of customers at the start of the process is not controlled by the operation.

The waiting line or queue effectively regulates the flow of customers into the process, and turns the uneven demand into a manageable flow.

We can see a good example of this in a theme park. Customers are free to walk around the theme park, and take a trip on any of the rides on offer. The customers will arrive at the rides in an irregular fashion, and so there will be peaks and troughs in demand all day long. If a roller coaster can accommodate 50 passengers on a ride that runs for 2 minutes and takes 3 minutes to load and unload customers per ride, and 1200 customers arrive, then they will be processed in 5-minute batches of 50, and the queue will be cleared in 2 hours. However, the customers will arrive in varying groups and batch sizes, in different timing.

The customers entering into the process are called the *calling population*. The number of customers may be known, where for example a quantity of tickets have been sold in advance, as for a theatre show; or they may be completely unknown, where there is no advance warning of arrival numbers: an example of this might be at a post office, where daily demand can be uncertain.

When arriving, a customer is not usually engaged in the process straight away. The customer is free to either join the queue or not: the latter is known as *baulking*. Or the customer may queue for a time, but then leave the queue: this is referred to as *reneging*. The operation itself can also prevent customers from entering the queue, if there is too much demand for the service at the given time: in this case the customer is *rejected* by the queue.

Figure 7.11 shows a simple queuing system.

The Process Servers

The points of sale, or *servers*, signify the start of the operation for most customers. They process each customer, and then the customer finishes this stage of the process. There are several ways of using servers:

> **Process servers:** are the points of sale or stations at the front of the queue where the customer is served.

- *There can be one main queue, facilitated by several servers.* An example of this could be the security check at an airport. This has a single, central queue that filters off at the front to the next available scanning

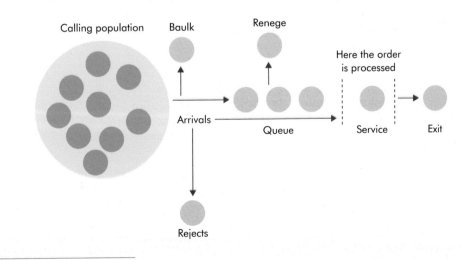

Figure 7.11 A simple queuing system

machine. This can result in a very long queue, but one that moves quite swiftly: a customer is not affected by a delay with another customer, as they are able to be seen by the next available server.

- *Each server can have its own queue, and therefore there will be several queues side by side.* This is common in supermarkets with the till checkout system. Here the customer has to select a queue and estimate the process time on order to find the shortest one. In this case the consumer has control over their selection, but this can lead to frustrations for customers if other queues move faster than the one they are in.
- *Lastly, there can be a sequential queue.* This is where the customer joins a queue, is served, and then moves on to the next part of the process in a continuing queue. An example of this could be in an accident and emergency department in a hospital, where the patient will join the queue to be seen by a nurse; is then moved to the second part of the queue to be seen by a doctor; and then may move on to a queue for an X-ray. If all the treatments take the same time, then the queue will flow evenly; if not, a bottleneck will occur.

For a queue to be effective, it must have clearly defined rules and layout. Each customer needs to be aware of how they are expected to queue, and in what sequence they are to be served. Customers boarding an aeroplane may expect to be seen on a *first come first served* basis, but may need to understand that there will be other passengers who are able to bypass the queue, such as disabled passengers or travellers with young children.

Customer involvement in the process can be part of queuing theory. If a customer queues, they wait to join the process, but if the queue becomes part of the process, then technically the customer is served sooner. Using the queue to collect information, such as pre-orders in a café queue, or collecting information relating to a process, such as personal details and requirements, engages the customer in the process, and may reduce reneging and frustration levels.

Queuing Calculations

There are many queuing *models* that can be used to calculate the effectiveness of a queuing system. The key factors are:

- *The population's source* – is it finite, where the potential customers are limited, or not finite, where arrivals are unrestricted?
- *The arrival rates and patterns of the calling population.* This is where the timing of customers arriving and how long it takes to serve each customer are variable, the system may be overloaded at times (hence the waiting): this can be described by a Poisson distribution.
- *The number of servers* – multi-server or single-server points.
- *The queuing discipline* – for example, is it a true first come, first serve model?

The most commonly used equations for a single-server distribution, where there is one queue and one service point, are shown below.

- The average number of customers waiting in a queue:

$$L_q = \frac{\lambda^2}{\mu(\mu - \lambda)}$$

- The average time a customer spends in the queue:

$$W_q = \frac{\lambda}{\mu(\mu - \lambda)}$$

- The server utilization, or the probability that the server is busy:

$$\rho = \frac{\lambda}{\mu}$$

where λ is the average arrival rate of customers per hour, and μ is the average number of customers served per hour.

Calculating Single-Server Queues

Problem: *A coffee shop has a single service desk, where customers order and pay for drinks and food. Throughout the day, customers arrive at an average rate of 55 customers per hour, and service times are distributed with an average rate of 40 customers per hour.*

Calculate:

(a) *The average number of customers waiting in the queue*

(b) *The average time a customer spends in the queue*

(c) *The probability of the barista being busy*

Approach: You will need to use the formulae to analyse the average time in the queue.

Solution:

$$\lambda = 40$$

$$\mu = 55$$

(a) The average number of customers waiting in the queue:

$$L_q = \frac{\lambda^2}{\mu(\mu - \lambda)}$$

$$= \frac{1,600}{55 \times (55 - 40)}$$

$$= \frac{1,600}{55 \times 15}$$

The average number of customers waiting in the queue is 1.9.

(b) The average time a customer spends in the queue:

$$W_q = \frac{\lambda}{\mu(\mu - \lambda)}$$

$$= \frac{40}{55 \times (55 - 40)}$$

$$= \frac{40}{825}$$

The average time a customer spends in the queue is approximately 0.05 hours (or nearly 3 minutes)

(c) The probability of the barista being busy:

$$\rho = \frac{\lambda}{\mu}$$

$$= \frac{40}{55}$$

The probability of the barista being busy is 0.73 therefore a 73% chance.

Customers' Perception of Waiting in Queues

The psychology of queuing, or 'waiting in line', has been a much discussed topic. An organization needs to know how its customers will react to a queue and, indeed, whether having queues damages its operation in any way by customers switching to competitors who do not have queues, or whether it affects satisfaction and repeat purchasing. It is also important to understand how the disadvantages of queuing can be minimized by considering the feelings of the consumer towards queueing.

There are several common factors that can be identified from customers' perceptions:

- Time spent in a queue is seen as idle or wasted time. A consumer will make a judgement to trade off the time spent in the queue against the perceived value of the service.
- Some consumers are prepared to pay a premium to reduce or avoid queuing time. This can clearly be seen at airport check-in desks, where first and business class have their own server, who does not support the main queue. Another example is paying for private health care, instead of waiting for state-provided services.
- The perception of the queue depends on the type of queue, and on whether the end result is worth waiting for. For example, the queues for a theme park can be several hours long, but the ride is valued highly, so there is a 'reward' for being in the queue.
- If the customer has information about the queue in relation to expected wait or position in the queue, there is a much lower level of anxiety. Informing a customer of their situation enables them to make a rational decision as to whether to remain in the queue or leave. Passing on this information often uses technology: for example, automated call centre queues regularly inform customers of wait time and queue position.
- A customer queuing to start the process will feel more dissatisfaction than a customer who has already started the process. This can be seen in the accident and emergency queue, where patients are seen by a nurse before they are seen by a doctor, thus beginning the process more quickly, but not necessarily shortening the wait time.
- Consumers have expectations for good service, and queues are often seen to detract from the quality of service.
- One of the lessons for operations managers is that customers dislike uncertainty. Waiting in a queue is an uncertainty.

Many things can affect happiness in the queue; it can be something as simple as good weather when queuing outside, to the mood of the individual customer in the queue, for example, if there is an individual complaining loudly, this will affect the whole queue.

It is important for an operation to be aware of and tackle frustration and irritation with the queue. Technologies have been devised to 'bust' queues: these include hand-held devices to take customers' orders while they are in the queue, and then give them an order number. These types of system are sometimes used in large shoe stores where the customer order number – the paper ticket picked up by the customer when entering the shop – is entered into a hand-held terminal by an assistant, with the selection and sizes of shoes the customer would like to try. When a qualified assistant becomes available the customer is then served; the shoes have, during the wait, been made ready for the assistant to collect from the store room. In this way customers are committed to the process, and are less likely to baulk or renege the queue. Many operations may take the customers' engagement in the process one step further, and provide entertainment in the queue: this can be an effective policy for queues for music concerts, sporting events or theme parks.

CRITICAL PERSPECTIVE

Are All Queues Bad?

Consumers generally are unhappy to wait for goods and services. As operations managers, we have come to see waiting and queuing as negatives in a process that involves customers. Queuing has become so much part of the life of a consumer, that it affects the way they make choices, plan purchases and allocate time to activities – but it has an important role to play in decision-making:

- A consumer may be prepared to wait longer in order to get a lower price, rather than pay a premium for a better service.
- A queue can also be an opportunity to encourage impulse buys, which keep the customer shopping for longer than they had initially intended.
- Queues can also act as a signal or give information to a consumer. A night club with a queue may indicate that there is a popular party going on inside, rather than a half-empty club with no atmosphere.

- A queue may also be part of the anticipation for an experience. The queue for a theme park ride can allow customers to view the ride, and see what they are about to experience themselves.

The key point is to consider what the customer expects from the queue, and aim to meet their expectations. A queue, in itself, isn't necessarily negative; but queues are negative if they are unexpected, there is a lack of information about the wait itself, or if they are particularly long.

SHORT CASE 7.4

Queuing for Wimbledon

Source: © Oli Scott/Getty Images Sport

As one of Britain's most popular sporting events, the Wimbledon Tennis Championships attract thousands of visitors a year. It is one of the few major events to offer a certain number of tickets to spectators for sale on the day, rather than in advance. There are around 500 premium tickets available for the 'show courts' and approximately 6,000 tickets for the grounds. The actual number varies according to previous sales, the weather, and the number of courts in play.

For a ground pass it is usually necessary to join the queue several hours before the grounds open. For a show court ticket, many people choose to queue overnight to maximize their chances of getting a ticket for the Centre, No. 1 or No. 2 Court. An area is created in Wimbledon Park for campers, and facilities are provided. In the early morning, campers are woken by stewards to pack up their kit and form a more regular queue.

There may be a wait of around 5 hours before the tickets then go on sale. Some members of the queue may be unsuccessful in their attempts, and leave empty handed.

The queue at Wimbledon has become part of the Championships themselves, and is known for being good natured and friendly.

Questions
1 What makes a queue for Wimbledon different from the normal approach to queuing?
2 What are the positive and negative aspects for a customer queuing for Wimbledon?

Source: http://aeltc2010.wimbledon.org/en_GB/about/tickets/queue.html

Summary

This chapter has introduced various approaches for dealing with everyday capacity problems. These should enable demand to be anticipated, and resources managed, in the light of actual variable customer demand.

Capacity management affects all areas of an operation. Capacity measures the *rate* at which the operation can transform inputs into outputs. Capacity is about the *quantity* of a product or service that can be made within a *given time period*. When measuring capacity, the unit of measure can be either an input to or an output from the process.

To assess the efficient use of the resources available, efficiency is calculated as output shown as a percentage of available capacity.

In planning capacity, the organization has three main choices: to build ahead of a forecast (*capacity leads demand*); to provide capacity as demand changes (*capacity matches demand*); or to respond after demand (*capacity lags demand*).

Demand can be volatile, and is something that tends to 'happen to' an operation. It exists outside the organization, and is therefore difficult to control. Demand may change due to a number of factors or circumstances.

Methods of forecasting can be quantitative or qualitative. These approaches can be used independently, but are not mutually exclusive. Qualitative methods use appraisal, judgement and experience to estimate demand swings.

There are three general strategies that can be used in the medium term in planning capacity: level production, chase demand, and demand management. These strategies are not mutually exclusive, and most organizations use a mix of the three, but it is likely that one method will dominate the strategy.

Where it is not possible to build a product in advance, *queuing theory* offers a more appropriate strategy. Queuing theory works on the basis that where the flow of consumers into a process is not regular, then there will be an element of waiting involved.

Key Terms and Theories

- **Resource mix** – this is the collection of inputs or resources into a process that can be adjusted to increase or decrease capacity.

- **Input and output measures of capacity** – it is possible to measure the capacity of an operation by analysing either inputs or outputs. Either method is correct; the selection of the method depends upon which measure is more logical. For example, the number of beds in a hospital is a logical input; barrels per day of oil from an oil rig is a logical output.

- **Design capacity** – is a top level and unachievable result as it presumes a 24/7 operation with no stoppages.

- **Effective capacity** – is the same as design capacity, but subtracts stoppages such as lunch breaks and maintenance.

- **Actual capacity** – is more of a working number; it looks at what is actually produced, and considers both planned and unplanned stoppages.

- **The theory of constraints** – created by Goldratt, suggests that capacity can be almost infinite if constraints or bottlenecks are identified and removed. The theory states that once a constraint is removed, capacity will increase, and another constraint will form.

- **Efficiency and utilization of capacity** – are ratios that show how well an operation is using its assets and resources to generate output. Efficiency looks at how much is produced, it considers what the operation would hope to make, taking into account planned stoppages. This allows the operation to establish how much unplanned problems are affecting the output. Utilization looks at output compared with design capacity, and demonstrates how well the processes are working.

- **Takt time** – is the rate at which a customer requires the operation to produce the product.

- **Yield management** – or revenue management, allows operations to maximize revenue if they have fixed capacity, by varying price from customer to customer depending on their willingness to pay. Higher-paying customers might receive additional features or benefits.

Key Equations

$$\text{Capacity} = \frac{\text{Time available}}{\text{Time of task}}$$

$$\text{Efficiency} = \frac{\text{Actual output}}{\text{Effective capacity}} \times 100$$

$$\text{Utilization} = \frac{\text{Actual output}}{\text{Design capacity}} \times 100$$

$$\text{Takt time, } T = \frac{T_a}{T_d}$$

The average number of customers waiting in a queue, $L_q = \dfrac{\lambda^2}{\mu(\mu - \lambda)}$

The average time a customers spends in the queue, $W_q = \dfrac{\lambda}{\mu(\mu - \lambda)}$

The server utilization, or the probability that the server is busy, $\rho = \dfrac{\lambda}{\mu}$

Suggested Answers to Stop and Think Question

1   To answer this question, consider what the advantages are to the customer who pays the higher price. A customer may benefit from a better view in the theatre, or a more comfortable seat on a plane. However, consider also the advantages to the customer paying the lowest price; they might not be able to afford the service if there was no differentiation in pricing, as the average price would most probably be higher.

Review Questions

1   What would be the most effective measure of capacity for:

   (a)   A car manufacturer?

   (b)   A music concert?

   (c)   An airport?

2   How could the capacity of a coffee shop be:

   (a)   Increased in the short, medium and long term?

   (b)   Decreased in the short, medium and long term?

3   When forecasting demand, what qualitative methods can be used? What are the advantages and disadvantages of these methods?

4   When an operation has a seasonal product, what strategies are available to it when planning capacity?

5   What must an operation consider when using historical data to predict future trends?

6   How can queues be managed effectively to reduce waiting time and customer frustration?

7   Using the theory of constraints, what are the most common constraints in:

   (a)   A car manufacturing plant?

   (b)   A post office?

   (c)   Dentists?

Discussion Questions

1   How can having multi-skilled staff increase the capacity of a hospital? Discuss what factors must be considered when increasing or decreasing a hospital's capacity.

2   If an operation adopts a level production strategy, what features must the product have for it to be successful? When may other strategies be more appropriate?

3   Discuss how an operation might manage demand in a restaurant.

Problems

1   A computer firm has a group of 50 computer consultants. These individuals either visit firms in the area on pre-arranged visits, or are called in for emergency repairs.

A call-out fee is charged that covers the first hour of their visit. Beyond the first hour they charge in minimum blocks of 30 minutes. The average call-out is 2 hours long.

The working day is usually 8 hours long, but allows two breaks of 15 minutes each and a half-hour lunch break, leaving a 7-hour day. If holidays and illness are accounted for at 25%, the 7 hours per day is actually a $5\frac{1}{4}$ hour day.

Required: *If actual work is only 500 hours billed in the week, then:*
   (a)   *What is the capacity utilization of the team?*
   (b)   *What is their efficiency?*

2   A student registration line has a working day of 6 hours. There are 25 members of staff working during induction week. These employees have a half-hour lunch break and two 15 minute tea breaks each day. At the start of each working day, the process takes 15 minutes to set up.

Required: *Calculate the total time available to work for the registration team, and the time that can be spent on each student application (the takt time) for 2,000 students per day.*

3   A beachside kiosk selling food has a single queue where customers order and pay for soft drinks and ice creams. On an average summer day, customers arrive at a rate of 160 per hour, according to a Poisson distribution, and the time it takes to serve each customer is distributed with an average rate of 130 customers per hour.

Required: *Calculate:*
   (a)   *The average number of customers waiting in the queue.*
   (b)   *The average time a customer spends in the queue.*

Visit the Online Learning Centre at
www.mcgraw-hill.co.uk/textbooks/paton for a range of resources to support your learning.

Further Reading

Aksin, Z., Armony, M. and Mehrotra, V. (2007) 'The modern call center: a multi-disciplinary perspective on operations management research', *Production and Operations Management*, **16**(6), 665–688

Bain, J. (2008) 'Future of revenue management: from the plane to the shelf', *Journal of Revenue and Pricing Management*, **7**(3), 302–306.

Goldratt, El. M. (1984) *Theory of Constraints*, North River Press, Great Barrington, MA.

Pinedo, M. (2009) *Planning and Scheduling in Manufacturing and Services*, 2nd edn, Springer, New York.

Rother, M. and Shook, J. (1998) *Learning To See: Value Stream Mapping to Add Value and Eliminate Muda*, The Lean Enterprise Institute, Brookline, MA.

8 Supply Chain and Supply Relationship Management

Learning Outcomes

After reading this chapter, you should be able to:

- Describe the management of supply chains
- Assess purchasing strategies for different types of item
- Identify key issues in managing supplier–buyer relationships
- Identify postponement strategies in supply chains
- Assess how demand uncertainties can be managed
- Compare various mechanisms for supply chain integration
- Compare different strategies for supply chain efficiency and responsiveness

Fun with LEGO Bricks

As you read this case, consider how LEGO toys are designed, distributed and sold internationally.

The LEGO Group is a Danish company, founded in 1932, which is globally known for its brick-based toys. As well as its strong brand name, it has a reputation for the product quality of its toys. In the past, the number of toys produced was based on demand forecasts from the retailers. However, the toy market is changing, and it has become more difficult to predict children's toy preferences. Consumers are shifting their preference to cheaper toys with added innovations. Retailers, too, are demanding lower purchase costs with greater supply responsiveness, in order to reduce the risk of lost sales.

Source: © Lego Group

Ten years ago, the LEGO Group felt an urgent need to reshape its overall strategy. It started to restructure its production strategies with recognized platform designs and updated facilities, and began initiatives to create more exciting experiences for children, with new games, theme parks and other, virtual, stimulations.

New products and product lines of LEGO bricks have been the key design strategy. There are about 2,350 different elements and 52 colours that have been mixed and matched into more than 7,000 products offered. The company grew from producing only a small variety of LEGO bricks to a large array of different bricks. It also started to partner with external partners to create innovative games. The partnership with Massachusetts Institute of Technology, for instance, resulted in the creation of the LEGO Mindstorms® family, allowing children to design their own robots. The package includes a computer, transmitter and receiver, software and sensor.

The company has production facilities in Denmark, the Czech Republic, Hungary and Mexico. Its products are sold in more than 130 countries via the LEGO Group's own sales channels, or through local distributors. Since 2006, a major part of the production has been outsourced to an external partner, Flextronics, in the Czech Republic. The new European distribution centre, also located in the Czech Republic, is operated by DHL. However, in 2008 the company started to in-source this operation, by taking over the Czech and Hungarian partners. The company also started to build a factory in Mexico.

LEGO has many initiatives to bring the company closer to its customers. For instance, lego.com, its official website, is a virtual universe where children of all ages and their parents can learn about the company's values and ideas through games and stories. Recently, the company launched LEGO Brickmaster, a membership club for children aged seven years and upwards. Consumers can build any toys they like, and order the bricks directly via LEGO Internet stores.

Consumers can have a selection of LEGO products supplied regularly to their homes. LEGO also offers recall services. When there is a concern about the safety of a toy, LEGO offers refunds in the form of a gift card to consumers who verify they are in possession of the recalled item.

Source: Juliana Hsuan, Copenhagen Business School

Introduction

The LEGO case shows how one company is changing its overall strategy, linking product development, production and customer experience to stay competitive in the toy industry. Remember that in Chapter 4 we looked at how supplier relationships are formed, and explored the different types of supplier relationship that may result. In this chapter we explore how such collaborations, once set up, can be managed, by taking a closer look at the various processes that link the firm to its suppliers and customers.

We'll learn that, before procurement decisions are made, it is crucial that the organization classify the purchased items in terms of their impact on the business, as well as on the supply risk and market complexity. This subsequently impacts on the nature of the supplier–buyer relationship, which can vary from an arm's length relationship to a strategic partnership.

Effective relationships depend on the extent to which firms are willing to share information. It is challenging to manage supply chains when we don't know the variation in demand. We need to understand why information about a customer's actual demand gets distorted all the way upstream along the supply chain.

As innovative products and services are continuously introduced to the market, all parties in the supply chain need to collaborate in devising flexible and efficient channels. A firm may combine efficiencies from logistics (e.g. collaborating with third party logistics companies), manufacturing (e.g. postponing customization), or supplies (e.g. combining the best solutions from lean and agile supplies). All these processes are supported by coordination efforts and information technology.

This chapter covers the key concepts and strategies related to the management of supply chains. We shall investigate the management of activities and processes that take place when goods and services are produced by suppliers and provided to customers. We'll also learn about how firms can organize their supply chains for operational efficiency.

Supply Chain Management

In Chapter 4 we learned that the term 'supply chain' is a metaphor used to describe a simple linear relationship between a series of different organizations, such as a raw materials supplier, a manufacturer, a distributor, and the end customer. Supply chains are concerned with the flow of three things – information, money and materials – between participating organizations. **Supply chain management (SCM)**, then, is the management of activities, organization and processes involving all stakeholders, from the end customers (downstream) to the supplier that produces the raw material (upstream). In order for goods or services to reach customers, the various processes have to be integrated.

> **Supply chain management:** the management of activities, organization and processes involving all stakeholders, from the end customers (i.e. downstream) to the supplier that produces the raw material (i.e. upstream).

SCM is built on the assumption that a company's supply chain (internal as well as external) is a resource to be exploited for market position. Strategic use of this resource requires companies to pay close attention to understanding customer needs, and how to fulfil them. The companies also need to pinpoint the inefficiencies in their processes that hinder cross-functional relationships with suppliers and customers. Many contemporary SCM concepts have been developed since the mass production era, such as third party logistics (TPL or 3PL), enterprise resource planning (ERP), and collaborative planning, forecasting and replenishment (CPFR). These concepts will be explored in later sections.

Managing Supplier–Buyer Relationships

Once an organization has achieved an appropriate supply network, with the correct number and type of suppliers in the correct locations, it must then decide how best to procure products and services from them on an ongoing basis. The type of relationship an organization shares with the supplier will depend on the types of items purchased, and their impact on the business, as illustrated by *Kraljic's matrix* in Figure 8.1. The strength of Kraljic's matrix lies in its simplicity: it shows four purchasing *tactics* that are contingent upon a product or service's complexity, risk and impact if it fails to be delivered.

The vertical axis of Kraljic's matrix is concerned with the impact on profit or the value obtained from a transaction for a buyer organization. These are the factors internal to the purchasing company, whereas the horizontal axis is concerned with market and supply risks – that is, external factors.

The ideal type of procurement process will depend upon the four contexts: routine, bottleneck, leverage, and critical.

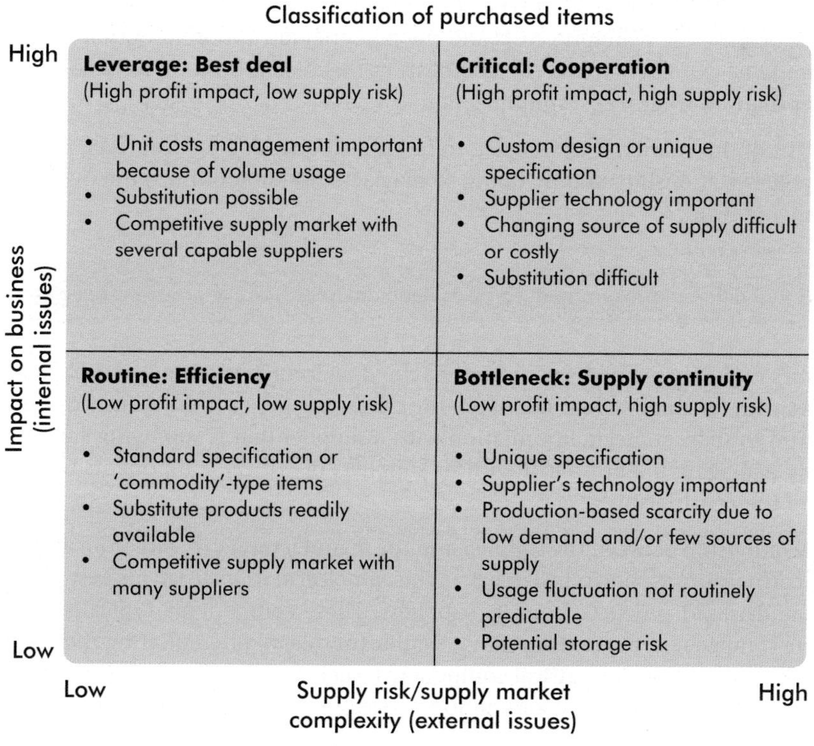

Classification of purchased items

Leverage: Best deal (High profit impact, low supply risk)	Critical: Cooperation (High profit impact, high supply risk)
• Unit costs management important because of volume usage • Substitution possible • Competitive supply market with several capable suppliers	• Custom design or unique specification • Supplier technology important • Changing source of supply difficult or costly • Substitution difficult
Routine: Efficiency (Low profit impact, low supply risk)	**Bottleneck: Supply continuity** (Low profit impact, high supply risk)
• Standard specification or 'commodity'-type items • Substitute products readily available • Competitive supply market with many suppliers	• Unique specification • Supplier's technology important • Production-based scarcity due to low demand and/or few sources of supply • Usage fluctuation not routinely predictable • Potential storage risk

Vertical axis: Impact on business (internal issues), High to Low. Horizontal axis: Supply risk/supply market complexity (external issues), Low to High.

Figure 8.1 Kraljic's tactical procurement matrix (adapted from Kraljic, 1983)

Routine: Efficient Process

When purchase items have a low profit impact and low supply risk, the procurement tactic should emphasize competition among suppliers to reduce transaction and unit costs. This requires high buyer power and multiple suppliers, competing primarily on a cost basis. Examples of this include low-value commodities such as nuts, bolts or rivets in manufacturing, or stationery for offices, or low-skilled, temporary labour for a building site.

Bottleneck: Reliable Process

When purchase items have low profit impact and high supply risk, suppliers tend to have very high power, because if supply is not available it will cause loss of production or service delivery to the end user. Examples could include processor chips for personal computers, or fuel deliveries to a petrol station, because without the supply of these products the end user has no product. To ensure constant availability, a long-term service contract is normally established between the buyer and supplier. In such cases it is normal to have a single supplier that makes very frequent and very reliable deliveries.

Leverage: Cost-effective Process

When purchase items have a high profit impact and low supply risk, the procurement tactic is often to liaise closely with a small number of suppliers to ensure that the product meets specifications and is sold at a reasonable cost. Consider, for example, the supply of seats for car manufacturers, or logistics providers for Internet-based retailers. These elements form a substantial part of the cost of the end product, which can often be tailored to customers' specific requirements. Leveraging can involve pooling together related products or services from within the buying organization (which may have previously been geographically dispersed) to increase the contract size and therefore the buyer's bargaining power.

Critical: Cooperative Process

Critical items have both high profit impact and high supply risk. Organizations often have key suppliers who account for the majority of the companies' purchasing costs, such as module engine manufacturers for aircraft manufacturers, or IT support for banks. This type of supplier is often single-sourced, and an in-depth, long-term relationship results, because the switching costs and the potential disruption to output if the product or service is not delivered would be extremely high. The emphasis in this case is on long-term collaboration and mutual dependence, rather than short-term cost minimization.

Despite the strengths of this matrix, it is designed to be applied only at a tactical level, and it seeks to optimize a single buyer–supplier relationship, and by doing so may actually sub-optimize the overall performance of an enterprise or supplier network.

> **The key point is** that different procurement contexts need different types of procurement tactics and processes.

As the characteristics of purchased items vary from having low to high profit and supply risks, the relationship that the firm shares with its suppliers should match the characteristics of these items. For instance, it would not be efficient for a firm to share strategic information with a supplier that is supplying simple commodity items. It would be equally damaging if a firm dealt with its suppliers of critical components without considering the long-term effects of their partnerships.

The nature of the relationship between the supplier and the manufacturer can vary from an arm's length relationship to a strategic partnership, as shown in Table 8.1. The *arm's length relationship* fits best when the manufacturer buys low-value, standardized products from its suppliers. These components typically are not related to the manufacturer's core competence, nor do they play a significant role in differentiating the buying firm's products. For example, sourcing of routine, non-critical components (such as nuts, bolts and washers) that can be bought in high volumes does not require much coordination between the manufacturer and the suppliers.

Strategic partnerships, on the other hand, are typically pursued when the manufacturer needs to have a close collaboration with its suppliers. This type of relationship tends to be pursued when the products are non-standard

Table 8.1 Characteristics of arm's length relationships and strategic partnerships

	Arm's length relationships	**Strategic partnerships**
Product/input characteristics	• Commodity/standardized products • Open architecture products • Stand alone (no or few interaction effects with other inputs) • Low degree of supplier–buyer interdependence • Low-value inputs	• Customized, non-standard products • Closed architecture products • Multiple interaction effects with other inputs • High degree of supplier–buyer interdependence • High-value inputs
Supplier management practices	• Single functional interface • Price benchmarking • Minimal assistance (minimal investment in inter-firm knowledge-sharing routines) • Supplier performance can be easily contracted *ex ante* • Contractual safeguards are sufficient to enforce agreements	• Multiple functional interfaces • Capabilities benchmarking • Substantial assistance (substantial investments in inter-firm knowledge-sharing routines) • Supplier performance on non-contractables (e.g. innovation, quality, responsiveness) is important • Self-enforcing agreements are necessary for optimal performance (e.g. trust, stock ownership.)

Source: adapted from Dyer *et al.* (1998).

or unique, with high-value inputs (e.g. rare materials, unique technologies, etc.), and critical items. Because of this, the supplier and the manufacturer both seek to enhance their capabilities. There is also substantial investment in fostering inter-firm knowledge sharing routines. The case study on Jeep's WIPER in Chapter 5, for instance, describes the strategic partnership shared between Chrysler and Motorola in order to make the silent-relay WIPER a success.

Suppliers and Product Life Cycle Effects

The strength of the relationship between members of a supplier network or enterprise changes over time, as shown in Figure 8.2, which illustrates the *partnership life cycle effect*. Initially, relationships may start off shakily but, if successful, move to a rapid growth stage and then into a mature phase as innovation and profitability

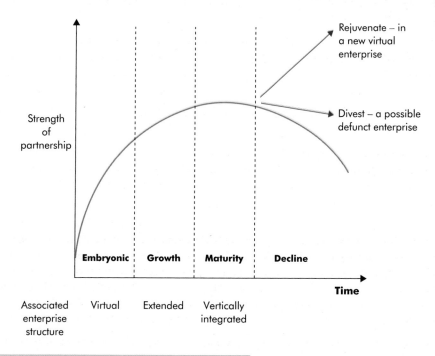

Figure 8.2 Partnership life cycle effect (adapted from Sako, 1992)

wane. At this point, tough decisions need to be made. Successful relationships can have a strong effect on product life cycles, and can affect whether a company decides to invest in rejuvenation, chooses to divest selected products, or falls into decline.

The figure also shows how the strength of the relationship relates to the type of enterprise structure. As the enterprise moves from a virtual to a vertically integrated structure, the strength of the partnership shifts from weak, at the embryonic stage, to strong, at the maturity stage.

BUSINESS INTEGRATION

CRITICAL PERSPECTIVE

Early Supplier Involvement

Many firms are convinced that having a relationship with their customers and suppliers is an important source of competitive advantage. As many firms continue to reduce their supplier base and rely more on system integrators, *early supplier involvement* (ESI) becomes crucial. ESI refers to a form of cooperation in which manufacturers involve suppliers at an early stage of the product or service development process. It is a means of integrating a supplier's capabilities into the manufacturer's supply chain and operations. In doing so, the manufacturer might gain from reduced development costs, improved overall performance, reduced development lead time, and access to the supplier's technical expertise and capabilities.

But involving suppliers early in the development process also imposes challenges, such as trust between the parties and difficulties in matching technical capabilities. It can be hard to gain supplier buy-in at the early stages before there is any financial incentive, and both parties need to provide a substantial investment of time and resources to develop and manage their business relationship.

The degree of supplier involvement needed depends on the complexity of the product or service being developed. The timing of involvement and competitive pressures among the suppliers also need to be taken into consideration. The firm needs to decide whether the supplier should be involved from the beginning of the project, and whether the supplier has the expertise and capability required to support the project all the way. If, for some reason, the supplier cannot support the project, the firm needs to find another qualified supplier, which might be extremely difficult.

Suppliers can be involved in the planning, design and production stages (Figure 8.3). In the automotive industry, the planning phase is often referred to as the *functional specification phase*, whereas the design

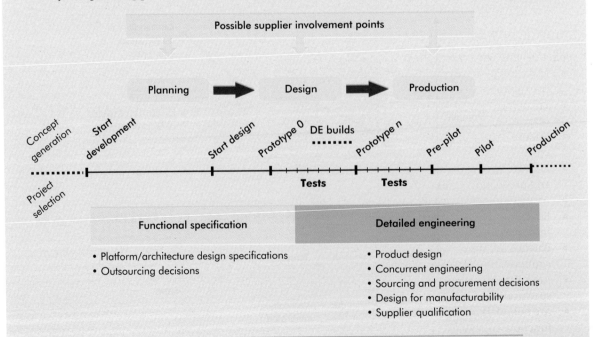

Figure 8.3 Supplier involvement points in new product development (Mikkola and Skjøtt-Larsen, 2004)

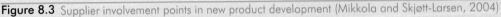

and production steps are often referred to as the *detailed engineering phase* (Clark and Fujimoto, 1991; Lamming, 1993). Involving suppliers requires that joint engineering processes be adopted (e.g. computer-aided design tools). Engineering expertise must also be shared.

> **The key point is** that most firms regard their ability to manage designs as their core competencies, and hence any involvement with the suppliers during the new product development process is carefully handled, often with strategic partnerships.

Challenges in Managing Supplier Relationships

Some factors have a negative impact on the success of supplier relationships. These might be:

- Changes in the supply base due to short-term, cost-oriented criteria rather than long-term value creation
- Late and insufficient involvement of suppliers in the development process
- Lack of open communication and information sharing.

These factors cause quality problems, increased costs and unforeseen changes, which can delay the start of production or service delivery (Binder *et al.*, 2008). The later changes take place, the more severe the impact will be.

Common reasons for switching suppliers change as a project matures. For example, during the early conceptual stages, technological and innovation issues are drivers for switching supplier. In the later stages, quality and time issues are more important. Ironically, this pattern increases time delays, quality problems and cost, which leads to a vicious circle of supplier switches and R&D ineffectiveness. Supplier managers believe this can be reduced by:

- Quick and early problem-solving through early collaboration
- Risk and reward sharing
- Less opportunistic behaviour through shared strategic thinking
- Increased communication and information sharing
- Joint definition of product and process specifications
- Clearly defined responsibilities and convergence of expectations
- Better responsiveness to critical issues through stronger integration.

Improving Supplier Relationships

Supplier relationships can be improved if *system integrators*:

- Make longer-term commitments to suppliers early on, with guaranteed return business for suppliers over a product's lifetime
- Encourage open-book accounting, where the target price of each product or service ensures a profit margin for suppliers, and is unaffected by renegotiations for unforeseen changes
- Endorse whole life cycle costing rather than just the short-term, upfront research and development costs
- Endorse open source standards for information sharing for things such as design data, time schedules and production volumes
- Assume the role of leader and coordinator within inter-firm R&D projects
- Balance internal and external know-how, as success is based on the effective exchange of technical information and the social interfaces between the members
- Balance the supply base to consider product attributes such as complex systems, standards and commonality, as well as supplier attributes such as R&D competence, high quality and low cost
- Are aware of customer needs and requirements, and translate these into technical functionalities and specifications for suppliers
- Are boundary spanning, transforming the traditional role of purchasing into a more strategic sourcing function involving a cross-functional and inter-organizational R&D committee composed of all the key members.

Supplier relationships will also improve if *suppliers*:

- Take more ownership, playing a more active role during inter-company R&D projects, by making investments in testing and tooling, actively setting quality standards and prices
- Offer exclusivity to the systems integrators in return for early and long-term commitment with potential return business, instead of aiming to standardize parts and services to sell to others
- Are more open to organizational agility, adjusting organizational structures and processes to adapt to working in inter-organizational relationships
- Develop their own integration competencies to manage their sub-suppliers, because inter-organizational R&D collaboration is increasingly being carried out at system and module levels.

The key point is that to develop sustainable supplier management and high-value outputs, a high level of trust is needed between all parties. This helps the transition from opportunistic behaviour in loose supplier networks to collaborative thinking in tight, strategically aligned enterprises.

🛈 Stop and Think

1 Preserving competition while encouraging cooperation is almost a contradiction. In addition to the above suggestions, how else can this be accomplished?

Third Party Logistics

Logistics refers to the process of planning and implementing the movement and storage of goods in the supply chain. As many companies expanded their operations to international markets, various logistics service providers began to emerge, often referred to as *third party logistics* providers. In the European logistics market, for instance, approximately 25% of the total logistics spend is outsourced to third party logistics providers (www.transportintelligence.com).

A *third party logistics* (TPL or 3PL) provider can be treated as an external supplier that performs some or all parts of a company's functions, especially logistics services. Examples of TPL services include facility management, transportation, warehouse management, call centres, and administration. The best-known TPL providers are UPS (United Parcel Service), FedEx (Federal Express), DHL and TNT.

There are several advantages of using TPL providers (Simchi-Levi *et al.*, 2008):

- *Focus on core strengths*: it allows a company to focus on its core competencies, leaving the logistics expertise to the TPL providers.
- *Provide technological flexibility*: often companies do not have the time, resources, or expertise to update their technology and equipment, such as RFID (radio-frequency identification). Many TPL providers have the capability to constantly update information technology and equipment in a quicker and more cost-effective way.
- *Provide other flexibilities*: increasingly, suppliers are demanding rapid replenishment, which may require regional warehousing. The TPL providers will provide services for this warehousing, so that the supplier can meet customer requirements without committing capital and limiting flexibility by constructing a new facility or committing to a long-term lease. TPL providers can also bundle customized services to fit companies' specific needs.

Depending on the required skills shared between the parties, TPL relationships can be classified into four types (Halldorsson and Skjøtt-Larsen, 2004):

- *Market exchange*: almost no specific assets or integration exist between the parties. No specific skills are required from the providers (e.g. shippers who buy transportation and logistics services on the 'spot market').
- *Customized logistics solutions*: the clients can customize the desired package of solutions, which can be bundled together from a broad range of standard services, such as transportation and warehousing services.
- *Joint logistics solutions*: the collaboration is seen as a win–win solution, as the two parties collaborate to find unique logistics solutions. For example, some companies provide a 'one-stop solution' for their clients, acting as the single interface between the clients and the multiple logistics service providers.

- *In-house logistics solutions*: logistics is considered the core skill for the TPL provider. A broad range of management and value-adding logistics services is offered. The collaboration also involves knowledge about system integration and inter-organizational teams from different management levels.

 Stop and Think

2 Would it be difficult for TPLs to provide customized services?

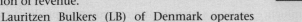

SHORT CASE 8.1

Lauritzen Bulkers

Did you know that around 90% of world trade is carried by ships? Do you know what happens when a global transportation network is disrupted? Recall the disruptions in air space caused by the ash from the volcanic eruption in Iceland on 15 April 2010. The International Air Transport Association (IATA) estimated that, within a week, it affected almost a third of global flights, costing airlines about US$1.7 billion of revenue.

Source: © Ron Niebrugge/Alamy

Lauritzen Bulkers (LB) of Denmark operates around 85 vessels, which specialize in ocean transport of dry bulk cargo – that is, commodities such as coal, grains, bauxite, iron ore aggregates, food products and steel products. These goods are typically transported from the Americas, Australia and Africa to Asia and Europe. With self-loading and discharge capabilities, LB can readily respond to almost any market. It also has one of the youngest fleets afloat, with an average vessel age of 5–6 years. It makes about 500 voyages per year, equivalent to 22,000 vessel-days, transporting more than 20 million tons of over 45 different commodities.

While shipping bears the stigma of being a big polluter, it is actually the least damaging form of transportation (Figure 8.4). LB is committed to reducing CO_2 and other exhaust emissions, such as NO_x and SO_x. The new generation of LB's fleet is 25% more energy efficient than the 10–15 year old vessels it is replacing. Recently, LB introduced Lab-On-A-Ship™ (LOAS), an on-board system that can analyse fuel and lubricants automatically, making significant contributions to the engine performance of the vessels. It not only helps to make the vessels more reliable and efficient, but also ensures compliance with environmental standards.

CSR

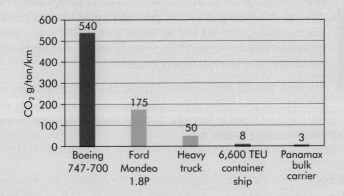

Figure 8.4 Comparison of CO2 emissions by different transport modes (European Shipowners' Association and International Chamber of Shipping)

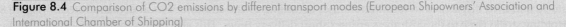

▶ As explained by the Senior Technical Manager:

Having more efficient ships is more attractive for the customers. Our customers, the charterers, are the ones who hire our ships to freight cargo from A to B. Having lower operational costs in terms of fuel consumption is a plus. Energy conservation, and subsequently lower fuel consumption, reduces the overall operating cost and negative environmental impact. If we can show that we can operate the ships very effectively in terms of fuel consumption, it's a benefit for the charter, as they are typically the ones paying for the fuel. This eventually will have a tremendous impact on the environmental reputation of the company, and sustain a 'green image'.

Questions
1. Why do you think disruptions in one mode of transportation, such as air, impact on the supply of and demand for goods across the world?
2. How would you decide on the right supply chain strategy and mode of transportation for your goods?
3. How would new environmental regulations impact on the transportation of goods between regions?

Source: Juliana Hsuan, Copenhagen Business School

The Impact of Product Design on Supply Chains

The way a supply chain is configured has an influence on how a manufacturer of complex products organizes and coordinates design activity. Nokia's supply chain, for instance, handles 100 billion components, 60 strategic suppliers, and 10 factories worldwide. New product introductions and variations are also impressive: one phone can have 170 handset variations and 250 sales package variants. To manage the supply chain, Nokia nurtures value-based strategic partnerships with suppliers, which are based on information sharing and flexibility. Companies such as Nokia design their new products and services while taking into consideration their supply strategies, such as mass customization and postponement.

Mass Customization and Postponement Strategies

In Chapter 5 we showed how mass customization provides products that meet customers' individual needs through combinations of modular components. There are various ways in which components can be combined, stored and assembled in order to create the desired customization. In Chapter 6, we learned that mass customization is a strategy for delivering different products or services at approximately the same cost as mass-producing them. It requires mass collaboration (in logistics, manufacturing, service delivery, etc.) along the supply chain.

Postponement: delaying the timing of crucial processes in which end products assume their specific functionalities, features and identities.

One central feature of mass customization is **postponement**. Postponement is about delaying the timing of crucial processes by which end products assume their specific functionalities, features and identities (Lee, 1998). It is a strategy that helps managers to achieve delivery of goods in a timely and cost-effective manner, by rearranging the production and logistics supply chains.

The logic behind postponement is that risk and uncertainty costs are tied to the differentiation of goods (i.e. form, place and time) that occurs during manufacturing and logistics operations, resulting in four types of strategy: full speculation, manufacturing postponement, logistics postponement, and full postponement (Figure 8.5).

Full Speculation Strategy

The *full speculation strategy* is the equivalent of mass production strategy, in the sense that the goods are made to stock, and then dispatched to local warehouses according to the amount of local demand forecast (Figure 8.6). Holding stocks close to the customers ensures short delivery times. This also means that products are distributed through a decentralized distribution system, requiring high inventory investment.

	Logistics	
	Speculation *Decentralized inventories*	Postponement *Centralized inventories and direct distribution*
Speculation *Make to inventory*	Full speculation strategy	Logistics postponement strategy
Postponement *Make to order*	Manufacturing postponement strategy	Full postponement strategy

Figure 8.5 The postponement and speculation matrix (adapted from Pagh and Cooper, 1998)

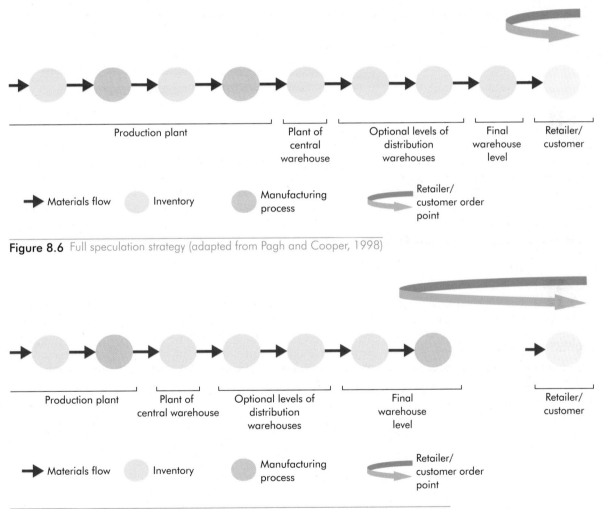

Figure 8.6 Full speculation strategy (adapted from Pagh and Cooper, 1998)

Figure 8.7 Manufacturing postponement strategy (adapted from Pagh and Cooper, 1998)

Manufacturing Postponement

With *manufacturing postponement*, the product retains its standard form in the manufacturing process for as long as possible. The differentiation is delayed until the latest possible point – normally when a customer order has been received (Figure 8.7). The final packaging of mobile phones, for instance, is often carried out by a TPL provider (after receiving the customer order), who has an inventory of handsets, manuals, SIM cards and accessories. Afterwards the package is shipped directly to the customer.

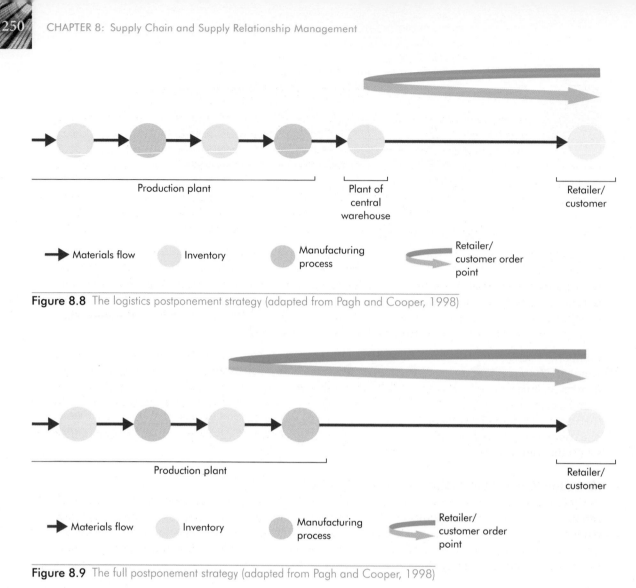

Figure 8.8 The logistics postponement strategy (adapted from Pagh and Cooper, 1998)

Figure 8.9 The full postponement strategy (adapted from Pagh and Cooper, 1998)

Logistics Postponement

With *logistics postponement*, a full line of anticipated inventory is stored at a few strategic locations (Figure 8.8). The changes in inventory location are delayed downstream in the supply chain to the latest possible point. The logistics operations begin after a customer order is initiated. For example, in order to improve the spare parts distribution for Ford, DB Schenker collects the required car parts from over 800 suppliers in Germany and Austria and brings them together in a consolidation centre in Cologne, where the car parts are repackaged and taken to the distribution centres of car factories.

Full Postponement

Full postponement takes place when both manufacturing and logistics activities, both customer order initiated, are postponed (Figure 8.9). For example, Bang & Olufsen, a Danish manufacturer of audio-video systems, can assemble, test and deliver customized products directly to the final customers in Europe within five days.

Component Design for Postponement and Mass Customization

CRITICAL PERSPECTIVE

Design for postponement refers to design of products or processes so that postponement is possible. It calls for a fundamental change of the product architecture, by using designs that standardize some of the components (hence changing the form of the product architecture) or process steps. In order for postponement to be successful, products or processes should be modular in structure (Lee, 1998). In other words, product modularity requires module interfaces to be redesigned so that they can easily be assembled and tested as a total unit. Furthermore, because postponement strategies involve many suppliers, collaboration becomes inevitable between multiple functions (e.g. cross-functional integration) and organizations (e.g. collaborative efforts among multiple firms).

One of the aims of the postponement strategy is to retain product commonality as far downstream in the supply chain as possible. Whereas the goal of mass customization is to produce customized goods at low costs, postponement strategy focuses on delaying customization as long as possible. The extent of customization and postponement of products is rooted in how modular the product architecture is. Taken together, postponement, mass customization and product modularity are dependent on supply chain strategies to facilitate assembly, logistics and outsourcing decisions.

Component design for postponement can take place in the following way (Figure 8.10). Let's assume that a mobile phone company sells two products, X and Y, to two markets: the US (market A) and Europe (market B). It needs to develop product specific components for each mobile phone – a component set for X and a component set for Y. The company then decides to redesign these products, and discovers with the advance of technology, that it is now possible to standardize the components for both phones X into one component set we can call Z. Now the company needs only to focus on producing one component set (Z) that can serve both markets A and B.

Mass Customization and Postponement Supply Management

We have learned that mass customization strategies are closely linked with postponement and modularization strategies. The various points at which customers can influence the degree of customization also require that firms manage their supply chains according to how the product platform can be modularized. The comparison of mass customization and postponement supply chains with respect to a traditional mass production supply chain is illustrated in Table 8.2.

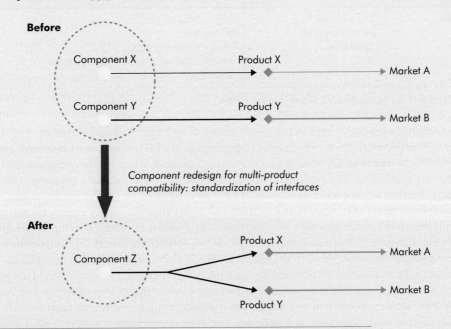

Figure 8.10 Component design for postponement (Mikkola and Skjøtt-Larsen, 2004)

Table 8.2 Mass customization and postponement supply chains

Modularization elements	Traditional supply chain	Mass customization supply chain	Postponement supply chain
Interface compatibility effects	• Integrated vertical structure • Long development lead time	• Modular product architecture • Reduction of development lead time • Vertical coordination	• Customer decoupling points • Accurate and short customer response time
Component customization	• Design and manufacturing focus • In-house product development • Standardized components	• Autonomous innovation in NPD • Customer focus • Design for manufacturability	• Process design • Design for postponement
Value inputs	• Economies of scale • Exploiting advantages of market mechanism • Standardization of operations • Consolidation of outbound logistics	• Outsourcing • Flexibility towards specific customer's needs • Economies of scale and scope	• Reduced inventory costs and risks of obsolescence • Increased flexibility towards market needs and changes • Economies of scale and scope
Supplier–buyer interdependence	• Arm's length • Supplier involvement in development not critical • Multiple sourcing	• Early supplier involvement in NPD • Strategic partnership • Supplier as system integrator • High interdependence	• Customer relationship management • Involvement of TPL providers in final manufacturing and logistics • Direct deliveries to customers through merge-in-transit
Examples	Ford's Model T Generic bicycles Light bulbs Tyres	Dell computers HP printers Oticon's hearing aids Bang & Olufsen's audio-video systems Smart cars	

Source: adapted from Mikkola and Skjøtt-Larsen (2004).

When modularizing a product platform for supply chain, the company should consider:

- *Interface compatibility effects*, which refer to the degree to which component interfaces are specified and standardized. Mixing and matching is possible when interface compatibility effects are minimized. The push nature of a traditional supply chain does not see interface standardization as important, as it tends to have an integrated vertical structure, with long development lead times. Mass customization and postponement supply chains, on the other hand, seek to maximize interface standardization as a means to reduce development lead time. With standardization it is also possible to decide the decoupling points for postponement.

- *Component customization* refers to the extent to which a component can be customized. Customized components, as opposed to standard components, are often dedicated to specific applications. The traditional supply chain does not give too much importance to customization, as it often focuses on efficiency of design and manufacturing processes, dictated by the production of components in high volumes. The mass customization supply chain focuses on customer needs, and encourages the new product development (NPD) group to innovate independently, owing to the modular nature of the product architectures. The engineers also have to consider how to design the products so that they can be manufactured (i.e. design for manufacturability). The postponement supply chain considers how to organize a company's processes to support the products that are designed for postponement.

- *Value inputs* refer to the value-adding inputs that differentiate the buyer's final system. The relevance of added value is relative to the structure of supply chains, such as the number of tiers of suppliers. First-tier suppliers play a more prominent role in creating value inputs, as they are more willing to invest in product and process developments, and are also responsible for coordinating the required supply of inputs from the second-tier and lower-tier suppliers. Parts supplied by the key suppliers often have higher strategic value. The traditional supply chain focuses on economies of scale, and tends to exploit the advantages of the market mechanism (e.g. many tiers of suppliers). The value inputs are often gained from standardization of operations, and consolidation of outbound logistics. Mass customization and postponement supply chains seek to gain both from economies of scale (i.e. high volume production) and from economies of scope (i.e. product differentiation through customization). Postponement supply chains also focus on how to reduce inventory costs, and how to manage risks of obsolescence, such as when accidents take place, disrupting the flow of the supply of the components.

- *Supplier–buyer interdependence* refers to the degree of supplier involvement in product development that leads to capabilities benchmarking, trust development and creation of inter-firm knowledge. The traditional supply chain tends not to involve suppliers in NPD. Multiple sourcing and arm's length relationships with suppliers are often the policy. The mass customization supply chain, on the other hand, sees key suppliers as partners for the success of platform development, especially with the system integrators, and this close collaboration leads to increased interdependence between the partners. The postponement supply chain takes a focus on customer relationship management in terms of services and logistics efficiency, by involving TPL providers in the manufacturing and logistics processes.

The key point is that when an organization is designing a new product, it should take supply chain strategies into consideration.

SHORT CASE 8.2   Did IBM Make the Wrong Move?

Until 1985, all of IBM's printed circuit boards (PCBs) were built in house. By the late 1990s it made only about 10% of its boards. Furthermore, it used to make 85% of the memory chips used in computers, but by 1999 the figure had dropped to 15%. IBM used to build its power supplies and keyboards, and assemble all of its own computers in house. Today, these tasks are outsourced to contract manufacturers, including PC assembly, manufactured notebook computers, lower-end servers and workstations, and mass storage devices. From 1986 to 1996 the proportion of IBM's revenue spent on outside suppliers increased from 28% to 51%. The economic outcome that resulted meant that IBM had reduced the overall costs by about 20% through outsourcing (Carbone, 1999). In 2005 IBM sold its PC division to Lenovo Group, the largest PC maker in China, formerly known as Legend.

Source: © Feng Yu/iStock

Questions

1 What had been the long-term effect of outsourcing for IBM?
2 What happened with the key suppliers of IBM components, such as Microsoft and Intel?
3 To what extent did this decision change the relationships IBM shared with its suppliers and customers?

Source: based on Carbone (1999).

ⓘ Stop and Think

3 Is there a limit to standardization?

Dynamics of Supply Networks

BUSINESS INTEGRATION

In Chapter 4 we learned how supply chain relationships can be organized. Here we present an alternative model, focusing on how products can be designed to shape the supply networks. As mentioned in Chapter 5, modular product architectures enable various specializations to take place independently of each other. This encourages innovation and technical advances to be developed in isolation. Any supplier can develop innovations, independent of other suppliers. This also means that suppliers compete with each other. Often the supplier with superior capabilities captures the market when its proprietary systems are established (such as Intel's microprocessor for IBM). Proprietary systems tend to encourage integration with other systems so that more value can be offered to the customers.

It is fair to say that it is extremely difficult for a firm to stay dominant in the marketplace for a long time. Vertically integrated firms are typically large corporations with hierarchical organizational structures, making them extremely rigid and unable to respond to rapid changes. These corporations face increasing competition from niche players that seek to have a share of the market. Eventually these corporations have to find ways to become more efficient, and be able to respond to market changes faster. The once-dominant integral product can no longer compete with the innovations from the niche players, either in price or in performance. This will force the company to modularize the product system (i.e. decompose the system into simpler portions). This will allow it to outsource portions of the system and have more supply options. When products become modular, and when there are many competing suppliers, the industry becomes horizontal.

Supplier relationships can change from a vertically integrated structure (with integral product strategies) to a horizontally fragmented structure (with modular product strategies), as shown in the *double helix model* in Figure 8.11.

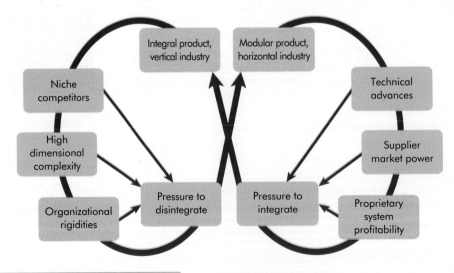

Figure 8.11 The double helix model (Fine, 1998)

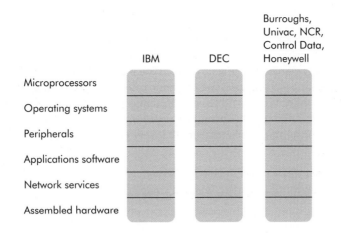

Figure 8.12 Computer industry structure, 1975–1985 (Fine, 1998)

Figure 8.12 provides an illustration of how the structure of the computer industry looked between 1975 and 1985. The industry was structured vertically with three main dominant players, each with its own integral product architectures and proprietary systems.

With IBM's decision to standardize its PC platform, the computer industry suddenly became fragmented, with a large number of players dominating in specific parts of the computer system. The industry structure had become less vertically integrated, owing to the modularity of product architectures (Figure 8.13).

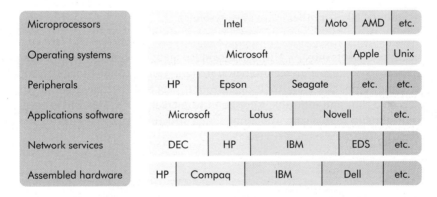

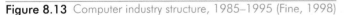

Figure 8.13 Computer industry structure, 1985–1995 (Fine, 1998)

The key point is that whatever decisions a company makes in order to optimize its supply chain, one of the most difficult challenges is to predict how the supply chain structure might change over time.

WORKED
EXAMPLE
8.1

Double Helix Model

There are twice as many bicycles as automobiles worldwide. Bicycles were introduced in the 19th century, and there have been few changes to its product architecture since then. The bicycle's inherently modular design allowed a large number of suppliers to compete in innovation as well as in price.

Shimano currently has approximately 50% of the market share in the global bicycle component market (such as drive train, brake, wheel and pedal components), and major control of the technological development of this industry. It gained this huge market share by integrating traditionally modular components into new components. For instance, the rear hub and cog set were integrated in a way that made other brands of cogs and hubs incompatible with Shimano's components. Shimano also integrated its shift levers into the braking system, requiring bicycle assemblers to purchase Shimano brake and shift levers as a single unit. Furthermore, bike makers that rely on Shimano parts also became distributors (Kerber, 1998).

Problem: *Apply the double helix model to describe the current bicycle industry, and predict what is going to happen in this industry. How might this affect Shimano's market share?*

Approach: Start by assessing whether the product architecture of the bicycle is modular or integral, and whether the industry structure is horizontal or vertical. In Figure 8.14, pick the starting point as either box 1 (modular product, horizontal industry) or box 6 (integral product, vertical structure).

Solution:

Step 1 Start with box 1: The modular design of bicycles and the huge number of suppliers suggest that the current bicycle industry has a horizontal structure, and the product architecture is modular.

Step 2 The Double Helix Model predicts that the technical advances (box 2 – e.g. integration of rear hub and cog set), supplier market power (box 3 – e.g. requiring bicycle assemblers to purchase Shimano brake and shift levers as a single unit), and proprietary system profitability (box 4 – e.g. 50% market share) enjoyed by Shimano are going to change.

Step 3 According to the model, the bicycle industry will face significant pressure to integrate (box 5) into a vertical industry structure, with bikes that are characterized by integral product architectures (box 6 – e.g. electric-powered bikes or other innovative systems).

Step 4 When this happens, the various component makers and assemblers will face competition from their respective niche markets (box 7). This will introduce many new dimensions of complexity (box 8 – e.g. capacity for market expansion, technological imitation from competitors, control of the supply chain, etc.). As these companies grow, their organization structures become rigid (box 9): that is, the organizations become slow and inflexible to respond to market needs. This will exert pressure for the industry to disintegrate (box 10) again into a horizontal structure, with bikes having modular product architectures (box 1). The cycle starts all over again.

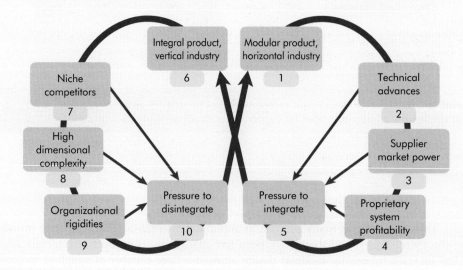

Figure 8.14

Tactics for Supplier Management

Functional Versus Innovative Products

Demand for products and services is difficult to predict, and supplier relationships are affected by this. In order to manage supplier relationships effectively, a company needs to understand the nature of the demand for the product or service it supplies. Uncertainties in demand for products can be better managed if we understand the type of product – that is, whether they are functional or innovative.

Functional products are products that have long product life cycles, a low contribution margin, low product variety, and predictable demand. For example, fast-moving consumer goods sold in grocery stores typically have stable, predictable demand and long life cycles. The low product variety makes accurate forecasting easier. Certainly the nature of demand for toothpaste and toilet paper can be quite different from those for high-speed cameras. Toothpaste and toilet paper are products that satisfy our basic needs, which don't change much over time. They are staples, with long product cycles, that people buy in a wide range of retail outlets. Their demands are predictable and stable. Functional products tend to have stable supply chains, and the focus for operations is on increasing efficiency through lean thinking, which is explored more in Chapter 10, or on gaining from economies of scale through mass production.

Innovative products, on the other hand, are products with short product life cycles, a high contribution margin, high product variety, and unpredictable demand. In comparison with toilet paper, high-speed cameras have shorter product life cycles, because the companies are forced to introduce innovations to counteract innovations from the imitators. The market ends up with a large variety of innovative cameras. The short life cycle and large variety make demand prediction difficult. Average stock-out rates tend to be high too. Other examples of innovative products are high-end computers, state of the art semiconductors, and mass-customized goods. The differences between functional and innovative products are shown in Table 8.3.

Services, too, face similar issues. For instance, standard services (such as those from McDonald's) can be more easily predicted than innovative services (such as Internet shopping for organic food).

Efficient Versus Responsive Supplier Relationships

In order to understand how to manage the supply chain for functional and innovative products, we need to understand the differences between efficient and responsive supply. Efficient supply is characterized by longer production lead times and larger batch sizes, which allow the firm to produce at a low unit cost. Responsive supply focuses on the ability to respond to wide ranges of quantities demanded, meet short lead times, handle a large variety of products, build innovative products, and meet a high service level.

Supply for innovative products should be responsive in order to deal with unpredictable demand – that is, innovative products should have a market-responsive supply chain. On the other hand, functional products require efficient and stable supply chains to maintain high utilization rates of manufacturing. These characteristics are illustrated in Table 8.4.

> ### ⓘ Stop and Think
>
> **4** Do all functional products have stable and mature supply processes? Do all innovative products have evolving processes? For example, how have the distribution channels for USB memory sticks changed during the past 10 years?

The Bullwhip Effect

BUSINESS INTEGRATION

The *bullwhip effect*, also referred to as the Forrester effect, is a term used to explain why information about the final customer's actual demand gets distorted from one end of the supply chain to the other: when there are disruptions in the ordering process, demand variability increases as we move upstream towards the supplier. Figure 8.15 shows the amplification of order variability from consumers to the supplier.

Table 8.3 Functional versus innovative products

Aspects of demand	Functional (predictable demand)	Innovative (unpredictable demand)
Product life cycle	More than 2 years	3 months to 1 year
Contribution margin*	5% to 20%	20% to 60%
Product variety	Low (10 to 20 variants per category)	High (often millions of variants)
Average margin of error in the forecast at the time production is committed	10%	40% to 100%
Average stock-out rate	1% to 2%	10% to 40%
Average forced end-of-the-season mark-down as percentage of full price	0%	10% to 25%
Lead time required for made-to-order products	6 months to 1 year	1 day to 2 weeks

* The contribution margin equals price minus variable cost divided by price, and is expressed as a percentage.

Source: adapted from Fisher (1997).

Table 8.4 Efficient versus responsive supply

	Physically efficient process	Market-responsive process
Primary purpose	Supply predictable demand efficiently at the lowest possible cost	Respond quickly to unpredictable demand in order to minimize stock-outs, forced markdowns, and obsolete inventory
Manufacturing focus	Maintain high average utilization rate	Deploy excess buffer capacity
Inventory strategy	Generate high turns and minimize inventory through the chain	Deploy significant buffer stocks of parts or finished goods
Lead time focus	Shorten lead time as long as it doesn't increase cost	Invest aggressively in ways to reduce lead time
Approach to choosing suppliers	Select primarily for cost and quality	Select primarily for speed, flexibility, and quality
Product design strategy	Maximize performance and minimize cost	Use modular design in order to postpone product differentiation for as long as possible

Source: adapted from Fisher (1997).

It shows the order patterns faced by each intersection in the supply chain, consisting of a supplier, a manufacturer, a wholesaler, a retailer, and consumers. The retailer places an order on the manufacturer that is based on the consumer sales data. The wholesaler plans its production based on the order it receives from the retailer; the manufacturer plans its production based on the order it receives from the wholesaler; and, finally, the supplier plans its production according to the order it receives from the manufacturer. As each party makes decisions based on the information it receives from the downstream member, the demand information gets distorted. The figure shows that the retailer's orders to the wholesaler display greater variability than the consumer sales; the wholesaler's orders to the manufacturer shows even larger variability; and, finally, the manufacturer's order to the supplier has the largest oscillations.

Imagine you are playing 'Chinese Whispers' in a party with your friends. One person (consumer) whispers a word or a phrase into the ear of the person next to him or her (retailer). The person who gets the whisper passes

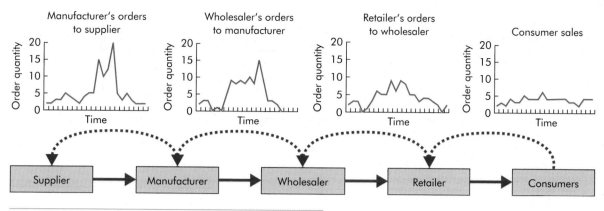

Figure 8.15 The bullwhip effect (adapted from Lee *et al.*, 1997)

it down to the next person, and so on, until the last person (supplier). The last person has to say what he or she thinks was whispered to him or her. There are always errors or misunderstandings during the retellings, and they accumulate as the whispers are passed: therefore the message received by the last person is often quite different from the message sent by the first.

There are four factors that lead to the bullwhip effect:
- *Inaccurate demand forecast updating*: forecasting relies on the order history from the company's immediate customers. When all parties in the supply chain add a percentage to their demand forecasts, the true customer demand becomes distorted.
- *Order batching*: customers place orders in batches at varying cycles. Some order daily, whereas others place orders weekly or monthly.
- *Price fluctuation*: distributors and manufacturers periodically offer special promotions such as price discounts, quantity discounts or coupons, in order to boost the order quantity. This encourages customers to buy in quantities that do not reflect their immediate needs. Often the customers will not place the next order until the inventory is sold.
- *Rationing and shortage gaming*: customers order more than they need when they know there will be a shortage in supply. Later, when demand is stabilized, excessive orders disappear and cancellations pour in. This 'game' that the customers play with the orders gives the supplier little information about the product's real demand.

Let's consider how the bullwhip effect can be controlled to improve supply chain performance. This requires the firms to find ways to coordinate the information flow and plan along the supply chain: namely, information sharing, channel alignment, and operational efficiency (Table 8.5). *Information sharing* is concerned with how demand information at the downstream site is transmitted upstream. *Channel alignment* refers to the coordination of pricing, transportation, inventory planning and ownership between the upstream and downstream sites of a supply chain. Finally, *operations efficiency* is concerned with activities that improve the performance of the supply chain.

Distorted information can lead to inefficiencies, such as excessive inventory investment, poor customer service, lost revenues, misguided capacity plans, ineffective transportation, and missed production schedules (Lee *et al.*, 1997).

Table 8.5 A framework for supply chain coordination initiatives

Cause of bullwhip	Information sharing	Channel alignment	Operational efficiency
Demand forecast update	• Understanding system dynamics • Use point-of-sale (POS) data • Electronic data interchange (EDI) • Internet • Computer-assisted ordering (CAO)	• Vendor-managed inventory (VMI) • Discount for information sharing • Consumer direct	• Lead time reduction • Echelon-based inventory control
Order batching	• EDI • Internet ordering	• Discount for truck-load assortment • Delivery appointments • Consolidation • Logistics outsourcing	• Reduction in fixed cost of ordering by EDI or electronic commerce • CAO
Price fluctuations		• Continuous replenishment programme (CRP) • Everyday low cost (EDLC)	• Everyday low price (EDLP) • Activity-based costing (ABC)
Shortage gaming	• Sharing sales, capacity, and inventory data	• Allocation based on past sales	

Source: Lee *et al.* (1997).

WORKED EXAMPLE 8.2

Estimating Demand Fluctuations

You work as a supply chain manager of a large clothing retail store. One of the best-selling items at your store is the latest fashion bag from a Brazilian manufacturer called Gorgeous. You have always ordered 200 bags every six months (in March and in September). Now other retail stores have started to sell competing fashion bags. You notice that the sale of Gorgeous bags is declining, so you decide to reduce the order by 5%, to 190 bags. Assume that the supply chain of Gorgeous bags has four tiers: the retail store, the wholesaler, the manufacturer, and the supplier. Let's also assume that each tier keeps one period's worth of inventory.

Problem: *Estimate the demand fluctuation across the supply chain due to the 5% drop in demand order. How many periods does it take until each tier is able to meet the new demand?*

Approach: Start by calculating the production stock needed for each tier in order to satisfy the consumer demand. This can be done with the grid shown in Table 8.6.

Period 1 is the base of your calculations, where there are no disruptions in the supply chain. Every tier is able to supply the 200 bags.

In Period 2, however, the drop of market demand to 190 bags requires the retail store (RS) to have a final stock [stock (f)] of 190 bags. However, RS still has 200 bags of initial (or starting) stock [stock (i)], which means that RS needs only to have a production rate of 180 bags (this becomes the demand rate for the wholesaler W).

The production rate is simply two times the demand (to account for actual demand in that period, and also assuming the same demand for the next period). This is because you need to keep one period's worth of inventory.

Table 8.6

Time (period)	Supplier (S) Production rate	Supplier (S) Stock (i) / Stock (f)	Manufacturer (W) Production rate	Manufacturer (W) Stock (i) / Stock (f)	Wholesaler (M) Production rate	Wholesaler (M) Stock (i) / Stock (f)	Retail store (RS) Production rate	Retail store (RS) Stock (i) / Stock (f)	Market demand
1	200	200 / 200	200	200 / 200	200	200 / 200	200	200 / 200	200
2	40	200 / 120	120	200 / 160	160	200 / 180	180	200 / 190	190
3	360	120 / 240	240	160 / 200	200	180 / 190	190	190 / 190	190
4	120	240 / 180	180	190 / 190	190	190 / 190	190	190 / 190	190
5	200	180 / 190	190	190 / 190	190	190 / 190	190	190 / 190	190
6	190	190 / 190	190	190 / 190	190	190 / 190	190	190 / 190	190

The production rate of W for Period 2 is 2(180) − 200 = 160 bags

Production rate of W = Demand for M = 160 bags

Follow the same logic for each period, until each tier is able to meet the new demand of 190 bags.

Solution: In this case, it took six periods. Graphically, the demand fluctuations (or the production rates) for the entire supply chain are illustrated in Figure 8.16. Notice how the fluctuations amplify towards the supplier.

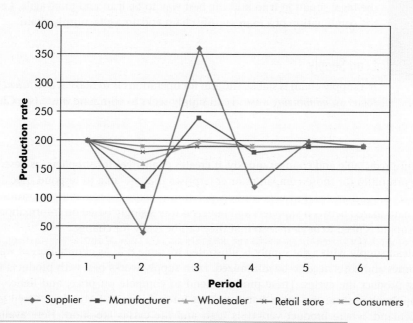

Figure 8.16 Demand fluctuation in the supply chain of fashion bags from Gorgeous

SHORT CASE 8.3

FitMe: New Solution for On-Line Apparel Shopping?

FitMe develops smart solutions for the apparel industry. It has size information on more than 300 brands of clothing. One of its products is Size Genie, which uses web-based software that allows individual shoppers to accurately determine their measurements. Its purpose is to enable consumers to purchase apparel with confidence. The Size Genie service can be used by retailers who wish to offer clothing purchases on line or at their retail stores.

With the increasing number of on-line retailers offering customized clothing, the information along the supply chain from the customer to the supplier should be as accurate as possible. Information technology and applications, such as Size Genie, align the supply chain by providing more accurate and on-time demand forecast updates. They also reduce order-batching problems, as customers can place orders whenever they wish, and the information is transmitted directly to the supplier. Price fluctuations as well as rationing and shortage gaming are also reduced, as customers do not have to purchase larger quantities than they need. In short, information sharing and collaboration between all parties in the supply chain can help reduce the bullwhip effect.

Questions

1. In what ways can information technology influence the bullwhip effect?
2. How can FitMe make sure that its products have the right supply chain?

Source: www.allbusiness.com

Leagile supply: combination of a lean supply chain and an agile supply chain.

Lean supply: seeks to develop a value stream to eliminate all waste.

Agile supply: use of market knowledge and the virtual corporation to exploit profitable opportunities in a volatile marketplace.

Leagile Supply

We have learned that variation in demand can be difficult to predict, and that companies need to match their products with the appropriate supply channels. The supply channel for mass-produced goods, for instance, would not be effective if the company wanted to be flexible, and to be able to respond to unique customer demand quickly. On the other hand, firms also seek to achieve efficiency by eliminating waste. In fact, the ideal situation is to find the best way to be lean and to be agile. **Leagile supply** is the combination of a **lean supply** chain and an **agile supply** chain.

Lean Supply

If a supply chain is stable, the aim for operations is to make it as *efficient* as possible, and focus on *minimizing waste*. Lean supply seeks to eliminate waste (see Chapter 10).

Agile Supply

When demand is unpredictable and changes quickly, it creates challenges for suppliers, as described above. But it also creates opportunities for those companies or enterprises that are able to respond quickly to changes in demand. *Agile suppliers* use market knowledge and cooperation to exploit profitable opportunities in a volatile marketplace. The data shared between suppliers and buyers is increasingly based on information technology. In order to be agile, suppliers need to be *flexible* so that they can be ready for change.

A comparison of lean supply with agile supply is illustrated in Table 8.7. As elimination of waste is central to being lean, lead times and costs need to be minimized. Lean supply works best with products with predictable demand and long product life cycles. These products tend to compete on price, and hence have low profit margins. Agile supply chains, on the other hand, fit best for fashion- or technology-based goods subject to volatile market demand, where product variety is high and life cycles are short. Here availability becomes the driver.

Table 8.7 Attributes of lean supply and agile supply

Distinguishing attributes	Lean supply	Agile supply
Typical products	Commodities	Fashion goods
Marketplace demand	Predictable	Volatile
Product variety	Low	High
Product life cycle	Long	Short
Customer drivers	Cost	Availability
Profit margin	Low	High
Dominant costs	Physical costs	Marketability costs
Stock-out penalties	Long-term contractual	Immediate and volatile
Purchasing policy	Buy goods	Assign capacity
Information enrichment	Highly desirable	Obligatory
Forecasting mechanism	Algorithmic	Consultative

Source: adapted from Mason-Jones *et al.* (2000).

Combining Lean and Agile

It is possible to combine the best of both the lean and agile approaches. The challenge is to balance efficiency and flexibility. To find the balance between lean and agile processes in supplier management, all parties involved need to understand the market requirements, such as product variety and demand variability (Figure 8.17). Whereas lean processes focus on developing a value stream to eliminate all waste, agile processes use market knowledge to find the value provided to the customers. Balancing the two processes means finding the best combination of efficiency of lean processes (early in the supply chain) and flexibility of agile processes (later in the supply chain). This also relates to mass customization and the types of order and related processes (e.g. make to order, make to stock or assemble to order – see more in Chapter 6). The point in the leagile supply chain that links these two processes is called the *decoupling point* (also referred to as the order penetration point).

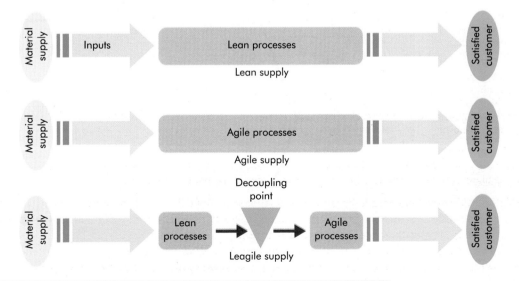

Figure 8.17 Lean, agile and leagile supplier management (Mason-Jones et al., 2000)

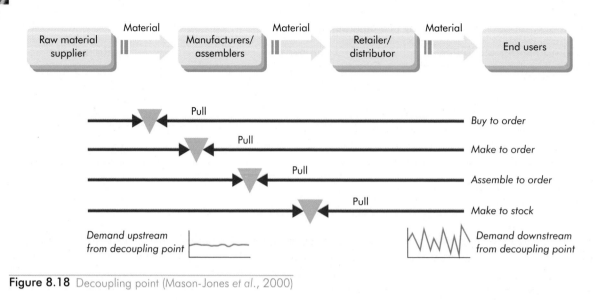

Figure 8.18 Decoupling point (Mason-Jones et al., 2000)

Decoupling Point

For optimal supplier relationship management, the *decoupling point* separates activities that are directly geared towards satisfying customer orders (i.e. pull strategy) from activities directly based on forecast demand (i.e. push strategy). With a 'pull' strategy, customer order information is acquired before production of the goods starts. Types of pull strategy include buy to order, make to order, assemble to order, and ship to stock. With a 'push' strategy, on the other hand, goods are produced first and then sold to the customer, which means that an organization has to have plenty of inventory ready for shipment. In order for the items to flow efficiently, the push and pull strategies should be aligned.

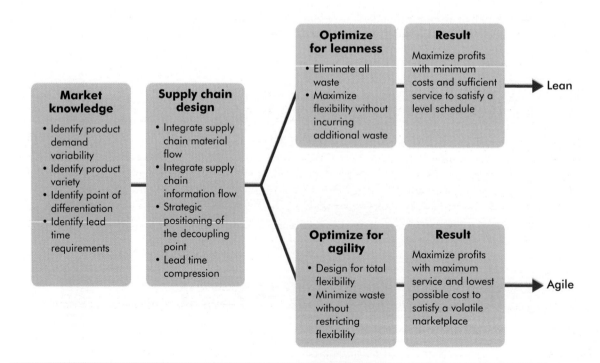

Figure 8.19 Route map for integrating lean and agile supply chains (adapted from Mason-Jones et al., 2000)

The decoupling point is where the buffer stock is held. This is to help safeguard against fluctuating customer orders, and simultaneously help to smooth production (Figure 8.18). It is also the point where product differentiation (from standardized goods into customized ones) takes place through postponement.

A route map for integrating leanness and agility is illustrated in Figure 8.19.

Coordination Efforts and Information Technology

BUSINESS INTEGRATION

As supplier relationships adapt to changes in supply and demand requirements, information must be shared with all suppliers. Information technology (IT) can be used so share information about forecasts, stock levels, production plans and order quantities. Two widely applied IT techniques are vendor-managed inventory (VMI) and collaborative planning, forecasting and replenishment (CPFR).

GLOBALIZATION

Vendor-managed Inventory

Vendor-managed inventory (VMI) is inventory that is managed by a supplier on behalf of its customers. It is also known as *co-managed inventory*. The buyer shares its inventory information with its vendors (or suppliers), so that the vendors can manage the inventory for the buyer, dealing with such things as inventory replenishment decisions regarding order quantities, shipping and timing. The purchase order still has to be initiated by the buyer, though. With VMI, the buyer's transaction costs related to ordering and order fulfilment are transferred to the vendor. This reduces the supply-side uncertainty, and gives the vendor a better chance to coordinate its inventory with the buyer's. This is a practice used widely by leading grocery stores such as Tesco.

Some of the benefits of VMI partnership are (Angulo *et al.*, 2004):
- Reduced costs due to better resource utilization for production and transportation
- Improved service levels due to better coordination of replenishment orders
- Reduced lead times and increased inventory turns
- Reduced inventory stock-outs achieved by increasing inventory visibility
- Higher selling space productivity obtained by optimizing inventory.

SHORT CASE 8.4

P&G's Pampers

One of the best-selling items made by Procter & Gamble (P&G) is Pampers nappies. The logistics executives could not understand why its sales at the retail stores were fluctuating, when it is well documented that the customer demand for nappies does not fluctuate significantly. The executives discovered that P&G was faced with a substantial degree of variability in orders from its retailers. After a close investigation, P&G found that the primary causes of this bullwhip effect were the demand

Source: © Gaby Kooijman/iStock

signals from its distributors, who would often place orders on an infrequent basis. Changes in prices by the manufacturer also changed the order demand. This was accentuated when distributors placing multiple orders were not certain that the manufacturer could meet the distributor's demand. Currently P&G employs VMI in its supply chain for nappies, starting with its supplier 3M and finishing with its customer Wal-Mart. This allows P&G to have access to the demand and inventory information from 3M and Wal-Mart, hence improving its demand forecasting.

Questions
1 Should Procter & Gamble implement VMI for other products? Why?
2 How can Procter & Gamble, through VMI, improve its relationship with its suppliers and customers?

Source: Lee *et al.* (1997).

Table 8.8 CPFR tasks

Retailer tasks	Collaborative tasks	Manufacturer tasks
Strategy and planning		
Vendor management	Collaboration arrangement	Accounting planning
Category management	Joint business plan	Market planning
Demand and supply management		
Point-of-sale forecasting	Sales forecasting	Market data analysis
Replenishment planning	Order planning/forecasting	Demand planning
Execution		
Buying/re-buying	Order generation	Production and supply planning
Logistics/distribution	Order fulfilment	Logistics/distribution
Analysis		
Store execution	Exception management	Execution monitoring
Supplier scorecard	Performance assessment	Customer scorecard

Source: adapted from VICS (2004).

Collaborative Planning, Forecasting and Replenishment

Collaborative planning, forecasting and replenishment (CPFR) is a business practice that combines the intelligence of multiple trading partners in the planning and fulfilment of customer demand. It links sales and marketing best practices to supply chain planning and execution in order to increase availability, while reducing inventory, transportation and logistics costs (www.vics.org). It establishes guidelines for companies to integrate their planning processes across corporate boundaries. The CPFR model comprises four collaborative activities, each complemented by business-to-business tasks: strategy and planning, demand and supply management, execution, and analysis. *Strategy and planning* activities include establishing the ground rules for the collaborative relationship, determining product mix and placement, and developing event plans. *Demand and supply management* activities include projecting consumer demand, ordering and shipment requirements. *Execution* activities include placing orders, preparing and delivering shipments, receiving and stocking products on retail shelves, recording sales transactions, and making payments. *Analysis* activities include monitoring, planning and execution activities for exception conditions, aggregating results, calculating key performance metrics, and sharing insights and adjusting plans for continuously improved results. Each of these tasks is linked to respective retailer and manufacturer tasks, as summarized in Table 8.8.

The Düsseldorf-based Metro chain, for example, implemented the CPFR process with Metro Cash & Carry in Germany, and its seven key suppliers of detergents and paper goods, among them Kimberly-Clark Corporation, Procter & Gamble Co., Johnson & Johnson, and Colgate-Palmolive Co. (www.internetretailer.com). The goal of the programme is to support joint workflow processes for promotion planning and promotional sales forecasting among the partners. Metro shares transactional data, sales forecasts and production schedules with its partners. This initiative has enabled a reduction of out-of-stock inventory by about two-thirds. Metro has also significantly reduced its end-of-promotion stocks (www.allbusiness.com).

🛈 Stop and Think

5   If the benefits of embracing VMI and CPFR are so great, why aren't there more companies working with these concepts?

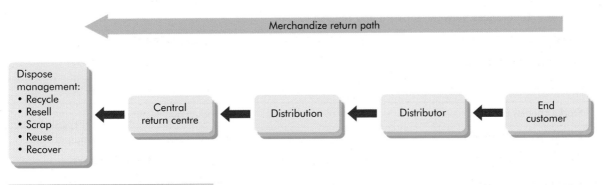

Figure 8.20 Reverse supply management

Contemporary Thinking: Reverse Supply and Logistics

Reverse Supply

Supplier management traditionally charts the path of raw materials as they are transformed into goods and sold to end consumers. *Reverse supply* also includes processes related to retrieving used products from a customer, to either dispose of them or reuse them (Figure 8.20). Managing product returns is essential and mandatory for many industries. For instance, some goods, such as washing machines, computers, batteries and tyres, are typically managed by government agencies after disposal. Depending on the type of product, it might be repaired and reused, refurbished, recycled (with or without disassembly), or incinerated.

A great deal of manufactured products such as refrigerators and aerosols contain hazardous substances, such as mercury, lead and arsenic. This creates a huge burden for the waste management authorities. Many governments and environmental groups are encouraging *product stewardship*, making the manufacturers responsible for collecting, recycling and disposing of their products after consumers have finished with them.

The management of a reverse supply includes the following tasks (Guide and Wassenhove, 2002):
- *Product acquisition*: the task of retrieving the used product, as the quality, quantity and timing of product returns are crucial for creating a profitable supply.
- *Reverse logistics*: the process of transporting the retrieved goods to facilities for inspection, sorting and disposition.
- *Inspection and disposition*: the task of testing, sorting and grading the returned products.
- *Reconditioning*: the task of extracting and reconditioning components for reuse, or re-manufacturing the product for resale.
- *Distribution and sales*: after reconditioning, the task of determining whether there is a market for the product.

Reverse Logistics

Forward logistics (or simply logistics) is a part of the supply chain process that plans, implements and controls the efficient flow and storage of goods from their point of origin to the point of consumption, in order to meet customers' requirements (Council of Supply Chain Management Professionals: www.cscmp.org). **Reverse logistics** reverses the flow of these activities. It addresses key issues related to how companies can become more environmentally efficient through recycling, reusing and reducing the amount of materials used (Carter and Ellram, 1998). Many companies in the world have started to include reverse logistics in their supply management. Some are forced by legislation or environmental regulations to embrace reverse logistics; others do it to reduce operational costs. Kodak, for example, has recycled more than 310 million cameras, and re-manufactures its single-use cameras after the film has been developed.

> **Reverse logistics:** addresses key issues related to how companies can become more environmentally efficient through recycling, reusing and reducing the amount of materials used.

Table 8.9 Differences between forward and reverse logistics

Forward logistics	Reverse logistics
Forecasting relatively straightforward	Forecasting more difficult
One-to-many transportation	Many-to-one transportation
Product quality uniform	Product quality not uniform
Product packaging uniform	Product packaging often damaged
Destination/routeing clear	Destination/routeing unclear
Standardized channel	Exception driven
Disposition options clear	Disposition not clear
Pricing relatively uniform	Pricing dependent on many factors
Importance of speed recognized	Speed often not considered a priority
Forward distribution costs closely monitored by accounting systems	Reverse costs less directly visible
Inventory management consistent	Inventory management not consistent
Product life cycle manageable	Product life cycle issues more complicated
Negotiation between parties straightforward	Negotiation complicated by several factors
Marketing methods well known	Marketing complicated by several factors
Real-time information readily available to track product	Visibility of process less transparent

Source: Tibben-Lembke and Rogers (2002, p. 276).

Although forward and reverse logistics are concerned with similar activities, they are not necessarily the same. It is much more challenging to manage reverse logistics. The differences between these processes are listed in Table 8.9.

It has been estimated that between 4% and 30% of products are returned by customers, and total UK retail returns are estimated to be valued at £6 billion per year. Despite the fact that it is costly and challenging to manage returns, they can have a significant impact on bottom-line performance as well as on environmental concerns. The major drivers for reverse logistics operations are listed in Table 8.10.

Table 8.10 Drivers of reverse logistics operations

Driver	Issues
Forecast accuracy and demand variability	One of the most recognized drivers of obsolete stock is caused by 'make to stock' or 'push' supply chains.
Promotional activity	In fast-moving consumer goods (FMCG) environments, marketing through the use of short-run promotional activity is prevalent, and this can lead to overstocking.
New product introduction	For some markets, the success of new product introduction is difficult to determine. For example, in the music industry, sales on the release of a new single may be almost impossible to predict accurately.
Product range and safety stock policy	Consumer expectations of choice mean that companies will provide a wide range of stock-keeping units (SKUs) within each product category. Brand extensions that drive additional SKUs require safety stock to be held for each SKU.
Product life cycles	Product life cycles are shortening, and the risk of obsolescence is becoming a major supply chain strategy for providing competitive advantages in markets such as electronics and high-technology products.

Table 8.10 *Continued*

Logistics trade-offs	For some products the economics are such that the costs of manufacturing and logistics are low, compared with lost revenue from not having on-shelf availability. This can lead to excessive stockholding in retail outlets, which has to be returned at some later date.
Purchasing policies	Purchasing by placing large orders to obtain quantity discounts may result in obsolete stockholding, and the benefits gained through bulk buying may be offset by the cost of dealing with returns.
High on-shelf availability	On-shelf availability is a prime measure of supply chain performance for retailers. In order to achieve superior performance, some retailers may keep high stock levels at both the retail outlet and the distribution centre. This may lead to high returns of obsolete stock.
Legislative factors	Emerging EU legislation, for example WEEE (European Union legislation on electrical and electronic equipment), is likely to have a significant impact on organizations planning their returns management policy.
Cash flow management	The trading terms that exist between retailers and manufacturers will include the commercial arrangements for managing returns. Liberal terms may exist, and some retailers may take advantage by returning goods to manufacturers for credit to enhance their cash flow position.
Liberal returns policies and customer returns	A liberal returns policy may allow customers to return unwanted goods for a refund within a defined period of time. Customer returns will inevitably be in a condition that very often renders them unfit to be resold, either because the product has been removed from its original packaging, or because there is a quality problem.
Customer 'no fault' policy	A significant number of products that are returned by customers are found to have no problem. The problem is linked to the liberal returns policies that companies offer to customers. For many 'no fault found' items, the costs involved in taking the product back to grade A for resale are uneconomical, and therefore it will be sold at a significantly reduced price.

Source: Bernon and Cullen (2007, p. 47).

Summary

In this chapter we focused on supply chain and supply relationship management. We took a close look at the issues that firms should consider when integrating their processes and activities with those of their suppliers and customers.

We started by analysing how purchased items can be classified according to their impact on business and supply/risk complexity. We showed that the ideal type of procurement process depends on four contexts: routine, bottleneck, leverage, and critical. As the characteristics and value of the purchased items vary, the relationship between the supplier and the buyer also varies. For instance, an arm's length relationship fits better when sourcing low-value, standardized products, but a strategic partnership is crucial when sourcing key components that require close collaboration with the supplier.

We looked at the role of third party logistics (TPL) as an external supplier of logistics services. Depending on the required skills shared between the firm and the TPL supplier, relationships can range between market exchange, customized logistics solutions, joint logistics solutions, and in-house logistics solutions.

We also learned that the configuration of supply chains can influence how a manufacturer of complex products organizes and coordinates its design and distribution activities. We looked at how postponement strategies can be applied in order to achieve delivery of goods in a timely and cost-effective manner, by rearranging the production and logistics supply chains. It is also important to note that the product architectures of product systems can potentially shape the structure of supply networks. Through the lens of the double helix model, we saw how the industry structure can change between vertical and horizontal, influenced by the technological changes embedded in product architectures (i.e. modular and integral).

Demand for products and services is difficult to predict. We learned that whereas functional products should have an efficient supply chain, innovative products should have a market-responsive supply chain. Furthermore, it is important for firms to be able to estimate demand fluctuations, and understand why demand information becomes distorted. Various industries are applying IT to reduce the information distortion, including vendor-managed inventory (VMI) and collaborative planning, forecasting and replenishment (CPFR).

Finally, as firms become more socially responsible towards the environment, especially in terms of product return, reuse and recycling, the supply chain management of reverse logistics operations is becoming one of the competitive advantages for many firms.

Key Theories

The key theories discussed in this chapter were:

- **Postponement** – delaying the timing of crucial activities by which end products assume their customer-specific functionalities, features and identities.

- **The bullwhip effect** – a concept used to explain why information about the final customer's actual demand gets distorted from one end of the supply chain to the other.

- **Fine's double helix model** – this theory describes how supply structure can oscillate between vertical integration and horizontal disintegration with respect to product architecture strategies (i.e. modular versus integral).

- **Leagile supply** – the combination of lean supply and agile supply.

Suggested Answers to Stop and Think Questions

1 **Competition versus cooperation:** The answer to this is not simple. Often it can be achieved only through legal contracts and intellectual property rights (IPR) protection. Unfortunately, there are many unethical organizations that will pretend to be working collaboratively when they only want to steal ideas and practices. Another answer is to use open source agreements (e.g. the Linux operating system for PCs).

2 **Customized TPL services:** It would be difficult if the TPL didn't understand its processes well. Before embarking on customization of services, it is crucial for the TPL to know how the information and services provided are being transformed across the supply chain. The type and amount of customization are also dependent on whether it is to take place in the upstream or downstream supply chain. Customization downstream (i.e. closer to the consumers) would be looking at how to optimize customization for increasing service variety. Customization upstream (i.e. closer to the suppliers), on the other hand, would have to take into consideration how the service is to be designed and configured.

3 **Limit to standardization:** Standardization creates common operating procedures for suppliers of goods and services, which make it simpler for everyone to collaborate. Standardization fosters economies of scale, though, and forces the market competition to focus on prices rather than on performance. When this happens, many firms find it difficult to survive on low profit margins.

4 **Functional products:** We should always apply frameworks with caution. There are functional products with evolving processes. Let's think about functional products that have innovation in them, and which require a responsive supply chain. Examples of these types of product include vitamin-fortified yogurts and milk products, and ready-made organic soups. Similarly, there are

innovative products with mature supply processes. In this case, think about innovative products that are supplied with efficient processes. Examples of these types of product include new versions of mobile phones, and new drugs. The dynamics of matching products with processes also change over time. The USB memory stick, for instance, was considered an innovative product when it was first introduced to the market. It required the market to be responsive. But, over time, it has become a standard product for data storage. Nowadays, USB sticks are considered functional products, with stable supply processes.

5 **VMI and CFPR:** The adoption of most process technologies tends to be slow, especially when they involve other parties outside the organization. VMI and CPFR allow the firm to share information with its suppliers. In order for both parties to access each other's systems, their systems have to be compatible. Compatibility issues are one of the most challenging barriers to manage. The firms also need to consider upgradability of the technology (i.e. one party cannot change its system without making sure it will not affect its supplier's system), the level of security, the costs incurred, the type of information to be shared with the other party (this means that there should be trust), and technology lock-in (once a particular VMI and CPFR system is adopted, it will be difficult and expensive to switch to another technology).

connect

Review Questions

1 Consider the opening case study again after reading this chapter. How has customization changed the competitive landscape of toy industries? What issues (internal as well as external) should LEGO consider when implementing mass customization? Give examples.

2 What supply strategies should product (or service) based firms consider when developing new products (or services)?

3 How can a firm decide where customization should take place in order to balance the push and pull strategies?

4 If you were a producer of standard bicycles, and decided to sell customized bicycles, how would you make this happen? How would you organize your suppliers?

5 You are in the fashion business, and it is extremely crucial that you have the latest fashion items in the retail stores. What can you do in order to match customer demand with production of fashion items?

Discussion Questions

1 Discuss the role of product design for supply chain management. Depending on the degree of technological complexity of the innovations, how should firms manage the relationships shared with suppliers and customers? Explain, and give examples.

2 Consumers are becoming more health conscious. The number of organic products and dairy products with added vitamins is growing at an astronomical rate. Discuss the benefits and challenges a dairy producer may face with the farmers and the grocery stores as a result.

3 Companies are becoming increasingly dependent on IT to share information. Discuss the challenges a firm might encounter when deciding which type of IT technology to adopt, and how this technology could impact on the firm's relationship with its suppliers.

4 Imagine you are the manufacturer of the world's most famous brand of customized tennis shoes. There are wholesalers and retailers in Asia, the USA and Europe. Discuss how and why the order information for this product could become distorted from downstream to upstream supplies.

5 Discuss why we sort our household waste into paper, glass, food, etc. Where does the waste go? What would the reverse logistics look like for this example?

Problems

1 The mouse for your PC has just broken. You desperately need to use it, so you go to an electronics store to buy a replacement. At the store you have many brands and options to choose from, ranging from a simple, plug-in mouse to fancy, multifunction ones. The prices are affordable, too. On the way home, you start to wonder how it's possible for producers to survive and compete on such devices. It is obvious that there are many mouse producers, and that they compete on price. You also notice that the producers of keyboards and monitors face similar challenges.

Required: *Apply the double helix model to describe the current structure of the PC industry. Can you predict what is going to happen?*

2 You are the manager of a supermarket chain. You notice that the sale of organic products is increasing, which means that the sale of non-organic products is decreasing. You want to promote the 'healthy food' image of the supermarket chain, so you have started to buy less of certain types of non-organic product. One such product is ordinary spaghetti. You have always ordered 500 kg every month. With the 'healthy food' initiative, you decided to reduce the order by 10% to 450 kg. Assume that the supply chain of spaghetti has four tiers: the supermarket chain, the wholesaler, the manufacturer, and the supplier. Assume that each tier keeps one period's worth of inventory.

Required: *Estimate the demand fluctuation across the supply chain due to the 10% drop in demand order. How many periods will it take until each tier is able to meet the new demand?*

Online **LearningCentre**

Visit the Online Learning Centre at
www.mcgraw-hill.co.uk/textbooks/paton for a range of resources to support your learning.

Further Reading

Clark, K.B. and Fujimoto, T. (1991) *Product Development Performance: Strategy, Organization and Management in the World of Auto Industry*, Harvard Business School Press, Boston, MA.

Fine, C. (1998) *Clockspeed: Winning Industry Control in the Age of Temporary Advantage*, Little, Brown and Company, London.

Lamming, R. (1993) *Beyond Partnership: Strategies for Innovation and Lean Supply*, Prentice Hall, New York.

Mikkola, J.H. and Skjøtt-Larsen, T. (2006) 'Platform management: implication for new product development and supply chain management', *European Business Review*, **18**(3), 214–230.

Sako, M. (1992) *Prices, Quality and Trust: Buyer Supplier Relationships in Britain and Japan*, Cambridge University Press, Cambridge.

Simchi-Levi, D., Kaminsky, P. and Simchi-Levi, E. (2008) *Designing and Managing the Supply Chain*, 3rd edn, McGraw-Hill, Boston, MA.

Skjøtt-Larsen, T., Schary, P., Mikkola, J.H. and Kotzab, H. (2007) *Managing the Global Supply Chain*, 3rd edn, Copenhagen Business School Press.

Stock, J.R. and Lambert, D.M. (2001) *Strategic Logistics Management*, 4th edn, McGraw-Hill, Boston, MA.

References

Angulo, A., Nachtmann, H. and Waller, M. (2004) 'Supply chain information sharing in a vendor managed inventory partnership', *Journal of Business Logistics*, **25**(1), 101–120.

Bernon, M. and Cullen, J. (2007) 'An integrated approach to managing reverse logistics', *International Journal of Logistics: Research and Applications*, **10**(1), 41–56.

Binder, M., Gust, P. and Clegg, B. (2008) 'The importance of collaborative frontloading in automotive supply networks', *Journal of Manufacturing Technology Management*, **19**(3), 315–331.

Carbone, J. (1999) 'Reinventing purchasing wins the medal for Big Blue', *Purchasing*, 16 September, 38–62.

Carter, C.R. and Ellram, L.M. (1998) 'Reverse logistics: a review of the literature and framework for future investigation', *Journal of Business Logistics*, **19**(1), 85–102.

Clark, K.B. and Fujimoto, T. (1991) *Product Development Performance: Strategy, Organization and Management in the World of Auto Industry*, Harvard Business School Press, Boston, MA.

Dyer, J.H., Cho, D.S. and Chu, W. (1998) 'Strategic supplier segmentation: the next "best practice" in supply chain management', *California Management Review*, **40**(2), 57–77.

Fine, C. (1998) *Clockspeed: Winning Industry Control in the Age of Temporary Advantage*, Little, Brown and Company, London.

Fisher, M. (1997) 'What is the right supply chain for your product?', *Harvard Business Review*, **75**(2), 105–116.

Guide, V.D.R. and Wassenhove, V.N.L. (2002) 'The reverse supply chain', *Harvard Business Review*, **80**(2), 25–26.

Halldorsson, A. and Skjøtt-Larsen, T. (2004) 'Developing logistics competencies through third party logistics relationships', *International Journal of Operations and Production Management*, **24**(2), 192–206.

Kerber, R. (1998) 'Bicycles: bike maker faces a tactical shift', *The Wall Street Journal*, 12 October, Sec. B, 1.

Kraljic, P. (1983) 'Purchasing must become supply management', *Harvard Business Review*, September–October, 107–109.

Lamming, R. (1993) *Beyond Partnership: Strategies for Innovation and Lean Supply*. Prentice Hall, New York.

Lee, H. (1998) 'Postponement for mass customisation: satisfying customer demands for tailor-made products', in *Strategic Supply Chain Alignment: Best Practice in Supply Chain Management*, J. Gattorna (ed.), Gower, Aldershot, pp. 77–91.

Lee, H.L., Padmanabhan, V. and Whang, S. (1997) 'The bullwhip effect in supply chains', *Sloan Management Review*, **38**(3), 93–102.

Mason-Jones, R., Naylor, B. and Towill, D.R. (2000) 'Engineering the leagile supply chain', *International Journal of Agile Management Systems*, **2**(1), 54–61.

Mikkola, J.H. and Skjøtt-Larsen, T. (2004) 'Mass customisation, postponement, and modularisation strategies in shaping supply chains', *Production Planning and Control*, **15**(4), 352–361.

Pagh, J.D. and Cooper, M.C. (1998) 'Supply chain postponement and speculation strategies: how to choose the right strategy', *Journal of Business Logistics*, **19**(2), 13–33.

Sako, M. (1992) *Prices, Quality and Trust: Buyer Supplier Relationships in Britain and Japan*, Cambridge University Press, Cambridge.

Simchi-Levi, D., Kaminsky, P. and Simchi-Levi, E. (2008) *Designing and Managing the Supply Chain*, 3rd edn, McGraw-Hill, Boston, MA.

Skjøtt-Larsen, T., Schary, P., Mikkola, J.H. and Kotzab, H. (2007) *Managing the Global Supply Chain*, 3rd edn, Copenhagen Business School Press.

Tibben-Lembke, R. and Rogers, D.S. (2002) 'Differences between forward and reverse logistics in a retail environment', *Supply Chain Management: An International Journal*, **7**(5), 271–282.

Inventory Planning and Management

Barilla: Managing Inventory

Barilla is the world's leading manufacturer of pasta products with 35% of the Italian and 22% of the European market, employing 18,000 people, selling 2.8 million tons in 125 countries and generating sales of €4.2 billion in 2007. Barilla was founded in 1877 when Pietro Barilla opened a small shop in Parma, Italy, selling his own bread and fresh pasta. It now owns over 20 brands selling 1,500 different products.

Manufacturing

Barilla has 54 production units throughout Italy and the rest of the world making pasta, bread, sauces, and various cakes and biscuits, as well as 10 flour mills producing much of the raw material. Making pasta is relatively straightforward, with flour, water and often eggs and spinach mixed together to form a dough. This is then rolled and forced through dies to shape before being cut to length. The pieces are then dried on a long conveyor in an oven where the conditions are carefully controlled for temperature and humidity to ensure quality. The drying process varies depending on the shape and size

Source: © Dušan Zidar/iStock

of the pasta, and so Barilla develops complex plans to ensure low set-up penalties. Barilla's plants specialize in terms of the type (flour and ingredients used), shape and size of pasta, and whether the product is fresh or dried. The largest plant can produce 900 tons of pasta a day.

Sales and Distribution

Barilla's products are sold in over 100,000 outlets in Italy alone. Dry products have a shelf life of around 2 years and make up 75% of Barilla's output, coming in approximately 800 different stock-keeping units (SKU) of different package sizes and products. Many of the biscuit products, about 200 SKUs, have a shelf life of 3 months, whereas fresh pasta lasts only 3 weeks. Fresh bread products have even shorter usable times of one day. As a result, Barilla needs different ways of distributing the products.

In Italy, fresh products are sent from the manufacturing units through two distribution centres which generally hold 3 days' supply. From here, the fresh products are sent out to 70 regional warehouses for distribution. The dry products are sold predominantly through supermarkets, and dispatched from the distribution centres to the supermarket's own distributors, called *grande distribuzione* (GD). The rest of the dried products go through the distribution centres to 18 Barilla depots before going out to independent distributors called *distribuzione organizzata* (DO) and eventually to shops.

Ordering and Inventory

The wide range of products at Barilla and the different handling and sales routes make it an interesting case to think about managing inventory – both the stocks of raw materials needed for manufacture and the finished products. For example, Barilla's raw materials and the GDs for the supermarkets have very regular and predictable demands, whereas the DOs need more reactive methods to cope with unpredictable events and consumption rates. There is no single way that can help Barilla and its distributors manage the ordering and delivery of products and raw materials. The demand at the DO stage is unpredictable, and managed on an ad hoc basis by local managers juggling the need for products in the shops. This is a different task from managing demand at Barilla and the GDs, where it is possible to predict accurately the amounts needed. This certainty means they can create a flow of materials and products to support a fixed production plan.

Sources: Barilla SpA (A) Harvard Business School case: 9-694-046, and Barilla website, http://www.barillagroup.com/, accessed 4 April 2011.

Introduction

Inventory management is about working out what to produce or deliver, and when. As a result, it is a key topic in operations management because firms such as Barilla, with good inventory control, can expect consistent deliveries to their customers, whereas weak inventory management reduces customer satisfaction and adds cost. Land Rover, for example, has a materials bill of about £2 billion per year and so a 1% saving in this bill gives an immediate profit of £20 million.

In service operations inventory may be harder to identify, but is just as important. Running out of a particular drug in a hospital could mean the death of a patient, and in retail the main assets are the products on the shelves and more people may be employed stacking shelves than dealing directly with the customer.

This chapter covers the tools available for inventory management and shows how managing the material flow can be used to control operations. Timing which material is needed and when it is available can serve as the main mechanism used to control the work within the firm, and this is discussed at the end of the chapter along with the implications that enterprise-wide systems have for management activity.

What Is Inventory?

Inventory: the materials and finished products that are present in the firm, and also in its supply chain.

Types of Inventory

Inventory represents the materials and finished products in the firm and supply chain. This includes:

- **Raw materials** – purchased but not processed
- **Work-in-process inventory** – being worked on
- Maintenance/repair/operating supplies (MRO) – for the plant
- **Finished goods inventory** – completed and waiting shipment
- Goods in transit – to warehouses and customers.

> **Raw materials:** materials purchased but not processed.
>
> **Work-in-process inventory:** materials that have started being worked upon but are not complete.
>
> **Finished goods inventory:** completed products awaiting shipment or built for stock.

❗ Stop and Think

1 Take a minute to think about an organization you know well. What represents its inventory, where is it kept, and what might happen if it got out of control?

The Valuable Functions of Inventory

Inventory has various different roles, the most obvious being to satisfy immediately customer demand. For example, blood supplies must be stocked as they cannot be ordered when a patient needs a transfusion; and food can only be sold if it is on the supermarket shelf. In other examples though, an immediate response is not always possible: BMW, for example, may expect us to wait for a car to be made if we want it in a colour that is not available on the garage forecourt. Here the inventory does not need to be immediately available. Therefore, as well as satisfying immediate demand, inventory has other roles in the smooth running of operations, as summarized in the following list.

The useful functions of inventory are:
- To provide immediate satisfaction for customer demand – some customers expect to walk in off the street and out again with the product
- To uncouple stages in the operation chain – inventory between manufacturing stages smooths fluctuations, allowing machines to operate independently
- To provide cover for uncertainty
  - Extra inventory prevents shortages which can otherwise cause operational problems and poor customer service
  - Inventory allows work to continue if there is a delay or breakdown elsewhere in the supply chain
- To reduce costs
  - It can be cheaper to buy things in bulk
  - Buying in advance can hedge against future price changes, but carries risk.

Problems Caused by Inventory

Despite the useful ways inventory can help a firm with its operations, the aim will always be to operate with the minimum inventory possible because excess stocks add cost and cause other problems, as summarized below:
- Inventory ties up working capital
  - What else could the firm do with the money invested in materials?
  - The firm will have interest charges if it borrows the money to buy the inventory
- Inventory takes up space
  - It costs money to store, monitor, document and manage the inventory
  - There is a lost opportunity of using the space, such as installing another machine
- Inventory is prone to:
  - Damage: if things are lying around then they can get broken
  - Pilferage: it can be stolen. For example, car makers used to install CD-radios at the factory, only to find them missing later. Now they are fitted just before delivery.
  - **Obsolescence**: changes in design may mean throwing away old parts, and other products, such as food, have a limited life.
- Inventory causes manufacturing errors to go undetected; reducing inventory can make it easier to see delays and uneven supply chains.

> **Obsolescence:** the state of becoming obsolete, or out of date.
>
> **Inventory turn:** the time taken for a firm's entire inventory to be used and replaced.

It is possible to measure firm performance with **inventory turn** – the time taken for the entire inventory to be used and replaced. The more efficient a firm, the faster its inventory turn. Accountants measure this as the ratio of annual cost of goods sold to annual inventory investment. Care should be taken when comparing these measures between firms within an industry as they are a very high-level and generalized guide because firms can have different scopes of operation. Comparisons of inventory in UK and Japanese car makers in the 1980s were sometimes made. However, because Japanese firms were not manufacturing high-value engines and gearboxes like their UK competitors, but instead only buying them from a supplier, the parts and assemblies that made up the inventory were not the same, resulting in an unfair comparison.

> ### ⓘ Stop and Think
>
> 2   Before we go into how we can model inventory systems mathematically and arrive at optimal solutions, it is important that we reflect on the nature of inventory. Thinking about your local supermarket, identify three different types of their inventory, and how they are useful to the company.

Service Inventories

Service inventory includes the steps that are completed before the customer arrives, and allows resources to be buffered from variable demand. For example, processing an existing customer's application for an additional credit card can be improved if the credit check has already been completed. In many cases, service inventories offer an advantage to the firm as they store the service in advance, improving quality, speed and customization, and cutting costs, as shown in Table 9.1.

Inventory Management

Most inventory changes take place with regular patterns, and therefore lend themselves to mathematical modelling. With a mathematical representation, managers can find solutions to minimize inventory cost. The simplest models order fixed amounts of parts and materials at fixed intervals but, in practice, variation – either in how much to order or when to order it – leads managers to use one of two different approaches, either ordering based on *fixed quantities* or ordering based on *fixed dates*.

A fixed order quantity approach, where the timing is adjusted and the quantity stays the same, is called a *continuous review* or *Q system*. The fixed date approach, where quantity is adjusted but timing stays the same, is called a *periodic* or *P system*.

Table 9.1 Reasons to build service inventories

Service attribute	Ways in which service inventory can improve performance	Reasons to build service inventory
Quality	Provides consistency Facilitates service recovery	Customers value transactional conformance Enables simple, standardized response to common service failures
Speed	Reduces the amount of work needed after customer arrival Allows provider to expand capacity Reduces handoffs	Allows for significant capacity expansion Eliminates need for handoffs
Customization	Applies standard process to individual inputs Allows greater customer control	Customers provide unique inputs to a standard process Customers value exercising greater control
Price	Facilitates self-service Allows use of cheaper resources Enhances resource productivity	Significantly reduces resource costs Increases staff productivity Allows higher resource utilization

Source: Chopra and Lariviere (2005, p. 95).

Stock Time Charts

Figure 9.1 shows a useful inventory management tool, the inventory chart or **stock time chart**. This plots the changing inventory level of a part over time.

> **Stock time chart:** chart showing how the inventory of a part or component changes over time.

In Figure 9.1, items are used at a constant rate and delivered in bulk. The steady usage of items is shown as the line of constant value in the left-hand chart. This would happen on a production line needing a constant supply of materials. The peaks on the second diagram show the instantaneous delivery of a new batch of stock. The delivery rate is zero for long periods of time; then, when a bulk shipment of parts is delivered, it is very high; it then returns to zero until the next delivery. Plotting the combination of these two elements on the right-hand chart shows the level of inventory. From the starting level, items are used at a constant rate, and the level drops gradually. When a batch of new materials is delivered, the stock level returns to the starting level, and is again used at the same rate. Repeating the cycle gives the sawtooth diagram.

This is the simplest representation of inventory delivery and use: large delivery of materials at a fixed time, with a constant rate of use. From this simple model there are several ways which the input and output can change, either regularly, as above, or unpredictably, and so there are different patterns and corresponding mathematical models.

Economic Order Quantity

One basic inventory management approach minimizes the costs associated with ordering fixed quantities of items (the Q-type system). Under the simple conditions shown in Figure 9.1 there is an optimum amount to order that minimizes the inventory costs. This is called the **economic order quantity (EOQ)**.

> **Economic order quantity (EOQ):** fixed order (or production) amount that minimizes the total costs over a whole year.

The total cost of the inventory system includes the holding cost plus the ordering cost, shown in Figure 9.2. These costs vary with the amount ordered, and with the order size. Obviously, the goal is the cheapest total cost.

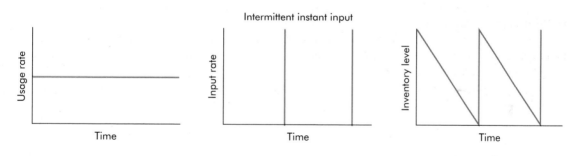

Figure 9.1 A basic inventory chart

Holding Costs: Pressure to Order Small Amounts

Figure 9.2 shows *holding costs* rising with order quantity. Ordering a large quantity of an item results in more parts being stored, which costs money in terms of light, heat and security for the warehouse, especially on

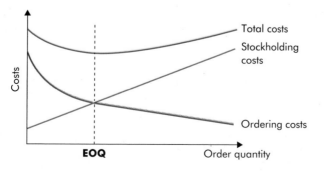

Figure 9.2 The economic order quantity (EOQ)

high-value items (e.g. precious stones) or items that are difficult to store (e.g. food). These costs, vary depending on what we are buying and how it needs to be kept. In a small shop the ice cream in the freezer will cost more to hold than the biscuits, because of the electricity used for the freezer. Similarly, a jeweller's shop needs expensive security, which in effect can be considered a stockholding cost.

Often the main cost of holding an item is the interest incurred in borrowing the money to buy it. Thus holding costs are often calculated as bank interest on the stored items' value.

Holding costs encourage parts to be bought in smaller batches, so less material is stored.

Ordering Costs: Pressure to Order in Bulk

Ordering costs are those charged by suppliers because they have to change a machine from making their normal product to the one ordered. This set-up takes time during which the machine is not producing. The longer it takes to set up the machine, the larger the cost associated with machine downtime (unproductive time). Normally the set-up time (and its associated cost) is a fixed amount, which needs to be recovered equally from all the items produced in the batch. This encourages large numbers of parts to be ordered because, once the machine is set up, a long run reduces the cost assigned to each item in the batch.

Total Inventory Costs

The two costs above – holding and ordering – therefore seem to be pulling in different directions, but managers are most interested in the *total cost*, calculated by adding the holding and order costs. The quantity to order that minimizes this total cost is the EOQ, and is given by the formula

$$Q = \sqrt{\frac{2DC_s}{C_h}}$$

where Q is the economic order quantity, D is the demand, C_s is the set-up cost, and C_h is the holding cost.

The EOQ says that the cheapest inventory costs will result if a firm orders this amount. Ordering more or less will cost more overall.

A good example of this formula in action is the amount of money you take out of an ATM. Your decision on the amount optimizes the frequencies of visits (the time you waste as the set-up cost of travelling to and from the ATM) against the risk of carrying too much cash (the holding cost of your taking extra care of the money).

WORKED EXAMPLE 9.1

Economic Order Quantity (EOQ)

The EOQ concept is very important, and fairly easy to implement in many situations, as the calculation is straightforward.

Problem: *The Corner Convenience Store (CCS) gets its drinks delivered by a wholesaler. At CCS, Light Cola sells at a rate of 860 cans per day. (The shop is open 250 days of the year.) A six-pack of Light Cola costs CCS $1.20. Annual holding cost is 10% of the cost of the cola. It costs CCS $25 to place an order, and this covers any delivery charge. What is CCS's EOQ?*

Approach: This calculation is simple, but take care to get the units consistent, such as using days or years, and cases or cans.

Solution:

$$D = 860 \times 250 = 215{,}000 \text{ cans/year}$$

$$C_h = 1.20/6 \times 10\% = \$0.02/\text{can/year}$$

$$C_s = \$25$$

$$Q = \sqrt{\frac{2DC_s}{C_h}}$$

$$= \sqrt{\frac{2 \times 215{,}000 \times 25}{0.02}}$$

$$= 23{,}184 \text{ cans or } 3{,}864 \text{ cases}$$

Therefore CCS should order 3,864 cases each time it needs some Light Cola. We can learn other things about this situation using the formulae used to derive the EOQ equation (see the Appendix to this chapter):

- The average stock held is $Q/2 = 11{,}592$ cans.
- The cost of holding this stock will be $Q/2 \times C_h = \$231.84$ per year.
- The number of orders they will place a year is $D/Q = 9.3$ times a year, or every 39 days (365 days in a year divided by 9.3 orders).
- The cost of placing all the orders in a year will be $D/Q \times C_s = \$231.84$ per year (note: by definition, this is the same as the annual holding cost).
- The total cost of operating the inventory system will be $\$231.84 + \$231.84 = \$463.68$ per year.
- CCS will spend $D \times$ Cost per can $= 215{,}000 \times 1.2/6 = \$43{,}000$ on buying the Light Cola per year.

CRITICAL PERSPECTIVE

Accuracy and the EOQ

In practice, we are unlikely to know the precise demand for an item or the exact holding/set-up costs, so we normally use estimates. Indeed, it is likely that any figures used are probably subject to variation as demand or other factors change. Luckily, the EOQ equation is relatively insensitive to any errors in our figures.

Look again at the EOQ equation. You can see that if any one of the estimated values (D, C_s or C_h) is out by 50%, the correct EOQ value would be out by only about 30%. (Try putting some example numbers into the equation to check this for yourself.)

The key point is that as long as the values are close, it is unlikely to make a big difference to the EOQ value, which means it is acceptable to round the EOQ to some convenient value, such as the nearest hundred, or a multiple of a whole truckload or full box.

Extending the EOQ Model

Inventory management techniques can be extended to take account of different situations. The EOQ equation is used when an order comes from a supplier, or for something we make ourselves. There is no difference mathematically, as identical set-up costs apply to our factory as apply to the supplier's factory.

An extension of the EOQ is the **economic production quantity (EPQ)**, sometimes called the **economic batch quantity (EBQ)**. This includes intermittent demand, where parts are consumed constantly but also produced in the factory at certain times. The stock time chart is slightly more complicated, but still cyclical and mathematically modelled. The EPQ generates an EOQ-type value that we can use to optimize the inventory costs of this system.

Economic production quantity (EPQ): extension of the EOQ that includes the effect of producing parts.

Economic batch quantity (EBQ): another name for EPQ.

Another example involves price-break discounts on ordering above a certain amount. The order costs C_s will therefore have multiple values, and the lowest total inventory costs could be found in one of a number of order volumes. In practice, therefore, we would calculate the EOQ at different volumes to find the cheapest.

Things get more complex when we adapt the model by adding statistical likelihoods to reflect variations in demand or production. Here we want to ensure that enough stock is available to meet any likely situations. Again, the EOQ model can be extended to reflect this variability and arrive at an optimal inventory model. However, these inventory models are all based on the EOQ.

🛑 Stop and Think

3 We should spend a little time thinking through the difference between the different models above, such as EOQ and EPQ. What are the major differences between the EOQ for bought-in items and those made in our factory? What other factors does the EPQ model take into account over the EOQ approach?

Reorder level (ROL): The trigger level used in the reorder point inventory system (Q type), which generates the ordering of a fixed amount (normally the EOQ) with an irregular interval.

Reorder point: level of inventory that indicates the time to order a batch of the EOQ in a reorder level system.

Safety stock: extra inventory used to cover uncertainty or delivery times so that the system can keep operating.

Cyclical review: inventory review system that determines the amount to be ordered at set intervals.

Inventory Systems in Practice

We have already noted two distinct main inventory control systems based on either fixed quantity (Q) or fixed period (P). These ideas are most often implemented as either:

- Q: the **reorder level (ROL)** system (sometimes called the **reorder point (ROP)**)
- P: the **cyclical review (CR)** or reorder cycle system.

The Reorder Level System

As an example, a simple reorder level system can be used for screws used on a production line. The bucket the screws are kept in has a line drawn around the inside to indicate the reorder level. When the level of screws in the bucket is down to the line, an order is placed, and there are just enough screws left in the bucket for the workers to use until the order is delivered. Normally there is a little extra (**safety stock**) in the bucket to cover any variation in the delivery time. The more safety stock, the less likely we are to run out. The cycle is then repeated, as shown in Figure 9.3.

The ROL system is sometimes implemented as the *two-bin system*. Instead of a line on one container, one bin is filled up to the ROL, and the rest of the batch is put in the second bin. An order is placed when the first bin is empty and the ROL is reached.

One problem with this system is that we need to keep track of how many parts we have in stock all the time. If we cannot use a simple visual tool, such as two bins, or the line on a bucket, it can be expensive to track the stock level continually to identify when the ROL is reached.

The manager designing a ROL system tries to balance the costs of running out against the costs of holding extra stock. This can be worked out mathematically, or may just be based on judgement if the cost of running out is small or the value of the parts is low. For example, if the stock-out cost involves sending someone off for

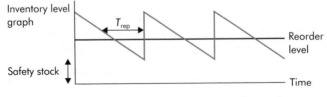

ROL = usage in replenishment time (T_{rep}) + safety stock

The amount of safety stock depends on:
  the variability in time to replenish
  the cost of a stock-out

Figure 9.3 The reorder point

2 minutes to the warehouse, then the safety stock need not be accurate or large. However, if the items are very expensive or have a long lead time, such as the gearboxes in a car factory, then managers need to be as accurate as possible, given the high cost of getting it wrong. If the car factory runs out of gearboxes, the production line stops and stands idle until the delivery.

WORKED EXAMPLE 9.2

Reorder Level System

A college radio station records a copy of its five hours per day broadcast stream onto CDs. Each CD records one hour. The stationery firm delivers CDs exactly three days after an order is received.

Problem: *What is the ROL for the CDs, and what is the ROL when a safety stock of 1 day's worth of CDs is used for reserve?*

Solution: The ROL for the CDs is 15, as they need 5 CDs per day for the 3 days until the order arrives. Mathematically, we can say that:

$$\text{ROL} = \text{Demand (per day)} \times \text{Delivery lead time (in days)}$$

In practice the radio station will want to make sure it has a few CDs left in case of a delay, or if a CD is faulty. A safety stock of one day's worth of CDs would be a sensible number as a reserve. The ROL is now 20 (15 to cover the normal usage for 3 days and another 5 for one day's safety stock):

$$\text{ROL} = \text{Demand per day} \times \text{Delivery lead time in days} + \text{Safety stock}$$

$$\text{ROL} = 5 \times 3 + 5 = 20$$

The Cyclical Review System

In the cyclical review (CR) system (an example of the P approach) inventory is reviewed at set intervals, and an order is placed each time for the amount needed to bring the stocks back up to a set level. A different amount is ordered each time. Again, safety stock is needed to cover the time taken to deliver the order, or for any likely delay. The main advantage of CR over ROL is that the firm does not need to keep track of how many parts are in stock, as they are counted each time an order is made.

CR is often used when several items come from one supplier, as the separate orders can be combined to cut costs. CR is common in retail, where stocks are checked at the end of the month and enough is ordered to bring the level back to that at the start. This system is easily automated with electronic point of sale systems (EPOS), or smart tills, which report sales at regular intervals.

WORKED EXAMPLE 9.3

Cyclical Review

The chemists' shop on the high street uses a cyclical review system for its toothbrushes. Typically, the shop sells 3,300 toothbrushes a year. An order is placed each month to bring the stocks up to the average monthly demand for the toothbrush. It takes a week for the delivery to arrive, and the chemists use a 10% safety margin to cover for any variation in demand.

Problem:

(a) *What is the target level of stock for the toothbrush?*

(b) *On counting the stock as part of the end-of-month review they find 120 brushes left on the shelf. How many should they order?*

▷ **Approach:**

Start by calculating the target stock. In this case it is the sum of average sales, lead time cover and safety stock.

Solution:

(a)   Target stock = Average sales + Lead time cover + Safety stock

$$= \frac{3{,}300}{12} + \frac{3{,}300}{52} + \frac{3{,}300}{12} \times 0.1$$

$$= 275 + 63.4 + 27.5 = 365.9$$

$$= 366 \text{ brushes}$$

(Note the rounding up, as this is a safety stock and we don't want less than the 10%.)

(b)   When counting the 120 bushes left as part of the end-of-month review, the chemists need to order 246 (366 – 120) to bring the stock up to the target level. It appears they have had a bad month, and have sold less than the usual 275.

Which System: Reorder Level or Cyclical Review?

Choosing between ROL and CR depends on several things:

- *Accuracy*: ROL systems can be more accurate as they monitor the level constantly; but some ROL systems capture only changes, and can get out of step with reality. As CR is forced to count all the stocks at regular intervals, its values are accurate, if not always up to date.
- *Consolidating orders*: CR groups orders from a single supplier, resulting in lower transportation and ordering costs. ROL systems will order each part as the need arises, and combining orders is difficult.
- *Safety stocks*: safety stocks with ROL cover a relatively short and fixed period – the delivery time. In CR sufficient stocks are needed not only for the delivery time, but also to cover the time before the next review.
- *Implementation costs*: counting the level of stock every review period may cost more than monitoring the changes in an ROL system, particularly if there is an accurate way of recording usage. EPOS systems, for example, know by the minute how many of each item is in stock, and orders are generated automatically.

Greater accuracy is provided by ROL systems, as they operate with a monitoring system to track the level of stock. Cyclical review systems can be cheaper to introduce, but by their nature are less accurate, as the stock level is checked only once per period. This means that firms have a higher risk of either having too much inventory or running out.

❗ **Stop and Think**

4   These systems are actually very simple to operate in practice, and a short exercise will show we knew them before we started this chapter. Can you think of any examples from your own home where you effectively use the systems above? Did you know you were practising inventory management?

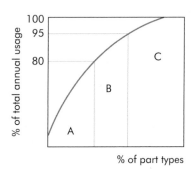

Figure 9.4 ABC inventory classification

ABC Inventory Classification: Choosing Inventory Control Methods

If we have only limited resources to manage our inventory, it makes sense to identify the parts that we should control closely with a sophisticated and accurate but sometimes expensive system, and separate them from those we can get away with controlling less accurately but more cheaply. **ABC** inventory classification analysis is a tool to help us do this.

> **ABC:** system for ranking inventory into parts to control closely and parts that don't merit undue effort in monitoring.

ABC analysis ranks inventory items to identify the amount of money that is spent on each during a year. This consists not only of how much the item costs, but also how many are used. The ABC ranking divides those we should control closely from those that are less important.

ABC produces a chart sorted by the cumulative annual usage value, as shown in Figure 9.4. Items are labelled A, B, C in accordance with their annual usage value, expressed as a percentage of the total annual usage value of all the items in inventory. Class A items constitute a small percentage of the items (normally about 10%) but contribute most of the total material spend (often around 80%). These can be high-value items with high unit costs or cheaper items used in large numbers. At the other extreme, class C items are plentiful (60%) but contribute only a very small amount (5%) of the total material bill. These tend to be small and cheap items such as nuts, bolts and washers which we only use infrequently. Class B is typically 30% of items, costing about 15% of the total material spend.

Class A items should be very closely controlled with a very accurate system, such as ROL using real-time tracking and barcode, whereas class C items need only cursory checks, as holding excess inventory is not going to add excessive cost. They are ideal for a long-interval CR system. Type B is somewhere in between, and managers need to decide for themselves how to control this class of inventory.

WORKED EXAMPLE 9.4

ABC Analysis

To perform ABC analysis, the first thing to do is calculate, for each item in the analysis, the annual usage value (how many we use and how much each costs):

Annual usage value = Unit cost × Quantity used per annum

Then rank the items in order of annual usage value and plot the cumulative percentages on a graph to classify them.

Table 9.2 shows the bought-in price and annual sales of the set of different types of garments that are held in stock by a wholesaler.

Step 1 is to calculate the annual usage value, as shown in Table 9.3.

Next, put the items in descending order of annual usage value, and work out the annual spend on each item as a percentage of the total (see Table 9.4). This is done because there could easily be thousands of parts, and so using percentages allows comparisons with other studies. Also add each of these percentages, item by item, to give the cumulative spend. This column in the table is needed, as it is plotted on the chart to analyse the results.

Table 9.2 Item usage and value

Item type	Purchase price (£)	Annual sales (items per year)
a	8	1,250
b	18	450
c	30	75
d	25	10
e	3	280
f	4	80
g	18	45
h	7	250
i	12	150
j	26	30

Table 9.3 Annual usage values

Item type	Purchase price (£)	Annual sales (items per year)	Annual spend (price × number)
a	8	1,250	10,000
b	18	450	8,100
c	30	75	2,250
d	25	10	250
e	3	280	840
f	4	80	320
g	18	45	810
h	7	250	1,750
i	12	150	1,800
j	26	30	780

From the table, plot the chart for the garments against the cumulative percentage of annual usage value (Figure 9.5). From this identify which to label A, B or C.

In this example we could use a strict rule, such as 'Class A are designated as the first 20%', but as we have only 10 items it is better to examine the values in the table to help identify items as A, B or C. Garments a and b are clearly very significant and should be type A. We could put c into type A as well, but its annual usage value is more similar to i, h, e and g, and so it seems sensible to group these together as type B. Again j, f and d all have similar annual usage values, and so they can be labelled type C. These divisions are shown on the graph. We can now find different inventory control procedures for each group.

Table 9.4 Ascending percentage usage values

Item type	Purchase price (£)	Annual sales (items per year)	Annual spend (price × number)	Percentage spend (%)	Cumulative spend (%)
a	8	1,250	10,000	37.2	37.2
b	18	450	8,100	30.1	67.3
c	30	75	2,250	8.4	75.7
i	12	150	1,800	6.7	82.3
h	7	250	1,750	6.5	88.8
e	3	280	840	3.1	92.0
g	18	45	810	3.0	95.0
j	26	30	780	2.9	97.9
f	4	80	320	1.2	99.1
d	25	10	250	0.9	100.0
			26,900	100.0	

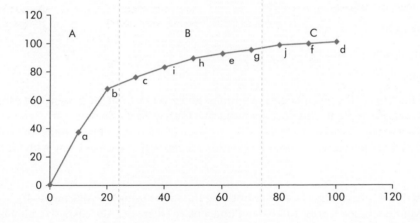

Figure 9.5 ABC chart showing classifications

- Type A items require very close monitoring and very tight inventory control procedures with real-time tracking and counting such as bar code scans and RFID.
- Type B items require formal inventory control, but less intense scrutiny and intervention than is the case with A items.
- Type C items require a minimum of formalized control. In manufacturing, type C parts are often provided on free issue, and reordered in long lead time cycles.

SHORT CASE 9.1 ABC: Cathay Pacific's Spare Parts Inventory System

Cathay Pacific Airlines has an alternative application of ABC analysis in managing its spare parts. Cathay Pacific spends HK$7,643 million (£596 million) on spares each year, and there is great pressure to reduce the bill. Managing airline spare parts is a highly complex task because of the time-critical nature of the business (it costs US$60 per minute to have an aeroplane on the ground), the large numbers of parts (Cathay Pacific has 380,000 spares coming from 2,300 different suppliers) and the special safety and quality regulations, which often vary from country to country.

Source: © Bostjant/iStock

One tool that Cathay Pacific uses to analyse and manage its spares is to grade them based on criticality rather than rate of usage. The grading system is as follows:

1　No Go: must be replaced before the plane can fly

2　Go If: there is an alternative solution to the problem not requiring replacement

3　Go: the part is not critical and can be fixed later

Another ABC-type analysis that Cathay Pacific uses is to classify the spare parts for the cabin by the class of passenger they affect:

1　first class VIP

2　first and business class

3　economy class

The reason behind this is the potential loss of business and revenue from the passenger having a less than perfect experience on the flight. This does not mean that Cathay Pacific does not carry spares for economy class, but that the systems it uses mean there are higher levels of safety stock for the more 'valuable' passenger classes, so that a first class passenger should never have a poor experience of flying with Cathay Pacific.

Questions

1　What risks does Cathay Pacific face by prioritizing the spares using the ABC method?
2　Think of your own experiences, and try and find a place where the ABC analysis would be useful. Perhaps you can think about the food you keep in your kitchen cupboards. Which would you like to monitor most closely to ensure you never run out?

Sources: Cathay Pacific website, www.cathaypacific.com/cpa/en_INTL/aboutus/investor/annualreports, accessed 20 July 2009; Hong Kong Aircraft Engineering Company Limited, www.haeco.com/about_haeco/group.html, accessed 20 July 2009; K. Lee and J. Pelosi, Asia Case Research Centre (ACRC), 2009, Case No. 609-012-1.

Manufacturing Control Systems: Dependent Demand

Independent demand: demand that is treated as unrelated to anything else.

In large organizations with complex, multi-part products, managers do not control inventory as single parts in isolation.

The ROL and CR approaches treat all items as having **independent demand**. This means that the demand for one item is not linked to or influenced by anything

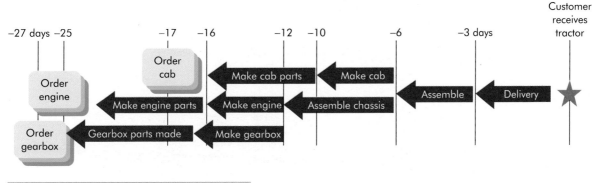

Figure 9.6 The backwards time tracing approach

else happening in the firm. In most production lines, though, very few components or raw materials are independent.

In car assembly the plant runs at a predetermined capacity, and so the materials planners will know how many parts they need. Making 3,000 cars in a week needs 3,000 engines, 3,000 gearboxes, 3,000 bodies, 15,000 wheels, and 6,000 front seats. The parts demand is dependent on finished car production.

When to place an order is also known, as it is based on the production lead time. For example, if it takes 3 weeks to make and ship an engine from the supplier to the assembly area, the plan for car assembly can be used to produce a schedule for ordering engines. **Dependent demand** and backwards ordering is shown in Figure 9.6 for a tractor; it starts with the finished product and works back, adding the time needed for each subassembly. The diagram also breaks the product down into the parts to be assembled in the finished product. A sensible plan would be to start placing an order for the gearbox 27 days before the finished tractor is to be delivered to the customer.

> **Dependent demand:** demand for a part that is normally directly related to that for some others, and ultimately to the aggregate production plan.

The implication of dependent demand is that, with enough information, managers can determine which parts to order, how many, and when, to make the products listed in the order book.

Material Requirements Planning (MRP)

There are several manufacturing control systems which make use of dependent demand, but the most widespread is **material requirements planning (MRP)**. This section explores MRP, and then looks at how the idea has been expanded to make more complex manufacturing control systems: **MRP II** and **Enterprise Resource Planning (ERP)**.

> **Material requirements planning (MRP):** a way of calculating the demand and timing for component deliveries in order to make the products listed in the master production schedule.

The MRP Process

MRP works out the timing and quantities to order to meet a given production schedule, as shown in Figure 9.7. It uses three pieces of information to generate a material plan: the master production schedule (MPS), the bill of materials (BOM) and the inventory record. MRP is nearly always done by a computerized system, as this is the only way that the necessary steps can all be carried out quickly and accurately enough.

Master Production Schedule

In developing a plan, MRP starts with a statement of the final outcome. This is the **master production schedule (MPS)**, a formal list of the products to be made, including delivery dates. Ideally, this information is composed of real customer orders that have already been paid for, but often it is a forecast of possible orders. This MPS is therefore a working refinement of the aggregate capacity plan (Chapter 5).

> **Master production schedule (MPS):** a formal list of the products to be sent to customers, plus detailed specifications and delivery dates; the start of the MRP calculation.

MPSs have fixed, firm and flexible periods. The fixed period is needed, as many parts have already been produced to be used in the short term. The firm part of the MPS can cope with limited changes, depending on what has

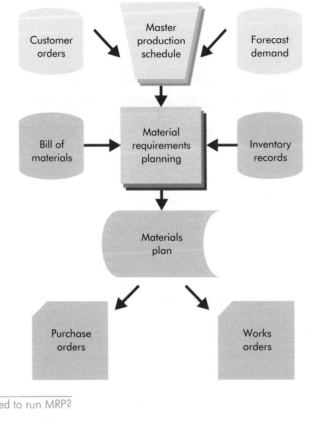

Figure 9.7 What is required to run MRP?

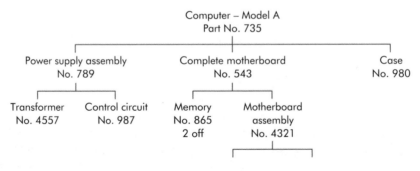

Figure 9.8 The bill of materials

already been ordered; and the flexible part of the MPS looks far enough ahead to allow changes to the schedule without negative consequences.

Bill of Materials

The bill of materials (BOM) lists, in a hierarchical structure, the individual parts and subassemblies needed to make finished products, as shown in Figure 9.8. It is developed during new product development (Chapter 5). The BOM processor is a computer program for generating and maintaining the BOM structure for all the products. It is important to ensure that design modifications are translated into an updated BOM structure in an accurate and controlled manner. Errors in the BOM will result in missing parts when it comes to building the product.

One important feature of a BOM for MRP is the way it is organized, with all entries for the same part being shown on the same level. It could be that the same part is used in different products or subassemblies; if so, then it is easier to work out the total demand for the part if all its instances are on the same level of the BOM. The manager then just needs to look across one row, rather than find all instances of the part.

Inventory Record File

Combining the MPS and BOM will give a list of the parts needed, but as some are already in stock, or orders have already been placed, more information than this is needed. Information on present and future stock also needs to be included in the MRP calculation, and this comes from the **inventory record file**. As well as recording the stock levels, this file introduces future demand not directly needed to satisfy the current MPS, such as orders for spares and service parts.

> **Inventory records file:** information about the part, including sources, and the stock levels. A key part of the MRP calculation.

Running the MRP Calculation

The core of MRP is combining the MPS, BOM and inventory records to compute (or explode) the parts required to satisfy the MPS. Starting with the MPS, MRP calculates whether there are enough finished products in stock to supply to the customer. If not, it identifies how many need to be produced, and when. The second level of the BOM is then included, using the results of the first step to see which parts are needed to make the finished products scheduled for production. Knowing how many of each part are already in stock helps to determine how many more are needed, and when to start making (or buying) them. The process continues to the next level of the BOM, and calculates how many of its parts are needed, and when. This process is repeated through all the levels of the BOM until all parts are taken care of.

Putting each part on only one level in the BOM makes it much easier to add together all the places where that part might be used. All requirements for the items higher up in the BOM need to be calculated before the requirements for the part concerned can be worked out.

Figure 9.9 shows the BOM for a kettle. Note the way that some parts appear more than once, but always on the same line.

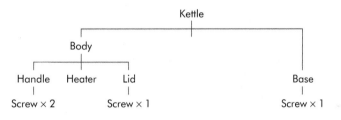

Figure 9.9 BOM representation for the kettle

Figure 9.10 shows the basic MRP calculation in operation for the kettle: Figure 9.10a is a blank record, and Figure 9.10b is the completed record. The top line in each table shows the week number, and below this is the demand for the part. The two bottom lines show the stock situation at the beginning and end of the week respectively. The remaining rows show what needs to be purchased, or produced, and when to send out this request in order to meet the demand on the top line.

Part: Kettle Week number	23	24	25	26	27	28
MPS demand	10	10	15	10	15	10
Orders delivered						
Orders released						
Starting stock	45					
Balance of stock	35					

Order size = 30 units, lead time = 1
(a)

Part: Kettle Week number	23	24	25	26	27	28
Forecast demand	10	10	15	10	15	10
Orders delivered				30		
Orders released			30			
Starting stock	45	35	25	10	0	15
Balance of stock	35	25	10	0	15	5

Order size = 30 units, lead time = 1
(b)

Figure 9.10 The basic MRP calculation in operation for the MPS (level 0 of the BOM)

The MRP process completes the table by moving forward and assessing the number of parts required, compared with the current stock level. A shortfall leads to an order for new stock, but if there are enough parts in stock, none are ordered.

The 'Orders delivered' row gives the extra parts needed, and the 'Orders released' row indicates when to place the order, based on the procurement lead time. This order release information is the manufacturing schedule for the item (or, if it is bought from a supplier, the schedule of parts that must be ordered).

Repeating this process for all the parts in the firm, as in Figure 9.11 for example, gives a coordinated plan of all the actions needed to achieve the MPS. Note the way that the orders released from a higher-level BOM item represent the demand for the next level, and the need to incorporate how many of each part is required to make the one above it in the BOM. In this example, the orders released for the kettle become the demand for the body and base. Demand for the screws comes from 2 for the handle, 1 for the lid and 1 for the base, and these are added together to calculate the total needed. Only then can the demand for more be calculated.

> ❗ **Stop and Think**
>
> **5** Why is it important to ensure a high degree of accuracy in the inputs to the MRP calculation?

Manufacturing Resource Planning

BUSINESS INTEGRATION

Early MRP systems were initially limited to planning first-level (finished product) requirements. These were then extended to other levels of the BOM, resulting in a materials plan for the whole 'tree' of parts. Increases in computing power led to MRP systems that could do more than just calculate future materials needs. More sophisticated systems were implemented, to cover the planning and control of production, including the production operations. This incarnation of MRP is called **manufacturing resource planning (MRP II)**. In addition to the inventory and purchasing calculations, it includes functionality for controlling:

> **Manufacturing resource planning (MRP II):** extension of MRP that not only identifies the amounts and times for delivery for components but also includes capacity checks, and extends the calculations to cover the scheduling of production.

- Production routeing data
- Shop floor tracking and control
- Batch traceability
- Capacity planning
- Business planning
- Sales analysis and forecasting
- Supplier contract management
- Work tool management
- Design/engineering change control
- Cost control
- Links to existing finance systems such as ledgers.

These days it is rare to find a simple MRP system; most systems have at least some MRP II functionality. Figure 9.12 shows a typical MRP II system, with top-level planning and detailed materials requirements (the original MRP elements we saw above), but also with new routines for capacity and routeing constraints, and the tasks for subsequent monitoring and execution of the plan.

Capacity Planning and Scheduling

> **Closed-loop MRP:** use of the MRP calculation to examine whether the plans it produces are achievable, given limits in capacity or supply times and other constraints.
>
> **Capacity requirements planning (CRP):** an MRP module that examines workloading on workstations to identify shortfalls.

Early MRP systems did not check whether the firm could complete the resulting plan. In effect they assumed that there was infinite capacity in the system, scheduled items based on due dates, and so often produced plans that overloaded some workstations. To deal with this issue, one of the first MRP II developments was the **closed-loop MRP** approach shown in Figure 9.13. Here the designed capacity of the production system is checked against the plan. The first check is at the aggregate planning level – the whole month's volume. Next is a rough-cut capacity plan looking at the viability of the MPS, checked against the available capacity on that day. As computing power developed, and the accuracy of MRP systems improved, **capacity requirements planning (CRP)**

BOM Level 0

Part: Kettle Week number	23	24	25	26	27	28
Forecast demand	10	10	15	10	15	10
Orders delivered					30	
Orders released				⌐30 ─┐		
Starting stock	45	35	25	10	0	15
Balance of stock	35	25	10	0	15	5
				Order size = 30 units, Lead time = 1		

BOM Level 1

Part: Body Week number	23	24	25	26	27	28
Forecast demand				30◄		
Orders delivered				40		
Orders released			┌ 40			
Starting stock	20	20	20	20	30	30
Balance of stock	20	20	20	30	30	30
				Order size = 40 units, Lead time = 1		

BOM Level 2

Part: Handle Week number	23	24	25	26	27	28
Forecast demand			40◄			
Orders delivered			20			
Orders released		20 ─┐				
Starting stock	30	30	30	10	10	10
Balance of stock	30	30	10	10	10	10
				Order size = 20 units, Lead time = 1		

BOM Level 2

Part: Heater Week number	23	24	25	26	27	28
Forecast demand			40◄			
Orders delivered						
Orders released						
Starting stock	100	100	100	60	60	60
Balance of stock	100	100	60	60	60	60
				Order size = 100 units, Lead time = 3		

BOM Level 2

Part: Lid Week number	23	24	25	26	27	28
Forecast demand			►40			
Orders delivered			15			
Orders released		┌ 15				
Starting stock	30	30	30	5	5	5
Balance of stock	30	30	5	5	5	5
				Order size = 15 units, Lead time = 1		

BOM Level 2

Part: Base Week number	23	24	25	26	27	28
Forecast demand				►30		
Orders delivered				30		
Orders released			30 ─┐			
Starting stock	20	20	20	20	20	20
Balance of stock	20	20	20	20	20	20
				Order size = 30 units, Lead time = 1		

BOM Level 3

Part: Screw Week number	23	24	25	26	27	28
Forecast demand		►55◄	30◄			
Orders delivered		30	30			
Orders released	30	30				
Starting stock	40	40	15	15	15	15
Balance of stock	40	15	15	15	15	15
				Order size = 30 units, Lead time = 1		

Figure 9.11 The complete MRP schedule for production of the kettle and all its subassemblies

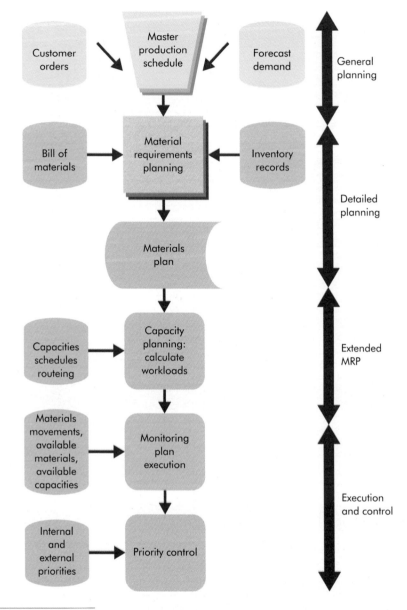

Figure 9.12 MRP II system elements

modules were developed that analysed at the individual part level, instead of aggregating parts using similar processes. The delivery date for the part allows the demand on each workstation for the given period to be calculated, and identifies any capacity problems. CRP identifies whether a work centre is going to be over- or underloaded and produces a *load report* that identifies where problems will occur.

Finite Capacity Scheduling

Finite capacity scheduling is a more advanced MRP II system which includes routines to try to solve the identified capacity problems. The computer reschedules the jobs in a structured and iterative manner, taking the available work centre capacities into account. Work is often rescheduled, giving preference to jobs with the earliest due dates, and so a more achievable plan can eventually be established. However, prioritizing jobs can be very complex, so few firms manage to make this work well. As a result, scheduling to infinite capacity, together with **rough-cut capacity planning**, and then adjusting the plan by hand when capacity issues are identified, is still common.

Finite capacity scheduling: advanced MRP II system including routines to try and solve any capacity problems.

Rough-cut capacity planning: CRP applied at the aggregate level to try and ensure the plan is close to achievable with existing capacity limits.

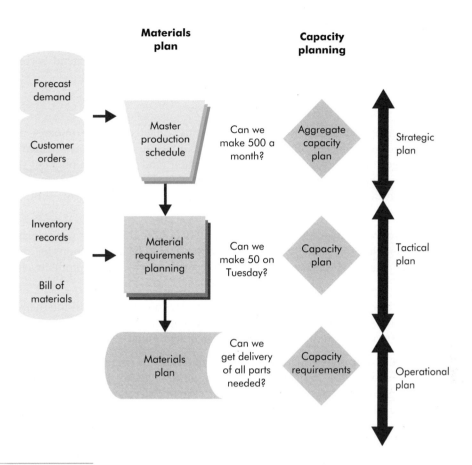

Figure 9.13 Closed-loop MRP

Evaluating MRP

CRITICAL PERSPECTIVE

MRP systems represent a way to schedule production and control inventory, and are in use in most firms. However, as for any large-scale project, there are problems introducing such systems to the organization. Common problems are:

- Inadequate training of production control staff
- Inadequate preparation and maintenance of the database
- Inadequate understanding of the system purchased
- Difficulties combining the new system with existing ones.

The key point is that the MRP system will only be as accurate as the data input, and the degree to which the resulting plan is followed.

❗ Stop and Think

6   As MRP II is an integrated planning process that is generated by computer, can you see how senior managers can direct and control the system?

Enterprise Resource Planning

BUSINESS INTEGRATION

Recently MRP II systems have been expanded into corporate-wide systems that extend beyond production, called **enterprise resource planning (ERP)**.

Enterprise resource planning (ERP): ERP systems are corporate-wide information systems that present data as if from a central single entity source.

Extending MRP II to ERP

Integrated organization-wide IT systems, called enterprise resource planning (ERP), are commercial software packages that integrate transactions-oriented data and business processes throughout an organization (and perhaps throughout the entire inter-organizational supply chain). Although ERP systems often have core MRP II workflow and planning modules, their wide coverage, as shown in Figure 9.14, means they are equally applicable to service organizations.

One significant ERP improvement over MRP is a single central data store that allows commonality of information between different modules. Traditionally, when the data was held in separate sections for each task, sharing it between the modules needed specialized, very complex software which was prohibitively expensive to develop.

In addition, ERP systems have Internet interfaces that make it easy to link data, both internally and also with customers and suppliers. These often enter and manage their own information directly, such as updating a delivery address in Amazon, or placing an order online.

Customer relationship management (CRM): ERP tools where all relevant information about a customer can be presented in one place, thus offering a transparent way of supporting customers.

ERP can present data in a single application to whoever needs access. In **customer relationship management (CRM)**, all the relevant information about a customer – previous orders (from the sales data), current order status (production schedules), service calls (from after sales), payment history and creditworthiness (accounts data), and any other contact the customer may have had with the firm – is presented on one screen, giving better customer service and more efficient operations.

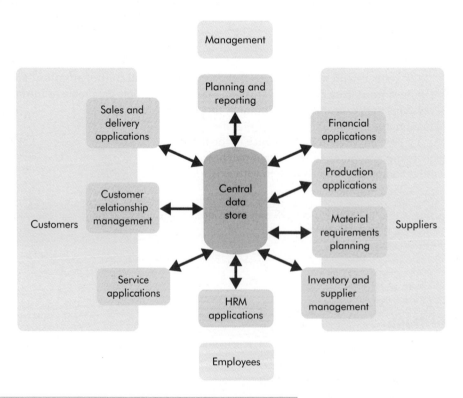

Figure 9.14 ERP systems with central data stores and processing modules

ERP Challenges

Successful ERP systems offer many benefits to the organization, including executive information systems to allow long-term planning, decision support applications for medium-term planning and control, and transaction processing. But there are problems, as ERP systems are normally purchased as standard packages, and it is the task of consultants and vendors to translate existing organizational processes into these predefined systems. This adaptation to the software adds considerable cost and risk to the adoption of ERP. However, as the systems are utilized within many firms, they can represent industry best practice, and so their adoption can lead to improved operational performance. Problems can also be caused by implementation issues, such as the management of the transition, the accuracy of data, people's resistance to change, and the difficulties of integrating legacy systems.

Contemporary Thinking: ERP Players and Scope

The leading purveyors of ERP solutions are shown in Table 9.5, together with their focus. The players chose different sectors, and can target large firms offering sets of solutions tailored to particular industries, as in SAP, or provide bespoke solutions for the unique business processes of smaller firms.

SAP organizes its R3 ERP modules under the following headings, giving an idea of the breadth offered:
- Financials
- Human resources
- Customer relationship management
- Supplier relationship management
- Product life cycle management
- Supply chain management
- Business intelligence.

More specifically, SAP has a portfolio of applications, some of which are listed in Table 9.6. Despite claims from vendors, the MRP elements are in the list, and so ERP is not something completely new.

The key point is that, as we saw in the discussion of MRP systems, the validity of the data and ensuring the systems are followed closely are very important to the correct running of ERP systems. There is also much choice in the market, and finding or developing a system that aligns closely with the firm' operations is a major factor in ensuring effective ERP.

Table 9.5 ERP firms and their focus

	SAP	**Oracle**	**Microsoft**	**Infor**	**Independents**
Market approach	Two brands: SAP/R3 and MySAP	Four brands	Four basic brands	Many products with diverse functions	Normally bespoke applications for smaller firms
ERP position	Market leader in top-level and complete systems	Number two, but catching up with SAP	Currently second tier, but making ground	Third largest, but based on IBM equipment leasing	Sage and Intuit have many customers, but do not offer fully integrated systems
Market scale	SAP deals mainly in integrated solutions	Has more standalone applications in place than SAP	Uses MS Office applications to sell add-ons, and CRM in particular	Large range of standalone applications	Thousands of examples
Industry-based approach	Offers 25 industry specific solutions	Main focus on standalone applications	Applicable in all areas	Core focus on supply chains	Thousands of examples

Table 9.6 The main SAP/R3 modules

FI Financial accounting	CO Controlling	AM Asset management
General ledger Book close Tax Accounts receivable Accounts payable Consolidation Special ledgers	Cost elements Cost centres Profit centres Internal orders Activity-based costing Product costing	Purchase Sale Depreciation Tracking
SD Sales and distribution	**HR Human resources**	**PM Plant maintenance**
Sales orders Pricing Picking (and other warehouse processes) Packing Shipping	Employment history Payroll Training Career management Succession planning	Labour Material Downtime and outages
MM Materials management	**QM Quality management**	**PP Production planning**
Purchasing Inventory management	Planning Execution Inspections Certificates	Capacity planning Master production scheduling Material requirements planning Shopfloor

 Stop and Think

7 We can now see that the MRP-based ERP systems are very pervasive, and employed in all areas of business, both services and manufacturing. But what gave the push for traditionally manufacturing-centred systems to be so widely adopted? Try the following question. How important do you think the Internet was for the recent explosion in ERP systems?

SHORT CASE 9.2

NIKE: ERP Implementation, from Failure to Success

One of the most-analysed examples of ERP introduction is Nike. Late 2001 saw an uncharacteristic 30% fall in profits, which Nike attributed to problems with a new ERP system introduced with i2 Technologies. The issues were a major worry for Nike and its shareholders, as the i2 system was only the first part of a move to adopt ERP based on SAP/R3.

The i2 system shortened the planning, ordering and production time of products, allowing real orders to drive the system rather than reliance on a forecast.

However, the i2 project, based on their established TradeMatrix Plan system for retail and supply, did not go well. One major issue that emerged was the high degree of customization Nike made to the i2 system, making it slow to update entries, and difficult to track down and rectify errors. The customization problems were compounded by i2's lack of experience in clothes and shoes, and Nike's changing operating conditions, which forced the adoption

Source: © Getty Images

of the system before it was ready. When first used, the system had poor integration with Nike's other systems. Nike and i2 quickly found solutions to the problems, but had already over-ordered on some products, leading to heavy discounting, and under-ordered on others, leading to shortages of some top sellers.

Nike learnt from the project, and the rest of the ERP programme with SAP has been far more effective. Nike now uses a third-party integrator to migrate data to new systems, and has reduced system customization. Increased testing of the system before going live ensures it works as expected.

Nike now has a single-instance, apparel industry focused SAP/R3 system (i.e. all data is held only once in the database) that gives a competitive advantage as it now operates with firm orders from retailers, rather than having to rely on a forecast. Nike's and their partners' learning will help with the next steps, which includes plans to capture orders from end customers.

The case shows the problems and benefits of ERP, where firms effectively replace the entire operating systems at the core of the firm with one system. Such a large-scale change carries very high risks, but can also generate great rewards if done properly.

Questions

1 What advantage does Nike get from having its single-instance ERP system?
2 What advice would you give to other firms embarking on ERP programmes, given the experience of Nike?

Sources: /www.computerworld.com/action/article.do?command=viewArticleBasic&taxonomyName=software&articleId=9130301&taxonomyId=18&intsrc=kc_feat; T.H. Davenport, Putting the enterprise into the enterprise system. *Harvard Business Review*, 1998, **76**(4), 121–131.

Summary

Managing inventory is a very important task for all firms, and there are many ways to ensure they tackle the problem effectively, such as ROL and CR. Although firms should normally try to reduce inventory whenever possible, they need to remember that inventory is not always a bad thing and has many uses, including uncoupling separate activities in the chain of operations.

We can apply mathematics to managing inventory levels, and there are many refinements to the EOQ formula that take in ever more accurate representations or statistical ideas to improve the accuracy of the models.

By controlling the flow of material, we can control the activities of the organization. MRP II systems schedule the activities of the firm to meet the planned orders for finished products, and so match output to demand. This can greatly reduce inventory and waste. Despite the claims of the systems providers, the complex ERP systems with their central data stores and web-integrated processes are an extension of MRP, and are equally valuable to service firms as well as to manufacturers.

In summary, we have:

- Contrasted the different roles of inventory

- Explained when inventory is useful and when it is problematic

- Explored the use of reorder level and cyclical review systems

- Shown how the ABC technique can help classify parts

- Witnessed the power of EOQ models

- Defined dependent and independent demand systems

▶
- Seen what is involved in an MRP system
- Described the extensions that lead to MRP II
- Defined the scope of ERP systems.

Key Theories

- **EOQ** – economic order quantity (EOQ) is a fixed order amount that minimizes the total costs over a whole year.

- **Reorder level** – reorder point inventory systems (Q-type) tell us when we need to order a fixed amount (normally the EOQ).

- **Cyclical review** – cyclical review inventory systems (P type) determine the amount to be ordered at a fixed time.

- **ABC** – ABC ranking tells us which parts we should control closely, and also those that we should not exert undue effort in monitoring.

- **Dependent/independent demand** – with independent demand, the demand for each part is treated as unrelated to anything else. Dependent demand makes use of the fact that demand for a part is normally related to that for others, or to the aggregate production plan.

- **MRP** – material requirements planning is a way of calculating the demand and timing for component deliveries in order to make the products listed in the master production schedule.

- **MRP II** – manufacturing resources planning is an extension of MRP that not only identifies the amounts and times for delivery for components, but also includes capacity checks, and extends the calculations to cover the scheduling of production.

- **ERP** – enterprise resources planning systems are corporate-wide information systems that present data as if from a central, single source.

Key Equations

Economic order quantity:

$$\text{Economic order quantity, } Q = \sqrt{\frac{2DC_s}{C_h}}$$

Reorder level system:

$$\text{ROL} = \text{Demand (per day)} \times \text{Delivery lead time (in days)}$$

Reorder level system with safety stock:

$$\text{ROL} = \text{Demand (per day)} \times \text{Delivery lead time (in days)} + \text{Safety stock}$$

ABC inventory classification:

$$\text{Annual usage value} = \text{Unit cost} \times \text{Quantity used per annum}$$

Suggested Answers to Stop and Think Questions

1 **Inventory control:** The answer depends on the organization you chose. In a hospital, say, the inventory would include the drugs, and losing control would mean that patients could not be treated if stocks were low. If inventory is too high, though, the costs can spiral, and the hospital they will have to throw some unused drugs away, as they will have passed their use-by dates. If you were thinking about a firm of builders, the inventory would be the materials they have at the yard. If they ran out of something, then they would need to get it in quickly, and that would cost more than a

normal order. If they had too much material in the yard, then it would be hard to find the right materials behind the piles of other stuff, and there the firm would have too much capital tied up in inventory.

2 **Function of inventory:** The functions of inventory can be summarized as meeting demand (anticipation), protection against stock-out (buffer), cutting costs by ordering in bulk, flexibility (buffer), covering delays (decoupling), taking advantage of price changes, and also as transit or pipeline, and cycle inventories. In a supermarket we can see the stocks on the shelves as anticipation (awaiting demand), decoupling in the materials held behind the counter whilst more are delivered, and work in progress in the bakery ovens at the rear of the store.

3 **EPQ:** EPQ models add a level of complexity, in that they also consider the fact that parts may also be produced in the factory at a set rate, and not arrive in the system by instantaneous delivery.

4 **Order systems:** Most of the foodstuffs we have in our homes effectively operate on some form of either reorder point or cyclical review. Some food we buy every time we visit the shops, such as milk and bread, and we decide how much to get based on when we will next go shopping (cyclical approach). Others we only buy when the jar or packet is empty, or we notice we are getting low – in effect a reorder point approach. These are not as formalized as they are in a manufacturing firm.

5 **Data accuracy:** Accuracy of data in the files is a major area of concern when introducing MRP, as the outputs of the system are used repeatedly in other calculations. If any mistakes are not identified in advance, then the firm will either run out of materials it needs, or else carry excessive stocks.

The Oliver Wight organization, which sells MRP consultancy, grades the implementations of systems in firms, and one of the criteria for getting its A grade is 99% BOM accuracy. This is particularly hard when you remember that products are constantly being developed and changed. Quite complex systems exist to ensure that such engineering changes are managed and timed through the supply chain in a coordinated manner. If, for example, the old steering wheel and the new steering column are not compatible, but come from different suppliers with different lead times and order quantities, you can imagine the potential problems this could cause.

6 **Design of MRP:** Top managers have a very important role in ensuring that the system works correctly. Rather than chasing day-to-day issues, their new focus is on the strategic roles of implementing and developing the system. Their biggest input is not in how the plan is carried out, as it once was, but in designing the parameters of the system and thinking forward. For example, they need to be aware of future capacity issues, and develop plans to alleviate them. At a more practical level, the managers are responsible for setting the MPS that drives the system, and this can be a very delicate task, trying to keep an eye on CRP outputs and sales performance.

7 **ERP and the Internet:** The Internet and the evolution of ERP occurred at the same time. As IT systems were just evolving that could manage the complex data operations fast enough for the ideas of MRP extension to become reality, so too was the development of wide-area networks. As these became faster with the explosion of the Internet, so the ERP systems could be distributed. The development of ERP would probably have happened without the Internet, but this made it available to a much wider range of firms, who could not have invested in their own fast wide-area networks. The universal availability of the Internet also helped ERP systems, and their web-based front ends, to enable the sales force and customers to interact with the processes directly. It is likely that many of the truly useful elements of ERP would have been very slow to emerge if the Internet had not developed at the same time.

connect

Review Questions

1 Write down the equation to determine the EOQ for a product. Why is the EOQ concept significant for a shop manager?

2 What tools exist to help managers control inventory levels?

3 Describe the processes in MRP II systems, paying particular attention to the organizational issues of introducing the system to a company with little previous experience of computerized production systems.

4 Describe the steps in introducing ERP systems, paying particular attention to the organizational issues.

5 What is ERP, and how does it differ from MRP?

Discussion Questions

1 Discuss, with examples from international firms, whether inventory is an asset or a liability.

2 How useful is the concept of EOQ to service operations?

3 Describe the difference between MRP and MRP II production control systems.

4 Giving examples, discuss the circumstances under which MRP systems are inappropriate. Also, discuss the choices that following such a strategy pre-defines.

5 With reference to theoretical frameworks, discuss whether firms can adopt MRP-based inventory systems for products with both low and high production volumes.

Problems

1 Pay a visit to the college shop, or one nearby, and see if you can calculate the EOQ for a popular soft drink. (Be sure to ask the shop manager for permission before you start.) You will need to estimate the daily demand (you can always watch for 30 minutes and use that as an estimate), stock order costs (you could work out how much it would cost to send an employee to the wholesaler, including wages and van mileage), and holding costs (try a bank loan rate of 10%). When you are done, see what the manager thinks about your figures, and find out exactly what stock control system they use.

As a more advanced task, you could try and work out the reorder level as well.

2 Look at the different stocks held in the library. There is probably a short or restricted loan section where books can be taken out for only a short time. How do you think the librarian knows which books to put in this section? How would you adapt the ABC method to help the librarian estimate better the books to hold on restricted loan? Perhaps you could see whether the librarian can find time to give you the information to help your calculations, and whether they know about ABC analysis.

3 Using the Internet, try to identify the different competitive strengths of the ERP suppliers listed earlier in Table 9.5. The introduction to their annual reports would be a good place to look. Which sectors of the industry would you recommend as good pickings for a small, start-up company to make its first move?

4 The demand for Tasty-Lick snacks at the college shop is constant at 2,000 a month. The snacks sell for £1.99 each, and the cost of placing an order with the supplier, Sticky Sweets Co. Ltd, is £10 an order (including delivery charges). The cost of storing items in the small storeroom is estimated to be £28 per snack per year.

(a) How many snacks should the shop order in each delivery?

(b) What is the total holding cost associated with Tasty-Lick snacks for the shop in a typical year?

(c) Why is the EOQ concept significant to the shop manager?

5   The demand for cans of Bernard's Baked Beans at the Cold Storage Supermarket in Egham is constant at 9,000 a month. The cans sell for 55p each, the cost of placing an order with Bernard (which also covers the delivery by Man-n-Van Co.) is £75, and the cost of keeping a can in the storeroom is estimated to be £2 per can per year.

   (a)   What are the most important limitations to the use of the EOQ formula in inventory management decision-making?

   (b)   Describe how the EOQ is different from the EBQ (Economic Batch Quantity).

   (c)   How many snacks should the shop manager order in each delivery?

   (d)   What is the total holding cost associated with Bernard's Beans for the shop in a typical year?

   (e)   Why is the EOQ concept significant to the shop manager, and what might happen if the items needed special care, such as refrigeration?

6   The demand for Munch-u-Like snacks at the college shop is constant at 500 a month, the snacks sell for £1.50 each, the cost of placing an order with Jones Snacks Co. (which also covers the delivery by Securicor) is £60, and the cost of keeping a snack in the small store room is estimated to be £18 per snack per year. How many snacks should the shop order in each delivery?

7   The demand for 2GB memory sticks at the Computer Centre is constant at 500 a month. It takes 3 days for an order for the EOQ to the supplier to be delivered.

   (a)   What is the reorder level for the memory sticks? (Note the units of days and months.)

   (b)   If the IT consultants add a 10% safety stock, what is the new reorder level?

8   The petrol station sells 1,200 litres of unleaded fuel per day. It takes 15 days for an order to the refinery to be delivered. The EOQ is 30,000 litres.

   (a)   What is the reorder level?

   (b)   If the managers add a 10% safety stock, what is the new reorder level?

9   If it takes half a day to deliver an order of milk to Starbucks in the city centre, and they use 20 bottles per day:

   (a)   What is the reorder level?

   (b)   If the managers add a 10% safety stock, what is the new reorder level?

10   The business school's stock of paper is operated using a cyclical review system, and an order is placed every month.

   (a)   If the school normally uses 64 packets of paper a day, and it takes 4 days for the delivery, what is the target stock level it should aim for?

   (b)   This month the business school finds it has 120 packets of paper left in stock. Using the information above, how many more should it order?

   (c)   The office manager at the business school is worried that it might run out of paper, and so adds a 10% safety stock. What is the new target level?

11   The supermarket uses a cyclical review system for its own-brand shampoo. Typically, it sells 4,500 bottles a week. An order is placed each week to bring the stocks up to the average weekly demand. It takes a day for the delivery to arrive, and the supermarket uses a 10% safety margin to cover any variation in demand. What is the target level of stock for the shampoo?

12   A farmer keeps his chickens in a shed in winter, heated by special bulbs. If he needs to replace 6 bulbs a week and it takes 4 weeks for the bulbs to arrive, how many should he aim to have ready to use when he counts the spares every Monday morning?

13   The table below shows the bought-in price and annual sales of the set of different types of garment that are held in stock by a wholesaler.

Item type	Purchase price (£)	Annual sales (items per year)
a	4	2,250
b	47	1,950
c	148	85
d	75	200
e	11	580
f	129	115
g	67	15
h	201	150
i	69	310
j	78	900

(a) Should inventory be seen as an asset or liability? Ensure you justify your views.

(b) Construct an ABC chart for the items above.

(c) Suggest, giving clear reasons, which items should be treated as classes A, B and C.

14 The table below shows the bought-in price and annual sales of the set of different types of garment that are held in stock by a wholesaler.

Item type	Purchase price (£)	Annual sales (items per year)
a	24	2,250
b	54	950
c	90	95
d	75	20
e	9	380
f	12	120
g	56	155
h	21	550
i	36	310
j	78	90

(a) Construct an ABC chart for these items.

(b) Suggest which items should be treated as classes A, B and C, discussing why, and what this means.

15 The table below shows the purchase price and annual sales for various items of stock.

Item type	Purchase price per unit (£)	Annual sales (items per year)
a	880	1,400
b	810	400
c	2,100	70
d	1,650	20
e	100	350
f	160	1,850
g	6,100	150
h	230	550
i	1,500	650
j	2,500	50

Construct an ABC chart for these items, showing which items you designated as class A, which as class B, and which as class C.

16 SPG Ltd produces a range of household products. Its top-selling cordless kettle is made of five subassemblies: lid, handle, body, heater and base. The assembly process has recently been streamlined, and now consists of push-fitting the heater into the body, and then fastening the lid and handle using three screws. The bases are a complete unit and do not need any work before packaging with the assembled kettle.

It is Monday morning at the start of week 7, and the sales director has the following orders for the kettle.

Week	8	9	10	11
Orders	150	260	220	190

You have the following information on stock levels and delivery times.

Part	Current stock level	Delivery/assembly time (weeks)	Batch size
Kettle	190	1	50
Base	150	1	50
Body	450	2	200
Heater	170	2	200
Lid	200	1	90
Handle	30	1	90
Screw	3,000	1	1,000

(a) Given the description above, construct a table or diagram of the BOM (Bill of Materials) for the kettle.

(b) Generate the MPS of the top-level demand for the kettle.

(c) Using the MPS, run through the MRP calculation to identify whether there are any supply problems for the firm to satisfy the sales orders. If you identified any problems, what advice would you give to the firm?

17 TVS manufactures satellite dishes from sheet metal components. It controls its material supply using a manually based MRP system. Each dish (part A001) is made of two subassemblies: a reflector assembly (part B001) and a mount assembly (part B002). Each reflector assembly requires one dish (C001), one arm (C002), and four screws, and each mount requires one pole (C003), one mount (C004), and two screws. The reflector assembly and mount assembly are fastened together using a further two screws. All the screws are the same design (F500).

The latest information available from the sales department shows expected orders of:

Week number	Predicted sales of dishes
1	100
2	400
3	600
4	300

The current stock level and ordering information is:

Part	Opening stock for week 1	Delivery time from placing order with supplier (weeks)	EOQ
Dish (A001)	360	1	100
Reflector assembly (B001)	600	1	300
Mount assembly (B002)	600	1	150
Dish (C001)	500	1	50
Arm (C002)	1000	1	300
Pole (C003)	600	2	80
Mount (C004)	500	1	200
Screws (F500)	1000	2	1000

(a) Draw a tiered representation of the BOM for an assembled dish (A001).

(b) Produce the MRP calculation requirements record cards for each part for the four weeks, including the demand, opening stock, closing stock, orders released and deliveries received.

(c) State whether the current production forecast is realistic. If you identified any problems, what might be done to solve them?

18 A company manufactures solid oak doors, and controls its material supply using a manually based MRP system. Each door requires one solid oak door panel, two brass hinges and two brass handles. Each hinge is fastened to the door using three screws, and each handle uses two screws of the same type as for the hinges.

The latest information available from the sales department shows expected orders of:

Week number	Predicted sales
1	70
2	20
3	40
4	30

The current stock level and ordering information is:

Part	Opening stock for week 1	Delivery time from placing order with supplier (weeks)	EOQ
Panels	90	1	50
Hinges	150	1	150
Handles	170	1	75
Screws	350	2	400

(a) Draw a representation of the BOM for an assembled door.

(b) Given the sales forecast, work out the weekly aggregate demand for each part used in the factory.

(c) Produce the requirements record cards for each part for the four weeks, including the demand, opening stock, closing stock, orders released and deliveries received.

(d) Identify whether the current production forecast is realistic. If you identified any problems, what might be done to solve them?

 **Online LearningCentre**   Visit the Online Learning Centre at **www.mcgraw-hill.co.uk/textbooks/paton** for a range of resources to support your learning.

Further Reading

Chopra, S., and Lariviere, M.A. (2005) 'Managing service inventory to improve performance', *MIT Sloan Management Review*, **47**(1), 56–63, 95.

Davenport, T.H. (1998) 'Putting the enterprise into the enterprise system', *Harvard Business Review*, **76**(4), 121–131.

Grubbstrom, R.W. (2006) 'Analysis of standard ordering policies within the framework of MRP theory', *International Journal of Production Research*, **44**(18/19), 3759–3773.

McCutcheon, D.M., Raturi, A.S. and Meredith, J.R. (1994) 'The customization–responsiveness squeeze', *Sloan Management Review*, **35**(2), 89–99.

McNurlin, B. (2001) 'Will users of ERP stay satisfied?', *MIT Sloan Management Review*, **42**(2), 13–13.

Orlicky, J. (1975) *Material Requirements Planning; The New Way of Life in Production and Inventory Management*, McGraw-Hill, New York.

References

Chopra, S. and Lariviere, M.A. (2005) 'Managing service inventory to improve performance', *MIT Sloan Management Review*, **47**(1), 56–63, 95.

Davenport, T.H. (1998). Putting the enterprise into the enterprise system. *Harvard Business Review*, **76**(4), 121–131.

Appendix

Mathematical Derivation of EOQ

There are several ways to find the EOQ. They are all based on the following argument.

$$\text{Total cost} = \text{Total holding cost} + \text{Total ordering (or set-up) cost}$$

$$\text{Total holding cost} = \text{Average number held} \times \text{Cost of holding one item per year}$$
$$= \text{Average inventory} \times C_h$$
$$= \frac{Q}{2} \times C_h$$

To see why the average inventory in the cyclical behaviour is $Q/2$, look at the sawtooth diagram in Figure 9.15. See how the top halves of the triangles fit in the gaps to give the same as a flat line at $Q/2$.

$$\text{Total ordering (or set-up) cost} = \text{How many times we need to order} \times \text{Cost per order}$$
$$= \text{Number of orders} \times C_s$$
$$= \frac{D}{Q} \times C_s$$

(If we need D per year, and order them in batches of Q, then we shall need D/Q orders in a year.)

The next step is based on looking back at Figure 9.2 and observing that the optimum order quantity occurs at the point where set-up costs and holding costs are equal. Mathematically, we can write this down using the formulae above:

$$C_s \frac{D}{Q} = C_h \frac{Q}{2}$$

Rearranging this formula:

$$2C_s D = Q^2 C_h$$

$$Q^2 = \frac{2DC_s}{C_h}$$

And therefore:

$$Q = \sqrt{\frac{2DC_s}{C_h}}$$

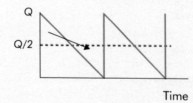

Figure 9.15

10 Lean Operations and Just in Time (JIT)

Learning Outcomes

After reading this chapter, you should be able to:

- Classify push or pull systems
- Explain how kanban works
- Describe the factors that are needed to support lean systems
- Identify the limits of lean management
- Employ the volume and variety model to identify which production control system is suitable for which operating conditions

Subway: Sandwiches Just in Time

We are all familiar with fast food, but perhaps we have never really looked at what is going on behind the counter. How can firms produce their products so cheaply and quickly, and yet still offer high quality and the choice from the menu we want every time? The answer lies in the fact that fast-food restaurants have whole-heartedly adopted the ideas of lean production and just in time.

The Subway sandwich chain is a good example of the application of lean production to service provision. In 2008 Subway operated more than 30,000 restaurants in 87 countries, and in North America and Australia they had more outlets than McDonald's. Part of this success comes from Subway's franchising approach, which means that local owners run the stores but use central advertising, design and logistics expertise. Subway plays on the current focus on health, quoting the healthy calorie and fat content of their food, and offering diet plans. Indeed the parent company is called Doctor's Associates, reflecting the founders who, in 1965, were a PhD and an aspiring medical student.

Source: © Stephan Zabel/iStock

The lean production of sandwiches at Subway is driven directly by the customer, who first chooses the bread, then chooses a filling and choice of cheese, and then selects the 'veggies' and sauces. The sandwich is assembled along a counter, and at busy times is passed from employee to employee (or 'sandwich artists' as Subway prefers to call them), who cut the bread, add one of the three elements, and wrap the finished sandwich. A sandwich is made in less than 60 seconds, and

Subway holds regular competitions where artists race one another; some artists can complete the process in less than 33 seconds.

The choice on the menu may seem complicated, but it is actually simple and well thought out. For example, the bread is one of just five options: Italian, nine-grain wheat, nine-grain honey oat, Italian herb and cheddar, and healthy Italian. These are made of two base doughs, but with different toppings added before baking.

So one key element of the lean system we can observe is late configuration of the product to **make to order (MTO)**.

Make to order (MTO): where planning, procurement and production wait until there is an order from a customer before starting.

The bread itself is delivered as frozen sticks, and prepared (proved and baked) on the premises in small batches using special machines that closely control the oven temperature and humidity. The proving machines automatically rotate the loaves to ensure a high consistency. The bread is always fresh, not just because it is baked locally, but also because it is allowed to stand for (at most) only three hours before being discarded.

The meat is also closely controlled, and comes pre-portioned in paper trays. This ensures the correct quantity, and also speeds up the preparation process as the employee does not need to count the slices. When stocks of meat run low, another container is fetched from the cold store to replenish the counter stocks. Again, freshness is ensured as the meat is only out of the cold store for a short time. The Subway approach is based on a set of core values and aims that permeate the operations of the franchises. The important elements of the Subway system are:

- *Simplicity*: the system is kept free of complexity by having tight control on the options available to customers.
- *Control*: the system has built-in controls, and material flow is fast, regular and very visible.
- *Made to order*: the customer is important not just as the source of cash, but also in defining the products to make.
- *Quality*: as the customer is impatiently waiting for lunch, there is no scope for Subway to make mistakes, run out of a filling, or provide substandard items.
- *Training*: the employees have clear instructions and direct training to ensure they operate the system exactly the way it was designed.

Sources: www.subway.com and www.ipcoop.com (Independent Purchasing Cooperative of Subway owners that runs the supply chain), accessed 6 April 2011; C. Munson, M. Rosenblatt and Z. Rosenblatt, 'The use and abuse of power in supply chains,' Business Horizons, 1999, **41**(1), 55–65.

Introduction

In Chapter 9 we examined inventory management, and saw how in most cases companies try to keep the levels of inventory as low as possible to reduce costs. One method of coordinating the supply of parts across the whole organization is to use dependent demand planning systems, such as MRP-based ERP (enterprise resource planning). These apply the EOQ (economic order quantity) to develop a realistic plan of material production and procurement to meet the master production schedule. However, as we can see at Subway, it is possible to ensure that exactly the right amounts are manufactured at exactly the right time, and these systems are often called **lean production**.

Lean system: a highly efficient process that produces products and services in the desired quantities, exactly when they are needed.

Just in time (JIT): the pull-based material control system used at Toyota, and the basis of developing the lean model.

In this chapter we shall look at implementing lean systems, and their approach to respond to variations in demand. So we can define a lean system as a highly efficient process that produces products and services in the desired quantities, exactly when they are needed. Lean systems are an extension of the **just in time (JIT)** approach, most clearly observed at Toyota, and so we start off by examining the Toyota Production System (TPS) before looking at the more widely applicable lean model, which is increasingly also being used in the service delivery practices of firms.

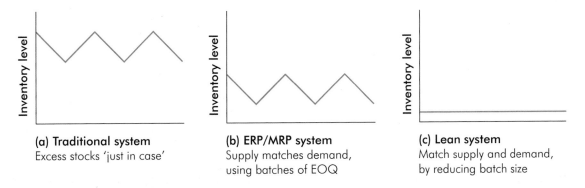

(a) Traditional system
Excess stocks 'just in case'

(b) ERP/MRP system
Supply matches demand,
using batches of EOQ

(c) Lean system
Match supply and demand,
by reducing batch size

Figure 10.1 Matching supply and demand: stock time charts for different systems

Inventory Control Classification

We have already seen the benefits of introducing control in the form of dependent demand systems such as ERP, but larger reductions in inventory can be obtained using lean systems.

Figure 10.1 shows the stock time charts for different systems. With traditional *independent demand* systems there is extra stock in the system to ensure there is always enough, and because managers may not accurately know the exact amount of material required (see Figure 10.1a).

With ERP systems, the MRP calculation sets production and delivery to match the demand, and so there is no excess stock left once the demand has been satisfied. However, as these systems normally utilize batching rules such as EOQ, parts are ordered as fixed quantities, and so we get the common sawtoothed pattern. The ERP approach helps to eliminate the problem of ordering excessive stock, and so it can be beneficial to organizations, but it can still result in stockholdings while parts wait to be used on the production line (see Figure 10.1b).

With lean systems, the EOQ rules are challenged to try and make parts in a *batch size of one* to further reduce the stockholding level. Reducing the batch size as far as possible gives a stock time chart showing a very low and constant inventory level. The inventory in a lean system is fixed, and is made up of in-process material directly driven by demand from the customer. This is a very efficient system, with very low or near-zero inventories being held (see Figure 10.1c).

Push and Pull Systems

In classifying the differences between inventory control systems in a more general manner, we can identify two different approaches: these are known as *push* and *pull*.

Figure 10.2 shows how systems such as ERP and MRP are often 'push' in their approach, as the activities in the firm are planned centrally, and instructions and materials are sent to individual workstations to push the product through production.

The lean approach operates in a different way, with customer orders starting activities in the factory. Thus this approach is called a 'pull' approach, as an operation responds to demand by pulling material (or people) through the operation from the customer end of the supply chain, see bottom of Figure 10.2.

The **push–pull inventory control** contrast in planning approaches is useful in helping us appreciate the basic nature of lean systems. In essence, the push system makes a plan, and then tries to coordinate the production of all the subassemblies and parts to achieve the plan. We saw this clearly in the MRP system in Chapter 9, where the task is one of coordination of quantities and timings to deliver the MPS. Pull systems normally develop similar plans, but they are carried out when an order for a product arrives from a customer, or is generated by the manager of the system. This means that the last production station is first to respond by making the finished product, and this prompts further workstations back up the chain to produce the parts that have been consumed.

Push–pull inventory control: in push systems there is a central planning system that generates and programmes orders for the production line. With pull, orders come from customers, and the line reacts to the demand.

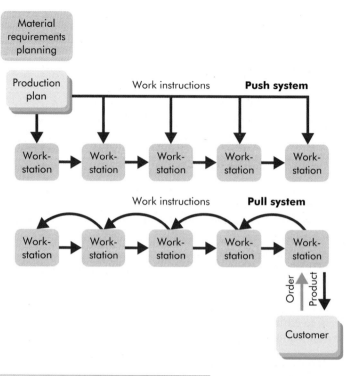

Figure 10.2 Differences between push–pull inventory control system

We can also see this in a service environment. For example, when a new bank account is opened, the customer-servicing department requests a credit check from the credit control department, and the issuing of ATM cards from elsewhere.

In summary, with pull the order initiates the flow of materials. However, there are many parts to a lean implementation, and we need to explore these in some detail to fully appreciate the way they operate, and exactly when each approach is suitable.

It is worth noting that the process of producing the product is the same whether a push or pull system is used. Push or pull refers purely to how production is initiated.

> **❗ Stop and Think**
>
> 1   Think of the different types of food outlet you use: fast food, help-yourself buffet restaurant, supermarket, college shop. Which approach – push or pull – do they use?

Lean Production

Lean production is based on a series of practices which are most popularly seen at Toyota as a management approach called *just in time* (JIT) which is part of a wider system called the *Toyota Production System* (TPS). Toyota developed TPS after studying Ford in the 1940s, and it has been generalized and extended to other industries to become known as *lean production*. At the heart of the approach is a focus on eliminating waste, the most evident of which is inventory, but it can also be seen as a general focus on continuous operational improvement. Waste in this context does not just mean that the parts that constitute the inventory will be wasted or thrown away, but that the time these parts spend in storage (i.e. not being worked on) is wasted lead time, and the storage space they occupy is wasted space.

History of Lean Systems

Lean systems are based on JIT, and most often cite the TPS work of Taiichi Ohno at Toyota. Ohno faced difficulties because of poor supply conditions. He could not plan ahead as he was not sure which parts would be delivered by the suppliers. This caused cash flow problems because the plant was forced to store more and more unfinished vehicles as they waited for late parts to come in to finish the vehicles, and of course the vehicles could not be sold until they were complete.

Holding excess inventory hides fluctuations in supply, and so, in order to identify which parts were missing, Ohno developed a system linking production stages closely together, which became just in time, using a technique called **kanban**. Toyota's solution was not developed as a super-efficient revolutionary production system, but to highlight material shortages quickly. From this base, the whole TPS system evolved. Even today, Toyota still claims it is developing and learning about the system. By his own account, Ohno (1988) thinks it took 35 years to realize the potential of the approach.

> **Kanban:** Japanese word for the card that is the essential vehicle for operation of the JIT system of production control.

The transfer of ideas about JIT, TPS and lean production gained popularity through a book by Womack *et al.* in 1990, called *The Machine that Changed the World*. Much of the TPS and the JIT approach had already been described in books by Monden (1983), Cusumano (1985), Shingo (1985) and Ohno (1988), but *The Machine . . .* spread the ideas to a wider audience.

It is best to think of the TPS, lean systems and just in time as parts of the same approach, implemented as production systems, business improvement philosophy or material control systems; this is the customer-driven, pull approach.

Confusingly, lean ideas are often given other names, including:
- Zero inventory
- Batch of one
- Continuous flow manufacturing
- Increased value manufacturing

Some of these titles are slightly misleading, as will become clear as we go into more depth in this chapter.

Just in Time

The TPS is concerned with making items only as and when they are required, and in the quantities that are needed to satisfy immediate requirements – or, in other words 'just in time' (JIT). The principle must be applied at every stage in the production chain, from raw material delivery through to the finished product. There are many techniques used in the JIT system, but at the heart of it is the kanban system.

The Kanban System

Kanban is a technique developed by Toyota to help implement JIT. Kanban is a Japanese word meaning 'card' or 'signal'. These 'kanbans' are the key element in a JIT operation. They are used widely throughout production and service delivery systems around the world today.

In its simplest form, a kanban is a way of indicating to a workstation whether it is required to produce something. If there is no signal, then there is enough stock in the system, and no more is needed. The signal can be an empty box (showing that the previous delivery of parts has been used), or a marked space on the floor where parts should be (showing that more can be delivered). If the box or space is empty, then more parts are needed; if it is full, then there is no need for more parts.

Therefore, if an operator sees an empty box or space, they should make some more parts. When the box is full or the outlined space is occupied, they stop. As the box empties, this indicates it is time to make some more parts or deliver more service. At McDonald's, a service process, you can see the kanban instruction as it is a metal tag in the row of burgers waiting to be served. The kanban process is represented in Figure 10.3.

A service example of kanban use, which is used to process people, is the line or marked space that travellers stand in at airports; when it is empty, this signifies that the security or immigration officer is ready to receive more people and deliver more service.

Figure 10.3 shows kanban operating. When parts are used by operation A, it pulls more from operation B. If operation B has a box to put the parts in, then it can produce. No box means that operation B has no instruction, and so makes nothing. When B uses parts, this generates an empty box and so an instruction for C to produce. Designing

1 Starting position

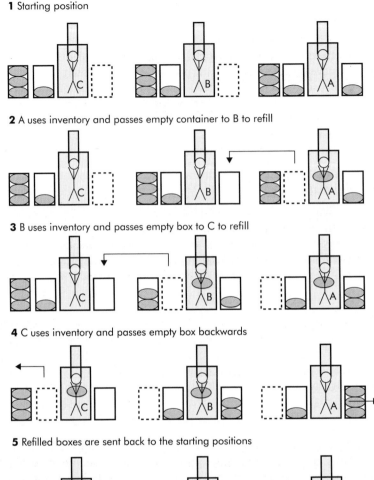

2 A uses inventory and passes empty container to B to refill

3 B uses inventory and passes empty box to C to refill

4 C uses inventory and passes empty box backwards

5 Refilled boxes are sent back to the starting positions

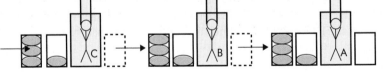

Figure 10.3 The kanban system

the system involves making sure that there is enough inventory in the system to keep working at the cell until the previous cell has replaced the box with a full one. Limiting the kanban stock is how the system limits inventory.

The original kanban system at Toyota employs two kanban cards: the *production kanban* (or *P kanban*) and the *conveyance kanban* (or *C kanban*). Parts are kept in standard containers, to which one of the two types of kanban are attached. The production kanban specifies the part number of the item, the quantity to be made and the tools required, and the conveyance kanban states the source of parts, and the work centre to which they should be conveyed. The use of two cards means that the different jobs can be divided between workers: production staff and material handlers.

Every workstation needs to have a kanban link with its neighbours. The final assembly line, because it is the ultimate downstream activity, initiates and effectively controls all upstream activities right back to the suppliers and subcontractors in a chain reaction. You can see the reasons why this type of system is referred to as a 'pull' approach.

With kanban, there will always be a set amount of inventory in the system that cannot be exceeded, and the system will only produce items used to make the customer's final product. In Subway they only pull the sandwich fillings from the cold store as and when they are required.

Kanban is more than just an inventory control system; it is a means by which continual pressure is exerted over the whole of the production system to achieve improved productivity.

Calculation of Kanban Quantity

The amount of stock held in the kanban loop between workstations needs to be sufficient to cover the time taken for the replacement parts to be both manufactured and then delivered to the workstation. This needs to be worked out for all the production workstations, and for each part.

The number of kanban containers placed between the workstations is given by the formula

$$N = \frac{D(T_w + T_p)(1 + c)}{a}$$

where:

$N =$ the number of containers for the part

$D =$ the planned usage rate for the part (parts per day).

$T_w =$ the average waiting time for replenishment of parts. This is the time that the conveyance part of the kanban takes – moving the empty container to the supplying workstation, and also moving the full container back to the demanding workstation (use a fraction of a day).

$T_p =$ the average time to produce a container of parts. This is the production kanban time needed to make a container's worth of parts (use a fraction of a day).

$a =$ the capacity of the container (number of parts). This should not be more than 10% of daily demand for the part; more than this, and the kanban can start to operate as a buffer between the workstations rather than signalling demand.

$c =$ a safety stock variable (expressed in the formula as a decimal fraction). Note how this value adds a safety margin to the calculation. It is set by the management and determined by company policy. It should not be set at more than 0.10, i.e. a 10% margin; more than this, and the kanban can start to operate as a buffer between the workstations rather than signalling demand.

WORKED EXAMPLE 10.1

Putting Kanban into Practice

A workstation undertaking the final assembly of a component has a planned daily usage rate of 240 parts per day, and receives unfinished parts from the preceding station in containers that hold 5% of the day's demand. It takes 1 hour for the preceding station to fill a bin, and 20 minutes for the filled bin to be delivered to the covering station.

Problem: *How many such bins are needed for the kanban loop to work efficiently in this production cell, given a single 8-hour shift per day and a risk factor of 8%?*

Approach: Kanban works by ensuring there is just sufficient stock between two stages in the production line so that, when the kanban request is issued, the replacement parts are delivered before the workstation runs out. It uses the formula

$$N = \frac{D(T_w + T_p)(1 + c)}{a}$$

Solution: In this example, the values to be used are:

$$D = 240 \text{ parts per day}$$
$$T_w = 20/(60 \times 8) = 0.04167$$
$$T_p = 1/8 = 0.125$$
$$c = 0.08$$
$$a = 5\% \text{ of } 240 = 12$$

And the calculation is therefore:

$$N = \frac{240 \times (0.04167 + 0.125) \times (1 + 0.08)}{12}$$
$$= \frac{240 \times 0.1667 \times 1.08}{12}$$
$$= 3.6$$

This means that the firm needs to have four containers of parts to make up the kanban stock. Having three containers would mean that there could be a delay, as parts might still be on the way when they were needed. This might not be a bad thing, as it would force the firm to look at the time taken to produce and deliver the parts, and so force them to improve the process.

> **The key point is** that having more kanban stock than needed is a waste, but less may result in parts being short, and so delay production.

Stop and Think

2   Think of three possible problems that adopting the JIT system might generate.

SHORT CASE 10.1

Primark uses JIT

In retail clothing operations there is a high risk that changing fashions can leave stores with high inventories of merchandise that is difficult to move. Traditionally, the problem has been dealt with by markdowns and clearance sales. In an effort to improve operating efficiency, companies such as the UK's Primark adopt a more flexible 'quick response' (QR) approach.

The basic concept of QR in retailing is similar to that of JIT in manufacturing: to provide the right products, in the right quantities, in the quickest

Source: © Christian Lazzari/iStock

time, with minimum holding of inventory, at the lowest cost. Primark delays purchasing decisions until the season's fashions become clear. This requires suppliers to employ QR manufacturing, and Primark employs combined weekly deliveries in order to compress lead times and provide maximum flexibility in adjusting the product mix. Sales information is shared across the suppliers and retailer, and so Primark uses electronic data transfer with suppliers. In this way it can respond quickly to what is happening in its stores by changing schedules to make larger or smaller numbers of particular products, styles, colours and sizes as current demand requirements dictate.

Operating a QR system imposes pressure on the manufacturers supplying Primark as it means they have to accommodate highly volatile production schedules, much smaller production quantities, and more frequent deliveries. Not surprisingly, not all manufacturers are up to the task, but those who have made the adjustment find that retailers such as Primark are prepared to pay premium prices for the QR service. This has given Primark a competitive edge over other cut-price suppliers who cannot match the QR requirement or get the latest fashions into the shops quickly enough.

Questions

1   How does QR help Primark achieve its corporate aims?
2   What problems will Primark face in trying to use QR as it expands its operations into Europe?

Sources: A. Jones, 'Primark seeks to replicate success with expansion in Belgium', *Financial Times*, 10 July 2009, 17; Z. Wood, 'Primark makes great strides with peg-leg trousers', *The Guardian*, 5 November 2008, 31; www.primark.co.uk/aboutus/FAQ, accessed 4 April 2011.

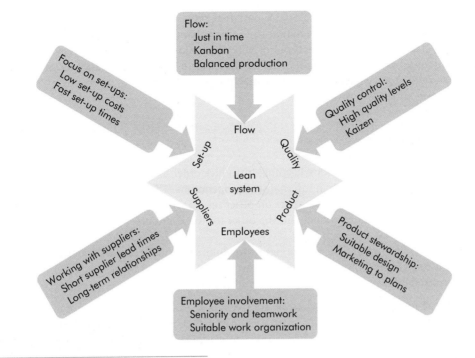

Figure 10.4 Elements of the lean production system

Characteristics of Lean Systems

There are several elements to lean systems, and all are necessary for the system to work. We can see evidence for this in the work of Ferdows and De Meyer (1990), who developed their *sand cone* principle. The sand cone idea states that some practices will work only if they are based on sound foundations laid by other practices that are already proven. The analogy is that a sand cone (or sand castle) will only stand up if it is standing on a solid foundation. In this context, Ferdows and De Meyer specifically argue that quality gives dependability, which allows speed, and these two together can enable flexibility – and only then can firms achieve efficient operations. Lean production follows the sand cone principle closely, as many elements are needed before a lean JIT system will work properly. If any one element is missing, then the system may not function to the best of its ability.

The elements of a lean system are summarized in Figure 10.4. Note how there are many elements needed to ensure the whole system works together, including not only production practices within the company, but also quality and supplier issues.

Focus on Set-Ups

As mentioned previously, lean systems are different from other forms of inventory control in that they do not assume that there are optimum economic order or economic batch quantities. Lean systems aim to produce all items in a batch size of one. This means that, in designing lean systems, managers need to examine the set-up activity for each operation in order to reduce the time associated with it. Remember: it is the cost of the set-up that makes it economical to produce in larger batches. There are several tools available to help with set-up reduction, but the most famous is **single minute exchange of dies (SMED)**. (Note: A 'die' is the part of a machine tool that is used to cut metal that will be part of the end product.) SMED follows Shingo's work at Toyota, where pressing machines were adapted to reduce changeover time from hours to seconds (Shingo, 1985).

> **SMED (single minute change of dies):** how to get a batch of one.

The concept has wide implications for both production and service delivery. Where firms have introduced these techniques effectively, batch sizes can be reduced towards a size of one: that is, the operator can press a button and the machine changes automatically to produce another type of part. We saw this in Chapter 7, where we talked about the difference between takt time and cycle time. The SMED approach seeks to make these the same, so reducing waste.

In a car factory, for example, expensive, specially designed press machines can make any type of car body demanded by a kanban within a short production run, quick changeover and short cycle time. An alternative approach also seen at Toyota is to use several old or very simple machines instead. It may be cheaper to have three simple machines set up for the three different parts, and switch from one to another as demanded by the kanban instruction rather than an expensive flexible machine. But whatever the approach, fast set-up is essential for the JIT system, and for smooth production.

The SMED Approach

Shingo presents a routine to implement SMED:

- Maintenance organization and housekeeping: introduce order to the existing system.
- Try to develop external rather than internal set-up operations. These can be performed offline, outside the production cycle, and have less impact on other set-up activities – for example, having two machines, one set up for one product and the other for the alternative. This removes the set-up activity from the production cycle.
- Examine every changeover element in an effort to eliminate, simplify, or reduce the time required.
- Examine the need for machine adjustment; it can normally be eliminated.
- Introduce automation to improve consistency and quality.

This is a specific list of things to do, and a scientific approach to re-examining the set-up of machines. The results of a SMED programme can be quite dramatic, with machine changeovers reduced from hours to seconds. These can be applied to services as well, such as when single venues are transformed to accommodate concerts, or ice hockey matches, or exhibitions.

Working with Suppliers

Much time is also lost in the delivery of items from suppliers, and so lean systems demand that the suppliers work closely, in terms both of cooperation and of physical location, with the manufacturer. The inability to reorganize suppliers to deliver smaller batches more rapidly is one of the main reasons for the poor success rate of JIT implementation in US and European companies. More specifically, lean supply requires focusing on reducing lead times by introducing frequent deliveries driven by kanban signals. The suppliers thus become an extension of the production line, delivering exactly what is required at very short notice, and with perfect quality. If you were to stand outside a factory with a well-designed lean system, you would see many small vans making frequent deliveries, instead of infrequent deliveries being made by just a few large trucks.

Flow and Synchronization

In addition to the delivery of parts using kanban outlined above, a JIT system demands specific operating practices for the production line. One key focus of the system is smooth flow, in terms both of volume (a constant flow) and of product mix (an even and predictable plan). In order for the line to operate consistently, managers often intervene and smooth out variations in the product mix that may arise from unpredictable, batch-of-one demand. For example, a large order of high work content cars, such as those with air conditioning, is split up and interspaced with normal vehicles to spread the workload on the production line more evenly. Manufacturing could not complete all the extra work of producing a long run of high work content products and keep to the average time taken per vehicle. In practice the work demanded by customers on the production line is manipulated to give a fixed repeating schedule: this is called *heijunka* in Japan.

Heijunka: a method for developing a repeating schedule that produces the correct mix of products. It is important to spread the launch of products into the production line evenly to smooth the amount of work required.

Other tools developed by Toyota to help ensure manufacturing flow and smoothness include *jidoka* or *autonomation*. This is the in-process application of technology to identify and correct mistakes. The production line self-corrects, and poor-quality parts are eliminated. With lean systems, poor quality quickly impacts on the next workstation, and jidoka is one tool for ensuring the constant flow of good parts.

Heijunka

Heijunka is a technique used to generate smooth, mixed production schedules. Using the heijunka technique, an assembly line or service can deliver output in a predetermined

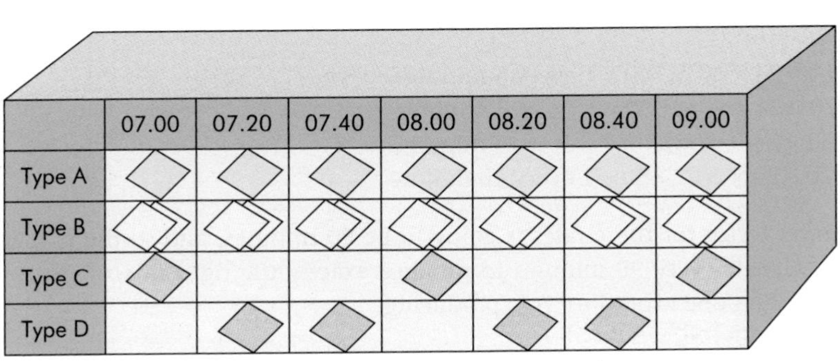

	07.00	07.20	07.40	08.00	08.20	08.40	09.00
Type A	◇	◇	◇	◇	◇	◇	◇
Type B	◇	◇	◇	◇	◇	◇	◇
Type C	◇		◇				◇
Type D		◇	◇		◇	◇	

Figure 10.5 A heijunka box to help sequence product mix in a lean JIT system

order volume and variety for many hours (e.g. a whole shift, or a working week), and then repeat this schedule over and over again. This gives the benefits of batch manufacture with economies of repetition and the predictability helps coordination of supply. However, designing a schedule that is able to produce customer orders in a repeating pattern is complicated. This process is simplified if the number of products and combinations of options offered are limited.

Despite the complexities in establishing the schedule, its implementation can be simplified by using a *heijunka box* (as shown in Figure 10.5). A heijunka box is effectively a box full of different slots. Each slot represents a different product or service variant (e.g. the 'types' at the side of the box), and the sequence (or time) at which they will need to be produced (shown across the top of the box). It provides a quick and easy visual signal. Sometimes, if the finished product is small, it is actually placed in the box to show that it has been completed (e.g. a hamburger in the heated metal racks of a fast-food restaurant, or some printing work rolled up in racks at a copy shop).

WORKED EXAMPLE 10.2

Heijunka: Smoothing Production Orders for Improved Flow

A production line runs a double 12-hour shift, which means it is working for 24 hours per day, 5 days a week, and has a 4-week month.

The orders come at irregular intervals, but on average arrive in a month as shown:

Product A = 5,760
Product B = 4,800
Product C = 3,200
Product D = 2,880

Problem: *(a) What is the total monthly production volume and respective production mix?*
(b) What is the production sequence schedule for products A, B, C and D?

Approach: Developing a production schedule from a list of known constraints is similar to working out the cycle time in line balancing. Managers work out how often to make a unit of each product, so that at the end of the schedule time they have made the right total number. With heijunka, the aim is to develop a repeating sequence that is able to produce the right quantities of products, but which mixes the orders up to smooth the demand on production, and limit work in progress.

Solution: From above, the total production for the month will be 16,640: this can be met by levelling the production volume to 4,160 per week (832 per day or 416 per shift). This smooths the factory volume and sets a constant speed for the assembly line, the cycle time for line balancing.

The next step considers the mix of production for each model. In order to make that number of each over the month, they will need to make them at the following rates (20 days × 24 hours × 60 minutes divided by the demand for each product):

Product A = 20 × 24 × 60/5,760 = 1 every 5 minutes
Product B = 20 × 24 × 60/4,800 = 1 every 6 minutes
Product C = 20 × 24 × 60/3,200 = 1 every 9 minutes
Product D = 20 × 24 × 60/2,880 = 1 every 10 minutes

The lowest common factor for these rates is going to be 90 minutes, and so the manager can develop a schedule which repeats every 90 minutes to produce exactly the right mix of parts. This list can be re-written (90/how often one is produced) as producing:

Product A = 18 every 90 minutes (90/5 = 18)
Product B = 15 every 90 minutes
Product C = 10 every 90 minutes
Product D = 9 every 90 minutes

The final schedule can be set by looking at the ratios between the products, and remembering that it will produce 416 per shift or 52 per 90 minutes. The sequence is developed by starting with an approximate sequence and then adjusting it to get the final proportions. In this case the start is 3A, 2B, 1C and 1D spread out as ABACABD and then repeated it 7 times to give 49 production slots. So a close approximation is going to be:

ABACABD ABACABD ABACABD ABACABD ABACABD ABACABD ABACABD

The full list of 52 needed above can be obtained by adding another 3 slots with the exact proportions achieved by adding 3Cs, 1B and 2Ds and removing 3As from the 49 slots above. This can be done by hand-picking equally spaced places through the sequence for the removals and additions. One result of the finished sequence might be:

ABACABDACBACBDABDACABCDABACBDABDACABDABCBABDCABACABD

However, the exact result depends on how the close approximation was generated, and where in the sequence products were added and removed. This sequence will be the basis for the positioning of holes in the heijunka box, and is repeated every 90 minutes.

Note: The above example shows the levelling of the variations in work and the generation of quite a complex sequence. Over the month the sequence will satisfy the volume and mix of orders, but at the same time it has generated an even and repeating production schedule. This is clearly more desirable than building a single large batch of A, followed by a single large batches of B, C and D, and changing the numbers of batches in each day.

Quality Control for Lean Systems

Within lean systems there is an emphasis on doing things quickly, with very limited stocks of materials. As a result there is no slack in the system, and the impact of poor-quality components or poor work is quickly felt further down the production line. Lean production therefore needs to have a clear focus on doing things right first time, and so needs a very effective quality system. This system is often called **total quality management (TQM)**; it is so important that some people often refer to lean production as *JIT/TQM* to stress the importance.

TQM is covered in more detail in Chapter 13, however, to understand lean production, some of the basic ideas are outlined here. The most important consideration is that production processes are made as robust as possible to ensure smooth flow. One approach to this is called **kaizen**, which can be translated as 'continuous improvement'. In practice, when quality problems occur, a new routine is developed to ensure that the problem cannot reoccur. Kaizen has already been mentioned in Chapter 6 in the context of value stream mapping.

Total quality management (TQM): quality system that is needed for effective lean production, and based on kaizen (continuous improvement)

Kaizen: continuous improvement approach to quality control.

Lean Quality Tools

Hansei, or 'reflection', is one key approach to quality which tries to ensure that managers and employees identify the root causes of any quality problem. This includes detailed forensic-style investigation, called *gemba*, to gather data from all sources, and not just opt for the first solution. Another quality term is *genchi genbutsu*, which means 'go and see for yourself', and stresses how employees must not rely on reports from others to identify solutions, but should go and look themselves. It is not uncommon in other organizations for oversimplified reports and conference calls to be used to try to solve problems, but these often miss something important as the manager making the decision hasn't been to see the machine in operation. Genchi genbutsu makes the investigation more robust and an incomplete solution less likely, thus promoting kaizen.

Another tool is the *5 Whys*. Instead of just identifying the first cause of a problem, employees ask the question 'Why?' as many times as is needed to get to the root cause. For example, if we find that the wheels fall off the vehicles, asking five whys might generate the following:

1 why – because of loose nuts

2 why – because of a badly calibrated torque wrench, which caused the nuts to be insufficiently tightened

3 why – because the tool for calibrating the torque wrench was worn

4 why – because it hadn't been maintained properly

5 why – because there was no procedure for carrying out maintenance on the calibration machines.

The real cause of the problem is established (i.e. maintenance procedures), and instead of just re-tightening the nuts at the end of the line, a new calibration procedure would ensure that this type of error could not happen again.

When a solution is implemented, lean organizations follow the principles of *poka yoke*, which is 'fail-safeing' or 'mistake-proofing'. Here the emphasis is on designing a process that can only happen in one way – the correct way – and so mistakes cannot be made. A good example of this is fitting steering wheels on the production line. Toyota includes a keyed slot as well as a hexagonal nut and bolt. The keyed slot will only fit in one position, and so it is impossible for the operator to fit the steering wheel in any other position than straight. Without the keyed slot, the wheel could be aligned with any of the six sides of the hexagonal nut. The same approach can be employed in services, when online forms automatically check to see whether data we have entered is correct. For example, if the form requires a telephone number to be entered in a particular box, it will check to see whether a valid set of characters has been entered.

Lean organizations take great care in looking after machines on the production line, and often employ **total productive maintenance (TPM)**. TPM ensures that the important measure of overall equipment effectiveness (the time spent producing) is maximized by making employees responsible for maintenance, and developing kaizen approaches to improving the reliability of machines. This is much more than preventive maintenance, and is another indispensible part of getting the lean system working.

> **Total productive maintenance (TPM):** the application of TQM ideas to ensuring that machines operate effectively, and are always available.

Another lean quality element worth noting is *andon*. So that workers know what is happening in the production area, a series of andon lights are used that warn of quality issues elsewhere on the line, and draw the attention of the nearby employees to help sort out the problem quickly. Some people criticize the use of andon, as one problem on a production line can cause the whole line to stop. However, the purpose of this is that all attention is given to this, so that it is solved quickly and permanently.

❗ Stop and Think

3 JIT converts say that 'a defect is a treasure'. What do they mean by this, and how does it relate to JIT?

Employee Involvement

Lean production and TQM demand the support and dedication of workers in quality activities, and place high emphasis on training. As the system is so precisely designed, and has no excess capacity, there is no place for people to learn on the job – such a notion is contrary to the ideas behind leanness. In the same way as we saw SMED externalizing set-up, so training takes place *off* the production line. Using someone in production who has not mastered their tasks is too big a risk. In addition, employees working within a lean system undergo far more training than those in companies that do not operate this way. This training enables employees to make their own decisions in developing kaizen and implementing quality solutions. The training includes many advanced quality tools to allow the reasons for quality problems and variation to be analysed. Working in a JIT lean system can be a high-pressure and stressful environment, that requires a high level of physical fitness and mental alertness. Workers on production lines in lean plants are relatively young, and are required to physically warm up before starting work.

Senpai–Kohai Authority System

The way lean firms manage the relationships between employees and their superiors, the mentoring process, is another important factor. The mentoring system at Toyota is called *senpai–kohai*. Senpai are the mentors and kohai the trainees. These relationships last beyond direct training, and continue when people have moved on to other roles in the organization. As a result, Toyota has a well-developed system of learning, as senior people remain connected to the organization and the kohai actively seek out their advice. It is common for organizations to keep trying the same things again and again, without learning from their mistakes: the senpai–kohai approach reduces this wasteful repetition. The same respect for seniority features in the gemba and genchi genbutsu approaches to investigating quality problems. Evidence of these practices can be seen in the way lean firms rely on teams and teamwork, where each member is valued for his or her contribution.

Product Stewardship

Lean firms employ *value stream mapping* (see Chapter 6) as a key planning tool to analyse the value-added network required in bringing a product to the consumer. In addition, when developing new products, lean organizations make use of *simultaneous engineering*, in which the people involved in producing the parts – even the suppliers – have a combined role. This means not only that a wider range of skills and resources can be employed in designing the product, but also that design decisions reflect future choices for production and service delivery processes. This is a closed-loop approach, and removes the need to redesign parts later when problems trying to manufacture emerge.

Also, at the design stage there should be a focus on product standardization and modularity (see Chapter 5). These not only make the product simpler by reducing the parts, but also ease the adoption of JIT and SMED. *The Machine that Changed the World* showed this by stating that Japanese firms could design a new car in half the time of their US competitors and using only half the resources.

 SHORT CASE 10.2

Apple's iPod

Apple's iPod has been a remarkable success since its introduction in 2001, reaching 200 million sales by October 2008. In 2005 Apple introduced the option for customers to order a customized iPod with an engraved cover design. The product is produced by one of its subcontractor factories in China (run by Foxconn) and shipped to the USA in 90 hours.

Achieving this employs many of the steps from the TPS – in particular the focus on looking at value-adding steps and set-up reduction/SMED. Apple uses SCM practices such as long-term sole supply contracts with component makers in China, and employs a specialist logistics operator (FedEx).

The iPod is particularly suitable for lean production, as it is high value, produced from standardized parts, and the customization can be carefully controlled. Given the fast-changing nature of

Source: © David Pearson/Alamy

the MP3 market, running with little or no stocks also makes sense to Apple, as it reduces the risk of having outdated stocks, and smooths out the introduction of new models.

This example illustrates that lean production is not just the application of one approach, but rather the adoption of an entire integrated toolbox of many techniques.

Questions
1 What advantages does Apple gain by operating its lean system?
2 How critical is the relationship with FedEx for the success of the customized iPod process?

Sources: A. Chakraborty, *Just-in-time Global Economy: A case of Apple*, ICFAI Case Study # 608-029-1, 2008; 'An iPod's quick journey from China marks arrival of just-in-time global economy', *Pittsburgh Post-Gazette*, 14 August 2005; www.redorbit.com/news/technology/207325/, accessed 11 April 2011; Apple website, www.appple.com

Contemporary Thinking: Extending Lean to Other Industries

Above we have concentrated on lean production. However, the original book by Womack *et al.* generated interest far beyond the car industry, and lean ideas have been applied to many other industries. An updated book, *Lean Thinking* (Womack and Jones, 1996), repackages and extends the ideas originally documented by Ohno and Shingo. This section examines some of the broader ideas or philosophies that have become known as the lean system. A more recent analysis is in Liker and Hoseus (2008).

The Five Principles of Lean Thinking

**BUSINESS
INTEGRATION**

Lean thinking focuses on improvement through five principles:
- *Concentrate on value for customers*: lean systems focus on reducing waste and satisfying the needs of customers
- *Appreciate the value stream*: a lean organization should understand which activities add value for the customer, and which are wastes to be eliminated
- *Concentrate on improved flow*; flow should be smooth and constant to ensure efficient operations
- *Adopt pull*: meet customer demand by reacting to them; pull systems do not produce unnecessary outputs
- *Perfect quality*: lean systems target right first time and use kaizen.

By implementing the five principles, managers gain a greater understanding of how to run the system more efficiently.

The Lean Focus on Reducing Waste

Along with a focus on value adding, the lean movement focuses on reducing waste at all levels. Ohno (1988) described three types of waste: *muda* ('non-value-adding work'), *muri* ('overburden') and *mura* ('unevenness'). This framework is central to many lean implementations:
- *Muri*: planning waste due to the poor design or implementation of the system. It represents things such as having to move heavy weights, or having to work harder than usual. The highly stressed lean system becomes more prone to variation, which generates waste.
- *Mura*: imbalance as a result of poor implementation of the design. Toyota tries to smooth production activities and eliminate fluctuation at the scheduling or operations level, such as quality and volume, and also imbalance within work tasks.
- *Muda*: non-value adding tasks. This has been the focus of attention for most lean advocates, who state that the role of management is to examine and reduce muda. This is where the practice of removing waste is most evident.

Ohno added more detail by identifying 7 muda wastes:

- *Transportation*: waste moving products in the manufacturing process. This does not add value to the product and, apart from final delivery, is unimportant to the customer.
- *Inventory*: any type of inventory (components, work-in-progress or finished goods) represents products not being processed, and leads to other problems, such as obsolescence and the hiding of quality issues.
- *Motion*: waste generated when people or equipment move or walk. This does not add value to the product.
- *Waiting*: such as inventory. Holding inventory does not add value.
- *Overproduction*: producing an item before it is needed is a waste, which generates waiting and inventory.
- *Overprocessing*: waste is generated if the equipment used is too complex or expensive for the task performed. Toyota uses the simplest machine for the job, which often means older but well-maintained equipment.
- *Defects*: inspecting and fixing defects does not add value.

Recently there have been attempts to extend Ohno's list to include other wastes. Womack added the underutilization or misdeployment of employees – in particular, the waste that results when employees are asked to carry out manual tasks, but their employers do not make use of the their ability to think about the task, and how to improve the job itself. Conversely, using expensive highly trained staff to do menial tasks is a waste: for instance, it would be wasteful to use a highly trained lawyer to work on a simple car insurance claim.

It was once thought that effective muda reduction led to improvements in muri and mura, and therefore many managers concentrated purely on the seven wastes. However, managers are now realizing that better planning and implementation can be more effective steps to take than just concentrating on eliminating waste.

❗ Stop and Think

4 It is important to stress that the lean system focuses the firm on thinking about the demands of the customer. Do you think that customers will define waste in the same way as the company? Think of a firm you use regularly. To you as a customer, what constitutes waste? Now put yourself in the position of the manager, and think about what constitutes waste for the manager, and for the firm. Are these the same? If not, why aren't they?

The 5S Lean Implementation Framework

Another framework which is used within lean management is 5S. This is a programme for reorganizing the workspace and workflow to improve efficiency by eliminating waste. 5S is an effective way to apply lean ideas to both production and service activities. They are Japanese terms that can also be translated into English words starting with S:

1 *Sort* (*seiri*): remove unnecessary items from the workplace.

2 *Set* in order (*seiton*): efficient and effective storage methods, including painted floors, and marked-off work areas, so that workers do not waste time looking for things.

3 *Shine* (*seiso*): make the workplace clean, so that things remain in place, and employees take pride in the area and in their work.

4 *Standardize* (*seiketsu*): encourage all employees in sharing and developing standardized best practices.

5 *Sustain* (*shitsuke*): the last step – continue to follow the other Ss.

Other Thinkers' Lean Ideas

CRITICAL PERSPECTIVE

The extension of lean production to a wider lean system is heavily dependent on Japanese ideas based on the Toyota-focused writings of Ohno (1988) and Shingo (1985), and has much in common with the quality gurus such as Deming, covered in Chapter 13.

Lean production ideas also came from Schonberger (1986), who studied and reported the sources of Japanese industrial power in the 1980s. At the University of Nebraska he based his ideas on observation of the Kawasaki motorcycle plant nearby. Schonberger's main thesis involved identifying nine lessons or practices that lay at the heart of the lean system. He described not only the operation of JIT, but also the rest of the system, along with TQM, the supply relationships and the role of employees. Shonberger showed the highly integrated nature of lean production, a message that was not appreciated at first, as many firms focused purely on kanban, and found the results of their efforts disappointing (Pilkington, 1998).

The key point is that some people claim that the lean approach is applicable to all firms, and focus purely on its its improvement and waste reduction approaches. But there are many additional elements that are necessary for it to work effectively as a production system, and these are often overlooked by some firms seeking a fast transformation. As a result, their new systems do not deliver everything as expected. Look again at Figure 10.4 and the elements of the lean production system.

! Stop and Think

5 How might JIT apply to a service like a hospital or department store?

Lean Services

Lean systems, and their presentation in terms of waste reduction strategies, make the approach appealing to non-manufacturing firms, and there has been a rise in service firms and not-for-profit organizations implementing lean projects. Good examples of firms adopting lean approaches in services include fast-food outlets such as Pizza Hut and McDonald's, logistics firms such as FedEx and DHL, e-businesses such as Amazon and Yahoo Shopping, the emergency services, and telecom firms for their repair activities. For these firms speed is an order winner, and so generates an advantage over competitors who do not follow.

When discussing the differences between manufacturing and service operations, we described the intangible nature of services and the way that services do not exist before consumption by the consumer, require the consumer to be present and cannot be made in advance. All these features show that services are ideal for making use of lean systems, which demand attention paid to the customer, and do not produce something until it is needed.

The main elements of lean systems can be applied to service environments with the lean thinking framework we saw earlier: customer value, the value stream, improve flow, use pull and perfect quality. Many firms choose the 5S framework, with its focus on basic housekeeping, as it is immediately applicable by managers, and offers a clear set of steps. Getting things tidied and set out in the 5S framework are valuable to service processes, which traditionally have not focused on designing efficient processes.

Following the lean method, and 5S in particular, generates sizeable improvements with little effort, and the spread of the resulting success stories has added more impetus to the lean movement. According to Spear and Bowen (1999), the four rules of lean thinking can be equally applicable to services as to production. They are:

1 All work shall be highly specified as to content, sequence, timing and outcome. This eliminates any ambiguities in a process

2 Every customer–supplier connection must be direct, and there must be an unambiguous yes-or-no way to send requests and receive responses. This eliminates poor hand-offs between people and departments

3   The pathway for every product and service must be simple and direct. This eliminates 'work-arounds' and extra work to compensate for poorly designed processes

4   Any improvement must be made in accordance with the *scientific method*, under the guidance of a teacher, at *the lowest possible level* in the organization. This means that decisions must be based on evidence and fact, rather than on 'gut feelings', and that those operating the process need to be actively involved in its improvement.

All the rules require that activities, connections and processes have built-in controls to signal problems automatically. It is the continual response to problems that makes this seemingly rigid system so flexible and adaptable to changing circumstances in service and production.

SHORT CASE 10.3

Lean Adoption in the NHS

The UK's National Health Service (NHS) has been working on lean ideas for several years, and is a good example of how lean systems can be employed in service environments.

The NHS has an Institute for Improvement and Innovation, tasked with 'helping all NHS organizations achieve the same levels of quality and efficiency as top-performing organizations'. One way has been through the adoption of service transformation teams, which employ the 5S framework to implement ideas on wards and in clinics.

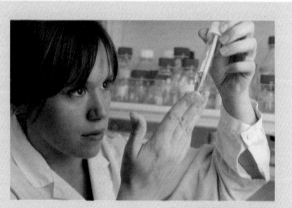

Source: Aricl Emtegren/iStock

At the Hereford Hospitals a major problem was identified in the time spent waiting for the results from the pathology department. A project was set up to understand and redesign the flow of work in the department, using lean principles.

The five-day project involved 50 staff, and centred on mapping the existing journey of samples through pathology. This was then examined using gemba and genchi genbutsu (go and see the actual source) to remove obvious sources of waste, duplication and delays. This practice of walking through the entire process enlisted the support and encouragement of the staff.

Previously, test samples had been batched, and so it was hard to identify the arrival order and provide consistent response times. Collecting samples from arrival was reduced from 13 minutes on average to just 1 minute by removing batching. Heijunka ideas of smooth flow meant that tests were then carried out immediately on arrival. Much time was found to be wasted looking for the right equipment: therefore simple visual tools such as putting taped outlines on the floor were employed to ensure that equipment had a clear location, and that it was replaced after use.

Overall, a 40% reduction in process time resulted, from 62 minutes on average (but ranging up to 2 hours) to a consistently lower 38 minutes. Working more effectively and removing duplicated activities, such as having to re-mark samples as they moved around the department, generated savings of £365,000 per year. A by-product is that the department finishes its work 15 minutes earlier each day, and can use this time to develop further quality improvements.

Questions
1   Which parts of the five principles of lean thinking have the improvement team employed?
2   Why do you think the pathology department were not able to introduce these changes themselves in the past?

Source: www.institute.nhs.uk/quality_and_value/lean_thinking/leean_case_studies.html

The Best System?

CRITICAL PERSPECTIVE

The attractions of lean systems make them tempting to all managers, but some care is needed, as there are elements that cannot be implemented in every case. This section tries to assess the conditions that are necessary for the full lean system to be suitable. Many of the lean elements can be applied to all situations, and so it is not uncommon for firms to state that they have adopted lean principles without following JIT. In particular, the general housekeeping of 5S and much of the TQM approach are readily transferable, whereas JIT can be harder.

Full Lean Is Not Always a Good Choice

Although we have seen that lean thinking has many benefits, and can be applied to many widely different situations, there are instances when JIT in particular, if it could be implemented at all, would be a poor choice. These issues may be related to difficulty in implementing elements such as worker empowerment or supplier cooperation, to the prohibitive expense of breaking the EOQ rules and reducing set-ups, or a lack of stable demand for the product. In these cases full lean production is not suited to the operations of the firm, and would not be a good choice, but these firms can still benefit from lean thinking and waste reduction. A good example is the Hoover washing machine plant in Merthyr Tydfil. It employs kanban and lean quality tools within the factory, but is driven by a make-to-stock system. The result is that the factory itself is efficient, and work moves smoothly and quickly, but the company does not have to invest in all the elements of the lean system, or force suppliers to adopt the new systems as well.

With push systems, changes in demand can be accommodated, as the plan can be changed to produce more items, or alter the product mix for the next production run. For example, many car makers have a 13-week MRP plan, and so this is the longest a customer must wait for a vehicle. However, lean producers do not have this flexibility, as the system is so highly stressed that the entire production facility needs redesigning to produce extra products, or change the heijunka mix. In this case, customer orders that cannot be accommodated in the lean system are added to the next available production slot, and this queue can extend indefinitely if there is too much demand for one product.

Similarly, in service firms the concepts of pre-producing inventory and batching do not exist. These firms focus on the lean philosophy and general housekeeping, and on the customer.

The Volume and Variety Model

If we consider the Hayes and Wheelright (1979) model of volume and variety, the choice between implementing production with batches or with JIT becomes easier to identify. This is illustrated in Figure 10.6,

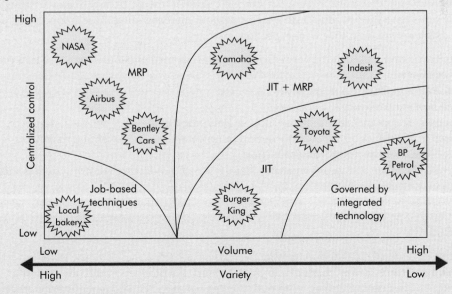

Figure 10.6 Hybrid JIT–MRP systems

which shows that the high volume and relatively low product varieties of Toyota and Burger King are suited to JIT.

With lower volumes, it is hard to justify the expense of setting up a dedicated, lean/JIT system, and so small firms such as the local bakery find it too expensive to adopt. Similarly, if an organization is already operating a lean system, increasing product variety necessitates large numbers of extra kanban loops, and increases stock, which adds cost. In these cases, batching and the push approach become more suitable, as can be seen in firms such as Bentley, or many in the aerospace industry, where the complex nature of the product excludes the adoption of JIT.

In practice, most companies employ a system that suits their own situation, and it is likely to be a combination of MRP, kanban and push. The Synchro MRP system developed and employed by Yamaha is one such example, where the JIT/kanban system is used on the shopfloor to move materials and products around, but an MRP system is used for the planning and push-style ordering of parts.

The key point is that the lean system has many elements that need to be in place for it to function properly. If any of these cannot be introduced, then perhaps the firm should consider whether another approach is more suitable.

Summary

This chapter has looked at lean production by exploring the lean production system and its just-in-time system of production control.

The lean system coordinates activities in a different way from the push systems normally used with the ERP/MRP approach we saw in the last chapter. One of the main aspects has to do with the initiation of the system, and hence the distinction between 'pull' (JIT) and 'push'.

Lean production can be a very efficient system, but it is not suitable for all products, services or markets, and we have focused on the need to select an appropriate delivery system. Lean/JIT is very expensive to design, not least in the set-up time reduction activities and getting the suppliers of materials to make frequent small deliveries. These features are not normally present, except in large manufacturing organizations; many firms have tried to adopt lean systems without understanding these ground rules, and found the results didn't deliver what they were expecting.

In this chapter we have looked at the very efficient systems adopted under the banner of lean production. Specifically we have:
- Dealt with how to classify pull systems
- Explored how kanban works
- Described the factors that are needed to support lean production
- Developed lean production to cover the notion of lean thinking and extension to services
- Identified some weaknesses of lean production
- Employed the volume and variety model to identify which production control system is suitable for which operating conditions

Key Theories

The key theories discussed in this chapter were:
- **Push and pull inventory control** – in push systems, the production activities follow a programme from a central system. With pull, the line reacts to demand requests from other production cells, which all ultimately respond directly to the customer.

- **Lean production** – a highly efficient management approach with repeated focus on waste reduction, and based on the ideas of the Toyota Production system and JIT.

- **Kanban** – the Japanese word for the card that is the essential signalling device for the operation of the JIT system of production and service delivery

- **Smooth production scheduling (heijunka)** – approach used to ensure an even and repetitive process when operating with small, short-run batch sizes that require frequent changeover

- **TQM (total quality management)** – a quality system that is needed for effective lean production, and is based on kaizen (continuous improvement)

- **Lean thinking** – extending lean production to broader ideas or philosophies through a focus on waste reduction

- **Sand cone principle** – records the importance of certain practices building on others in predetermined order. This is important to ensure that lean systems work as intended

- **Volume, variety and control** – the best practice for controlling production and delivery processes.

Suggested Answers to Stop and Think Questions

1 Push and pull: The choice of push or pull depends on a range of factors, such as customer demand patterns and processing time. Fast food uses a pull approach, as the demand is constant and the preparation times are short. A traditional restaurant will employ a combination of both push and pull, as some preparation is completed in advance, and the food finished to the specific orders of the customer. That is why they often run out of popular dishes when they are busy (as experienced particularly in a 'help yourself'-style buffet restaurant). The supermarket and college shop will use a push approach, as the customers cannot wait for the products to be delivered if the shop runs out. There may well be some pull elements, as in the reorder level system we saw in Chapter 9, where a certain level of stock triggers (or pulls) a replenishment of the stocks.

2 JIT implications: Adopting the JIT system can produce many problems for managers. If we consider the kanban system first, there is a need for the manager to be certain about the level and consistency of demand for the product. As this is a pull system, it needs orders to generate reactions, and so a constant demand is necessary. Other problems appear if the firm has a weak control of quality, as it needs to be able to use every part being produced. Running out of parts because some are unusable scrap will create problems. In practice, there are many different elements that need to be in place for the system to work properly, and these are covered in the next section.

3 Quality in lean systems: When people talk of 'a defect as a treasure' they mean it forces them to improve the system. Something going wrong shows a situation that shouldn't be allowed to repeat, and so the system can be redesigned to prevent the problem recurring. The correction makes the system less likely to generate faulty products, and so becomes more robust, which is the aim of continuous improvement.

4 Waste: As systems become leaner, the excess resources are squeezed out of the system, and so managers need to focus more closely on exactly meeting the needs of their customers. So whereas a manager may see excess staff as a waste, the customer looks at this as an extra cost they need to pay. Another example is the way that managers will see processing delays in production as costing staff time, whereas the customer sees this as an unmet delivery.

5 Lean services: JIT has been employed in many service environments. Becoming leaner, and so using fewer resources and delivering services exactly in the right amounts and quantities, can benefit everyone in the health care industry, as it improves quality of care and reduces costs. Similarly, in the department store, starting the lean journey leads to lower operating costs and so a more efficient process for customers. It can also improve product availability, as the accuracy of the stocks held increases, and deliveries can be satisfied more quickly.

connect™

Review Questions

1   Describe the supporting factors needed for a kanban system to function effectively.

2   What conditions are needed for a JIT system to work, and do these prohibit the adoption of lean production in your country?

3   Discuss the merits and limitations of push versus pull approaches to managing inventory.

4   Describe the volume–variety model of Wheelwright and Clark. With examples, explain whether you think the model is valuable to practising managers in selecting between MRP and lean production.

5   Use the volume and variety model to choose a production system for the following products and processes. Be sure to explain why you make your choice.

(a) Car manufacturing

(b) Washing machine production

(c) Optician's workshop

(d) Producing canned soup

(e) A bakery

(f) Sandwich bar

Discussion Questions

1   Visit a nearby fast-food restaurant (McDonald's would be a good choice). Take time to watch what happens behind the counter, following the production of both the fries and the burgers. What controls the work, and how is an order for more food from the kitchen initiated? (If you cannot visit somewhere, take a look at www.inventorymanagementreview.org/2005/11/mcdonalds_a_gui.html for more information.)

2   Use the Internet to find out about the car firm NUMMI, which produces cars under the Saturn brand in North America. How was the company started, and why? Draw up a list of features of the TPS, and see if you can work out how much of the system NUMMI have used. (A good place to start is www.nummi.com.)

3   If you can, watch the video on Dell's Global Fulfilment System (type 'Dell factory tour' into a search engine, or try www.youtube.com/watch?v=EEhNkzdKyrw). How similar to the TPS is this system? (Try and develop a list of your own features of lean systems.) What advantages does the approach give Dell over its competitors?

4   Go to the Subway case at the start of the chapter. Look at the list of important elements of the Subway lean system, and try and see how many are similar to those of the TPS. Compare the preparation process at Subway with another fast-food chain you know. Which do you think is the most lean, and why? As Doctor's Associates is a purely franchised operation, what risks does this present for maintaining its brand?

5   'To be competitive today, companies must adopt just in time.' Discuss the validity of this statement by considering several different industry sectors.

6   Discuss, with examples, whether you think JIT can be used in a service environment.

7   Briefly describe the key components of MRP and JIT systems. Why must they be fully understood before selecting an appropriate production control system for a small manufacturing company?

Problems

1   The kanban system uses bins containing a fixed, small amount of WIP. The number of such bins of each part used in the production system depends on the usage, replenishment time and size of the container.

(a) Produce the formula for the number of bins needed for one kanban loop between two cells.

(b) A workstation covering seats for cars just-in-time has a planned daily usage rate of 320 seats per day, and receives uncovered seats from another station in containers that hold 4% of the day's demand. It takes 1 hour for the preceding station to fill a bin, and 30 minutes for the filled bin to be delivered to the covering station. How many such bins are needed for the kanban loop to work efficiently in this production cell, given a single 8-hour shift per day and a risk factor of 7%?

(c) What changes to the system would be needed if the company were to start producing a racing-style seat in addition to the existing design?

2   A workstation binding books just-in-time has a planned daily usage rate of 600 books per day, and receives leabound books from another station in containers that hold 5% of the day's demand. It takes 1 hour for the preceding station to fill a bin, and 30 minutes for the filled bin to be delivered to the covering station.

(a) How many such bins are needed for the kanban loop to work efficiently in this production cell, given a single 8-hour shift per day and a risk factor of 8%?

(b) What changes to the system would be needed if the company were to start producing a ring-bound version in addition to the existing design?

3   A workstation assembling the cases for pocket calculators just-in-time has a planned daily usage rate of 1,320 calculators per day, and receives the insides of the calculators from another station in containers that hold 1% of the day's demand. It takes 1 hour for the preceding station to fill a bin, and 15 minutes for the filled bin to be delivered to the casing station. How many such bins are needed for the kanban loop to work efficiently in this production cell, given a single 8-hour shift per day and a risk factor of 8%?

4   A workstation making water fountains just-in-time has a planned daily usage rate of 100 fountains per day, and receives uncovered seats from another station in containers that hold 5% of the day's demand. It takes 2 hours for the preceding station to fill a bin, and 1 hour for the filled bin to be delivered to the covering station. How many such bins are needed for the kanban loop to work efficiently in this production cell, given a 10-hour day?

5   A production line runs an 8-hour shift for 5 days per week. The orders come at irregular intervals, but on average arrive as shown in a month:
Product A = 400
Product B = 600
Product C = 600
Use heijunka to develop a smoothed production schedule for the products.

6   A production line runs a 12-hour shift for 5 days per week. The orders come at irregular intervals, but on average arrive as shown in a month:
Product A = 200
Product B = 400
Product C = 300
Use heijunka to develop a smoothed production schedule for the products.

7   A production line runs an 8-hour shift for 5 days per week. The orders come at irregular intervals, but on average arrive as shown in a month:
Product A = 150
Product B = 200
Product C = 150
Use heijunka to develop a smoothed production schedule for the products.

Online
Learning Centre

Visit the Online Learning Centre at **www.mcgraw-hill.co.uk/textbooks/paton** for a range of resources to support your learning.

Further Reading

Bartezzaghi, E. (1999) 'The evolution of production models: is a new paradigm emerging?', *International Journal of Operations and Production Management*, **19**(2), 229–250.

Chapman, C.D. (2005) 'Clean house with lean 5S', *Quality Progress*, **38**(6), 27–32.

Hines, P., Holweg, M. and Rich, N. (2004) 'Learning to evolve: a review of contemporary lean thinking', *International Journal of Operations and Production Management*, **24**(10), 994–1011.

Liker, J.K. (2004) *The Toyota Way: 14 Management Principles from the World's Greatest Manufacturer*, McGraw-Hill, London.

Swank, C.K. (2003) 'The lean service machine', *Harvard Business Review*, **81**(10), 123–129, 138.

Wu, Y.C. (2003) 'Lean manufacturing: a perspective of lean suppliers', *International Journal of Operations and Production Management*, **23**(11–12), 1349–1376.

References

Cusumano, M.A. (1985) *The Japanese Automobile Industry: Technology and Management at Nissan and Toyota*. Harvard University Press, Cambridge, MA.

Ferdows, K. and De Meyer, A. (1990) 'Lasting improvements in manufacturing performance: in search of a new theory', *Journal of Operations Management*, **9**(2), 168–184.

Hayes, R. and Wheelright, S.C. (1979) 'The dynamics of process-product life cycle', *Harvard Business Review*, **57**(2), 15–22.

Liker, J. and Hoseus, M. (2008) *Toyota Culture: The Heart and Soul of the Toyota Way*, McGraw-Hill.

Monden, Y. (1983) *Toyota Production System: Practical Approach to Production Management*, Industrial Engineering and Management Press, Norcross, GA.

Ohno, T. (1988) *Toyota Production System: Beyond Large-Scale Production*, Productivity Press, Cambridge, MA.

Pilkington, A. (1998) 'Manufacturing strategy regained: evidence for the demise of best practice', *California Management Review*, **41**(1), 31–42.

Schonberger, R. (1986) *World Class Manufacturing: The Lessons of Simplicity Applied*, Free Press, New York.

Shingo, S. (1985) *A Revolution in Manufacturing: The SMED System*, Productivity Press, Stamford, CT.

Spear, S. and Bowen, H.K. (1999) 'Decoding the DNA of the Toyota Production System', *Harvard Business Review*, Sep–Oct.

Womack, J.P. and Jones, D.T. (1996) *Lean Thinking: Banish Waste and Create Wealth in Your Corporation*, Simon & Schuster, New York.

Womack, J.P., Jones, D.T. and Roos, D. (1990) *The Machine That Changed the World*, Rawson Associates, New York.

Project Management

Learning Outcomes

After reading this chapter you should be able to:

- Define the scope of activities involved in modern project management

- Use the basic tools available to plan and deliver projects on time, within budget and to specification

- Appreciate the move towards project-based organizations, and the use of project management frameworks such as PRINCE and PMBOK

- Describe the role of leadership in helping organizations adapt and change, to understand and meet the business challenges they face

- Describe various approaches to organizational design and consider the tensions between functional capabilities and project capabilities

- Outline the role and competencies of a project manager

Crossrail: A 21 Kilometre Tunnel under London

The Crossrail project is the largest civil engineering project in the UK, and the largest single addition to the London transport network for over 50 years. After many years of planning and false starts, work began in 2009, with major construction commencing in 2010. A series of underground tunnels and stations will extend the mainline services from the west of England and Heathrow Airport through the centre of the city, allowing direct access to key areas without the need to change train services. It will also connect the West Coast services to the East Coast services and the Channel Tunnel. It will take eight years to complete the work, with passenger services scheduled to begin in late 2017.

Source: © Keremk/iStock

In 2009 Gordon Brown, the then Prime Minister, said: 'Many people said it would never be built, but today we are celebrating a defining moment for London as Crossrail's construction gets under way. Crossrail will not only mean faster journey times across the capital and beyond, it will also bring a massive economic boost to the city, creating thousands of jobs and adding at least £20 billion to our economy.'

The project is largely publicly funded. The two main contributors are Transport for London, which will pay £7.7 billion, and the Department for Transport, which will pay £5.6 billion. There are also smaller partners who have a stake in the project, including airport operator BAA, providing £230 million, and the Corporation of London, providing £200 million. In addition, Crossrail is creating a Tunnelling Academy to tackle the shortage of people with the necessary skills to work on the project, by providing training on the key skills required to work in and around a tunnel excavation and build environment.

Given the size of Crossrail, its organization is every bit as complex as the project itself. Three companies – Bechtel, Halcrow and Systra – have been selected as project delivery partners, and have contracts to complete major parts of the project. These companies will be overseen by Crossrail, but will also have to work together where their parts of the projects overlap. They also have their own project management teams who will work out how their individual parts of the project should be delivered, and will employ a multitude of other contractors as they are needed.

So there are several layers of project management, spanning several companies, which all need to be coordinated if the project is to be completed successfully. This hints at the complexity of the management of the project, but says nothing of the engineering difficulties that will be faced in designing and building not just one of the longest railway tunnels in the world, but one that passes through the complex network of existing tunnels and utilities in one of the busiest and most densely populated cities in the world.

Sources: www.railway-technology.com/projects/crossrail/; www.crossrail.co.uk/news/press-releases/construction-crossrail-begins-as-foundations-laid-for-new-canary-wharf-station, accessed 7 April 2011.

Introduction

With increasing pressure on organizations to complete work more rapidly and cost-effectively, the modern manager is expected to have a variety of skills that his or her predecessors may not have thought necessary. One fundamental change is the way in which initiatives and new developments are introduced through project management. It used to be enough to allow individual departments to introduce changes in an ad hoc way, but the advent of company-wide, process-dependent initiatives means that more rigorous methods of managing change are needed. The initiatives that a manager may now have to deal with require accurate control and co-ordination, and so demand formal project management techniques. These were originally developed for projects in manufacturing, construction and civil engineering.

However, many projects that make full use of formal techniques still fail, often with very serious consequences. Projects can fail in different ways. Some fail when they are first used, such as the baggage-handling system at Heathrow's Terminal 5; some suffer long delays, such as the Airbus A380, or the large hadron collider at CERN; and others, such as the London 2012 Olympics, need ever-increasing sums of money to meet their deadlines. Why is this? There is no simple answer; projects fail for many different reasons. But regardless of the complexity or size of a project, three features are fundamental to success: **cost, performance and time**. There are many tools available for managing these three, and we shall see a few of these in this chapter.

Cost, performance and time: projects are normally subjected to these three performance criteria.

Care is needed; the employment of sophisticated project management tools and techniques alone is not enough to guarantee success. Project success can be measured using cost, performance and time, but project management is concerned with managing people within changing environmental and organizational contexts. These all have a profound and often unpredictable bearing on the project itself. Successful project managers are also project leaders, and have well-developed strategic and interpersonal skills. These are needed in addition to the technical skills associated with scheduling, resource allocation and decision-making in optimizing the three variables of cost, performance and time.

This chapter will focus on both tools and techniques, and will consider the challenges facing practising managers in order to help them understand the difficulties and complexities of managing projects by looking through multiple lenses and considering overlapping subjects. In particular, the chapter will first consider the strategic

Possible project management focus:

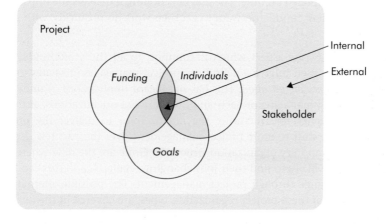

Figure 11.1 The two perspectives of project management

aspect of projects, such as project stakeholders, and the ways in which we can structure projects within the organization. It will then focus on the tools, by looking at the sequence of steps typically found in project management – the tools needed to develop plans, monitor project progress, manage the individuals in the project team, and ensure completion.

Alternative Views of Project Management

At one level, project management processes and techniques can be used to coordinate resources to achieve predictable results. However, it is important to understand that project management is not totally a science; there is no straightforward formula for success. Since projects involve people, there are always uncertainties that cannot be absolutely controlled, and so project management is partly an art that requires flexibility and creativity.

Projects are owned by a multiplicity of stakeholders, whose needs and aspirations must be accommodated. Organizational 'politics', the external environment, marketing pressures and the needs and objectives of a large number of individuals must be considered. Hence there must be regular interaction, especially when a project team is being set up, with 'commissioning executives', other stakeholders and interested parties. The purpose of this interaction is to define the boundaries of the project, and to keep its core objectives in focus. The significance of the motivation and commitment of individual team members should be recognized. Teamwork is vital because projects involve not only internal specialists but also external suppliers, subcontractors and end users.

Figure 11.1 shows how we can view project management from two alternative perspectives. The first is *inside* the project, looking outwards, where detail will dominate the life of the project manager and he or she is likely to be thinking mainly of the three project goals of time, performance and cost. Here the project manager is concerned with detail in planning and controlling the project.

The project manager may be responsible for achievement of the goals of the project, but normally his or her direct authority is often limited as he or she is responsible for just one project. Resources and support have to be negotiated with a wide network of more senior people inside and outside the organization. Often the project manager's authority is low at the outset, and must be built up and maintained if the project is to progress well and achieve its goals.

Our second perspective on project management is from *outside* the project looking in: here the stakeholders' views become more evident, and communications and relationships dominate. These views are from suppliers, commissioning managers, and other interested parties such as the general public. They tend to want to see the big picture, and how the project's progress will impact on them.

Think about how different your views on and involvement with the Crossrail project would be if you were the project manager, a building contractor, the Mayor of London, or a commuter: The views on when a project can be considered a success or failure also change with the perspective taken. The project manager will focus on the three performance criteria of cost, performance and time, whereas the commuters want as little disruption as possible and the work to be completed on time. The mayor is hoping it delivers the improvements promised and within budget, whereas individual contractors want to get their work done quickly, with as few complications as possible, while making a profit.

Stakeholders: the people who have a say in or are influenced by a project.

There is one aspect which is common to all the **stakeholders**, though, and which can be used to give a definition: project management relates to the management of a *temporary organization*. This has significant implications in understanding the task and tools of managing projects and the nature of organizations, as there are many different approaches to structuring the organization to deliver the project. One major and consistent development in the shift to more project management over the past few decades has been a move towards more dynamic and temporary organization structures. Gone are the days where people used to have a job for life; they are now more likely to find their jobs changing regularly, and this can be directly attributable to organizations managing change through project management. The possible alternative structures, and the advantages and disadvantages of these project organization types, are covered in the next section.

SHORT CASE 11.1

Airbus chief executive resigns

A series of problems at Airbus during the early manufacturing of the A380 super jumbo left the European firm struggling, and so the board appointed the deputy chief executive of glass maker Saint-Gobain to lead an aggressive turnaround. However, Christian Streiff lasted only 100 days before the board took up his threat of resignation. He had issued the warning after he failed to gain the autonomy to carry out his €5 billion cost-savings plans.

Source: © AFP

Production problems had put the A380 project two years behind schedule, and left the firm facing millions of euros in compensation to customers as a result, and also led to it losing its lead over US rival Boeing. In response, Streiff developed a turnaround project called Power8 which sought €2 billion annual cost savings, a 30% cut in overheads, and a 20% rise in productivity.

However, Streiff's rescue plans managed to anger both French and German political leaders, who had significant state funding stakes and, with them, a major say in the running of Airbus. Particular problems came from Streiff's plans to move A380 production from Hamburg – most of the production delays had been blamed on the German plant – to Toulouse. In addition to the state owners, Streiff was also criticized by workers and unions for the scale and speed of potential job cuts and plant closures of the Power8 programme.

Questions

1 Identify the stakeholders in the Airbus A380 project.
2 What do you think was Streiff's mistake in believing he was in sole control of the company and its major project?
3 What advice would you give to his successor about managing the stakeholders as well as the firm?

Source: www.guardian.co.uk/business/2006/oct/09/money3

The key point is that project management is about more than just applying some tools to ensure that cost, time and performance are met. It involves a wider strategic/organizational appreciation, and a range of skills that bring all the many players' and stakeholders' concerns together.

Towards the Project-based Organization (PBO)

Once the stakeholders are identified, and their different needs are made clear, project managers can start to think about the strategic issues in completing the project. As a project is a temporary organization, the managers need to consider a range of different organizational structures that can be employed to deliver the project. Some organization structures are better suited to projects than others. This section explores these different structures and identifies their benefits, with particular reference to accomplishing projects.

Designing a Project-based Organization

An organization can be defined as *the arrangement of people in a business so that they can act as one body*. The conventional approach to company management is the *line and staff* or functional approach, which separates skill sets such as product design, production, sales, marketing and accounting. This is the traditional hierarchical structure of organization as shown in Figure 11.2. It is possibly the oldest structure, and its persistence is due partly to its simplicity, and partly, for many years, to the apparent absence of a better alternative. We now see that the conventional pyramidal hierarchy is considered unnecessarily authoritative. Several studies have highlighted weaknesses in the line and staff approach. There is a slow flow of information; the approach is impersonal, because of its inherent bureaucracy; it is slow to change, because of the inflexible and complex nature of the structure; an ever increasing use and application of technology is required to assist organizational communication; and younger people are less keen on rigid line and staff authority.

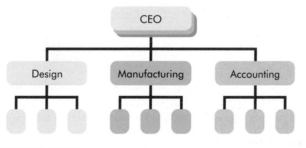

Figure 11.2 Functional organization structure

Many organizations – Scandinavian Airlines (SAS), for example – have moved to a more customer-oriented organization. They believe that organizations should be focused on the workers who are in contact with the customer, and that these are supported at the sharp end by management. The next step is to try to 'flatten' the layers between the decision-makers and the front-line employees who actually deliver the service or add value. This increases the speed of communication between the customers and the managers.

With projects, the hierarchical and functional boundaries in the organization also act as constraints on communication, and so hinder the performance of the project. Instead of carrying out the project using whatever skills are needed at the time, projects operating within a functional organization require negotiation with the functional managers for access to the skills and resources. For example, if a manufacturing-based project needs access to the sales computer system, the project manager has to enlist support from his superior to clear the way to talk to his opposite number in sales. Carrying out work for the manufacturing department is not what sales staff are there to do, and so there is understandable resistance and a delay in completing the work until it has been agreed by both departments.

As a result, it is usually possible to operating a project within a functional structure only if it is established as a separate part of the organization, temporarily staffed by the required experts drawn from the functions. This is shown in Figure 11.3. These project teams are normally championed by one function to provide the support and line management needed, as there is no other place for the organization to locate the project in its hierarchy. These types of project are often weak in their impact, as the members are still focusing on their functional responsibilities, and are easily distracted by the needs and activities back in their home function. As a result, they are not always working towards the aims of the project.

There are alternatives to the functional organization that are more suited to managing projects. Figure 11.4 shows the **matrix organization**, which has staff reporting to two

> **Matrix organization:**
> combined organization structure that overlays functional and project-based styles.

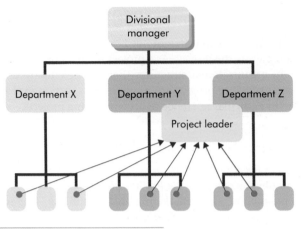

Figure 11.3 Typical cross-functional project team or task force

managers. The (vertical) responsibility is to the functional role, and the other (horizontal) responsibility is to a specific project. This structure can be stressful for staff, because working for more than one boss can result in divided loyalties and ambiguous lines of authority. However, it can help cross-functional teams to form ownership of a project.

Practitioners consider the matrix structure to be a two-dimensional system, where each project represents a potential *profit centre* and each functional department represents a *cost centre*. This interpretation can create conflict, because functional departments may feel they no longer have an input to corporate profits.

Generally there are three types of matrix structure:
- A *weak matrix arrangement*, where the project manager acts as a coordinator of the work, and chairs meetings with the representatives of other departments involved in the project. Resources are allocated by consensus, and the project manager is reduced to administering the project rather than leading it.
- A *middling matrix*, where there is an attempt to balance the power of the project manager with that of the line manager. The administration of the organization is such that the line manager applies resources to the activities that need to be carried out by project: that is, the project provides a source of income for the functional department.

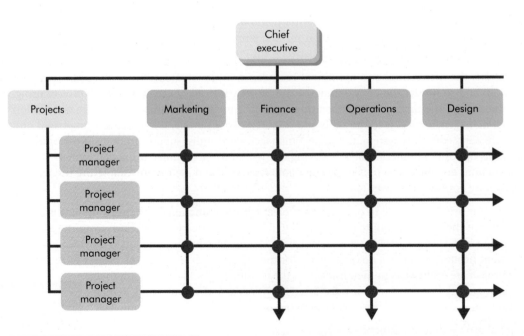

Figure 11.4 The matrix organizational structure

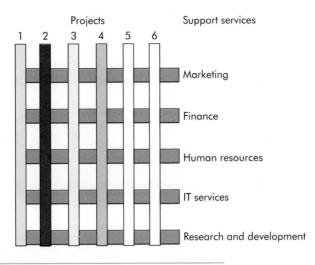

Figure 11.5 A strong matrix structure with hierarchy only for support staff

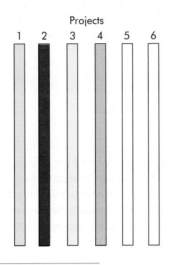

Figure 11.6 Wholly project-based organization

- A *strong matrix*, where functional departments have the role of providing resources through seconding people on a full-time basis to the project team. This arrangement operates only when the project is vitally important to the organization. There are drawbacks, as it may isolate an individual from their normal promotion or career development path. However, here the aims and needs of the project are paramount, and so it is likely to be successful.

Some organizations take the matrix even further, and lose the direct functional hierarchy, leaving just ancillary central roles such as personnel, accounting and training. This can be seen in Figure 11.5.

Recently, some firms have taken this approach still further into what is known as the **project-based organization** structure. As its name suggests, this organization is structured purely around projects; each is self-contained, with all its own staff and support skills (see Figure 11.6). The move towards virtual organizations and the emergence of new technologies allows this structure to operate, and the only permanent staff are the senior executives and the project managers. The other staff are on fixed contracts, and so are hired and used as needed. This allows the project to be the focus of the organization, and offers greater flexibility to the firm as it can take on projects in a wide range of areas, just by recruiting staff with the necessary skills, and not having to worry about how to use its employees.

> **Project-based organization:** a shift from functional organization structure, via the matrix organization, to one where the project is the focus of attention.

The problems with this approach are that there is greater duplication of roles across projects owing to a lack of central coordination. Also there are problems with learning, as there is no guarantee that the staff from one project will be used in any others; and that acquiring the right skills may be difficult or expensive in times of shortages. Take, for example, the simultaneous Crossrail project (discussed in the opening case study) and the London 2012 Olympics. Both are looking for staff with similar skills for short-term temporary contracts in what are already shortage trades in London. This can only mean that the costs are higher than they could be if their staff were permanently employed. However, neither organization will exist after the completion of each project, and so does not need to appoint these staff permanently.

The key point is that the format of an organization is important for carrying out the project, and there are certain structures that make managing projects easier than others. However, it is important to remember that projects, by definition, are only temporary. Therefore the project-based organization is not ideal for those firms where projects are used purely for occasional activities.

! Stop and Think

1 You are setting up a new company that delivers training courses over the Internet. Which organization type would you use for the following activities in the firm?

(a) The head office, including the sales, IT and accounting departments.

(b) The commissioning department, which arranges for different experts to produce a package of materials.

(c) After five years of growth, a project to relocate to a new building with more space.

Managing the Project Life Cycle

So far we have seen the complexity of managing projects effectively, and the strategic considerations of different stakeholders, as well as the way projects fit into existing organization structures. Now we shall start to look at some of the approaches that can help us deliver the project on time, in budget, and to specification. We have already defined a project as a temporary structure that is focused on delivering one objective. This can become more complicated if we think about how some firms have to co-manage the delivery of several projects with varying objectives at once. A good starting point, though, for the techniques of project management is that every project goes through the same phases: definition, planning and resourcing, implementation, and wind-up or handover to the customer.

There are many frameworks that help us structure the way we manage projects. The best way to describe a project management framework is to think of a cookbook. If you are unsure of how to manage a project, simply refer to the cookbook. There are two well-known structures (cookbooks) for managing projects. The first, *PRINCE* (Projects in Controlled Environments), is promoted by the UK government, and the second, *PMBOK* (Project Management Body of Knowledge), is supported by the US-based Project Management Institute.

PRINCE Methodology

PRINCE is a project management methodology developed by the UK's Office of Government Commerce (OGC), which is an independent office of HM Treasury. OGC manages PRINCE and has adopted an 'open' strategy that makes it publicly available so that it can be used without the need for a proprietary licence or royalty payments of any kind. It has been revised several times, and should more accurately be referred to as PRINCE2 2009, reflecting the current version.

Numerous major organizations currently use PRINCE. They include The AA, Aviva, British Rail, BT, Camel, GlaxoWellcome, Hitachi, HM Land Registry, the Home Office, Hong Kong Telecom, London Underground, the Danish Government, NatWest, the NHS, Philip Morris, the RAF, Reading Borough Council, Royal Mail, Tesco, TSB, Unilever, RBS and GCHQ. Many of these organizations use only some elements of the methodology rather than the full package. The use of a cookbook doesn't guarantee a perfect meal; nor does it include all the information that might be needed. PRINCE is a framework within which to operate, and represents a set of guidelines

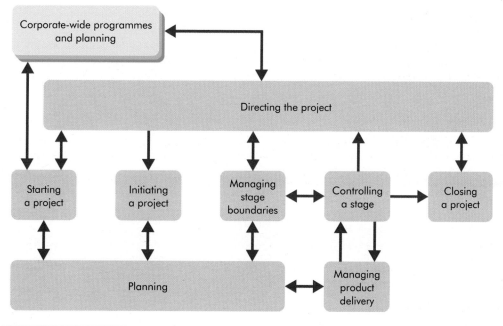

Figure 11.7 The PRINCE process

and knowledge of best practice, in a similar vein to the ISO 9000 quality management system, which is covered in Chapter 13.

PRINCE is not intended to include all the subjects relevant to project management. Project management techniques and tools such as network planning are adequately covered elsewhere, and are considered to be tried and tested techniques. PRINCE focuses on the management of the project, and the resources involved in carrying out all the activities of that project. Thus PRINCE is a process-oriented approach to project management, and it separates the management of a project into various key processes. Each is clearly defined, and contains the essence of a system: inputs, outputs, objectives and feedback control. Figure 11.7 shows the key processes of the PRINCE methodology. Note the way that the processes themselves are linked in a certain rigid way.

In more detail, PRINCE2 defines 45 separate activities, and groups these under the eight processes as shown in the diagram. Each process has a clear list of outputs, which represent key timing or decision points for a project. These are summarized in Figure 11.8, showing the different management levels that are responsible for each. The *directing* process is the responsibility of the *project board*, which is charged with an overview and integration with the rest of the business. The middle layer is concerned with *delivering* the project and is the responsibility of the team members, and the last line of the diagram shows the role of the project manager.

PRINCE Elements

PRINCE defines a programme as:

> *A portfolio of projects selected, planned and managed in a coordinated way which together achieve a set of defined business objectives. Programme management methods and techniques may also be applied to a set of otherwise unrelated projects bounded by a business cycle.*

PRINCE is designed for an environment where there are products, supported by a business case, commissioned by a customer and produced by a supplier, that are intended to produce benefits and are operated by a user. These terms are important, because they show the concerns and motivation of PRINCE, along with its focus.

- *Business case*: a formal document that contains the information necessary to justify the project. It describes the costs and benefits of the project, and answers the question 'Why should this project be undertaken?' It should also contain the criteria for reviewing the progress of the project, and criteria for measuring satisfactory progress or terminating the project.

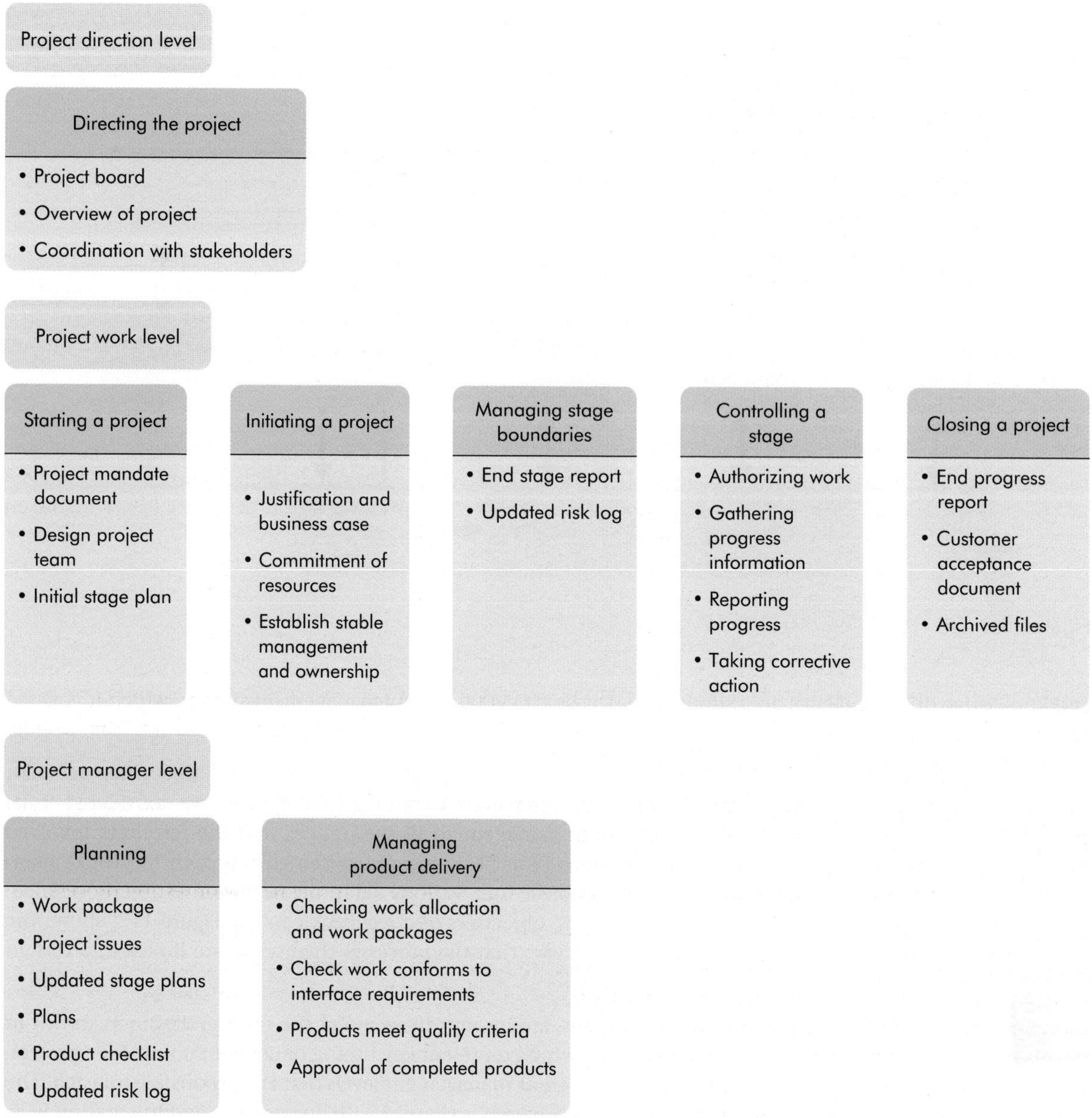

Project direction level

Directing the project

- Project board
- Overview of project
- Coordination with stakeholders

Project work level

Starting a project	Initiating a project	Managing stage boundaries	Controlling a stage	Closing a project
• Project mandate document • Design project team • Initial stage plan	• Justification and business case • Commitment of resources • Establish stable management and ownership	• End stage report • Updated risk log	• Authorizing work • Gathering progress information • Reporting progress • Taking corrective action	• End progress report • Customer acceptance document • Archived files

Project manager level

Planning	Managing product delivery
• Work package • Project issues • Updated stage plans • Plans • Product checklist • Updated risk log	• Checking work allocation and work packages • Check work conforms to interface requirements • Products meet quality criteria • Approval of completed products

Figure 11.8 PRINCE process contents and level of responsibility

- *User*: this defines those who will ultimately operate the final product and should be identified separately from the customer.
- *Customer*: the person(s) who commissioned the project, and who should ultimately receive its benefits.
- *Product*, *deliverable* and *outcome*: these words are used interchangeably to describe project end points. They describe what has been or what should be achieved. Results of projects may vary enormously, from tangible items such as buildings to intangibles such as a culture change.
- *Project issues*: things that may adversely affect the successful outcome of the project – also known as problems.
- *Supplier*: a person or group providing specialist skills and resources to the project in order to create the project outcomes required by the customer and users.
- *Subcontractor*: a person or group who provides products and/or services to the supplier.

So PRINCE is about managing all projects in a programme or organization in a controlled manner. The cookbook has clear statements about how a project is initialized and recorded in the *project initiation document* (PID). This defines what the project will deliver, and a mechanism for managing the changes if the client wants additional work carried out.

The running of the project is also clearly defined, with a *project board* that manages the project for its whole duration. It consists of several members, each representing a major project interest. This is useful, as it generates cross-ownership of the project between the interested parties.

Under PRINCE, projects are monitored by a *project assurance team* for the duration of the project. This covers both technical and administrative responsibilities. This ensures the continuity and integrity of the project are maintained, and involves a focus on the user.

Project managers are appointed for day-to-day management of the project, and PRINCE gives guidance on deciding how their duties should be allocated. A project manager may be appointed for the duration of the project, to plan the project and define responsibilities for each stage manager. Thereafter, the job involves ensuring that the project progresses to time and budget, managing the interface with other projects, reporting to the project board, and initiating any corrective action as necessary.

A *stage manager* may be appointed for each stage, and is given the task of ensuring that stage products are produced on schedule to acceptable quality standards and within budget. The stage manager is supported by the *stage team(s)* responsible for producing the products of the stage. At the discretion of the project board the same person may manage more than one stage, or the roles of project manager and stage manager may be undertaken by the same person. *Teams* are created during each stage to implement the project. The team organization, responsibility definitions and the allocation of those responsibilities to individuals will depend upon the size and nature of the project, and on the skill mixes available.

PRINCE helps ensure that a project is fully defined and scoped, by using *product breakdown structures* (PBS) to identify all necessary products, whether they are to be produced within the project, already exist, or are to be produced by another project. The structure has as its *origin* the product that the project has been commissioned to produce. This reflects the PRINCE distinction between management and technical activities, and the need for the quality control process to be independently auditable.

The project manager, the project board and the senior users have to put effort in 'up front' to make more of the project visible right from the start. But the effort put in at the beginning is repaid by a reduction in work later, both for the board and for the project team overall. It helps the project planners and auditors to identify, earlier rather than later, whether specific individuals or special tools need to be involved in the review or testing process.

Once the major products and the necessary activities to produce them have been defined, the project can be divided into stages. Each stage will end at a *key control point*, where a formal decision must be taken whether to proceed to the next stage, or to abandon (or suspend) the project. These key points will usually coincide with the completion of a major product, or product set, which then becomes the baseline for moving forward. Such a key point might be: when detailed user requirements have been established, and these need to be confirmed formally, with a commitment to meet them; or where tenders have been received, and acceptance of one of them will introduce a new set of circumstances and new commitments.

PRINCE requires a structured set of technical and resource plans to achieve effective technical and managerial control of a project, including:

- technical plans
- resource plans
- exception plans.

A *stage technical plan* is prepared for each stage of the project, and shows all products and technical activities within that stage. The stage technical plan is produced at the same time as, and to complement, the stage resource plan. Detailed technical plans will probably be necessary in all but the smallest projects. Typically, they are used for detailed planning and control of major activities (e.g. system test).

Individual *work plans* are produced as necessary from the stage and detailed technical plans to allocate detailed activities to specific people within a stage team. Actual progress is reported against these plans for later compilation of control reports.

Resource plans are used to identify the type, amount and period of use of the various resources required during the life of the project. The *project resource plan* is mandatory for all projects. It is a top-level plan produced during the initiation stage to quantify the resources needed for succeeding stages of the project. The *stage resource plan* contains details of all the required resources for a stage. It may be produced at two levels of detail: the first in summary form for approval by the project board; the second in more detail for the stage manager, and against which actuals are recorded. The initiation stage plan is prepared as early in the project as possible. Plans for each subsequent stage are prepared before the stage commences, in time for submission to the end stage assessment meeting of the previous stage.

The detailed resource plans are created as necessary to plan the required resources for a particular activity (e.g. system test).

The *exception plan* is required only when a significant deviation from the plans, in terms of cost or elapsed time, has exceeded or will exceed tolerances previously defined by the project board (e.g. if a significant request for change has to be implemented). It shows the action proposed to meet the deviation, and the consequences of the deviation and of the corrective action.

PRINCE provides a *control structure* to be applied during each stage. The control components cover all aspects of project activity, and allow the project board to assess project status before committing to further expenditure and/or a revised timescale. Controls are applied via meetings of project management and project staff as required, each meeting producing a set of predefined documents. There are five types of control meetings following comprehensive reporting and change control procedures.

PRINCE includes guidance on getting the project firmly under control at the outset, and recognizes that this cannot usually be done in the context of a single meeting. What needs to be in place before any development starts – the project initiation document (PID) – is described in detail, as well as how to assemble the information required. The *mid* and *end stage assessments* (MSA and ESA) are mandatory management controls that occur at the midpoint and end of each stage. They consist of formal presentations by the project manager to the project board of the current project status, and requests for approval of the resource and technical plans for the next stage. Approval by the project board is needed before the project can proceed to the next stage.

The final stage of the PRINCE method is *project closure*. This addresses what needs to be handed on from the project to those who will be using, running and maintaining the system in the future; receives a project valuation report that reviews the conduct of the project and considers what lessons can be learnt; arranges for a post-implementation review to be held at the appropriate time and formally closes the project; and hands the resulting system over to the service manager and the users.

Managing all products as a single configuration is referred to generally as *configuration management*. This approach allows all participants to see the entire project as a configuration, where there is structure to the management of all information relating to the project. Configurations could be loaded onto databases and accessed by both internal and external staff. This presents the possibility of knowledge capture and ultimately knowledge management.

GLOBALIZATION

PRINCE Alternative: PMI PMBOK

PRINCE is not alone in offering a structured framework for managing projects. An equally popular approach giving advice on the successful completion of projects comes from the Project Management Institute (PMI). PMI offers its *Project Management Body of Knowledge* (PMBOK), which lists the roles and skills of project managers in much the same way as PRINCE lists the steps for effective project management. The PMI cites its mission as advancing the profession of project management, and was recognized by the US ANSI as an Accredited Standard Developer in 1988.

In PMBOK, PMI has a framework for professional development that describes the clusters of knowledge, skills, abilities, and other personal characteristics relevant to most, if not all, types of project. These skills can be acquired and improved through training and development programmes for project managers. PMI promotes project management as an individual skill, which must be based on a sound body of knowledge, and is directed towards the development of professional standards of both ability and conduct. PMI qualifications are available to employers as an indication of the fitness of an individual to manage projects.

The *PMBOK Guide's* fourth edition was released in 2008, and was a significant update as the body of knowledge had grown substantially. Like PRINCE, the PMBOK document seeks to spread and standardize project management practices, and since mid-2007 nearly a half-million *PMBOK Guides* have been purchased from the PMI website, or distributed to PMI members. The Institute of Electrical and Electronics Engineers has adopted the *PMBOK Guide* as IEEE Standard 1490 to further promote its adoption.

CRITICAL PERSPECTIVE

Project Management Frameworks

The description of PRINCE gives some idea of the meaning of a project management framework or cookbook. It shows the extent of the detailed descriptions and approaches contained within PRINCE and similar frameworks such as PMBOK.

Some organizations adopt the PRINCE approach in full, whereas others apply only parts which they integrate with internal procedures. This is due largely to the complete nature of PRINCE, as it can be seen as a sledgehammer to crack a nut; smaller, simpler projects do not need the complete formal framework for successful completion. Experienced project managers know the importance of the key steps that PRINCE and PMBOK represent, and so they intuitively manage their projects well. Without this experience, projects can and often do go astray.

Another criticism often levelled at systems such as PRINCE is that they do not address the nature of management structures, nor what software to use for project planning. They cover only the broad approach to the management of a project, and the stages and processes necessary to bring a project to completion. Such aspects of the organizational design and which specific tools are needed to meet the key elements in the framework must be addressed separately and decisions made by the project board. This detail of guidance is beyond PRINCE, but is often needed in organizations inexperienced in project management.

Similarly, the frameworks ensure only that a firm covers the necessary steps; they do not offer the most elegant solution for a particular project.

The key point is that complex projects require a formal process to ensure that all aspects are covered, but often a project is too small to warrant the full application of PRINCE or PMBOK.

SHORT CASE 11.2

The Human Genome Project

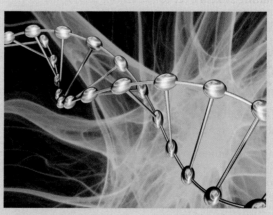

Source: © Science Photo Library

One of the most remarkable scientific undertakings in recent years has been the human genome project (HGP). 'The ultimate goal of this initiative is to understand the human genome' and 'knowledge of the human as necessary to the continuing progress of medicine and other health sciences as knowledge of human anatomy has been for the present state of medicine.' The aim is to establish a map of the human genes, and then enable the identification of common variations that could be linked to the increased likelihood of specific diseases such as cancer or diabetes.

The $3 billion project, formally started in 1990, was a 13-year US National Institute of Health and UK Welcome Trust funded initiative involving many international collaborators in universities and research centres from the United States, the United Kingdom, Japan, France, Germany, and China, as well as private firms. Initially the project was to last 15 years, but this was shortened as new technologies accelerated progress.

The specific goals were to:

- Determine the sequence of the 3 billion chemical base pairs in human DNA (consisting of protein combinations made up of four types, labelled A, T, C and G).
- Identify and appreciate the role of the 20,000–25,000 genes in human DNA (genes are the active significant part of the complete DNA sequence)

- Store and make available this information in accessible databases
- Develop tools to analyse the databases
- Involve private firms in developing the sequence and exploiting its potential
- Address the major ethical, legal and social issues arising from the project

Benefits of the project emerged even before the work was complete, as new tests were established for common genetic diseases such as breast cancer, liver disease and cystic fibrosis.

Organizing the work has been a major undertaking in project management, not only in determining who carries out what work, but also in how it is funded and how it might be exploited commercially.

Questions

1 How do you think the project goals set out above were developed into a more complete plan?
2 What problems do you think the project planners had in establishing their plan at the start, when they knew that the technologies they would employ needed to be developed as part of the project itself?

Source: US Department of Energy Genome Program, http://genomics.energy.gov.

Project Management Tools

Project management frameworks such as PRINCE ensure that all the steps in the project life cycle are completed in a controlled and organized way. This is valuable in the management of a project, as it clearly identifies the relevant players and key milestones for the project. However, PRINCE does not go into the detail of planning the work for the project – just the major processes of the project itself. To enable the detailed planning and management of the project, there is a set of specific project management tools that can be employed. All of these involve generating plans and ensuring they are followed, or at least make the managers aware of when the plan is not being followed so that appropriate action can be taken.

This section will look at these project planning and monitoring techniques.

Project Planning

At the heart of project management is planning or – more accurately – coordinating activities in terms of timing and understanding the associated costs.

Planning should be considered only as a tool, as the project still has to be controlled and managed using appropriate measures and monitoring systems to ensure that the timings established in the plan occur.

Developing project plans is essentially a process of continuously opening up boxes to reveal more and more detail about the project – a bit like peeling back the layers of an onion. The PRINCE methodology gives us the outer layer, but we need to keep delving ever deeper until we have sufficient detail to map all the steps needed to complete the project. This is rarely simple; as there are often different ways to tackle an activity, each option may change the other activities needed to complete the project. For example, in building a bridge it is possible to choose to pour concrete sections on site as needed, but these take time to set. If the sections are made off site, they can be used as soon as they are delivered. The project manager needs to consider a wide range of things in deciding which route to adopt.

Work breakdown structure (WBS): statement of all the work that has to be completed in a project.

Developing a project plan is often made more complex when projects span several different organizations and involve many individuals and parties. The planning process can become unstructured, as plans often need to be updated as the work progresses.

The **work breakdown structure (WBS)** is a statement of all the work that has to be completed in a project. The project manager works closely with the other members of

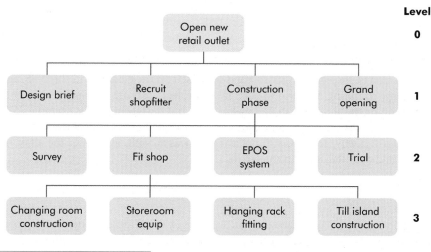

Figure 11.9 Work breakdown structure (WBS)

Table 11.1 Responsibility matrix for Smart Togs shop opening (extract of fit shop phase)

Phase/tasks (partial)	Responsible staff				
	Mike	**Jane**	**Harry**	**Melvin**	**Wendy**
3. Construction phase					
3.1 Survey					
3.2 Fit shop					
3.2.1 Changing room construction	R			I	
3.2.2 Storeroom equip			R	C	A
3.2.3 Hanging rack fitting			I		R
3.2.4 Till island construction		R		C	A
3.3 EPOS system					
3.4 Trial					

R = responsible; C = consult; A = assist; I = inform.

the project team to identify all work tasks. Major work elements are broken down into smaller components, and another level of detail is added: see Figure 11.9, which is for the Smart Togs company's opening of a new shop. Perhaps the most important contributor to delay in projects is the omission of work that is essential to the successful completion of the project. The WBS is essential for the project, as it is the document that lists the packages (or chunks) of work which need to be done for the project to be completed.

Each work package will consist of activities. An *activity* is the smallest unit of work effort, consuming both time and resources, that a project manager can schedule and control. Each package of work in the WBS must have an *owner* who is responsible for doing the work. Each task, in turn, must also have an owner. Ownership avoids confusion in the execution of activities, and assigns responsibility for timely completion. If an activity is without an owner, it is unlikely to get done. This also helps the PM track the project as it crosses between different organizations or functional groups that may be the source of conflict. The WBS can be redrawn as a *responsibility matrix* (Table 11.1) to show who is responsible for each activity, and when it changes hands. The project manager can focus on these interfaces, once they are identified; they are often sources of problems, as communication may not be perfect across the organization units. PRINCE highlights these through its stage boundary process.

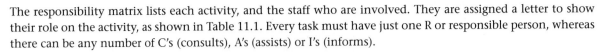

The responsibility matrix lists each activity, and the staff who are involved. They are assigned a letter to show their role on the activity, as shown in Table 11.1. Every task must have just one R or responsible person, whereas there can be any number of C's (consults), A's (assists) or I's (informs).

Once defined, the WBS becomes the basis of the project, and so it must be accurate; any errors or omissions will have serious knock-on effects. Project budgets are then set, based on the elements in the WBS, and so the impact of errors relates not only to timing, but also to cost. If the project costs are unreliable, then the impact on the contracting organization or the sponsor can be catastrophic, and far reaching. For example, Wembley Stadium was the subject of long delays as the main contractor and subcontractor for the steel work argued about who was responsible. Both suffered greatly, and it is still unclear who was at fault, even after the affair had degenerated into a series of claims and counterclaims in the courts.

Developing Budget Plans

Budgets are very important for project management. Because of the temporary nature of projects, there is no source of funds other than those assigned to the project and the activities in the WBS, and so the process of budgeting is more than just estimating the possible total cost of the project. Some firms have highly developed methods for estimating budgets, depending on their experience and the nature of what needs estimating. Architects, for example, can take the area of a building and multiply by a figure to give a very good approximation of the costs for normal construction. Similarly, software producers' estimates of budget are based on the number of lines of code required, and are calculated using standardized values.

As a project continues, a common method for monitoring progress is to compare the money spent on each activity against the budget allocated for that activity. Failure to assign the right funds to an activity at the beginning of the project means that later it may overspend. Then it either has to be completed in a different (cheaper) way, or needs to be funded from the budget of another activity. If the entire project has been underbudgeted at the outset, then this will lead to a cost overrun.

There are two ways for developing budgets: top-down and bottom-up.

Top-down Budgeting

One approach to setting budgets is to ask the senior managers to predict the cost. They draw on their experience, and formulate an overall guide figure for the project as a whole. This can then be given to others to divide the total amounts into ever-finer detail, and allocate them to work packages and activities. This is called breaking down the cost, and results in a *cost breakdown structure*. This is similar to developing the work breakdown structure mentioned earlier, and the two activities often happen at the same time.

A problem with this approach is that often it amounts to little more than senior management guesswork, and even if the overall budget is approximately correct, errors may creep in as the budget is broken down and allocated to work packages and activities.

Bottom-up Budgeting

With bottom-up budgeting, the individual elements of the work breakdown structure are costed separately. The overall project budget can then be calculated. These budgets can be very accurate, as each element represents a well-defined piece of work. Another benefit is that there are many people involved in developing these budgets, ensuring activities are not neglected. Also, there are benefits from including stakeholders early on, as their support and investment of time help the smooth running of the project itself.

However, developing a complete list of the tasks involved in the project can be difficult, and there is often pressure from senior management to cut budgets after they have been set. This can cause problems later in delivering all the stages of the project.

Top-down is more common than bottom-up, as senior managers see the importance of controlling the budgeting process and the organization as a whole. Also, it is such an important task that responsibility is rarely delegated to juniors.

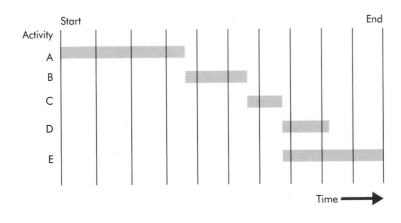

Figure 11.10 Gantt chart

Scheduling Projects

Project Visualization Tools

Sometimes known as bar charts, **Gantt charts** are the simplest representation of project timing. Time is shown across the bottom of the chart, and the vertical axis lists the activities of the WBS. The activity start and durations are shown as coloured bars running across the chart, as shown in Figure 11.10. Gantt charts are easy to follow, but have one major drawback, in that they do not show relationships between activities, giving purely a picture of the timing.

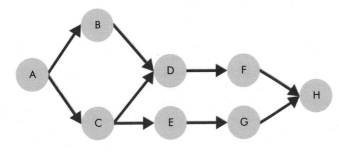

Figure 11.11 Network activity diagram: activity on node representation

Network Approaches

Gantt charts can be annotated to include information on the order of relationships between the project tasks. There are different ways of showing this information, but, regardless of the method used, the plan should show the interaction or dependence of events, and allow distinctions to be made between activities (things that need to be done), events (things that happen) and milestones (project-tracking or control points).

A *network diagram* representing a project is shown in Figure 11.11. The activities are represented by the nodes, and are given letters to identify them, but the order in which they need to be completed is shown by the lines. For example, activity A can start at once, and proceed without waiting for any other activity. Activities B and C, though, cannot start until activity A is finished, and similarly activity D needs both B and C to have completed before it can be started. The project will be finished only when all the activities are complete, with H being the last. This representation of the activity order is logical, as some jobs cannot be started before others are finished. If the project is to build a new house, the walls cannot be built until the foundations are laid, and similarly work on the roof cannot start until the walls are built.

There are two different sorts of notation used in network approaches: *activity on node*, as in Figure 11.11, and *activity on arrow*, as shown in Figure 11.12. This chapter will use both types of diagram, but the method of calculation is the same; it is just the notation that differs. It is very important that you know which one you are using, and do not mix them up.

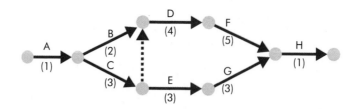

Figure 11.12 Network activity diagram: activity on arrow representation showing dummy activity

For some networks, dummy activities need to be used when there are two different paths in the network which are separate but dependent on one another. For instance, in Figure 11.12, activity D cannot start until both B and C are finished. To show this dependence, a dummy link needs to be shown, using a dotted line.

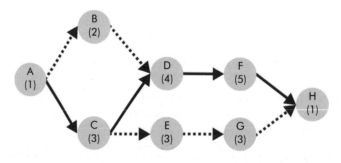

Figure 11.13 The critical path for a project network

The Critical Path Method

The *critical path method (CPM)* is a project management tool that makes use of the network diagram. The first valuable role of the CPM technique is to identify the longest train of activities through the project network. As we saw above, some activities cannot start until others are finished, and if we add these together end to end, they show us the time needed to complete these tasks. The longest path through the network is known as the **critical path**, as it will determine the total time taken for the project to be completed. Activities that lie on the critical path need careful monitoring, as any delay will extend the end date for the whole project.

> **Critical path:** the chain of activities that determines the total duration of a project from start to finish.

Figure 11.13 shows a network, with the times for each activity. If the times are added together through the network, it is easy to see that the longest path is A C D F H, and it needs 14 days to complete these activities. The possible paths and their times are shown in the following table.

Path	Times	Duration of path
A B D F H	1 + 2 + 4 + 5 + 1	13
A C D F H (critical path)	1 + 3 + 4 + 5 + 1	14
A C E G H	1 + 3 + 3 + 3 + 1	11

> **Float:** the spare time an activity has before it becomes part of the critical path. Allows rescheduling without impact.

> **Slack:** the spare time an activity has before it will become on the critical path.

Note the way the critical path is highlighted in the diagram. Activities not on the critical path have what is called **float** (or **slack**) time, which can be used without affecting the total length of the project. We need to be careful because if a non-critical path activity is delayed too much, it will then form a new critical path and so impact the entire project duration.

The critical path can be identified by inspection, but there is a rule that takes away any chance of our missing a path in the network. We start by working out the *earliest start times* (EST) for the activities through the network: work forwards from the first activity,

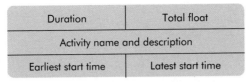

Duration	Total float
Activity name and description	
Earliest start time	Latest start time

Figure 11.14 A node layout showing useful data on a network diagram

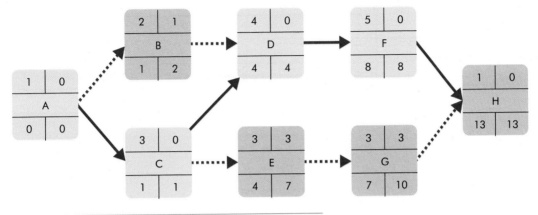

Figure 11.15 Network diagram showing critical path and activity float

adding the times for each of the activities and recording them. This gives the earliest possible start times for the activities. This calculation is then repeated backwards, starting with the completion time for the last activity, based on the longest path through the network. This gives the *latest start time* (LST) for each activity – the latest time it can start without affecting the total project duration. The critical path is the route through the network which has matching LST and EST times, and this is of course the longest path. Activities on the critical path have no slack or spare time, and must start when the previous activity is finished, otherwise the project will overrun.

Figure 11.14 shows the way we can now redraw the nodes of the network diagram to show all the information we would like to see at a glance, including the name of the activity, its duration, EST, LST and float. Using the convention in Figure 11.14, the network example from Figure 11.13 can now be redrawn, and is shown in Figure 11.15. It becomes clear which activities lie on the critical path and also how much slack or float time is available for each activity.

The forward and backward calculation approach effectively determines the float of activities – the amount of slack time between having to start the activity and getting the project finished on time, and the earliest possible time the activity could be started. This is useful for balancing the demand on resources without disturbing the total project time. For example, we might have two activities needing bricklayers scheduled for the same week. However, if one of the activities had a week of slack, then we could delay its start and use the same team for one run of two weeks instead of having to recruit two sets of bricklayers. This would be cheaper and less complex for us.

CPM: Crashing Times and Costs

Another important use of CPM is in exploring *trade-offs* between project time and cost. It is common for the duration of an activity to be reduced by extra investment (perhaps in more people, or in more or better machines), and CPM allows the project manager to balance this extra cost and total project time. A term used in this approach is *crashing* an activity. A crashed activity cannot be reduced further, no matter how much extra money is spent. For example, there is nothing we can do to cut the time for baking biscuits in the factory once we have invested in a new production line and ovens; biscuits need time to bake. Similarly, you cannot put more female resources together to help gestate a human baby quicker than 9 months.

A common example is when cost penalties arise as projects exceed certain dates and the manager has to determine whether it is worth spending money on crashing the project or taking the penalty.

University Gas Pipe

The table below describes a project to lay a new gas pipe across the university campus:

Activity	Precedes	Normal time (days)	Crash cost per day	Crash time (days)
A	B, C	10	50	6
B	D	6	30	3
C	E	2	–	2
D	F	4	40	3
E	D	6	80	4
F	–	8	100	5

Problem:

(a)   Construct the activity-on-node network diagram.

(b)   Determine the ESTs, the LSTs, slack, the project duration and the critical path activities.

(c)   Use the crash cost information to redesign the project so that the work will be completed two days earlier, in time for the start of term.

Approach:

(a)   Draw the network diagram so that the precedence of the activities can be established.

(b)   Record the duration, calculate the forward and backward path lengths, and hence the EST, LST and floats. The critical path is where there is zero float.

(c)   Concentrating on the critical path, try and reduce individual activity times using the cheapest option, taking care that the critical path is not extended to another route through the network.

Solution:

(a)   Draw the diagram (Figure 11.16) by starting with the first activity and working forwards so that the logic shown in the table is transferred to the diagram. So, from above, activity A is first, and must be completed before B and C can start. D has to follow B and E, and E follows just C. F follows D alone.

(b)   The duration of each activity is written in the node as shown (A lasts 10 days, etc.). Use these times to work out the EST for each activity/node. So the earliest B and C can start is when A is finished, i.e. after 10 days. D can start after B, which would be 16 days (10 for A and 6 for B), but actually D cannot start until E is finished, which cannot be until 18 days (10 for A, 2 for C and 6 for D). F starts 4 days after D (D starts after 18 and takes 4 days itself). The total duration of the project is 30 days, as we need to add the 8 days for F to its start time of 22. This completes the forward pass.

To work out the LST, start at the end of the project with F and work backwards. As the project will take 30 days in total, the latest that F can start without the end time changing is 22 (30 less the 8 days for F). The LST for D is 18 (4 days before F needs to start). E must start at latest 6 days before D starts, which is 12 (18 for D, less 6 for E), and similarly for C and A: their LSTs are the same as their ESTs – they are on the critical path, as we can see. B, on the other hand, has an LST of 12, as it has to be finished for D to start, and D has to start at latest on day 18. Hence B can start on day 12 and still be finished without delaying D.

Where the EST and LST are the same, this is the critical path, shown in Figure 11.16 in bold.

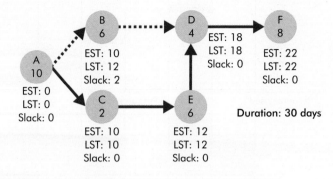

Figure 11.16 Network diagram before crashing, showing the critical path

(c) The project duration needs to be reduced by 2 days. The cheapest and so the first choice to reduce the critical path is D, which is reduced by 1 day at a cost of £40. We should check and see whether the critical path has changed, in this case whether B has lost its float. Figure 11.17 is the new network diagram. B still has its 2 days' slack, so there is no change in the critical path. Now we can look for the next day to take out of the project.

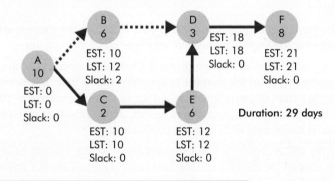

Figure 11.17 First step: showing network reduced by 1 day from D

D cannot be reduced any further, and so we need to look for the next cheapest on the critical path, which is A, which can be reduced by 1 day at a cost of £50. The new network is shown in Figure 11.18.

Final result: the project has been reduced by 2 days, at a total cost of £90.

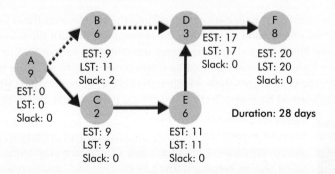

Figure 11.18 Solution showing the crashed network

The key point is that we can nearly always change the duration of an activity by spending money. However, the project manager has to know whether this is a good use of his or her limited funds.

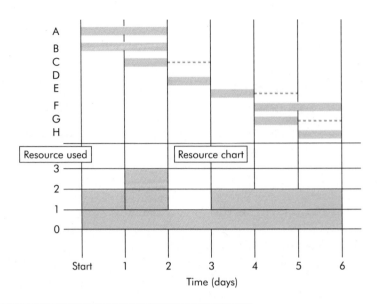

Figure 11.19 GANTT chart showing slack times and resource utilization

Resource Allocation

As well as defining the timing of activities and the overall length of the project, another important activity in scheduling is planning which resources are needed, and how much of each one.

If we think again about the London 2012 Olympics and Crossrail projects, in both cases it was realized early on that they would be unable to recruit the number of specialist trades that they needed. As a result, both project teams set up apprentice schemes to ensure they had sufficient trained resources to complete the project plan. An alternative approach to acquiring or training the necessary skilled resources is to examine the project plan and see whether changes to it might help with resource constraints.

Figure 11.19 shows how Gantt charts can be extended to show the loading of resources, or in this case the number of employees needed for the project. The table at the foot of the bar chart uses the same time axis to show the resource demand throughout the project.

The load diagram shows the usage of the resources as the project develops, and some constraints can be easily identified. In Figure 11.19 it is clear that we need three workers on the second day, but the rest of the project could be completed with one or two per day.

Resource Levelling

The above example is based on resource allocation against the earliest start times for the activities, but given the slack in the project it may be possible to schedule the activities to smooth the resource demand. The reason why we expressly calculated the float or slack time before was not only so that we could establish the critical path, but also to help identify when activities could be rescheduled to help with the loading of resources. Looking again at Figure 11.19, the dotted lines show which activities can be rescheduled within their float or slack time. Moving these activities would have no effect on the critical path or total length of the project.

> **Resource levelling:** the practice of using float to improve the resources needed in a project.

Figure 11.20 shows that by considering the timing of one activity we can level the resource needed. By delaying the start time of activity C, the project can now be completed with a level resource usage of just two employees. **Resource levelling** has the advantage of keeping staffing levels constant, and so reducing the number of resources that need to be moved on and off the project.

❶ Stop and Think

2   How might the ideas covered in this chapter on project scheduling help you complete a group project for your course?

SHORT CASE 11.3

Bolshoi Ballet Renovation

The world famous Bolshoi Ballet Company was founded in 1776 as the Imperial Bolshoi Theatre of Moscow. Its home is now in Theatre Square, Moscow, and the current building was designed by architect Andrei Mikhailov and built in 1824 to replace the Petrovka Theatre, which was destroyed by fire in 1805.

The Bolshoi Theatre was closed for a planned four-year restoration in 2005, but the project was beset with numerous problems. The theatre has been renovated several times in its history, but this project was the largest, and was initially budgeted at a cost of 15 billion roubles ($610 million). However, once engineers started work, they identified significant weaknesses with the existing foundation, which meant that 75% of it needed to be replaced. Additionally they discovered a river flowing through the foundation, which needed to be diverted.

Source: © Getty Images

Much of the extra work on the foundation was the result of the unexpectedly poor condition of previous restoration work.

The renovation is intended to restore the theatre to its original acoustics, which were substantially changed during Soviet era renovations, and to do this the theatre's interior has been totally removed. This includes the 19th-century wooden fixtures, silver stage curtain and red velvet banquettes, which have all been removed for repair. The two-headed eagle of the original Russian coat of arms has been reinstalled in place of the Soviet hammer and sickle that was there before.

The project was further complicated by the involvement of the Russian authorities, who funded the work, with their sense of national pride and artistic perfection adding to the stringent quality standards the project had to meet. These stakeholders have insisted that the main purpose of the project is to create an international treasure with excellent acoustics and performance ambience. As a result, the project saw important changes to the specification as it developed. Each change meant a significant rethink of the project, which in some cases led to the reworking of completed stages. Best estimates are that the total cost of the project is likely to have exceeded the original cost at least tenfold, and to have taken twice as long as planned.

Questions

1 What were the sources of changes to the project plan? Think about both those from the uncertain nature of the work itself and also those from artistic and governance interventions.
2 Which of the changes you have identified could have been managed, and which were beyond the realm of the project manager?
3 How might the project manager have kept track of how the project was developing, and what would you like to see reported on a regular basis if you were in charge?

Sources: http://rt.com/news/bolshoi-theatre-restoration-delay/; www.bolshoi.ru/en/theatre/reconstruction/

Managing Project Progress

Given that there are three objectives for effective project management – to meet time deadlines, to stick to the costs set in the budget, and to meet the requirements set out in the specification – and given that the project may consist of a number of work packages, each with numerous activities, it can be difficult to report progress against this complex situation without giving long, detailed explanations.

For example, consider a project with a budget of £4 million, lasting 24 months, and with four goals set in the project specification. If the project is about halfway in month 12, the firm has spent £3 million, and one objective has been

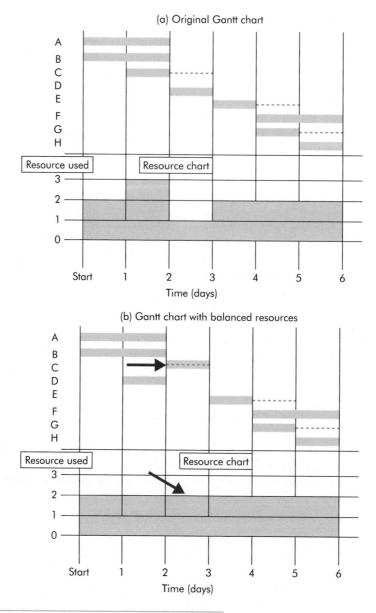

Figure 11.20 Balancing resources by moving activities within slack

reached: is the project on time, within budget, and to specification? It's not possible to say with this informa-

tion. To be able to give a clear explanation, the project manager must concentrate on the stakeholder group being addressed. Each group may have a different view of how the project's progress should be expressed. An internal audience may focus on cost, an external stakeholder may focus on more on time, and the customer on all three objectives. In order to avoid ambiguity and information overload, there is a method that attempts to clarify the situation objectively: it is referred to as **earned value reporting (EVR)**.

Earned value reporting (EVR): a means of monitoring projects, based on key measures of completion against estimated cost or schedule.

Variance and Earned Value

Earned value is a tool to report how much work has been accomplished on a project, and can be used as a simple way to monitor progress. The term *variance* is used to describe deviation from the planned schedule or budget. Both the schedule and budget need to be considered simultaneously because:

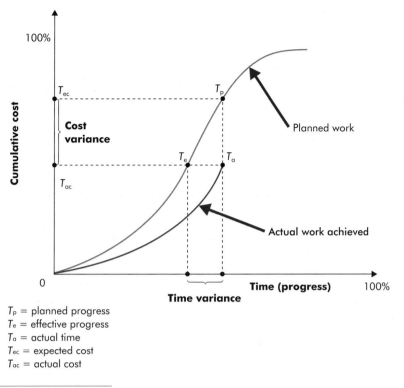

T_p = planned progress
T_e = effective progress
T_a = actual time
T_{ec} = expected cost
T_{ac} = actual cost

Figure 11.21 Cost–schedule comparison

- *Cost variance* refers only to the budget, and does not measure the differences or variances between scheduled work to be completed and actual work completed
- *Schedule variances* provide a comparison between planned work completed and actual work completed, but do not report on cost.

These are shown in Figure 11.21, which compares the cost of the project with the time the project has been under way. The figure reviews progress at time T_a, and shows the project is currently behind schedule, as progress is less than planned. However, the expected cost to date (T_{ec}) was forecast in the project plan, and is less than the total actual cost (T_{ac}), as shown in the diagram. If we take the curve and extend it to the end, as in Figure 11.22, the project may be looking at late delivery, and in this case it looks like it may not be able to stick to the budget either. This is only speculation, but it shows how the EVR tool provides early warning of problems.

A difficulty in comparing actual and budgeted expenditure is that, for a given period, the comparison fails to take into account the amount of work achieved in relation to the cost incurred. To help with this problem, the earned value of the work done (often expressed as the *value completed*) is found by multiplying the estimated percentage completion of work for each task/activity in progress by the planned cost of those tasks/activities. This can then be used to make an estimate of overall completion of the project, by adding all these calculations for all tasks completed plus those in progress.

In practice, there are some important questions to ask about a project, that help in understanding the relationships between cost and work:
- Actual costs are less than the budget. Is the project doing well, or is it behind schedule?
- The project's actual costs are higher than budgeted, and the project is only halfway complete. What is the project likely to cost at completion?
- The project manager continually tells us not to worry about the cost overruns. The rest of the work will cost less than budgeted. Is this probable?

EVR charts can be used to derive certain measures that allow us to quickly identify project status and so answer these questions. Earned value is accurately measured as *budgeted cost of work performed* (BCWP), and is normally

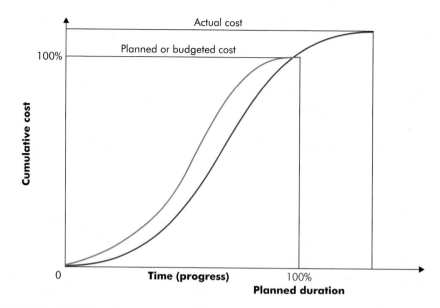

Figure 11.22 Cost–schedule speculation

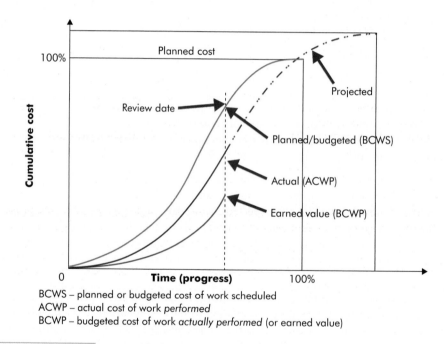

Figure 11.23 Earned value chart

compared with the *actual cost of the work performed* (ACWP) and *budgeted cost of work scheduled* (BCWS), as shown in Figure 11.23.

Typically, variances are defined so that they will give a negative number when the project is behind, or over budget. It is also possible to project the actual costs forward, with the assumption that if the performance continues, this is how the overall project might turn out. We can see that we are able to calculate the cost variance, as it is the difference between the amount budgeted for the work and that performed to date: budgeted cost of work performed or earned value (BCWP) minus the actual work performed (ACWP):

$$\text{Cost variance (CV)} = \text{BCWP} - \text{ACWP}$$

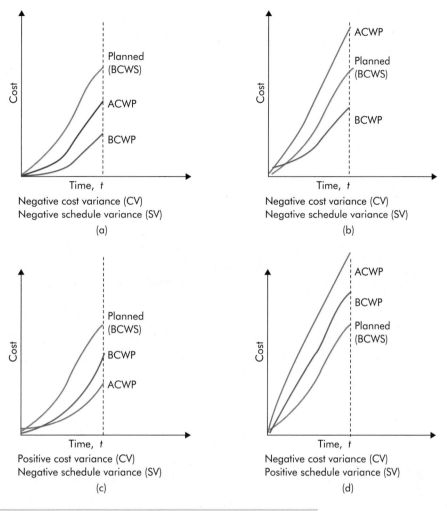

Figure 11.24 Possible arrangements of ACWP, BCWP and the planned (BCWS)

Similarly, we would also be interested in the variance in schedule, calculated as the difference between the budgeted cost of work performed or earned value (BCWP) and the budgeted cost of work scheduled (BCWS):

$$\text{Schedule variance} = \text{BCWP} - \text{BCWS}$$

The different situations relating to the variances are shown in Figure 11.24. Note the way that the different measures give an indication not only of the source of the problem but also of its severity.

Tracking Project Ratios

Combining the values of variance into index values tells us even more quickly how the project is progressing. In general, indices of 1.0 show the project to be on schedule, whereas values below 1.0 are unfavourable. Again, as above, we are interested in both the cost and the schedule and so have one index for each, and also an overall measure for the project. These are:

$$\text{Cost performance index (CPI)} = \frac{\text{BCWP}}{\text{ACWP}}$$

$$\text{Schedule performance index (SPI)} = \frac{\text{BCWP}}{\text{BCWS}}$$

$$\text{Cost–schedule index} = \text{CPI} \times \text{SPI}$$

With these indices there is no need for a long, detailed explanation of progress, and the trend in value taken over time can be tracked. If the values are within accepted limits, then there is no need for managerial action.

EVR: Project Management Tracking Indices

Given a project with:

ACWP = £1,500

BCWS = £1,000

BCWP = £800 (earned value)

Problem: *Calculate the CSI index, and determine whether it is managerially satisfactory.*

Approach/solution:

$$CSI = \frac{£800}{£1,500} \times \frac{£800}{£1,000}$$
$$= 0.427$$

So CSI < 1, indicating a problem. We can see that we have spent nearly twice as much as planned for the work performed so far (CPI), and also that we are running behind schedule (SPI).

The key point is that while we may have the most elaborate project plans and budgets, we need to be able to track progress, and tie this directly into what we expected to have achieved. Failure to do so means that the project is effectively out of control.

Managing People

This chapter started by talking about how many companies are re-engineering their functionally oriented organizations in order to focus on key business processes, and enable project-based working. Companies such as General Electric have stressed the need to promote flexible organization: 'The challenge, for us, is to strip and break down walls that cramp people, inhibit creativity and waste time' (GE's Annual Report, 2010). Companies such as DuPont, IBM, Hewlett-Packard, Renault and GM have launched major efforts to create high-performance teams using techniques such as kaizen and Six Sigma (explored in more depth in Chapter 13).

Within project-based organizations the pressure to perform is even greater, as each project is temporary and so needs to quickly set up, define its own structure and style, and then begin to perform. This section will look briefly at the ideas surrounding building and managing effective teams, as these are highly important to project managers trying to accomplish their three performance criteria of cost, time and specification.

Project Teams

Teams are groups of individuals who cooperate to carry out a joint task. They may be assigned to specific work roles, or operate a more flexible system where roles are shared. A *project team* is a group organized to work together to accomplish a set of objectives that cannot be achieved effectively by individuals. Organizational barriers, such as infrastructure, policies and procedures, all have an impact on how the team performs.

Forming Teams

There are some basic principles in team formation, and these are referred to as the *team paradigm*:
- Teams are task oriented rather than functionally focused
- Teams hold a single organization view, which promotes unity rather than conflict
- Teams have participative leadership rather than remote supervision
- In teams, power, conflict and emotion are seen as anti-productive forces.

So lines of command and control are replaced by links based on influence and common interest.

Three attributes are usually considered when building membership of a project team:
- Technological, business or commercial skill (professional orientation)
- Time and cost consciousness (goal orientation)
- Ability to work with different types of people (team orientation).

In choosing members of a team, technical skill is usually the first consideration, with the second attribute time and cost consciousness. It is often the case with operations managers and engineers that business or organizational skills are a poor relation to their armoury of technical skills. Indeed, 'soft' or people-related skills are often viewed with less enthusiasm than the 'harder' technical skills, but we have already seen the nature of projects, and the focus on a single goal demands that these are all equally important.

Team Roles

As a team is made up of a number of individuals, they typically include many patterns of behaviour, and a key aspect of success is ensuring the members interact effectively. This can be described as creating a *team spirit*, and is a source of synergy. Successful teams refer to themselves and colleagues in complimentary terms, as together they can achieve more than the sum of their individual contributions. There are four interlocking principles that guide team designers:
- There is a balance between functional roles and team roles
- Members of teams are able to adjust themselves to the relative strengths within the team, both in expertise and in specific team roles
- Personal qualities make team members suited to some team roles and weak in others
- A team can deploy its technical resources to best advantage only when it has a full range of team roles to ensure efficient teamwork.

There are a number of frameworks used to identify the roles. One of the most useful is that of Belbin (1981), which defined the characteristics of team members. These frameworks argue that most of the roles need to be present for a team to be effective. For example, a team made up solely of manager types, who are strong on coordinating, managing resources and monitoring the project, will not make progress without the creative and diligent types that design and carry out the work.

Belbin's team roles:
- *Plant*: creative, imaginative, unorthodox . . .
- *Resource investigator*: enthusiastic, communicative, extrovert . . .
- *Coordinator*: mature, confident . . .
- *Shaper*: challenging, dynamic, thrives on pressure . . .
- *Monitor evaluator*: sober, strategic and discerning . . .
- *Teamworker*: cooperative, mild, perceptive . . .
- *Implementer*: disciplined, reliable . . .
- *Completer*: painstaking, conscientious, anxious . . .
- *Specialist*: single-minded, self-starting . . .

Leading Teams

Leadership is crucial in projects for inspiration, motivation and direction. At its purest it generates an emotional connection between the leader and the team. There are various interpretations of leadership, which are summarized in Figure 11.25.

The difference between a manager and a leader is that leadership implies inspiration and directing from the front, whereas management is concerned with control. There are many examples of leadership, with the best political leaders able to mobilize support around their ideas and visions. They rarely instruct their colleagues, but inspire support based on the ideas they communicate.

Leaders have been shown to adopt a combination of the following roles when needed:

Directing: autocratic style, appropriate to use with people who lack competence but are committed to their work

Coaching: appropriate to use with people who have competence but lack commitment. A project manager should encourage decision-making, although the style would be directional. Explanations for decisions would be given, and suggestions would be solicited.

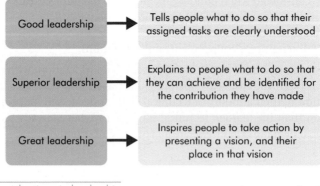

Figure 11.25 Suggested graduations in leadership

Supporting: appropriate to use with people who have competence but lack motivation. A project manager need not always give direction, as an expert in a discipline will always know better, but support is important to boost confidence.

Delegating: appropriate for people who have both competence and commitment.

Positive leadership is the single greatest factor contributing to a project's success or failure; therefore leadership is one of the most important competencies of a project manager. There are some fundamental leadership qualities among effective project managers:

Style: use of a combination of directive and supportive relationships as appropriate. This is especially useful, because project teams consist of individuals of widely varying expertise.

Analytical: in order to achieve technical project goals, the project manager needs to be analytical, to understand the technical subtleties.

Collaborative: to surmount the boundaries between the organizational units in order to accomplish something in the interest of the larger organization. Avoiding negative criticism; always preferring constructive criticism.

Organizational know-how: project managers need to be sensitive to the needs of the senior managers, recognize cultural barriers, build networks, and develop an organizational insight.

Negotiative: project managers should be accomplished negotiators. They are required to negotiate with the functional department managers for resources – both people and material. They must also negotiate when overcoming obstacles, driving towards project goals, and dealing with poor performance.

Affable: in general, if you are to work with people, then you must be able to get on with them. Getting on means being a good listener, understanding differing points of view, and above all being culturally sensitive. Cultural sensitivity addresses issues of differences and ensuring thoughtfulness and inclusiveness.

❶ Stop and Think

3   Think of a person you regard as a great leader. Do they exhibit all or just some of the roles seen above? Do they need to be exemplary in all to complete their job?

Ending Projects

We have already seen in the PRINCE methodology that the end of a project is equally as critical as the other stages. Ending a project is about ensuring that all the objectives have been met, that the resources and contractual obligations have been completed, that personnel have found new projects to work on, and that the organization has recorded the important aspects learnt in carrying out the project. A key part of this is the *project audit*, which is a formal inquiry into the project to validate the original business feasibility studies, to reassure top management of the completion and effective running of the project, and to confirm the organization's readiness to move on to the next project or phase. An organization needs to stores the lessons learned from one project to apply to another, and prevent making similar mistakes again.

Projects by their nature are temporary, and so each one will have its own measure of success. The primary measure is to what extent it has achieved it objectives. Again, PRINCE makes this exercise of reviewing success an explicit part of the project process. A major reason why projects fail is called *scope creep*; this happens when stakeholders keep changing the specification of the project as it progresses, as demonstrated earlier in the Bolshoi Ballet case. There are many public sector projects where changes in political leadership mean that the aims or content of the project often change. Such revisions to the project goals make managing the work itself virtually impossible, and often work packages become distorted and do not fit together, and so the project eventually becomes unmanageable. An example of this was the UK's attempt at electronic patient records in the National Health Service, where the original aim of digitizing records was constantly revised as the original needs of the family doctor were changed to accommodate hospitals and the changing layers in management systems of the health service.

The key point is that as organizations move towards project-based work, they need to introduce ways to capture and learn experiences for future work, as the individuals may not stay within the firm.

SHORT CASE 11.4

Mr Chai's SQ318 Team and Singapore Airlines

When Mr Jones got on flight SQ318 from Singapore's Changi Airport to London Heathrow after a successful business trip, he was thinking about how he might best run the new luxury hotel project he had just signed. As the trip unfolded, he was given much inspiration.

At first glance, the work of a super-jumbo cabin crew may not seem a good example of a project, which can be defined as a temporary organization with one purpose. However, as the crew members are all brought together for just one trip, and each trip may have a different number of passengers and route, it could be called a project.

What struck Mr Jones most about his flight was the way the In-flight Supervisor, Mr Chai, set a tone of professionalism and focus on service that permeated his crew of 24 and made the trip exceptional. Right from the start, it was clear that this crew was working well as a team, with each knowing their own tasks, but also freely helping each other, and being relaxed and confident in providing for the needs of the customers. Mr Chai came on the intercom as the plane taxied, and as well as the usual safety messages, he introduced the key team members in each cabin, welcomed his guests and in particular the newlyweds in 33E and F, and thanked the passengers for choosing Singapore Airlines.

Mr Chai's leadership style was to lead by example, as he seemed to be all over the plane, serving the food, collecting rubbish and crockery, and chatting with nearly every one of the 450 passengers on the packed flight. Mr Chai's demeanour spread through his colleagues, who all followed his lead – from the very attentive and personal service for the passenger in seat 51C, who didn't get the choice of meal he wanted, but was showered with extra bread rolls and desserts to take his mind off it, to the help given to the families with babies, making the trip as comfortable as possible for them, and also for their neighbouring passengers.

As the plane landed in London, Mr Chai was again on the intercom, passing on the wishes of his crew to the passengers, leaving no one out from those returning home, going on holiday, returning to study after the break, undertaking business, and of course the honeymooners. He received a round of applause from both the passengers and his crew as he finally signed off.

Mr Jones was impressed, and then remembered that Singapore Airlines has received numerous awards for its standard of service, and claims to be 'The World's Most Awarded Airline'. He now understood how they had achieved this, with a focus on service that was epitomized by Mr Chai and delivered by his team.

Questions
1 Think about Belbin's list of team roles, and list which of them relate to the different jobs of the cabin crew.
2 Which of the list of fundamental leadership styles did Mr Chai use on the flight?

Source: written by Alan Pilkington, Royal Holloway; www.singaporeair.com/mediacentre/pacontent/news/NE_5307.jsp

Summary

This chapter has examined project management, an area of growing importance in operations management. It started with a definition that projects are temporary organizations, tasked with carrying out just one purpose. It is important for people involved in projects to appreciate that there is more than one way to look at the project. Often people focus on purely the internal view of achieving the cost, time and performance targets of the project, but neglect the importance of thinking like an outside stakeholder. Looking at the project from the point of the outside stakeholders allows the project management team to meet its commitments to those whom the project ultimately serves.

Projects make unusual demands on the organization, as there are alternative ways in which the firm can be organized to deliver the project. Many organizations are looking to adopt flatter structures, which focus the power to make decisions on front-line staff, and moving towards the project-based organization is one way to achieve this.

Successful project managers need a high level of both technical and leadership skills, including familiarity with scheduling and resource allocation techniques. But while tools such as PRINCE ensure that all the key steps in projects are completed in a controlled manner, project management involves much more than step-by-step problem-solving. There is a high degree of complexity and uncertainty involved in all but the simplest of projects, and understanding teams and developing leadership skills are vital for handling complexity and overcoming uncertainty.

Key Theories

The key theories discussed in this chapter were:

- **Project-based organization** – a shift from functional organization structure, via the matrix organization, to one where the project is the focus of attention.

- **Project management framework** – a structured approach, such as PRINCE or PMBOK, to ensure that all steps are covered and stakeholders considered in completing a project.

- **Critical path management** – an approach to managing projects that focuses on the activities that determine the total length of the project.

- **Belbin's team roles** – a list of team member characteristics, the inclusion of which ensures a balance between doers and planners.

Key Equations

$$\text{Float for an activity} = \text{Latest start time} - \text{Earliest start time}$$

$$\text{Cost variance (CV)} = \text{BCWP} - \text{ACWP}$$

$$\text{Schedule variance} = \text{BCWP} - \text{BCWS}$$

$$\text{Cost performance index (CPI)} = \frac{\text{BCWP}}{\text{ACWP}}$$

$$\text{Schedule performance index (SPI)} = \frac{\text{BCWP}}{\text{BCWS}}$$

$$\text{Cost–schedule index} = \text{CPI} \times \text{SPI}$$

where BCWS = planned or budgeted cost of work scheduled; ACWP = actual cost of work *performed*; and BCWP = budgeted cost of work *actually performed* (or earned value).

Suggested Answers to Stop and Think Questions

1 **Different organization forms for different situations:** (a) The head office, including the sales, IT and accounting departments, are very functionally focused, and so this kind of structure is probably more suited. (b) The commissioning department, which arranges different experts to produce a package of materials, is effectively managing a number of projects simultaneously, and so a matrix structure would work well. (c) Relocating to a new building is a pure project activity, with its temporary structure and single purpose.

2 **Applying project scheduling to an assignment:** Being able to develop and produce a plan for the project, including a schedule to complete by the deadline, is useful in monitoring progress. Regular meetings will show when something is running late and some more resource might be needed to get back on track.

3 **Identifying leadership style:** Leaders come from many different walks of life, and some can be successful with only a few of the roles. Charismatic and autocratic style can be sufficient for political leaders, whereas business leaders normally need to exhibit technical skills to be able to control their organization, and maintain the support and respect of others.

connect™

Review Questions

1 Name the organization styles as they move from the functional to pure project-based form.

2 List the eight processes of the PRINCE framework, and give an example for each one.

3 Why does EVR have both schedule and cost variance elements?

4 List Belbin's team roles, and identify which one(s) you most regularly carry out in class work. Discuss your thoughts with a close colleague.

Discussion Questions

1 Why would an 'outside looking in' approach provide a useful perspective on project management?

2 Discuss three projects you are aware of that have not been delivered on time, or within budget, or have not met the planned outcome or specification. Why did they fail?

3 Why are matrix structures difficult to manage?

4 Are PRINCE and PMBOK the same or very different? Discuss.

5 Using EVR to monitor and report project progress is dependent on the accuracy of the information fed into the measures. Is this an accurate critique?

6 Of all of the competencies and preferred behaviours of a project manager, which do you think are the most difficult to develop or achieve?

Problems

1   Table 11.2 shows a list of activities, with their immediate predecessors and their durations.

Table 11.2 Activity precedence and durations

Activity	Immediate predecessors	Duration (days)
A	–	2
B	–	3
C	A	4
D	A	5
E	C	6
F	D	3
G	D and B	4
H	E	7
I	F	2
J	F and G	3

(a)   Using the information in Table 11.2, construct a Gantt chart.

(b)   Use the information in Table 11.2 to:
   (i)   Draw a critical path network for these using the 'activity on arrow' notation.
   (ii)   Calculate the earliest start times.
   (iii)   Calculate the latest start times.
   (iv)   Calculate slack time.
   (v)   Define the critical path.
   (vi)   Calculate the float time. Given the resource available in Table 11.3, state how the resource requirement could be smoothed by 'floating' some of the activities.

Table 11.3 Resource available

Activity	Number of people
A	2
B	3
C	3
D	4
E	5
F	4
G	5
H	6
I	4
J	4

(c) Table 11.4 shows the times by which the activities in Table 11.2 can be crashed (e.g. A cannot be reduced at all, whereas B can be reduced by 1 day maximum), and the cost of doing so. Is it possible that the project can be finished in 17 days, and if so, how much more would that cost?

Table 11.4 Details of crash times possible and cost

Activity	Days to crash	Cost per day (£)
A	0	–
B	1	60
C	2	80
D	0	–
E	1	40
F	0	–
G	1	90
H	2	90
I	0	–
J	1	20

2 Table 11.5 shows a list of activities, with their immediate predecessors and their durations:

Table 11.5 Activity precedence and durations

Activity	Immediate predecessors	Duration (days)
A	–	3
B	A	2
C	A	4
D	A	5
E	B and C	2
F	C	3
G	D	6
H	E F and G	4
I	H	5

(a) Using the information in Table 11.5, construct a Gantt chart.
(b) Using the data in Table 11.5:
   (i)   Draw a critical path network for these, using the 'activity on node' notation.
   (ii) Calculate the earliest start times.
   (iii) Calculate the latest start times.
   (iv) Calculate slack time.
   (v)   Define the critical path.
   (vi) Calculate the float time. Given the resource available in Table 11.6, state how the resource requirement could be smoothed by 'floating' some of the activities.

Table 11.6 Resource available

Activity	Number of people
A	4
B	2
C	2
D	3
E	5
F	1
G	2
H	4
I	1

(c) Table 11.7 shows the times by which the activities in Table 11.5 can be crashed (e.g. A can be reduced by 1 day maximum, and B not at all), and the cost of doing so. Is it possible that the project can be finished in 20 days, and how much more would that cost?

Table 11.7 Resource available

Activity	Days to crash	Cost per day (£)
A	1	20
B	0	–
C	2	50
D	1	70
E	0	–
F	0	–
G	2	40
H	1	30
I	0	–

3 Table 11.8 shows a list of activities, with their immediate predecessors and their durations.

Table 11.8 Activity precedence and durations

Activity	Immediate predecessors	Duration (days)
A	–	2
B	–	3
C	A	1
D	B	4
E	C and D	1
F	D	3
G	E	2
H	F	4
I	G and H	3

(a) Using the information in Table 11.8, construct a Gantt chart.
(b) Using the data in Table 11.8:
   (i)   Draw a critical path network for these, using the 'activity on node' notation.
   (ii) Calculate the earliest start times.
   (iii) Calculate the latest start times.
   (iv) Calculate slack time.
   (v)   Define the critical path.
   (vi) Calculate the float time. Given the resource available in Table 11.9, state how the resource requirement could be smoothed by 'floating' some of the activities.

Table 11.9 Resource available

Activity	Number of people
A	10
B	20
C	10
D	30
E	40
F	50
G	10
H	30
I	10

(c) Table 11.10 shows the times by which the activities in Table 11.8 can be crashed (e.g. A can be reduced by 1 day maximum, and C not at all), and the cost of doing so. Is it possible that the project can be finished in 15 days, and how much more would that cost?

Table 11.10 Resource available

Activity	Days to crash	Cost per day (£)
A	1	90
B	1	80
C	0	–
D	1	70
E	0	–
F	1	90
G	1	90
H	1	80
I	0	–

4 Based on the project information in Table 11.2 (question 1 above), after 7 days the project should have activities A, B, C and D completed, and 1/6 (16.7%) of activity E completed. Using the budgeted costs, actual costs and percentage completion for each activity given in Table 11.11:
(a) State the BCWS, ACWP and BCWP.
(b) Calculate the schedule variance. Comment on your findings.
(c) Calculate the cost variance. Comment on your findings.

(d) Calculate the CPI. Comment on your findings.
(e) Calculate SPI. Comment on your findings.
(f) Calculate CSI. Comment on your findings.

Table 11.11 earned value information

Activity	Days' duration	Budget (€)	Actual costs (€)	% complete
A	2	600	680	100
B	3	300	270	100
C	4	800	On budget	80
D	5	400	On budget	25
E	6	400		0

5   Based on the project information in Table 11.5 (question 2 above), after 7 days the project should have activities A, B, and C completed, and 4/5 (80%) of activity D completed. Using the budgeted costs, actual costs and percentage completion for each activity given in Table 11.12:
(a) State the BCWS, ACWP and BCWP.
(b) Calculate the schedule variance. Comment on your findings.
(c) Calculate the cost variance. Comment on your findings.
(d) Calculate the CPI. Comment on your findings.
(e) Calculate SPI. Comment on your findings.
(f) Calculate CSI. Comment on your findings.

Table 11.12 Earned value information

Activity	Days' duration	Budget (€)	Actual costs (€)	% complete
A	3	500	300	100
B	2	700	790	100
C	4	300	On budget	80
D	5	400	On budget	80

6   Based on the project information in Table 11.8 (question 3 above), after 5 days the project should have activities A, B, and C completed, and 2/4 (50%) of activity D completed. Using the budgeted costs, actual costs and percentage completion for each activity given in Table 11.13:
(a) State the BCWS, ACWP and BCWP.
(b) Calculate the schedule variance. Comment on your findings.
(c) Calculate the cost variance. Comment on your findings.
(d) Calculate the CPI. Comment on your findings.
(e) Calculate SPI. Comment on your findings.
(f) Calculate CSI. Comment on your findings.

Table 11.13 Earned value information

Activity	Days' duration	Budget (€)	Actual costs (€)	% complete
A	2	9,000	12,000	100
B	3	10,000	21,000	60
C	1	8,000	On budget	100
D	4	20,000	On budget	0

Online **LearningCentre** Visit the Online Learning Centre at **www.mcgraw-hill.co.uk/textbooks/paton** for a range of resources to support your learning.

Further Reading

Andersen, E.S. (2008) *Rethinking Project Management: An Organisational Perspective*, FT Prentice Hall, Harlow.

Davies, A. and Hobday, M. (2005) *The Business of Projects*, Cambridge University Press, Cambridge.

Ensworth, P. (2001) *The Accidental Project Manager: Surviving the Transition from Techie to Manager*, John Wiley, Chichester.

Kerzner, H. (2007) *Project Management: A Systems Approach to Planning, Scheduling and Controlling*, 9th edn, John Wiley, Chichester.

PMI (2008) *A Guide to the Project Management Body of Knowledge (PMBOK Guide)*, 4th edn, Project Management Institute, Newtown Square, PA.

Schmidt, T. (2009) *Strategic Project Management Made Simple: Practical Tools for Leaders and Teams*, John Wiley, Hoboken, NJ.

References

Belbin, M. (1981) *Management Teams*, Heinemann, London.

Davies, A. and Hobday, M. (2005) *The Business of Projects*, Cambridge University Press, Cambridge.

Improving

Contents

JOBS

WANTED
Strategic Operations Development Director

We are a global company undergoing tremendous growth. As Strategic Operations Development Director, you will have a vital role in executing policy and strategic development in our organization. You will be responsible for improvement projects – such as the adoption and implementation of new technology and world-class practices.

This position has responsibility for developing and implementing innovative operations strategy, including: (1) developing and maintaining systems to measure key performances against established standards; (2) liaising and cooperating with management, external providers and standards bodies (e.g. ISO, government bodies); (3) establishing necessary communication strategy for the improvement and awareness of quality and innovation across all departments; (4) coaching and mentoring operations staff; and (5) being responsible for the constant improvement of organizational performance.

The right candidate will have a relevant master's degree with a minimum of five years of experience in an engineering, manufacturing, service, or performance and quality improvement management role. They are likely to have professional qualifications and a chartered status. They should have a successful track record in process improvement, have effective coaching skills, and be able to integrate change management activities within large teams and inspire others.

What does it take to become an Operations Director?

We speak to Martijn De Lange at TNT Post to find out.

Name: Martijn De Lange

Age: 32

Current position: Operations Director, TNT Post UK

Years in role: 1

How did you get into Operations Management?

I was always interested in managing people. During my master's degree in public administration, I was chairman of various student activities, which I really enjoyed and learned a lot from. In my first job I managed 50 postmen directly, and then got into people/operations management.

What about the career attracted you?

It's interesting to get the best out of people. In the end, operations management is all about getting people motivated to do a good job, and I find people interesting.

What other jobs have you done?

Next to the various operational jobs, I also had brief experience as an HR adviser, and I've managed a salesforce and a customer service department.

What was the most useful experience that prepared you for your current role?

In my teenage years and early twenties, I trained to become a professional tennis player. That taught me discipline, and that in the end you will only succeed through hard work.

What's a typical day in the life of an Operations Director?

That's difficult to answer, as this role is so different every day. I might have a board meeting at head office, go to one of my depots, have a meeting on the progress of a main project, and look at the operational results on cost and quality.

What aspects do you like most about your job and why?

As Operations Director you are, on the one hand, directly involved in the day-to-day running of the business. On the other hand, you also have to think about the strategic developments that are needed in the future. All of this involves people, and the combination of this all makes my role very interesting.

What do you consider the ideal skills for your job/role?

You have to be able to combine directness with being interested in people. If I walk through the depots, I always try to show an interest in what everyone is doing, as they all contribute to the overall result.

What are the biggest challenges in your role?

Combining cost savings (always important in operations) with superior quality and looking after people. Every day you need to strike the right balance.

If you weren't an Operations Director, what would you be?

A professional tennis player, hopefully, otherwise I should like to run my own company.

What changes have you seen in your time in the industry?

Mail/post is now a declining market (because of electronic substitutions), which means there is a lot of price pressure. TNT Post UK, though, has been successful in growing in a declining market, and coming up with new initiatives.

Where do you see yourself in ten years' time?

Earlier on in my career I was busier thinking of the next step than I am now, but of course I still have a lot of ambitions. I would like to either become the CEO or run my own business.

12 Performance Management

Learning Outcomes

After reading this chapter, you should be able to:

- Examine the role of performance management in ensuring effective business performance

- Consider how a culture of suitable measurement can be established, and how sustainable performance can be embedded

- Demonstrate a systematic understanding of the processes involved in the development and implementation of performance management systems

- Devise and use performance measures to inform the performance management system

- Assess the benefits and drawbacks inherent in the implementation of performance management systems

- Analyse and evaluate different performance management methodologies

- Synthesise and analyse data and information, and evaluate their relevance and validity in the context of any given organization

W.L. Gore & Associates: Gore-Tex Manufacturer

BUSINESS INTEGRATION

Operational excellence usually means that an organization is doing more with less, and doing it right every day. From supply chain to customer service relationships, the organization is providing superior products or services, or a combination of both. It's also beating the competition with superior operations using its people, assets and technology to compete more effectively in the marketplace.

Overview

W.L. Gore & Associates (UK) Ltd employs nearly 400 associates at sites in Livingston and Dundee, Scotland. Best known as the manufacturer of the

Source: © Jacom Stephens/iStock

Gore-Tex® fabric that provides protection from the elements and enable wearers to remain comfortable across a broad range of activities and conditions, the company actually focuses on four main areas: electronics, fabrics, industrial and medical products.

Founded in 1958 by Americans William and Vieve Gore in the basement of their home, the company was established nine years later in Scotland, in 1967. Virtually all of the company's products are based on just one material, a versatile polymer called ePTFE (expanded polytetrafluoroethylene), which was discovered by the couple's son, Bob, in 1969. Today, the company is still in private hands and has over 9,000 employees worldwide.

Organizational Structure

William Gore first introduced the concept of a *matrix* organization in 1967. He later presented what he termed *cultural principles*. Unlike more traditional management structures, he proposed a flatter organization structure, where everyone shared the same title of 'associate'. He advocated that there should not be chains of command, nor predetermined channels of communication, and leaders should replace the idea of bosses. Associates could then choose to follow leaders, rather than have bosses assigned to them.

Organizational Culture

William articulated four guiding principles for organizing work in the company. He called them fairness, freedom, commitment and 'waterline' (taking risks, but not sinking the ship):

- Fairness to each other and everyone with whom we come in contact
- Freedom to encourage, help, and allow other associates to grow in knowledge, skill, and scope of responsibility
- The ability to make one's own commitments and keep them
- Consultation with other associates before undertaking actions that could impact on the reputation of the company.

In a matrix organization, associates are encouraged to communicate directly with each other, and are accountable to fellow members of their teams. Teams typically organize themselves around opportunities, new product concepts, or businesses. This unusual organizational structure and culture has been shown to be a significant contributor to associate satisfaction and retention.

Corporate and Operational Performance

In March 2010, for the seventh year in a row, the company was named the best company to work for in Scotland, and ranked seventh in the *Sunday Times* list of the Top 100 Companies to Work For in the UK. The *Sunday Times* list is based mainly on the attitudes of almost 150,000 employees from more than 600 UK companies, and assesses a wide range of factors, ranging from employee satisfaction and well-being to company policy on a wide range of benefits.

The continued success of Gore & Associates is attributed to its associates and its unique company culture. There are no line managers, supervisors or operatives at Gore – associates, as employees are called, are all part of strong teams, and are accountable to each other rather than answering to a traditional line manager. Associates are expected to do what is needed to make the whole organization successful. The company measures its success by its ability to make a profit, and by the number of patents it registers. It is so confident of its ability to sustain innovation that it has a policy of not moving out of product areas once their patents expire and other companies begin to compete on price.

Ann Gilles, an associate from the HR team, commented that achieving the *Sunday Times* accolade in such a competitive field is due to the strength of the corporate culture's fundamental beliefs, where trust in the individual engenders engagement and accountability – and delivers results:

> *The innovation that results in our world-leading products comes from the great people in our company, who work together as a team every day. Our corporate philosophy recognizes that it is the associates that deliver successes for the company. Our associates play a very important role in developing products and systems that make a huge contribution to the company's success globally. To top the poll once is an achievement, but to top it seven years in succession is a testament to the associates in our business, who operate in a unique culture.*

Individual Performance

Because individuals are relied on to exercise their own judgement, often after consultation with colleagues, it is crucially important that staff are highly skilled and well informed. It is also vital that the links between individual achievements and business performance are transparent. At Gore, this is achieved through a system of payment that is 100% performance related. Individual earnings are determined by a process of evaluation conducted by colleagues. They are asked to rank each other in terms of their respective contribution to company performance, which then determines their earnings. Additionally, money above agreed objectives is shared amongst all associates globally. Each associate also has a stock option, which represents a proportion of their earnings. In this way the commitment of the associate towards the success of the company is rewarded directly and unambiguously. In order to ensure that the resultant pay is competitive, each year the pay of a number of associates, from a range of roles and functions, is compared with peers in other companies.

Source: www.gore.com/en_gb/news/1266706363585.html; www.gore.com/en_gb/aboutus/index.html; Sung and Ashton (2005).

Introduction

The principles of **performance management** can be practised in a number of different ways. The W.L. Gore & Associates case illustrates how one company manages its performance. High performance across a wide arena, both internal and external, is created through this holistic approach, encompassing the over-riding purpose, the organizational strategy, culture, leadership and people. There is a clear alignment of purpose to outcome – from its guiding principle of innovation flow the structure, the operating model, the management of people and performance, and the reward system.

> **Performance management:** systematic measuring, monitoring and decision-making geared towards fulfilling organizational objectives through operations management.

Perhaps the majority of companies are not as innovative and dynamic as W.L. Gore & Associates across the entire spectrum, but what is clear from this case is how performance management can influence the shape of the business, and vice versa. There is a strong link between performance management and business strategy, and how an organization approaches the development and application of measures impacts on the realization of both.

The purpose of this chapter is to introduce the concept of performance management as a conduit for the proactive achievement of organizational objectives. The first step in managing performance successfully is to know what it is that you are trying to achieve. To do that, managers must know the over-riding purpose of the organization, and how their role fits into it. To manage performance successfully, a basic requirement is that managers know what the ultimate objective is, and how that objective is broken down so that it makes sense to people wherever they are in the organization, and whatever their role is. If you know specifically what is expected of you, you have a greater chance of doing it.

Defining and articulating the objectives of the business helps to reveal operational requirements through which goals can be set at increasing levels of detail. Planning, organizing, setting targets and agreeing objectives are fundamental parts of defining performance. Having suitable reporting on each of these aspects means that managers can analyse outputs and outcomes, devise and assess remedies to unsatisfactory situations, and put forward actions plans to address them.

What this means in practical terms is that people within an organization need to understand, for the level at which they work, the processes, skills and knowledge required to make sure they can fulfil what is needed of them.

What Is Performance Management?

By its very nature, performance management is a diverse subject that is difficult to categorize. We want to know how people and organizations will perform, yet we can only know what has happened in the past. So what you do, how you do it, and – most importantly – who you do it with have a direct causal effect on outcomes. It is the desire to bridge the gap between the past and the future that has made the field of operational performance management such a challenging arena, and it's why so much management and systems effort is expended on it.

To an extent, there is confusion as to what exactly is required. The main reasons for developing a systematic method to manage performance are the desire to get measures, the perceived need for targets, and the requirement for control.

Sometimes demands for the collection of as much performance data as possible can become so onerous that it feels as if it has taken over the core business (see Case Study 12.1 for an example of this). Some organizations focus on target-setting, which can inadvertently cause conflict. Later in the chapter we highlight how conflicting targets lead to dysfunctional behaviours and undesirable outcomes. And, finally, some organizations appear disciplined and clear about the required performance, specifying precisely what the immediate focus is. The problem with this is that too much rigidity and too narrow a focus can actually cause confusion – in one month for instance, there is a drive to increase sales and the following month the requirement is to increase efficiency. Such inconsistency puts unnecessary pressure on employees and managers alike. Moreover, it can divert attention from any attempt at customer orientation.

If the purpose of management is to create a continuous flow of value, then it is a natural corollary that judgement will tend to focus on results. Since results come from every facet of the business, it is logical that a systematic and structured approach to analysing and assessing what happens in an organization is adopted. This can guide alignment, and ensure conformity of policy deployment. At the same time, it is important to differentiate between what you can and what you cannot influence. For instance, the collapse of Lehman Brothers in 2008 led to the closure of many other businesses, some of which were among the best performers in their sector; fitness centres, florists and dry cleaners may have been well managed and profitable, but if a huge part of your customer base disappears overnight, the number of actions available to mitigate this loss are severely limited.

CRITICAL PERSPECTIVE

Performance Management Sustaining Competitive Advantage

Every aspect of a business links together to create the overall picture of performance. The *strategic focus* of the company provides the *guiding principle that differentiates one company from another*. The strategic focus drives the way a company markets its products and services, determines how resources are allocated, and sets the context for everything from company-side initiatives to the performance management system.

Treacy and Wiersema (1993) propose that highly successful companies narrow their focus for superior performance onto one of three *Value Disciplines* – operational excellence (cost), customer intimacy (satisfaction), or product leadership. Superior results cannot be delivered on all fronts. There are tensions between them, and companies can spread themselves too thinly if they try to become champions in all disciplines.

Making this possible operationally means breaking things down simply from the chosen business focus, which in turn derives from the strategic focus. This also creates a link from objectives to accountabilities (Figure 12.1).

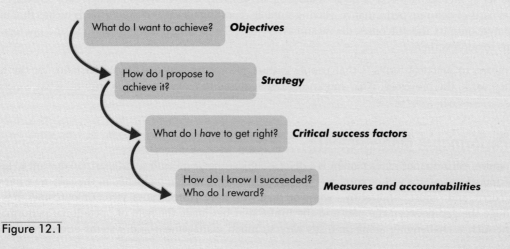

Figure 12.1

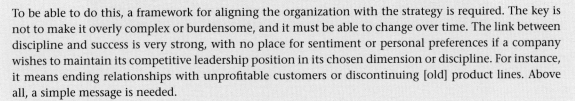

To be able to do this, a framework for aligning the organization with the strategy is required. The key is not to make it overly complex or burdensome, and it must be able to change over time. The link between discipline and success is very strong, with no place for sentiment or personal preferences if a company wishes to maintain its competitive leadership position in its chosen dimension or discipline. For instance, it means ending relationships with unprofitable customers or discontinuing [old] product lines. Above all, a simple message is needed.

A strategy is analogous to a map, and breaking it down into 'bite-size chunks' provides signposts on the journey, pointing to the right direction. Performance management provides the tools to plot the course from where you are, to where you want to be. Measuring performance, in itself, delivers little value. What's required is that the data gathered is analysed and acted upon. This proactive behaviour, making decisions based on the information gleaned from all aspects of the business and taking action, is what drives an organization towards its goal.

Management system standards are important, because they guide alignment and ensure conformity of policy deployment.

Performance management entails getting an appropriate balance across four main perspectives:
- The way people are encouraged to behave in ways that allow the business to prosper
- The thinking behind investment and return on investment to ensure success
- The way work and productivity are managed
- Measuring performance to inform the decisions made in the other three areas.

The key point is that performance management is the process of telling you what is going to happen (in advance), what action you need to take, and whether that action was effective. The core of performance management is to help us know as best we can, with the tools we have available, where we are on the continuum of performance.

! Stop and Think

1 What would you have to consider if you wanted your business to have a focus on customer intimacy (satisfaction)?

Performance Management's Contribution to Continuous Improvement and Competitive Advantage

One of the major challenges for management today is to establish coherence between long-term objectives and daily operations. In practice, what tends to happen is that senior management is clear about corporate objectives, but the rest of the workforce is less well informed. Generally, the objectives are reflected in a company's mission statement. However, by the time the stated goals reach individual departments, managers there see little connection between what they have to do on a daily and weekly basis and the corporate strategy. Indeed, in many companies, setting strategy and setting budgets are distinct activities, not directly part of everyday business as they are in what are known as **high performance organizations** (CIPD, 2005). The reason is a disconnect between strategic ambition and the operational targets that are designed to direct the daily operations.

More immediate operational problems take priority, and each department feels as if it is doing its best, with its employees working as hard as they can, all to little avail, as there is a lack of support and understanding from other departments. The result is that companies do not have inter-departmental coherence when it comes to pulling together to

High-performance organizations (HPOs): organizations deemed to excel at all aspects of performance, as recognized through the use of an integrated performance management system, whereby people, process and outcome are all performing at high levels.

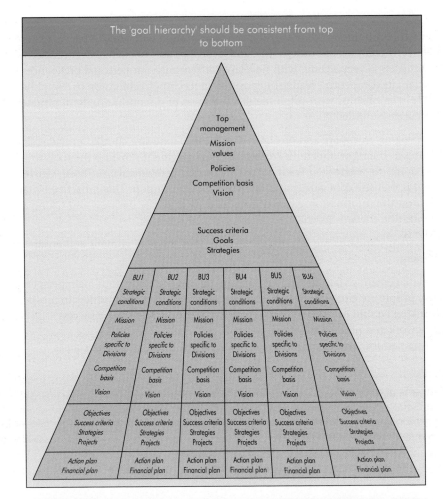

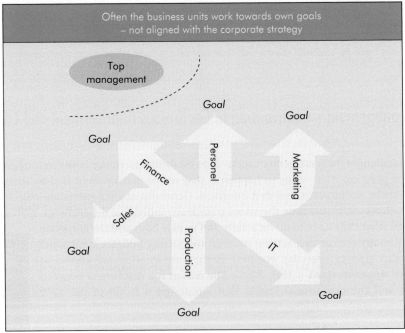

Figure 12.2 Strategic ambition and operational reality

achieve goals and objectives. Immediate targets appear more important. From this, it may appear that managers and directors of departments are 'doing well' – they are meeting their targets, for instance, rework is low, and throughput is high. These can all be indications that the department is successful. The real question is: successful at what? Are they in effect working to their own agendas? Figure 12.2 demonstrates how companies work when there is a disconnect between corporate goals and business unit goals. Instead of working together to achieve what was intended for the business, individual business units appear to have developed their own goals, which appear to bear little if any connection to the corporate strategy.

Coherence, or alignment, is a major need for any business if it is to be successful and do more than just survive. Coherence is achieved through structure and discipline. Part of that discipline is to break down the strategy into operational parts, and to understand clearly what it is that must be measured in order to:

- Understand whether the strategy is ultimately being met
- Understand whether what was planned in the more immediate term is being met
- Understand what tools and information should be used to rectify the situation, if what was planned is not happening.

Wade and Recardo (2001) have developed a model to help managers try and rectify this situation. Their framework, shown in Figure 12.3, demonstrates how the organization can become aligned with the strategy. They take as their starting point the *theory of business*. At its simplest level, businesses have two market mechanisms that drive efficiency and innovation: the *profit motive*, and *competition*. If we refer back to the introductory case study, we can see how W.L. Gore & Associates have thrived and become a high-performance company by having a firm grasp on both these market mechanisms, and by handling the issues around each of them.

The strategy is formed, and a *corporate scorecard* is developed to ascertain the 'what is required'. A *gap analysis* follows, where managers assess what the current capabilities and skills are, and the level of performance reached with that combination. An assessment is then made to see whether this falls short for the requirements of the new strategy. This then provides the backbone of the *business plan*, which differs from a strategy because it turns the strategic corporate goals into operational language, providing the first expression of the 'what' in terms of the 'how'. Converting the 'what' into the 'how' means that managers know which departments and which processes are going to be required, and can quantify this into 'how many'. As this thinking is broken down into greater levels of detail, individual *performance profiles* can be established, which in turn enable *compensation* and benefits to be determined.

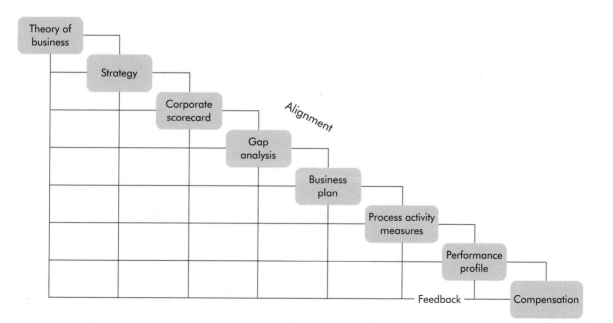

Figure 12.3 Organizational alignment model (Wade and Recardo, 2001, p. 47)

The key is not to make the performance management system (PMS) overly complex or burdensome. Being rigid and prescriptive hinders responsive decision-making. In other words, the content of the framework must be able to change over time. It is the use of feedback that identifies the process as iterative and not prescriptive, and it is that which in practice makes the model work.

Clearly designed processes with well-defined process activity measures are important, because they enable standards to be set and relevant timeframes decided. It is through measuring and monitoring agreed standards that an organization guides alignment and ensures conformity of policy deployment, beginning the journey of continuous improvement. If you cannot measure an activity, you cannot improve it. As well as helping an organization to direct resources at the most attractive improvement activities, measurement also provides a direct stimulus to action, because it highlights what was done versus what was planned. Discussing facts supported by numbers reduces subjectivity, and makes constructive problem solving possible. Managers are thus simultaneously monitoring progress, giving feedback, and reinforcing required behaviour.

Performance measurement: quantification of business activities, enabling comparison and discussion.

The impact of **performance measurement** on organizational behaviour depends on the organizational context of the measurement, the use made of measurements, the degree of agreement between measurements and organizational objectives, and the individual's motivational response to measurement.

The key point is that successful performance management influences behaviour in a positive way, which in turn improves performance.

Components of Performance Management

Now that we have ascertained the pivotal role of performance management in the success of any organization, it is time to consider the practicalities. How does an organization create a performance management system (PMS) that will provide all the information required, so that managers can make informed and timely decisions to steer the organization in the right direction? Consider Figure 12.4 – a boat sailing towards a specified target point, with its overall direction of travel indicated by the red line, but the effect of the waves and the wind means the boat cannot sail in a straight line. To get to the end point, many small directional adjustments must be made along the way, by constant monitoring of direction and course corrections made. When organizations agree on their strategy and set their goals and objectives, they are stating their end goal. Planning maps the steps required to achieve that goal. Then staff and managers are tasked with actually making sure this happens.

So most managers, weekly and daily, agree a destination, establish required performance, and make many alterations in order to reach the destination. Alterations are made as a result of monitoring what is done against what was thought would be done – comparing actual against plan. To be able to monitor activity you have to be able to measure it and record it. In other words, you are collecting data. Making decisions is the purpose and outcome of collecting data. Too much data means too much time has to be spent sifting through it looking for what is pertinent. As in many other instances, the saying 'less is more' applies here too.

So, there is a dynamic relationship between action and destination. There is also a dynamic relationship between the culture of the organization (which influences how people think and behave in the workplace) and success (Bititci et al., 2006), where success is expressed in terms of how well the organization has achieved its goals.

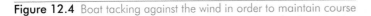

Figure 12.4 Boat tacking against the wind in order to maintain course

Table 12.1 Levels of performance management

Level/outcomes	Objectives	Design	Indicator perspectives
Organization	• The overarching strategy • Value creation • Organizational alignment • The business plan	• Strategy-driven functions • EVA or CVA value of functions • Permeability of boundaries • ABC/ABM-driven	• Financial • Customer • Organizational • Growth and innovation
Process	• Conformance to customer standards	• Process owner • Inputs • Outputs • Service level agreements • Boundary crossings	• Cost • Cycle time • Quantity • Quality • Conformance to standards
Job	• Report cards • Easy access • Motivation • Selection	• Process maps • Function charts • Task analysis	• Activities • Outcomes • Target measures • Data sources

Source: adapted from Wade and Recardo (2001, p. 13).

For years, financial results have been used to indicate company performance. Of course, for certain people – such as shareholders – this information is still vital. However, for customers and employees alike, on a day-to-day basis, financial results are not informative enough for hands-on operational decisions. As noted in Chapter 3, Enron provides a very public lesson of what the outcomes can be when there is an over-reliance by decision-makers on financial indicators. More recently, the Indian software company Satyam appeared to repeat Enron's behaviours, and as a consequence had to deal with similar issues.

Since Drucker (1955) first discussed the requirement for managers to have a clear picture of the whole organization's performance by looking at multiple aspects, there have been numerous attempts to devise the 'best' indicators. There has been a move from measuring financial effectiveness towards examining a broader spectrum of performance. Table 12.1 categorizes the levels of performance management that now need to be incorporated into management's portfolio of information required for decision-making.

The indicators vary, depending on what level of scrutiny is being carried out. The column on the left lists the level of detail, from whole company to individual task, for which *job cards* are provided to workers. Each level has its own distinct objectives, which require a defined set of considerations when monitoring tools are being designed. It is at this stage that what you intend to measure becomes important. This is specified in the final column, *indicator perspective*. Note how the granularity of detail necessary to understand what is going on becomes greater.

In order for the PMS to work properly, i.e. to enable managers to successfully fulfil their own roles and ensure their departments are contributing in the right way to the company's goals, five *key components* must exist:
- Understand your model for success
- Identify performance measures for success
- Cascade the performance measures and their application
- Establish performance reporting for relevant measures
- Coach, incentivize and reward success with a transparent approach.

SHORT CASE 12.1

Performance Management Crisis

On 18 March 2009, the *Daily Telegraph* ran with the front page headline 'Targets blamed for 1,200 deaths at hospital', and a BBC-televised news programme opened with the same story. There has probably not been a more damming headline implicating targets in organizational failure with such catastrophic consequences.

Patients admitted for emergency treatment at an NHS Trust in the UK were subjected to 'shocking and appalling' care that included untrained receptionists carrying out medical checks and heart monitors being switched off, a newspaper report stated.

The Healthcare Commission, the NHS standards watchdog, contended that evidence suggested that as many as 400 deaths at Mid Staffordshire NHS Foundation Trust could have been prevented, and may have been the result of poor care. The commission's investigation, based on more than 300 interviews and an examination of more than 1,000 documents, uncovered inadequately trained staff who were too few in number, junior doctors left in charge at night, and patients left without food, drink or medication as their operations were repeatedly cancelled. The Commission heard that some patients were in pain or needing the toilet, sat in soiled bedding for several hours at a time, and were not given their regular medication. Receptionists with no medical training were also expected to assess patients coming into A&E.

Describing the episodes as a 'gross and terrible breach of trust of the patients the NHS seeks to serve', Sir Bruce Keogh, medical director of the NHS, said the report showed there had been a 'complete failure of leadership' at the Trust. He added that: 'I'm proud of the NHS but actually I'm really saddened by this report.'

A consequence of this performance was that the trust's chief executive, Martin Yeates, and its chairman, Toni Brisby, resigned.

The Healthcare Commission's chairman, Sir Ian Kennedy, said the investigation followed concerns about unusually high death rates at the Trust. Those in charge of the Trust, which runs Stafford Hospital and Cannock Chase Hospital, appeared to fail to provide an adequate explanation of these figures, prompting the Commission to launch a full investigation.

One of the most fundamental criticisms of this situation was that, in order to achieve coveted Foundation status, the Trust management had become obsessed with meeting government targets rather than looking after the sick in its care. David Kidney, the MP for Stafford, suggested that the hospital was too enthusiastic in cost-cutting. He stated that people had died because they did not get the care that they should have done in their local hospital.

The Commission stated: 'An analysis of the trust's board meetings from April found discussions were dominated by finance.'

Questions

1 What key performance indicators (KPIs) were management focusing on?
2 What should the managers have been focusing on more?
3 How do you think managers could have prioritized their many performance measurements?
4 Which factors might be most important to the various hospital stakeholder groups? Write down who you think are the key stakeholder groups.

Sources: *The Times*, 17 March 2009; *Daily Telegraph*, 22 March 2009.

🛈 Stop and Think

2 What steps in managing performance could have been taken to avoid this situation?

BUSINESS INTEGRATION

Developing a Performance Management System

There are five generally accepted operations performance objectives (Table 12.2). Yet when performance management is the primary consideration, a slightly different perspective on these parameters perhaps better serves the practising manager.

Table 12.2 Operations performance objectives

Objective	Definition
Quality	*Do things right* – external and customer satisfaction, high process capability and reduced costs
Speed	*Do things fast* – service-enhancing factor, reduces inventory, reduces risk of obsolescence
Dependability	*Do things on time* – long-term selection criterion, increases availability, saves money, provides stability
Flexibility	*Change what you do* – customization, speed of response, saves time, maintains dependability
Cost	*Do things cheaply* – efficient processes, influenced by performance objectives
Innovation	*Adapt and develop* – respond to customer and market changes, develop new processes and products

Source: adapted from Slack *et al.* (2007).

In more recent years a sixth objective has been added to better reflect the prevailing business environment, in which change and adaptability is accepted as a normal part of 'business as usual': *innovation.* This means innovation in its generally accepted guise, but it also reminds managers to think about competencies, skills, responsiveness to customers and colleagues, and continued personal development. Adaptability, and the ability to develop knowledge and skills, enhance individuals' as well as corporate **capability**. Recognizing this through measurement means that progress can be gauged and thereby influenced accordingly.

> **Capability:** maximum amount of a product that can be made within a specified time.

By their very nature these objectives are *competitive priorities*. Organizations should therefore aim to maximize performance in these areas in order to maximize competitiveness. However, as resources are unlikely to allow improvement in all areas, organizations should concentrate on maintaining performance in *qualifying* factors and improving *competitive edge* factors. Qualifying factors are those that ensure an organization can continue to operate in its chosen business area. For instance, if you're a car manufacturer, you would probably need to ensure that you have a number of models that appeal to customers, and that you have a reputation for quality. Without these basics you would probably not be able to continue in business. Competitive edge factors are those that make you different from the other companies, or special in some way. You could be more innovative, cheaper, have better delivery times, or offer more customer-defined options – anything that will give you an advantage, appeal to more people, and be unique to your company in some way.

Competitive priorities change over time, and must therefore be reviewed. The main considerations always boil down to *people, processes and systems* in operational terms, or *time, cost and quality* in project management terms (see Chapter 11). All of these, however they are examined, impact on quality in one way or another, and echo the customer intimacy thinking of Treacy and Wiersema (1993).

When developing a performance measurement system (PMS) these performance objectives, in themselves composite or aggregate measures, must be taken into account. In a perfect world, managers would be able to design an optimum PMS that would have:

- Few measures
- Non-financials that would predict financial performance
- The same measures throughout the whole organization
- Clear connections to people performance, for compensation purposes
- Stability

Why do these features make the potential PMS ideal? Few measures make the PMS simple to construct, understand and use. Non-financial data, particularly those related to the objectives in Table 12.2, readily link actual operations to eventual financial performance on a daily and weekly basis, whereas financial performance is usually reported monthly and quarterly. For instance, a large number of returns in a manufacturing or retail environment will indicate a fall in revenue for that time period, because sales figures will ultimately be reduced. Creating the same measures throughout the organization enables comparison of teams, departments or business units. Connecting desired performance through the people who carry out the work with actual performance makes compensation and reward fact-based when it comes to appraisal time. This allows for the complexity inherent within organizations, provides a structure to satisfy the desire for perceived control, and provides a conduit for equating control and recognition with volume of measures. Stability, although desirable, is notoriously difficult to achieve, given that we all accept that business is carried out in a fast-changing environment, and it is through composite measures that this tends to be sought, since composite measures permit a level of comparability both against each other and against targets.

> **The key point is** that there is a disconnect between how many measures people can create and disseminate, and how many we can actually deal with, both practically and at a cognitive level.

Principles of a PMS

In operational terms, the principles of a PMS must be inclusivity, alignment and flexibility, as depicted in Figure 12.5.

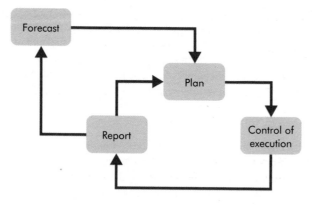

Figure 12.5

A *forecast* includes all departments, all areas, and all composite indicators. A forecast is generally a view on a period of 12–24 months. Sometimes a 12-month forecast can also be referred to as a *master schedule*. However, the two should not be used interchangeably; the difference lies in the fact that the master schedule includes manpower details. It links volumes to people, thereby helping make the *plan* more operationally meaningful. It is from this that measurements such as productivity, rework and errors are able to be estimated, and then used to inform the plan. The plan takes the forecast figures, breaking the forecast down from company level to department, to section and team, translating as it does so estimated generic volume to more granular items to which people carrying out the work can relate their day-to-day work. The work is then carried out in a controlled fashion by each department and subsequently *reported* upon. The key feature of any performance management system as outlined is that the measures used are *sensible*, and *compared against the plan*.

Without knowing where it was expected that performance would be, it is impossible to judge whether actual performance was good, bad or indifferent. For instance, in a call centre, if the planned achievement was 90% of calls answered within 15 seconds, and the result at the end of the working day showed that 91% of calls had been answered in 15 seconds, the first reaction would probably be a feeling of satisfaction at a job well done. However, if it was subsequently revealed that
- The nearest competitor consistently achieved 95%
- Last month's performance showed the call centre average had been 92%
- Customers expected all (100%) calls to be answered within the 15 seconds,

what would be a reasonable reaction? Clearly, the spread of reactions would vary. It is for this reason that it is important to be clear about your goals. The absolute level of achievement, on its own, does not necessarily tell you anything about your performance. But compare it against a defined goal and you are able to assess whether you are doing well or not (remember Figure 12.4). Once you decide where and how you wish to focus, then that is what you should do.

It is important to understand from this the need for and relevance of the process of management control. This is outlined in Table 12.3.

Table 12.3 Management control process

Forecast	Plan	Control of execution	Report
Expected outcomes Trends Agree and publish	Detailing of forecast into shorter time frames Agree and publish	Review at an appropriate interval	Use to indicate achievement against targets Merchandise success
Vision Objectives Balance demand and output	Regulate activities Eliminate bottlenecks Smooth workflow Track, adjust, refine Establish sequence and priorities	Feedback performance Surface problems Initiate action to rectify, recover, prevent Track, adjust, refine	Performance data only Indicate trends/patterns Achievement improvement

Each of the principles of the PMS as depicted in Figure 12.5 is listed in the table, with an explanation of how it is relevant for managers, as well as how each principle should be implemented and used. For the reporting to be of value, essential components are a clear organizational structure of people and information, and a disciplined review process. The greater the timescale, the higher the level of management to which the information pertains. For example, a board of directors would be concerned with annual or quarterly targets, whereas a supervisor or team leader would need to know and understand hourly and daily targets and results.

Creating a PMS

- *Step 1*: Define an appropriate hierarchical organization structure for the reporting system. This has the added benefit of clarifying what the performance goals ought to be for the business/department/section/team.
- *Step 2*: Identify the key variables that determine performance. Examples of these might include people, customers, suppliers, a production constraint or bottleneck process.
- *Step 3*: Develop **key performance indicators (KPIs)** for the areas that can and should be monitored. Differentiating between what you can measure and what you should measure makes the difference between an easy-to-use PMS and a complex one that ends up not being used. Too many KPIs make it difficult to track whether performance is really aligned with the overall strategic objective of the organization, because attention is spread too thinly over too many aspects. A working example of this would be the CEO of an airline wanting to know how the airline had performed the previous day. At the pinnacle of the organization, the CEO needs a KPI that is comprehensive, meaningful and readily obtained. This kind of KPI provides focus, gives purpose to decisions and actions.

> **Key performance indicator (KPI):** a specific aspect of measurement, the identification and quantification of which enhances management knowledge about a particular part of the business.

- *Step 4*: Set and agree objectives, plans and targets. These must be derived from the corporate strategy if they are to be an aid to achieving success rather than a managerial distraction.
- *Step 5*: Decide how to obtain timely and accurate information defining the achievement of objectives, plans and targets. No matter how good the definitions are, if capture and collation are difficult, once again the measures and management tools will be of little if any use.
- *Step 6*: Implement focused *action review meetings* at which managers identify problems and constraints that prevent achievement, and take appropriate remedial action. This reinforces that the data captured from meaningful measures can encourage problem solving and decision-making.

❶ Stop and Think

3 What is *the* KPI for an airline's CEO?

Thus performance measurement is a means to an end, not an end in itself. The real benefits of managing operational performance in this way come from closing the management loop, through ensuring that appropriate improvements in business performance take place. The *management report* is used to summarize the overall performance of each section or department within the business, against predetermined KPIs. The management

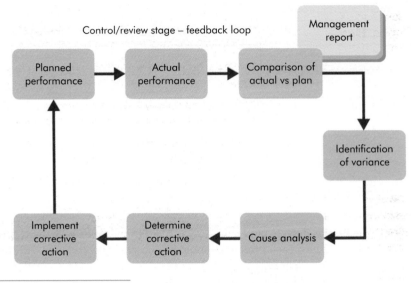

Figure 12.6 Action review meeting process

report is the focus of the management weekly *review meeting*, used to highlight problem areas and to enable corrective actions to be developed and assigned.

To ensure the PMS is comprehensive and fit for purpose, managers must confirm that it includes a number of elements. Measures should be aligned with the strategy, and be able to be directly matched, individually or by aggregation, with the recognition and reward scheme. This should use multiple input sources, so that appraisals stop being seen as a discrete event and instead become an integrated part of a continuous process of operational and individual performance management, designed to be relevant, accurate, fair and effective in inculcating the desire among employees for continuous improvement. This would serve the purpose of being able, through behaviour and reward, to change culture if necessary.

The number of measures contained is important. As stated earlier: too many become irksome to collect and act upon; too few and not enough information is obtained. Either way, managers are not readily able to act upon the information.

Another complication arising from too many measures is that the greater the number of measures, the greater the danger of their conflicting. For example, targets to 'increase customer acquisition' and 'improve customer retention' (getting new and keeping existing customers) may conflict. Discounts might be offered to new customers and not be available to existing customers, who might then complain and leave. So the discounts have increased the number of new customers but decreased the number of existing customers (which is called *churn*, and is also a unit of measure, a KPI, in some companies).

Another example of conflicting measures would be two call centre KPIs: 'customer satisfaction' and 'number of calls per hour'. Generally speaking, customers are satisfied if they have their query dealt with fully, so that they know where they are and what they need to do, and do not have to ring back about the same subject (*rework*). Call centres tend to state this as an objective, and measure it. However, they also measure the number of calls per hour (this is a productivity measure). Individuals may wish to manage their own performance and make sure they answer the targeted number of calls. In order to do so, though, they may well end up cutting a customer short, passing the customer on to someone else, dropping the call, or simply giving them the wrong answer. Not only might this result in rework, it usually ends up with an unhappy customer.

Both these examples show how easy it is to inadvertently encourage dysfunctional behaviours and undesirable outcomes – thus negatively influencing performance, for which managers then have to make directional adjustment, as explained with Figure 12.4.

There needs to be a balance across the types of measure, between internal and external and between financial and non-financial. All of this helps to provide managers with a holistic view of the organization, their department, or specific team.

The final level of granularity is that of individual measures of performance. Considerations here are around which and why, how easy (therefore cost-effective) to collate, and what purpose they serve. Measuring something just because you can may not be useful in the longer term.

Devising and Using Performance Measures

'You get what you measure'

'You get what you inspect not what you expect'

Productivity

Productivity expresses the relationship between results and the time it takes to accomplish them, usually in the form of a ratio or a percentage, which is calculated by taking the outputs (results in the form of goods and services) divided by the inputs (resources used to accomplish the outputs):

> **Productivity:** amount produced in relation to one or more of the resources used.

$$\text{Productivity} = \frac{\text{Output(s) from the operation}}{\text{Input(s) to the operation}}$$

Productivity tends to be used as a measure of the efficiency with which the resources employed by the organization (i.e. human resources, materials or capital resources) are converted into the goods or services sold by the company. Increasing organizational efficiency, in terms of improving the output achieved for a similar input, is the most common way in which productivity will be raised.

There are two ways to achieve and improve productivity:
- Decrease the inputs but maintain the outputs
- Increase outputs with the same inputs.

WORKED EXAMPLE 12.1

Calculating Productivity

A furniture manufacturer currently makes 100 tables a week for a national retailer. There are four carpenters in the department, working a 40-hour week. The customer wishes to increase the order to 135 tables a week.

Problem:

(a) *Calculate current productivity in the department.*

(b) *What is the new productivity level required?*

(c) *How can the department achieve the higher rate of productivity?*

Approach:

(a) Use the following formula in order to calculate the productivity:

$$\text{Productivity} = \frac{\text{Output(s) from the operation}}{\text{Input(s) to the operation}}$$

So current productivity = 100 tables (output) ÷ 160 person-hours × 100 (to make it a percentage figure):

Solution = 0.63 or 63%

This tells us that each carpenter can make one table in 1 hour and 38 minutes.

(b) Use the same formula to calculate the new productivity:

$$\text{Productivity} = \frac{\text{Output(s) from the operation}}{\text{Input(s) to the operation}}$$

So the new production level required = 135 tables (output) ÷ 160 person-hours × 100 (to make it a percentage figure)

Solution = 0.84 or 84%

This tells us that each carpenter is now required to make a table in 1 hour and 9 minutes to meet customer requirements, if all other conditions remain the same.

(c) What can be done to achieve higher productivity?

Consider the two bullets about how you can improve productivity:
- Decrease the inputs but maintain the outputs
- Increase outputs with the same inputs.

In this example the furniture manufacturer would first consider whether to increase outputs with the same inputs if he is to fulfil the customer order without making any other changes. This is a 40% increase in production, and therefore in productivity. How can the improvement be done?

First, management need to understand the table-making process (all the steps and activities). The process must be analysed to see whether it can be refined or streamlined in any way. Unnecessary steps should be removed, and the remaining steps should be made shorter if possible, including any waiting or handover time from one carpenter to another – depending on the production process in use. This may result in some improvement in productivity.

If redesigning the process produces some efficiency gains, and productivity can be improved, for instance by 20%, but not by the full amount required, then management may consider hiring another carpenter. This would mean that each carpenter can now make a table in 1 hour and 20 minutes. To make the 135 tables required with the productivity increase gained from the process redesign, then 202.5 hours are required (135 tables × 90 minutes per table/60). However, this would in theory still leave the manufacturer with a shortfall of 2.5 hours, which they could try to make up by increasing the working week by half an hour per person, by asking the carpenters to work overtime half an hour a week, or looking again at the process to find further efficiencies.

Another option might be to buy a machine to improve the process in some way (to automate the table-making process, or parts of it). Although this might appear to be increasing inputs, a process analysis and costing might demonstrate that buying such a machine and redesigning the process might result in an overall decrease in inputs relative to the increase in outputs. This potentially higher productivity improvement might then lead management to considering further options. Further options would broaden the scope of the decision-making, because it would incorporate thinking such as trying to increase the order even more, selling to other customers, or reducing the workforce.

As you can see from the worked example above, there are several layers of decision-making that may well emerge as a result of a simple-to-calculate ratio such as productivity. Other ratios also apply to measuring performance, and in the same way that productivity measures performance, they too adhere to the philosophy around measuring achievement against the target to be achieved.

There are too many different types of measure to create an exhaustive list, but some examples of different measurement ratios are given below:
- Actual units sold for the period ÷ Planned sales for the period (× 100 to give the %)
- Error rate ÷ Volume produced (× 100 to give the %)
- Invoices processed per manhour
- Number of telephone calls taken per manhour
- Actual time taken ÷ Planned elapsed time (indicates delays or throughput times)
- Available hours × Standard planned units per hour (indicates *capability*)
- Sales (£) ÷ labour costs (£)
- Sales (volume or value) ÷ Salespeople
- Number of complaints ÷ Number of transactions (can be an indicator of quality, customer satisfaction or productivity, for instance)

<table>
<tr><td>SHORT
CASE
12.2</td></tr>
</table>

The Consequences of Managing Measures not Performance

Severn Trent Water is the world's fourth largest privately owned water company. Its stated aim is to be the best water and waste services company in the UK. The challenge presented by this vision is to deliver the highest possible service standards for customers, while also offering the lowest prices.

Source: © Lisa Valder/iStock

Yet in October 2007 the company was charged by the Serious Fraud Office (SFO) in relation to data it provided to Ofwat (the water services regulation authority in England and Wales). The SFO did not charge any individual with an offence, but brought three charges against Severn Trent Water of providing false information concerning leakage data in the company's June returns of 2000, 2001 and 2002. The charges stem from an investigation Ofwat carried out after a Severn Trent employee made allegations in 2004 concerning false reporting at the company. Ofwat subsequently referred one strand of that investigation – the strand concerning leakage data – to the SFO. In 2005, the SFO told Severn Trent it was facing a criminal investigation into the matter, which led to fines imposed in 2008. The 2000 instance was eventually dropped.

Separately, Ofwat brought two fraud charges over another issue: misstated customer relations data. Severn Trent Water apologized to customers, and credited their accounts. Severn Trent Water's customer relations department deliberately misreported some of its customer service data to hide its true performance in 2005 and in earlier years. This issue, not subject to any criminal procedures, was a problem that Severn Trent itself uncovered in 2006, and to which it drew the regulator's attention. The company identified that it had provided false information to Ofwat regarding customer service data, such as information on how quickly the company dealt with supplier interruptions and customer queries or complaints. In a monopoly industry, where the majority of customers have no choice of supplier, the only protection that they have is from the regulator. Reliable, accurate and complete information is fundamentally important if Ofwat is to be able to protect consumers. By deliberately misrepresenting its performance, Severn Trent Water prevented Ofwat from identifying failures in the company's customer service and taking action to improve that service.

This deception, combined with poor internal processes and controls within the company, meant that customers of Severn Trent Water received a service that was far below that reported, and in many cases was below the statutory minimum standards. The outcome was that Severn Trent was fined 2.9% of its 2006/2007 turnover (£34.7 million) for deliberately misreporting some key customer service information, and 0.1% of its 2005/2006 turnover (£1.1 million) for providing sub-standard services to customers in 2005–2006 by failing to meet guaranteed standards of service.

Note: The regulator sets restrictions on how much water companies can charge customers, based on how effectively they treat their customers. By overstating its customer service performance, the company was allowed to charge higher prices than if it had provided correct figures.

Questions
1   Are the vision and the operational performance aligned at Severn Trent Water?
2   Why did the company misrepresent data to Ofwat?
3   How would you describe Severn Trent Water's customer orientation?
4   What would you say was the key performance driver for this company?

Sources: *Financial Times*, by John O'Doherty, 22 November 2007, http://cachef.ft.com/cms/s/0/ad46048a-98ca-11dc-bb45-0000779fd2ac.html; Times Online, 8 April 2008, http://business.timesonline.co.uk/tol/business/industry_sectors/utilities/article3703915.ece; Severn Trent Water website, News section, www.stwater.co.uk/server.php?show=ConWebDoc.3403

People in organizations respond to measures. The Severn Trent Water case is just one of many stories of how individuals and teams are doing well yet are actually harming the business. Toyota, Thames Water, EDF Energy and RBS are all examples of companies that have been fined in the recent past for 'multiple failings' in one or more of their processes related to customer service delivery. In October 2008 BT was fined £1.3 million after its staff had been found calling each other to meet call-answering targets, which were part of BT's contract to service the Armed Forces' telephone system. Similarly, call centre staff are known to end calls prematurely to stay within their target call times, and to reach target volumes.

GP surgeries and hospitals in the UK provide another pertinent example of the law of unintended consequences. Government set targets: a 48-hour maximum wait for a GP appointment by 2004, and a four-hour maximum wait in A&E (Accident and Emergency) prior to admission, transfer or discharge by 2005. The consequence of this well-intentioned, customer-focused idea was to make matters worse, as staff expended time and energy meeting, and misinterpreting, those targets. Patients would telephone to make an appointment, and if they wanted a 'future' booking, which meant anything more than two days in advance, they would be asked to call back within the 48-hour time span. At hospitals, patients would be moved from one waiting area to another within the four-hour time, while not actually having their case resolved. By engaging in this behaviour the staff were often meeting the targets, but letting down the patients. In June 2010 the newly elected coalition government in the UK abolished these targets, in an attempt to signal the end of what it labelled a 'target culture'. These examples provide readily available examples of how measures lead to inappropriate employee behaviour, because the target rather than the underlying business need is the reason for the indicator.

What these examples show is that measures contain messages about what matters and how people should behave. When the measures are consistent with the organization's strategies, they encourage behaviours that are consistent with the strategy. It is perhaps important to consider the following quotation:

Not everything that can be counted counts, and not everything that counts can be counted.

Albert Einstein

WORKED EXAMPLE 12.2

Using Data for Performance: Control and Review in Action

Your company has too many product lines. This is causing quality problems in both production and distribution. Sales are also falling. The salesforce say this is because the product range is too disparate, and customers are hearing through word of mouth of the quality problems. There is an urgent need to improve performance. Senior management have decided that rationalizing the product line is the first step in managing this process.

Table 12.4 summarizes the range of products and shows each product's ranking against the others by both sales value and total contribution.

Problem: *Select the products that are to be discontinued, explain the rationale and consideration in your decision-making.*

Approach: To decide which products are to be retained, more than just profit must be considered. Some sort of rational selection criteria must be applied.

Your initial reaction is probably that the company is earning an awful lot of money from three or four items, and therefore in the interests of improving performance through simplification of product lines, the remainder can be stopped. That is a big mistake. Much more consideration and applied thinking is needed before you decide on what can and should be done. Factors that need to be explored, for instance, are:

(a)   At what stage of the product life cycle is each product (because newly launched products may not yet be making money, owing to development costs still to be recouped)?

(b)   Are obsolete products still being sold as part of product bundles? What, if any, are the implications of unbundling them?

Table 12.4 Product range ranked by total sales value and total contribution

Rank/item	Cumulative total value of sales last year		Rank/item	Cumulative total contribution last year	
	(£)	(%)		(£)	(%)
1/F	100,000	50	1/H	29,000	48.4
2/H	160,000	80	2/F	42,000	70
3/A	174,000	87	3/A	52,000	86.7
4/I	184,000	92	4/C	54,000	90
5/C	190,000	95	5/B	55,500	92.5
6/B	193,000	96	6/D	56,700	94.5
7/D	195,000	97.5	7/G	57,700	96.2
8/G	197,000	98.5	8/J	58,700	97.8
9/J	199,000	99.5	9/I	59,500	99.2
10/E	200,000	100	10/E	60,000	100

(c) Which products are important for our key customers?

(d) By product line, the following questions need to be asked:
   (i)   Should (and can) we reduce costs?
   (ii) Should (and can) we increase prices?
   (iii) Should (and can) we increase sales?

(e) Is staff training an issue, in either production or sales – or both?

This is not an exhaustive list, but indicative of cause analysis embarked upon by managers before determining corrective action that inevitably has implications for the future performance of the organization.

Solution: Further exploration of the data reveals that selecting the first four products on the basis that they form 90% of the business can be seen to probably be a rash choice, given the considerations.

So the recommendations you make to the senior team would either happen after a significant amount of further research had been carried out (based on the example considerations), *or* you would state the obvious from the data, and advise them that at this stage it is inconclusive, because of the shortcomings in this level of data (based on the example considerations).

Devising Measures

Performance measurement is the process of quantifying the **efficiency** and **effectiveness** of past action, so that informed decisions can be made about future activity, shaped by current performance. In simple terms, measures can tell you how far you have come. Managers also need to know how far there is still to go – and in identifying this shortfall, managers can formulate action plans to close this gap. There are two straightforward requirements:

> **Efficiency:** ratio of actual output to possible output.
>
> **Effectiveness:** describes how well goals are achieved.

- *A PMS infrastructure*, which indicates what is going to be done when and how
- *A set of suitable metrics*, providing the actual measures that will be used to populate the PMS.

For any business, the critical variables that provide the core measurements are:

- Employee satisfaction
- Customer satisfaction
- Cash flow.

Employee satisfaction tells management about productivity; customer satisfaction influences market share; and cash flow confirms that everything is working as it should, because the business has money in the bank to pay employees and suppliers, and thereby continue to create goods and services to continue satisfying customers. In many ways these performance parameters are non-negotiable, being thresholds below which survival may be threatened. Every single operational indicator devised is a sub-set of one of these composite measures. A composite measure is one made up of any number of more detailed indicators. For instance, the KPI of *speed*, being one of the operations performance objectives, could be made up of delivery time, order processing, throughput time, and so on.

So it is crucial that a measurement system provides an *early warning signal* that can highlight the approach of a breach of target or objective.

> ### ❶ Stop and Think
>
> **4** What is it that makes a performance measure useful?

Implementing a PMS

Top-level indicators are established with reference to business objectives. They should pinpoint the key drivers that have the greatest impact on whether or not the business objectives are achieved. For example, you would measure productivity at hourly, daily or weekly frequencies, headcount monthly or quarterly, and staff turnover perhaps quarterly or annually.

There are several questions around practicalities that need to be asked when choosing KPIs and deciding to implement a PMS:

- How will the data be collected, and by whom?
- Who will collate the data?
- Who analyses all the information captured?
- Who ensures compliance?
- Who makes decisions?
- Who takes the actions?
- How are decisions and actions reported, and fed into the KPIs and the PMS?

These questions are not just about the detail of execution. There is another aspect too – that of *manageability*. If a PMS becomes cumbersome, employees will stop using it, and if the KPIs are irrelevant, the usefulness of the PMS is reduced. For any organization, the balance between the cost of obtaining the information and the benefit of having that information is key. The mechanics and practicalities also need to be specified. Each component of the measure must have a clearly defined definition. The targets for each component need to have been set in line with corporate strategy, and managers need to know the status of the target – whether it is a *stretch* target, for instance.

During this development for implementation, it is also necessary to consider which performance drivers are the most important, and to be clear about which KPIs they appear in. Getting the answers to these questions right means the organization is well on the way to achieving buy-in from managers and supervisors, particularly if they have been involved in the development and selection of the KPIs. Some interesting questions can be posed to establish the usefulness of an indicator to be used in a PMS:

- The *truth test*: Is the measure definitely measuring what it's meant to measure?
- The *focus test*: Is the measure measuring only what it's meant to measure?
- The *consistency test*: Is the measure consistent, whenever it's measured or whoever measures?
- The *access test*: Can the data be readily communicated and easily understood?
- The *clarity test*: Is any ambiguity possible in interpretation of the results?

- The *so what test*: Can, and will, the data be acted upon?
- The *timeliness test*: Can the data be analysed soon enough for action to be taken?
- The *cost test*: Is it going to be worth the cost of collecting and analysing the data?
- The *gaming test*: Will the measure encourage any undesirable behaviours?

The answers may not all be what is expected. However, because KPIs play an important role in driving the operational culture of an organization, it is important to spend considerable time on *due diligence* (thoroughly checking and exploring the issue at hand; trying to make sure that things are being done correctly), to ensure the KPIs are specific to a department and to a moment in time, and are acted upon (through the action review steps outlined in Figure 12.6). Finally, it should be remembered that all indicators should be *refreshed*. In other words, they are relevant only as long as they are used, and they will be used only if they inform rather than simply record.

Performance Management Models

From Taylor (1911) to Skinner (1974), and through the quality gurus (Oakland, 1993; Kelemen, 2003), the imperative to measure has increased throughout business. Although in the main this is helpful to businesses and managers, it has nevertheless led to the *unanticipated consequences of measurement* (Ridgway, 1956). The concept of a balanced set of measures was first mooted by Drucker (1955) as a potential solution to the issues raised by these same themes. However, many years passed, and various iterations of models evolved, until a coherent framework was developed that could be put to use by any kind of organization. This section introduces several models that historically have been practised. Developments in both thinking and practice can be traced through the models, as each one appears to build on its predecessor. Each of these approaches attempts to overcome the limitations of reporting mainly on financial measurements, and to respond to the need to provide balanced measurements collected into a framework, where all the measurements can be considered. The models discussed are:

- The Performance Pyramid
- The Balanced Scorecard
- The Performance Prism
- EFQM
- Benchmarking.

Each approach provides its own unique perspective and reflects the major concerns prevalent at the time it was developed. Each approach still remains valid, and provides management with a lens through which to examine the activities and outcomes within their organization. The choice of model, and how it is adapted, rests on the personal or corporate preferences of the management team, based on organizational requirements and culture.

The Performance Pyramid

This framework displays the organization performance measures in the form of a pyramid, with a hierarchy of measures cascaded down from the vision, reflecting coherence and alignment within the business (Figure 12.7). The underpinning premise is that in theory these articulated targets are also *SMART*: specific; measurable, meaningful and motivational; achievable and action-oriented; relevant and results-oriented; and, finally, timely and trackable.

This pyramid illustrates how objectives are cascaded down the business hierarchy in such a way that they become operational – and therefore measurable – targets. The framework encourages the creation of a cycle of activity, accountability and responsibility.

Its basic assumption is that of combining customer-oriented principles with financial and non-financial figures. It shows the company at four different levels, and provides a structure for two-way communication.

Strategy and operations are linked together by translating objectives from the top down, based on customer priorities and reporting measures from the bottom up. You will note that no measures are specifically mentioned here. This is because *what* you measure is contextual, and specific to each organization.

The Balanced Scorecard

Perhaps the most ubiquitous of performance management models is Kaplan and Norton's Balanced Scorecard (Kaplan and Norton, 1996, 2008), which measures the achievement of the business strategy. It communicates

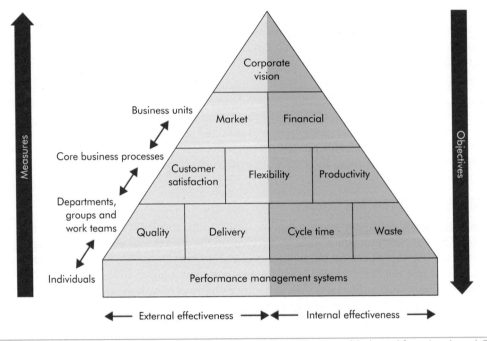

Figure 12.7 The strategic measurement and reporting technique (SMART) pyramid (adapted from Lynch and Cross, 1991)

strategic direction, and establishes key performance measures and performance targets at the organizational level. It is both a process and a tool. As a *thinking process* it defines what constitutes a thriving business, and what matters most to it. As a *communications tool* it articulates what people need to do to achieve success, and as a *management tool* it provides traceability of performance problems to their cause.

The Balanced Scorecard helps an organization keep track of the things it has to do in order to thrive. The discipline of linking strategy to individual needs and responsibilities clarifies understanding, and helps to develop measures that help identify what is going well and what is not.

The Balanced Scorecard also provides assistance with the vital task of communicating a corporate strategy to the rest of the business through identifying the vital aspects that must be 'got right', and turning often vague statements of strategy into concrete, practical requirements and actions. It does all this by measuring performance through four perspectives, where for each perspective one to five key measures are developed for a particular purpose, strategy or objective (Figure 12.8).

Kaplan and Norton suggest using the scorecard for a year or so to have confidence in the indicators, so that you are sure the measures are correct. Once you are satisfied with the measures, you can use the scorecard to also appraise and compensate performance. In reality, the search for 'the right measures' is flawed, since a PMS should contain indicators suitable for a particular time and purpose, with the emphasis being that a performance culture is driven not through the choice of the *right measures* per se, but for the choice of measures for a particular purpose, strategy or objective. Figure 12.9 shows the Balanced Scorecard with its four perspectives, and how the framework is built with the indicators.

How do customers see us? Customer perspective

In this perspective the company needs to depict the way in which the internal and external customers value the company's products and services. Here performance measures for customer satisfaction are evaluated. Customers concerns tend to relate to time, quality, performance, service and cost. The focus here is on customer needs and satisfaction as well as on market share. Most organizations make general statements about their customers, and believe their satisfaction is critical to the future prosperity of the business. So market share shows that customers are either being attracted or retained, and it would be fair to assume that this is because customers are having one, all or a combination of their needs met, based on the measures of time, quality, performance, service and cost.

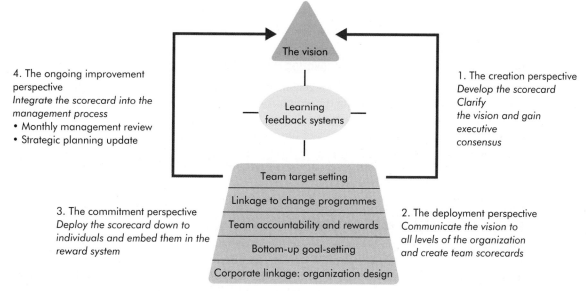

Figure 12.8 Using the scorecard to drive a performance culture (Kaplan and Norton, 1996)

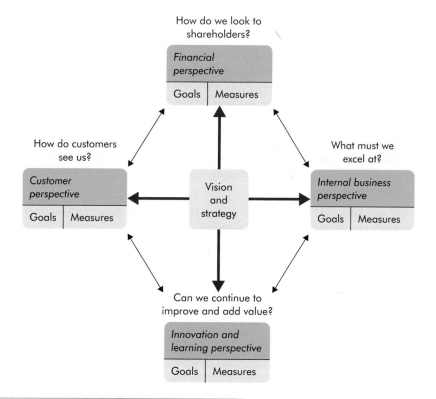

Figure 12.9 The Balanced Scorecard (Kaplan and Norton, 1996)

How do we look to shareholders? Financial perspective

In this perspective, the company identifies how and what individual functions contribute to the accomplishment of its overall mission and strategic goals. Moreover, performance measures for plans and processes are also considered. Typically, goals have to do with profitability, growth and shareholder value. The measures are composed of the results that the business ultimately delivers to its shareholders. In addition, financial results are crucial to confirm whether the focus in the other three perspectives has delivered results. These indicators can influence future performance by applying revenue and expense indicators in less traditional ways, such as on key processes, or tracking the costs of reports.

Can we continue to improve and add value? Innovation and learning perspective

In this perspective, the company emphasizes the design and application of business management initiatives that foster increased innovation and learning among the workforce. Included here can be measures to increase sales of new products, and measures to improve yield, defect rates, customer satisfaction or position in competitor ranking. The indicators direct attention to the basis of future success by focusing on continuous improvement of products and processes. Measures are typically around the introduction of new products, and improvement in adverse measures such as scrap rates and levels of rework. Also common in this perspective are indicators around the organization's people and infrastructure.

What must we excel at? Internal business perspective

Companies must decide which core competencies they wish to excel at. Usually there is a focus on critical internal operations that enable them to satisfy customer needs. The internal measures should stem from business processes and key factors such as quality levels, on-time delivery, customer relations, employee skills, improvement levels and productivity. The main area of attention is on the key internal processes that drive the business, with managers asked to define goals and measures around key processes, actions and core competencies that will have the greatest impact on customer satisfaction. These indicators are often split out further and deployed down through the organization to create alignment of activities at all levels.

The Performance Prism

The Performance Prism (Figure 12.10) is a three-dimensional model developed by the Centre for Business Performance at the Cranfield School of Management in the UK.

The advantages of this so-called 'second generation' PMS over older systems, such as the Performance Pyramid and the Balanced Scorecard in particular, is that it applies to all stakeholders in the organization – principally investors, customers, employees, suppliers, regulators and communities. It does this by considering both the needs of these stakeholders and what the organization needs from them. In essence, it examines the reciprocal relationship with each stakeholder, and then addresses each of the strategies, processes and capabilities required to satisfy these two sets of needs (Neely *et al.*, 2002).

The Performance Prism adopts a stakeholder-centric view of performance measurement. It reflects the need for an organization to identify and satisfy each of its key stakeholders.

So the first and fundamental perspective on performance is the stakeholder satisfaction perspective: organizations need to identify and measure whether or not they are satisfying the wants and needs of their stakeholders.

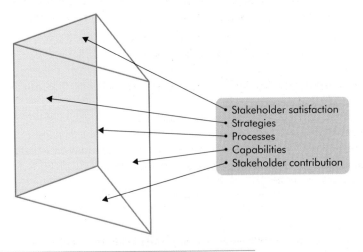

- Stakeholder satisfaction
- Strategies
- Processes
- Capabilities
- Stakeholder contribution

Figure 12.10 The five facets of the performance prism (Neely *et al.*, 2002)

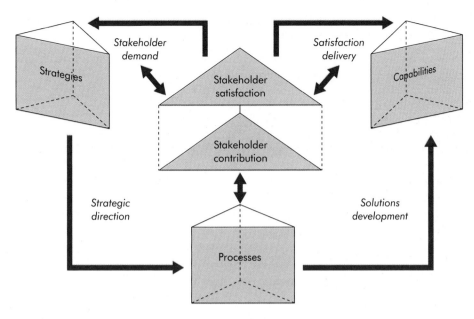

Figure 12.11 The Performance Prism (Neely et al., 2002)

The other side of that coin is that all organizations, to a greater or lesser degree, expect to have a symbiotic relationship with their stakeholders. So there has to be a quid pro quo: what can they do for the organization? What does the organization need from the stakeholders so that they contribute to success?

Once the wants and needs of the stakeholders have been identified, the organization has to turn to the other perspectives on performance: strategy, processes and capabilities. The Performance Prism's framework is constructed with three further critical facets or measurement sub-categories: these are strategies, processes and capabilities (Figure 12.11). Each facet of the prism represents a critical category of performance measurement and management focus. If this broad perspective on performance is not adopted, then there is a significant risk that the organization will fail to satisfy the wants and needs of a particular stakeholder, or stakeholder group.

First it is necessary to consider the strategies an organization is going to use to ensure the satisfaction of its stakeholders. Measurement of strategies considers whether the strategy is being implemented, communicated, encouraged and challenged. The company then needs to put measures in place to assess the processes that are designed to deliver the strategy, and the capabilities necessary to perform the processes.

This should help to avoid one of the key reasons for strategic failure, which is that often the organization's processes and capabilities are not aligned with one another, or with the organization's strategies. Like a DNA chain, there are linkages and interdependencies, connectivity and influences between the facets. The relationships are linked in a cause and effect relationship: what happens in one area has an immediate impact elsewhere.

The differences between the Performance Prism and other performance systems can be summarized as follows:
- It addresses all stakeholders – not just investors and customers, i.e. shareholders – and makes them the focal point for measurement design.
- It identifies critical strategy realization measurement issues – including metrics for challenging its assumptions and checking its dependencies.
- It focuses on measuring the key process architecture and design elements.
- It ensures that essential capability development components get included.
- It allows 'drilling down' to a framework providing further selection prompts at greater levels of detail.
- It is three-dimensional, and implicitly suggests cause and effect linkages between the measures selected for each facet of the framework.

EFQM

The EFQM Business Excellence framework is covered in greater detail in Chapter 13. However, it is pertinent to mention it briefly in this chapter because of the influence it has on managing performance within an organization.

The very fact that it is a non-prescriptive tool for managing performance by examining performance criteria means that managers must consider in greater depth what and how they want to measure, and for what purpose.

The detail of how each criterion contributes to performance management thinking is listed below:
- *Leadership*: how business leaders behave in support of excellence
- *Policy and strategy*: how plans are produced and made to happen
- *People*: how people are recruited, trained, developed and involved
- *Partnership and resources*: how resources are managed and used
- *Processes*: provide a clear, easily understood depiction of how the business is carried out
- *Customer results*: are customers' needs being met? Are they satisfied?
- *Society results*: is the business meeting the needs of the community? Is the community satisfied?
- *Performance indicators*: are targets met?

Benchmarking

Benchmarking came to prominence in the 1980s (Oakland, 1993; Johnston and Clark, 2008) as a way of measuring performance outside the firm. There was widespread interest in understanding an organization's performance relative to others, which gave companies insights into how much they had to improve, *as well as* ideas on how they might improve. Companies can have very different businesses but the same processes – invoicing, payments, and supply chain, for example. Finding out who does what in the best way is a step to finding out with which company you would want to carry out a benchmarking exercise.

The UK government keeps lists of organizations willing to be involved in benchmarking exercises.

You can benchmark for all sorts of things in a variety of ways. Internal and external benchmarking provides comparison between functions. Non-competitive benchmarking provides comparison of operations with best in class for a particular category of process. Competitive benchmarking (usually via anonymous benchmarking clubs) provides comparison of operations against competitors, where you might compare call centre processes and performance across the banking sector, for instance. The objectives of benchmarking generally all stem from the desire to improve performance through managing something differently – whether that improvement is current operational performance, copying new ideas or practices, or understanding better how to serve customers.

Generally all organizations involved benefit, as do each company's customers.

BUSINESS INTEGRATION

SHORT CASE 12.3

Managing for Results

Four Seasons Health Care owns and operates over 350 nursing and care homes and specialized care centres in England, Scotland, Northern Ireland, Jersey and the Isle of Man, with an average of 60 staff in each home.

The company is one of the largest independent providers of care services in the United Kingdom. Four Seasons' origins date back to the late 1980s. For over 20 years the company has achieved growth through acquisitions and the construction of care facilities.

Four Seasons cares for over 17,500 people in its care homes, nursing homes and specialist units, and employs over 21,500 staff.

Almost 80% of the care home sector is fragmented, made up of 24,000 operators in small, domestic-type home environments. The remaining 20% of the sector in the UK is made up of four relatively large organizations. In such a fragmented industry it is hard to drive change; it is heavily regulated, because of its nature, and it is very hard to manage costs because it's a people-intensive industry. Quality control is key, because one mistake can affect a

Source: © Kirby Hamilton/iStock

resident's general comfort and well-being as well as contravene the stringent regulations. Staff costs are 60% of the cost base, with most being minimum-wage employees. The business is about people looking after people; it is a low-tech, high-touch business. The remainder of the cost base is around 20% on food and 15% on utilities, with the balance relating to consumables, medical supplies and so on. Fixed overheads are high, and margins are tight. EBITDA. Margins are in the region of 2%.

If good performance management stems from understanding your business drivers, then this business is given a clear message by the way revenue is generated. About 80% of the revenue comes from the public purse. In the current economic climate, local authorities and primary care trusts are seeking to cut expenditure by 15–20%, thereby reducing their fees. Historically, the large companies have grown their business through acquisition. The focus now is to grow the bottom line through doing what they do well as a core business even better than before. Being able to do this is made possible by knowing what success looks like, and knowing what the end goal is. Having good measurement and recognizing where you need to improve is the first step in performance improvement. This is made possible by having a good performance management system and accepting the difficult messages that come from that. There is no acquisition programme that can deliver bottom-line results the same way as performance improvement.

The business has to reconcile conflicting tensions in its daily operations as well as in legislative requirements. The business is about providing homes to people – fundamentally, care homes rent out rooms. Residents are a primary stakeholder – they are not necessarily the customer, though. Sometimes the customer is a relative of the resident, and their perception of the service required is different from the person receiving it. As a regulated industry, the sector must conform to a myriad of quality standards and requirements, and any home can be subjected to random checks with no notice. Staff and management work in small homes, even though they are part of a large organization. At the operational level, the strategic objective of the business, as articulated in the vision, can be realized only through recognizing that in practical terms there are a number of business operations converging into one company. Hospitality and catering, just as in hotel management, is a core part; housekeeping and cleaning services is another business element; medical and pharmaceutical is another. Purchasing and the supply chain are an important component in standardization of materials. The main component of the business is service – and that is something the company strives to personalize, not standardize.

Questions

1 How does the management team draw all the knowledge from each home to establish best practice?
2 Where should knowledge be stored, managed and transferred?
3 How can benchmarking play a role in improving performance in the individual care homes?
4 How do the corporate objectives translate into operational reality for this company?

Source: www.fshc.co.uk/company-information/about-four-seasons

Contemporary Thinking

New pressures and external demands have led managers to both refine and enlarge the search for meaningful ways to measure and manage performance.

Techniques and Approaches

For instance, the proliferation of *enterprise performance management* (EPM) systems has helped management think about the practicalities of what and when to measure in order to be able to better manipulate the levers of performance to deliver the desired results. Gartner, Inc. (NYSE: IT) is the world's leading information technology research and advisory company, and they confirm that EPM systems provide real-time access to critical business performance indicators to improve the performance and effectiveness of the business, with companies showing strong interests in *business activity monitoring* (BAM) systems. BAM and EPM are interchangeable terms. Real-time access to key performance indicators or business process information is one of the core elements for a successful

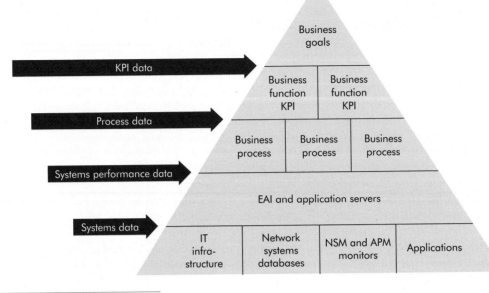

Figure 12.12 Real-time data collection

process and people management system. Since performance measurement cannot be managed independently of business processes, BAM systems monitor performance metrics in terms of business processes, and through this comes the link with people performance.

Once again the triangle image demonstrates how the approach is all-encompassing at all levels throughout the organization, showing alignment with strategic objectives. From a technical point of view, the lower two arrows in Figure 12.12 refer to actual system and data performance. The two larger arrows refer to the issues that operational managers concern themselves with – how processes are being executed, and what the KPIs are showing. These two are the ones that together create a picture for all managers of how the business goals are being created.

Figure 12.13 uses the same triangle image to highlight how people and managers are involved in these systems, along with the appropriate level of detail in line with an organizational hierarchy. Again, the lowest two arrows indicate IT support and involvement. This is about making sure the data is being collated accurately and in a timely manner, and that the systems work properly to ensure this happens. The top three arrows indicate operational manager involvement, where the process manager, or departmental or section manager, or even team leader will be concerned at a greater level of detail, more specifically interested in knowing what is happening; the senior manager is looking at his function, directorate or division, and the executive needs to know about the big picture, the high-level indicators aggregating the various detailed indicators.

Although this kind of comprehensive automation of a PMS is becoming widespread, there is a mounting body of evidence (Neely *et al.*, 2008a, 2008b) which indicates that, no matter what the possibilities are for EPM to deliver organizational benefits, there are many problems that prevent companies from achieving the full potential of their systems and their knowledge. Enterprise performance management systems, appropriately designed and implemented, can overcome all the nine identified gaps that hinder the realization of significant value through EPM. The gaps are depicted in Figure 12.14.

Work to date shows that the journey to a world-class enterprise performance management system is neither simple nor straightforward, and it is a journey that companies are likely to continue to pursue for a number of years to come.

Rampersad (2005) has researched a new blueprint for creating a learning organization in which personal and organizational performance and learning mutually reinforce each other on a sustainable basis. His starting premise was that traditional business management concepts are insufficiently committed to learning, and rarely

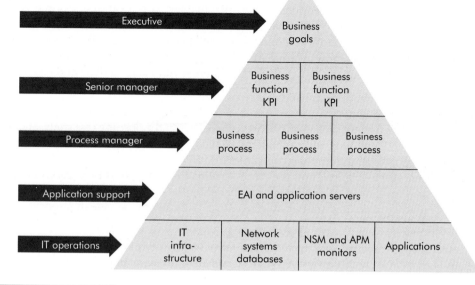

Figure 12.13 Real-time visibility

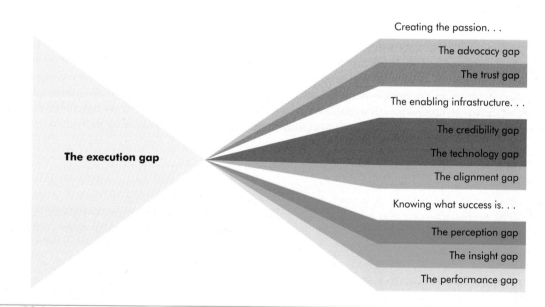

Figure 12.14 What drives the execution gap in EPM (Neely et al., 2008a, p. 3)

take the specific personal ambitions of employees into account. The misalignment with organizational strategy is starkly evident when the evidence is considered that this kind of behaviour results in a plethora of superficial improvements, marked by temporary and cosmetic changes, and coupled with failing projects that lack sufficient buy-in by personnel, and in some cases even have an adverse effect. To counteract this, he has developed a new business management concept, called the *total performance scorecard*. This approach stresses the importance of and the need for developing an organizational structure and philosophy that combine the goals and aspirations of the individual with those of the company. It is a melding process, which results in a corporate culture that is both individually and organizationally driven. In keeping with current thinking about sustainability and employee engagement as well as customer orientation, this new tool may gain credence over the coming years, if not in its entirety then through the adoption by organizations of aspects of this concept to continue to help them in the quest for improved performance.

Concepts and Measures

Another interesting direction that has been identified is the analogy with sport and sporting achievements to help managers enhance organizational performance. Adcroft and Teckman (2008) assert that understanding the outcome of contests is a complex business. Contests are not always won by the best-performing team, but rather are won by the team with the most appropriate blend of competitiveness and performance. Applied to businesses, this thinking can help enliven and confirm the requirement to align activity and target-setting with organizational objectives, so that companies can be confident in their own combination of competitiveness and performance.

High-performance organizations (HPOs), such as W.L. Gore & Associates in the opening case study, are increasingly being studied with a view to identifying what a modern HPO looks like, and providing the characteristics that managers need to focus on in order to turn their companies into HPOs (Sung and Ashton, 2005; de Waal, 2007). The key thing about these developments is how they show the link to people – how they work and behave – and how the appraisal system for individual performance is therefore part of the overall PMS. HPOs are shown to demonstrate that the practice of linking strategic objectives to activity and to individuals results in alignment of purpose and outcome.

CSR

Measurement is increasingly required for *corporate social responsibility* (CSR) and *sustainability* as governments and organizations become more keenly aware of the social and environmental impacts of their activities. This is partly legislation driven, and partly market driven. The outcome appears to be that organizations need to add two further dimensions to their PMS – those of *social* and *environmental impact*. This requirement appears to have arisen as the belief became widespread that an organization's ultimate success is dependent on the overall fulfilment of obligations to communities, as well as to employees, suppliers and customers. This can, and should, be measured and calculated. Sometimes this is referred to as the *triple bottom line* (3BL).

Large organizations have absorbed this as a principle, although as yet there is not enough evidence to demonstrate whether organizations are being driven by it. Compliance with the philosophy is complicated by the fact that there is a multiplicity of legislation around it. For instance, in the UK all companies over a given size must report carbon usage using a nationally imposed calculation. China, the USA and Europe also all have their own legislative requirements around this. Standardization for comparative purposes is therefore not routinely possible, and the complexities raised around this are not yet fully understood for global trade or for individual companies.

BUSINESS INTEGRATION

SHORT CASE 12.4

Integrated Performance Management Delivering Success

Overview

Tesco, the British-based international grocery and general merchandising retail group, operates 4,331 stores across 14 countries, employs around 470,000 people, and in 2009 generated £59.4 billion in sales. Since its inception as a 'pile it high, sell it cheap' market trader, Tesco has become the largest private sector employer in the UK, and is currently the second-largest global retailer, based on profit.

Organizational Culture

Tesco's mission and over-riding philosophy is *'every little helps'*, from which two key values emerge, creating the central code of conduct. These are: 'No-one tries harder for customers' and 'Treat people how I like to be treated'. The aims are to instil a customer focus in everything people do, and to have well-managed people working in an environment that is based on trust and respect, believing that well-motivated and well-managed staff will give customers a better service.

Source: © Craftvision/iStock

Figure 12.15 Tesco's corporate steering wheel

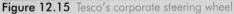

Corporate and Operational Performance

Tesco's performance and business success hinge on the right strategic objectives communicated effectively to all staff, so that everyone in the company is actively and continuously engaged in trying to improve company performance, and having the data and analytical skills to test ideas, and turn insight into relevant customer and business actions. Even in the current global recession, Tesco saw 5% growth in sales and 5% growth in profits in 2009.

Upon joining Tesco, CEO Sir Terry Leahy made it clear that the company needed a clear direction, a map and a compass. The management team decided to create a PMS that would provide the map and outline the key strategic objectives. They then created the KPIs to act as the compass, enabling the organization to check whether it was on track or not.

The *corporate steering wheel* (Figure 12.14) provides strategic focus for Tesco by communicating what matters the most, in a simple and easy-to-understand framework. It includes 20 corporate objectives across five perspectives, arranged in a circle around the two values, with the mission at the core of it all. The CEO says that having objectives across these five perspectives allows a balanced approach to performance. The steering wheel analogy also 'creates a shared language, a shared way of thinking and a common blueprint for action.'

Individual Performance

Every store has its own steering wheel to manage performance, engage staff, facilitate local discussion, and capture local challenges, so that everybody feels responsible for performance. To this end, Sir Terry closed the strategy department, because he wanted everyone to understand strategy.

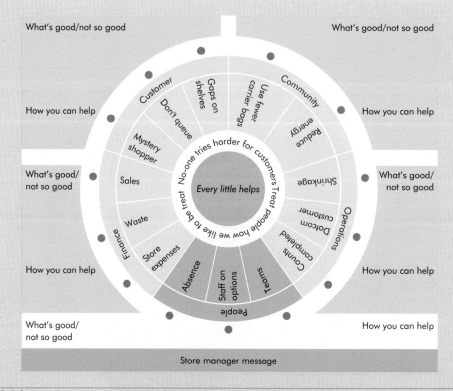

Figure 12.16 Tesco's corporate steering wheel – control/review stage, action review template for stores

There are many performance indicators, but because of the danger of looking at them in isolation and out of context, the company pays regular attention to those that matter most to the business. Tesco's philosophy is to analyse only the data that help answer the critical and most important questions. Tesco always stresses the need for practical insights. Pragmatism ruled when building the PMS, and the goal was to build the smallest data storage that would give useful information. For example, the company looks at a 10% sample of the data to identify key issues, and then investigates it further using larger data sets for the questions that matter to customers and the business. It does not try to answer every conceivable performance question with data, managing by exception not by data overload.

The keys to good management insights and evidence-based decision-making are having the right data and the ability to analyse that data. They help answer the 'big' questions and put performance data into context.

Tesco has an internal team responsible for analysing the data, creating information, and extracting insights. That is how it ensures the continued relevance of its PMS as insights, and decisions made, reflect the shifting priorities. Tesco has been able to amend the steering wheel in line with strategic objectives. For instance, a recent evolution was the addition of the community perspective, when Tesco realized the issues of climate change and the impact its presence has on a local community created challenges. The introduction of the community perspective has led to initiatives such as reducing the use of carrier bags by 50%, providing more locally sourced products, and gaining a reduction in the company's carbon footprint.

Questions

1 How is Tesco's mission expressed?
2 How are Tesco's values encouraged in its employees?
3 What are the five key business perspectives that inform strategy and actions?

4 How has Tesco used its PMS to achieve business success?
5 What were the critical success factors in implementing the PMS?
6 How did Tesco develop its KPIs?

Source: B. Marr, *Delivering Success: How Tesco is Managing, Measuring and Maximising its Performance*, Management Case Study, The Advanced Performance Institute, 2009 (www.ap-institute.com)

Summary

In this chapter we have introduced the concept of performance management as a conduit for the proactive realization of organizational objectives. We have examined the role of performance management in ensuring effective business performance, and how culture and measurement are linked, the one influencing the other and vice versa. We considered how a culture of suitable measurement can be established so that sustainable performance can be embedded. The emphasis throughout has been on the importance of the management contribution to the PMS's and thereby the organization's success.

In summary, the components of a PMS, regardless of the precise model or framework used, are that goals and objectives need to be articulated into observable and measurable parts; metrics need to be actionable and tangible, and support the tracking of achieving the objects; and targets reflect performance-level expectations set against the strategic plan.

The real test of any performance management system is its ability to discriminate good from bad performance. To do this in a balanced way the PMS *must* combine financial and non-financial measures into an overall appraisal and compensation system. No matter what managers choose to do within their organization, these two points are irrefutable. As long as the PMS being used has the characteristics listed throughout this chapter, and as long as judgements on performance can be fulfilled, the chosen PMS will work for the organization.

All other details are organization dependent, set in the context of the configuration of events, demands and culture within that organization.

As it becomes more readily accepted that the 21st century organization needs to have top-down direction to motivate self-directed, thinking-intensive employees, working with one another horizontally across the company, companies nevertheless need to acknowledge that *hierarchical leadership is important* and still exists. They also need to recognize that it is equally important to enable *large-scale collaboration across the enterprise*. No matter what systems are in place, however sophisticated they may be, whether vertical and horizontal information flows are provided, the struggle for the most relevant and applicable PMS boils down to *what you do with it*.

The practical, operational implication of this simple statement is that it is the people aspect that is the most important, because it is through the people that continuous improvement and corporate objectives can be achieved.

Key Theories

The key theories discussed in this chapter were:

- **Organizational alignment**
- **Operations performance objectives**
- Components of a **performance management system**

- **Performance management frameworks:**
  - The Performance Pyramid
  - The Balanced Scorecard
  - The Performance Prism
  - EFQM

- **Benchmarking** as a tool for managing performance

- **Continuous improvement** through performance management. There are many ways to improve performance, and using the tools of quality can help (see Chapter 13)

Performance Indicator Examples

Performance indicator	Example
Sales performance	Customer satisfaction – i.e. warranty claims, service level incidents Conversion rate – i.e. number of customers seen for one sale
Quality performance	Error rate Customer complaints (as an absolute number or as % of units sold or as % of total customer transactions) Rework Customer retention levels
People performance	Productivity: – Invoices processed per manhour – Number of telephone calls taken per manhour Days absence compared with total annual workdays Utilization Volumes processed Headcount/hours available/hours worked
Process performance	Backlog items Training days Skills flexibility Maintenance or system downtime

Key Equations

Sales performance:

$$\text{Sales performance} = \frac{\text{Actual units sold for the period}}{\text{Planned sales for the period}} \ (\times \ 100 \text{ to give the \%})$$

$$\text{Sales performance} = \frac{\text{Sales (£/€)}}{\text{Labour costs (£/€)}}$$

$$\text{Sales performance} = \frac{\text{Sales (volume or value)}}{\text{Salespeople}}$$

Quality performance:

$$\text{Quality performance} = \frac{\text{Error rate}}{\text{Volume produced}} \ (\times \ 100 \text{ to give the \%})$$

$$\text{Quality performance} = \frac{\text{Number of complaints}}{\text{Number of transactions}}$$

Productivity:

$$\text{Productivity} = \frac{\text{Output(s) from the operation}}{\text{Input(s) to the operation}}$$

$$\text{Productivity (or customer satisfaction)} = \frac{\text{Number of complaints}}{\text{Number of transactions}}$$

People performance:

$$\text{Utilization} = \frac{\text{Hours used}}{\text{Hours available}}$$

Process performance:

$$\text{Delay/throughput time} = \frac{\text{Actual time taken}}{\text{Planned elapsed time}}$$

$$\text{Capacity} = \text{Available hours} \times \text{Standard planned units per hour}$$

$$\text{Capacity} = \text{The resource} \times \text{Units per resource} \times \text{Availability}$$

Suggested Answers to Stop and Think Questions

1 **Customer intimacy:** If customer satisfaction is the main business focus, then managers need to consider all aspects of operations from the customer perspective. This includes product design and marketing. Questions at the forefront of the manager's mind should be: 'What is it that the customer would like?', 'How would the customer like to receive this?', 'What is important to the customer?' and so on. This is not so that the company is organized around customer whims, but so that managers and staff alike understand that trying to satisfy customer requirements is paramount. In practice this means designing processes and systems around this rather than around internal drivers.

2 **Performance management crisis:** Managers could have thought about outcomes (i.e. patients cured, patient requirements), and with that as a starting point could have avoided much of the 'extraneous' work required by the focus on matters other than what they were there to achieve. Managers could have approached the planning and target-setting process as outlined in Figure 12.2. This would have helped them establish a link directly between patient care targets and efficiency targets. They could then have considered the alignment model in Figure 12.3 to help them work out what they could actually do, and what they couldn't readily achieve. Having the results of this gap analysis would then have enabled them to make a series of decisions as to what service they could deliver, and how they could deliver it, without the dramatic unintended results that were actually achieved.

   The steps could be:
   - Determine organizational objectives
   - Ascertain which objectives satisfy which stakeholder requirements
   - Establish any stakeholders not covered, and any operational aspects omitted
   - Cascade through the organization the requirements for each, through communication and reporting
   - Ensure management and staff understand their own specific roles to ensure goal fulfilment (not just attainment) is delivered
   - Monitor, through the PMS.

3 **Airline CEO KPI:** The number of delayed flights is the key performance indicator here. This simple indicator uncovers significant performance details of the airline for any given period. Knowing the number of delayed flights enables the CEO to have a better grasp of customer service issues, employee issues, financial issues and capacity issues. This is because each delayed flight will have repercussions for the number of complaints the airline will receive from its passengers. It tells the CEO that

▶ overtime has to be paid, and that scheduling problems for other flights may exist, since crew are subject to strict time and location factors. Fines are incurred for landing outside the specified slots, as well as for overstaying in a slot, and are payable to the airport authorities. It indicates how the potential knock-on effects can impact on future performance because of flights that have not happened, and passengers who have not moved to planned destinations. This creates a backlog, which has to be dealt with while avoiding further repercussions, and doing so with a fixed number of crews and planes, taking into account airports' provision of landing slots and so on.

This indicator shows how one performance measure, relevant across all geographical sectors for instance, is clearly aligned to and derives from the strategic objectives.

4 **Useful:** A performance measure is useful only when it has a target against which it can be compared. In its own right it is meaningless, because it cannot be compared against what was planned, and can rarely be linked back to the overall performance objectives.

connect

Review Questions

1 What are the five key components of a performance measurement system (PMS)?

2 What is the difference between performance management and performance measurement?

3 What is meant by the term 'integrated PMS'?

4 Why is an integrated PMS useful for an organization?

5 What is the difference between efficiency and effectiveness?

6 How does benchmarking help in managing performance?

7 What are the two new dimensions that organizations need to start thinking about for their PMSs?

Discussion Questions

1 Discuss why performance management must be a top-down process.

2 Discuss how using a PMS such as the Balanced Scorecard, the Performance Prism or the EFQM model is a better tool for managing performance than a measure such as productivity.

3 What are the cultural and people challenges that organizations face when attempting to introduce an integrated performance measurement system?

4 Discuss the linkage between performance measurement and performance management, and their impact on continuous improvement.

5 Explain how performance management can be an enabler for an organization's corporate sustainability?

Problems

1 A machine is rated at 10 units an hour, is available for 2×9 hour shifts, is used for 7 hours a shift, and produces 55 units a shift.

(a) Calculate the production capability of the machine.

(b) Calculate the planned utilization of the machine.

(c) Calculate the planned total production of the machine.

(d) Calculate the planned productivity of the machine

(e) What is the efficiency rating for this machine at the given levels?

2   A call centre employs 500 agents (the resource) 7 hours a day, 5 days a week (availability). The call centre staff are required to answer 8 calls (the unit) per hour, and be on the telephone 5 hours a day (hours used).

(a)   Calculate the capacity of the call centre.

(b)   Calculate the weekly planned utilization of an agent.

(c)   One agent successfully answers 10 calls an hour every day, and is on the phone 5.5 hours instead of 5 each day. Calculate the planned and actual productivity of this agent.

Online Learning Centre

Visit the Online Learning Centre at **www.mcgraw-hill.co.uk/textbooks/paton** for a range of resources to support your learning.

Further Reading

Axson, D.A.J. (2007) *Best Practices in Planning and Performance Management: From Data to Decisions*, 2nd edn, Wiley, Hoboken, NJ.

Dale, B.G., van der Wiele, T. and van Iwaarden, J. (2007) *Managing Quality*, 5th edn, Blackwell, Malden, MA.

Eccles, R.G. (1991) 'The performance measurement manifesto', *Harvard Business Review*, January–February, 131–137.

Eckerson, W.W. (2005) *Performance Dashboards: Measuring, Monitoring, and Managing Your Business*, Wiley, Hoboken, NJ.

Latham, G.P. (2005) 'New developments in performance management', *Organizational Dynamics*, **34**(1), 77–87.

Lynch, R.L. and Cross, K.F. (1991) *Measure Up: The Essential Guide to Measuring Business Performance*, Mandarin, London.

Marr, B. (2006) *Strategic Performance Management: Leveraging and Measuring Your Intangible Value Drivers*, Butterworth-Heinemann, Oxford.

Neely, A. (2007) 'Performance: the search for meaningful measures', *Management Services*, **51**(2), 14–17.

Neely, A., Yaghi, B. and Youell, N. (2008) *Enterprise Performance Management: The Global State of the Art*, Cranfield University, School of Management.

Parmenter, D. (2007) *Key Performance Indicators: Developing, Implementing and Using Winning KPIs*, Wiley, Hoboken, NJ.

Pongatichat, P. and Johnston, R. (2008) 'Exploring strategy-misaligned performance measurement', *International Journal of Productivity and Performance Management*, **57**(3), 207–222.

Varma, A., Budhwar, P.S. and DeNisi, A. (eds) (2008) *Performance Management Systems: A Global Perspective*, Routledge, London.

References

Adams, C. and Neely, A. (2002) 'Prism reform', *Financial Management*, May, 28–31.

Adcroft, A. and Teckman, J. (2008) 'A new look at the sports paradigm for business: performing isn't enough', *Journal of Business Strategy*, **29**(5), 38–43.

Bititci, U.S., Mendibil, K., Nudurupati, S., Garengo, P. and Turner, T. (2006) 'Dynamics of performance measurement and organisational culture', *International Journal of Operations and Production Management*, **26** (12), 1325–1350.

CIPD (2005) *High Performance Work Practices: Linking Strategy and Skills to Performance Outcomes*, Chartered Institute of Personnel and Development, London.

De Waal, A.A. (2007) 'The characteristics of a high performance organization', *Business Strategy Series*, **8**(3), 179–185.

Drucker, P.F. (1955) *The Practice of Management*, Heinemann, London.

Johnston, R. and Clark, G. (2008) *Service Operations Management: Improving Service Delivery*, Pearson Education, Harlow.

Kaplan, R.S. and Norton, D.P. (2008) 'Mastering the management system', *Harvard Business Review*, **86**(1), 62–77.

Kaplan, R.S. and Norton, D.P. (1996) *The Balanced Scorecard: Translating Strategy into Action*, Harvard Business School Press, Boston, MA.

Kelemen, M.L. (2003) *Managing Quality*, Sage, London.

Neely, A., Adams, C. and Kennerly, M. (2002) *The Performance Prism: The Scorecard for Measuring and Managing Business Success*. FT Prentice Hall, London.

Neely, A., Yaghi, B. and Youell, N. (2008a) *Enterprise Performance Management: The Global State of the Art*, Cranfield University, School of Management.

Neely, A., Yaghi, B. and Youell, N. (2008b) *Enterprise Performance Management: The UK State of the Art*, Cranfield University, School of Management.

Oakland, J.S. (1993) *Total Quality Management: The Route to Improving Performance*, Nichols, East Brunswick, NJ.

Rampersad, H.K. (2005) 'Total performance scorecard: the way to personal integrity and organizational effectiveness', *Measuring Business Excellence*, **9**(3), 21–35.

Ridgway, V.F. (1956) 'Dysfunctional consequences of performance measurements', *Administrative Science Quarterly*, **1**(2), 240–247.

Skinner, W. (1974) 'The focused factory', *Harvard Business Review*, **52**(3), 113–121.

Slack, N., Chambers, S. and Johnston, R. (2007) *Operations Management*, Financial Times Prentice Hall, Harlow.

Sung, J. and Ashton, D. (2005) *High Performance Work Practices: Linking Strategy and Skills to Performance Outcomes*, Department of Trade and Industry, London.

Taylor, F.W. (1911) *The Principles of Scientific Management*, Harper, New York.

Treacy, M. and Wiersema, F. (1993) 'Customer intimacy and other value disciplines', *Harvard Business Review*, January–February, 84–93.

Wade, D. and Recardo, R. (2001) *Corporate Performance Management; How to Build a Better Organisation through Measurement-Driven Strategic Alignment*, Butterworth-Heinemann, Woburn, MA.

13 Quality Management

Coca-Cola's Dasani

Dasani is the Coca-Cola Company's bottled water, which first launched in the US in 1999 to compete with Pepsi's Aquafina brand. It was described as bottled, purified water that was 'enhanced with minerals for a pure, fresh taste'. It had appealing packaging, with attractive recyclable light-blue tinted bottles. Dasani's promotional campaign carried the punch line 'Treat yourself well. Everyday', as the company wanted to emphasize the emotional and physical satisfaction provided by a healthy lifestyle. Dasani quickly captured a huge market share in bottled water, second only to Aquafina.

Coca-Cola spent £7 million launching Dasani in the UK on 10 February 2004, with the rather unlikely punch line 'The more you live life, the more you need Dasani.' It was a huge investment.

Within five weeks of its launch, Coca-Cola voluntarily recalled its entire stock of Dasani bottled water – about 500,000 bottles. The recall was made after a potentially harmful chemical, bromate, was found to exceed local legal standards. The UK's food quality regulator, the Food Standards Agency (FSA), claimed that long-term exposure to high levels of bromate could increase the risk of cancer. The limit for

Source: © DNY59/iStock

bromate in bottled and tap water differs across countries. In the UK the limit is 10 parts per million (ppm), whereas the limit in Europe is 25 ppm. Dasani was tested to be between 10 and 22 ppm, too high for the UK.

A reporter discovered that the source of Dasani was actually tap water, not natural spring water. The water came from Thames Water, and was processed at Coca-Cola's factory in south-east London. The story quickly made it to the leading newspapers, which accused Coca-Cola of selling processed, bottled water to the public for 95 pence (for a half-litre bottle), so making a profit of 3,166 times!

The FSA stated that Dasani did not comply with British labelling guidelines on the use of the term 'pure', as it should be used only with reference to 'single ingredient foods or to highlight the quality of ingredients.' Since Dasani added calcium (according to UK regulations), magnesium and sodium bicarbonate to the water to improve its taste, it could not be labelled or advertised as 'pure'. The FSA further accused the company of misleading consumers through erroneous advertisements: if bottled water was not labelled as mineral water or spring water, it was considered simply bottled drinking water.

When the story broke, Coca-Cola's marketing department explained that the tap water they used went through four stages of production before it was bottled. The purification process (adopted from NASA) removed any impurities, such as bacteria, viruses, salts, minerals, sugars, proteins, and toxin particles. This process would make the water tasteless: so, in order to enhance the taste of the purified water, minerals were added.

To support Coca-Cola's claim, it was stated that Dasani water had passed 99.92% of quality tests conducted by the Drinking Water Inspectorate of England and Wales. Coca-Cola worked closely with all regulatory bodies to solve the controversy, and was fully confident that Dasani complied with all guidelines and regulations in the UK. Canadean, an independent beverage research company, stated that at least two out of every five bottles of water sold around the world were like Dasani's 'purified' water, albeit with different purification processes. Canadean emphasized that the purity treatments were exactly the same as the treatments that normal tap water undergoes to satisfy public health requirements.

Coca-Cola had to halt the launch of Dasani in France and Germany, but despite the recall, the company remained adamant about the high quality of its bottled water: 'In the packaged water business, people pay for a product because they know it is safe, high quality, available, and convenient. When the Coca-Cola Company sells drinking water in its various forms, it is not charging for the water per se, but rather for the value we add to the water to make it a branded beverage.'

Source: K.Y. Aparna, 'Coca-Cola's Dasani in the UK', ECCH case study, ref no. 505-040-1, 2005.

Introduction

We can see from the Dasani case that even large corporations such as Coca-Cola can make quality management mistakes. In the eyes of customers, any mistake committed by a firm can cause dissatisfaction. From a company's perspective, customer dissatisfaction is a quality problem. No organization can be 100% sure that it can provide the quality that the customers expect. Many firms also realize that quality has become a central issue for value creation and competitiveness. However, quality standards are challenging to manage.

There are several interpretations of what 'quality' means. In this chapter we shall show that there are different approaches that an organization can adopt in order to raise quality levels and prevent defects and failures occurring in its processes, products and services.

We'll explore how quality management paradigms have been changing in order to comply with competitive challenges shaped by innovation, technology and services. We'll address the dilemmas that many firms face when choosing the most suitable quality management approach. We'll also show how quality performance can be measured, monitored and controlled.

Quality management can contribute to improved profitability by helping companies to design products and services that conform to specifications that define exactly what the customer wants. Quality products, processes and services also create greater value for customers, thus obtaining increased market share and revenue growth for the company. All this can lead to improved profitability, as shown in Figure 13.1.

Defining Quality

'Quality' is a highly subjective term. If you went around and asked a number of people to articulate what quality is, you would probably get many different answers. You would probably hear comments such as 'things that don't

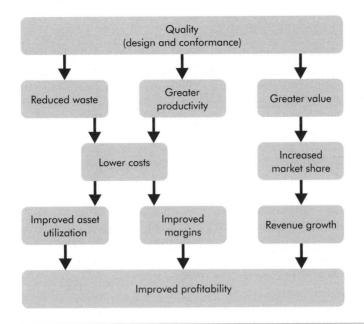

Figure 13.1 Quality's contribution to profitability (adapted from George and Weimerskirch, 1998)

break', 'right the first time', 'customer value', 'conformance to standards', 'customer satisfaction' or 'no defects', for example. There are also short-, mid- and long-term quality expectations of products. For instance, it is acceptable that clothes might fade within a year if worn and washed a lot, but you would expect your washing machine to last at least 5 years. The perceived quality of a product might also depend on what the product is made from; after all, a silk shirt feels nicer than polyester, and organic vegetables supposedly taste better than non-organic ones.

Our perception of service quality is even more subjective. It's likely that we all have been sick, or have required help from a doctor or hospital, at some point in our lives. In that situation, we would obviously prefer not to wait too long for consultations or treatment. Our perception of the experience is also affected by the behaviour of the doctors and nurses – whether they seem caring, and are able to give us enough attention.

Quality is one of the most critical issues in satisfying the customer. Given the variations in expectations of quality, an organization has to make decisions about what level of quality it will aim to provide for its customers.

An initial challenge for improving quality levels is to define what is meant by quality. Garvin (1987) identifies five different approaches:

- The *transcendent approach* views quality as synonymous with innate excellence. This is the traditional dictionary definition. Examples might be a Rolex watch, or a British Airways first class flight
- The *manufacturing-based approach* assumes that quality is all about making or providing error-free products or services, and is also known as the *production perspective*. Examples might include the Japanese car industry.
- The *user-based approach* assumes quality is all about providing products or services that are *fit for their purpose*, and is also known as the *customer perspective*. For instance, a watch needs to keep time, and a plane needs to fly from one destination to another.
- The *product-based approach* views quality as a precise and measurable set of characteristics, and is also known as the *engineering perspective*. For example, watches need to keep time, but may have many other features designed in.
- The *value-based approach* defines quality in terms of value to the customer, and is also known as the *economic perspective*. Some may consider a cheap product or 'no-frills' service to be better than an expensive one if it delivers value for money. For instance, Ryanair could be better than British Airways, or a Swatch watch better than a Rolex.

The key point is that quality is always defined by the customer, and a product should be fit for purpose and should conform to specification.

Philosophical Approaches to Quality

The notion of quality management started in the 1950s in Japan. During that time, Japan employed consultants from the US and Europe to assist in the process of its industrial reconstruction after the Second World War. The best known of these consultants were W. Edwards Deming and Joseph Juran. Later, Western organizations also embraced quality, using approaches advocated by Philip Crosby and Armand V. Feigenbaum. The philosophies of these four Americans, often referred to as the *quality gurus*, have considerably influenced the development of quality management in organizations across the world.

Deming's Philosophy

Deming's approach to quality is considered as the cornerstone of modern quality management. He saw quality as a way to satisfy customers – not merely to meet their expectations, but to exceed them. He stressed the need for organizations to stay ahead of customers. The means to improve quality rests with the organization's ability to control and manage systems and processes properly. Deming emphasized that it is management's responsibility to take care of changing processes. The management should establish clear standards that are considered acceptable, and also provide tools to carry out that work.

Deming's philosophy is mostly associated with the *PDCA* (plan, do, check, act) cycle of continuous improvement shown in Figure 13.2:

Plan (P): The cycle starts with the planning stage, when the necessary objectives and processes are established in order to deliver the results according to the expected output.
Do (D): Once the plan has been agreed, the next stage is the implementation of the processes, when the plan is tried out in the operation.
Check (C): The next stage of the cycle is when the processes are measured and the results are compared against the expected performance improvement.
Act (A): This is the last stage of the cycle. During this stage, the differences between the trials and expected performance are analysed to determine their cause. Once the cause is determined, the cycle starts again until the desired performance improvement is achieved.

In addition, Deming advocated the use of *statistical process control* (SPC) to ensure that processes were robust and in control.

Deming (1986) expressed his philosophy towards quality through his famous 14 management principles:

Principle 1: Create consistency of purpose to improve products and services – take a longer-term view, and innovate.
Principle 2: Adopt the new philosophy – accept the management style that promotes constant improvement.
Principle 3: Cease dependence on mass inspection – concentrate on improving processes.
Principle 4: End the practice of awarding business on price tag alone; build up relationships with fewer suppliers to understand jointly specifications of and uses for materials and other inputs.

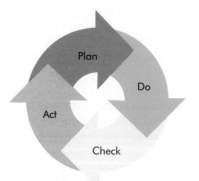

Figure 13.2 The PDCA Cycle

Principle 5: Constantly and forever improve the system – search continually for problems in all processes. It is management's job to work on the system.

Principle 6: Institute modern methods of training on the job – for all, to make the best use of every employee.

Principle 7: Institute modern methods of supervision – managers to focus on quality, not numbers.

Principle 8: Drive out fear – so that people work more effectively.

Principle 9: Break down barriers between departments – teamworking to tackle problems.

Principle 10: Eliminate numerical goals for the workforce – eliminate slogans and exhortation; make reasonable requests of the workforce.

Principle 11: Eliminate work standards and numerical quotas – focus on quality, and provide support.

Principle 12: Remove barriers that rob workers of pride in their work – for example, defective materials, poor tools, lack of management support.

Principle 13: Institute a vigorous programme of education and training – for continual updating and improvement.

Principle 14: Create a top management structure to push every day on the above 13 points. Top management commitment is where it begins and ends.

We can see that these principles all fit together, and lead managers and employees to change the way they deliver quality to the customer.

Juran's Philosophy

For Juran, quality begins with who will use the company's products or services, and how and why these customers will use them. All improvement activities should be customer focused. Juran defined quality as 'fitness for purpose or use', which has five major quality dimensions: quality of design, quality of conformance, availability, safety, and field of use:

Quality of design is concerned with how well the design concept and its specifications match the intended use of the product or service.

Quality of conformance deals with how well the actual product or service delivery matches the design intended.

Availability also includes how the company manages reliability and maintainability.

Safety is concerned with whether there is any risk to the customer when they use the product or receive the service.

With **field of use**, the company seeks to understand how well the product conforms to specifications after it reaches the customers.

> **Quality of design:** concerned with how well the design concept and its specifications match the intended use of the product or service.
>
> **Quality of conformance:** deals with how well the actual product or service delivery matches the design intended.
>
> **Availability:** The actual amount of time that a resource can be used for its intended purpose
>
> **Safety:** concerned with whether there is any risk to the customer when they use the product or receive the service.
>
> **Field of use:** the company seeks to understand how well the product conforms to specifications after it reaches the customers.

Juran introduced the idea of a quality trilogy: *planning*, *control* and *improvement*. Like Deming, he emphasized the importance of management involvement and the need for a supportive infrastructure. Juran, however, argued that quality is not free, and that companies must reduce the cost of quality. His philosophy of quality is summarized in the following 10 points (Juran, 1988):

Point 1: Build awareness of the need and opportunities for improvement.

Point 2: Set goals for improvement.

Point 3: Organize to reach the goals, such as establish a quality council, identify problems, select projects, appoint team, and designate facilities.

Point 4: Provide training throughout the organization.

Point 5: Carry out projects to solve problems.

Point 6: Report progress.

Point 7: Give recognition.

Point 8: Communicate results.

Point 9: Keep the score.

Point 10: Maintain momentum by making annual improvement part of the regular system and processes of the company.

For Juran it is all about developing a planned approach to managing quality in the organization.

Crosby's Philosophy

Philip Crosby (Crosby, 1979) advocated the philosophy that 'quality is free'. He defined quality as *conformance to requirements*. He argued that organizations should seek to produce zero defects – that is, to make the product right the first time. Higher-quality products reduce costs and raise profits. It is much more expensive to correct errors or to pay for scrap, rework, or failures in the field.

Crosby's programme has 14 steps that focus on how to change the organization, and offers action plans for implementation (Ghobadian and Speller, 1994, p. 60).

Step 1: *Management commitment* – make clear where management stands regarding quality.

Step 2: *Quality improvement team* – set up a team to run the quality improvement programme.

Step 3: *Quality measurement* – provide a display of current and potential non-conformance problems in a manner that permits objective evaluation and corrective action.

Step 4: *Cost of quality evaluation* – define the ingredients of the cost of quality, and explain its use as a management tool.

Step 5: *Quality awareness* – provide a method of raising the personal concern felt by all personnel towards product/service conformance and the reputation of the company.

Step 6: *Corrective action* – provide a systematic method of resolving quality problems that have been identified through the previous steps.

Step 7: *Zero-defect planning* – examine, identify and implement the actions necessary prior to the launch of a zero-defect programme.

Step 8: *Employee education* – identify and introduce the training that employees need in order to carry out their part in the quality improvement process.

Step 9: *Zero-defects day* – create an event that will let all employees know, through personal experience, that there has been a change.

Step 10: *Goal setting* – turn pledge and commitment into actions, by encouraging individuals to establish improvement goals for themselves and their groups.

Step 11: *Error cause removal* – give the individual employee a method of communicating to management the situations that make it difficult for the employee to meet the pledge to improve.

Step 12 *Recognition* – appreciate those who actively participate.

Step 13: *Quality councils* – bring together the professional quality people for planned communication on a regular basis.

Step 14: *Do it over again* – emphasize that the quality improvement process never ends.

For Crosby, quality is all about *right first time*.

Feigenbaum's Philosophy

Armand V. Feigenbaum saw quality as the 'total composite product and service characteristics of marketing, engineering, manufacture and maintenance through which the product and service in use will meet the expectations of the customers' (Feigenbaum, 1986). To him, quality is a way of managing an organization, and it is everyone's responsibility. He believed that effective management of quality represented the best return on investment for the firm.

One of Feigenbaum's major contributions is on the cost of quality. He identified three categories of quality costs:

Failure costs: these are costs caused by defective materials and products that do not meet company quality specifications.

Appraisal costs: these are costs related to maintaining company quality levels by means of formal evaluations of product quality, such as inspection, testing and quality audits.

Prevention costs: these are costs related to keeping defects from occurring in the first place, such as quality control engineering, employee quality training, and quality maintenance of patterns and tools.

He also identified 10 benchmarks for quality success:

1   Quality is a company-wide process.

2   Quality is what the customer says it is.

3   Quality and cost are a sum, not a difference.

4   Quality requires both individual and team zealotry.

5   Quality is a way of managing.

6   Quality and innovation are mutually dependent.

7   Quality is an ethic.

8   Quality requires continuous improvement.

9   Quality is the most cost-effective, least capital-intensive route to productivity.

10   Quality is implemented with a total system connected with customers and suppliers.

Feigenbaum was first to coin the term *total quality*, suggesting that quality is responsibility of all in the organization and so needs a high degree of coordinated effort.

The Evolution of Quality Management

Managing quality can be extremely challenging, depending on the situation and the tasks being controlled. The practice of quality management has evolved over recent decades. Modern operations management is considered to have evolved since the 1920s. The evolution has progressed, beginning with inspection, before moving on to quality control, and then quality assurance, before reaching total quality management, and Six Sigma (see Figure 13.3). Each subsequent evolution has subsumed those that have come before it. The characteristics of these evolutionary steps are summarized in Table 13.1, and are explored further in this section.

Inspection

Inspection is the simplest process of a quality system. One or more characteristics of a product, service or activity are examined to assess and identify sources of non-conformance in relation to specification or performance standards. For example, in a manufacturing plant, incoming goods and materials are checked (sometimes visually or sometimes with more sophisticated tools) to make sure they are defect-free before they are transported to the assembly line. The incoming goods and materials that do not meet the specifications may be returned, salvaged, scrapped, reworked, or modified.

Service industries, too, can use inspection. For instance, all food establishments must comply with health and sanitation standards. These establishments are regularly inspected by governmental bodies to check whether they have violated the standards.

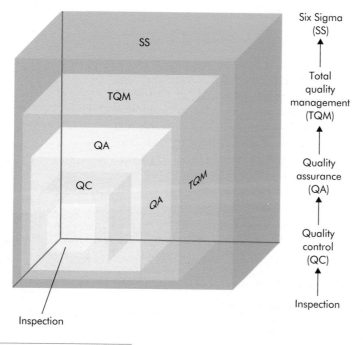

Figure 13.3 The evolution of quality management

Table 13.1 Main tasks of quality management stages

Level of quality management	Characteristic actions of this level
Inspection – retrospective checking for quality after tasks have been completed. This is mainly done just by quality inspectors	• Salvage • Sorting, grading, re-blending • Corrective actions • Identify sources of non-conformance • Limited to a small number of police-like inspectors
Quality control (QC) – a system to detect quality problems as they occur, normally limited to operations	• Develop quality manual • Process performance data • Self-inspection • Product testing • Basic quality planning • Use of basic statistics • Paperwork controls
Quality assurance (QA) – a systems that is proactive with some emphasis on improvement, normally limited to operations and directly related areas	• Quality systems development • Advanced quality planning • Use of quality costs • Failure mode and effect analysis (FMEA) • Statistical process control (SPC) • Use of quality as a unique selling point for marketing
Total quality management (TQM) – a proactive approach involving everyone in an organisation.	• Policy deployment • Involve suppliers and customers • Involve all operations • Process management • Performance measurement • Teamwork • Employee involvement throughout the organization
Six Sigma – a proactive approach involving everyone in an organization, which has low failure rates	• Linkage to personal performance reviews and career progression • Emphasis on the reduction of errors • Application of Six Sigma tools to reduce process variation

Source: adapted from Dale *et al.* (2007, p. 24).

SHORT CASE 13.1

Beer Tasting Is a Serious Business

Three times a week, at 11 o'clock in the morning, a quality assurance tasting panel, comprising nine or ten specially trained tasters, sit in Carlsberg's Research Centre (CRC) in Copenhagen, Denmark, to ensure that a Carlsberg beer tastes like a Carlsberg, regardless of where it is brewed. Every company that brews Carlsberg beers under licence has to send samples once a month to the tasting panel. They have to submit samples of every type of beer, especially if the beers are packaged in different bottles or cans, or brewed to different strengths.

The panel measure the beers against an international beer 'flavour wheel', which itemizes and numbers 140 different base flavours and aromas, ranging from fruits and flowers to nuts and grains. Lene Bech, CRC's panel manager, explains: 'In a Carlsberg, we're looking for flavours of hops, malt, summer apples and pine, and a good balance between sweetness and bitterness. If the tasters recognize any other flavours, then we can identify the faults in the beer and report back to the individual brew master.'

Source: © Mikhail Kotov/iStock

The tasters are chosen from within the company. New tasters are required to attend seven training sessions, where they are taught to recognize different flavours, beers and aromas. They also have to score at least 60% in all their taste tests, and participate in panels on a trial basis for their first 3–6 months. Interestingly, the flavour receptors that are most sensitive to beer are at the back of the tongue, which means that the tasters have to swallow the beer being tested!

Questions

1   How difficult is it for Carlsberg to monitor and control the taste of its beers?
2   Should there be other standards and/or procedures to ensure quality at Carlsberg?

Source: www.carlsberggroup.com

Quality Control

With *quality control* (QC), a more sophisticated approach is used to manage quality. At this level quality standards are set, and quality manuals with detailed product and performance specifications are developed. Basic statistics are also used in quality control measures in order to achieve greater process control and lower incidences of non-conformance. Self-inspection against internationally recognized standards (such as those of the International Organization for Standardization) is also used.

We often take standards for granted in our daily lives. However, if standards were absent, we would soon notice. For example, it would be frustrating if your favourite chocolate drink tasted different every time you bought it. We also rely on standards to ensure that we aren't harmed by things we are not capable of noticing, such as contamination in our drinking water, or electromagnetic radiation from high-voltage power cables. Standards make sure that the characteristics of products and services, such as quality, environmental friendliness, safety, reliability, efficiency and interchangeability, meet desired specifications.

The **International Organization for Standardization (ISO)** is the world's largest standards organization, and has 162 members worldwide. Since 1947 it has published more than 17,500 standards. Perhaps the best-known ISO standards are the ISO 9000 series. ISO 9000 certifies that a company meets certain industry standards. Its objective is to give customers assurance that the quality of the products and services provided by a supplier meets their requirements. It also ensures that organizations have a quality policy, with standardized procedures to ensure that defects are monitored, there are corrective and preventive action systems, and all systems are reviewed by the management.

> **International Organization for Standardization (ISO):** the world's largest standards-developing organization.

The ISO 9000 series consists of the following main standards:

* *ISO 9000: Quality Management Systems – Fundamentals and Vocabulary*: describes the fundamentals of quality management systems.
* *ISO 9001: Quality Management Systems – Requirements*: provides the requirements that an organization needs in order to achieve customer satisfaction through consistent products and services that meet customers' expectations.
* *ISO 9004: Quality Management Systems – Guidelines for Performance Improvements*: provides guidance on how an organization can plan for continual improvement.

CRITICAL PERSPECTIVE

Advantages and Disadvantages of ISO Standards

In order to attain ISO accreditation, an organization has to prove that every step of a process is documented and subsequently adhered to. The process of recording and documenting can be tedious and extremely frustrating for companies that do not have a standard way of doing things. ISO accreditation can be obtained only through an approved certifying body by paying a

▶ fee. Although the fee is relatively small, the cost of obtaining accreditation can be relatively expensive, because a lot of time and effort can go into developing a comprehensive quality system.

However, many organizations are willing to invest in getting ISO certification. Although it is not a legal requirement, it is becoming a requirement of doing business in the European Union. One of the biggest advantages is that the third party audit ensures that the quality management of the organization is on a par with the rest of the industry. As ISO certification is the most common type of certification, implementation of new systems becomes easier. The process of certification forces the organization to analyse its internal processes objectively, resulting in more efficient and cost-effective processes.

The key point is that although quality accreditation is important, it can be onerous and expensive to gain.

Quality Assurance

Quality assurance (QA) embraces activities that provide confidence that the organization will fulfil the requirements of quality. Whereas inspection and quality control focus on the detection of mistakes, QA aims to prevent them from occurring.

BUSINESS INTEGRATION

Finding and solving a problem is not enough to ensure quality excellence; the root causes of the problem need to be eliminated too. The focus at this stage shifts from detection to the prevention of non-conformance. This requires the support of top management, to encourage all departments and functions to work together. Here we see the biggest impact of the quality gurus, who were all concerned not just that existing systems should be made to work the way they were designed to, but that managers should be constantly working on a systematic approach for improvement. QA therefore represents an advance over QC, as it includes all parts of the firm, not just the operations, in delivering the service or producing the product.

QA is often seen as little more than a step in the journey towards total quality management.

Total Quality Management

Total quality management (TQM) embraces all aspects of inspection, quality control and quality assurance. TQM is an approach that involves the whole organization, with the focus on producing high-quality goods and services. It is a quality management approach based on the participation of all its members, aimed at the long-term success of an organization through customer satisfaction. Because of this, teamwork and employee involvement become a crucial part of the TQM process, although customers and suppliers are also involved. Successful TQM implementation brings benefits to all members of the organization and society.

There are eight TQM principles (Dale *et al.*, 2007, p. 30):

1   *Customer focus*: organizations depend on their customer needs, meet customer requirements, and strive to exceed customer expectations.

2   *Leadership*: leaders establish unity of purpose and the direction of the organization. They should create and maintain the internal environment in which people can become fully involved in achieving the organization's objectives.

3   *Involvement of people*: people at all levels are the essence of an organization, and their full involvement enables their abilities to be used for the organization's benefit.

4   *Process approach*: a desired result is achieved more efficiently when activities and related resources are managed as a process.

5   *Systems approach to management*: identifying, understanding and managing interrelated processes as a system contributes to the organization's effectiveness and efficiency in achieving its objectives.

6   *Continual improvement* (kaizen): continual improvement of the organization's overall performance should be a permanent objective of the organization.

7   *Factual approach to decision-making*: effective decisions are based on the analysis of data and information.

8   *Mutually beneficial supplier relationships*: an organization and its suppliers are interdependent, and a mutually beneficial relationship enhances the ability of both to create value.

Properly implemented TQM systems have improved the performance of many firms, resulting in fewer defects, lower inventory levels, reduced lead times, higher flexibility, and increased employee satisfaction. However, the implementation of TQM can be very challenging. In a study of American companies, Salegna and Fazel (2000) identified the following obstacles:

- A lack of a company-wide definition of quality
- A lack of a formalized strategic plan for change
- A lack of a customer focus, poor inter-organizational communication
- A lack of real employee empowerment
- A lack of employee trust in senior management
- A view of quality programmes as a quick fix
- A drive for short-term financial results, politics and turf issues
- A lack of strong motivation
- A lack of time to devote to quality initiatives
- And lack of leadership.

Why TQM Doesn't Always Work

CRITICAL PERSPECTIVE

Is TQM a fad or just a buzzword? Japanese companies seem to have been more successful in implementing TQM than Western companies. So what are the underlying reasons for the successful implementation of TQM? TQM was based primarily on Japanese experiences in the automotive and electronic industries. Today, the aim of TQM is to increase external and internal customer satisfaction with fewer resources (Hellsten and Klefsjö, 2000), regardless of the type and nationality of the companies.

TQM transformation is a long-term process, often requiring a fundamental shift in management practice and organization culture, which needs a huge investment in money and time. Senior management in many firms feel that quality improvement efforts have not boosted their capacity to compete, have not resulted in implementation of a significant number of practices associated with TQM, and have not focused TQM improvements on providing better products and services (Beer, 2003).

Top management adopts TQM programmes typically with the goal of improving performance. However, TQM will fail if they are not committed or if they lack understanding of the programme. Hence it is essential that the senior team has the capacity to (Beer, 2003, p. 623):

1   Develop commitment to the new TQM direction and behave and make decisions that are consistent with it

2   Develop the cross-functional mechanisms, leadership skills, and team culture needed for TQM implementation

3   Create a climate of open dialogues about progress in the TQM transformation that will enable learning and further change.

The key point is that TQM needs top management support even though it is primarily delivered by all employees.

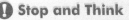 **Stop and Think**

1   Should all companies (regardless of their size or reputation) adopt TQM?

Six Sigma

Six Sigma is an evolution of TQM that was pioneered by Motorola in the 1980s. A senior engineer there introduced the concept in response to increasing complaints from the field salesforce about warranty claims. The Six Sigma methodology made Motorola one of the first companies to win the Malcolm Baldrige National Quality Award in 1988, a prestigious award that is given to US corporations that have demonstrated outstanding quality in their products and processes. Since then, many companies have tailored the Six Sigma method to their own programmes, including General Electric (GE), Texas Instruments, Kodak, Xerox and Ford. GE, for example, launched its Six Sigma programme in 1995, and over a four-year period was able to achieve a 20% margin improvement and a 12% reduction in headcount per year (Basu, 2004).

In essence, Six Sigma is a quality concept with the goal of value creation through quality improvement. Many objectives in Six Sigma are similar to those in TQM, such as customer satisfaction, continuous improvement, team-based activities, education and training, and problem-solving methodologies. One distinct characteristic of Six Sigma, though is that it places statistical analysis centrally in quality management. The Greek letter σ is the symbol for standard deviation, and Six Sigma is represented as 6σ. The aim of Six Sigma is to reduce defects to less than 3.4 per million opportunities/outputs **(DPMO)**.

> **DPMO:** defects per million opportunities

The DMAIC Cycle

Six Sigma is a continuous improvement, or kaizen methodology, based on the DMAIC cycle (Figure 13.4), which is an extension of Deming's PDCA wheel. This cycle can be broken down as follows:

Define (D): The cycle starts with the problems, project goals and processes being defined. Here the organization identifies the customers and their priorities, as well as its business objectives. Often the target for performance is determined at this stage.

Measure (M): This stage determines how to measure the process and its performance. Relevant data are collected. The quality gurus stressed how we need to measure performance in order to know whether anything is improved by our actions.

Analyse (A): Once the measurements are set, they can be analysed. It is here that cause-and-effect relationships and the most likely causes of defects are revealed. It becomes crucial to identify the key variables that create process variation, and in turn result in product and service delivery variation, which can cause dissatisfaction in customers.

Improve (I): Once the causes of defects are identified, work can begin to improve the processes to remove these causes. At this stage the maximum acceptance ranges of the key variables, and how to measure the deviations of the variables, are set.

Control (C): This is the final stage of the cycle. The improved process needs to be continuously controlled and monitored, to make the improvements sustainable. Then the process starts all over again, to achieve further improvements or redesign the process as customer requirements change.

As with previous approaches to quality management, for Six Sigma to succeed it is crucial that there is support from all levels of the organization. The management needs to provide strong leadership, define performance

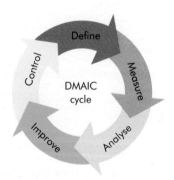

Figure 13.4 The DMAIC cycle

metrics, select projects that have a high probability of yielding good business results, and provide appropriate training for all employees. Depending on the level of expertise attained, practitioners or employees are known as: green belts, black belts, or master black belts:

Green belts: these are professionals with at least three years of experience using the Six Sigma methodology and tools, who wish to lead a process improvement or quality improvement team.

Black belts: these are experts in Six Sigma philosophies and principles. They also have basic knowledge of lean enterprise concepts, so they are able to identify non-value-added processes and activities. They have team leadership skills, and act as coaches for the green belts.

Master black belts: these are the ultimate experts in the methodologies, tools, and applications in strategic implementation of Six Sigma within an organization. They have extensive training in statistics and the use of quality tools. They are also qualified to train the black belts and the green belts. These are usually full-time quality professionals.

Training and certification for Six Sigma belts can be obtained from external bodies.

Contemporary Thinking: Lean Six Sigma

BUSINESS
INTEGRATION

Lean Six Sigma is the most comprehensive level of quality management. It includes key concepts from lean management and Six Sigma tools.

Traditional quality management systems have worked well for many firms. However, with increasing outsourcing activities and globalization, the role of quality management has to be redefined. Many firms are combining Six Sigma with lean production methodologies, resulting in Lean Six Sigma, in order to improve process capability and eliminate waste. The integrated approaches should enable firms to become faster and more responsive to customers, to operate with lower costs of poor quality, and to achieve greater flexibility throughout the business (Antony *et al.*, 2003). Table 13.2 compares the tools used by the two methodologies.

It is worth noting that there is some overlap between these methodologies, and ideally they should be used together for the best results. Practitioners and academics are still trying to agree on the best way of doing this.

> ## 🛈 Stop and Think
>
> **2** What do you think TQM is lacking, and why do you think it has been usurped by Lean Six Sigma?

European Foundation of Quality Management (EFQM) Excellence Model

There are several alternative frameworks to Lean Six Sigma that aim to help firms implement quality improvement in a structured way. The *EFQM model* was formed by 14 leading western European companies in 1988 to recognize quality achievements, especially for public sector organizations and SMEs (small and medium enterprises). In 2004 a study by Basu revealed that EFQM had 19 partner organizations in Europe, and over 20,000 member companies, which include 60% of the top 25 companies in Europe.

Table 13.2 Tools used by Six Sigma and lean production

Six Sigma tools	Lean production tools
• Belt system (green belt, black belt, and master black belt) • DMAIC cycle • Statistical process control • Process capability analysis • Quality function deployment • Failure mode and effect analysis • Root cause analysis • Process mapping • Change management tools	• Workplace management • Pull system (kanban) • Total Productive Maintenance • 5S practice • Value stream mapping • Just-in-time • Production flow balancing • Waste identification and elimination • Kaizen • Change management tools

Source: adapted from Antony *et al.* (2003).

The EFQM model (see Figure 13.5) is a non-prescriptive framework based on nine criteria. Five of these criteria are *enablers* (leadership, people, policy and strategy, partnership and resources, and processes) and four are *results* (people, customer, society, and key performance). Whereas the enablers cover what an organization *does*, the results cover what an organization *achieves*. Innovation and learning help to improve enablers that, in turn, lead to improved results. The EFQM model is used for self-inspection, allowing firms to rate their performance, and the EFQM criteria are very similar to those used in competitions to rate firms' quality systems. In North America, for example, the prestigious Baldridge Award is given to one firm per year to recognize their efforts, and Japan has an equivalent, called the Deming Prize.

Table 13.3 shows an example of how EFQM is applied by a care provider. The weighting for each of the results and enablers may vary for each application.

SHORT CASE 13.2

Harley-Davidson for Women

Harley-Davidson, the motorcycle company, is facing some challenges to stay competitive and grow. Registration of new motorcycles has fallen 36% for Harley since 2007. Its production level has also sunk to 2001 levels. Since Keith Wandell became the CEO in May 2009, he has made a several changes, including reworking labour contracts at Harley's plants, and streamlining the Harley-Davidson brand.

Harley bikes have typically appealed to middle-aged, rich, white males. In a riders' event in Orlando in May 2009, Wandell realized that a bike more suitable to women is something that Harley customers have long been asking for. As he recalls, 'Ten questions were asked and nine of them were from women, and all of them were really asking the same thing: When are you going to design a bike that's more suitable for women riders?'

Harley is definitely taking the new market potential for women seriously. It hired Marisa Miller, a model who appeared in *Sports Illustrated*'s swimming suit edition, as a spokesperson. The company also doubled its spending on marketing activities, including the introduction of the Super Low.

Source: © Nat Ulrich/iStock

However, while much work is being done on marketing, the key issue here is actually operational. Most of the bikes are designed for male bikers, and as men and women have considerably different physiologies – women tend to be shorter, weigh less and have wider hips than men – the customer requirement is therefore different. This means that a bike designed to a specification based on a woman's physiology will be different from one designed to a specification based on a man's physiology. Selling a bike designed for a man to a woman therefore leads to a quality problem. Essentially, the bike and the customer do not fit together properly!

Questions

1 Can Harley-Davidson benchmark its current practices to enhance the appeal of new bikes for women?
2 What challenges should Harley-Davidson consider in order to ensure that the same quality standards (in both the bikes and the service levels) are maintained?

Source: *Bloomberg Businessweek*, 4–10 October 2010.

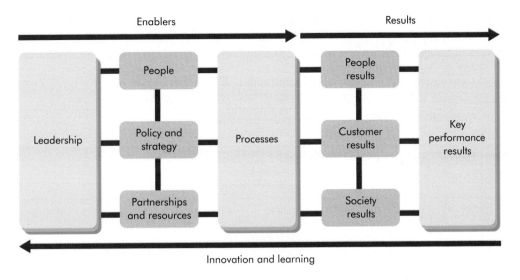

Figure 13.5 The EFQM excellence model

Dimensions of Quality

Over the years, various concepts and tools have been developed to help companies improve their operations. When a firm designs a product or service, certain performance characteristics and features need to be handled carefully in order to make sure that they can fulfil customers' expectations.

Product Quality

Quality has many dimensions, including performance, features, reliability, durability, conformance, serviceability, aesthetics and perceived quality (Garvin, 1987). Table 13.4 lists eight dimensions, and provides examples of these dimensions in a car.

Service Quality

Many aspects of quality are subjective, and depend on the customer's expectations, but it is easier to meet the expectations for products than for services. Customers can see and touch most products before buying them, and manufacturers can inspect the quality of the products before releasing them for purchase. Many aspects of a product's quality can be subjective, though. For example, how long you expect your mobile phone to work may depend on how quickly you plan to switch to a newer model, but manufacturers can influence customers' expectations by the length of guarantee they offer.

Services differ from products in four ways:
- *Intangibility*: most services cannot be counted, measured, inventoried, tested or verified in advance of sale to ensure their quality, as in having a consultation with a doctor, for example. Services cannot be protected through patents, and prices are difficult to set.
- *Heterogeneity*: the performance of services differs between producers, and what the firm intends to deliver might be entirely different from what the customer receives.
- *Inseparability*: the production and consumption of services occur simultaneously.
- *Perishability*: services cannot be stored or inventoried. For example, an empty seat in a bus or airplane is a sale lost forever.

Because of these differences there are additional dimensions that we might use to judge the quality of products and services (Parasuraman *et al.*, 1985, p. 47):

Reliability: involves consistency of performance, and dependability. It means the firm performs the service right first time. It also means that the firm honours its promises.

Table 13.3 Application of EFQM by a care provider

Criteria		Example
Results	Key performance	Key outcomes: • Outcomes for adults, carers, children and families • Performance against national and local targets
	Customer	Impact on people who use our services: • Experience of individuals, children and their parents and carers who use our services
	People	Impact on employees: • Motivation and satisfaction • Employees' ownership of vision, policy and strategy
	Society	Impact on the community: • Community perception, understanding and involvement • Impact on other stakeholders • Community capacity
Enablers	Processes	Delivery of key processes: • Access to services • Day-to-day planning and resource allocation • Assessment, care management and statutory supervision • Risk management and accountability • Personalized approaches • Inclusion, equality and fairness in service delivery • Joint and integrated delivery of services
	Policy and strategy	Policy and service development, planning and performance management: • Development of policy and procedures • Operational and service planning • Strategic planning including partnership planning • Involvement of users, carer and other stakeholders • Range and quality of services • Quality assurance and continuous improvement
	People	Management and support of employees: • Recruitment and retention • Employee deployment and teamwork • Development of employees
	Partnership and resources	Resources and capacity building: • Financial management • Resource management • Social work information systems • Partnership arrangements • Commissioning arrangements
	Leadership	Leadership and direction: • Vision values and aims • Leadership of people • Leadership of change and improvement Capacity for improvement: • Global judgement based on evidence of all key areas, in particular, outcomes, impacts and leadership direction

Source: adapted from EFQM (2003).

Responsiveness: concerns employees' willingness or readiness to provide service.
Competence: means possession of the required skills and knowledge to perform the service.
Access: involves approachability and ease of contact.
Courtesy: involves politeness, respect, consideration, and friendliness of contact personnel.

Table 13.4 Dimensions of product quality

Dimension	Meaning	Example in a car
Performance	A product's primary operating characteristics	Acceleration; braking distance; steering; handling
Features	The 'bells and whistles' and secondary characteristics	Power options; CD player or iPod adaptor; antilock breaking system; leather seats
Reliability	The probability of a product operating over a specific period of time under stated conditions of use	A car's ability to start on cold days; frequency of failures
Durability	The amount of use one gets from a product before it physically deteriorates, or until replacement is preferable	Corrosion resistance; the long wear of upholstery fabric.
Conformance	The degree to which a product's design and operating characteristics meet established standards	All electronics components in a car have to work within −40°C and +85°C.
Serviceability	The speed, courtesy and competence of repair work	Access to spare parts; the number of miles between major maintenance services; the cost of servicing
Aesthetics	How a product looks, feels, sounds, tastes or smells	A car's colour; instrument panel design; control placement; the 'feel of the road'
Perceived quality	Past performance and reputation	A customer might be influenced by their personal experience and that of acquaintances, as well as written reviews by other users

Source: adapted from Crosby *et al.* (2003).

Communication: means keeping customers informed in language they can understand, and listening to them. It may mean that the company has to adjust its language for different consumers – for example, increasing the level of sophistication with experienced users but speaking simply and plainly with a novice.

Credibility: involves trustworthiness, believability, honesty. It means having the customer's best interest at heart.

Security: is the freedom from danger, risk, or doubt.

Understanding/knowing the customer: involves making the effort to understand the customer's needs.

Service quality deals with the company's ability to meet customers' expectations. However, as service quality can be hard to measure, a useful method is to look at the difference between what we expect and what we actually receive. So if the service we receive is less than we were expecting, we shall be disappointed. Similarly, if the company exceeds our expectations we are likely to be pleased. Word of mouth, personal needs and past experience shape our expectations of the quality of services (ES). We tend to be satisfied when perceptions exceed the expectations of a service (ES < PS), but unhappy when the expectations are not met (ES > PS).

The *service quality model* (Figure 13.6) illustrates various possible sources in the process of service delivery that may result in gaps between customers' expectations and the quality of the services delivered:

Gap 1: Consumer expectation/management perception gap: The managers of service firm do not always know what features to provide to consumers in advance, and what levels of performance on those features are needed in order to deliver high-level service.

Gap 2: Management perception/service quality specification gap: It is often difficult for managers to match or exceed consumer expectations, often because there is an absence of management commitment to service quality.

Gap 3: Service quality specifications/service delivery gap: There is no guarantee that high-quality service performance can be attained, even when guidelines exist and the personnel treat the consumers correctly. Service firms' employees often exert a strong influence on the quality of the service delivered. Because employees are human beings, their performance cannot always be standardized.

Gap 4: Service delivery/external communications gap: The media, advertising and other communications channels can affect consumer expectations. When a firm promises more than it can deliver, it raises initial expectations. However, when it can't fulfil the expectations, the perceptions of quality will be significantly lower.

Gap 5: Expected service/perceived service gap: The key to ensuring good quality of service is meeting and exceeding what consumers expect from the service. This gap is arguably the most important, as it is the resulting effect of all the others, and is judged by the customer.

SHORT CASE 13.3

7-Eleven, Japan

There are 7-Eleven convenience stores in many different countries around the world, but the experiences we expect as consumers vary from country to country. For instance, in Asian stores one can get kimchi-flavoured rice balls, one of the store's most popular items. Kimchi is a traditional Korean fermented dish, typically made with napa cabbage, chilli and garlic, but rice balls would probably not be very popular items in Europe or North America.

The Japanese 7-Eleven stores focus on providing good-quality service to customers. As early as the 1980s, 7-Eleven introduced computers that displayed graphic data and interactive registers in order to transmit information between the headquarters and the stores to ensure that high-selling items would not go out of stock. For instance, popular items such as cooked rice could be delivered to the stores as frequently as three times a day.

By the mid-1990s it was possible for customers to pay for mail order purchases at the stores. Stores also started to offer all kinds of innovative services, including sales of ski-lift vouchers, international phone cards, colour photocopying, games software, and more.

Source: © Getty Images

In 2007, 7-Eleven introduced a web shopping service, which combined Internet shopping with existing store services and infrastructure. The corporation's goal is to create products and services that provide new value for customers and franchises, and by doing this service quality is also enhanced. With innovations in information technology, 7-Eleven is able to fulfil customers' expectations and create better shopping experience for the customers at its stores.

Questions

1. How difficult it would be for 7-Eleven stores worldwide to be as good at ensuring quality as 7-Eleven in Japan?
2. Which factors enable 7-Eleven Japan to grow and continuously satisfy its customers?

Source: www.sej.co.jp

Quality Tools

Quality philosophies, approaches and frameworks are high-level ways of thinking about quality issues. At a more practical level, quality managers need tools and techniques to collect, analyse and fix operational problems. There are many tools; this section highlights some of the most popular and effective ones.

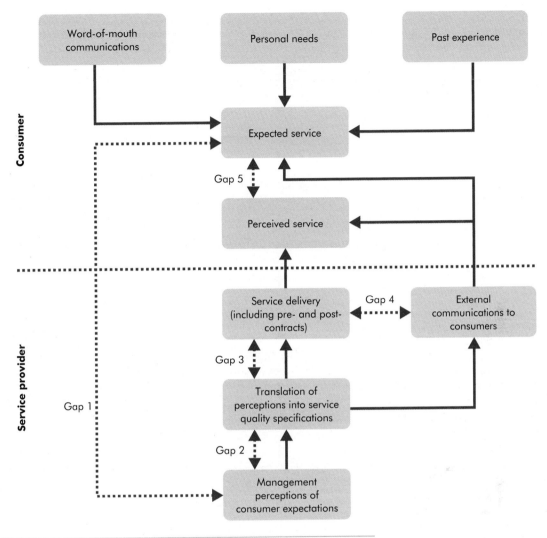

Figure 13.6 The service quality model (adapted from Parasuraman *et al.*, 1985)

The Seven Basic Tools of Quality

SIPOC Diagram

SIPOC (supplier–input–process–output–customer) diagrams are used to map operational processes. Figure 13.7 shows a simple SIPOC diagram for making coffee. The diagram allows us to record and then analyse the different roles, parties and processes involved in the operation.

Flow Chart

A **flow chart** is a series of connected supplier–input–process–output diagrams. It provides a visual representation of the different steps in a process. Flow charts can provide a common language or decision plan for a process. Figure 13.8 shows a flow chart for getting out of bed.

Histogram and Measles Chart

Histograms are used to record the type and frequency of data occurring. They can be used in connection with data capturing tools such as 'measles charts'. Figure 13.9 shows a spanner being produced, which is then inspected

> **SIPOC (supplier–input–process–output–customer) diagram:** maps the processes a company (or a person) goes through in order to satisfy a customer's requirements in the context of the supply chain.
>
> **Flow chart:** provides a visual representation of all major steps in a process.

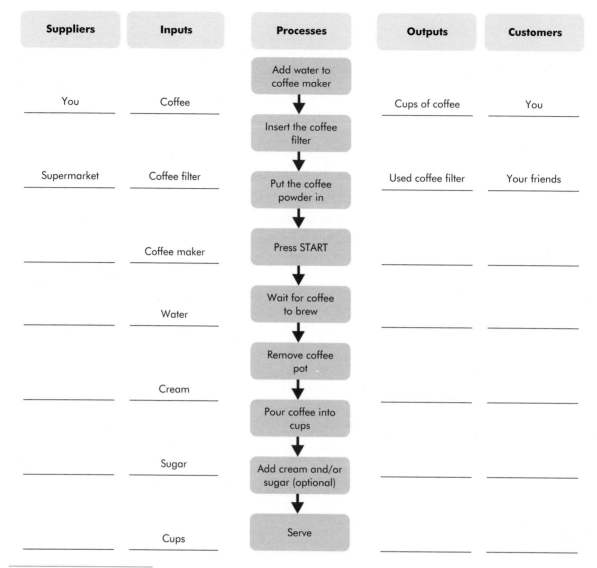

Figure 13.7 SIPOC diagram

for faults. If a fault is found it is then marked with a 'measle' to show exactly where the error has occurred. The frequency of each type of fault occurring is then recorded on the histogram.

This simple tool helps us to identify patterns. If all the defects are focused in one area a root cause may then be revealed.

Pareto Analysis

Pareto diagram: arranges categories from highest to lowest frequency of occurrence.

A **Pareto diagram** arranges categories from highest to lowest frequency of occurrence. A Pareto analysis of quality problems would start by listing the problems identified, then recording the number of times each occurred (the *frequency*), and then ordering them, with the most frequent problem listed first so that addressing this problem could be prioritized. For instance, there are many reasons why luggage gets lost by airlines: flight delays, meaning that passengers miss connecting flights; luggage tags accidentally getting torn off; or simple loss through human error).

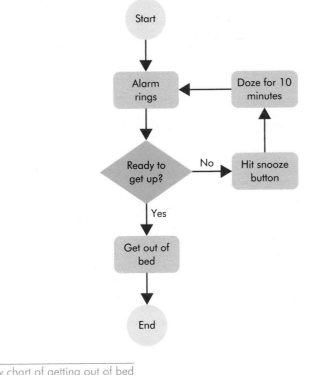

Figure 13.8 A flow chart of getting out of bed

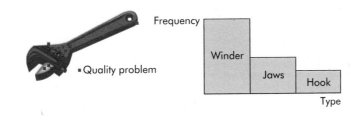

Figure 13.9 A histogram and a measles chart

Table 13.5 Pareto analysis of reasons for lost luggage

Problem	Percentage of incidences	Cumulative percentage
Missing connecting flight	40	40
Passengers arriving late	25	65
Luggage being misplaced	15	80
Tags that are accidentally torn off	10	90
Security delays	8	98
Other	2	100

Figure 13.10 is a Pareto diagram for luggage lost by an airline. Table 13.5 displays the percentage of incidents that can be attributed to each cause, and the cumulative percentage. In this example, although there are perhaps many different reasons for luggage getting lost, as described above, an airline could prevent 65% of instances of luggage loss if it addressed the two most common reasons – those caused by passengers arriving late or missing connecting flights.

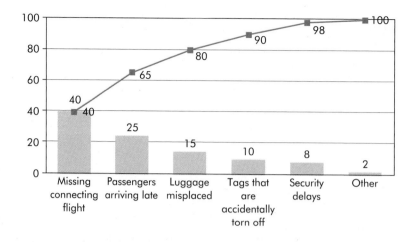

Figure 13.10 Pareto diagram showing reported reasons for lost luggage.

Scatter Diagram

Scatter diagram: shows the degree and direction of the relationship between two variables.

Scatter diagrams show the correlation between two variables – for example, the correlation between customer satisfaction in a five-star restaurant and variables such as waiting time and presentation of food, as shown in Figure 13.11. Here it can be seen that there is a high degree of correlation between presentation of food and satisfaction (Figure 13.11b), but much less correlation between customer satisfaction and waiting time (Figure 13.11a). These relationships may be very different in a different context. For instance, in a fast-food restaurant the relationships may be reversed, as customers prefer speed over presentation.

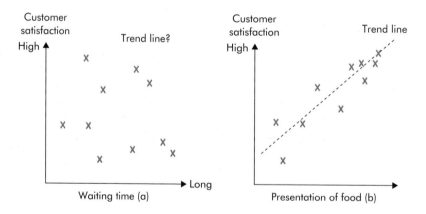

Figure 13.11 Scatter diagram correlating customer satisfaction with waiting time (a) and presentation (b)

Cause-and-Effect Diagram

Cause-and-effect diagram: structural approach to finding of possible cause(s) of a problem.

The **cause-and-effect diagram** (also known as an *Ishikawa* or *fishbone diagram*) is a structured approach to finding the possible cause(s) of a problem. Figure 13.12 shows the causes for lack of responsiveness to customers. Consider an IT company that supplies printers and related services (such as maintenance) to a university. Recently, the marketing department received lots of complaints from customers for its 'lack of responsiveness to customers'. The top management asked the marketing and sales managers to look into possible reasons for the customer complaint (the effect). A cause-and-effect diagram was drawn consisting of a 'backbone' and 'fish bones', e.g. manpower, machines, methods and materials, to identify possible causes. Each of the fish bones may have more bones. For instance, manpower was identified as one cause that needed further investigation. One of the reasons might be related to having too few trained staff.

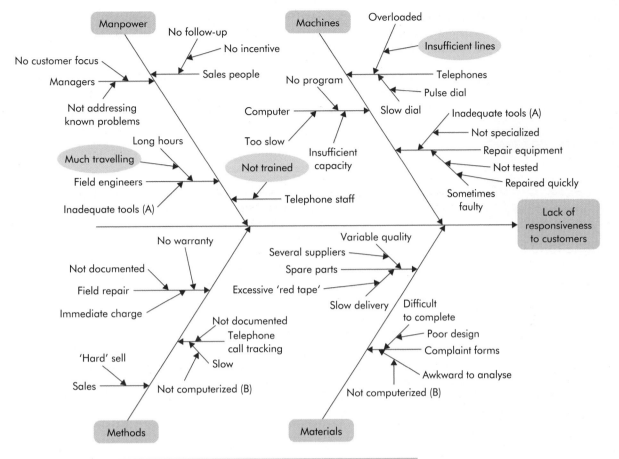

Figure 13.12 Cause-and-effect diagram (source: *The Improvement Encyclopedia*)

Run and Multi-Vari Charts

A **run chart** shows trends in data over time and can be used to identify evolving changes to the system, or differences that repeat or occur at certain times. Figure 13.13a shows readings from two machines making drinking straws over a three-day period. The blue line shows that this machine is operating in a similar pattern to the machine producing the output displayed by the red line, but that it is producing, on average, longer straws, which are in general further away from the target length. In Figure 13.13b a *multi-vari* diagram is shown displaying the same information in a different way: it shows the difference between the longest and shortest output (the range) for each machine, for each day.

> **Run chart:** shows the trends in data over time.

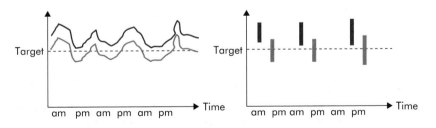

Figure 13.13 A run chart of straw lengths produced on two different machines

Benchmarking

Benchmarking originated from the Rank Xerox Corporation in the 1980s as an improvement method to compare performances. It is a popular technique that has been widely adopted into a wide range of business processes and performance metrics. Today, benchmarking is widely used by companies to compare best practices. Its goal is to provide knowledge in different specific areas about which company is the 'best in class', and how its performance compares with that of other organizations (Basu, 2004).

Benchmarking can be classified into three categories (Dale, 1999):

- **Internal benchmarking**: provides a comparison among similar operations or processes within a company's organization.
- **Competitive benchmarking**: compares the company's performance with that of the competitors.
- **Functional benchmarking**: compares specific processes and functions across different industries to find the 'best in class'.

For example, the Rover Group employed internal benchmarking to compare its three manufacturing sites' reject rates, and so allow them to share practice ideas. The same firm also used functional benchmarking to compare its machine spare parts inventory system with the approach used by Marks and Spencer.

The process of benchmarking involves the steps shown in Figure 13.14.

> **Internal benchmarking:** provides a comparison among similar operations or processes within a company's organization.
>
> **Competitive benchmarking:** compares the company's performance against that of the competitors.
>
> **Functional benchmarking:** compares specific processes and functions across different industries to find the 'best in class'.

Failure Mode and Effect Analysis (FMEA)

The technique of FMEA was developed by the aerospace and defence industries in the 1960s as a method of identifying possible failures that might occur in a product while in service (the *failure mode*), predicting what effect the failure might have should it occur, and then analysing the severity of that failure. Work can then be done during the design phase to stop that failure from occurring.

Essentially, the team identify what could go wrong with the product and then rate these failures by likelihood and severity. They can then use this information to prioritize solving or preventing the event happening.

FMEA involves the following steps (Basu, 2004, p. 149):

Step 1: Form a team and flow-chart the relevant details of the product, process or service that is selected for analysis.

Step 2: Assign each component of the system a unique identifier.

Step 3: List all the functions that each component of the system performs.

Step 4: Identify potential failure modes for each function listed in step 3.

Step 5: Describe the effects of each failure mode, especially the effects perceived by the user.

Step 6: Examine and summarize the causes of each failure mode.

Step 7: Identify and assess current controls to detect a potential failure mode.

Step 8: Determine the severity of the potential hazard of the failure to personnel or system, on a scale.

Step 9: Estimate the relative likelihood of occurrence of each failure.

Step 10: Estimate the ease with which the failure might be detected.

Step 11: Determine the risk priority number (RPN) for each failure, which is attained by multiplying the numbers obtained in steps 7, 8 and 9. The potential failure modes in descending order of RPN should be the focus of the improvement action to minimize the risk of failure.

Step 12: Monitor the recommendations and corrective actions that have been put in place to eliminate or reduce failures, for continuous improvement.

Figure 13.15 provides an illustration of FMEA used on assessing the hotel service provided at the Special Olympics.

Quality Function Deployment

Quality function deployment (QFD) is sometimes referred to as the House of Quality (because the diagram looks like a house). It helps to build in quality, as defined by the customer at the beginning of the design process. This tool is applicable whether a service or a product is being designed.

QFD is typically used at the beginning of a design process to help capture customer requirements for a new product or service. QFD is said to capture the *voice of the customer* (VOC) by producing a detailed list of what the

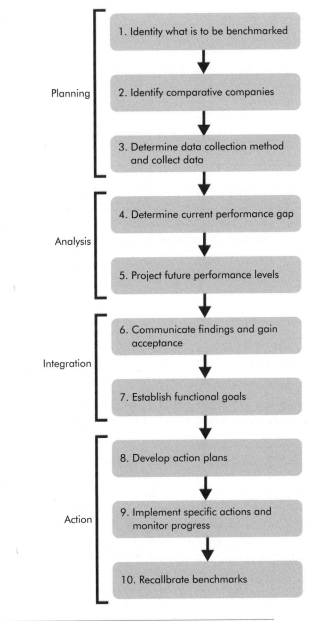

Figure 13.14 Benchmarking processes (adapted from Chen and Paetsch, 1998)

customer wants. These WHATs are then prioritized in terms of relative importance, possibly benchmarked against competitors, and then the design team has to decide HOW they could deliver what the customer has asked for. The final – and perhaps the most important – step is then to see how well the solutions (the HOWs) correlate with WHAT the customer has asked for, overall.

It comprises the following elements, as shown in Figure 13.16:

The WHATs: creates a list of customer requirements. Their importance is scored and prioritized on a scale.

The HOWs: compiles a list of design requirements necessary to achieve the customer requirements listed as WHATs.

Relationship matrix: shows the relationship between the WHATs and the HOWs.

Correlation matrix: is the roof of the house. It captures the interrelationship between the design requirements. This is important when design features are being bundled together (e.g. a new mobile phone can be used to make calls, access the Internet and take pictures).

Process responsibility: FMEA date: [Revi:

Process function requirement	Potential failure mode	Potential effect(s) of failure	Severity	Class	Potential cause(s) mechanism(s) of failure	Occur	Current process central	Occur	RPH	Recommended action(s)	Responsibility and target complete date	Action taken	Severity	Occurrence	Detection	R P H
Service desk	Service desk	Complaints	5		Lack of language and communicaton skills support of volunteers and sufficient	4	No plan on training content: training and volunteer support and sufficient	3	72	Make complete training plan, implement personnel training and provide enough volunteers						
	Lock of barrier-free facility	Inconvenience and injury	10		Cannot provide barrier-free facility	3	Providing barrier-free facility	7	210	Add barrier-free facility						
Good support	Unclear signs	Can't find the room			Signs out of date and overdue; identificaton not removed	4	Post new signs			Periodic inspection and maintenance						
	Poorly planned equipment	Personal injury			Inappropriate equipment	3	Move, replace and/or improve equipment			Periodic inspection and repair						
Food service	Substandard food items	Diease or injury	5		No supplier control system, procedure or method of purchasing and/or inspection	3	Random purchasing and random inspection	3	72	Establish inspection procedure and method; strenghen outgoing product control						
					Food-preserving equipment and environment inconsistent with requirement	4	No requirements for storage equipment, maintenance or periodic cleaning of warehouse	7	210	Set requirements for storage equipment and environment; provide periodic maintenance						
	Food goes bad	Disease or injury	10		Raw material past shelf life	6	No control on the raw material	8	240	Periodic inspection						
					Packing damage		No control of packaging	3	120	Regular loading/unloading						
Medical service	Service not in time	Illness changes for the worse	10		No 24-hour service		12-hour service	3	180	Provide 24-hour service						

Figure 13.15 A FMEA of a hotel service at the Special Olympics (source: www.qualitydigest.com)

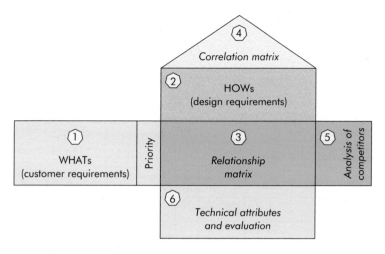

Figure 13.16 Quality function deployment

Analysis of competitors: determines how the customers perceive competitors' abilities to meet the requirements.

Technical attributes and evaluation: ranks the technical importance of each design requirement (usually shown as an absolute score, and a relative ranking).

Let's consider the QFD function of the Apple iPhone (Figure 13.17) and ask ourselves what it is that consumers want from an iPhone. Some of the requirements – the WHATs – are size, technology, features, storage capacity, battery life and price. Consumers also value these requirements differently. Price, for instance, means more (priority 10) than being environmentally friendly (priority 5). From the technical design's perspective, Apple needs to evaluate the design requirements for iPhones (the HOWs), such as technical requirements for case, screen, memory, software, camera and battery.

Once the HOWs and WHATs are gathered, Apple need to find out the relationship between them. The Relationship Matrix shows, for instance, that the size of the iPhone has a strong relationship with the camera, but a weaker relationship with the case, screen, and battery.

The roof shows that there is a *strong positive* correlation between case and screen (i.e. a design improvement in the case will contribute strongly to the improvement of the screen, and vice versa), whereas the correlation between battery and camera is only *positive* (i.e. a design improvement in the battery will contribute to the improvement of the camera, and vice versa, but not significantly). There is no correlation between screen and camera (i.e. a design improvement in the screen will not contribute to improvement of the camera, and vice versa).

The right-hand side of the matrix indicates how the competitors perform in satisfying the WHATs. The iPhone is superior to its competitors in terms of technology, design and features, but it is considerably more expensive than other phones in the market. This high-tech product also has a superior case, screen, memory and software elements (ranked the best in technical evaluation). The QFD provides a comparative analysis of the iPhone in relation to the competitors' products.

QFD matrices can be linked together to show how customer attributes flow through and influence other parts of the operation, such as the production process. The HOWs of one matrix become the WHATs of the next matrix (Figure 13.18). For a manufacturing plant, the engineering characteristics of House 1 become the customer attributes of House 2 in order to understand their influence on parts deployment. The design requirements need to be assessed in relation to the parts characteristics. The houses can be interlinked with as many houses as the company sees fit.

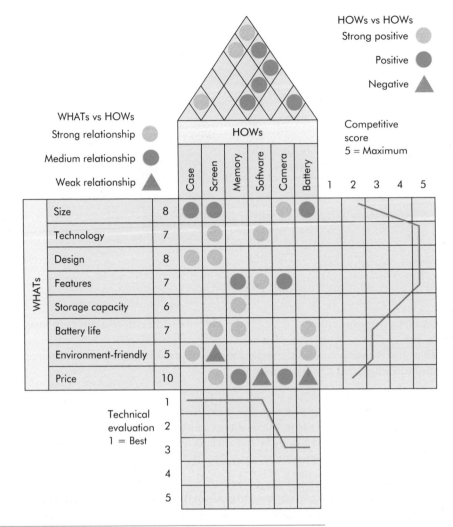

Figure 13.17 Example of iPhone (source: http://blogs.warwick.ac.uk/ssanchez)

Statistical Process Control

So far, we have seen some of the many tools which help firms focus and improve the quality of their products and services. In this section we focus on an approach which can be used to control the quality of the process, called *statistical process control* (SPC).

All processes exhibit some degree of variability in their outputs (e.g. a product or a service). This is because machines, tools, methods, materials and people are inconsistent. A mistake or variation in how any one part of a process is carried out might result in the product being faulty, or the service not meeting customer expectations. Rather than wait to identify defective products or substandard service by inspection or through customer complaints, SPC aims to detect the variation occurring within a process. More standardized processes with less variation should result in fewer defects and higher-quality outputs.

In order to manage process variation, we need to know the source of the variation, and whether the variation can be controlled or not. There are two types of process variation that commonly occur): random and non-random. *Random variation* cannot be controlled, but *non-random variation* has a cause that can be identified and assigned. Non-random variations are always caused by events that are not inherent in the production process. For quality management, we are concerned mostly with variations that can be identified and controlled. In order for the quality of a process to be improved, management needs to understand the nature of the variation (i.e. whether it is random or non-random), and take the corrective action to reduce or remove the variation.

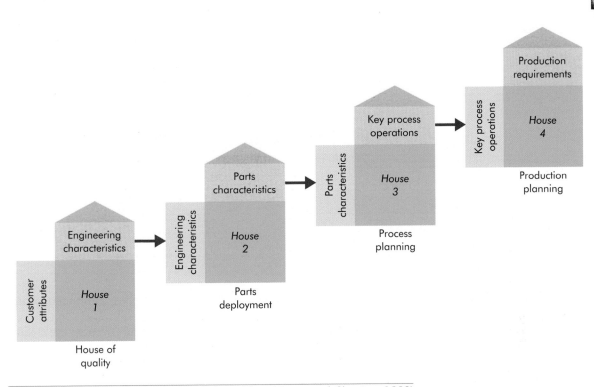

Figure 13.18 Linked houses of quality (adapted from Hauser and Clausing, 1988)

Before we can start controlling variation, it helps to understand how variation occurs. Statistical models help us predict likely patterns of variation, and decide how much variation is acceptable, and what change is likely to be a symptom of a faulty process. SPC is concerned with checking the quality characteristics of a product or service while it is being produced, through the use of statistics or statistical methods. It identifies the natural variation of the process, and sets the limits for what is and is not acceptable. Any variation beyond the acceptable level indicates a non-random or assignable cause that needs attention. There are four main uses of SPC (Basu, 2004):

- To achieve initial process stability
- To provide guidance on how the process may be improved by the reduction of variation
- To assess the performance of a process and increase process capability
- To provide information to assist with management decision-making.

Normal Distributions

SPC models are based on measurements that vary according to a statistical distribution. The exact statistical distribution depends on whether we are measuring *attributes* or *variables*.

Let us initially deal with measuring variables, which follow a *normal* (or bell-shaped) distribution. In a normal distribution, measurements are distributed continuously, but tend to cluster around a set point, with more extreme measurements being less likely to occur. This produces a bell-shaped curve called the *normal curve*, such as those shown in Figure 13.19.

Two key characteristics describe the **population** in a normal curve: the *mean* (μ) and the *standard deviation* (σ). The mean (μ), pronounced 'mu', is the average of the population measurements. The population is defined as every member of a *set* – for instance, all students currently registered at your university, or all the invoices sent to customers in a particular month, or all eggs produced by a farm in a week. The standard deviation (σ), pronounced 'sigma', is a measure of the variation of the population measurements. A small sigma, as exhibited in the blue curve, means that most of the data are centred on the mean, and hence have less variation than the red curve, which has a larger value of sigma.

Population: in a statistical distribution, the entire set of things that make up what is being measured.

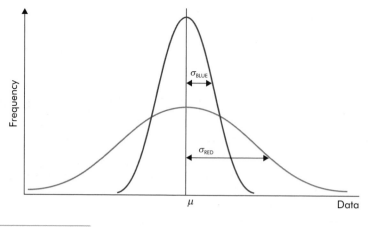

Figure 13.19 Normal distribution curves

If a population has mean μ and standard deviation σ, and is described by a normal curve, then the following empirical rules apply, as illustrated in Figure 13.20:

- *Rule 1*: 68.26% of the population measurements are within one standard deviation (1σ) from the mean in either direction. Therefore 31.74% of the data is more than one standard deviation from the mean. That is, 15.87% of the data will fall below −1 standard deviation, and 15.87% will be above +1 standard deviation.
- *Rule 2*: 95.44% of the population measurements are within two standard deviations from the mean in either direction. Therefore 4.56% of the data is more than two standard deviations from the mean. That is, 2.28% of the data will fall below −2 standard deviations, and 2.28% will be above +2 standard deviations.

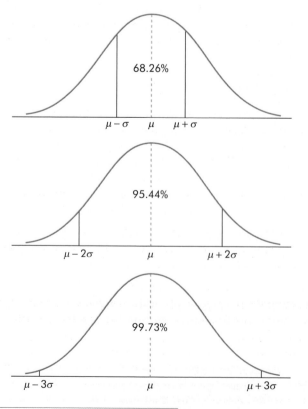

Figure 13.20 Empirical rule for a normally distributed population

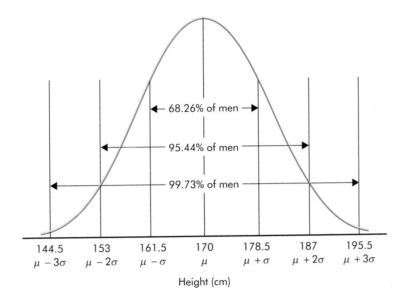

68.26% of men

95.44% of men

99.73% of men

| 144.5 | 153 | 161.5 | 170 | 178.5 | 187 | 195.5 |
| $\mu - 3\sigma$ | $\mu - 2\sigma$ | $\mu - \sigma$ | μ | $\mu + \sigma$ | $\mu + 2\sigma$ | $\mu + 3\sigma$ |

Height (cm)

Figure 13.21 Example of empirical rule

- *Rule 3*: 99.73% of the population measurements are within three standard deviations from the mean in either direction. Therefore 0.27% of the data is more than three standard deviations from the mean. That is, 0.135% of the data will fall below −3 standard deviations, and 0.135% will be above +3 standard deviations.

These proportions are fixed, and are described in statistical tables: so once we know the mean and standard deviation of a measurement, we know what proportion of the population is likely to fall within any particular range of measurements. Suppose that the distribution of heights of men between the ages of 18 and 26 is approximately normal, with a mean of 170 centimetres ($\mu = 170$ cm) and standard deviation of 8.5 centimetres. Using the empirical rule, we would have the following statistics, as shown in Figure 13.21:

- 68.26% of men are between 161.5 and 178.5 cm tall
- 95.44% of men are between 153 and 187 cm tall
- 99.73% of men are between 144.5 and 195.5 cm tall

We often interpret the three sigma interval ($\pm 3\sigma$) to be the interval that contains almost all the measurements in the population, and this has traditionally been considered an acceptable quality level. In practice, this means that if the specification limits of a product are set equal to $\pm 3\sigma$, we could expect 0.27% defective parts, or 2,700 defective parts per million (ppm), to be produced. *Six Sigma* is so called because it aims to reduce the variability of a process so that outputs that lie within $\pm 6\sigma$ of the mean fall within the specification limits. This means that only 3.4 parts per million will be beyond the specification limits, which for most operational purposes is as close to zero as is required.

In Six Sigma the terms *defects per million opportunities* (DPMO) is used, which means the number of defects a process would produce if there were a million opportunities to do so. This is slightly different from defects per number of parts produced, as each part may have more than one way in which it can be defective.

For any company these tighter tolerances mean that there are fewer faulty products being made, and this in turn means lower costs of rework and scrap. For example, if the designers of a product state that all the good, non-defective parts need to be within specification range, and the process producing the parts needs to operate within 6σ limits, then we have a process that should produce only 3.4 parts per million that we cannot use. This is a very low scrap rate. It is shown in Figure 13.22, where the process described by the bottom curve is less likely to produce faulty parts. The top curve, however, shows a higher likelihood of producing unusable parts – those that fall outside the specifications – and so we should continuously need to inspect the parts. The lower curve needs less monitoring, as there is less variation or change in the process. This situation is the ultimate aim of the Six Sigma approach: the reduction of variation in a process's output.

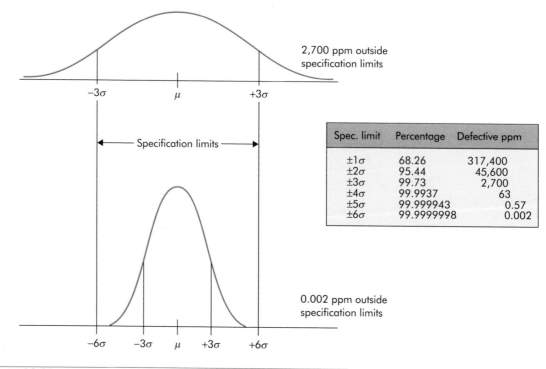

Spec. limit	Percentage	Defective ppm
±1σ	68.26	317,400
±2σ	95.44	45,600
±3σ	99.73	2,700
±4σ	99.9937	63
±5σ	99.999943	0.57
±6σ	99.9999998	0.002

Figure 13.22 Comparison of curves within and outside specification limits

Is Six Sigma 3.4 Defects per Million Opportunities?

CRITICAL PERSPECTIVE

The table in Figure 13.22 lists the 6σ defect rate as 0.002 DPMO, but the Six Sigma philosophy indicates that a 6σ process will produce 3.4 DPMO. This is because the architects of Six Sigma built a 1.5σ shift into their statistical calculations, believing that over time the process would drift, so eroding its integrity from 0.002 DPMO to the more realistic 3.4 DPMO. This shift of course alters the process integrity for all σ values, as shown in Table 13.6.

Table 13.6 DPMO, defect and yield percentages with a 1.5σ shift incorporated

+ and −	DPMO	Defect percentage	Yield percentage
1σ	691,462	69%	30.9%
2σ	308,538	31%	69.1%
3σ	66,807	6.7%	93.3%
4σ	6,210	0.62%	99.38%
5σ	233	0.023%	99.977%
6σ	**3.4**	**0.00034%**	**99.99966%**
7σ	0.019	0.0000019%	99.9999981%

The key point is that regardless of the absolute values used, a 6σ process is the ultimate goal for a process designer.

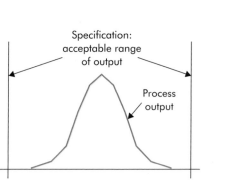

Specification:
acceptable range
of output

Process
output

Figure 13.23 A process output curve fitting well between the specifications set by the designer

Using SPC

If we apply the information above, we can ensure our process is producing only good parts by ensuring that the output curve of the process fits within the tolerances set by the engineers designing the product, as shown in Figure 13.23.

In practice, ensuring the output is always within tolerance needs two steps. The first step is to ensure that the output is stable and producing within tolerance as shown in Figure 13.23. When we first turn on a hot tap, for example, the water temperature may vary before becoming stable; this is because there may be cold water in the pipe between the hot water tank and the tap. So we need to run the process to ensure it is stable before testing if it is producing within tolerance. The second step uses SPC charts to monitor the process and see whether there is any evidence that the mean or standard deviation is changing as a result of assignable causes. If there is no indication that the process is varying, then we can continue operating it and use the parts it produces with confidence. As the parts were within specification when we started, there is no evidence that the process has changed and so the parts will still be within specification. We repeat this second check frequently to be sure we catch any change in the process as soon as it occurs.

Measuring Process Capability

Process capability measures how much yield (output) a process can produce within pre-specified tolerance limits. Traditionally, a process is capable if all its outputs as measured using 3σ limits fall within the specified tolerance limits. However, using 6σ thinking, we know that this may not be good enough for today's quality requirements and so some firms choose the tighter measure by insisting production measured at the 6σ level is within specification. Whether a process is capable or not can be determined by visual inspection (from a chart), or by calculation.

Customers normally state their requirements in terms of a target value with some specified *tolerances* (also called *specifications*), to give a range of what would be acceptable. For example, the output voltage specification of many semiconductors is set at 5 volts ±5%, which means that as long as the voltage measurements are between 4.75 and 5.25 volts, the semiconductors meet the specifications, and hence are acceptable.

To measure the process capability we use an index number called Cp calculated as shown in the Process Capability Ratio below. This compares the width of the tolerance range to the width of the process output. Note that the 6σ process output shown as the denominator in the equation below is the plus or minus 3σ level: 3σ either side of the mean equals a total of 6σ – not to be confused with the 6σ process we have been discussing, which would be $+6\sigma$ or -6σ either side of the mean, totalling 12σ.

$$\text{Process capability ratio, } C_{\text{p}} = \frac{\text{Upper specification level (USL)} - \text{Lower specification level (LSL)}}{6\sigma}$$

Referring to Figure 13.24, a ratio of less than 1 ($C_{\text{p}} < 1$) indicates that outputs will be outside the predefined specification or tolerance limits. (As the width of the process output is wider than the range specified by the designers). A ratio greater than 1 ($C_{\text{p}} > 1$) indicates that the outputs are within the specification, as shown. However, we would not want the ratio to be too close to 1.0, as this implies a tight fit, and would leave little margin for error. Typically, the process aim is set at 1.33, to allow some leeway. A ratio of 2 would signify that 6σ levels (as defined by the quality philosophy) have been reached.

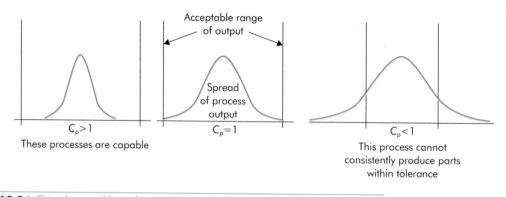

Figure 13.24 Cp values and how they compare process output and specification limits

The C_p ratio takes into account only the variance or width of the process output; it does not measure the location of the values. To measure location and variance we need to use a more sophisticated measure, known as the C_{pk} ratio. This takes into account whether the process output is central to the specification or, if it isn't, how far from central is it. We can see in Figure 13.25 that it is possible to have a good C_p value but still produce many defective parts if the process output is too far from the centre of the acceptable values as set in the specification.

The C_{pk} ratio is calculated as follows. Note that the 'min' and the square brackets indicate we are interested in the minimum value of either possible calculation:

$$C_{pk} = \min \left[\frac{\bar{X} - \text{LSL}}{3\sigma}, \frac{\text{USL} - \bar{X}}{3\sigma} \right]$$

where $\bar{X}$ is the average of the process output (its centrality); LSL and USL are the lower and upper specification limits (set by the designers); and 3σ is the process output range over 3 standard deviations. If:

$C_{pk} = C_p$ the process mean is centred between the specification limits

$C_{pk} > 1.0$ the process is capable

$C_{pk} < 1.0$ the process is not capable

For example, assume a manufacturing process that produces the above-mentioned semiconductors has a mean of 4.9 volts and a standard deviation of 0.1 volts:

$$C_{pk} = \min \left[\frac{4.9 - 4.75}{3 \times 0.1}, \frac{5.25 - 4.9}{3 \times 0.1} \right]$$

$$= \min(0.5, 1.17)$$

Hence the lowest value of C_{pk} is 0.5, which means that the process is not capable of always producing semiconductors that are within the specification. – the situation that is represented in the left-hand diagram of Figure 13.25.

So C_p and C_{pk} are indices that tell us whether the process is producing all its output (or, rather actually 99.73% or more, as we have adopted the 6σ limit) within specification. This means the process is producing only good parts.

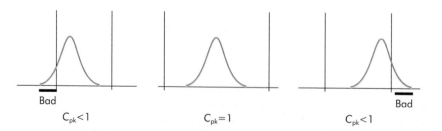

Figure 13.25 Representation of possible C_{pk} results

SPC Charts

An SPC chart is a **control chart** that graphically presents samples of output taken from the total output (the population) being produced by the process. Its job is to test the output and see whether this has varied from when the process was capable (i.e. passing both the C_p and C_{pk} tests). If the SPC chart reveals a variation in the output of the process, then we no longer have the same output, and so could be producing faulty parts.

> **Control chart:** used to plot sample means, average means and ranges over time; indicates the lower and upper control limits.

Our reaction is to stop using the process and find out what has changed. As there are different types of measurement we can apply to samples, there are therefore different types of chart. The process of establishing which control chart to use is determined by the following steps:

- *Step 1*: Consider whether you are collecting variable data or attribute data. *Variables* refer to data that are measured on a continuous scale, such as weight, height, volume, or time. *Attributes* refer to situations, such as yes/no, on/off, or right/wrong.
- *Step 2*: Choose the type of chart to be used. A variables chart is used to control individual, measurable characteristics. Attribute charts are used to control the number of defective units or defects in a unit. You also need to also consider whether the sampled population or sample space is constant, or varies. Figure 13.26 shows a decision tree for choosing which chart to use to measure a process.
- *Step 3*: Once the type of chart to be used is established, one can take samples and calculate means of samples, and upper and lower control limits using the appropriate formula. The principles for every chart are the same; however the formulae vary due to different distributions being used (attributes follow a binomial distribution whilst variances follow a normal distribution).

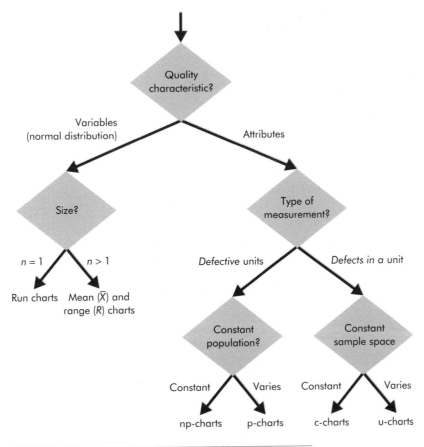

Figure 13.26 Which control chart to use? (adapted from Bicheno, 2002, p. 38)

SPC Charts for Variables: $\bar{X}$ and Range

If the process can be measured using a continuous variable such as length, height or time, the chart employed is the $\bar{X}$ and range chart. An example is shown in Figure 13.27, which identifies the top part as showing the mean

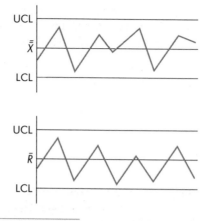

Figure 13.27 The main parts of the $\bar{X}$ and range chart

($\bar{X}$, or average) and how it varies over time, and the lower part the same for the range (spread or standard deviation). Both charts have a central line to help us record the data and assess how it is changing, and they also have upper and lower control limits. These are there to warn us if something unexpected happens. If either chart suggests that the process has varied from its previous (capable) state, then we need to take action. If there is no evidence of any change to the process, then we can continue to operate the process, confident that the output is still within specification.

The $\bar{X}$ (or X-bar) chart monitors the average (mean) of the samples being measured, and the range (or R) chart the variance (standard deviation) in the samples. The $\bar{X}$ and R charts are used together in a sampling plan to monitor repetitive processes and see whether the output curve has changed.

An $\bar{X}$ chart plots the means of the samples taken from the outputs of a process. Each sample mean will be an approximation to the population mean (μ). The larger the sample is, the more closely it will represent the population (e.g. a sample of 10 football diameters from a total population output of 1,000 will give a less accurate approximation of the population mean than if 100 were sampled). This potential error is corrected using pre-calculated values from a table such as Table 13.7.

The centre line of an $\bar{X}$ chart is the average of the sample means, $\bar{\bar{X}}$ (this is known as the *grand mean* or as X-bar-bar), or a target value for the process.

$$\text{Mean of the sample, } \bar{X} = \frac{\sum_{i=1}^{n} X_i}{n}$$

$$= \frac{X_1 + X_2 + \ldots + X_n}{n}$$

where i is the item number, and n is the total number of items in the sample.

$$\text{Average of the means of the samples, } \bar{\bar{X}} = \frac{\sum_{j=1}^{m} \bar{X}_j}{m}$$

$$= \frac{\bar{X}_1 + \bar{X}_2 + \ldots + \bar{X}_m}{m}$$

where j is the sample number, and m is the total number of samples.

$$\text{Average range, } \bar{R} = \frac{\sum_{j=1}^{m} R_j}{m}$$

$$= \frac{R_1 + R_2 + \ldots + R_m}{m}$$

where R is the difference between the maximum and minimum values of each sample.

The upper and lower control limits for $\bar{X}$ charts are:

$$\text{Upper control limit for } \bar{X}, \text{ UCL}_{\bar{x}} = \bar{\bar{X}} + A_2\bar{R}$$

$$\text{Lower control limit for } \bar{X}, \text{ LCL}_{\bar{x}} = \bar{\bar{X}} - A_2\bar{R}$$

The upper and lower control limits for range charts are:

$$\text{Upper control limit for } R, \text{UCL}_R = D_4\bar{R}$$

$$\text{Lower control limit for } R, \text{UCL}_R = D_3\bar{R}$$

The process standard deviation can be estimated (again as we only have a small sample and not the whole population, using Table 13.7) as:

$$\text{Standard deviation, } \sigma = \frac{\bar{R}}{d_2}$$

Table 13.7 Factors for determining control limits for $\bar{X}$ and R charts.

No. of observations in subgroups, N	Factor for X̄ chart	Factors for R chart		
		Lower control limit	Upper control limit	Divisor estimate of standard deviation
	A_2	D_3	D_4	d_2
2	1.880	0	3.267	1.128
3	1.023	0	2.574	1.693
4	0.729	0	2.282	2.059
5	0.577	0	2.114	2.326
6	0.483	0	2.004	2.534
7	0.419	0.076	1.924	2.704
8	0.373	0.136	1.864	2.847
9	0.337	0.184	1.816	2.970
10	0.308	0.223	1.777	3.078
11	0.285	0.256	1.744	3.173
12	0.266	0.283	1.717	3.258
13	0.249	0.307	1.693	3.336
14	0.235	0.328	1.672	3.407
15	0.223	0.347	1.653	3.472
16	0.212	0.363	1.637	3.532
17	0.203	0.378	1.622	3.588
18	0.194	0.391	1.608	3.640
19	0.187	0.403	1.597	3.689
20	0.180	0.415	1.585	3.735
21	0.173	0.425	1.575	3.778
22	0.167	0.434	1.566	3.819
23	0.162	0.443	1.557	3.858
24	0.157	0.451	1.548	3.895
25	0.153	0.459	1.541	3.931

The values for A_2, D_3 and D_4 vary with the number of observations in subgroups, as listed in Table 13.7. Essentially, as the values change and the more observations we have, the more true the value, and so we can see smaller variations before needing to take action.

WORKED EXAMPLE 13.1

Grommets: Calculating Sample Carton

A materials inspector wants to know whether a special component called a grommet meets the length specification required for manufacturing. The specification limits for the grommet are between 24 and 36 mm. He collects 25 samples with 4 observations in each, as shown in Figure 13.28.

Problem: *Are the samples in control? Should the inspector be concerned?*

Approach: Figure 13.28 provides an example of how $\bar{X}$ and R charts are used. The chart shows the data collected from the measurements of the process. There are 25 samples ($m = 25$) with 4 observations each ($n = 4$). The mean of each sample, $\bar{X}$, and range R are calculated for each sample. The centre line, upper limits and lower limits for each of the charts are calculated as follows:

$$\bar{\bar{X}} = \frac{\sum_{j=1}^{m} \bar{X}_j}{m} = \frac{\bar{X}_1 + \bar{X}_2 + \ldots + \bar{X}_m}{m}$$

$$= \frac{731.25}{25} = 29.250$$

$$\bar{R} = \frac{\sum_{j=1}^{m} R_j}{m} = \frac{R_1 + R_2 + \ldots + R_m}{m}$$

$$= \frac{217}{25} = 8.680$$

Using Table 13.7, and knowing that $n = 4$, we have $A_2 = 0.73$, $D_3 = 0$ and $D_4 = 2.28$. So:

$$\begin{aligned} \text{UCL}_{\bar{x}} &= \bar{\bar{X}} + A_2\bar{R} \\ &= 29.25 + (0.729 \times 8.68) \\ &= 35.578 \end{aligned}$$

$$\begin{aligned} \text{LCL}_{\bar{x}} &= \bar{\bar{X}} - A_2\bar{R} \\ &= 29.25 - (0.729 \times 8.68) \\ &= 22.922 \end{aligned}$$

$$\begin{aligned} \text{UCL}_R &= D_4\bar{R} \\ &= 2.282 \times 8.68 \\ &= 19.808 \end{aligned}$$

$$\begin{aligned} \text{LCL}_R &= D_3\bar{R} \\ &= 0 \end{aligned}$$

Solution: The chart shows that there are four samples that require further investigation, as they are outside the control limits: samples 3, 8, 22, and 25. This could be due to machine, material or human error, or some other factor. Note that each point plotted on the X-bar chart is the average of a mean, and each point plotted on the range chart is the range of a sample.

Any point outside the control limits would not normally occur, and so would indicate that the process had changed in some way. If we had already tested C_p and C_{pk}, any variation would tell us that we were now possibly producing parts out of specification.

Variables Control Chart (X and R)

			Part number		Chart number
Part name (product) **Grommet**		Operation (process)			
Operator	Machine	Gauge	Specification limits **24–36**		
			Unit of measure **0.0001**	Zero equals	

n = 4

Date Time	1	2	3	4	5	6	7	8	9	10	11	12	13	14	15	16	17	18	19	20	21	22	23	24	25
Sample measurements 1	24	29	38	24	33	28	30	28	24	26	25	28	31	30	26	24	25	26	27	28	24	18	29	20	14
2	27	30	42	28	36	28	28	24	27	27	26	24	26	31	25	36	35	30	31	33	24	42	30	36	25
3	28	29	36	27	31	28	27	29	33	38	27	29	38	33	24	24	25	28	29	30	32	36	31	34	36
4	33	31	35	32	28	26	26	30	28	26	28	30	24	32	36	36	35	32	33	34	32	30	28	32	35
5																									
Sum	112	119	151	111	128	112	111	111	112	117	106	111	119	126	111	120	120	116	120	125	112	126	118	122	110
Average, X̄	28	29.75	37.75	27.75	32	28	27.75	27.75	28	29.25	26.5	27.75	29.75	31.5	27.75	30	30	29	30	31.25	28	31.5	29.5	30.5	27.5
Range, R	9	2	7	8	8	0	4	6	9	12	3	6	14	3	12	12	10	6	6	6	8	24	3	16	22
Notes																									

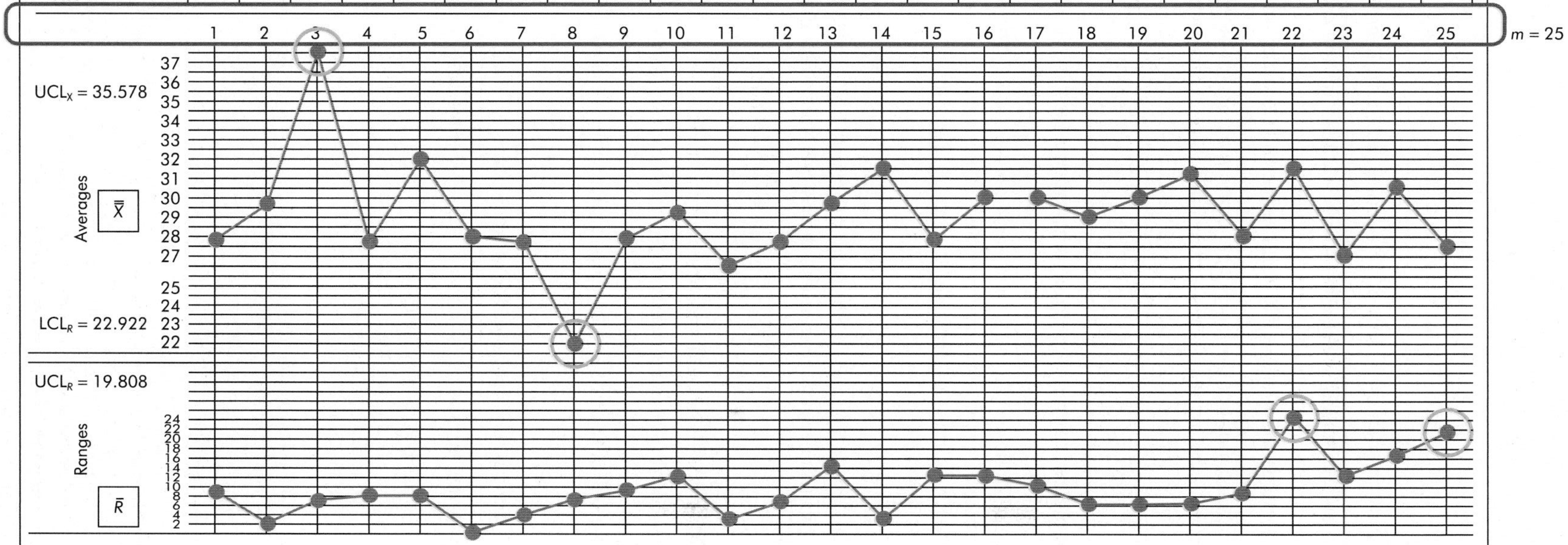

m = 25

Averages
$UCL_{\bar{X}} = 35.578$
37
36
35
34
33
32
31
30
29
28
27
26
25
24
23
22

$LCL_R = 22.922$

Ranges
$UCL_R = 19.808$
24
22
20
18
16
14
12
10
8
6
4
2

Figure 13.28 An example of completed X̄ and R charts (Foster 2010, p. 369)

SPC Charts for Attributes

When we are recording attribute data such as counts or proportions, rather than variables such as height or length, we need to use different charts.

The *p*-chart is used to illustrate the *proportion of defectives* (or percentage non-conforming) in each subgroup – for example, the proportion of dissatisfied customers in a survey of train commuters. It is the most universal chart, based on the proportion of non-conforming items within a chosen set of items. Other possible applications of *p*-charts include late deliveries, incomplete orders, accounting errors, typing errors, or misspellings.

A *np*-chart plots the *number of defectives* (or the number of non-conforming items) in each subgroup (using the same sample size each time). The use of an *np*-chart is essentially the same as the use of a *p*-charts, except that *np*-charts use integer numbers (e.g. 0, 1, 2) rather than proportions (e.g. 0.5, 1.1, 2.5).

A *c*-chart is used to monitor the *number of non-conformities* (or defects) in a discrete unit, *not* the number of items found to be conforming. It requires a constant sample space, which means that the space for finding defects must be the same for each unit. Typical situations when a *c*-chart is used include flaws in a specific length of fabric, flaws in an auto finish (for a particular model), defects in a paint finish (if all cars are of the same size), the number of flaws in a standard A4 paper, or number of incorrect responses on a standardized test.

When the sample space varies (such as in inspection for flaws in different models of car within a model family), a *u*-chart is used. In this case the *average number of non-conformities* is charted. For instance, you might decide to inspect the end-of-line scratches in the paint on all cars of differing sizes in a production line – for example a saloon, an estate or a coupe. Consider in this example that the car is the unit. As all cars (units) are of different sizes (i.e. different surface area of paint to check), checking *defects per unit* is a far more useful measure than just the *number of defects*.

As for $\bar{X}$ and R charts, for all these charts the upper control limit (UCL) and lower control limit (LCL) are usually established at ±3 standard deviations from the centre line (unless Six Sigma tolerances are being used, in which tolerance limits will be set at ±6 standard deviations from the centre line). The formulae for the attribute data are listed in Table 13.8.

Interpretation of Charts

In addition to identifying data points outside the control limits, we need to keep an eye for unusual patterns on SPC charts, such as data points that exhibit non-random variation in the process. These indicate that the process may be going out of control and becoming incapable – a capable process passed C_p and C_{pk} and is only able to

Table 13.8 Control limit formulas for attribute data

Chart type	Data type	Centre line	Upper control limit	Lower control limit
p	Percentage non-conforming, where p is proportion defective, $\bar{p}$ is average proportion defective	$\bar{p}$	$UCL = \bar{p} + 3\sqrt{\dfrac{\bar{p}(1-\bar{p})}{n}}$	$LCL = \bar{p} - 3\sqrt{\dfrac{\bar{p}(1-\bar{p})}{n}}$
np	Number of non-conforming items, where p is proportion defective, $\bar{p}$ is average proportion defective	$n\bar{p}$	$UCL = n\bar{p} + 3\sqrt{n\bar{p}(1-\bar{p})}$	$LCL = n\bar{p} - 3\sqrt{n\bar{p}(1-\bar{p})}$
c	Number of non-conformities, where c is number of defects	$\bar{c}$	$UCL = \bar{c} + 3\sqrt{\bar{c}}$	$LCL = \bar{c} - 3\sqrt{\bar{c}}$
u	Number of non-conformities per item, where u is process average number of non-conformities or defects per unit, n is average sample size	$\bar{u}$	$UCL = \bar{u} + 3\sqrt{\dfrac{\bar{u}}{n}}$	$LCL = \bar{u} - 3\sqrt{\dfrac{\bar{u}}{n}}$

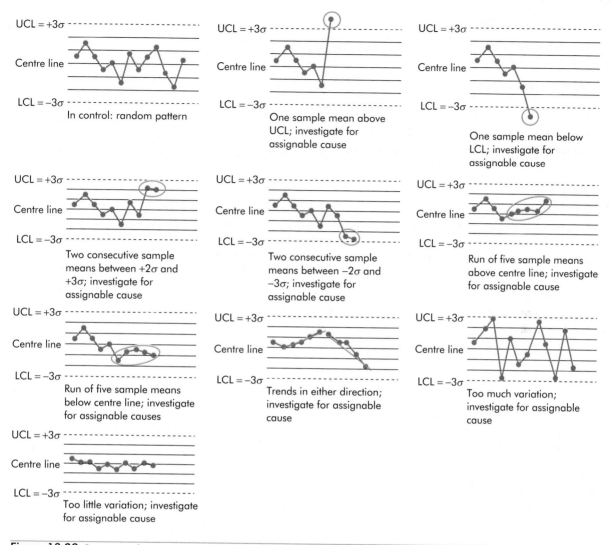

Figure 13.29 Scenario of non-random variation in processes (adapted from Hansen, 1963, p. 65).

produce parts within specification. Figure 13.29 illustrates various scenarios of non-random variation that can occur, and which can be identified using an SPC chart.

Cost of Quality

Managing quality is not cheap. It has been estimated that in 2001 it cost General Electric (GE) somewhere between $11 billion and $16 billion to implement its quality management strategy (www.isixsigma.com). As quality management evolves from being reactive (i.e. fixing problems after detection) to proactive (i.e. preventing failures from occurring in the first place), the nature of what constitutes quality costs is changing as well. Quality costs can be classified into three categories: *prevention costs*, *appraisal costs* and *failure costs* (internal and external), as detailed in Table 13.9.

The traditional view of the costs of quality was that there was an optimum level of investment in quality prevention and appraisal, after which there were diminishing returns to failure reduction, as shown in Figure 13.30.

The modern view of the cost of quality is shown in Figure 13.31. This demonstrates that investment in cost of quality prevention and appraisal will always result in some improvement – i.e. some reduction in internal or external failure.

Traditionally, the costs of quality were perceived by many manufacturing companies as costs related to running the quality assurance department and costs relating to scrap. Similarly, it was estimated that companies in the

Table 13.9 Definitions of quality costs

Category	Description	Examples
Internal failure costs	Costs related to deficiencies discovered before delivery that are associated with the failure to meet explicit requirements or implicit needs of customers	Scrap, rework, lost of missing information, failure analysis, 100% sorting inspection, re-inspection, re-testing, redesign of hardware and software, and downgrading
External failure costs	Costs related to deficiencies that are found after the customer receives the product. The costs also include lost opportunities for sales revenue	Warranty charges, complaint adjustments, returned material, allowances, penalties due to poor quality, rework on support operations, revenue losses in support operations, and customer defections
Appraisal costs	Costs incurred to determine the degree of conformance to quality requirements	Incoming inspection and test, in-process inspection and test, document review, examination of accounts, product quality audits, maintaining accuracy of test equipment, inspection and test materials and services, and evaluation of stock
Prevention costs	Costs incurred to keep failure and appraisal costs to a minimum	Quality planning, new products review, process planning, process control, quality audits, supplier quality evaluation, and training

Source: adapted from Gryna *et al.* (2007).

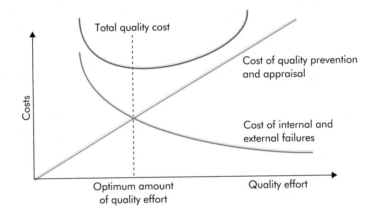

Figure 13.30 Traditional view of the cost of quality

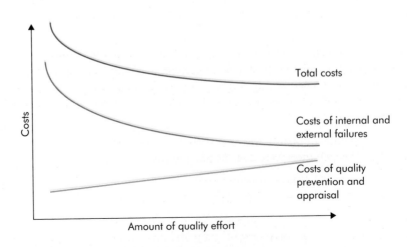

Figure 13.31 Contemporary view of the cost of quality

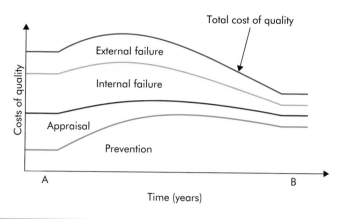

Figure 13.32 The changing profile of quality costs

1980s typically spent between 5% and 25% of their annual sales turnover on quality-related costs, and 95% of this was spent on appraisal and failures (Dale and Plunkett, 1990).

Today, we know that quality costs extend to all levels of the organization, including the costs incurred in designing, implementing, operating and maintaining a quality management system. Figure 13.32 shows that the profile of quality costs changes as the practice of quality management becomes more proactive. At point A on the diagram, when a quality programme is just starting, costs will focus predominantly on failure rectification. Investment should then move towards prevention, which at point B should result in lower overall costs of quality.

Contemporary Thinking: Quality Control and Corporate Social Responsibility

Recently, firms have started to consider the quality costs related to environmental factors, and how they impact on sustainable operations management practice. Various organizations are developing standards for corporate social responsibility (CSR). ISO 26000 is an ISO initiative for CSR standardization. It is intended for both the public and private sectors in developed and developing countries. Its purpose is to:

- Develop an international consensus on what social responsibility means, and the CSR issues that organizations need to address
- Provide guidance on translating principles into effective actions
- Refine best practices that have already evolved, and disseminate the information worldwide for the good of the international community.

In addition to ISO 26000, two other prominent standards are AA 1000 and SA 8000. The *AA 1000 standard* has been developed by the Institute of Social and Ethical Accountability, with the purpose of improving the accountability and overall performance of organizations through increased quality in social and ethical accounting, auditing and reporting, through management of the system, individual behaviours and the impact on stakeholders.

SA 8000, developed by Social Accountability International, is a social accountability standard for child labour, forced labour, health and safety, freedom of association and the right to collective bargaining, discrimination, working conditions, and workers' rights. It specifies requirements for social accountability so that a company can develop, maintain and enforce policies and procedures in order to manage those issues that it can control and influence.

---

❶ Stop and Think

3 Is compliance with ISO standards a sufficient criterion to guarantee that a company can produce products and services of a desired quality? Does it guarantee that the company is ethical?

Summary

In this chapter we have explained how difficult it is to define quality, and have highlighted the importance of quality performance for organizations. Quality is embedded in all aspects of our lives, ranging from the physical products we use to the services we consume.

The philosophies of quality management have been outlined, and its fundamental principles indicated. The evolution of quality management over recent decades was explained. It is important to understand this, as it mirrors the 'quality journey' that many organizations undertake as they strive to practise better-quality management and raise their standards.

As well as philosophies there are also many operational tools that managers can use to assess and improve quality, such as FMEA, QFD and SPC. The tools are typically structured into a methodological approach such as TQM or Six Sigma.

Views about quality management have changed in recent decades, and this can be demonstrated by the different way in which the costs of quality are assessed. The contemporary view is that it is always good to continuously invest in quality.

An emerging issue is the role that corporate social responsibility is playing, which adds another dimension of complexity to quality management.

Key Theories

The key theories discussed in this chapter are:

- **Total quality management (TQM)** – a quality management approach centred on the participation of all its members, aiming at the long-term success of an organization through customer satisfaction.

- **European Foundation of Quality Management (EFQM)** – a framework for quality management based on nine criteria: five are enablers (leadership, people, policy and strategy, partnership and resources, and processes) and four are results (people, customer, society, and key performance).

- **Quality function deployment (QFD)** – sometimes referred to as the House of Quality; a tool to capture customer needs in product designs.

- **Six Sigma** – a method for standardizing the way defects are counted. It applies statistical methods to achieve no more than 3.4 defects per million opportunities in any process, product or service.

- **Failure mode and effect analysis (FMEA)** – an advanced method to conduct reliability analysis. It provides detailed insights into the system's interrelationships and potential sources of failures.

- **Lean Six Sigma** – the integrated approach of combining Six Sigma with lean production methodologies to improve process capability and eliminate waste.

Key Equations

Measuring process capability:

$$\text{Process capability ratio, } C_p = \frac{\text{Upper specification level (USL)} - \text{Lower specification level (LSL)}}{6\sigma}$$

$$C_{pk} = \min\left[\frac{\bar{X} - \text{LSL}}{3\sigma}, \frac{\text{USL} - \bar{X}}{3\sigma}\right]$$

$\bar{X}$: the average of the process output (its centrality)
LSL: lower specification limit
USL: upper specification limit
σ: standard deviation

$\bar{X}$ and range charts:

$$\text{Mean of the sample, } \bar{X} = \frac{\sum_{i=1}^{n} X_i}{n}$$

$$= \frac{X_1 + X_2 + \ldots + X_n}{n}$$

i: the item number
n: the total number of items in the sample

$$\text{Average of the means of the samples, } \bar{\bar{X}} = \frac{\sum_{j=1}^{m} \bar{X}_j}{m}$$

$$= \frac{\bar{X}_1 + \bar{X}_2 + \ldots + \bar{X}_m}{m}$$

j: the sample number
m: the total number of samples.

$$\text{Average range, } \bar{R} = \frac{\sum_{j=1}^{m} R_j}{m}$$

$$= \frac{R_1 + R_2 + \ldots + R_m}{m}$$

R: the difference between the maximum and minimum values of each sample
Upper control limit for $\bar{X}$, $\text{UCL}_{\bar{x}} = \bar{\bar{X}} + A_2 \bar{R}$
Lower control limit for $\bar{X}$, $\text{LCL}_{\bar{x}} = \bar{\bar{X}} - A_2 \bar{R}$
Upper control limit for R, $\text{UCL}_R = D_4 \bar{R}$
Lower control limit for R, $\text{LCL}_R = D_3 \bar{R}$

Standard deviation, $\sigma = \dfrac{R}{d_2}$

A_2, D_3 and D_4 : factors for $\bar{X}$ chart and R chart.

Answers to Stop and Think Questions

1 **TQM:** TQM is a management approach centred on quality that is based on the participation of the organization's people, aiming at long-term success. If an organization seeks to follow the eight quality management principles (customer focus, leadership, involvement of people, process approach, system approach to management, continous improvement, factual approach to decision-making, and mutually beneficial supplier relationships), then it should adopt TQM. In fact, we can say that virtually all organizations (small and large) apply these principles. However, more recent developments in quality management, such as Lean Six Sigma, claim to be more effective.

2 **Lean Six Sigma:** For firms trying to use TQM as an approach to quality, it is often criticized for a lack of structure. As TQM is a collection of the ideas of the quality gurus, it is not owned or defined by any individual or organization, and so there is no blueprint to follow. Along with TQM, Lean Six Sigma shares the benefits of a focus on continuous improvement and the many tools available for zero defects and right first time, but includes a more prescriptive framework from the many consultants offering advice. This means that firms may find it easier to implement Lean Six Sigma.

3 **ISO standards:** ISO certification has become the minimum requirement for many organizations to be accepted in an industry. It provides a certain level of reputation for organizations. However, no quality manuals or procedures are comprehensive enough to guarantee that an organization

▶ can provide defect-free products and customer satisfaction 100%, all the time. The organization needs to match its quality objectives with the appropriate quality management tools. Although ISO certification is seen as a minimum standard by many, the downside is that it can also stifle any future changes, because of the extensive documentation and procedural constraints it introduces,

connect™

Review Questions

1   Would you consider poor service as a failure? How would you go about getting rid of the failures and improve the service?

2   Name five products that, in your opinion, have a high degree of quality. Are these products produced by large corporations? How do the corporations ensure the high degree of quality?

3   Should companies consider ISO 9000 as the first step to approaching quality management? If so, why?

4   You are helping your best friend to plan his/her wedding. How are you going to make sure that nothing goes wrong? Which decision tools can you use to ensure a successful wedding?

5   Describe your decision criteria for buying your most recent mobile phone. Would you replace your phone soon? Discuss how the next generation of phones can be best developed. Apply the quality function deployment framework.

Discussion Questions

1   Describe a recent event where you were not satisfied with the service. Identify where the gaps between your expectation and perception might have occurred.

2   Discuss Six Sigma and lean production methodologies. Can you apply Lean Six Sigma to services?

3   Describe your holiday experiences from various countries and cities. What kinds of transportation mode did you use (e.g. taxis, buses, rental car)? Did the taxi ride experience, for instance, differ from those in your home country? Discuss the different aspects of an experience such as a taxi ride (e.g. the interior technologies installed, smell, cleanliness, comfort, safety) and compare them with the quality standards you might expect in your country.

Problems

1   Suppose that $\bar{p} = 0.3$ and $n = 200$. Calculate the upper control limit (UCL) and lower control limit (LCL) of the corresponding p-chart.

2   Suppose that $\bar{c} = 26$. Calculate the upper control limit (UCL) and lower control limit (LCL) of the corresponding c-chart.

3   An organization wants to study the fraction of incorrect sales invoices that are sent to its customers. A random sample of 100 sales invoices for 40 weeks is collected. It reveals that the total number of incorrect sales invoices from all samples is 97.

   (a)   Calculate the fraction of incorrect sales invoices.

   (b)   Calculate the centre line (CL) for the p-chart.

   (c)   Calculate the upper control limit (UCL).

   (d)   Calculate the lower control limit (LCL).

4 The manager of a printing shop wishes to monitor the number of non-conformities (missing characters, miscolouring, smearing, etc.) produced by a high-speed printing machine. The manager inspects 3 pages of the text output from the printing machine every day for 40 days. The recorded non-conformities are listed in Table 13.10.

(a) Construct a c-chart for the printing machine's non-conformities.

(b) Discuss whether the manager should be concerned about the situation.

Table 13.10

Inspection unit	Number of non-conformities	Inspection unit	Number of non-conformities
1	0	21	3
2	2	22	2
3	2	23	1
4	0	24	0
5	0	25	0
6	3	26	0
7	5	27	2
8	1	28	3
9	1	29	4
10	0	30	3
11	3	31	1
12	0	32	0
13	0	33	0
14	1	34	0
15	1	35	2
16	2	36	0
17	2	37	1
18	2	38	1
19	0	39	3
20	1	40	0

Visit the Online Learning Centre at **www.mcgraw-hill.co.uk/textbooks/paton** for a range of resources to support your learning.

Further Reading

Hayler, R. and Nichols, M.D. (2007) *Six Sigma for Financial Services: How Leading Companies Are Driving Results Using Lean, Six Sigma and Process Management*, McGraw-Hill, New York.

Juran, J.M. and Godfrey, A.B. (1999) *Juran's Quality Handbook*, 5th edn, McGraw-Hill, New York.

Martin, J.W. (2007) *Lean Six Sigma for Supply Chain Management: The 10-Step Solution Process*, McGraw-Hill, New York.

Rampersad, H.K. and El-Homsi, A (2007) *TPS-Lean Six Sigma: Linking Human Capital to Lean Six Sigma*, IAP, Charlotte, NC.

References

Antony, J., Escamilla, J.L. and Caine, P. (2003) 'Lean Sigma', *Manufacturing Engineer*, April, 40–42.

Basu, R. (2004) *Implementing Quality: A Practical Guide to Tools and Techniques*, Thomson, UK.

Beer, M. (2003) 'Why total quality management programs do not persist: the role of top management quality and implications for leading a TQM transformation', *Decision Sciences*, **34**(4), 623–642.

Bicheno, J. (2002) *The Quality 75; Towards Six Sigma Performance in Service and Manufacturing*, PICSIE Books.

Chen, I.J. and Paetsch, K. (1998) 'Benchmarking: a quest for continuous improvement', in *Handbook of Total Quality Management*, C.N. Madu (ed.), Kluwer Academic, London, pp. 409–424.

Crosby, P.B. (1979) *Quality is Free*, McGraw-Hill, New York.

Crosby. L.B., DeVito, R. and Pearson, J.M. (2003) 'Manage your customers' perception of quality', *Review of Business*, Winter, 18–24.

Dale, B.G. (1999) *Managing Quality*, Blackwell, Oxford.

Dale, B.G. and Plunkett, J.J. (1990) *The Case for Costing Quality*, Department of Trade and Industry, London.

Dale, B.G., van der Wiele, T. and van Iwaarden, J. (2007) *Managing Quality*. 5th edn, Blackwell Publishing.

Deming, W.E. (1986) *Out of Crisis*, MIT Press, Cambridge, MA.

Feigenbaum, A.V. (1986) *Total Quality Control*, 3rd edn, McGraw-Hill, New York.

Foster, S.T. (2010) *Managing Quality: Integrating the Supply Chain*, 4th edn, Prentice Hall, Boston, MA.

Garvin, D.A. (1987) 'Competing on the eight dimensions of quality', *Harvard Business Review*, November–December, 101–109.

George, S. and Weimerskirch, A. (1998) *Total Quality Management*, John Wiley & Sons, New York.

Ghobadian, A. and Speller, S. (1994) 'Gurus of quality: a framework for comparison', *Total Quality Management*, **5**(3), 53–69.

Gryna, F.M., Chua, R.C.H. and DeFeo, J.A. (2007) *Juran's Quality Planning and Analysis*, 5th edn, McGraw-Hill, New York.

Hansen, B.L. (1963) *Quality Control: Theory and Application*. Pearson Education, Upper Saddle River, NJ.

Hauser, J.R. and Clausing, D. (1988) 'The House of Quality', *Harvard Business Review*, May–June, 63–73.

Hellsten, U. And Klefsjö, B. (2000) 'TQM as a management system consisting of values, techniques and tools', *TQM Magazine*, **12**(4), 238–244.

Juran, J.M. (1988) *Quality Control Handbook*, 4th edn, McGraw-Hill, New York.

Parasuraman, A., Zeithaml, V.A. and Berry, L.L. (1985) 'A conceptual model of service quality and its implications for future research', *Journal of Marketing*, **49**(Fall), 41–50.

Salegna, G. and Fazel, F. (2000) 'Obstacles to implementing TQM', *Quality Progress*, **33**(7), 53–57.

www.efqm.org

www.isixsigma.com

14 Future Directions in Operations Management

Learning Outcomes

After studying this chapter, you should be able to:

- Summarize current themes and topics in operations management
- Discuss the challenges faced by operations managers
- Discuss future directions for operations management
- Evaluate the future of the operations management role.

BUSINESS
INTEGRATION

Beth's Chocolate Ambitions

Beth is a recent university graduate with a degree in business and technology management, which included a placement year with a large international company producing a variety of confectionery products. She took the operations management themed electives in her degree, including operations management, supply chain management, operations research, e-business, and IT for businesses, and passed with distinction. She is now working as an assistant operations manager with a small but ambitious company that makes boutique-style chocolate products, which it sells

Source: © Nancy Louise/iStock

online and through magazines to customers all around the world. As the food and drink industry is the largest part of the UK manufacturing sector (14.6% when Beth graduated), she saw a 'tasty' future ahead of her.

During her placement year in the confectionery company she spent short periods in the strategic planning, purchasing, sales and marketing, and production departments, which gave her a great overview of how important operations management is to everything that a company does. For instance, on one occasion while she was working in sales, an unexpectedly large order for Sticky Lollies was received from a large and important chain of high street stores, and she was tasked with making sure that the order was fulfilled correctly to the customer's wishes. However, because the order had not been anticipated by strategic planning, there was a shortage of ingredients. This meant she had to talk to the purchasing department to get suppliers to amend their delivery volumes at short notice. It also meant that she had to talk to the production manager and warn him that he should take on some more short-term staff from a temping agency. After resolving these urgent issues, she also let strategic planning know that the situation could happen again the following year, as the order had seemed to coincide with the store's new Back to School promotions.

She had initially found it ironic that even though she was in the Sales Department at the time, she had been very involved in many production and operations management decisions. Her experience stood her in good stead for her job interview after graduation, where she described how she had been so crucial in bringing in and delivering such a big order.

Now working as assistant operations manager for the small chocolate company, she had a strong grasp of the similarly complex and challenging issues that they faced. She knew that she was in a key role, and that she had to be a quick thinker, a good communicator, a good planner, a team player and a leader. She found opportunities to demonstrate these skills soon after starting, which got her noticed by the operations director, who had given her a new project to set up the production line for a new chocolate cake product.

She was very excited about this, because it would be an interesting challenge – and would obviously mean testing and eating a lot of chocolate cake to ensure that quality levels were just right! Also, she knew that the current chief executive officer had started out in just the same way, and had been promoted after making several new product launches operational successes. After many other successes, such as his adoption of online technologies, his development of new overseas markets, becoming a chartered manager and completing a part-time MBA, he had eventually got the top job. Over coffee one day Beth found out that he put most of his success down to understanding the operations of the company, its capabilities, and how to deliver what the customer had asked for. As Beth was ambitious to get to the top, she saw this as valuable advice . . . and if she followed it perhaps one day she too would get to run her own little chocolate factory!

Source: Ben Clegg, Aston Business School.

Introduction

The opening case demonstrates how demanding the role of an operations manager is, the wide variety of skills needed, and how rewarding it can be when good products and services get delivered to happy customers. The role of operations managers is rapidly changing as more demands are placed on them by macro trends in the social, environmental, political, economic, legal and technological areas. As a result, we believe that the role of the operations manager will become increasingly strategic over the forthcoming decades. In addition to being aware of external macro trends, operations managers also require an appreciation of all the other organizational functions if they are going to be able to make effective operations decisions.

In the past, the operations manager's job was perhaps seen as the least glamorous of the managerial functions in industry, with poor working conditions, limited career prospects, and low pay. Operations managers were not well qualified, and the operations role failed to attract ambitious people. The current position is changing as operations managers are now becoming more highly qualified and highly paid, and find their jobs challenging and interesting.

This chapter looks ahead to the future of operations management, and outlines the likely changes to this role and the new skills it will require. Operations management jobs will require higher levels of conceptual, interpersonal and analytical skills. These requirements have significant implications for management education. Graduating students from schools of business management or engineering disciplines will need knowledge in core areas of business, along with mathematics, computer and communication skills. Business schools are likely to respond by increasing the number of field trips, internships and industry-based projects to form part of their business programmes. Students will need to develop a greater understanding of strategy and technology. Along with subjects in the operations management area, newer subjects such as inter-organizational and international enterprise management, CSR, and the management of workforce diversity may become important parts of the core curriculum. In tandem, companies may also encourage apprenticeship schemes for school leavers and graduates.

In this chapter we pick up on the three themes threaded throughout the book, and explore them in more detail. These themes are important; they touch upon many different topics and, therefore, cannot be limited to single chapters. They epitomize what is currently happening in operations management, and point towards what will happen in the future. These themes will make operations more demanding, and require more educated and skilful operations managers.

- *Globalization* – which addresses the fact that companies increasingly have to adopt common standards and practices throughout the world, but takes cultural differences, commercial and technical histories into account.
- *Business integration* – which includes the use of information technology, structure and strategy issues, function-to-function integration within an organization, and integration between different organizations.
- *Corporate social responsibility (CSR)* – which considers environmental, ethical and social issues.

This chapter will briefly explore each of these themes, point to how they are relevant to previous chapters, discuss their current impact on operations management and, where possible, discuss the implications for the future. In doing so we shall show how important it is for operations managers to continually learn and develop themselves, and to contribute towards developing the practice and the theories of operations management.

This chapter also contains a short section specifically on operations managers and their careers. This is because many new graduates start off in an operations management role, even though they may not actually be called operations managers. The intention of this section is to help you become more successful in your career more quickly. It will help you realize what personal skills are valued by potential employers, and to become more aware of wider trends in operations management, so that you can prepare for the future directions operations management may take.

Globalization

GLOBALIZATION

Globalization is increasing global connectivity, integration and interdependence in the economic, social, technological, cultural, political and ecological spheres. The globalization of industry should allow for better worldwide production networks to provide broad access to goods and services for consumers, and the globalization of financial institutions should allow for better access to funds and credit for consumers, companies and government agencies. Similarly, the globalization of transportation and communication systems should allow for a better flow of goods, people and information among nations.

Throughout this book the theme of **globalization** and global issues has been prominent. Part One discussed how strategy and innovation is becoming increasingly global. Part Two discussed how operations design should achieve an appropriate portfolio of competencies in suitable geographic locations; how operations are influenced by supply and demand forces; and how operations managers are becoming accountable for more than just delivering products and services. Part Three highlighted why capacity and work are assigned to particular locations, the risks of distributing suppliers across the globe, efficiency and effectiveness, and the issues associated with globally sized projects. Part Four looked at how performance measurement systems, and quality and performance improvement, can affect business units, regions and nations.

> **Globalization:** increasing global connectivity, integration and interdependence in the economic, social, technological, cultural, political and ecological spheres.

The negative side of globalization and interconnected operations systems is that any disruption propagates through nations at a very rapid rate. For instance, any unscheduled blockage of ships at one of the world's major ports, such as Hong Kong, Amsterdam, Singapore or Dubai, can affect the availability and prices of many essential goods around the world. Similarly, any changes in currency exchange rates (e.g. the euro against the dollar) can affect both the demand for and the supply of goods and services across the world. The credit crunch is probably the most high-profile example of globalization gone wrong, where poor-quality, 'toxic' financial products were circulating in the global financial supply chain, damaging all economies that they touched, regardless of location.

The positive effects of globalization mean that we can benefit from efficient production and distribution systems; we get the benefits of using goods manufactured at locations around the world that have been delivered to us in a cost-effective manner. Also, advances in information and communications technology are now allowing companies to deliver a wide range of services, from financial transactions to customer service to medical diagnostics, to customers all around the world. While there are costs and risks associated with managing and operating a globalized organization, globalization is also attractive to organizations for a variety of other reasons:

- *Access to cheaper labour and operating costs*: US and European companies are now setting up in China, Malaysia, India and South Africa
- *Access to knowledge and skills*: some firms locate in Germany, the UK and Japan to gain access to knowledge in these countries despite higher labour costs
- *Access to natural resources*: certain companies locate facilities in African nations to draw upon their natural resources
- *Access to new markets*: by locating facilities in new countries, firms can market their products and services to a new set of customers. For example, Dyson and Black & Decker moved their production to China, partly to access the Chinese market
- *To establish facilities at strategically international locations* so that logistic and distribution costs can be reduced. Intel has a distribution centre in Amsterdam that serves the whole of Europe
- *To take advantage of tax and financial incentives* provided by local governments. For example, Honda moved into South Wales and Nissan to the North-East of England.

In addition, globalization is sometimes driven by other political and industry-specific reasons. For example, by locating a production facility in a country, providing employment and participating in community activities, a firm can be perceived as local rather than foreign – as in the US company Ford's move to the UK, for example.

Approaches and Stages of Globalization

According to Ghemawat (2007), when firms globalize, they can consider three different approaches: adaptation, aggregation or arbitrage. Each of these approaches has a slightly different purpose, and is suitable for different strategic and operational scenarios. A firm uses:

Adaptation (in a globalization context): boosting revenue and market share by maximizing local presence in a country.

Aggregation (in a globalization context): achieving economies of scale by creating regional or global operations.

Arbitrage (in a globalization context): the exploitation of differences among national or regional markets, often by locating separate parts of supply chains in different places.

- **Adaptation** to boost revenue and market share by maximizing its local presence in the country. In doing this, the firm will try to adapt its products and services to be more in tune with the new host nation. It will, however, retain its overall, global strategy, corporate identity, core competencies and values. For example, Tesco adapts the look and feel of its stores as it seeks to globalize its operations, in Thailand they are called 'Tesco Lotus', and in the USA they are called 'Fresh and Tasty'.
- **Aggregation** to achieve economies of scale by creating regional or global operations. In doing this, the firm tries to boost the size its output. There is little attempt to adapt to local cultures and values, and companies can sometimes be criticized for being too powerful and too insensitive to local needs, or have been accused of exploiting natural resources and local workforces. For example McDonald's has in the past been accused of destroying Brazilian rainforests to raise beef cattle for its burgers sold elsewhere in the world.
- **Arbitrage** to exploit the differences among national or regional markets. This is achieved by locating separate parts of supply chains in different places. For instance, two different sources of coal (Australian and South American) may be used to ensure that prices remain competitive.

Further differences between and features of these approaches are shown in Table 14.1.

In reality, firms tend to use a mixture of these three approaches. However, the aggregation approach has to be used sensitively, as nations are becoming increasingly aware of the negative effects that large globalizing organizations can have. In contrast, the adaptation approach is currently seen as more politically correct.

Another different view of globalization is provided by Farrell's (2004) five-stage model. Farrell takes a different view, based upon the *level* of globalization that a company wants to achieve, as it must be remembered that not all companies will want to 'conquer the world', and will settle for a less global presence. Farrell's model suggests five stages, which are not necessarily sequential, but achieve various levels of globalization: these are shown in Figure 14.1. Stage 1, the lowest level of globalization, achieves entry into a new market. Stage 2 involves relocating part of a company's operations to a new country. Stage 3 involves the development of an extended supply network spanning several countries. Stage 4 is reached when companies become reliant on their core processes operating across the globe. Stage 5, the most advanced level of globalization, allows new products and services

Table 14.1 Features of different approaches to globalization

	Adaptation	**Aggregation**	**Arbitrage**
Competitive advantage Why should we globalize at all?	To achieve local relevance through national focus while exploiting some economies of scale	To achieve scale and scope of economies through international standardization	To achieve economies through international specialization
Configuration Where should we locate operations overseas?	Mainly in countries that are similar to the home base, to limit the effects of culture, administrative, geographic and economic distance		In a more diverse set of countries, to exploit some elements of distance
Coordination How should we connect international operations?	By country, with emphasis on achieving local presence within boarders	By business, region, or customer, with emphasis on horizontal relationships for cross-border economies of scale	By function, with emphasis on vertical relationships, even across organizational boundaries
Controls What types of extreme should we watch for?	Excessive variety or complexity	Excessive standardization, with emphasis on scale	Narrowing or fragmentation of activities spreads
Change blockers Whom should we watch out for internally?	Entrenched countries	All-powerful unit, regional, or account heads	Heads of key functions
Corporate diplomacy How should we approach corporate diplomacy?	Address issues of concern, but proceed with discretion, given the emphasis on cultivating local presence	Avoid appearance of homogenization or hegemonism (particularly Americanization by the USA)	Address the exploitation or displacement of suppliers, channels or intermediaries that are potentially most prone to political disruption
Corporate strategy What strategic levers do we have?	Scope selection Variation Decentralization Partitioning Modularization Flexibility Partnership Recombination Innovation	Regions and other country groupings Product or business Function Platform Competence Client industry	Cultural (country-of-origin effects) Administrative (taxes, regulations, security) Geographic (distance, climate differences) Economic (differences in prices, resources, knowledge)

Source: adapted from Ghemawat (2007).

to be designed by drawing on the whole global network of resources and skills, and which can be delivered to new markets in a timely and efficient manner.

As with Ghemawat's model, Farrell's model is only indicative of what organizations may do. The stages can occur in different sequences, and the model could be deployed differently for any nation that an organization chooses to include in its globalization strategy.

Functions Commonly Globalized

As a result of globalization, many activities can now be performed at locations far from an organization's home country.

Manufacturing

Manufacturing products and their components at locations far from the home country is perhaps the most common function of a global firm. This can be done to remain competitive: for instance, firms often locate their factories close to a source of cheap labour, such as Taiwan or Poland, or a source of inexpensive raw material.

The five stages of global restructuring				
Industries and companies tend to globalize in phases; at each stage, there are different opportunities for creating value. In the first three stages, value comes from the basic improvements to typical business practices. In the last two stages, it comes from true process innovations and market expansion. The stages are not necessarily sequential.				
1. Enter new markets	2. Move production abroad	3. Disaggregate the value chain	4. Re-engineer the value chain	5. Create new markets
Companies use production models similar to the ones they deploy at home to enter new countries and expand their customer bases	Companies relocate their production processes to take advantage of cost differentials; they export finished goods globally	Companies' individual product components are manufactured in different locations or regions; countries may specialize in component manufacturing, assembly, or both	Companies redesign their production processes, taking into account, to maximize efficiencies and cost savings	Given lower costs due to globalization, companies can offer new products at lower prices, and can penetrate new market segments or geographies, or both

Less global ⟵————————————⟶ Highly global

Figure 14.1 Farrell's globalization stages (Farrell, 2004)

Procurement

In a non-globalized environment, a firm buys materials and components from suppliers located close to production facilities. However, the ease of transportation and the reduction in other associated purchasing costs in a global economy make it possible for companies to purchase their supplies from vendors located far from their home countries.

Maintenance and Monitoring

Advances in information technology mean that it is becoming possible to monitor and maintain manufacturing and products remotely. For instance, the Rolls-Royce engines of an aircraft can be monitored while in-flight from service centres (e.g. Singapore), which liaise with destination airports anywhere in the world to ensure, if necessary, that spare parts are readily available when the aircraft lands.

Logistics and Distribution Services

As companies, products and services are becoming spread around the world, logistics and distribution services have become more important. For instance, TNT, the Dutch logistics company, was once a part of the Dutch national postal services, but now is a global business in its own right, moving and managing other organizations' products around the world.

Customer Service

Customer service and support provided by telephones or via the Internet (chat, talk, instant messaging, and emails) has seen an explosion in globalization during the last decade; it is now common to talk to someone in India or South Africa if you ring a help desk in Europe.

Technical Expertise

With the advance in information technology and the spread of *education* worldwide, it is now possible to locate facilities for complex and knowledge-based business processes internationally. For example, using the Internet, health care facilities can make patients' records available to medical experts who might be located far from the home country. Similarly, many complex financial and legal functions can also be performed remotely.

Research and Development

Many companies are increasingly locating their own facilities, or outsourcing production activities, in foreign countries to facilitate product development and innovation. As mentioned in Chapter 5, product development in goods and service industries is a long-term and complex process. However, effective product development is essential for a firm's long-term success. Globalization has allowed many firms to locate product development activities abroad. For example, Microsoft, IBM, Oracle and many other Western companies have located their facilities in several different countries to take advantage of the local talent pools for their product development efforts.

Globalization is a strong theme in operations management, and this is likely to continue for the foreseeable future. Smart operations managers will ensure global forces are used to their advantage.

CRITICAL PERSPECTIVE

Is Globalization a Good Thing?

Globalization poses a dilemma for most organizations. On the positive side, they must globalize to be able to gain benefits from standardization (lower costs, speedier delivery, and enhanced reliability), foster and integrate new knowledge to raise industry standards (without eroding competitive advantage), reach new markets, and achieve strategic change (by adopting new practices and discontinuing old ones). However, on the negative side, those who seek to globalize must:

- Reach the right balance between local specialization achieved by integrating knowledge into local activities and maintaining a global product or service (e.g. McDonald's now tries to adapt its products, depending on the country or region it is in, but still have standardized processes).
- Maintain ethical issues about work allocated to lower-wage economies. Typically dirty, dangerous or highly repetitive work is given to developing nations; is this right? People with a social conscience want to make sure that people of developing nations are not exploited. (e.g. in 2006, the clothing giant GAP was found to be using child labour in one of its 'unapproved' subcontractors).
- Work with local trade unions, who often oppose the 'exportation of jobs' from their countries.
- Minimize the negative social impact of products (e.g. Nestlé caused problems when it introduced powered baby milk into African nations), and assess whether the trade is 'fair'.
- Fit products and services correctly to different cultures and religions (e.g. financial products in Islamic cultures must be Shariah compliant, and beef products cannot be made or consumed in Hindu nations).
- Ensure the safety of workers and nearby residents in developing nations, which is not always done (e.g. the Union-Carbide chemical disaster at the Bhopal plant in India, which killed or seriously injured thousands).
- Minimize language and interpretation misunderstanding (e.g. UK call centres moving to India has not been totally successful because accents cannot be understood by customers).
- Familiarize themselves with data security laws. For instance, law in the USA is very tight, but in India it is not (e.g. personal data does not have the same level of protection).
- Steer clear of bribery and corruption (e.g. payments to local officials in host nations who claim to 'ease' deals).

The key point is that many of these global issues are complex, as they have problematic ethical and social dimensions.

❶ Stop and Think

1   Why do some organizations choose to globalize and others choose not to? In the opening case, how do you think globalization will affect Beth's career?

GLOBALIZATION

Business Integration

Business integration is an operations management theme that covers systems (including IT systems), staff, style (cultural, personal), skills, strategy and higherlevel superordinate goals such as philanthropic aspirations, or wider industrial or national contributions. This is applicable to all levels of operations, from an individual's fit within a department, to departments fitting together in an organization, to organizations fitting together in wider supplier relationships. Put simply, it is about getting the various parts, people, processes and systems to work together better.

The theme of business integration is prominent throughout this book, and is important at all levels in and beyond single organizations. It must be practised in temporary teams, functional departments, entire companies and company-to-company relationships if systems and processes are going to work effectively and efficiently.

For instance, in Part One of this book we highlighted how customer requirements should drive the strategy and systems of the organization, and that a holistic view needs to be taken that neither sub-optimizes an organization nor neglects to incorporate the right competencies within its extended suppliers and partners. In Part Two of the book we discussed how information systems (e.g. enterprise resource planning – ERP) must join together seamlessly; and how products and processes need to be designed with ease of delivery in mind. In Part Three of the book we demonstrated why business integration is essential to plan capacity, integrate suppliers, practise lean thinking and just-in-time operations, and deliver projects successfully. Part Four of the book shows why and how performance, quality and improvement initiates are affected by the degree of business integration.

McKinsey's 7S Framework Applied to Business Integration

Many different facets of business integration can be put forward; we are going to use an adapted version of the McKinsey 7S framework (Waterman *et al.*, 1980) to show why business integration is so important at all levels. Figure 14.2 shows the 7S framework, which considers strategy, structure, systems (including IT systems)/processes, staff, style, skills, and superordinate goals as important strategic factors. All these factors affect individuals, departments, companies and inter-company structures to some extent.

Table 14.2 shows how each of the 7S factors relates to operations management and success factors for maximizing business integration. If an organization fails to apply the correct level of business integration, at best it can result in organizational inefficiency and ineffectiveness. At worst an organization can make dangerous and fatal mistakes. For instance, lack of business integration in hospitals has seen patients mistreated, and even accidently killed. Lack of integration in government has seen illegal activities such as immigration go undetected. Similarly, lack of business integration in chemical and scientific organizations has resulted in large-scale explosions such as the Chernobyl nuclear power plant disaster in Russia.

The Role of Information Technology in Business Integration

Over recent years developments in information technology (IT) have dominated discussion about business integration, and are likely to continue to do so in the foreseeable future, so it is worth looking at IT and its role in business integration in more detail. The use of IT has particularly increased since the advent of the Internet, as it has allowed e-business and e-commerce to develop.

E-business: electronically mediated information exchanges, both within an organization and with external stakeholders, supporting the entire range of business processes.

E-business allows:

- *Business-to-business (B2B) integration*: this implies that both sides are businesses, non-profit organizations or governments. This usually involves the linking up of core operational ERP systems that process manufacturing or service delivery transactions

Table 14.2 Application of the 7S framework in an operations management context, with key success factors for business integration

Element of 7S model	Relevance in an operations management context	Key success factors for business integration
Strategy	The contribution of operations management in influencing and supporting organizations' strategy	<ul><li>Make all departments' roles clear in delivering or supporting customer-facing process</li><li>Define what the company is going to do, and what it is going to outsource</li><li>Budget provided for integrative activities with other functions (e.g. marketing and purchasing)</li></ul>
Structure	The modification of organizational structure to support operations	<ul><li>Be predominantly process dominated, not functionally dominated</li><li>Be as flat as possible</li><li>Multi-site companies are clear on their individual roles and interdependences</li></ul>
Systems (including IT systems)/process	The development of specific processes and information systems to support operations management	<ul><li>Lean and agile processes</li><li>Driven by customer-pull signals using the value stream concept</li><li>Information systems (e.g. ERP – Chapter 9) use single-point real-time data, which is available to all those that need it, including those outside the organization when necessary</li><li>Well-designed supply and demand chains</li><li>Just-in-time thinking is used</li><li>Performance measurement systems encourage integrative behaviour</li><li>Unifying reporting</li></ul>
Staff	The characteristic of staff in terms of their background, age and sex and characteristics such as engineering background or service background, use of contractors/consultants	<ul><li>Well informed through good communication channels up and down between all levels of management</li><li>Willingness to work with suppliers, customers and partners to make whole supply chain better</li><li>Recruit good staff; train and retain them</li><li>Role of operations manager becomes enlarged</li></ul>
Style	Includes how key managers behave in achieving the organization's goals and the cultural style of the organization as a whole	<ul><li>Culture should include teamworking</li><li>Need joint reward systems for productivity</li><li>High levels of trust and professionalism</li><li>Clear leadership</li><li>Shared values and beliefs</li></ul>
Skills	Distinctive capabilities of key staff, but can be interpreted as specific skill-sets of teams	<ul><li>Are teams multi-skilled and cross-functional?</li><li>Are team players at all levels?</li><li>Strong project management practices</li><li>Endorse the quality management ethos</li></ul>
Superordinate goal	The guiding concepts of the organization which are also part of shared values and culture. The internal and external perception of these goals may vary	<ul><li>Organization looks to partner with external organizations to form multi-company structures to complement its own core competencies</li><li>Have joined-up information systems (e.g. inventory management, and sales, ordering processes)</li><li>Use the enterprise management concept</li><li>Develop integrative capabilities</li></ul>

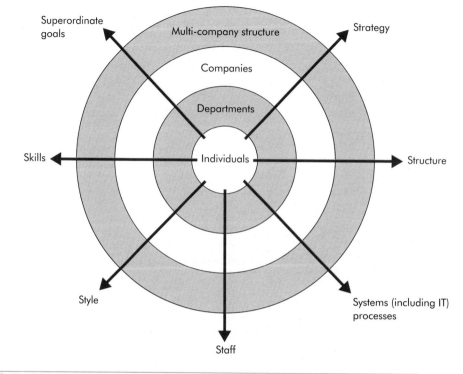

Figure 14.2 The 7S model applied to business integration (adapted from Waterman *et al.*, 1980)

- *Business-to-employee (B2E) integration*: used by an organization to communicate with its employees for activities such as scheduling work, communication, and provide shared workspace for common work files. Such systems are sometimes known as a *staff intranet*.

E-commerce: electronically mediated information exchanges between an organization and its external stakeholders, concerned predominantly with buying and selling.

E-commerce allows:
- *Business-to-consumer (B2C) integration*: facilitating transactions in which buyers are individual consumers
- *Consumer-to-consumer (C2C) integration*: a scenario in which consumers sell directly to other consumers (e.g. eBay) via a neutral third-party organization
- *Consumer-to-business (C2B) integration*: where individuals make business propositions to businesses (e.g. Priceline's 'name your own price' facility).

E-business and e-commerce helps achieve higher levels of integration by developing:
- *Channels to sell a product or service through*: such as Amazon.com, which sells exclusively through the Internet
- *Supplementary channels*: where traditional 'click and mortar' retailers have extended their catchment areas through the Internet
- *Technical support*: customers can solve problems regarding the products or services they have purchased
- *Enhancements to existing services*: customizing product or services, or tracking orders
- *A means to convey further information*: such as product/service details, customer accounts or supplier ratings.

Mobile/M-commerce: electronically mediated information exchanges using mobile electronic devices.

Higher levels of integration are achievable by using employees' and consumers' mobile electronic devices through what is known as **mobile commerce** (or M-commerce) so that people can be reached when they are away from their normal personal computer.

The capabilities of the Internet have transformed many traditional operations into e-operations when it has been feasible and desirable to do so. For instance, an organization that has a dynamic and interactive website is able to market, integrate, operate, trade, engineer and exchange more effectively with its suppliers, customers and partners. A successful example is the Driver and Vehicle Licensing Agency in the UK. It has a system that allows you to buy car tax online, and the system is clever

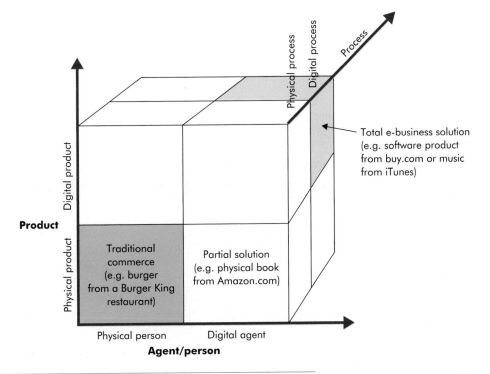

Figure 14.3 Information intensity cube (adapted from Negroponte, 1995)

enough to check whether you have a valid roadworthiness certificate and motor insurance policy by automatically linking up with other organizations' systems before issuing the tax. This saves the government lots of time and money, and reduces fraud.

To decide which aspects of an operation are best suited to become an online e-operation, the information intensity of the operation needs to be considered in respect to the agents or people operating it, the way the process is delivered, and the type of product or service being delivered.

Figure 14.3, the information intensity cube, shows three main types of business integration in respect to their information technology:

- *Traditional commerce*, with low information intensity, which involves a real person dealing with a physical product using a physical process that involves machines, cash payments and interfacing face to face with a customer. This is what we might see in a fast-food restaurant (e.g. hamburgers). In a situation like this the use of customer-facing IT is limited, although we are beginning to see some restaurants having self-ordering and payment machines. The back-end supply systems, though, are likely to use sophisticated electronic ordering systems.
- *Total e-business* with a high information intensity, such as a digitized product like a music mp3 file, delivered automatically through a programmed IT system using a standard process. This is a perfect solution for e-business, because it has taken what once was a physical product (a CD or record) and made it into a digital computer file, which can then be sold online without any physical transaction. Taking this to a more advanced level can allow companies to integrate their automated processes and sell complementary products and services together – for instance, the purchase of travel tickets, hotels and car hire from different companies through a single online travel company such as Expedia.
- *The partial solution*, with medium information intensity, where physical products are delivered to the customer but ordering and payment are carried out online. This partial solution, pioneered by companies such as Amazon, is fast being adopted by all retailers of easily movable goods.

Although it needs to be stressed that information technology is not the only thing that has contributed to business integration, it has been the most significant in recent years, and it is generally thought that this will continue to be the case in the near future. Therefore operations managers need to be aware of the *information intensity* of their operation, products and services if they wish to apply IT appropriately.

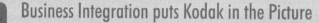

❶ Stop and Think

2 In the opening case, how would Beth's placement year job have been easier if the confectionery company had had more integrated processes and IT systems?

BUSINESS INTEGRATION

SHORT CASE 14.1

Business Integration puts Kodak in the Picture

Eastman Kodak was founded by George Eastman in 1880. The Eastman Kodak Company is a global leader in imaging technology, supplying photographic, imaging and scanning products and services to industry and general consumers. The commercial and medical sectors account for about half of Kodak's revenues. In 2009 the company employed over 80,000 staff in more than 30 countries, and achieved revenues of over US$13 billion.

During the mid-1990s Kodak had more than 200 different order-entry systems that were used by its various operating units. In order to improve productivity and reduce costs, Kodak decided to

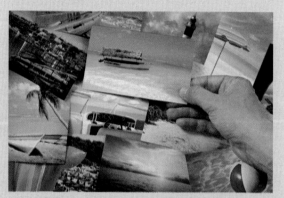

Source: © Online Creative Media/iStock

adopt the R/3 enterprise resource planning (ERP) solution from the German company SAP. This was to be used to streamline and connect a variety of business functions, including accounting, production and management, plant maintenance, and sales and distribution. Kodak also aimed to integrate its e-business systems, which according to Duane Cook (Kodak's e-business process manager) were slow, error-prone, and expensive to maintain separately. Kodak wanted to implement a new, real-time system that could link its e-business operations with the ERP system to improve invoicing, payments and other transactions with corporate customers.

After a rigorous selection process, Kodak selected GXS (an IT consultancy company) to implement the SAP certified product. The results were as follows:

- Batch processes that used to take an average of four hours were now completed in minutes, improving Kodak's responsiveness to its customers, suppliers and carriers
- More than 150,000 transactions a month could be processed, with customers using the web to send orders, receive invoices, and request information about products and pricing
- Previously around 1,400 trading partners used the old, non-Internet-based system, with other customers relying on phone and fax to communicate with Kodak. Now, over 2,600 customers use a standard Internet browser to access Kodak's ERP system
- Response times have improved remarkably, and replies to customer and partner queries are now immediate, which has led to increased transaction capabilities.

Questions

1 What were the problems caused for Kodak by having many different systems that do the same thing?
2 What are the advantages for Kodak's partners and customers in having an Internet-based system?
3 Do you think even more integration will help the company further? Why?

Source: adapted from 'e-Business puts Kodak in the Picture, case study, GXS website, 29 July 2010.

CSR

Corporate Social Responsibility

Corporate social responsibility (CSR) in operations management means having an operations strategy that will meet the requirements of current needs without compromising the ability of future generations to meet their own needs. This means considering environmental, ethical and social issues on a par with financial and more traditional operational performance metrics. Companies have traditionally focused their aims on creating profit for their shareholders, and other performance metrics relating to CSR issues have typically been much less important. However, the shareholders and stakeholders of companies have currently become much more interested in the factors that impact on wider social and environmental issues.

The shareholders are those individuals or companies that legally own one or more shares in a company. Stakeholders are those individuals or organizations who are influenced, either directly or indirectly, by the actions of the company. This expanded view of organizational accountabilities means that the scope of a firm's strategy must not only include economic viability but should also consider the natural environment and social impact on its stakeholders.

Throughout this book CSR has been a prominent theme. For instance, in Part One we highlighted increasing customer concerns about ethical practices and the exploitation of vulnerable nations and people. In Part Two we highlighted how ethical and environmental issues are more important in product design and service delivery. In Part Three we explained how CSR can add to industry and planetary sustainability. Part Four of the book describes how ethics is becoming an increasingly important part of performance measurement and quality management systems.

The Triple Bottom Line

To capture an expanding view of stakeholders and their expectations concerning CSR, the phrase the **triple bottom line** has been coined (Elkington, 1994): see Figure 14.4.

The triple bottom line evaluates the firm's performance against social, economic and environmental criteria. The following expands on the meaning of each dimension of the triple bottom line framework.

> **Triple bottom line:** considers the social and natural environmental impact of a company's strategy as well as the more conventional economic impact.

Social

This pertains to fair and beneficial business practices towards labour, the community, and the region in which a firm conducts its business. A triple bottom line company seeks to benefit its employees, the community, and other social entities that are affected by the firm's existence. A company should not use child labour, should pay fair salaries to its workers, should maintain a safe working environment with tolerable working hours, and should not otherwise exploit its community or labour force. A business can also give back by contributing to the community through health care, education and other special programmes. But consumers must also play their part, ensuring that items and services that they purchase are used, maintained and reused suitably, and are recycled once they are no longer usable. Land Rover (based in the UK), which make off-road sport utility vehicles (SUVs), is often criticized for making fuel-inefficient vehicles, but over 60% of the Land Rovers ever made (over the last

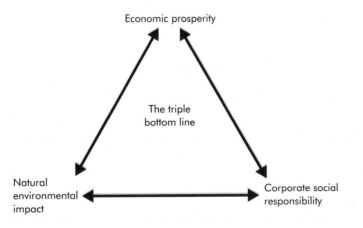

Figure 14.4 The triple bottom line (Elkington, 1994)

60 years) are still on the road. Therefore Land Rover, and its owners, claim that they are excellent at conserving the raw materials from which they are made, in contrast to the manufacturer of an average vehicle that might last only 10 years.

Economic

The firm is obligated to compensate shareholders who provide capital through stock purchases and other financial investments via a competitive return on their investment. Company strategies should promote growth and increase long-term value for this group in the form of profit. Within a sustainability framework, this dimension goes beyond just profit for the firm, and should also provide lasting economic benefit to society, such as through local and national tax payments to government. This is so important that in many countries economic CSR is carefully defined in law and regulated (e.g. the Sarbanes-Oxley Act in the USA, which came into being after the collapse of Enron). So, is a company really practising CSR if it just adheres to the basic requirements? Some people certainly think so, but they also think that extra voluntary steps should also be taken, such as protecting pension schemes for employees and making prompt payment to smaller suppliers.

Natural Environment

This refers to the firm's impact on the natural environment. The company should protect the environment as much as possible. Managers should move to reduce a company's ecological footprint by carefully managing its consumption of natural resources, and by reducing waste, as well as ensuring that the waste is not harmful before disposing of it in a safe and legal way. Many businesses now conduct 'cradle-to-grave' assessments of products to determine what the true environmental costs are – from the processing of the raw materials, to manufacture, to distribution, and to eventual disposal by the final customer. For instance, all wood- and paper-based products in the UK must now conform to Forest Stewardship Council (FSC) regulations to show they have come from sustainable sources.

Another emerging standard in recent years has been ISO 14000, from the International Organization for Standardization. This is a three-section environmental management system that covers initial planning, implementation, and objective assessment. Although it has had some impact, it has largely been limited to Europe. ISO 14000 makes a number of specific requirements, including:

- A commitment by top-level management to environmental management
- The development and communication of an environmental policy
- The establishment of relevant legal and regulatory requirements
- The setting of environmental objectives and targets
- The establishment and updating of a specific environmental programme, or programmes, geared to achieving the objectives and targets
- The implementation of supporting systems such as training, operational control and emergency planning
- Regular monitoring and measurement of all operational activities
- A full audit procedure to review the working and suitability of the system.

CRITICAL PERSPECTIVE

Is CSR Really Any Good for Business?

Conventional operations strategy focuses on just the economic part of the triple bottom line. But because many of the processes that fall under the domain of operations and supply chain management have social and environmental impacts, it is important that these are also considered. Therefore the whole topic of CSR is rising swiftly up the corporate agenda. In 2008 the Economist Intelligence Unit found that the majority of managers surveyed believe CSR is of either 'high' or 'very high' importance, which contrasts with 2004, when the majority of managers surveyed thought it was of 'moderate', 'low' or 'very low' importance. The likelihood is that it will grow to be even more important in the future. It is estimated that around 35% of the world's largest corporations publish reports on their environmental policies and performance (Kolk, 2000). This may be partly motivated by an altruistic desire to save the planet. However, what is also now clear to companies is that 'green reporting' also makes sound business sense.

Although most strategists believe that improving society and preserving the environment are good things, some still disagree, citing the potential loss of profit or efficiency. Others argue that companies operating in rich countries can afford to contribute to society and the environment, whereas a company in a poor or developing nation must focus purely on survival. In the developing world the economic benefit realized by the use of abundant local resources may be viewed as worth their destruction. For example, cutting down trees in the Amazon rainforest to sell for timber and clear space to graze cattle may seem reasonable to the Brazilian government, but currently unreasonable to Europeans, who in the past have cut their own forests down to power their industries.

Some people believe that CSR is nothing more than just *greenwash* (a term used to describe practising CSR for cynical or disingenuous reasons, because it is currently fashionably do to so, rather than because one actually believes in its genuine purpose), and that CSR is being used as a marketing strategy to increase brand value and sell more products and services, which results in greater consumption of scarce resource and ironically may make the situation worse.

The key point is that the jury still seems to be out on whether CSR is good business sense, or whether it is one step too far in 'political correctness'.

! Stop and Think

3 Is corporate social responsibility just a cynical marketing ploy to make us think organizations care about us and the planet, or is there some real substance to it? In the opening case, how does CSR affect Beth's job?

SHORT CASE 14.2

Good Wood?

Source: © Jerry Moorman/iStock

CSR

GLOBALIZATION

Royal Houthandel G. Wijma & Zonen BV is a Dutch timber company established in 1897. The company has a long tradition in managing the supply chain from timber harvested in the forest, via timber processing and trade to the final user. Approximately 70% (by volume) of the wood traded by Wijma comes from its own production facilities (sawmills). The other 30% is purchased from third parties, particularly from West Africa, where Wijma has been active for many years. As a result of redevelopment after the Second World War, there was a large demand for hardwood in Europe. Azobé timber was introduced by the Dutch government as a good, cheap alternative to European oak. In 1968 the supply of this timber from West Africa was secured for them by establishing a purchasing office in Cameroon.

However, since the 1990s, Wijma has been involved in a conflict between the timber industry and various environmental organizations calling for a boycott on the use of tropical timber. Later Wijma changed its position, and the emphasis was placed on promoting certified sustainable forest management based on the principles of the FSC (Forest Stewardship Council). For various reasons the implementation of sustainable forestry takes place very slowly. Many countries in the Southern hemisphere lack the experience, knowledge and financial resources found in Western countries that make this type of activity possible. In addition, developing countries find it difficult to understand the reasons why this action is necessary, mainly because of the diversity of opinions held by the various stakeholders, such as scientists, politicians and pressure groups in various countries.

In 2001 Wijma gained an area of long-term concessions in Cameroon (currently a total of 190,000 hectares for the next 30 years), with areas designated as 'production forests' by the government. A management plan was required to state how the forest manager will operate it in a sustainable way, taking into consideration the sociocultural, economic and ecological aspects of the forest.

By 2005 Wijma had completed the pioneering work of full FSC certification in Africa. Mark Diepstraten, the CEO, explained the lesson learned by Wijma from the above experiences as follows: 'We should not turn down social discussions, but participate in them. We must communicate our chosen path clearly and transparently. You must, as a company, communicate what you do, why you do it and how you are going to achieve it . . . The new director in Cameroon is more open, because he understands how important it is to make a link between the market requirements in Europe and timber extraction in Cameroon'.

Questions

1 Why should companies in developed countries care about where their raw materials come from and how they are produced?
2 Are governments right to intervene in business and operations practice?
3 Could companies in developing countries take a different approach, rather than exporting raw materials as demonstrated in this case?

Source: adapted from J. Cramer, 'Timber extraction by Koninklijke Houthandel Wijma in Cameroon', in *Corporate Social Responsibility and Globalisation: An Action Plan for Business*, Greenleaf Publishing, 2006, pp. 81–84.

Operational Learning for Operations Managers

During the past two decades significant changes have occurred in the job of the operations manager, mainly in response to the introduction of new process technologies and management philosophies. Trends indicate that the operations manager will have a much greater role to play in setting the strategic direction of the company, and in defining competitive priorities. The ability to gather and interpret information from the external environment will become more critical. Competitive and consumer pressure will force operations managers to concentrate on improving CSR and sustainability.

As globalization continues to increase, there will be greater choice over where to buy, produce and sell goods and services. Globalization has blurred the economic distinctions between countries and companies, creating an increasingly 'borderless' or 'flat' world in which economic decisions are made without reference to company or country boundaries (Friedman, 2005). The ability to manage people and resources within and across national boundaries will become an important part of the operations manager's role. Organizations will increasingly focus on core competencies, and outsource most of the non-core activities. In addition, organizations will focus more on the management of their supplier relations to improve profitability. To achieve a balance between costs and consumer satisfaction, operations managers will have to think more about the integration of organizations. Operations managers will also have to recognize that business processes, not functions, create value for the customer, and that such processes typically transcend functional units and organizational boundaries.

In the future, sustainability issues will become more important, and operations managers will be required to design and implement ecologically sound manufacturing and service delivery practices. Operations managers will play an increasing role in deciding the types of product to manufacture and the materials that should be used, and will increasingly help to design processes that can reduce waste and harmful emissions.

As more firms embrace the goal of lean and agile manufacturing, technology will play a more prominent role in the future. Flexible automation, computer-integrated manufacturing, computer-aided design, artificial intelligence and the use of robots are a few examples of new technology. Technological improvements in communications over the Internet have greatly improved relationships between an organization and its customers.

All this implies that, in the future, operations managers will have to be more highly trained, and should have the ability to understand and use complex manufacturing technologies and systems. It may be more important to become a member of a professional institution that can help disseminate the latest changes in the field. In terms of job content, operations managers will have more opportunities to exercise personal initiative, improve efficiency, and be innovative.

As cross-functional linkages between manufacturing, marketing, engineering and human resources increase, operations managers will be required to possess an increasing breadth of management knowledge. With the increasing focus on lean and agile thinking, the span of control of operations managers will inevitably increase. In addition, the rapid move towards the use of the Internet has resulted in the growth of **knowledge workers**, who are highly educated and skilled. Thus the traditional function of *supervision and control* is likely to change to that of a *specialist* providing assistance to employees and teams. This implies that organizations will have to spend a considerable amount of time and money to enhance the managerial skills of operations managers. Currently, it is generally thought that most operations managers need more training in business and management in order to be more successful in their future careers. However, on the positive side, these changes will inevitably provide new and more exciting career paths for operational managers.

> **Knowledge workers:** employees whose skills are based more on what they know than on what they can physically do.

In summary, the rapid increase of technology and the advent of the knowledge worker will require highly qualified individuals to manage the operations of organizations effectively. As companies increasingly focus on their manufacturing and service delivery operations to gain competitive advantage, the operations manager of the future will play a key strategic role in enhancing organizational performance.

SHORT CASE 14.3

Could You Be Hired by Lord Sugar?

Lord Alan Sugar was originally famous for building up the Amstrad group, and lately – and perhaps more widely known – for fronting the hit TV show *The Apprentice* in the UK. He is a charismatic leader, who has always known the value of good operations management. He left school at an early age to set up his own business, selling things such as boiled beetroot, car aerials and related electronics products. His entrepreneurial drive has led to the development of innovative home computing and entertainment products. His value proposition to the consumer has always been 'innovative products at reasonable prices'. To deliver these, he focused on low costs of manufacture by using innovative manufacturing processes, ensuring that components were bought at competitive prices, and adopting a no-nonsense management style. As someone who has risen from humble beginnings to head an £800 million business operation he has always known the value of good operations management, and *The Apprentice*, believe it or not, is very much aimed at, amongst other things, developing excellent operations management skills!

Questions
1. What personal skills does a good operations leader, such as Lord Sugar, require?
2. What operational principles has Lord Sugar adopted?
3. Do you think you could become a successful operations director or manager? Why and how might you do this?

---

❶ Stop and Think

4. There can be a lot of pressure on operations managers to 'get everything right first time'. What do you think they should do to prepare themselves for such challenges?

Table 14.3 Summary of the key themes in this book

Chapter topic area	Business integration	CSR	Globalization
Strategy and customer orientation	Customers' requirements drive overall organizational strategy	Increasing customer CSR concerns are addressed	Used to positively affect all stakeholders
Operations strategy	Holistic systems perspective is taken of the business	Does not exploit vulnerable workers, natural resources or developing nations	Correct balance of centralization versus decentralization and duplication versus robustness
Innovation and competitive advantage	Incorporate a network of research and development competencies	Does not exploit vulnerable workers or developing nations	Seeks to reduce unnecessary waste for the planet
Supply network and enterprise design	ICT is used to connect operations together	Does not exploit vulnerable workers or developing nations	Appropriate portfolio of competencies is built, and these are in the right geographical location
Product and service design	Correct level of duplication and robustness is built into the product service delivery system	These are designed with ethical and environmental issues in mind	Organization has units at points of natural resource, human resource, knowledge bases and end markets, and draws upon them appropriately
Designing and managing processes	Process are customer facing and lean	Delivers financial gain while preserving natural resources	Demonstrates responsible management, accountability towards and empathy with all stakeholders
Capacity planning and management	Work allocated to suitable business unit, depending on volume and competencies	Does not exploit vulnerable workers, natural resources or developing nations	Work allocated to suitable business unit depending on volume and competencies and proximity to end market
Supply chain management	Supply chains highly integrated, and tend towards enterprises	Does not exploit vulnerable workers, natural resources or developing nations	Draws upon production and service delivery networks and minimizes logistics risks
Lean operations and JIT	Customer-driven processes, with continuous flow and levelled loading	Improves business and sector sustainability	Lean thinking extends to partners, suppliers and customers.
Inventory planning and management	Minimum inventory, made to order whenever possible	Accurate accounting, storage, transportation and use of recycled materials	No overproduction
Project management	Establish core competencies and commonality between projects	Meet all project stakeholders' criteria – not just traditional time, cost and quality	Drawn on global resources as necessary
Performance measurement	Accurate, real-time data available to all	Ethical and environmental impact is measured	Net effects for nations and business units is known
Quality and performance improvement	Organization has a 'total quality management' philosophy and people have a 'right first time' attitude	Meet all organizational stakeholders' criteria – not just traditional time, cost and quality	Globalization should enhance overall sector standards while maintaining competitive advantage

Summary

This final chapter has concentrates on the main cross-chapter themes of the book. These are all themes that are too significant to be left to just one or two chapters, as they epitomize the current state of operations management and point towards its future. Table 14.3 picks out the main points from each chapter.

Now that you have studied this book, we hope that you are a great deal more prepared in terms of your knowledge, skills and personal aspirations to go forth and become an excellent operations manager.

Suggested Answers to Stop and Think Questions

1 **Globalization:** It is appropriate for some companies to globalize if their products and services are generic and widely marketable, have high set-up costs, and will benefit from a large scale of economy. Globalization can be part of market development for successful mature products and services (e.g. Coca-Cola, Fedex, Tesco). However, some products and services are not well suited to globalization, particularly those that serve niche markets, and are difficult or expensive to transport (e.g. real ale, health services).

The chocolate products in the opening case could be part of a globalization strategy. From an operational point of view it would mean that the chocolates had to conform to international standards for content and production. It may be the case that new production facilities are set up abroad, or that the products are made under licence by another company, if production and transportation costs are prohibitive.

2 **Information technology:** Good IT integration should facilitate better communication within and between organizational departments, as well as between different organizations that work closely together (e.g. retailers and manufacturers). If the chocolate company had had an IT system that linked up prospective and actual sales orders, accessible in real time by the purchasing, production and strategic planning departments, the shortfall in ingredients and staff might have been avoided, and the customer might have been served better. In addition, an advanced system might have been able to detect trends like this occurring throughout the annual demand pattern, and forewarn the strategic planners.

For Beth, such an IT system (sometimes known as a sales ordering process system, as part of a larger enterprise resource planning – ERP – system) could have made her job a lot less stressful; it might have meant that instead of spending time correcting things that had gone wrong or not thought of, she could have concentrated on developing exciting new products and processes.

3 **Corporate social responsibility:** Looking after our natural environment and resources is unquestionably an important thing to do. Similarly, it is also important to respect cultural, political and social differences. Both of these, along with making sustainable profit, are necessary for organizations. However, CSR can sometimes be used for marketing purposes without actually having any real impact; you should consider how companies' and governments' CSR claims would actually make a difference. For instance, is putting more tax on petrol or air flights really going to stop people travelling? Will people stop buying cheap products if they know workforces are being exploited?

Beth, working in the chocolate factory, would need to consider the following factors. Are ingredients obtained from sustainable forests? Are suppliers treating their workforces ethically? Are developing countries getting a fair share of the profits? And are machines using power economically? Wider issues involve customers' health and marketing messages (e.g. is chocolate really good for you, or should it contain health warnings?).

▶   **4   Right first time:** To have a successful career, operations managers must always be aware of all the latest developments in management thinking, tools, techniques and technology. This usually requires a combination of continuing professional development and the implementation of competitive practices.

However, even the best operations managers get it wrong at times. The important point is not to hide or ignore problems, but to resolve them as a team within the organization, to learn from them, and not to make them again. In this way organizations and practice will continually improve, and organizations will become more competitive and sustainable.

connect

Review Questions

1   Describe the key success factors for business integration.

2   Explain why some businesses are more appropriate to be supported by information technology than others, and why some will never be pure online businesses.

3   Consider whether you think the benefits of globalization outweigh the negative issues in respect to: (a) individual companies; (b) nations; (c) Planet Earth.

4   Can globalization really be practised at the same time as corporate social responsibility?

5   Is corporate social responsibility adding to unnecessary organizational costs and complexity?

6   How can we ensure that the workforce of the future is adequately prepared for the future challenges of operations managers?

Discussion Questions

1   Imagine that credit cards, online shopping and large department/supermarket stores didn't exist, and that we, as consumers, had to travel around visiting individual independent stores to acquire our goods and services. In other words, our personal suppliers were poorly integrated, and had no IT support. Discuss with your colleagues what the impact on our lives would be.

2   Look at the mission statements of HSBC (bank), Orange (mobile phone operator), the John Lewis Partnership (retailer) and Starbucks (coffee houses). State the similarities and differences. Why do you think Starbucks and HSBC have been the targets of anti-globalization activities?

3   Characterize the personal consumer behaviour of your peer group. How do you think you can influence the corporate social responsibilities of large organizations?

4   Look at job recruitment sites such as www.monster.com, and see the skill sets that are required by operations managers. Do you think you have them?

 Online **Learning**Centre

Visit the Online Learning Centre at **www.mcgraw-hill.co.uk/textbooks/paton** for a range of resources to support your learning.

Further Reading

Benedettini, O., Clegg, B., Kafouros, M. and Neely, A. (2010) *The Ten Myths of Manufacturing*, AIM executive briefing paper (www.aimresearch.org).

Binder, M. and Clegg, B.T. (2010) *Sustainable Supplier Management in the Automotive Industry: Leading the 3rd Revolution through Collaboration*, Nova Science Publishers, New York.

Burcher, P.G., Lee, G.L. and Sohal, A.S. (2004) 'The changing roles of production and operations managers in Britain from the 1970s to the 1990s', *International Journal of Operations and Production Management*, **24**(4), 409–423.

Cramer, J. (2006) *Corporate Social Responsibility and Globalisation: An Action Plan for Business*, Greenleaf Publishing, Sheffield.

D'Netto, B. and Sohal, A.S. (1999) 'Changes in the production manager's job: past, present and future trends', *International Journal of Operations and Production Management*, **19**(2), 157–181.

The *Sunday Times*, *The Independent* and other quality newspapers: job advertisements for operations managers and directors.

References

Economist Intelligent Unit (2008) *Why CSR?*, Economist Intelligent Unit, London

Elkington, J. (1994) 'Toward the sustainable corporation: win-win-win business strategies for sustainable development', *California Management Review*, **36**(2), 90–100.

Farrell, D. (2004) 'Beyond offshoring: assess your company's global potential', *Harvard Business Review*, **82**(12), 82–90.

Friedman, T. (2005) *The World is Flat: A Brief History of the 21st Century*, Farrar, Straus and Giroux, New York.

Ghemawat, P. (2007) 'Managing differences: the central challenge of global strategy', *Harvard Business Review*, **85**(3), 58–68.

Kolk, A. (2000) *The Economics of Environmental Management*. FT Prentice Hall, Harlow.

Negroponte, N. (1995) *Being Digital*, Vintage Books, New York.

Waterman, R.H., Peters, T.J. and Philips, J.R. (1980) 'Structure is not organization', *Business Horizons*, **23**(3), 14–26.

Glossary

ABC – system for ranking inventory into parts to control closely and parts that don't merit undue effort in monitoring.

Actual capacity – the expected output of an operation, considering both planned stoppages and unplanned stoppages.

Adaptation (in a globalization context) – boosting revenue and market share by maximizing local presence in a country.

Aggregate planning – a top-level look at demand for the operation as a whole; does not differentiate between different products and services.

Aggregation (in a globalization context) – achieving economies of scale by creating regional or global operations.

Agile supply – use of market knowledge and the virtual corporation to exploit profitable opportunities in a volatile marketplace.

Andon – series of lights to warn the whole factory of quality issues when they occur.

Arbitrage (in a globalization context) – the exploitation of differences among national or regional markets, often by locating separate parts of supply chains in different places.

Assemble to order (ATO) – production system in which parts are ordered and subassemblies made, but final assembly waits for a customer order, to allow customization of the specific product.

Back-office activities – activities that are hidden from the customers.

Back-order – production to replenish inventory stock.

Batch of one – a key element of the lean approach, which seeks to produce individual products, as this is normally what the customer orders.

Bill of materials (BOM) file (or product structure or product tree file) – lists the description of the product (such as the material, components and quantity) and the sequence in which the product is to be assembled.

Business process – sequence of tasks to get things done.

Capability – the maximum amount of a product that can be made within a specified time.

Capacity requirements planning (CRP) – MRP module that examines workloading on workstations to identify shortfalls.

Capacity – the maximum goods or services that an operation can produce.

Cause-and-effect diagram – structural approach to finding of possible cause(s) of a problem.

Centre of gravity method – approach that uses the physical analogy of a 'balancing point' to determine the geographical location of an operation relative to others that it has a direct relationship with.

Chase demand – capacity strategy in which the operation expands and contracts its capacity to follow demand changes.

Closed-loop MRP – use of the MRP calculation to examine whether the plans it produces are achievable, given limits in capacity or supply times and other constraints.

Collaborative enterprise governance – method of controlling parts of many different organizations simultaneously, in order to deliver products and services with agility and efficiency.

Collaborative planning, forecasting and replenishment (CPFR) – business practice that combines the intelligence of multiple trading partners in the planning and fulfilment of customer demand.

Competitive advantage – what sets a firm apart from its rivals, making it the supplier of choice for customers within a particular market.

Competitive benchmarking – compares the company's performance against that of the competitors.

Constraint – a restriction on the running of an operation.

Continuous flow manufacturing – another name for the Toyota Production System.

Continuous innovation – the ability to repeatedly generate new ideas.

Control chart – used to plot sample means, average means and ranges over time; indicates the lower and upper control limits.

Conveyance kanban – one part of the two-bin system.

Core competencies – competencies that contribute directly to business goals.

Corporate responsibility – the awareness, acceptance, and management of the wider implications of management decisions.

Cost, performance and time – *projects are normally subjected to these three performance criteria.*

Critical path – the chain of activities that determines the total duration of a project from start to finish.

Customer contact – refers to the physical presence of the customer in the system, or the percentage of the time that the customer is in the system relative to the total service time.

Customer relationship management (CRM) – ERP tools where all relevant information about a customer can be presented in one place, thus offering a transparent way of supporting customers.

Customer value elements – factors that, when combined, define the value proposition.

Customer value proposition – statement of precisely what the customer values and will therefore buy in the form of a product.

Customization point – the point where a process output becomes linked to a specific customer order.

Cycle time – the actual time a process or task in a process takes to produce a unit of output.

Cyclical review – inventory review system that determines the amount to be ordered at set intervals.

Degree of interaction and customization – the customer's ability to affect the nature of the service being delivered.

Degree of labour intensity – the ratio of employee cost to capital cost.

Demand management – capacity strategy in which the operation attempts to manipulate demand to smooth the peaks and troughs; used in conjunction with the marketing department.

Demand – the quantity of goods and services demanded by consumers.

Dependent demand – demand for a part that is normally directly related to that for some others, and ultimately to the aggregate production plan.

Dependent demand – reasonably predictable demand, linked or associated with another factor, which may have a clearer future pattern.

Design capacity – the expected output of an operation when there are no stoppages.

Development – activity that involves systematic but non-routine technical work directed towards producing new or improved materials, products or services.

Distinctive competencies – competencies so unique that they create competitive advantage.

DPMO – defects per million opportunities.

Dynamic capability – a firm's ability to upgrade and reconstruct its capabilities in response to the changing environment, therefore attaining and sustaining its competitive advantage.

Earned value reporting (EVR) – a means of monitoring projects, based on key measures of completion against estimated cost or schedule.

Early supplier involvement (ESI) – form of cooperation in which manufacturers involve suppliers at an early stage of the product development processes.

E-business – electronically mediated information exchanges, both within an organization and with external stakeholders, supporting the entire range of business processes.

E-commerce – electronically mediated information exchanges between an organization and its external stakeholders, concerned predominantly with buying and selling.

Economic batch quantity (EBQ) – another name for EPQ.

Economic order quantity (EOQ) – fixed order (or production) amount that minimizes the total costs over a whole year.

Economic production quantity (EPQ) – extension of the EOQ that includes the effect of producing parts.

Economies of scale – doing things on a large scale to make them economically viable.

Economies of scope – having capability to be able to deliver a variety of outputs.

Effective capacity – the expected output of an operation considering planned stoppages for maintenance, shift changeovers etc.

Effectiveness – describes how well goals are achieved.

Efficiency – ratio of actual output to possible output.

Efficiency – actual output shown as a percentage of the operation's effective capacity; demonstrates how well the operation is working to expectations.

Employee involvement – essential part of the Toyota Production System, where employees play a significant role in the management system.

Endogenous theories – theories about an organization that focus on the organization and its links to the business environment.

Engageability – the ability to attract partners and the means to deliver value.

Enterprise – group of different companies, or group of parts of different companies, working together to deliver a product or service in a highly integrated way.

Enterprise integrator/orchestrator – organization that takes the lead role in transforming a loose supply network into a tightly integrated enterprise.

Enterprise resources planning (ERP) – ERP systems are corporate-wide information systems that present data as if from a central single entity source.

Enterprise – group of different companies, or group of parts of different companies, working together to deliver a product of service in a highly integrated way.

e-Service – the delivery of service using online media, which can be delivered in a virtual environment with little or no human interaction.

Exogenous theories – theories about an organization that focus on its internal workings, resources and skills.

Extended enterprise – semi-permanent group of organizations working towards joint strategic objectives.

Field of use – the company seeks to understand how well the product conforms to specifications after it reaches the customers.

Finished goods inventory – completed products awaiting shipment or built for stock.

Finite capacity scheduling – advanced MRP II system including routines to try and solve any capacity problems.

Fixed position layout – layout in which all activities cluster around the product or service being delivered.

Flexibility – the ability to respond quickly with little penalty in time, cost or value.

Float – the spare time an activity has before it will become on the critical path, and so allowing rescheduling without impact.

Flow chart – provides a visual representation of all major steps in a process.

Flow diagram – a drawing used to analyse the flow of people and materials.

Front-office activities – activities where there is direct customer contact, whether face to face, or by email, telephone, or letter.

Functional benchmarking – compares specific processes and functions across different industries to find the 'best in class'.

Gantt chart – horizontal bar diagram showing activities and their duration.

Gemba – quality approach demanding the gathering of data from all sources.

Genchi genbutsu – quality approach to 'go and see for yourself'.

Globalization – increasing global connectivity, integration and interdependence in the economic, social, technological, cultural, political and ecological spheres.

Globalization – the increasing integration of internationally dispersed economic activity, and the extension of an organization's operational activity to cover the whole world.

Hansei (reflection) – problem-solving approach used in lean systems.

Heijunka – method for developing a repeating schedule that produces the correct mix of products. It is important to spread the launch of products into the production line evenly to smooth the amount of work required.

High-performance organizations (HPOs) – organizations deemed to excel at all aspects of performance, as recognized through the use of an integrated performance management system, whereby people, process and outcome are all performing at high levels.

Holistic thinking/holism – considering a system to be more than a sum of its parts.

Increased value manufacturing – another name for the Toyota Production System.

Incremental innovation – change that moves things on in small steps.

Independent demand – a less predictable demand pattern than dependent demand; not easily linked to other factors.

Independent demand – demand that is treated as unrelated to anything else.

Innovation outcome – the output that is new or different.

Innovation process – the sequence of activities that generates an idea.

Interface specifications – define the protocol for the fundamental interactions across all components constituting a technological system.

Internal benchmarking – provides a comparison among similar operations or processes within a company's organization.

International Organization for Standardization (ISO) – the world's largest standards-developing organization.

Inventory records file – information about the part, including sources, and the stock levels. A key part of the MRP calculation.

Inventory turn – the time taken for a firm's entire inventory to be used and replaced.

Inventory – the materials and finished products that are present in the firm, and also in its supply chain. In general, inventory represents a waste, and should be avoided if possible.

Jidoka – implementing self-checking to ensure a consistent flow of production.

Just in time (JIT) – the pull-based material control system used at Toyota, and the basis of developing the lean model.

Kaizen – continuous improvement approach to quality control.

Kanban – Japanese word for the card that is the essential vehicle for operation of the JIT system of production control.

Key performance indicator (KPI) – a specific aspect of measurement, the identification and quantification of which enhances management knowledge about a particular part of the business.

Knowledge push – innovation driven by advances in technology that create new products.

Knowledge workers – employees whose skills are based more on what they know than on what they can physically do.

Layout – the physical configuration of departments, work centres, and equipment in an operation.

Lead time – the time it takes to design, make and deliver a product or service.

Leagile supply – combination of a lean supply chain and an agile supply chain.

Lean production – highly efficient management approach with repeated focus on waste reduction, and based on the ideas of the Toyota Production System and JIT.

Lean supply – seeks to develop a value stream to eliminate all waste.

Lean system – a highly efficient process that produces products and services in the desired quantities, exactly when they are needed.

Lean thinking – extending lean production to broader ideas or philosophies. Based on five-step framework: concentrate on value for customers, appreciate the value stream, concentrate on improved flow, adopt pull, perfect quality.

Level production – capacity strategy in which the operation produces to a consistent level; unsold product is stored, and sold when demand peaks.

Line balancing – assigning tasks to workstations so that they are approximately equal.

Lot-for-lot – batching routine that ignores the EOQ; instead of a fixed batch being ordered, the exact number needed is used.

Make to order (MTO) – where planning, procurement and production wait until there is an order from a customer before starting.

Make to stock (MTS) – where production happens before an order has been received.

Manufacturing resource planning (MRP II) – extension of MRP that not only identifies the amounts and times for delivery for components but also includes capacity checks, and extends the calculations to cover the scheduling of production.

Market-based view – the strategic approach that prioritizes what the market wants in its decision-making.

Mass customization – system to produce high volumes of customized output at a low price, in response to customer orders.

Mass production – system to produce high volumes of standardized products.

Master production schedule (MPS) – a formal list of the products to be sent to customers, plus detailed specifications and delivery dates; the start of the MRP calculation.

Material requirements planning (MRP) – a way of calculating the demand and timing for component deliveries in order to make the products listed in the master production schedule.

Matrix organization – combined organization structure that overlays functional and project-based styles.

Mobile/M-commerce – electronically mediated information exchanges using mobile electronic devices.

Muda, muri, mura – focus on waste at the heart of lean systems.

Need pull – customer identification of gaps in the market that provide an opportunity to innovate and create a product.

Net change MRP – approach that recalculates requirements as an update of the previous plan, but only for those parts that involve a change.

Newsboy problem or single period model – specific inventory problem that balances stock-out costs against the possible wastage costs in addition to the holding costs in the EOQ.

Obsolescence – the state of becoming obsolete, or out of date.

Operations strategy – the set of major decisions about core competencies, capabilities and processes, technologies, resources and key tactical activities necessary in the function or chain of functions that create and deliver product and service combinations.

Optional replacement systems – inventory control situations in which both period and quantity are changed.

Order-qualifying criteria – the required standards that, if not achieved, will disqualify a product or service from consideration by the customer.

Order-winning criteria – the key reasons to buy a product or service.

Outsourcing – process of giving part of your operations to another organization.

Overall equipment effectiveness (OEE) – actual capacity when applied to individual machines; tells the operation how well the equipment is being used.

Overall professional effectiveness (OPE) – actual capacity when applied to individual workers; tells the operation how well the employee is performing.

Pacemaker task – the task that dictates the speed of the overall process.

Pareto diagram – arranges categories from highest to lowest frequency of occurrence.

Performance management – systematic measuring, monitoring and decision-making geared towards fulfilling organizational objectives through operations management.

Performance measurement – quantification of business activities, enabling comparison and discussion.

Performance measures – factors that the customer will use to judge the performance of a product or service.

Poka yoke – 'fail-safing or mistake-proofing'.

Population – in a statistical distribution, the entire set of things that make up what is being measured. Samples are taken from a population.

Postponement – delaying the timing of crucial processes in which end products assume their specific functionalities, features and identities.

Process chart – tabulated chart that uses symbols to analyse the flow and movement of people and materials.

Process dominant layout – physical arrangement focusing on the optimization of a process rather than the production of any particular product or service.

Process servers – the points of sale or stations at the front of the queue where the customer is served.

Product life cycle – generalized model of the buying behaviour of customers over time; used to predict demand for a product or service.

Product platform – set of interconnected subsystems that form a common structure, from which a stream of derivative products can be developed and produced.

Production – total amount of a product that is made.

Production kanban – one part of the two-bin system.

Productivity – amount produced in relation to one or more of the resources used.

Productization of services – the process of convergence of services to include product content.

Product–service dominant layout – physical arrangement focusing on delivering a particular product or service.

Project-based organization – represents a shift from functional organization structure, via the matrix organization, to one where the project is the focus of attention.

Push–pull inventory control – in push systems there is a central planning system that generates and programmes orders for the production line. With pull, orders come from customers, and the line reacts to the demand.

Quality of conformance – deals with how well the actual product or service delivery matches the design intended.

Quality of design – concerned with how well the design concept and its specifications match the intended use of the product or service.

Quick response (QR) – implementation of JIT in clothing manufacture.

Radical innovation – extreme, game-changing progress.

Raw materials – materials purchased but not processed.

Reductionism – seeing parts of a system as more important than the whole.

Regenerative MRP – system in which the complete material requirements plan is recomputed on a regular basis.

Reorder level (ROL) – The trigger level used in the reorder point inventory system (Q type), which generates the ordering of a fixed amount (normally the EOQ) with an irregular interval.

Reorder point – level of inventory that indicates the time to order a batch of the EOQ in a reorder level system.

Research – scholarly or scientific investigation or inquiry; generally categorized as either basic or applied.

Resource levelling – the practice of using float to improve the resources needed in a project.

Resource-based view – the strategic approach that prioritizes the capability of the firm in its decision-making.

Reverse logistics – addresses key issues related to how companies can become more environmentally efficient through recycling, reusing and reducing the amount of materials used.

Rough-cut capacity planning – CRP applied at the aggregate level to try and ensure the plan is close to achievable with existing capacity limits.

Run chart – shows the trends in data over time.

Sand-cone principle – records the importance of certain practices building on others in a predetermined order.

Safety stock – extra inventory used to cover uncertainty or delivery times so that the system can keep operating.

Safety – concerned with whether there is any risk to the customer when they use the product or receive the service.

Scatter diagram – shows the degree and direction of the relationship between two variables.

Scheduling – committing the demand that has been ordered to the operation so that it can be made and delivered.

Senpai-kohai – Toyota mentoring system of personnel development.

Sequencing – the order in which things are processed (e.g. assembly).

Service – any activity or benefit that one party can offer to another that is essentially intangible, and does not result in the ownership of anything.

Service blueprinting – process-mapping technique specifically suited to services.

Service level – percentage of service requests or product orders delivered to specification.

Servitization of products – the process of convergence of products with service content.

SMED (single minute exchange of dies) – approach to reduce machine changeovers to achieve batch size of one.

SIPOC (supplier–input–process–output–customer) diagram – maps the processes a company (or a person) goes through in order to satisfy a customer's requirements in the context of the supply chain.

Slack – the spare time an activity has before it will become on the critical path.

Stakeholders – the people who have a say in or are influenced by a project.

Stock time chart – chart showing how the inventory of a part or component changes over time.

Stockless production system – another name for the Toyota Production System.

Strategic alignment – the alignment of all decisions made at different levels of the organization with the overall strategic goals.

Supplier network – loose group of organizations that collectively delivery parts and services to an end customer.

Supply base rationalization – reduction of suppliers in order to become more efficient.

Supply chain management (SCM) – the management of activities, organization and processes involving all the stakeholders, from the end customers (i.e. downstream) to the supplier that produces the raw material (i.e. upstream).

Sustainable competitive advantage – competitive advantage that is based on a valuable, rare, imperfectly imitable and non-substitutable resource that is specific to the company, and cannot be transferred.

Swim-lane diagram – process depiction technique that has function and time dimensions.

Synchro MRP – system developed and employed by Yamaha using kanban to implement an MRP-derived plan.

System – a complex whole, the functioning of which depends on its parts and the interactions between those parts.

Systems integrator/orchestrator – organization that takes a lead role in transforming a loose supply network into an a tightly integrated enterprise.

Systems thinking – considering a system to be more than a sum of its parts; same as holism/holistic thinking.

Takt time – the time allowed by the customer for each unit of output to be produced.

Third party logistics (TPL) – a TPL provider can be treated as an external supplier that performs some or all parts of a company's functions, especially logistics services.

Threshold competencies – competencies that allow the firm to exist and operate, but provide no competitive advantage.

Total productive maintenance (TPM) – the application of TQM ideas to ensuring that machines operate effectively, and are always available.

Total quality management (TQM) – quality system that is needed for effective lean production, and based on kaizen (continuous improvement).

Toyota Production System (TPS) – the model for lean systems as developed at Toyota by Ohno and using JIT.

Trade-offs – factors that cannot exist concurrently in their best state; the optimization of one necessitates a compromise in another.

Transaction costs – the price associated with buying or selling goods or services.

Transformed resources – materials to be converted into products for sale, and information.

Transforming resources – facilities such as buildings, equipment and tools and process technology; all the staff involved in the conversion process; and the capital that is needed to buy materials, and pay for the facilities and staff.

Triple bottom line – considers the social and natural environmental impact of a company's strategy as well as the more conventional economic impact.

Two-bin system – Toyota's version of the kanban system, which employs two cards/bins, one to initiate production and the other to move the parts for use.

Utilization – proportion of available capacity that is used.

Utilization – actual output shown as a percentage of the design capacity of the operation; shows the percentage of time the facility is in actual use, and therefore demonstrates how well the resources are working.

Value disciplines – generic operations strategies that focus on a single approach that directs the set-up of the operation in support of that approach – either operational excellence, product leadership or customer intimacy.

Value matrix – a framework of generic operations strategies called value propositions that informs the set-up of the operation.

Value stream map – a technique used in lean thinking which can help eliminate non-value adding activities.

Value stream mapping – analysing the flow of materials and information required to bring a product to the consumer in order to remove waste.

Variety – differing outputs.

Vendor managed inventory (VMI) – a partnering initiative for improving multi-firm supply chain efficiency, where the buyer shares inventory information with its vendors (or suppliers), so that the vendors can manage the inventory for the buyer.

Vertically integrated enterprise – almost permanent and extremely well-integrated group of organizations; very similar to a single legal entity.

Virtual enterprise – temporary group of organizations exploiting a short-term, high-risk opportunity.

Volume – the amount of output.

Wagner–Whitin – inventory procedure in which separate demand periods are joined to reduce set-up costs.

Weighted score technique – technique for comparing the attractiveness of alternative operational locations that allocates a weighted score to each relevant factor in the decision.

Work breakdown structure (WBS) – statement of all the work that has to be completed in a project.

Work cell – specialized unit with people, machines and knowledge to perform a particular set of activities or events (e.g. sales rooms, inspection units).

Work cell layout – physical arrangement that focuses on delivering an efficient work cell.

Work-in-process inventory – materials that have started being worked upon but are not complete.

Yield management – a group of methods that assist an operation with fixed capacity to maximize its revenue and utilize the capacity it has to best advantage.

Zero inventory – another name for JIT, which focuses on reduced inventory.

Index